EDUCATION LAW

AUSTRALIA AND NEW ZEALAND
The Law Book Company Ltd.
Sydney : Melbourne : Perth

CANADA AND U.S.A.
The Carswell Company Ltd.
Agincourt, Ontario

INDIA
N. M. Tripathi Private Ltd.
Bombay
and
Eastern Law House Private Ltd.
Calcutta and Delhi
M.P.P. House
Bangalore

ISRAEL
Steimatzky's Agency Ltd.
Jerusalem : Tel Aviv : Haifa

MALAYSIA : SINGAPORE : BRUNEI
Malayan Law Journal (Pte.) Ltd.
Singapore and Kuala Lumpur

EDUCATION LAW

An outline of the law
relating to the public system
of education in England and Wales

by

K. P. Poole, M.A.
Solicitor, Honorary Senior Research Fellow in Public
Administration at the University of Kent at Canterbury

LONDON
SWEET & MAXWELL
1988

Published in 1988 by
Sweet & Maxwell Limited of
11 New Fetter Lane, London
Computerset by Promenade Graphics Ltd., Cheltenham
Printed in Great Britain by Adlard & Son Ltd.,
The Garden City Press, Letchworth, Herts.

British Library Cataloguing in Publication Data
Poole, Kenneth P.
Education law: an outline of the law
relating to the public system of education
in England and Wales.
1. Educational law and legislation—
England
I. Title
344.204'7   KD3600

ISBN 0–421–32830–4

PREFACE

Mr. R. A. Butler (later Lord Butler of Saffron Walden) as former Minister of Education opened for the Opposition in the Second Reading debate on the Bill for the Education Act 1946. The official report for February 1, 1946 (vol. 48, col. 1259) records him thus:

> "I make this appeal to the government. When lawyers or educational administrators, directors of education or members of education committees have to interpret this measure [the 1946 Act] in the future they will unfortunately have to read it with the Act of 1944, and they may find it easier to understand the Act of 1944 if they read it in conjunction with what will be the Act of 1946. I think it would be more satisfactory to have some form of codification of the two Acts in one."

Mr. Hardman, the Parliamentary Secretary, replied:

> ". . . unfortunately there are heavy demands on parliamentary time and on parliamentary draftsmen, and however much all of us may desire a consolidating bill that has been found to be impossible."

Governments have found time to innovate but not to consolidate. In 1970 the Labour Party manifesto[1] promised legislation to replace the principal 1944 Act, but having lost the 1970 election the party failed to renew their pledge. So more than forty years on Mr. Hardman's answer seems to remain in point; and there are now 25 Education Acts to be read as one. The principal Act is moth-eaten and threadbare. Even some of the patches have had to be replaced to meet changing needs and fashions. Much of current further education provision may be *ultra vires*,[2] and there are other shortcomings. The need for legislative renewal is manifest.

By odd comparison, Scottish education law has been consolidated on two occasions since its renewal after the Second World War. Equally odd, it may be thought, has been the absence in advance of this volume (apart from Halsbury's Laws) of a narrative account of the law; but it would be ungenerous not to pay tribute to the long-standing and invaluable collection of statutory and other materials brought out in successive editions by the "other" law publisher, the contributions of the Society of Education Officers, and several substantial works prepared as aids for teachers by the late Mr. G. R. Barrell and others. And among the many

---

[1] See F. W. S. Craig, *British General Election Manifestos 1900–74* (1975) p. 353.
[2] See below at para. 3–10.

publications of the Advisory Centre for Education are some useful expositions of the law.

The present attempt is to provide a reasonably full work of reference. The material falls naturally under seven chapter headings, and each chapter is divided, following introductory remarks, into sections and, usually, subsections (as indicated in the table of contents). Three appendices contain documents that should help to meet working needs. Although some topics that cannot be omitted altogether are treated lightly (for example, administrative and employment law) there recourse is easily had to specialist authorities. There are other imbalances. The account of the School Sites Acts and of the law relating to mandatory further education awards, for instance, may seem unduly laboured, but this is deliberate in the belief that extended treatment will be found helpful by the practitioner. Imbalance in part reflects the state of the law itself. On further education in general it is sparse, but the awards regulations leave little to speculation: Regulation 22(6) of S.I. 1986/1306 specifies that "a day shall be reckoned as a seventh of a week." "Week," unguardedly, is left undefined. It is regrettable that few words could be spared to convey how the law comes to be as it is, since it springs to life only as an echo of its times[3] and of the legislators' intentions. The reader will look in vain for an account of the controversy over the organisation of secondary education that was marked by the passing of the Education Act 1976 and its repeal in 1979, or of the more recent disputes that led up to the Teachers' Pay and Conditions Act 1987.

Because the solicitor in local government service with administrative as well as legal responsibilities is the reader whose needs have been held most in mind, circulars and administrative memorandums from the Department of Education and Science are cited, together with Welsh Office equivalents where they exist.[4] Prescription, however, is avoided, and the hope is that lawyers in private practice will find the work of equal value. Only fifteen years ago it was a plausible contention that "in

---

[3] e.g. Mathew, J. in *Hunter* v. *Johnson* (1884) 13 Q.B.D. 225 at 227: "we are compelled to deal with the matter of education as a statutory interference with the liberty of the subject"; and the distressing inhumanity of a local education authority's decision, righted by the court, to dismiss a teacher because (with her head's approval) she extended her lunch hour to take leave of her future fiancé who was bound for the trenches in France (*Martin* v. *Eccles* [1919] 1 Ch. 387). At the present day exemption from V.A.T. (Value Added Tax Act 1983, Sched. 6, Group 6) perhaps reflects the uniqueness of education as a commodity.

[4] The Department of Education and Science surpasses other departments by publishing an annual bound volume of circulars and administrative memorandums, but has failed since 1979 to provide an annual index to those still current; so it is possible that despite advice sought from within the Department some of the material cited is anachronistic. The Welsh Office publishes circulars (a) setting out policy that applies to Wales and England equally: these, and similar circulars published up to April 1, 1978 by the former Welsh Education Office, are noted in the text with their English equivalent, (b) on specifically Welsh issues, especially language, and (c) that have a slightly different emphasis from their English counterparts (*e.g.* on education support grant and in-service teacher training) to acknowledge language and cultural differences.

general the courts have not had much to do with educational administration[5]" but in more recent years the practice of public administration has become subject to an increasingly critical public opinion, of which there is evidence in reported cases and in the files of the Parliamentary Commissioner for Administration and the local ombudsmen.

For the practitioner a textbook can be no substitute for reference to the letter of the law when a difficult or contentious matter arises, but it can provide a quick entry to the relevant material and it may perhaps draw attention to an aspect that might otherwise be overlooked. Moreover most of what is written will be accessible not only to lawyers but to members of local education departments and informed members of the public who need to know how the law stands. Academic lawyers may be disappointed at the uncritical and untheoretical approach; nevertheless they may find the book a convenient starting point for their own conjectures, and there is no lack of critical material in the footnoted articles. An exegesis of legislation cannot be passed off as a work of literature, but it will be enough if the message has been made plain. Only experience in using the book will show whether the balance has been properly struck between precision and readability.

In the preparation of this book I have received help from many sources, and express my gratitude to officers of the teachers' unions, the local authority associations, the Welsh Joint Education Committee, the Local Authorities' Conditions of Service Advisory Board, the Welsh Office and the Department of Education and Science, Assistant Librarian. The former Solicitor to the Department, Mr Peter Harvey C.B., gave me help and encouragement at the outset, and subsequently Miss Arabella Wood, went to a great deal of trouble on my behalf. Mr. J. Jeffries and Ms. Sarah Carter, Assistant Librarians at the Univeristy of Kent at Canterbury, also helped the work along. I have benefited by the comments of, and information received from Mr. J. D. Hill (University of Bristol), Mr. I. H. Ward (Under Secretary (Finance) of the Association of County Councils), Mr. S. A. Mercer (lately Senior Assistant Treasurer, Kent County Council), Mr. M. R. Hyde (lately Secretary of the Commission for Local Administration in England), and Mr. H. F. Jones (Commissioner for Local Administration in Wales). Mr. I. K. Widdison of C.L.E.A. volunteered much helpful information as well as meeting all my importunate requests. My friends Dr. J. M. Benn C.B., Professor J. A. Craven and Mr. D. L. Stewart gave me advice which I took in spirit if not wholly to the letter.

Mr. B. D. Harrold (lately Deputy Town Clerk and Solicitor, London Borough of Enfield) read the whole of the draft (except for the passages relating to recent legislation) and his constructive comments saved me from error and enabled me to make both statute and case law more

[5] See B. Schwartz and H. W. R. Wade, *Legal Control of Government* (1972) p. 51.

intelligible. I am also much in debt to Mr. C. A. Cross, whose name is a byword in the field of local government law, and who suggested in the first place that I should take on this task. He too read and commented on the whole of the draft (with the same exception) and he supported me throughout with advice and encouragement, as did my publishers.

For the typing and retyping of the manuscript my thanks are due to Miss Carol Wilmshurst of Keynes College secretarial staff, aided from time to time by her colleagues, and in the concluding stages to Mrs. Barbara Green. Remaining errors and omissions are of course entirely my responsibility.

Many of those named bring back to mind more or less distant periods in my working life, and I maintain the note of nostalgia by dedicating the book to Mr. L. W. K. Brown C.B.E., sometime Deputy Secretary (Education) of the County Council Association and Education Officer of the Association of County Councils, whose cheerful company in the shadowy world between Department and local education authority I was once fortunate to keep.

Canterbury   K. P. Poole
October 1987

NOTE

The law stated is that in force on April 30, 1987, but where possible later changes have been recorded. By April 30, most of the provisions in the Education (No. 2) Act 1986 had not been brought into force, but with one exception noted in the text appointed day orders (S.I. 1986 No. 2203 and S.I. 1987 No. 344—see Circulars 8/86 and 7/87) will have brought the whole Act into force by the date of publication. There are, however, important transitional provisions to which reference is made at appropriate places in the text.

The Government formed in June 1987 announced the intention to make further legislative change: to establish a national school curriculum, to give schools greater autonomy by control of their budgets or by opting out of local authority control (so as to be funded by the Department of Education and Science), to reform the structure of education in inner London, to give greater independence to polytechnics and some other colleges, to support the establishment of city technology colleges, and to clarify the circumstances in which local education authorities may impose charges.

A supplement to this book will be published following the passage of the new legislation.

CONTENTS

CHAPTER 2 SCHOOLS

CONTENTS

TABLE OF CASES

*[Paragraph references in **bold** type indicate where a case is dealt with in greater depth.]*

TABLE OF STATUTES

*[The Acts in **bold** type are the Education Acts 1944 to 1986. Note that sections 4 and 5 of the Further Education Act 1985 are not part of the Education Acts; and that the Teachers' Pay and Conditions Act 1987 is to be construed as one with the Education Act 1944. In the text a reference to, for example, the 1980 Act is a reference to the Education Act of that year, except where the context otherwise requires.]*

TABLE OF STATUTORY INSTRUMENTS

xlv

1

li

TABLE OF ABBREVIATIONS

A.C.—Appeal Cases (Law Reports)
A.M.—Administrative Memorandum
All E.R.—All England Law Reports
App.Cas.—Appeal Cases (Law Reports)
B. & Ald.—Barnewall and Adolphus (Law Reports)
B. & P.—Bosanquet & Puller
Car. & P.—Carrington & Payne
Ch.—Chancery (Law Reports)
C.I.P.F.A.—The Chartered Institute of Public Finance and
              Accountancy
C.L.E.A.—Council of Local Education Authorities
C.L.J.—Cambridge Law Journal
C.L.Y.—Current Law Year Book
C.M. & R.—Crompton, Meeson & Roscoe
C.M.L.R.—Common Market Law Reports
Crim. L.R.—Criminal Law Review
D.L.R.—Dominion Law Reports
E. & B.—Ellis and Blackburn (Law Reports)
E.H.R.R.—European Human Rights Reports
F. & F.—Foster and Finlason (Law Reports)
Fam. Law—Family Law
H.C. Deb.—House of Commons Debates
H.L. Deb.—House of Lords Debates
H.M.S.O.—Her Majesty's Stationery Office
H.M.I.—Her Majesty's Inspectors
I.C.R.—Industrial Cases Reports
I.R.L.R.—Industrial Relations Law Reports
J.P.—Justice of the Peace Reports
J.P.J.—Justice of the Peace and Local Government Review
J.P.N.—Justice of the Peace Journal
J.S.W.L.—Journal of Social Welfare Law
K.B.—King's Bench
L.A.G. Bull.—Legal Action Group Bulletin
L.G.C.—Local Government Chronicle
L.G.R.—Local Government Reports
L.G. Rev.—Local Government Review
L.J.—Law Journal Newspaper
L.J.K.B.—Law Journal, King's Bench
L.Q.R.—Law Quarterly Review
L.S. Gaz.—Law Society's Gazette
L.T.—Law Times

Lit.—Litigation
Ll.L. Rep.—Lloyd's List Reports (before 1951)
M. & S.—Maule & Selwyn (Law Reports)
N.Z.L.R.—New Zealand Law Reports
New L.J.—New Law Journal
P.L.—Public Law
Q.B.—Queen's Bench
Q.B.D.—Queen's Bench Division
R.R.C.—Ryde's Rating Cases
R.T.R.—Road Traffic Reports
S.A.S.R.—South Australia State Reports
S.C.—Sessions Courts
SCO.L.A.G. Bull.—Journal of the Scottish Legal Action Group
                              Bulletin
S.J.—Solicitors Journal
S.L.T.—Scots Law Times
S.T.C.— Simon's Tax Cases
Stark N.P.—Stark (Law Reports)
T.L.R.—Times Law Reports
W.H.S.C.—Welsh Health Service Circular
W.L.R.—Weekly Law Reports
W.O.—Welsh Office

CHAPTER 1

THE FRAMEWORK

THE Education Acts[1] promote and regulate the public system of edu- **1–01**
cation in England and Wales. In this book the attempt is made to
expound them. It will not do, however, to ignore any of the sources of
law—statute, subordinate legislation, European legislation and the
common law—that provide a context for the education system or materially affect its operation.

By the public system of education is meant the provision of school- **1–02**
ing and further education, through teachers and other staff, by local
education authorities and, in conjunction with them, churches and
voluntary bodies, subject to the exercise of the powers of the
Secretaries of State for Education and Science and for Wales. This
definition must be extended to include supplementary functions of
local education authorities and of the Secretaries of State; and reference has also to be made to the role of parents and governors, which
has recently been emphasised, and to the statutory relationships that
exist between public authorities and independent schools. With some
very limited exceptions,[2] the powers and duties of the Secretaries of
State, local education authorities and parents are of general application.

The present chapter gives an account of the law on central and **1–03**
local administration; the role of subordinate legislation; some general
rules of interpretation and administrative law; some of the requirements, based on general principles, that govern the operation of the
substantive law; and the law relating to the provision of finance and
land.

---

[1] The Education Acts appear in bold type in the table of statutes towards the front of this book.
With the very few exceptions noted where necessary in the text, later Acts are to be construed as
one with the 1944 Act. (As to "construed as one" see Craies on *Statute Law* (7th ed. 1971), p.
138). The principal, 1944, Act was preceded by a White Paper, "Education Reconstruction," published in July 1943 (Cmd. 6458). A concise chronological account of education legislation from the
19th century onwards is contained in Chartered Institute of Public Finance and Accountancy,
"Financial Information Service," *Education*, Vol. 20, Chap. 1.

[2] The exceptions are (a) where the Secretary of State certifies that the exercise and performance of
these powers and duties is unnecessary in the case of a child or young person in Crown service by
reason of arrangements made for their education (1944 Act, s.115. No certificate remains in force;
see A.M. 17/72. (b) where a person is detained by a Court Order or Prison Commissioners' recall
order (but a local education authority have power to make arrangements to provide educational
facilities for him) (1944 Act, s.116 as amended by 1948 Act, s.11 and Sched. I, Pt. 1, and by 1970
Act, s.2 and Sched.).

MINISTERS AND THEIR DEPARTMENTS

1–04   The first government grants to school promoters were made in 1833 by the Treasury. The next landmark in the development[3] of state concern with education was the establishment in 1839, by Order in Council, of the Committee of the Privy Council on Education, consisting of four senior cabinet Ministers, to administer the distribution of grants voted by Parliament for the provision of education for the poor. Grants were paid subject to the conditions attached to them, including standards of building being met, and inspectors of schools were appointed. In 1856 the Committee gave way to an Education Department whose functions grew when elementary education[4] was made compulsory by the Elementary Education Act 1870. In 1900 a Board of Education came nominally into existence, its President in effect the Minister for Education; and, marking in particular the growth of secondary and technical education, the department's powers were further expanded under the Act of 1902. The expansion continued as responsibilities diversified.

1–05   The Act of 1944—still the principal Act—which repealed[5] most pre-existing education legislation formally established a Minister of Education in place of the President, and the shadowy existence of the Board was ended.[6] Twenty years later the functions of the Ministers of Education and of Science were transferred by order[7] to the Secretary of State for Education and Science, and the Ministry of Education was superseded by the Department of Education and Science.[8] It was provided that "Secretary of State"[9] should be substituted for "Minister" in existing statutes and instruments; and to preserve the coherence of

---

[3] See, *e.g.* K. Fenwick and P. McBride, *The Government of Education* (1981); K. Brooksbank *et al.*, *Education Administration* (2nd ed. 1984) P. H. J. H. Gosden, *The Development of Educational Administration in England and Wales* (1966); *The Education System Since* 1944 (1983); H. C. Dent, *Education in England and Wales* (2nd ed. 1982); J. S. Maclure, *Educational Documents: England and Wales 1816 to the present day* (5th ed. 1986); and Chartered Institute of Public Finance and Accountancy, "Financial Information Service" *Education*, Vol. 20, Chap. 20.

[4] Elementary education was the principal part of the education given at an "elementary school" (which is otherwise undefined in 1870 Act, s.3). It corresponds, more or less, to primary education in current terminology (see 1944 Act, ss.8 and 120(1) and below at para. 2–03).

[5] With savings for subsisting subordinate legislation (as to which, see below paras. 1–41 *et seq.*). See 1944 Act, s.121 as amended by 1973 Act, s.1(4) and Sched. 2, Pt. 1; and as to amendment of enactments upon the coming into force of the 1944 Act, *ibid.* s.120 as amended by 1980 Act, s.1(3) and Sched. 1, para. 14 and by the Statute Law (Repeals) Act 1978.

[6] See 1944 Act, s.2, under which property and functions were transferred from Board to Minister and references in subsisting statutes and instruments were to be interpreted accordingly.

[7] The Secretary of State for Education and Science Order 1964 (S.I. 1964 No. 490) made under the Ministers of the Crown (Transfer of Functions) Act 1946 (now repealed and replaced by the Ministers of the Crown Act 1975).

[8] The current organisation of the Department is described at Chartered Institute of Public Finance and Accountancy, "Financial Information Service" *Education*, Vol. 20, Chap. 20, paras. 26–62.

[9] The preamble to S.I. 1964 No. 490 indicates that where "Secretary of State" appears in the Order, reference is intended to the Secretary of State for Education and Science. Where "Secretary of State" appears in subsisting statutes and instruments (and in subsequent Education Acts since they are ordinarily to be construed as one with the 1944 Act) "Secretary of State for Education

sections 1 and 3 explicit reference to the Secretary of State for Education and Science was substituted in those sections, to which attention is now turned.

The Secretary of State for Education and Science

Under section 1(1) of the 1944 Act, as amended: **1–06**

"it shall be the duty[10] of the Secretary of State for Education and Science to promote the education of the people of England and Wales and the progressive development of institutions devoted to that purpose, and to secure the effective execution by local authorities, under his control and direction,[11] of the national policy[12] for providing a varied and comprehensive educational service in every area."

The ringing terms of this opening subsection suggest that it is to be read as an inspirational declaration of intent rather than as an operational provision; but in its time it was significant in indicating that there was indeed to be a national policy (though "state" education has been a misnomer) and that the Minister had a duty to promote it, whereas the pre-existing Board was "charged with mere superintendence."[13] The first fruits of national policy were the provision up to the age of 15 of free secondary education for all; but the inclusion of the word "comprehensive" has nothing to do with its organisation: its customary use as a term of art was ten or more years away.

Though section 1 gave the Secretary of State no specific powers it did **1–07** give notice of his intention to take particular powers to influence the course of educational provision, and these, with his duties, are recorded in the pages that follow according to their subject matter. The very existence of powers may sometimes be as significant as their use, in colouring the decision-making of the providing bodies. Decision-making is

---

and Science" is, therefore, to be understood, but without prejudice, it may be, to the general rule (Interpretation Act 1978, Sched. 1) that "Secretary of State" means any of Her Majesty's Principal Secretaries of State, so that one may act for another (*Harrison* v. *Bush* (1855) 5 E. & B. 344 at 352).

[10] The duty of the Secretary of State under this provision is not directly enforceable in the courts (E.C.S. Wade & A. W. Bradley, *Constitutional and Administrative Law,* (10th ed. 1985), p. 30). To accord with constitutional practice statutes (*e.g.* 1980 Act, s.36) provide that expenses incurred by the Secretary of State in carrying out his functions are to be defrayed out of moneys provided by Parliament. The Statute Law (Repeals) Act 1978 repealed spent provisions in that form (*e.g.* 1944 Act, s.107).

[11] As to the relationship between Secretaries of State and local authorities see the remarks of Lord Diplock in *Secretary of State for Education and Science* v. *Tameside Metropolitan Borough Council* [1977] A.C. 1014 at 1063; K. Fenwick and P. McBride, *The Government of Education* (1981); J. A. G. Griffith, *Central Departments and Local Authorities* (1966); M. Kogan, *Educational Policy-Making* (1975); D. Regan, *Local Government and Education* (1975); W. D. Pile, *The Department of Education and Science* (1979); K. Young (ed.), *National Interests and Local Government* (1983); and S. Ranson, in S. Ranson *et al., Between Centre and Locality* (1985).

[12] The "national policy" is presumably the policy promoted by the Secretary of State for the time being within the context of government policy generally, if only because there seems no means by which it can otherwise be determined. See *R.* v. *Ponting* [1985] Crim.L.R. 318.

[13] Mr. R. A. Butler, President of the Board, 396 H.C. Deb. 209, January 19, 1944, (2nd reading debate on the Bill for the 1944 Act). See also the debate in committee on clause 1 at cols. 1647 *et seq.*

also influenced by circulars, administrative memorandums and other advice, more or less formal,[14] from the Department of Education and Science and other departments. In form, circulars are not legislation and so have as such no binding effect,[15] but they may be used to convey ministerial decisions; and the boundary between executive decision and legislation is not always clear.[16] Even when a circular is advisory in character it may convey more or less directly an indication that the Secretary of State is prepared to use collateral powers to achieve his policy. Circulars and administrative memorandums may be used for diverse purposes, including explaining legislation and obtaining information from local education authorities.

1–08 The second subsection of section 1 provides that the Secretary of State shall for all purposes be a corporation sole: an artificial person having perpetual succession and with the property rights enjoyed by an individual together with the capacity to enter into contracts and to sue and be sued. Civil servants in the Department of Education and Science (as in other departments) are servants not of the Secretary of State but of the Crown, and the Crown is liable for torts committed in the course of employment, though civil servants may be sued personally. A Crown servant who enters into a contract does so as the Crown's agent and proceedings are not taken against him personally for breach.

1–09 The formal acts of corporations are done under seal, and section 3 states that the Secretary of State for Education and Science shall have an official seal[17] which is to be authenticated by his signature or that of a secretary[18] to his department or of any person he authorises for that purpose. The seal is to be "officially and judicially noticed" and every instrument the Secretary of State makes or issues is in legal proceedings to be deemed to be authentically sealed or signed by a secretary or other authorised person unless the contrary is shown. A certificate signed by

---

[14] *e.g.* Building Bulletins, Design Notes, Broadsheets and "Dear C.E.O." letters—all, as it happens, mentioned in A.M. 2/81.

[15] See *Colman (J.J.) Ltd.* v. *Commissioners of Customs and Excise* [1968] 1 W.L.R. 1286 at 1291; and H. W. R. Wade, *Administrative Law* (5th ed. 1982), p. 745. "Any disregard of the requirements of a circular may be evidence, but no more than evidence, that a local education authority is acting unreasonably"—*per* Wolf J. in *R.* v. *Inner London Education Authority, ex p. Bradby*—unreported, but see P. Liell & J. B. Saunders, *The Law of Education* (9th ed. 1984), p. E1. On the other hand, that " . . . ministerial statements of policy and circulars to local authorities may have a practical effect which falls little short of modifying the law" (E. C. S. Wade & A. W. Bradley, *Constitutional and Administrative Law* (10th ed. 1985), p. 625) is borne out by the remarks at May L.J. in *R.* v. *Oxfordshire Education Authority, ex. p. W, The Times*, November 22, 1986.

[16] See *Blackpool Corporation* v. *Locker* [1948] 1 K.B. 349; *Lewisham Borough Council* v. *Roberts* [1949] 2 K.B. 608; *Patchett* v. *Leatham* [1949] 65 T.L.R. 69 and *Acton Borough Council* v. *Morris* [1953] 1 W.L.R. 1228. See also para. 1–42, and H. W. R. Wade, *Administrative Law,* (5th ed. 1982), pp. 745–746.

[17] The Secretary of State for Wales also has a corporate seal—see the Secretary of State for Wales . . . Order 1965 (S.I. 1965 No. 319) art. 8.

[18] "Secretary" is undefined but the provision derives ultimately from the 1870 Act where reference was made in s.85 to "some secretary or assistant secretary." So presumably, it includes all senior administrative civil servants down to the rank of Assistant Secretary (now Grade 5).

the Secretary of State certifying that he did make or issue any instrument is conclusive of that fact.

The Secretary of State's obligation under section 4 to appoint Central **1–10** Advisory Councils[19] for England and for Wales, which he had not discharged for nearly two decades was repealed[20] by the 1986 (No. 2) Act, as was his obligation to make an annual report to Parliament on his duties, and on the composition and proceedings of the Advisory Councils. The Secretary of State continues to take advice both from formal advisory bodies such as the Secondary Examinations Council and informally from a variety of educational interests including the associations of teachers and local authorities; and he is, of course, accountable to Parliament, notably in recent years through the Select Committee on Education, Science and Arts.

The Secretary of State for Wales

From 1907 there existed a Welsh department of the Board of Edu- **1–11** cation with its own permanent secretary and inspectorate. In the years following the Second World War, education in Wales gained a growing autonomy,[21] and following the appointment in 1964 of a Secretary of State for Wales, in 1970 the department[22] in Cardiff became responsible for the administration of functions relating to primary and secondary education, which were transferred[23] to him from the Secretary of State for Education and Science. In 1978 more functions, relating to further education and teachers, were transferred[24] to the Secretary of State for Wales. The allocation of functions between the two Secretaries of State took shape as follows.

In addition to transferring primary and secondary education functions **1–12** in relation to matters affecting only Wales, and making concurrent functions (now withdrawn) relating to educational trusts, the 1970 Order provided for the joint making of regulations relating to primary and secondary education,[25] joint determination of the upper limit of compulsory

---

[19] The Central Advisory Councils acted after the fashion of *ad hoc* committees of inquiry rather than standing advisory bodies.

[20] See the 1986 (No. 2) Act, ss.59 and 60. Reasons are given in "Second Government Response to the Second Report from the Education, Science and Arts Committee" (1981–82) (Cmnd. 8648) p. 11.

[21] See H. C. Dent, *The Education System of England and Wales* (1961), p. 38.

[22] From April 1, 1978, transferred to the Welsh Office and known as the Welsh Office, Education Department.

[23] See the Transfer of Functions (Wales) Order 1970 (S.I. 1970 No. 1536) and Circ. 18/70, (W.O. 108/70). Monmouthshire was treated as part of Wales and it is now incorporated in the Welsh county of Gwent.

[24] See the Transfer of Functions (Wales) (No. 2) Order 1978 (S.I. 1978 No. 274) and Circ. 5/78, (W.O. 47/78).

[25] Also, with the Home Secretary, regulations for the purposes of s.30 of the Child Care Act 1980 (superseding s.21 of the Children Act 1948), (allocation of functions as between local authorities and local education authorities). See S.I. 1951 No. 472 as amended by S.I. 1965 No. 654, art. 4 and Circ. 232.

school age,[26] joint involvement in the composition and administration of the (now defunct) Central Advisory Council for Wales and transfer to the Secretary of State for Wales of functions relating to the registration of independent schools. This last provision apart, the Secretary of State for Education and Science retained functions in relation to the qualifications (including disqualification), training, supply and remuneration and superannuation of teachers and the appointment of Her Majesty's Inspectors (H.M.I.s). The 1978 Order transferred to the Secretary of State for Wales functions in relation to further education and the training and supply of teachers for primary and secondary education in Wales; and the power to make regulations jointly that had been conferred by the 1970 Order was superseded by enabling the Secretary of State for Wales to make regulations regarding primary and secondary education in Wales in his own behalf. He was also empowered to make regulations under section 3(*a*), (*c*) and (*d*) of the 1962 Act,[27] and payments due under the regulations, but not otherwise to exercise functions under that Act. The Secretary of State for Education and Science retained as respects Wales functions relating to the qualifications (including medical fitness), probation, misconduct, remuneration and superannuation of teachers, and the appointment of H.M.I.s.

1–13   Throughout the book references to the Secretary of State must be taken to signify the Secretary of State for Education and Science or the Secretary of State for Wales as is appropriate having regard to the division of functions described; and exceptionally, in context, other Secretaries of State.

Local Education Authorities

1–14   Under the Elementary Education Act 1870, school boards were locally elected to administer elementary education[28] in areas where church school provision was inadequate. By the 1902 Act the boards were superseded by county and county borough councils as local education authorities, whose responsibilities extended to the provision of secondary and further education[29] and the training of teachers. The larger non-county borough and urban district councils were made local education authorities for elementary education. The 1918 Act abolished fees for elementary education and further extended the powers and duties of local education authorities. County and county borough councils

---

[26] Under 1944 Act, s.35. See below at para. 1–81.
[27] See below at paras. 3–67 and 69 (grants to teacher training students and certain mature students). s.3(*d*) has been repealed.
[28] See above at para. 1–04.
[29] 1902 Act, s.2, referred to "education other than elementary."

again had their functions extended under the 1944 Act but most of the more populous non-county borough and urban district councils retained limited powers as "excepted districts," and some county primary and secondary county education functions might be delegated to divisional executives on which members of county district and non-county borough councils within the division might serve.[30] The Local Government Act 1972 brought about a radical change[31] by its abolition of county boroughs and redrawing of county boundaries. Outside the six provincial conurbations county councils remained local education authorities and the councils for the new county districts were not granted any education powers. Divisional administration ended.[32] In the six new metropolitan areas district (metropolitan borough) councils became local education authorities. During their brief existence, 1974–1986, the metropolitan county councils were not concerned[33] with education.

In London, the county council were education authority until super- **1–15** seded in 1965. Then within the area of the former county their successors, the Greater London Council, became the local education authority, acting through an *ad hoc* committee, the Inner London Education Authority.[34] In the remainder of the Greater London Council area, the outer London boroughs became local education authorities,[35] at the expense of the home counties, which lost territory to the Greater London Council. Middlesex ceased to exist as an administrative county.

At present there are 104 local education authorities[36] in England and **1–16** Wales: 39 (shire) county councils in England and eight in Wales; 36 metropolitan district councils within the areas of the former metropolitan county councils; 20 outer London borough councils and the Inner London Education Authority.[37] Additionally, the council of the Isles of Scilly are the local education authority for those islands.[38]

---

[30] 1944 Act, Sched. 1, Pt. III (repealed).

[31] See Circ. 1/73 (W.O. 22/73).

[32] Some counties have appointed area committees under Local Government Act 1972, s.102. Their functions are purely advisory.

[33] But see *Manchester City Council* v. *Greater Manchester Metropolitan County Council* (1980) 78 L.G.R. 560 (H.L.) and below at para. 5–30.

[34] As to the status of the I.L.E.A. before April 1, 1986, see *I.L.E.A.* v. *Secretary of State for the Environment, The Times*, May 26, 1984. Its members were those Greater London councillors who represented inner London boroughs, together with one representative of each inner London borough and of the Common Council of the City of London (as to which see para. 1–31, n. 85).

[35] See London Government Act 1963, s.30(1)(*a*).

[36] See the definitions in 1944 Act, s.114(1) as amended, *ibid.* s.6 (repealed in part) and Local Government Act 1972, s.192. Both the last-mentioned sections contain provisions transitional from the systems of administration they superseded. For the duty of authorities generally to publish information about the discharge of their functions, see Local Government, Planning and Land Act 1980, s.2 as amended.

[37] As to London, see below at paras. 1–28 *et seq.*

[38] 1944 Act, s.118, and the Isles of Scilly (Local Education Authority) Order 1945 (S.R. & O. 1945/360) as amended by the Local Authorities, etc., (Miscellaneous Provisions) Order 1977 (S.I. 1977 No. 293) art. 4(5). 1944 Act, s.88 (appointment of chief education officer) does not apply to the Isles of Scilly.

Committees

1–17   At the heart of local education administration are the education committee of the local education authority and their sub-committees. Every local education authority are to establish an education committee[39] or committees as they think expedient for the efficient discharge of their functions. The arrangements for establishing education committees are subject to the approval[40] of the Secretary of State, who has indicated[41] that so far as they are made at discretion he does not consider it appropriate to approve them. There are, however, certain statutory requirements. Every education committee are to include "persons of experience in education and persons acquainted with the educational conditions prevailing in the area for which the committee acts."[42] The Secretary of State expects a reasonable proportion of persons other than councillors to be appointed[43] and that they should not be representatives as such of particular organisations but be eligible because of their personal experience or knowledge and interest. Among the sources of recruitment are the churches and the teaching profession, who commonly nominate members. It is not, however, mandatory for teachers to be co-opted on to an education committee: it was established in *R.* v. *Croydon London Borough Council, ex p. Leney*[44] that "persons of experience in education" does not exclude those who do not hold a teaching qualification or have not had teaching experience. By the Local Government Act 1972, section 104(2)(*a*), teachers may serve on the education committee of their employing authority, but may not be members of the authority as such.[45]

---

[39] 1944 Act, Sched. 1, Pt. II, para. 1. Membership is not compulsory: a person appointed against his wishes may resign (*R.* v. *Sunderland Corporation* [1911] 2 K.B. 458. As to the power of a council to remove a person once appointed see *Manton* v. *Brighton Corporation* [1951] 2 K.B. 393 and *R.* v. *Newham London Borough Council, ex p. Haggerty, The Times*, April 11, 1986. See Circ. 8/73 (W.O. 86/73).

[40] By the Local Government (I.L.E.A.) Order 1985 (S.I. 1985 No. 1341) the Secretary of State modified s.98(4) of the Local Government Act 1985 so that existing arrangements for I.L.E.A Committees did not continue as approved arrangements after December 31, 1986.

[41] See Circ. 8/73, paras. 5–8. At discretion are, *inter alia*, terms of office of members, frequency of meetings, quorum and filling of casual vacancies. See D. Lanham. "The Quorum in Public Law" [1984] P.L. 461.

[42] 1944 Act, Sched. 1, Pt. II, para. 5. See Circ. 8/73 paras. 12–13.

[43] The power to co-opt is not an "education function" and may not be delegated to the education committee themselves, though they may make recommendations to the local education authority. Co-opted persons are entitled not to attendance allowance but to financial loss and other allowances in relation to attendance at committee meetings and other "approved duties." See Local Government Act 1972, ss.173–178 as amended and *Encyclopedia of Local Government Law*, 1980. If a co-opted member of an education committee becomes an elected member of the same council he must resign as a co-opted member of the committee.

[44] *The Times*, November 27, 1986.

[45] Local Government Act 1972, s.80(1)(*a*) and (3) and see s.81(4)(*a*). I.L.E.A. teachers may no longer serve as members of inner London Borough councils (*ibid.* s.80(6) inserted by Local Government Act 1985, s.84 and Sched. 14, para. 3(2), and s.81(3) having been repealed by Local Government Act 1985, s.102(2) and Sched. 17).

"At least a majority of every education committee of a local edu- **1–18**
cation authority shall be members of the authority."[46] Arrangements
may comply with this requirement by expressing the number of council
members as lying between a given minimum and maximum. There is no
impropriety in the appointment of all members of a council to their education committee. The chairman of the committee must be an elected
council member and elected members must form a majority of members
present and voting at an education committee meeting.

Except in urgent cases "every local education authority shall consider **1–19**
a report from an education committee of the authority before exercising
any of their functions with respect to education."[47] A decision made in
breach of this requirement is *ultra vires*. A report must not only be made
to the local education authority, it must be properly "considered" by
them (*R. v. Brent London Borough Council, ex p. Gunning*[48]). It
"should either make some recommendation or should at least . . . set
out the arguments for and against a particular course of action," *per*
Forbes J. in *R. v. Liverpool City Council, ex p. Professional Association
of Teachers.*[49] And a recommendation alone is inadequate. A report has
to involve an evaluation and "to be an account of issues relevant to making the decision,"—*per* Mann J. in *R. v. Kirklees Metropolitan Borough
Council, ex p. Molloy.*[50]

"A local education authority may authorise an education committee **1–20**
of the authority to exercise[51] on their behalf any of their functions with
respect to education except the power to borrow money or to raise a
rate." Delegation of a function does not prevent the authority from continuing to exercise the function themselves,[52] but they remain under
obligation before doing so to consider a report from the committee; and
should a committee act without express powers of delegation, their

---

[46] 1944 Act, Sched. 1, Pt. II, para. 6 and see Circ. 8/73, paras. 10–11.
[47] *Ibid.* para. 7. "Functions with respect to education" are presumably those substantive functions
that flow from the Education Acts (listed above at pp. xxviii *et seq.*) and include personnel matters
regarding teachers and other education staff (*e.g.* applications to attend courses). Para. 7 applies
to action contemplated by a local education authority under s.111 of the Local Government Act
1972 (see below at para. 1–39) which is incidental to the exercise of an education function. Where
a matter which has been before an education committee is subsequently considered by another
committee of the same council it does not need to be reconsidered by the education committee in
advance of a council decision (unless the education committee expressly sought the other committee's views before reaching a conclusion). As to allocation of child care functions see Local
Authorities and Local Education Authorities (Allocation of Functions) Regulations 1951 (S.I.
1951 No. 472) and Circ. 232.
[48] 84 L.G.R. 168, and see below at para. 1–45.
[49] 82 L.G.R. 648 at 654.
[50] *The Times*, November 5, 1986. The decision was upheld in the Court of Appeal (*The Times*,
August 17, 1987).
[51] 1944 Act, Sched. 1, Pt. II, para. 8. It is not clear whether s.101 of the Local Government Act 1972
supplements this provision so as to enable a local education authority to delegate to an education
committee other than education functions (see note 47 above) or whether the maxim "*expressio
unius exclusio alterius*" applies. It is in any event open to a local education authority to seek without restriction the opinion of their education committee.
[52] *Huth v. Clarke* [1890] 25 Q.B. 391.

1–20

action may, subject to the same obligation, lawfully be ratified by the local education authority.[53]

1–21 "Every education committee . . . may subject to any restrictions imposed by the local education authority or the order of the Secretary of State . . . appoint . . . sub-committees constituted . . . as the committee may determine; and authorise [them] to exercise any of the functions of the committee on their behalf."[54] Delegation to a sub-committee is therefore lawful: delegation to the chairman of the education committee is not.[55] A matter which is referred under statute to another committee of a council, for example a social services committee, does not need to be referred additionally to their education committee or a sub-committee.[56]

1–22 A local government elector[57] for the area may on payment of up to 5 pence, inspect education committee minutes and make a copy or extract.[58] Meetings of education committees and sub-committees (as well as of local education authorities) are open[59] to the public subject to exclusions in specified circumstances. Public notice of meetings must be given and agendas and connected reports made available. A general power of public inspection of minutes and other documents is granted.

Joint committees and boards

1–23 Where the Secretary of State considers it expedient that two or more local education authorities should combine to exercise some, but not all, of their functions he may, after consulting them, by order establish a joint education committee[60] of the authorities to whom specified functions are to be referred. The order may authorise the committee to exercise functions on behalf of the authorities. *Mutatis mutandis* the law in relation to education committees set out above applies and the order may deal, *inter alia*, with the appointment and functions of sub-

---

[53] *Firth* v. *Staines* [1897] 2 Q.B. 70.

[54] 1944 Act, Sched. 1, Pt. II, para. 10. As to the relationship between local education authority committees and sub-committees, see *Young* v. *Cuthbert* [1906] 1 Ch. 451 and *Richardson* v. *Abertillery Urban District Council; Thomas* v. *Abertillery Urban District Council* (1928) 138 L.T. 688.

[55] See *R.* v. *Liverpool City Council, ex p. Professional Association of Teachers* 82 L.G.R. 648 and *R.* v. *Secretary of State for Education and Science, ex p. Birmingham District Council & Another,* 83 L.G.R. 79. There cannot be a "committee of one"; see *R.* v. *Secretary of State for the Environment, ex p. Hillingdon London Borough Council* [1986] 1 W.L.R. 192. As to delegation to officers see below at para. 1–27.

[56] 1944 Act, Sched. 1, Pt. II, para. 11. See also note 54 above.

[57] Defined in 1944 Act, s.114(1) by reference to Local Government Act 1933, s.305 (repealed by Local Government Act 1972—see now *ibid* s.270(1)).

[58] 1944 Act, Sched. 1, Pt. II, para. 9 as amended by Decimal Currency Act 1969, s.10(1). As to the operation and extent of this provision, see the notes to s.228 of the Local Government Act 1972 in *Encyclopedia of Local Government Law* (1980).

[59] Local Government Act 1972, ss.100A–100K inserted by the Local Government (Access to Information) Act 1985.

[60] 1944 Act, Sched. 1, Pt. II, para. 3.

committees. A joint committee may also come into existence by agreement between local education authorities.[61]

Joint committees have been set up to administer polytechnics, colleges of education and other instutions. A special case is the Welsh Joint Education Committee established by order of the Minister of Education in 1948. Their constitution is now contained in the Schedule to the Order Further Varying Order 1974 made by the Secretary of State for Education and Science and the Secretary of State for Wales under section 111 of the 1944 Act. The Committee consist of 116 members: 84 members of county councils (all Welsh county councils being represented) and 32 appointed mainly to represent teachers, the University of Wales, chief education officers and industrial interests, including trade unions. To the Joint Committee are referred in particular, co-ordination of provision of special educational treatment, availability of boarding facilities and schools, provision and co-ordination of provision of further education, co-ordination of provision for recreation and social and physical training, provision of agricultural education, school curriculum with special reference to Welsh language and culture, in-service training and refresher courses, and research. The Order provides for the appointment of a sub-committee to express views on behalf of local education authorities in Wales and an examinations sub-committee to conduct secondary school and further education examinations; and it contains various other administrative provisions. The appointing councils may authorise the W.J.E.C. to exercise on their behalf any of their education functions except the power to borrow money or raise a rate.

The Secretary of State may, by order, constitute a joint board[62] as **1–24** local education authority for the areas of two or more county councils, if it appears to him that its establishment "would tend to diminish expense, or to increase efficiency or would otherwise be of public advantage." A local inquiry is to be held before the Secretary of State constitutes a joint education board unless all the county councils have consented to the order. A joint board consist of members appointed by the county councils affected and are a body corporate with perpetual succession and common seal. The order establishing the joint board, which must be laid before Parliament[63] as soon as may be, settles the mode of appointment and term of office of members and other, mainly administrative, matters.

---

[61] Formerly authorised by 1944 Act, Sched. 1, Pt. II, para. 2 (repealed by Local Government Act 1972, s.272(1) and Sched. 30). Statutory authority now rests on Local Government Act 1972, s.101(5), and see also s.103 (expenses of joint committees) and the Accounts and Audit Regulations 1983 (S.I. 1983 No. 1761) as amended.

[62] See 1944 Act, Sched. 1, Pt. I as amended by Charities Act 1960, s.48(2) and Sched. 7, and by 1980 Act, s.38(6) and Sched. 7. Para. 5 of Sched. 1, Pt. I is anachronistic, and no statutory provision appears to be made for constituting joint boards in relation to other than county areas.

[63] "Laid before Parliament"; see Laying of Documents Before Parliament (Interpretation) Act 1948.

1–25   Joint committees and their sub-committees and joint boards and their
committees and sub-committees are subject to the same access to information requirements as are local education authorities and their
committees and sub-committees.[64]

Chief education officer

1–26   The Local Government Act 1972 relieved local authorities of the obligation to appoint certain named officers, such as clerk and treasurer,
and also withdrew the Secretary of State's power to prohibit the
appointment of a person as chief education officer. The duty placed
upon local education authorities to appoint a fit person to be chief education officer,[65] without prejudice to general obligations[66] regarding the
appointment of officers, was however retained, presumably to ensure
that every authority employed a chief officer with responsibility exclusively for the education service, at a time when some councils, encouraged by the Bains Report,[67] were experimenting with combining the
administration of separate functions in one department. It remains permissible for a local education authority to appoint, for example, a
"director of educational and leisure services" superior in their administrative hierarchy to their chief education officer, but the normal practice
is for the chief education officer to head a separate education department.

1–27   Section 101(2) of the Local Government Act 1972 enables a local
authority committee established under section 101(1) to delegate to an
officer, functions that have been delegated to them. But education committees must be established under Part II of Schedule I to the 1944
Act,[68] and enjoy no such power (*R.* v. *Birmingham City Council, ex p.
National Union of Public Employees*[69]). It is however, open to a local
education authority themselves, upon the recommendation of their education committee, to delegate any function to the chief education officer
(or to any other officer) under section 101(10) of the 1972 Act.

London

1–28   As has been stated above, outer London boroughs are local education
authorities and the Inner London Education Authority (I.L.E.A.), succeeding the Greater London Council, is the local education authority
for inner London. As part of the reorganisation of London government

---

[64] See Local Government Act 1972, s.100E and 100J inserted by Local Government (Access to Information) Act 1985.

[65] 1944 Act, s.88 as repealed in part by Local Government Act 1972, s.272(1) and Sched. 30. Auth-orities are free to describe the chief education officer as they wish: director of education is a usual title.

[66] Local Government Act 1972, s.112 and see below at para. 4–02.

[67] *The New Local Authorities: Management and Structure*, H.M.S.O., 1972.

[68] See above at paras. 1–17 *et seq.* and Circ. 8/73, para. 9.

[69] *The Times*, April 24, 1984, (purported delegation of power to determine contract of service).

in 1965 provision was made in the London Government Act 1963 for further education schemes subsisting under the predecessor authorities to remain in force[70] and for the outer London boroughs to submit[71] a restatement of their schemes to the Minister. Maintained schools were ordinarily transferred[72] to the new local education authority for the area in which they were situated and arrangements for school government and religious education remained in force[73] at least for the time being.

From April 1, 1986, the Inner London Education Area continued to **1–29** consist of Greater London exclusive of the outer London boroughs and the I.L.E.A. became the local education authority for that area.[74] The Authority consists of between 48 and 58 members[75] elected[76] for a period of four years[77] by the local government electors of the Inner London Education Area. The Inner London Education Area is divided[78] into electoral divisions each returning two members at the first, 1986, elections. A separate election is held for each electoral division. The electoral divisions in 1986 were the Parliamentary constituency areas, but they are subject to review by the Local Government Boundary Commission for England to enable the second and subsequent elections to be held on the basis of single member divisions.

The I.L.E.A. is to appoint[79] a chairman and vice-chairman from **1–30** among its members as the first business at its annual meeting.[80] Both may be paid an allowance[81] the Authority thinks reasonable to meet the expenses of office. They remain in office[82] until their successors are appointed unless they resign or become disqualified. If there is a tie in voting for the appointment of a chairman the person presiding is to give a casting vote,[83] in addition to his vote as a member of the authority if he remains a member.

---

[70] s.31(1)(*c*).

[71] s.31(4).

[72] s.31(5) as amended by 1980 Act, s.16(4) and Sched. 3, (6) as amended by Local Government Act 1985, s.102 and Sched. 17, and (7).

[73] s.31(7), repealed in part by 1986 (No. 2) Act, Sched. 6.

[74] Local Government Act 1985, s.18(2) and (3). By *ibid.* s.45 the I.L.E.A. also became responsible for the Horniman and Geffrye Museums. As to committees of the I.L.E.A. see above at paras. 1–17 *et seq.*

[75] See Local Government Act 1985, Sched. 9, para. 2(8).

[76] *Ibid.* s.18(4) and the Representation of the People Act 1983 as amended by 1985 Act, Sched. 9, Pt. I. (Under s.18(5) until the first election the members of the former I.L.E.A. continued in office as the Interim I.L.E.A.—see above at para. 1–15.) As to qualification and disqualification for office see Local Government Act 1972 as amended by Local Government Act 1985, Sched. 14.

[77] *Ibid.* s.19(1) and (2).

[78] *Ibid.* s.19(3)–(5) and Sched. 9, Pt. II of which amends the Local Government Act 1972 and specifies election arrangements.

[79] *Ibid.* s.20(1)–(3).

[80] The holding of an annual meeting is required by Sched. 12 to the Local Government Act 1972 as applied by 1985 Act, Sched. 14, para. 35.

[81] Local Government Act 1985, s.20(4).

[82] *Ibid.* s.20(5)–(7).

[83] *Ibid.* s.20(8) and (9). See H. W. Clarke, "Electing a chairman of a principal council" (1978) L.G.C. p. 1051.

1–31   In each financial year[84] the Authority is to consult inner London borough councils and the Common Council[85] (of the City of London) about its proposals for expenditure[86] in the next financial year and how the expenditure is to be financed. This must be done[87] before it determines its estimates for precept purposes.[88] The Authority must also consult the same councils about its main policy objectives,[89] and if it decides during any financial year to alter any of them it must consult[90] any council likely to be significantly affected. Information reasonably required is to be supplied[91] for the purposes of consultation, which is to be carried out[92] in a manner agreed between the Authority and the councils mentioned or, in default of agreement, as the Secretary of State directs. Regard is to be had[93] to any guidance[94] given by the Secretary of State as to the matters to be regarded as main policy objectives, and generally as to consultation.[95]

1–32   The Secretary of State may before March 31, 1991 review[96] the Authority's exercise of its education functions and by that date is to lay a report on any review before Parliament.

1–33   Part VI[97] of the Local Government Act 1985 is concerned with the consequences for staff of the abolition of the Greater London Council (and metropolitan counties). Greater London Council staff formerly working under the direction of the I.L.E.A. were ordinarily transferred[98] to the employment of the Authority on April 1, 1986 under subsisting contracts of service. Part VIII[99] contains financial provisions. In common with other new ad hoc authorities the I.L.E.A. is financed by precept,[1] subject to limitation of the amount raised for its first three financial years, and it is brought into the rate support grant system[2] and

---

[84] The period of 12 months ending with March 31, in any year. See Local Government Act 1985, s.105(2), and Local Government Act 1972, s.270(1).
[85] Defined in Local Government Act 1972, s.270(1) as applied by Local Government Act 1985, s.105(2).
[86] Local Government Act 1985, s.21(1)(*a*).
[87] *Ibid.* s.21(2).
[88] Under General Rate Act 1967, s.11. Under s.12 it must issue its precept not less than 21 days before the start of the financial year. As to precepts see below at para. 1–33.
[89] Local Government Act 1985, s.21(1)(*b*).
[90] *Ibid.* s.21(3).
[91] *Ibid.* s.21(5).
[92] *Ibid.* s.21(4).
[93] For the significance of this expression see below at para. 1–46.
[94] Local Government Act 1985, s.21(5).
[95] As to consultation regarding schools, under *ibid.* s.21(6), see below at para. 2–14 n. 58.
[96] *Ibid.* s.22.
[97] *Ibid.* ss.50–56.
[98] *Ibid.* s.52.
[99] *Ibid.* ss.68–83. s.83 is concerned with the London rate equalisation scheme.
[1] *Ibid.* s.68 and see below at para. 1–121. The I.L.E.A. precepts on the rating authorities in the Inner London Education Area: the inner London borough councils, the Common Council of the City of London, the Sub-Treasurer of the Inner Temple and the Under-Treasurer of the Middle Temple.
[2] *Ibid.* s.69 and see below at paras. 1–122 *et seq.*

made eligible for block grant. The provisions regarding borrowing, lending and funds[3] which apply to local government generally are extended to the new authorities, as are those relating to accounts, audit[4] and the proper administration of financial affairs,[5] for which one of the Authority's officers is to have responsibility.

The content of Part IX of the Local Government Act 1985 is miscel- **1–34** laneous and supplementary. It applies[6] to the new authorities provisions of the Local Government Act 1972 relating, *inter alia,* to members and proceedings and discharge of functions, application of capital money, allowances to members, legal proceedings, documents and notices and the making of by-laws; and other statutory provisions are amended so as to apply them to the new authorities. In particular the I.L.E.A. is given power to provide entertainments[7] for the benefit of persons under 26 years of age. The exercise[8] of the functions of the new authorities during the first three years is subject, as provided, to intervention by the Secretary of State.

Other provisions in Part IX include the vesting[9] in the I.L.E.A. of **1–35** charity property formerly held by the Greater London Council, where the I.L.E.A. were formerly the charity trustees, upon the same trusts; and the Secretary of State was empowered[10] to transfer property, rights or liabilities generally to the I.L.E.A.

Representative bodies

To represent the interests of local authorities to central departments **1–36** there exist voluntary associations of local authorities. It does not reflect on their significance in the working of the local government system that they have no formal place in the legal framework except to the extent that local authorities are empowered[11] to pay reasonable subscriptions to them, allowances are payable for attendance at their meetings and conferences[12] and they are among the representative organisations to which reference is sometimes made in statute.[13] Local education authorities are represented by the Association of County Councils, the

---

[3] Local Government Act 1985, s.70, applying with amendments Local Government Act 1972, Sched. 13, para. 22.
[4] *Ibid.* s.72.
[5] *Ibid.* s.73.
[6] *Ibid.* s.84 and Sched. 14, Pts. I and II.
[7] *Ibid.* Sched. 14, para. 16, applying Local Government Act 1972, s.145 (in which the entertainments are specified).
[8] *Ibid.* s.85.
[9] *Ibid.* s.90(1).
[10] *Ibid.* s.100.
[11] By Local Government Act 1972, s.143.
[12] See *ibid.* s.175 as amended. As to conferences organised by local education authorities see below at para. 5–41.
[13] See, *e.g.* Education (No. 2) Act 1986, s.29(2) and *R.* v. *Secretary of State for Social Services, ex p. Association of Metropolitan Authorities* [1986] 1 W.L.R. 1 (as to which see below at para. 1–45 n. 32.

Association of Metropolitan Authorities and the Council of Local Education Authorities, a body jointly established by the two associations in 1974 and consisting of representatives of those associations.

1–37   The councillors who serve on those bodies[14] and their education committees attempt to formulate opinion on behalf of local education authorities, to urge their views upon the Secretary of State and his officers, and to persuade central government to moderate its proposals so as to make them, or at least the manner of their implementation, so far as possible acceptable to local education authorities. The standing of the associations is such that they can expect to be represented on, or to be invited to nominate representatives for appointment to, advisory committees and committees of inquiry established by government, and to be consulted on departmental circulars, etc., before they are issued.

1–38   The division of functions between the two local authority associations and C.L.E.A. has never been clearly drawn and C.L.E.A. has no formal constitution. The negotiation of teachers' conditions of service[15] has been a major function of C.L.E.A., while general policy issues and parliamentary, financial and politically sensitive matters have largely been retained for consideration by the two associations. But this generalisation has only to be stated for its weakness to be apparent at a time when the content of the teachers' contract of service has been a live issue[16]; and relatively non-contentious financial matters, for instance, the formulation of advice on further education tuition fees,[17] have been dealt with by C.L.E.A. rather than by the associations.

LAW AND ADMINISTRATION

1–39   The British constitution, whatever that may be, is grounded in the rule of law, and this, though also ill-defined, certainly includes the proposition that ministers and public authorities enjoy only those powers that are granted them by statute or, exceptionally, by the royal prerogative.[18] The functions of local education authorities are statutory and specific, but the rigours of the *ultra vires* doctrine[19] are tempered by two provisions in the Local Government Act 1972. By section 111 there is a

---

[14] The Welsh Joint Education Committee (see above at para. 1–23) has some of the characteristics of an association and may be drawn into the processes of consultation. The Committee were represented on the Burnham Committees (see below at para. 4–113).

[15] But not including remuneration and pensions. See below at paras. 4–20 and 4–98 to 4–99.

[16] See below at paras. 4–50 *et seq.*

[17] See below at para. 3–13.

[18] Prima facie an uncontentious statement but see *Malone* v. *Metropolitan Police Commissioners* [1979] Ch. 344 (telephone tapping authorised by Minister).

[19] A notable early exemplification of the *ultra vires* doctrine in the field of education was *R.* v. *Cockerton, ex p. Hamilton* [1901] 1 K.B. 726.

power "to do any thing . . . which is calculated to facilitate, or is conducive or incidental to, the discharge of any of their functions"; and by section 137 "a local authority may . . . incur expenditure which is in the interests of their area or any part of it or all or some of its inhabitants . . . ," where they are not otherwise empowered to incur it, up to the product of a 2 pence rate. The conditions and qualifications attached to these two provisions[20] moderate their use by authorities seeking to rely on them in the absence of other, more explicit, statutory recourse.

This section explains how statute gives latitude to the Secretary of **1–40** State by enabling him to make subordinate legislation, and how the courts constrain both him and local education authorities and grant rights of redress against them. It is also concerned with the role of ombudsmen—the guardians of the administrative process—because to the obligation to act *intra vires* has in recent years been added another, unenforceable in the courts—not to be guilty of maladministration.

Subordinate legislation

As will become apparent, subordinate legislation made by the Sec- **1–41** retary of State and therefore readily amendable, generously supplements the Education Acts. Regulations[21] are to be laid before Parliament[22] as soon as may be after they are made. Most are subject to the negative resolution procedure[23]—they cease to have effect if either House resolves that they be annulled, but without prejudice to anything done under them or to new regulations being introduced. Regulations are statutory instruments,[24] as, with the exceptions noted below, are orders and rules also made under the statutory authority of Education and other Acts.

There are a number of provisions in the Education Acts which give **1–42** power to the Secretary of State and to local education authorities to make orders[25] or give directions that are mostly of local or personal effect and (like by-laws—another form of subordinate legislation) are not statutory instruments. Sometimes the power is exercisable only in specified circumstances or subject to conditions. These orders and

---

[20] s.111 cannot be used to extend the scope of a function, but only to support its exercise. (See *R. v. Oxfordshire Education Authorities, ex p. W, The Times*, November 22, 1986). s.137 has been heavily amended by subsequent local government legislation.
[21] See 1944 Act, s.112. Similar provision is made in other Education Acts, *e.g.* 1981 Act, s.19 under which regulations may make different provision for Wales and for different cases or circumstances, and may contain incidental, supplementary or transitional provisions. Sometimes regulations must be laid in draft; see, *e.g.* 1980 Act, s.35(2) below at 6–36 n. 41.
[22] See above at para. 1–24 n. 63.
[23] An example where the affirmative procedure is required are those made under 1980 Act, s.17(6) in relation to the assisted places scheme (see below at para. 6–37).
[24] See Statutory Instruments Act 1946, s.1.
[25] As to service of orders and other documents see 1944 Act, s.113 as amended by 1946 Act, s.14 and Sched. II, Pt. I.

directions may be varied or revoked by a further[26] order or direction subject to the same requirements that applied to the making of the original instrument. It is not clear whether such instruments are to be regarded as legislative or administrative.[27]

1–43   Regulations and other instruments in force under legislation repealed by the 1944 Act continued in force[28] until revoked, and, generally, where a repealed Act is in effect replaced by new legislation, statutory instruments under the repealed Act continue[29] in force if they could have been made under the new Act; otherwise they lapse, ordinarily without prejudice[30] to action already taken under them.

Constraints on administration

1–44   The Education and other Acts contain characteristic forms of words which condition the exercise of functions by the Secretary of State and local education authorities or confer an explicit discretion whether to perform them. Where those formulations appear in these pages the reader should refer to the following paragraphs for a brief account[31] of how the courts have construed them.

1–45   Statute may require consultation[32] with representative bodies before the Secretary of State makes subordinate legislation or takes administrative action, or he may be obliged (as may a local education authority) to give persons affected the right to object or the opportunity of making representations in advance. Requirements of this kind may be held by the courts to be mandatory and if so must be honoured in substance: failure to comply with them may render the decision procedurally[33] *ultra vires* with the consequence that it may be quashed. Unless adequate and accurate information is provided as a basis for consultation or for making objections or representations, and sufficient notice given of what is

---

[26] 1944 Act, s.111. See *Lee and Others* v. *Department of Education and Science* 66 L.G.R. 211.

[27] See H. W. R. Wade, *Administrative Law* (5th ed. 1982), p. 734.

[28] 1944 Act, s.121 proviso (*a*).

[29] Interpretation Act 1978, s.17.

[30] Interpretation Act 1978, s.16.

[31] For fuller treatment see, *e.g.* Wade, *Administrative Law* (5th ed. 1982).

[32] See *e.g. Bradbury* v. *Enfield London Borough Council* [1967] 1 W.L.R. 1311 (failure of council to give notice of proposal to cease to maintain school—below at para. 2–31); *Lee and Others* v. *Department of Education and Science* 66 L.G.R. 211 (failure of Secretary of State to give more than four days for representations on orders amending articles of government—below at para. 2–72 n. 40). *Legg & Others* v. *I.L.E.A.* [1972] 1 W.L.R. 1245 (I.L.E.A. gave inadequate particulars of proposals for school closure, so Secretary of State's approval invalid—see below at para. 2–14 n. 60); *Coney* v. *Choyce and Others* [1975] 1 W.L.R. 422 (minor failure to comply with requirements about notice to be given of proposals to reorganise schools did not invalidate proposals: requirements were not mandatory but directory—see below at para. 2–14 n. 59); and *R.* v. *Secretary of State for Social Services, ex p. Association of Metropolitan Authorities* [1986] 1 W.L.R. 1 (failure to give representative body adequate time to consider proposed amendments to regulations: the court exercised its discretion and the amended regulations were not revoked).

[33] See below at para. 1–53.

proposed and time allowed for consideration, the terms of the statute will not be satisfied. " . . . any right to be consulted . . . should be implemented by giving those who have the right an opportunity to be heard at the formative stage of proposals—before the mind of the executive becomes unduly fixed"—*per* Sachs L.J. in *Sinfield and Others v. London Transport Executive*[34]; and according to Hodgson, J. in *R. v. Brent London Borough Council, ex p. Gunning and Others*[35] parents of school children whose schools are threatened with closure or amalgamation "have a legitimate expectation to be consulted in advance," and accordingly "they have the same legal right to consultation as they would have if it had been given to them specifically by statute."[36]

A local education authority may be required to "have regard to," for **1–46** example, guidance given by the Secretary of State.[37] In *Ishak v. Thowfeek*[38] it was held that a duty to have regard was not a duty to comply. Matters for which regard is to be had must be taken into account, considered and given due weight but an ultimate discretion remains.

There are various words and expressions associated with the exercise **1–47** of discretion, for example "may," "have power to," "consider necessary," "are satisfied," "is of the opinion," "thinks fit," "if it appears to." Although the use of subjective language might seem to convey an unfettered discretion the courts have shown that it is limited. "May" generally confers an unqualified discretion but a power becomes a duty[39] if prescribed circumstances come into existence or if failure to exercise a discretion would frustrate a statutory provision. In recent years the courts have been unwilling[40] to regard the other terms exemplified as granting an unqualified discretion, and are ready to question whether the Secretary of State or local education authority could reasonably have been "satisfied"[41] (or as the case may be) as well as to investigate whether the action—or inaction—complained of was taken on proper grounds and in good faith.

---

[34] [1970] Ch. 550 at 558.
[35] 84 L.G.R. 168 at 187, and see C. Grace and S. Morgan, "Legal lessons from Brent's school defeat" (1986) L.G.C. p. 450.
[36] This conclusion was doubted by Webster J. in *R. v. London Borough of Sutton, ex p. Hamlet* (unreported but see P. Liell and J. B. Saunders, *The Law of Education* (9th ed. 1984), F7). See also, as to expectation of consultation, *Council of Civil Service Unions v. Minister for the Civil Service* [1985] A.C. 374.
[37] See Local Government Act 1985, s.21(5).
[38] [1968] 1 W.L.R. 1718 at 1725.
[39] See *Julius v. Bishop of Oxford* (1880) 5 App.Cas. 214 at 225, S. A. de Smith, *Judicial Review of Administrative Action* (4th ed. 1980), at pp. 283–285 and H. W. R. Wade, *Administrative Law* (5th ed. 1982), at pp. 228–231.
[40] See S. A. de Smith, *Judicial Review of Administrative Action* (4th ed. 1980), pp. 362–364, and H. W. R. Wade, *Administrative Law* (5th ed. 1982), pp. 393–400.
[41] See *Secretary of State for Education and Science v. Metropolitan Borough of Tameside* (below at para. 6–11) and *R. v. Secretary of State for Education and Science, ex p. Chance* (below at para. 6–16).

Redress: courts and tribunals

1–48   Proceedings for breach of contract and in tort may be brought against the Secretary of State and against local education authorities; legislation specifies rights of appeal by parents and others from their decisions; and as public authorities their actions may be subject to judicial review.

1–49   There are express provisions in the Education Acts for redress[42] and for settlement out of court of questions,[43] in particular disputes between local education authorities and between a local education authority and governors; and the courts may require[44] powers so conferred to be used. The general rule[45] is that express provision, together with the powers granted to the Secretary of State when an authority are alleged to have acted unreasonably[46] or are in default,[47] exclude application to the courts. But there may be a right of appeal to the High Court from a tribunal on a point of law[48]; and where a person suffers special damage as a result of a failure by a public authority to carry out their duty, and there is no special statutory remedy or it is inadequate, he may apply to the courts for a remedy.[49]

1–50   Circumstances may exist when in the absence[50] of an alternative remedy redress may be sought by application for judicial review. There is no room here[51] to attempt to define the scope of the *ultra vires* doctrine or discuss the remedies[52] the courts may grant on finding an administrative act or decision *ultra vires* or in breach of the rules of natural justice, but reference is made below and elsewhere[53] to decisions concerning the Secretary of State and local education authorities. Whether or not

---

[42] *e.g.* regarding admissions to schools (see below at para. 2–178) and conduct of independent schools (see below at para. 6–32).

[43] See 1944 Act, s.67 as amended, 1968 (No. 2) Act, s.3(3)(*a*) and below at para. 6–08.

[44] See *Board of Education* v. *Rice* [1911] A.C. 179.

[45] See de Smith *op. cit.* pp. 531–532 and H. W. R. Wade *op. cit.* pp. 626–629.

[46] See 1944 Act, s.68 below at paras. 6–10 *et seq.* and the cases there cited.

[47] See s.99 below at para. 6–15 and the cases cited at 6–17 n. 62.

[48] *e.g.* from an independent schools tribunal—see below at para. 6–32.

[49] See *Gateshead Union* v. *Durham County Council* [1918] 1 Ch. 146. *Thornton* v. *Kirklees Metropolitan Borough Council* [1979] 2 All E.R. 349, *Meade* v. *Haringey London Borough Council* [1979] 1 W.L.R. 637 (C.A.) below at para. 2–11, and the cases cited at n. 32 above and below at paras. 7–39 *et seq.* (breach of statutory duty).

[50] In *R.* v. *Secretary of State for Education and Science, ex p. Talmud Torah Machzikei Hadass School Trust, The Times,* April 12, 1985, judicial review was refused because there was no clear error of law or approach: an independent schools tribunal was better equipped to make findings of fact and degree.

[51] See. *e.g.* de Smith and H. W. R. Wade *op. cit.* and as to the general obligations of public authorities in judicial review cases the remarks of Sir John Donaldson M.R. in *R.* v. *Lancashire County Council, ex p. Huddleston* [1986] 2 All E.R. 941 at 945.

[52] The prerogative orders of *mandamus*, requiring an authority to act where they are under a duty to do so, prohibition, forbidding a prospective excess of jurisdiction; and *certiorari* rendering a decision invalid. The other remedies are a declaration that an authority's conduct is unsupported by law and an injunction ordering an authority to refrain from acting *ultra vires*.

[53] See, *e.g. R.* v. *Secretary of State for Education and Science, ex p. Inner London Education Authority* (action for a declaration), below at para. 1–133 n. 27. *R.* v. *Hampshire County Council, ex p. Martin* (*certiorari*) below at para. 3–73 n. 21. *R.* v. *Burnham Primary and Secondary Committee, ex p. Professional Association of Teachers,* below at para. 4–113 n. 55 and *R.* v. *Liverpool City Council, ex p. Coade and Another,* below at para. 4–134 n. 3.

jurisdiction is accepted or a remedy granted is always at the discretion of the court.

In *R.* v. *Liverpool City Council, ex p. Ferguson and Others*; *Same* v. **1–51** *Same, ex p. Grantham and Others*[54] the court granted declarations to the applicants, and to the National Union of Teachers and the National Association of Head Teachers, that the decision of the council to issue notices dismissing all primary, secondary and special school teachers was unlawful. The notices were void, because the decision was the direct consequence of fixing an illegal rate, was not taken for educational purposes and its consequences would be a breach of statutory duty under section 8 of the 1944 Act. A decision by the same council (*R.* v. *Liverpool City Council, ex p. Ferguson and Ferguson*[55]) to pay on a "day of action," only those teachers who actually worked, to the exclusion of those who reported for work but found their school was closed, was also found to be *ultra vires,* and made the subject of an order of *certiorari* and a declaration that all teachers who were ready, willing and able to work on the day should be paid.

In *R.* v. *Inner London Education Authority, ex p. Westminster City* **1–52** *Council*[56] the court found that the I.L.E.A. had exceeded their powers under section 142 of the Local Government Act 1972 when they had retained an advertising agency to conduct a campaign to inform the public of the effect of rate capping[57] and to persuade them to adopt the view of the I.L.E.A. regarding that practice. Section 142,[58] it was held, authorised the giving of information but not persuasion.

As mentioned above procedural error[59] may also give rise to success- **1–53** ful application to the courts.

The rules of natural justice are *nemo judex in sua causa* (a man may **1–54** not be judge in his own cause) and *audi alteram partem* (he must be fairly heard in his own defence and know what is alleged against him). " . . . persons acting in a capacity which is not on the face of it judicial but rather executive or administrative have been held by the courts to be subject to the principles of natural justice."[60] "Natural justice" may

---

[54] *The Times*, November 20, 1985. *Ferguson and Another* v. *Liverpool City Council, The Times*, July 22, 1985, established the *locus standi* of the branch secretary of the Liverpool division of the N.U.T.; and see also *R.* v. *Liverpool City Council, ex p. Ferguson and Ferguson* [1985] I.R.L.R. 501.
[55] [1985] I.R.L.R. 501.
[56] *The Times*, December 31, 1984.
[57] See below at para. 1–121.
[58] See now Local Government Act 1986, Pt. II.
[59] See above at para. 1–45. See *R.* v. *Birmingham City Council, ex p. National Union of Public Employees and Another, The Times*, April 24, 1984, and above at para. 1–27; *R.* v. *Secretary of State for Education and Science, ex p. Birmingham District Council and Another, The Times*, July 18, 1984, and above para. 1–21 n. 55; and *R.* v. *Secretary of State for Education and Science, ex p. Chance* (see below at para. 6–16). See also *Lewis* v. *Dyfed County Council,* 77 L.G.R. 339 where a procedural defect was condoned (below at para. 4–114 n. 56). As to whether a procedural requirement is mandatory or discretionary see de Smith *Judicial Review of Administrative Action* (4th ed. 1980), p. 142 and H. W. R. Wade, *Administrative Law* (5th ed. 1982), pp. 218–9.
[60] Lord Hodson in *Ridge* v. *Baldwin* [1964] A.C. 40 at 130.

arouse in the layman's mind misleading notions of equity and natural law, and it has been stated alternatively in relation to administrative functions that when the rights or interests of individuals are at risk authorities are under obligation to "act fairly." This formulation enjoys the advantage of suggesting, correctly, that while the rules must be applied in substance adherence to judicial forms is not as such part of the obligation. But it is by no means always clear when the rules, or the duty to act fairly, apply.[61]

1–55   In *Central Council for Education and Training in Social Work* v. *Edwards and Others*[62] it was held that an educational institution, in considering an application for admission as a student, did not have to give an oral hearing or reasons for the decision; but the court claimed jurisdiction to review the process by which the application had been refused because the polytechnic concerned was a publicly funded educational establishment, the applicant's career would be seriously affected by the decision not to admit him, and details of the proper procedure had been published and a copy given to the applicant. On the facts of the case the treatment of the applicant had been unfair and his rejection had been invalid; so the court directed that the application be properly considered.

1–56   Fair treatment (again not necessarily including an oral hearing) is also obligatory in the case of a decision to expel a student for unsatisfactory work[63] or for misconduct,[64] but the courts will not investigate the conduct of an examination.[65] There is no breach of the rules of natural justice where an education officer acts as complainant before a disciplinary tribunal concerned with proceedings against teachers,[66] but it is undesirable for a clerk to a tribunal to retire with the tribunal if he is closely connected with the complainant as a member of his staff.

1–57   The duty to "act fairly" may extend beyond compliance with the rules of natural justice to require consistency of treatment of persons in similar circumstances and the proper exercise of discretion,[67] but it is not to

---

[61] A breach of the rules was established in *R.* v. *Department of Education and Science, ex p. Kumar* (below at para. 4–19 n. 58) and in *R.* v. *Brent London Borough Council, ex p. Assegai* (below at para. 2–78 n. 56) but not in *Haddow and Others* v. *I.L.E.A.* [1979] I.C.R. 202, *R.* v. *Secretary of State for Wales and Clwyd County Council, ex p. Russell* or in *R.* v. *Gwent County Council, ex p. Perry* (both unreported, but see P. Liell and J. B. Saunders, *The Law of Education* (3rd ed. 1984), F 80 and F 192 respectively). See also *R.* v. *Bradford Metropolitan Council, ex p. Professional Association of Teachers, The Independent*, December 16, 1986, and generally, de Smith, *op. cit.* pp. 175 *et seq.* and 276 *et seq.* H. W. R. Wade, *op. cit.* Chaps. 14 and 15 and P. Jackson, *Natural Justice* (2nd ed. 1979).
[62] *The Times*, May 5, 1978.
[63] *Brighton Corporation* v. *Parry* 70 L.G.R. 576 and *Herring* v. *Templeman* [1973] 3 All E.R. 569 (C.A.).
[64] *Ward* v. *Bradford Corporation*, 70 L.G.R. 27.
[65] *Thorne* v. *University of London* [1966] 2 Q.B. 237.
[66] *Ellis and Others* v. *I.L.E.A.*, 75 L.G.R. 382.
[67] See *H.T.V. Ltd.* v. *Price Commission* [1976] I.C.R. 170 and *R.* v. *Hertfordshire County Council, ex p. Cheung & R.* v. *Sefton Metropolitan Borough Council, ex p. Pau, The Times*, April 4, 1986, (below at para. 3–74), and, as to discretion, *R.* v. *West Glamorgan County Council, ex p. Gheissary, The Times*, December 18, 1985 (below at para. 3–74 n. 25).

be regarded as giving *carte blanche* to a complainant as a basis for proceedings.

Redress: ombudsmen

The Department of Education and Science is among the departments **1–58** and authorities subject to investigation by the Parliamentary Commissioner for Administration.[68] Local education authorities and school admission appeal committees[69] are within the jurisdiction of the Local Commissioners for Administration.[70] Commissioners are by usage referred to as "ombudsmen." Their task is to investigate written complaints of injustice sustained in consequence of maladministration,[71] which is undefined in legislation but taken to include "bias, neglect, inattention, delay, incompetence, ineptitude, perversity, turpitude, arbitrariness and so on."[72] Investigation of instruction in maintained schools and further education establishments, and conduct, curriculum, internal organisation, management and discipline are outside the jurisdiction of the local ombudsmen.[73] Their role is thus a limited one. Ombudsmen have discretion whether or not to pursue a complaint.[74] They may not question the merits of a decision taken without maladministration.[75]

Complaints to the parliamentary ombudsman about maladminis- **1–59** tration by the Department of Education and Science must be raised through a member of Parliament.[76] A complaint may be investigated by a local ombudsman only after the local authority concerned have had an opportunity to investigate and reply,[77] and must be raised through a local councillor, but if he fails to refer it may be made direct by the complainant.[78] When a complaint is made direct to a local ombudsman without a prior request to a councillor it is the practice of local ombudsmen in England to refer it to the civic head of the authority (notifying the chief executive), with a request to settle it locally or refer it to the local ombudsman if local settlement proves impossible. A similar, but not identical, procedure is followed in Wales. When the complainant has a

---

[68] Parliamentary Commissioner Act 1967, s.4 and Sched. 2. See *e.g.* H. W. R. Wade *Administrative Law* (5th ed. 1982), pp. 73 *et seq.*
[69] In respect of county and controlled schools only.
[70] Local Government Act 1974, s.25 as amended in particular by 1980 Act, s.7(7), as to which see Circ. 1/81, para. 26. England is divided into three areas for each of which there is a Local Commissioner. There is one Local Commissioner for Wales. See H. W. R. Wade, *op. cit.* pp. 123 *et seq.*
[71] 1967 Act, s.5(1)(*a*); 1974 Act, s.26(1).
[72] See 734 H.C. Deb. 51 (the "Crossman Catalogue") and *R.* v. *Local Commissioner for Administration for the North and East Area of England, ex p. Bradford Metropolitan City Council* [1979] Q.B. 287.
[73] 1974 Act, s.26(8) and Sched. 5, para. 5 (as amended by 1986 (No. 2) Act, Sched. 4, para. 5).
[74] 1967 Act, s.5(5); 1974 Act, s.26(10).
[75] 1967 Act, s.12(3); 1974 Act, s.34(3).
[76] 1967 Act, s.5(1).
[77] 1974 Act, s.26(5).
[78] *Ibid.* s.26(2) and (3).

right of appeal to a Minister or tribunal, or may apply for a remedy to a court, ombudsmen will not act[79] unless "satisfied that in the particular circumstances it is not reasonable to expect the person aggrieved"[80] to resort to any of those sources. Complaints may not be raised by public authorities or bodies.[81] When, after investigation, an ombudsman upholds a complaint there is no formal requirement for the department or local education authority to provide a remedy, but it is exceptional for one to be withheld, even though it may on occasion amount to no more than an apology. The activities of ombudsmen are hedged by elab-orate procedural provisions to which reference cannot be made here.

1–60 The role of the Department of Education and Science has been largely regulatory and appellate. Its contact with the public is limited, and it is not surprising, therefore, that by comparison with some other departments the Department of Education and Science receives little attention from the parliamentary ombudsman, whose annual reports for the years 1983, 1984 and 1985 together record only three complaints upheld and one further instance in which its administration was criticised. Over the same three years 43 complaints were rejected by the parliamentary ombudsman, or his investigations were discontinued, mostly[82] because the complaint was not properly referred or was not about administration, or because it concerned personnel matters, which are specifically excluded[83] from the jurisdiction of both parliamentary and local ombudsmen.

1–61 The following are some of the few selected cases published by the parliamentary ombudsmen in recent years[84] that have concerned the Department of Education and Science. An allegation that maladministration by the Department had contributed to an applicant's failing to secure a mandatory award for a university place from a local education authority was not upheld.[85] The Department was found to have reviewed the evidence in full and without bias and to have taken a consistent view. A complaint concerning the closure of rural schools was found not to disclose inconsistency of treatment by the Department or other maladministration.[86] The Department was, however, found guilty of delay, confusion and replying inadequately to a letter on a complaint about the administrative arrangements made to compensate parents with children in full time advanced education for the loss of child tax allowances[87]; and maladministration was also found by way of delay in

---

[79] 1967 Act, s.5(2); 1974 Act, s.26(6).
[80] "Person aggrieved"—defined in 1967 Act, s.12 and 1974 Act, s.34(1) as extended by s.26(11).
[81] 1967 Act, s.6(1); 1974 Act, s.27(1).
[82] Under 1967 Act, s.5(1).
[83] *Ibid.* s.5(3) and Sched. 3, para. 10; 1974 Act, s.26(9) and Sched. 5, para. 4.
[84] But see the earlier reports summarised in G. Marshall "Technique of Maladministration" (1975) 23 Pol. Studies pp. 307–8.
[85] H.C. 1979–80 693—C 451/79.
[86] H.C. 1980–81 250—C 697/80.
[87] H.C. 1981–82 132—C 120/81.

fulfilling an undertaking given to consider amending a clause in the instrument of management of a voluntary controlled school.[88]

Failure on the part of the Secretary of State to give directions to local   **1–62**
education authorities under section 68[89] of the 1944 Act on complaints by parents regarding allocation of children to schools has given rise to subsequent complaints to the parliamentary ombudsman,[90] and these have drawn attention to the thinness of the Secretary of State's powers under that section as well as occasionally to maladministration. Fewer such complaints may be expected now that new procedures and appellate provisions[91] have been introduced by the 1980 Act and recourse may be had to the local ombudsman.[92]

The first case reported[93] by an English local ombudsman following the   **1–63**
establishment of the Commission in 1974 was indeed concerned with the allocation of a pupil to a secondary school, and in the year ending March 31, 1983, 42 out of 155 complaints about education properly referred to the local ombudsmen were against appeal committees established under the 1980 Act; in 1983/84, 49 out of 170 and in 1984/85, 84 out of 221. In 1985/86, education complaints fell to 176.[94] Maladministration by local education authorities has taken so many different forms that it is impossible to select typical examples,[95] but it has included delay; failure to take all material facts into account; improper, mistaken and inconsistent procedure; misinforming and misleading parents and others; and failure to give reasons for decisions.

Eighteen of the 310 reports by the local ombudsmen for England in 1985/86 concerned education, and maladministration, mostly accompanied by injustice, was found in 13 of them. Comparatively few of the complaints considered by local ombudsmen, it should be added, become the subject of a formal investigation report: in 1985/86, 310 out of 3,134. Investigations are not pursued because complaints are outside jurisdiction, plainly contain no element of maladministration or (an increasing number) are settled locally; or they are terminated, mostly for the last two reasons,[96] following comments received from the authorities concerned.

---

[88] H.C. 1983–84 190—C 118/83. "Voluntary Controlled School"—see below at para. 2–02.
[89] See below at para. 6–10 and D. Foulkes, "Tameside and the Education Act 1944" 126 New L.J. 649.
[90] See report from the Select Committee on the Parliamentary Commissioner for Administration H.C. 1972–73 379 paras. 39–41 and Government Observations, Cmnd. 5527; and H.C. 1982–83 312—C 90/82.
[91] See below at paras. 2–178 *et seq.*
[92] See P. Meredith "Executive Discretion and Choice of Secondary School" 1981 P.L. 52 at 80, and D. Bull, "Monitoring Education Appeals" (1985) J.S.W.L. 189.
[93] Commission for Local Administration in England, Report for the Year ended March 31, 1975.
[94] Commission for Local Administration in England, Reports for years ended March 31, 1984, 1985 and 1986. See also below para. 2–185.
[95] See the annual reports of the Commission for Local Administration in England (Welsh examples would be similar).
[96] By exercise of discretion under 1974 Act, s.26(10).

1-64   The local ombudsman for Wales has received relatively few complaints concerning education: only six in both 1984/85 and 1985/86. Of the 12, two were settled satisfactorily and the remainder were not investigated for various reasons.

GENERAL PRINCIPLES

1-65   The powers and duties of those concerned in the provision of education are exercised in accordance with general principles mostly laid down in the Education Acts and other statutes. As will appear these principles may be indicative of the objects to which specific legislative provisions are addressed; or they may underlie or constrain the methods by which the objects are to be achieved. This section both identifies general principles and explains how some of them are carried into practice. It does not purport to be comprehensive. Other general principles, for example the degree of autonomy enjoyed by schools and teachers, will be seen to emerge from specific provisions in the Education Acts—or even from their absence.

Stages and purposes of the statutory system

1-66   Section 7 of the 1944 Act prescribes that "the statutory system of public education shall be organised in three progressive stages to be known as primary education, secondary education[97] and further education. . . . "[98] These requirements have been moderated to the extent that middle schools[99] have been established straddling the primary and secondary stages; and, as is contemplated in the following section of the Act, education for senior pupils[1] may be provided as part of further education.

1-67   By the second limb of the section:

> "it shall be the duty of the local education authority for every area, so far as their powers extend, to contribute towards the spiritual, moral, mental, and physical development[2] of the community by securing that efficient education throughout those stages [*i.e.* primary, secondary and further] shall be available to meet the needs of the population of their area."

In *re Belling (decd.) London Borough of Enfield* v. *Public Trustee and Others*[3] it was decided that the powers do not give a local education

---

[97] See 1944 Act, s.8 as amended and below at para. 2–03.
[98] For definition see s.41 and below at para. 3–03.
[99] See 1964 Act, s.1 as amended and below at para. 2–03.
[1] For definition see s.114(1) and see below at para. 2–03.
[2] As to physical training see below at para. 5–27.
[3] [1967] Ch. 425. It is uncertain whether the provision in s.222 of the Local Government Act 1972 authorising local authorities to bring proceedings in the interests of the inhabitants of their area enhances their powers so as to upset this decision.

authority any *locus standi* to bring proceedings for the purposes of establishing that a testamentary document creates a charitable trust for educational purposes. Beyond this decision, of very limited scope, the courts have had little opportunity to explain these general duties placed upon local education authorities and how far, if at all, extra-curricular activities[4] are to be regarded as part of education. The whole of the section follows fairly closely the second sentence in paragraph 23 of the White Paper, *Educational Reconstruction,*[5] which did not elaborate on the types of "development of the community" to which it refers. The attribute "spiritual" does not derive from the White Paper but was added by amendment of the House of Lords[6] where the view was expressed that "spirituality" was to be distinguished from "morality," and the Government agreed that its omission from the clause was mistaken. But in both Houses, Government spokesmen described the clause as declaratory, from which it is to be understood that its purpose is to indicate (in the same way as does section 1[7] of the Act) the principles underlying substantive provisions in the Act. This view is supported by the use of the words "so far as their powers extend" to which attention was drawn in *re Belling*. The "duty" imposed by the section is in such general terms as unlikely to be enforceable in the courts, and it is difficult to envisage who might have *locus standi*. More specific provisions[8] are available upon which an aggrieved parent may proceed.

That the clause was merely declaratory was questioned in the House **1-68** of Commons,[9] and the addition of "spiritual" was challenged by a Welsh university member[10] as "the most numinous word one could possibly find," upsetting the balance of the Act; but the fact remains that the section as enacted is one of few in the 1944 Act that has escaped amendment; and this together with the absence of litigation[11] bears out its declaratory nature and, on that account, the absence of any political incentive to amend it. It is not, therefore, necessary to speculate on the construction to be placed on, for example, "moral education"; rather should attention be directed to those provisions in the Act, tenuous

---

[4] This may be material, *e.g.* in connection with the powers of local education authorities under 1944 Act, ss.59 (restriction of employment) and 61(1) (prohibition of fees)—see below at paras. 5–35 *et seq.* and 1–87 *et seq.* respectively. To the extent that "extra-curricular" activities are not part of education they may be taken alternatively to be "incidental" activities under s.111 of the Local Government Act 1972 (see above at para. 1–39).

[5] Cmnd. 6458, 1943.

[6] See 132 H.L. Deb. 773 (July 11, 1944). The government preferred "spiritual" to "religious" (also proposed) because of the absence of provision for religious education in further education institutions.

[7] See above at para. 1–06.

[8] See below at para. 1–79.

[9] See 397 H.C. Deb. 95 (February 15, 1944).

[10] See 402 H.C. Deb. 921 (July 27, 1944).

[11] But absence of litigation might also be due to the fact that the enforcement of a duty under the Education Acts should ordinarily be by way of complaint to, and action by, the Secretary of State under s.99 as amended (see below at para. 6–15).

though they mainly are, and those in the 1986 (No. 2) Act,[12] that relate to the determination of the school curriculum.[13]

Respect for wishes of parents

1–69   Opportunities exist under the Education Acts for parents to influence the course of their children's education, for instance, as regards religious instruction,[14] but the Bill for the 1944 Act contained no general form of words requiring the wishes of parents to be taken into account. The Government acceded to pressure in the House of Commons, however, and introduced an amendment, based on a provision in the Education Act 1921 (repealed), to what is now section 8. The adequacy of the amendment was challenged in the House of Lords and the Government later substituted what is now section 76 of the 1944 Act. The section reads as follows:

> "In the exercise of all powers and duties conferred and imposed on them by this Act the Minister [now Secretary of State] and local education authorities shall have regard to the general principle that, so far as is compatible with the provision of efficient instruction and training and the avoidance of unreasonable public expenditure, pupils are to be educated in accordance with the wishes of their parents."

1–70   By section 114(1) of the 1944 Act "parent . . . includes a guardian and every person who has the actual custody of the child or young person"[15] and thus could include, according to the *dicta* of Lord Goddard C.J. in *Plunkett* v. *Alker*,[16] an aunt or grandparent if the child were in their actual custody. The courts do not appear to have considered cases in which the wishes of one parent are at variance with those of the other. In *Woodward* v. *Oldfield*[17] Shearman J. remarked *obiter* "where both husband and wife are living together the person having the actual custody would no doubt be the husband" but this decision may lack persuasive force when set against section 1(1) of the Guardianship Act 1973, (as amended), which provides that "in relation to the legal custody or upbringing of a minor . . . a mother shall have the same rights and authority as the law allows to a father and the rights and authority of mother and father shall be equal and be exercisable by either without the other." The law, though not clear, is perhaps adequate to support the practice of local education authorities in sending school reports[18] to the parent exercising actual custody and causing a child to attend school,

---

[12] Especially s.46, relating to sex education (see below at paras. 2–135—2–136).
[13] See below at paras. 2–128 *et seq.*
[14] See below at para. 2–158.
[15] Reg. 2(2) of The Education (Areas to which pupils belong) Regulations 1980 (S.I. 1980 No. 917) elaborates the definition of "parents" for limited purposes. For definition of "child" see s.114(1) and below at para. 2–04. By s.114(1) "young person" means a person over compulsory school age (see below at para. 1–81) who has not attained the age of 18 years.
[16] [1954] 1 Q.B. 420.
[17] [1928] 1 K.B. 204 (a case concerning school attendance).
[18] As to school reports see below at para. 2–145.

and to the other parent on request provided that he or she has not been deprived of legal custody by order of the court. It is, moreover, possible so to interpret "parent" as to exclude the proviso.

Like section 7, considered above, section 76, significantly, remains **1–71** unamended, but unlike section 7 it has been much cited in the courts; and it has been asked to bear (perhaps, more strictly, to impose upon local education authorities) burdens for which it appears not to have been designed. To be obliged to "have regard to" a general principle[19] is not onerous: it may be difficult to show that a local education authority have not discharged the obligation—that regard has not been paid to parental wishes in the course of reaching a decision to override them. And the reference to compatibility with the provision of efficient instruction and training and avoidance of unreasonable public expenditure further abates the rights of the parent: where there is no such compatibility even the obligation to have regard to the general principle lapses. Moreover, it will be difficult for a parent successfully to challenge the view of a local education authority as to what constitutes "efficient" instruction or training or "unreasonable" public expenditure. Decisions of the courts[20] bear out, or fail to upset, these propositions.

In *Watt* v. *Kesteven County Council*[21] the plaintiff, a Roman Catholic, **1–72** declined on religious grounds to send his twin sons to an independent secondary grammar school with which the authority, having no places available in schools of their own, had made arrangements,[22] and at which they were prepared to pay the boys' tuition fees. He sent them instead to a Roman Catholic boarding school at which the tuition fees were lower, and claimed repayment in full from the county council (who were willing to pay a grant towards the fees on an income scale).[23]

The plaintiff's claim was based on section 76, mistakenly in the view **1–73** of the court. The effect of the section, it was held, was that there must be read into each provision of the Act conferring a power or imposing a duty, an obligation in the exercise of that power or performance of that duty to have regard to the general principle. In the instant case the duty was that contained in section 8 of the 1944 Act—to secure that there

---

[19] See above at para. 1–46. A different view about the force of "general principle" was taken regarding the Scottish equivalent of s.76 in *Huckstep* v. *Dunfermline District Education Sub-Committee* [1954] S.L.T. (Sh.Ct.) 109. See A. Wharam, "Parental Choice in Education" (1973) 3 Fam. Law 118.
[20] See A. E. Hart, "Parental Rights and State Education" (1967) 111 S.J. 822; P. Meredith, "Executive Discretion and Choice of Secondary School" (1981) P.L. 52; R. J. Buxton, *Local Government* (2nd ed. 1973) Chap. 8; A. Wharam, "Parental Choice in Education" (1973) 3 Fam. Law. 118; A. Samuels, "Parental Choice in Education" (1966) 116 New L.J. 1511; M. Freeman, "Children's Education and the Law. 1. Parents' Rights" (1980) L.A.G. Bull. 61 and M. C. Dutchman-Smith, "Parental Rights in Education" (1975) 119 S.J. 158.
[21] [1955] 1 Q.B. 408. See [1955] C.L.J. 140. *Watt* and other cases referred to in the text are discussed by B. Harvey in "Comprehensive Education and Parental Rights" (1975) 120 L.G.C. 691.
[22] Pursuant to 1944 Act, s.8. See below at paras. 2–08 and 5–32.
[23] Under 1944 Act, s.81. See below at para. 5–31.

should be sufficient schools available—as extended by section 9 which gave authorities the power to fulfil their duties in ways which included making arrangements with independent schools of the kind entered into by Kesteven.[24] But there was no obligation upon the local education authority to provide free education at any other independent school, and the plaintiff had not shown that the authority had failed to have regard to the "general principle." The section left it "open to the county council to have regard to other things as well, and also to make exceptions to the general principle if it thinks fit to do so. . . . If they paid the full fees in this case, it would mean that every parent in the county who sent his boys to boarding school could come and ask the county council to pay the tuition fees, no matter how rich he was" (*per* Denning L.J., who in the course of his judgment also pointed out that the religious views of the parent were irrelevant: the question would have been the same had a member of the Church of England declined for any reason to send his child to the school nominated by the authority and had sent him elsewhere).

1–74   In *Watt* the court also considered whether a breach of section 76 in the exercise of section 8 gave rise to an action for damages, and reached the conclusion that had there, contrary to the decision reached, been an obligation to pay full tuition fees at the school of the parent's choice then an action would have lain.[25] But the only duty under section 8 was to secure that facilities were available, and the remedy for alleged breach would be application to the Minister under section 99.[26]

1–75   In *Wood and Others* v. *Ealing London Borough Council*[27] parents contended that the authority were in breach of section 76 in having failed to pay any, or proper, regard to the wishes of parents in formulating their proposals to introduce comprehensive secondary schools.[28] The court, following *Watt,* held that breach of section 76 could not of itself, independently of any substantive breach of duty under the 1944 Act, give rise to any head of claim; that the general principle was only one consideration to be taken into account; and that in any event the general principle was "confined to the wishes of particular parents in respect of their own particular children and does not refer to the wishes of parents generally." Moreover, (*per* Goff J.) "education" in section 76 referred "to the curriculum and whether it includes any, and if so what, religious instruction, and whether co-educational or single-sex and matters of that sort and not to the size of school or the conditions of entry." But in a subsequent case[29] section 76 did not avail "particular parents" who complained that they had not been consulted about the course of

---

[24] 1944 Act, ss.8 and 9. See below at paras. 2–08 and 5–32.
[25] Following *Gateshead Union* v. *Durham County Council* [1918] 1 Ch. 146.
[26] See also *Meade* v. *London Borough of Haringey* [1979] 2 All E.R. 1016, and below at para. 2–11.
[27] [1967] 1 Ch. 364.
[28] See below at para. 2–09.
[29] See *Times Educational Supplement,* May 2, 1980, p. 3.

studies available to their children. The court held that the school and county council had not acted unreasonably in adopting a particular system of options without prior consultation.

In *Lee and Another* v. *Enfield London Borough Council*[30] it was **1–76** claimed that transferring pupils to a secondary school without giving parents an opportunity to express their wishes was contrary to section 76 as well as to an article of government[31] which also required their wishes to be taken into account. The court upheld this claim but only, it appears, so far as it was based on the articles; and thus it is possible to reconcile *Lee* with the preceding cases. The court also upheld its own jurisdiction, consistently with remarks made in *Wood & Others,* on the ground that the implementation of the authority's scheme was an act of malfeasance; had it merely amounted to nonfeasance then the exclusive remedy would have been under section 99.

Another illustration of the reasoning in *Watt* v. *Kesteven* is contained **1–77** in *Cumings and Others* v. *Birkenhead Corporation*[32] where it was claimed, unsuccessfully, that wishes of parents were disregarded by virtue of a circular sent them by the local education authority indicating that, otherwise than in exceptional cases, because of the demand on places in non-Roman Catholic secondary schools, pupils from Roman Catholic primary schools would be considered only for Roman Catholic secondary schools. "There are many other things to which the education authority may have regard and which may outweigh the wishes of the parents" (*per* Lord Denning M.R.). The appropriate recourse of the parents would have been under section 68.[33]

It was held in *Winward and Another* v. *Cheshire County Council*[34] **1–78** that there is no scope for the operation of section 76 when because an authority decide to exclude[35] a child from a particular school the question arises at the instance of the parent whether that school is suitable for him.

Although section 76 is central to the rights of parents they have **1–79** other[36] and some sharper-edged forms of recourse. The parental preference[37] provisions in the 1980 Act as regards the admission of children to school and the rights of appeal in the 1981 Act in relation to handicapped pupils[38] are examples (which post-date the cases reviewed

---

[30] 66 L.G.R. 195.
[31] "Articles of government"—see below at para. 2–107.
[32] [1972] Ch. 12.
[33] See below at para. 6–10.
[34] 77 L.G.R. 172. See also *Darling and Jones* v. *Minister of Education, The Times,* April 7, 1962 and R. G. Lee, "Parental Choice of School" (1980) 10 Fam. Law 44.
[35] As to the right to exclude see below at paras. 2–118 and 122 *et seq.*
[36] In addition to those mentioned below see the subsections on redress (above at paras. 1–48 *et seq.*) ss.68 and 99 of the 1944 Act (below at paras. 6–10 and 6–15) and the European Human Rights Convention (below at paras. 1–110–12).
[37] See 1980 Act, ss.6 and 7 and below at paras. 2–176 *et seq.*
[38] See below at paras. 2–195 *et seq.*

above); but section 76 governs all powers exercised by the Secretary of State and local education authorities under the Education Acts, so that in exercising their functions under post-1944 Act legislation they remain bound by it.[39]

Parental duty to secure education

1-80   By section 36 of the 1944 Act (as amended by section 17 of 1981 Act) it is "the duty of the parent of every child of compulsory school age to cause him to receive efficient full-time education suitable to his age, ability and aptitude and to any special educational needs he may have, either by regular attendance at school or otherwise."[40] The section calls for word by word analysis. The interpretation of "parent" has been considered above.[41] Here it is sufficient to add the reminder that under the Interpretation Act 1978 the singular includes the plural. A child[42] means a person who is not over compulsory school age.

1-81   Compulsory school age is defined in section 35 of the 1944 Act as any age between five years and 16[43] years. As soon as he becomes[44] 16 a person is over compulsory school age. For practical reasons the period is modified at both ends. By the 1948 Act, section 4(2), there is no obligation to admit a child as a registered pupil[45] except at the beginning of a school term,[46] unless the reason for his non-attendance then is:

(a) illness or other circumstances beyond the parent's control; or
(b) the parent's having not then been resident at a place reasonably accessible to the school.

A parent is not in breach of section 36 for failing to send his child to school between the child's fifth birthday and the beginning of the following term. Local education authorities may give governors of maintained schools general directions[47] about the normal time of admission—where (a) and (b) above do not apply. If a registered pupil[48] at a school (or a person who was a registered pupil within the previous twelve months) attains the upper limit of compulsory school age between the beginning

---

[39] See P. Marson, "Parental Choice in State Education" (1980) J.S.W.L. 193.
[40] See 1944 Act, s.56 and below at para. 5–29 as to a local education authority's power to provide education otherwise than at school; also B. Strachan, "Compulsory Education" (1965) 129 J.P.N. 344; M. Freeman, "Childrens Education and the Law, 2. Parents' Duties" (1980 L.A.G. Bull. 135; M. Dutchman-Smith "The Parental Duty to Educate" (1970) 114 S.J. 921 and A. Khan, "Parents' Duty to Secure Regular School Attendance" (1986) 130 S.J. 776.
[41] Above at para. 1–70.
[42] 1944 Act, s.114(1). As to proof of age see below at para. 2–240.
[43] "16" was substituted for "15" by the Raising of the School Leaving Age Order 1972 (S.I. 1972 No. 444). See Circ. 8/71 (W.O. 139/71).
[44] A person attains a particular age at the start of the anniversary of date of birth (Family Law Reform Act 1969, s.9).
[45] For definition see 1944 Act, s.114(1) as amended by 1948 Act, s.11 and Sched. 2 and below at para. 2–109.
[46] "Term" is undefined but see below at paras. 2–140–2–142. In practice children may be admitted at the beginning of the term in which they reach their fifth birthday.
[47] 1948 Act, s.4(3) as amended by 1980 Act, s.1(3) and Sched. 1, para. 19.
[48] Registration of pupils—see below at para. 2–109.

of September and the end of January he may not leave until the end of the school's spring term. If he attains that age after the end of January but before the beginning of the following September the leaving date is the Friday before the last Monday in May.[49]

Full-time education is not, as such, defined in the Act, but there are **1–82** requirements[50] about the length of the school day and year at maintained schools. Age, ability and aptitude are questions of fact, more or less difficult to ascertain, as are "special educational needs," defined in section 1 of the 1981 Act.[51] Attendance at school to be "regular"[52] must be at the times prescribed for the school—late arrival will not do[53]—and in compliance with school disciplinary requirements.[54] A father who persistently sent his daughter to school in trousers, there being no evidence of medical reasons for doing so, was found to have failed to secure her regular attendance at school when she was refused admittance by lawful order of the headmistress.[55]

Whether education is "efficient" is a matter for the local education **1–83** authority which is responsible for enforcement[56] of the parental duty. It seems to follow that a school maintained by that local education authority is for this purpose at least *ipso facto* efficient. It is for the Secretary of State to decide whether an independent school is efficient. Formerly, it was his practice to recognise as efficient, schools which complied with (non-statutory) Rules 16, but that practice was ended in 1978. The fact that an independent school is registered under section 70 of the 1944 Act is not evidence that the education it provides is efficient.[57]

In practice the efficiency of education has been challenged in the **1–84** courts mainly where parents have taken advantage of the provision (or, mostly, corresponding provisions in repealed legislation) that full-time education may be received otherwise[58] than at school. In *R. v. Walton and Other Justices, ex p. Dutton*[59] comparison was made between the standard of achievement reached by boys who had been educated at home and that expected of boys of the same age in regular attendance at a public elementary[60] school. The boys were tested on behalf of the local

---

[49] 1962 Act, s.9, as amended by 1976 School Leaving Dates Act, s.1 and Sched. See Circ. 4/76 (W.O. 58/76).

[50] See the Education (Schools and Further Education) Regulations 1981 (S.I. 1981 No. 1086) below at paras. 2–140 to 2–142.

[51] See below at para. 2–194.

[52] See T. I. McLeod, "Aspects of school attendance reports" (1981) 145 J.P.N. 133.

[53] See *Hinchley* v. *Rankin* [1961] 1 W.L.R. 421.

[54] As to school discipline see below at paras. 2–115 *et seq*.

[55] See *Spiers* v. *Warrington Corporation* [1954] 1 Q.B. 61; and see *Walker* v. *Cummings* (1912) 107 L.T. 304 and below at paras. 1–93 n. 94, 2–118 and 2–226.

[56] See below at para. 2–234.

[57] See A.M. 557. Circ. 6/78 (W.O. 60/78) and below paras. 6–27 *et seq*.

[58] As to provision by a local education authority "otherwise than at school," see 1944 Act, s.56, below at para. 5–29; and as to an (unsuccessful) application under the European Human Rights Convention, below at para. 1–112.

[59] (1911) 75 J.P. 558.

[60] The predecessor of the "primary" school. See 1944 Act, ss.9(3), 114(7) and 120(1)(a).

education authority and, the comparison being unfavourable, the home education was held on the evidence to be inefficient. (It is, equally, open to a parent to bring evidence to show that he is efficiently educating his child outside school[61]). But in *Bevan* v. *Shears*[62] it was held that while comparison with an elementary school might provide a most useful guide it was not conclusive: "efficiency" in education had not been defined by reference to particular standards or curricula. Nevertheless, in *Osborne* v. *Martin*[63] Avery J. expressed the opinion that "efficient instruction in some other manner" meant efficient instruction in the curriculum approved for elementary schools. In this case the court also held that it was not open to a parent to withdraw his child from school for one hour a week to attend piano lessons. "A parent is not obliged to avail himself of the free education provided by the state if he prefers to provide privately for his child's education; but if he does avail himself of it he must take it as a whole," (*per* Salter J.). In *Baker* v. *Earl*,[64] decided on the 1944 Act provision, the duty under section 36 was in breach because children were found to have had no lessons or prescribed course of study. They were encouraged by their mother, who possessed no educational qualifications, to follow any subject in which they were interested (and in practice occupied themselves mostly in non-academic tasks).

1–85   It is not possible wholly to reconcile these decisions if only because previous cases are not discussed in later judgments, but it does appear that evidence of comparative standards of attainment will be relevant, and while perhaps (preferring *Bevan* to *Walton* and *Osborne*) it is not conclusive, yet there must be at least some evidence of systematic full-time study before efficient education outside school can be established.

1–86   How the parental duty under section 36 is enforced will appear on consideration of the law relating to school attendance.[65]

Fees and charges

1–87   By section 61(1) of the 1944 Act, a local education authority may not charge a fee for admission to a maintained school or for the education[66] provided there. Thus, for example, the fees for a field trip which forms part of a geography curriculum must be met by the school and ultimately

---

[61] *R.* v. *West Riding of Yorkshire Justices, ex p. Broadbent* [1910] 2 K.B. 192. See also *Bevan* v. *Shears* n. 12 below.

[62] [1911] 2 K.B. 936.

[63] (1927) 91 J.P. 197.

[64] [1960] Crim.L.R. 363. See also *Tweedie* v. *Pritchard* [1963] Crim.L.R. 270 where a school attendance order (see below at para. 2–231) was made on refusal by parents to permit the local education authority to inspect home provision.

[65] See below at paras. 2–222 *et seq.* and also Circ. 2/86 (School attendance and the education welfare service).

[66] As to examination fees see below at para. 2–139 n. 9.

by the local education authority[67]; but excursions, cruises, etc., which fall within the category of extra-curricular activities[68] are not a charge upon public funds.

Authorities have a wide discretion over the curriculum,[69] and it may **1-88** include the giving of individual tuition on the playing of a musical instrument. So it was held in *R. v. Hereford and Worcester Local Education Authority, ex p. Jones*[70] and, in consequence, that the authority were not entitled to charge fees for the clarinet and violin lessons given to Helen and Ruth Jones respectively, which, before a change of policy by the authority, they had received free of charge. But equally, the authority were entitled to cease offering individual music tuition as part of the school curriculum. It may be that if local education authorities provide this tuition (or, for instance, dancing lessons) as an extra-curricular activity, especially outside school sessions,[71] fees may still be charged[72]; but the extra-curricular category is ill-defined, and whether or not a school activity does form part of the curriculum may be arguable in the particular case. Again, while fees for cookery or swimming lessons within the curriculum are *ultra vires*, it is less certain that charges for the cost of materials or transport to the swimming bath cannot properly be made.

The express prohibition against fees is limited to schools, so it might **1-89** seem to follow that fees may be charged in respect of senior pupils who are in attendance not at school but a further education institution, unless the Secretary of State considers this practice unreasonable under section 68[73] of the 1944 Act, but the issue has not been tested.

Fees specified by the authority are payable[74] for board and lodging at **1-90** a maintained school, but not if the authority cannot otherwise provide suitable[75] education for a pupil (for example if he attends a boarding special school[76]); and if they are satisfied that payment of full fees would

---

[67] The local ombudsman (see above at paras. 1–58 *et seq.*) found, as maladministration, failure to pay the tuition fees for a residential field course which was organised as an essential part of an "A" level course (Commission for Local Administration in England. Report for year ended March 31, 1986).

[68] Authorised, perhaps, by s.111 of the Local Government Act 1972, as conducive or incidental to education functions (see above at para. 1–39).

[69] See below at paras. 2–128 *et seq.*

[70] [1981] 1 W.L.R. 768 (D.C.). See Second Report from the Education, Science and Arts Committee 1981–82 (H.C. 116–1) *The Secondary School Curriculum and Examinations* pp. xci–ii, and A. L. Polak, "Facing the Music," (1981) 145 J.P.N. 234.

[71] See below at paras. 2–140—2–141.

[72] See A.M. 15.

[73] See below at para. 6–10.

[74] 1944 Act, s.61(2) as amended by 1980 Act, s.30(1) and (2), s.38(6) and Sched. 7, and by 1981 Act, s.21 and Sched. 3, para. 5. As to the recovery of the cost of board and lodging otherwise than at a boarding school see 1944 Act, s.52, as amended, below at para. 5–14, and as to education at non-maintained schools see below at paras. 5–30 to 5–33 and 6–35 *et seq.*

[75] See 1944 Act, s.8, as amended, and below at paras. 2–06 to 2–08.

[76] See below para. 2–207.

cause hardship to a parent they must remit them to the extent necessary to avoid hardship.[77] Fees are recoverable summarily as a civil debt.[78]

1–91   In *East Riding County Council* v. *Pratt*[79] the local education authority successfully claimed damages in the county court for breach of contract against a parent who withdrew his son from a grammar school before the age up to which the parent had agreed to keep him there. The parent had entered into an agreement to pay liquidated damages in default of doing so. The agreement was held not to conflict with the local education authority's duty to provide free education because grammar schools "were considerably more expensive to run than ordinary secondary schools" and "the duty under section 76[80] was qualified by considerations of unreasonable public expense." It seems doubtful whether this decision would be followed today.

Sex discrimination

1–92   The White Paper *Equality for Women*[81] was the basis for the Sex Discrimination Act 1975 (which is also underpinned by a European Community Directive[82] and the European Convention[83] on Human Rights). The Act applies[84] equally to protect men,[85] and so in the exposition that follows reference to discrimination against women must, as appropriate, be read as applying to discrimination against men. Local education authorities are bound[86] by the general provisions in the Act, as is the Crown.[87] With appropriate exceptions[88] the Act makes discrimination in employment[89] and in the provision of goods, facilities (including facilities for education[90]), services and premises,[91] and also other discriminatory practices[92] (in particular discriminatory advertisements and instruction or inducement to discrimination) unlawful.[93]

---

[77] Where a child is in the care of a local authority he is to be treated as a child of a parent without resources and accordingly the local education authority must remit the whole of the fees (see the Local Authorities and Local Education Authorities (Allocation of Functions) Regulations 1951, (S.I. 1951 No. 472) reg. 6 and Circ. 232).

[78] See Magistrates Courts Act 1980, s.58.

[79] (1955) 105 L.J. 620.

[80] See above at paras. 1–69 *et seq*.

[81] Cmnd. 5724.

[82] Directive 76/207—see below at para. 1–117.

[83] See below at para. 1–110.

[84] 1975 Act, ss.2, 3(2), 4(3).

[85] "Men" and "women" include males and females of any age (1975 Act, s.5(2)).

[86] As to exemptions as respects acts done under statutory authority see *ibid.* s.51 as amended by 1986 (No. 2) Act, Sched. 4, para. 6 in relation to instruments and articles of government (as to which see below at paras. 2–70 *et seq*.

[87] 1975 Act, s.85 as amended.

[88] See especially Pt. V of the Act.

[89] Pt. II, ss.6–21 as amended. See below at paras.4–62 to 4–67.

[90] s.29(2)(*d*). But by s.35(3), s.29 does not apply to discrimination which is rendered unlawful by ss.22 or 23 (see below at paras. 1–94 to 1–95).

[91] Pt. III, ss.29–36.

[92] Pt. IV, ss.37–40.

[93] For cases decided outside the field of education (which may, nevertheless, bear upon educational administration) see *Encyclopaedia of Labour Relations Law* (1972).

By section 1, a person discriminates against a woman if on the **1–93** grounds of her sex he treats her (according to marital status or otherwise) less favourably than he treats or would treat a man. This is conventionally termed "direct" discrimination. Comparison of treatment must be such that the relevant circumstances are in each case substantially the same.[94] "Indirect" discrimination arises if he applies to her a requirement or condition which applies or would apply equally to a man, but relatively fewer women can comply with it, and he cannot show it to be justifiable irrespective of sex, and to her detriment she cannot comply with it. Section 3 provides that discrimination may also take place, in analogous circumstances, against married persons in the employment field. The foregoing are sex discrimination.[95] Section 4 makes unlawful discrimination by way of victimisation of a person who asserts her rights under the Act or under the Equal Pay Act 1970.[96]

By section 15(2) there must be no discrimination in the careers advice **1–94** and assistance given by local education authorities,[97] and the Act makes other special provision against discrimination in education[98] as follows. Except as explained below, it is unlawful under section 22[99] for a local education authority to discriminate against a woman in the terms on which they offer to admit her to an educational establishment[1] maintained by them; or by refusing or deliberately omitting to accept an application for her admission as a pupil; or, where she is a pupil, by treating her detrimentally as regards access to benefits, facilities or services or by excluding her from the establishment, or otherwise. Thus, for example, a quota on the number of girl entrants to a co-educational school would be unlawful discrimination; and boys and girls have equal rights of attendance at classes traditionally reserved for one or the other (but single-sex schools may lawfully be carried on, and subjects such as woodwork and home economics are unlikely to be offered as part of the curriculum of girls' and boys' schools respectively). The same constraints apply to other responsible bodies, namely governors of maintained educational establishments, proprietors of independent schools and of special schools not maintained by local education authorities, and the governing bodies of other establishments providing full-time or

---

[94] 1975 Act, s.5(3). From this provision it may follow that it would not be unlawful to prescribe different school uniform dress for the sexes and forbid the wearing of trousers by girls.

[95] *Ibid*. s.5(1)(*b*).

[96] See below at para. 4–62.

[97] Under s.8 of the Employment and Training Act 1973 (as to which see below at paras. 5–42 *et seq*.).

[98] "Education" for the purposes of the 1975 Act includes any form of training or instruction (s.82(1)). See Circ. 2/76 (W.O. 20/76) and M. A. Richards, "The Sex Discrimination Act—Equality for Women" (1976) 5 I.L.J. 35.

[99] As amended by 1980 Act, s.1(3) and Sched. 1, para. 27. As to modification of trust deeds so as to advance education without sex discrimination see below at para. 6–46.

[1] Not defined, but in context including schools and the other institutions referred to in this paragraph.

part-time education which are designated[2] by the Secretary of State and are either polytechnics,[3] establishments in receipt of grants payable out of money provided by Parliament,[4] are assisted by local education authorities in accordance with schemes under section 42 of the 1944 Act,[5] or provide full-time education for persons aged 16 to 18 inclusive.[6]

1–95   It is also unlawful, under section 23,[7] for a local education authority to do any act that constitutes sex discrimination in carrying out any other of their functions, for example in making discretionary awards to students.[8] And in *R*. v. *Secretary of State for Education and Science and Another, ex p. Keating and Others*[9] an authority's proposal to close the only single-sex county boys school, while continuing to maintain two single-sex girls schools, was held unlawful.

1–96   Section 25 imposes a general duty on local education authorities and most[10] other responsible bodies mentioned in the penultimate paragraph to provide facilities for education and ancillary benefits or services without sex discrimination.[11] The only sanctions for breach of this duty are the exercise of the powers of the Secretary of State to require reasonable exercise of functions, or in default.[12] He may use the same sanctions to enforce sections 22 and 23, but without prejudice to the other means of enforcement of those sections referred to below.

1–97   Section 28[13] exempts further education[14] physical training courses from the provisions of sections 22, 23 and 25; and section 36(5) exempts from those provisions benefits, facilities or services outside Great Britain except on British registered ships.

---

[2] Under 1975 Act, s.24 and the Sex Discrimination (Designated Educational Establishments) Order 1975 (S.I. 1975 No. 1902) as amended by the Sex Discrimination Designated Educational Establishments (Amendment Order) 1980 (S.I. 1980 No. 1860). Designation remains in force until revoked, notwithstanding that an establishment ceases to fall within one of the specified categories (s.24(3)).

[3] See below at para. 3–01. Five polytechnics (all in London) have been designated.

[4] Some 70 further educational establishments and five nursery schools, all in receipt of grants by the Secretary of State payable under s.100 of the 1944 Act as amended (see below at para. 6–19), have been designated. *Cf.* the list of establishments in the Education (Schools and Further Education) Regulations 1981 (S.I. 1981 No. 1086) Sched. 3—see below at para. 3–05 n. 23.

[5] Seven have been designated. For 1944 Act, s.42 see below at para. 3–10.

[6] 17 have been designated.

[7] As amended by 1981 Act, s.21, Sched. 3, para. 11.

[8] Under s.2 of the 1962 Act as substituted by Sched. 5 to the 1980 Act (see below at para. 3–65).

[9] *The Times*, December 3, 1985.

[10] But not including the proprietors of independent schools or the governing bodies of those designated establishments (a) in receipt of grants payable out of money provided by Parliament otherwise than under s.100 of the 1944 Act, or (b) providing full-time education for persons aged 16 to 18 inclusive.

[11] See s.46 as to exemptions in the case of communal accommodation.

[12] See ss.68 and 99, as amended respectively of the 1944 Act, below at paras. 6–10 and 6–15.

[13] Para. (*b*) of s.28 was repealed by s.4 of the Further Education Act 1985 so that courses for *teachers* of physical training are no longer exempt.

[14] "Further education" by s.82(1) means full-time and part-time education for persons over compulsory school age. See 1944 Act, s.41(1) and below at para. 3–03.

By section 26(1), section 25 and the provisions relating to the **1–98** admission of pupils in section 22 do not apply to single sex establishments. (These include establishments which admit pupils of the opposite sex only exceptionally or in comparatively small numbers to particular courses of instruction or teaching classes). Nor (by section 26(2)) do those provisions apply to the admission of boarders to a co-educational day and boarding school which takes boarders of one sex only (disregarding comparatively small numbers of the opposite sex); and at such a school neither do section 25 nor the provisions of section 22(c)(i) regarding access to benefits, facilities and services apply. By section 26(3), section 25 and the last-mentioned provisions are not to be taken as contravened in an establishment which is single sex by reason of its admission of comparatively small numbers of the opposite sex to a particular course of instruction or teaching classes, and pupils of one sex are confined to those courses or classes.

Provision is made in section 27 for exemptions from contraventions of **1–99** the Act relating to admission when a single-sex establishment is turning co-educational and the responsible body has applied for or obtained a transitional exemption order[15] in accordance with Schedule 2[16] from the Secretary of State, or from the Equal Opportunities Commission in the case of wholly independent establishments—those not falling within the categories next specified. The Secretary of State has made a regulation[17] regarding the contents of an application for an order in respect of single-sex special schools as defined in section 26(1), special schools falling within section 26(2), single-sex further educational establishments other than those designated under section 24 and in receipt of grants under section 100 of the 1944 Act, and (a separate regulation[18]) grant-aided single-sex establishments not provided by a local education authority. The major requirement in the application is a statement of the stages by which the establishment is to become co-educational and the period over which the continuance of discriminatory admissions is proposed.

Contraventions of the Act may be enforced only[19] as provided in the **1–100** Act, by industrial tribunals[20] as regards the employment field and, as respects sections 22 and 23, as a claim in tort to be pursued in a county court in accordance with section 66[21] of the Act. By section 41

---

[15] Not a statutory instrument (see above at para. 1–42).

[16] As amended by 1980 Act, ss.16(4), 33(3), 38(6) Sched. 3, para. 18 and Sched. 7.

[17] Reg. 9 of the Education (Schools and Further Education) Regulations 1981 (S.I. 1981 No. 1086) as amended by Amendment Regulations (S.I. 1983 No. 262).

[18] See reg. 31 of the Education (Grant) Regulations 1983 (S.I. 1983 No. 74) made under 1944 Act, s.100 as extended by 1975 Act, s.27 and Sched. 2 para. 3.

[19] s.62 as substituted by Race Relations Act 1976, Sched. 4, para. 3; and see also ss.74–76 as amended. The prerogative orders (see above at para. 1–50 n. 52) may also be available.

[20] See ss.63–65 as amended, and below at para. 4–66.

[21] As amended by Race Relations Act 1976, Sched. 4, para. 5. Under s.66(5) civil proceedings may be instituted only after giving prior notice to the Secretary of State of (presumably) Education and Science and awaiting his response for up to two months.

employers are liable for the contraventions of their employees in the course of employment,[22] and principals for those of their agents. Employers may raise as a defence proof that they took such preventive steps as were reasonably practicable.[23] By section 42 knowingly[24] to aid an unlawful act is to do that act unless the person aiding reasonably relied upon the statement of the person aided that the act was not unlawful.

1–101   The Sex Discrimination Act 1975 also established the Equal Opportunities Commission with various powers and responsibilities.[25] In particular under section 57 they may conduct formal investigations[26] into possible contraventions of the Act by, *inter alios*, local education authorities; and if the Commission become aware of acts that appear to be in breach of section 25 they must give notice of them to the Secretary of State, under section 67(6). Less formally, complaints have been received from parents, and representations made to local education authorities; and the Commission have been active in explaining the provisions of the Act in relation to education and publicising their views about good practice.[27]

Racial discrimination

1–102   The Race Relations Act 1976, based on the White Paper *Racial Discrimination*,[28] follows the pattern of the Sex Discrimination Act 1975. It makes discrimination unlawful[29] in the same areas of activity,[30] and racial discrimination is defined by analogy with sex discrimination. By

---

[22] "Employment" by s.82(1)" means employment under a contract of service or of apprenticeship or a contract personally to execute any work or labour, and related expressions shall be construed accordingly."

[23] "Reasonably practicable." See *Stroud's Judicial Dictionary*, (5th ed. 1986).

[24] "Knowingly." see *ibid*.

[25] See Pt. VI, ss.53–61, as amended (under s.56A has been made the Sex Discrimination Code of Practice Order 1985 (S.I. 1985 No. 387)); and, as to enforcement, ss.67–75 as amended.

[26] The Commission has conducted formal investigations into (a) equal provision of secondary education as between the sexes in Tameside (Report 1977), (b) Sidney Stringer School and Community College, Coventry (Report undated), and (c) Ebbw Vale College of Further Education (Report 1984). In (a) the Commission found no evidence to establish the existence of unlawful sex discrimination; in (b) although there was no evidence to substantiate the allegations of unlawful sex discrimination in relation to the particular appointments and promotions investigated, it found substantial and frequent departures from authorised appointment and promotion procedures; and in (c) there had been shortcomings in the promotion system of the College not all of which had been remedied.

[27] See, *e.g.* the following among the Commission's publications: "Do you Provide Equal Educational Opportunities?"; "Ending Sex Stereotyping in Schools"; "Promotion and the Woman Teacher; Equal Opportunities in Post-School Education"; and, "Annual Reports."

[28] Cmnd. 6234. See Circ. 4/77 (W.O. 87/77).

[29] For cases decided outside the field of education (which may, nevertheless, bear upon educational administration) see I. A. Macdonald *Race Relations. The New Law* (1977) and as to discrimination in the employment of teachers, below at paras. 4–65 to 4–67.

[30] See (as amended) Pt. II, ss.4–16 regarding employment (see below paras. 4–65 to 4–67) and especially s.14(2) which follows s.15(2) of the Sex Discrimination Act 1975 (above at para. 1–94), Pt. III, ss.20–26 (goods, facilities, services and premises) and Pt. IV, ss.28–33 (other unlawful acts). Pt. IX makes incitement to racial hatred an offence.

section 1, a person discriminates ("directly") for the purposes of the 1976 Act if on racial grounds he treats one person less favourably than he treats or would treat others[31]; or ("indirectly") if he applies to a person a requirement or condition which applies or would apply equally to persons not of the same racial group but relatively fewer members of the person's racial group can comply with it, and it cannot be shown to be justifiable irrespective of racial considerations, and he cannot, to his detriment, comply with it.[32] "Racial grounds" means colour, race, nationality (which, by section 3, includes citizenship) or ethnic or national origins, and, under section 78, "racial group" means a group of persons defined by any of those characteristics. Victimisation of a person who asserts his rights under the 1976 Act is also unlawful discrimination, under section 2.[33]

The special provisions in sections 17 and 18 against discrimination in   **1–103** education follow corresponding provisions in sections 22 and 23 of the Sex Discrimination Act 1975,[34] as does section 19 the general duty in section 25 of the 1975 Act to provide facilities without discrimination.[35] The same sanctions[36] are available to the Secretary of State. Section 71 places a duty upon local authorities in performing all their functions to have regard to the general objectives of the Act.

General exceptions[37] make lawful what would otherwise be discrimi-   **1–104** natory practices. These exceptions include giving a particular racial group access to educational facilities[38] to meet their special needs, and also giving persons not ordinarily resident,[39] and not intending to remain in Great Britain,[40] access to educational facilities.[41] Discrimination, as respects further education tuition fees, hostel charges, admissions and discretionary awards has been required or authorised by the Secretary of State.[42]

---

[31] See as to comparison of treatment s.3(4), which follows s.5(3) of the Sex Discrimination Act 1975 (see above at para. 1–93 n. 94).

[32] See *Orphanos* v. *Queen Mary College* [1985] 2 All E.R. 233 in which the college's policy in 1982 of charging a higher "overseas students' rate" to persons not ordinarily resident in the European Economic Community (see below at para. 3–14) was held to be in breach of ss.1(1)(*b*) and 17(*a*) but s.57(3) protected them from a damages claim. As to admissibility of evidence see *Chattopadhyay* v. *The Headmaster of Holloway School* [1981] I.R.L.R. 487.

[33] See *Kirby* v. *Manpower Services Commission* [1980] 1 W.L.R. 725.

[34] And by s.27(1) and (5), ss.17–19 do not apply to benefits, facilities or services outside Great Britain except on British registered ships and so as not to break the law of another country in its territorial waters.

[35] See the passages relating to those sections at paras. 1–94 to 1–96 above, and s.58(6).

[36] See 1944 Act, ss.68 and 99 as amended, and below at paras. 6–10 and 6–15.

[37] See Pts. V and VI of the Act, ss.34–42.

[38] "Education" by s.78 includes any form of training or instruction.

[39] "Ordinary residence." Not defined in the Act but see *R.* v. *Barnet London Borough Council, ex p. Shah* [1983] 2 A.C. 309, *Levene* v. *Inland Revenue Commissioners* [1928] A.C. 217, other cases cited in *Stroud's Judicial Dictionary* (5th ed. 1986) and below at paras. 3–73 to 3–75.

[40] England, Scotland, Wales and, by s.78(1), adjacent territorial waters.

[41] ss.35, 36 and 40.

[42] Under s.41. See Circs. 8/77 and 5/79 (but the amounts of tuition fees there specified are anachronistic) and also the 1983 Act (see below at para. 3–75).

1–105   In *Mandla* v. *Dowell Lee*[43] it was held, applying the dictum of Richardson J. in *King-Ansell* v. *Police*,[44] that:

> "a group is identifiable in terms of its ethnic origins if it is a segment of the population distinguished from others by a sufficient combination of shared customs, beliefs, traditions and characteristics derived from a common or presumed common past, even if not drawn from what in biological terms is a common racial stock. It is that combination which gives them an historically determined social identity . . . ."

Sikhs were thus a group defined by ethnic origins, and a requirement that a Sikh should not wear a turban in school was not justifiable.

1–106   The "bussing" of children of a particular racial group is probably not justifiable unless it can be shown to meet their educational needs[45]; but immigrant children may properly be denied access to voluntary aided schools on religious grounds. Segregation in separate classes of children of a particular racial group might be justified to meet their distinctive educational needs such as language tuition but is otherwise probably unlawful.[46]

1–107   The means of enforcement of the 1976 Act are similar to those in the 1975 Act. They are generally restricted[47] to industrial tribunals[48] as regards the employment field or, as regards sections 17 and 18, to claims in tort[49]; and sections 32 and 33 of the 1976 Act substantially follow sections 41 and 42 of the 1975 Act[50] in relation to the liability of employers and principals and the aiding of unlawful acts respectively.

1–108   In parallel with the Equal Opportunities Commission the 1976 Act established a Commission for Racial Equality[51] (succeeding the Race Relations Board), with similar powers of investigation and responsibilities[52]; and the aggrieved citizen may also have recourse to the

---

[43] [1983] 2 A.C. 548. See A. Hofler, "Religious Discrimination. A loophole to be closed" 80 L.S. Gaz. 1043.

[44] [1979] 2 N.Z.L.R. 531 at 543.

[45] See report of Race Relations Board for 1974 (H.C. 409, 1974–75), paras. 27, 28 and 29 and *Commission for Racial Equality* v. *London Borough of Ealing* [1978] 1 W.L.R. 112 (C.A.). On the *Ealing* case see Report of the Commission for Racial Equality, 1978, (H.C. 128, 1979–80) at p. 101.

[46] For further examples of the implications for local education authorities of the racial discrimination legislation see Annual Reports of the Commission for Racial Equality and its predecessor the Race Relations Board (H.C. Papers), Commission for Racial Equality publications such as "Local authorities and the Educational Implications of s.71 of the Race Relations Act" (1981) and the Race Relations Code of Practice Order 1983 (S.I. 1983 No. 1081) pursuant to s.47.

[47] See s.53.

[48] See ss.54–56 as amended.

[49] See s.57, especially sub-section (5), and s.68.

[50] See above at para. 1–100.

[51] See Pt. VII of the Act.

[52] But see in particular s.58(6). The Commission have made formal investigations: on secondary school allocations in Reading (Report 1983) they found that while there was no discrimination the authority had failed to take sufficient account of their duties under Race Relations Act 1976, ss.19 and 71; on suspension of pupils in Birmingham (Report 1985) they found that black

European Commission on Human Rights and the law of the European Community. Discrimination in education, very widely defined, is also the subject of a Convention[53] adopted by the General Conference of the United Nations Educational, Scientific and Cultural Organisation to which the United Kingdom adhered; and a Protocol[54] supplementary to the Convention has instituted a Conciliation and Good Offices Commission responsible for seeking the settlement of any dispute which may arise between the states which are party to the Convention.

European law

British membership of the Council of Europe and of the European   **1–109** Community brings with it international obligations in connection with the provision of education and the granting of rights to parents over and above those contained in domestic legislation. From the Council derive the European Convention on Human Rights signed in 1950, and the means of enforcement of those rights by the European Commission of Human Rights,[55] to whom individuals may apply for redress, and the Court of Human Rights, who consider those applications which are considered well-founded by the Commission. More surprisingly perhaps, the Treaty of Rome, which established the European Economic Community in 1957, has ramified so as to have an impact on the British education system.

The most (but not exclusively[56]) relevant provisions of the Human   **1–110** Rights Convention are Article 3: "No-one shall be subjected to torture or to inhuman or degrading treatment or punishment"; Article 14: "The enjoyment of the rights and freedoms set forth in this Convention shall be secured without discrimination on any ground such as sex, race, colour, language, religion, political or other opinion, national or social origin, association with national minority, property, birth or other status"; and Article 2 of Protocol 1: "No person shall be denied the right to education. In the exercise of any functions which it assumes in relation to education and to teaching, the State shall respect the right of parents to ensure such education and teaching in conformity with their own religious and philosophical convictions."

---

pupils were more likely to be suspended than white pupils; and they found that Calderdale's arrangements for teaching English as a second language (Report 1986) amounted to indirect discrimination in that children in the English Language Teaching Service could experience a regression in their learning process when they transferred out of it.

[53] Treaty Series no. 44 (1962) Cmnd. 1760.

[54] Treaty Series no. 23 (1969) Cmnd. 3894.

[55] See European Convention on Human Rights, Collected Texts (published periodically by the Council of Europe) and published as Cmd. 8969 and (the Protocol) Cmd. 9221, and *e.g.* R. Beddard, *Human Rights and Europe* (2nd ed. 1980), A. H. Robertson, *Human Rights in Europe* (2nd ed. 1977), and F. G. Jacobs, *The European Convention on Human Rights* (1975).

[56] Art. 9 was considered in *Ahmad* v. *I.L.E.A.*—see below at para. 4–49.

1–111   It might reasonably be supposed that the Education Acts and the practices of local education authorities conform to those articles, but all three have given rise, or potentially give rise, to problems, under Article 3 in relation to corporal punishment, under Article 14 to improper discrimination[57] and under Article 2 of Protocol 1, which seems to be of very wide scope.

1–112   Failure by Scottish education authorities to undertake to refrain from physically punishing children whose parents had "philosophical convictions" against corporal punishment was found by the Court of Human Rights[58] to be in breach of Article 2 of Protocol 1. In other cases[59] Article 3 has also been adduced. The Court have considered Article 2 of Protocol 1 in relation to obligatory sex education (in Danish state schools) and have upheld that practice.[60] Applications to the Commission by British parents, under the same Article and under Article 14, in protest against comprehensive secondary schools[61] and in support of claims to educate their children outside schools, have been unsuccessful.[62] British education law and practice seem vulnerable, however, in relation to the provision of education in accordance with religious convictions in what has become a nation of many distinct faiths, especially in London and some other major cities. But, as if in anticipation of this potential challenge, United Kingdom ratification of Article 2 of Protocol 1 in 1952 was made subject to a reservation[63] (under Article 64 of the

---

[57] See above at paras. 1–92 *et seq.* and paras. 1–102 *et seq.* (sex and racial discrimination respectively).

[58] See *Campbell and Cosans* v. *U.K.* (1982) 4 E.H.R.R. 293 and for the response of the British government, below at para. 7–51.

[59] *Application No. 8566/79, Mr. & Mrs. X and their Son* v. *U.K.* (1983) 5 E.H.R.R. 265, *Application No. 9114/80* v. *U.K.* (1985) 7 E.H.R.R. 409, *Application No. 9471/81, Mrs. X and Ms. X* v. *U.K.* (1985) 7 E.H.R.R. 450, *Application No. 9119/80* v. *U.K.* (1986) 8 E.H.R.R. 47 and Secretary to the European Convention on Human Rights, *Stocktaking on the European Convention on Human Rights* (Strasbourg, 1982) p. 217.

[60] See *Application No. 5926/72, Pedersen* v. *Denmark* [1973] Yearbook of the Convention on Human Rights 340 and Secretary to the Convention, *Stocktaking on the European Convention on Human Rights* (Strasbourg, 1982) p. 152.

[61] "Comprehensive secondary schools"—see below at para. 2–09. In *Application Nos. 10228 and 10229/82, Medland and Irvine* v. *U.K.* (1984) 7 E.H.R.R. 141, the Commission held that there was "no positive obligation on the State in relation to the second sentence of Art. 2, to provide for or subsidise any particular form of education in order to respect the philosophical convictions of parents. However, [as in *Campbell and Cosans*—note 58 above] once the state has entered upon the provision of public education it is under some positive obligation . . . to ensure respect for parents' philosophical convictions." Nor do "all differences in treatment constitute discrimination contrary to Art. 14 of the Convention. The test is whether the difference in treatment has a reasonable and objective basis proportionate to the aim pursued and its effects achieved." See also *Application No. 9461/81* v. *U.K.* (1983) 5 E.H.R.R. 465—an unsuccessful application under Art. 2 of Protocol 1 for financial support to educate children at the Rudolf Steiner school.

[62] As to domestic cases in relation to these two issues see above at paras. 1–75 and 1–84 respectively. As to an unsuccessful application to the Commission regarding education of children outside school see *Application No. 10233/83 (Harrison).*

[63] See European Convention on Human Rights, Collected Texts (published periodically by the Council of Europe).

Convention[64]) to the effect that "in view of certain provisions of the Education Acts in force in the United Kingdom, the principle affirmed in the second sentence of Article 2 is accepted by the United Kingdom only so far as is compatible with the provision of efficient instruction and training, and the avoidance of unreasonable public expenditure."

European Community law which affects educational administration in **1–113** Britain stems from the Treaty of Rome,[65] and in particular[66] from Article 7 of that Treaty which in general terms prohibits discrimination on grounds of nationality (against a state's own, as well as other Community, nationals) and Article 49 which enables the Council of the Community to issue directives and make regulations to facilitate freedom of movement of workers within the Community. Relevant Community legislation[67]—directives (which are binding as to the result to be achieved but are ordinarily given British legislative form) and regulations (which are directly applicable as such)—together with decisions of the court are as follows.

Council Regulation 1612/68[68] on Freedom of Movement of Workers **1–114** within the Community provides by Article 7(3) that a worker who is a national of a member state shall "by virtue of the same right and under the same conditions as national workers have access to training in vocational schools[69] and retraining centres." And by Article 12[70]:

> "the children of a national of a Member State who is or has been employed in the territory of another Member State shall be admitted to that State's general educational, apprenticeship and vocational training courses under the same conditions as the nationals of that State, if such children are residing in its territory. Member States shall encourage all efforts to enable such children to attend these courses under the best possible conditions."

In *MacMahon* v. *Department of Education and Science and Others*[71] it **1–115** was held that the effect of Article 7(3) was to override a discriminatory provision in the Local Education Authority Awards Regulations 1979 so as to entitle the plaintiff to an award in respect of a teacher training course to which, but for that Article, he would not have been entitled.

---

[64] Art. 64 does *not* permit "reservations of a general character:" it is not easy to construe the U.K. reservation as other than general.

[65] March 25, 1957. See *Encyclopedia of European Community Law* Pt. B 10 and, generally, European Parliament Secretariat, *Europe Today* (Luxembourg, 1983).

[66] Also Art. 41 (vocational training of farmers), Art. 57 (mutual recognition of diplomas, etc.) and Art. 118 (vocational training generally).

[67] See Art. 189.

[68] October 15, 1968, (J.O. 1968 L 257/2 (O.J. 1968 475); made pursuant to Art. 49 of the Treaty). See J. Kwodo Bentil, "Equality of Educational Opportunity under EEC Law" (1977) 121 S.J. 327 and 349 and "Educational Discrimination in the EEC" (1985) 129 S.J. 744.

[69] In *R.* v. *Inner London Education Authority, ex p. Hinde* [1985] 1 C.M.L.R. 716, Taylor J. said that "vocational school did not refer only to establishments offering manual and technical courses or where vocational training was the main activity, but extended to establishments providing professional training on a substantial and continuing basis." See *Casagrande* v. *Landeshaupstadt Munich* [1974] 2 C.M.L.R. 423.

[70] See annex to Circ. 1/81.

[71] 1982 3 W.L.R. 1129. See also below at para. 3–45 n. 72.

1–115 As a result of the decision the Secretary of State included a provision in the Education (Mandatory Awards) Regulations 1983[72] to bring British practice into conformity with the *MacMahon* decision.

1–116 *Forcheri* v. *Belgium*,[73] decided not on the Council Regulation but on Article 7 of the Treaty itself, provides another example of how community law protects workers within the community from discrimination. The European Court of Justice held that it is a breach of Article 7 of the Treaty to require a national of a member state who is lawfully established in another member state to pay a fee for a course which is not required of the nationals of that other state.

1–117 Council Directive 76/207[74] is designed to implement the principle of equal treatment for men and women as regards access to employment, vocational training and promotion, and working conditions. Account was taken of the draft Directive in preparation of the Sex Discrimination Act 1975[75] and no elaboration of its terms here is necessary.

1–118 Council Directive 77/486[76] on the education of the children of migrant workers applies by Article 1, "to children for whom school attendance is compulsory under the laws of the host State who are dependants of any worker who is a national of another Member State, where such children are resident in the territory of the Member State in which that national carries on or has carried on an activity as an employed person." By Article 2 children must receive free tuition in the language of the host state, and teachers be trained to provide it. Under Article 3 "Member States shall, in accordance with their national circumstances and legal systems, and in cooperation with States of origin, take appropriate measures to promote, in co-ordination with normal education, teaching of the mother tongue and culture of the country of origin for the children referred to in Article 1." The Secretary of State has advised local education authorities regarding compliance with this Directive.[77]

1–119 As a member of the European Community Britain has also acceded[78] to the 1957 Statute of the European School, and there are now a number of such schools for the children of officials of Community member states. They have had conferred on them the legal capacities of a body corporate.[79] The schools offer a European Baccalaureate.[80]

---

[72] S.I. 1983 No. 1135 (now superseded by S.I. 1986 No. 1306) reg. 9. See below at para. 3–45 n. 72.

[73] [1984] 1 C.M.L.R. 334, and see also *Gravier* v. *Ville de Liège* [1985] 3 C.M.L.R. 1.

[74] February 9, 1976, (O.J. 1976 L 39/40, made pursuant to Art. 235 of the Treaty which grants wide powers to attain the objectives of the Community). See *R.* v. *Secretary of State for Education and Science, ex. p. Schaffter, The Times*, August 18, 1986, (below at para. 3–57 n. 41).

[75] But see *Commission of the European Communities* v. *U.K.* [1984] I.R.L.R. 29 in which the European Court of Justice held that the 1975 Act did not wholly meet the requirements of the Directive.

[76] July 25, 1977, (O.J. 1977 L 199/32 made pursuant to Art. 49 of the Treaty).

[77] Circ. 5/81 (W.O. 36/81).

[78] Treaty Series 120 (1972) Cmnd. 5145.

[79] See The European Communities (European Schools) Order 1972 (S.I. 1972 No. 1582). As to taxation of salaries of teachers at a European School see *Hurd* v. *Jones* [1986] S.T.C. 127.

[80] See Annex to Statute, as amended by agreement of June 19, 1978, (T.S. 1 1981, Cmnd. 8083).

Finance

The funds of local education authorities are those which are allocated   **1–120**
for expenditure on education functions, mandatory and permissive, by
councils who (with the exception of the Inner London Education Authority) are authorities for many purposes of which education is but one.
So it is necessary to give a general outline of the sources and system of
local government finance as well as to draw attention to those aspects of
the law that are peculiar to education.

Revenue expenditure and its sources

Local authority revenue expenditure—day-to-day spending—derives   **1–121**
from three main sources: the income drawn from rates,[81] central
government grants, and charges (where authorised) for services. Borrowing for revenue expenditure is not ordinarily permissible.[82] Local
authorities are free to determine the amount of their income from rates
(or, in the case of county councils, precepts upon district councils) subject to the terms of the Local Government Finance Act 1982, and to the
exercise by the Secretary of State for the Environment of his powers
under the Rates Act 1984. Part 1 of the 1982 Act abolishes the power to
levy a supplementary rate (or precept) during a financial year. The 1984
Act enables the Secretary of State to set a limit to the rate call of (*i.e.*
"rate-cap") some or all local authorities under specified circumstances.

Grant aid to local authorities derives mostly from the rate support   **1–122**
grant,[83] which is calculated on an annual basis. After consultation with
the local authority associations, and if thought desirable individual authorities, the Secretaries of State for Environment and Transport present
to the House of Commons an annual rate support grant report[84] in
which their proposals for grant in relation to the forthcoming financial
year are specified. No payment of rate support grant may be made until
the House of Commons has passed a resolution approving the report.
The aggregate amount of rate support grant for all authorities is determined[85] as a proportion of their "relevant expenditure"—the greater
part of their current expenditure—after consultation as above. The
(non-statutory) Consultative Council on Local Government Finance provides a forum for consultation between Ministers and local councillors,

---

[81] A tax, levied annually, on the occupation of property. As to London rate equalisation schemes see
London Government Act 1963, s.66, as amended, and Local Government Act 1985, s.83.

[82] But see Local Government Act 1972, Sched. 13, para. 10 (temporary loans).

[83] See s.53 and Pt. VI, generally, of the Local Government, Planning and Land Act 1980, as amended,
Local Government Finance Act 1987, Rate Support Grants Act 1987, and the commentary thereon
in the *Encyclopedia of Local Government Law*. See also Chartered Institute of Public Finance and
Accountancy, "Financial Information Service," *Education*, Vol. 20, Chap. 2, para. 28.

[84] As required by s.60, as amended, of the Local Government, Planning and Land Act 1980, *e.g.* The
Rate Support Grant Report (England) 1983–84 (H.C. 1982–3 149). Separate reports are made by the
Secretary of State for Wales. See also s.61, supplementary reports.

[85] In accordance with s.54, as amended, of the Local Government, Planning and Land Act 1980.

but preliminaries (as regards expenditure on education) are conducted by senior education officers and treasurers from local authorities and Department of Education and Science officials in the Expenditure Steering Group (Education).[86] The total of relevant expenditure is reduced by,[87] *inter alia*, expenditure on awards for university and comparable courses[88] and postgraduate teacher training.[89]

1–123   The greater part of rate support grant is "block grant."[90] (The other constituent is domestic rate relief grant). The amount of block grant available for distribution to local authorities in England and in Wales is adjusted[91] to take account of the extent to which education expenditure by local education authorities in the one country benefits people in the other. All local authorities and the Inner London Education Authority are eligible to receive a share of block grant. The amount of grant receivable is in principle the difference between the product of a grant-related poundage[92] specified by the Secretary of State at a level the same for all authorities of a particular class (for example, metropolitan districts, non-metropolitan counties) and the authority's relevant expenditure in a financial year. The Secretary of State also makes annually for each authority a grant related expenditure assessment which is his estimate, having regard to specified objective "indicators," of their expenditure needs in relation to their various functions. Hence the education expenditure needs[93] of a particular authority are calculated having regard, *inter alia*, to the number of pupils of different age groups in the area and to the social and environmental problems of the area which may give rise to additional educational needs.[94] The expenditure needs of an authority are the aggregate of the needs in relation to the functions and services which give rise to relevant expenditure; and they are no more than the Secretary of State's best estimate. The authority are not obliged to allocate funds to particular services in the proportions indicated by the way in which the assessment is calculated; and the estimate

---

[86] This Group is concerned with the level of relevant expenditure. Another group, the Grants Working Group, consider the methodologies of grant distribution. See also the Second Report from the Education, Science and Arts Committee of the House of Commons (1981–82), *The Secondary School Curriculum and Examinations* (H.C. 116–1) paras. 9.22–9.26 and Government responses thereto (Cmnd. 8648 pp.15–16 and Cmnd. 8551, pp. 13–14). See also Chartered Institute of Public Finance and Accountancy, "Financial Information Service" Chap. 2, paras. 29–32.
[87] See Local Government, Planning and Land Act 1980, s.54(5) and (6), as amended, referring to 1962 Act, ss.1(1) and 2(3), as to which see below at paras. 3–41 to 3–43, and 3–65.
[88] The courses include initial training courses for teachers. See 1962 Act, s.1(1) and below at para. 3–43.
[89] See 1962 Act, s.2(3) and below at para. 3–65.
[90] See Local Government, Planning and Land Act 1980 ss.56–59 (as amended).
[91] See *ibid.* s.63 and Sched. 10, Pts. I and III, as amended by 1986 (No. 2) Act, Sched. 4, para. 7 and by the Local Government Act 1987, s.2.
[92] The "poundage" is a specified rate in the pound. See Local Government, Planning and Land Act 1980, s.57 as amended by Rate Support Grants Act 1986.
[93] See *Grant Related Expenditure 1983–84, How the expenditure needs of local authorities are assessed for block grant*, Department of the Environment, 1983.
[94] See Chartered Institute of Public Finance and Accountancy, "Financial Information Service," Chap. 2, paras. 13–27.

does not bind the authority, who may spend more or less than their assessed needs, but with consequences for the amount of grant they receive, because there is a schedule of grant related poundages for different levels of expenditure in relation to the grant related expenditure assessment. This schedule (or "tariff") is designed to make it relatively more expensive, in terms of levying a rate, for authorities if they spend significantly above the grant related expenditure assessment.

This is no more than the barest outline of the way in which block grant   **1–124** is settled and allocated to authorities. The system of calculation is extremely elaborate and is replete with arcane "fine-tuning" arrangements which include "multipliers," "thresholds" and "safety-nets"— safeguards against abrupt reductions in the amount of grant received by an authority year-by-year. Moreover,

(a) the grant aggregate is made subject to particular adjustments in relation to expenditure on education[95];

(b) from the aggregate there is deducted expenditure incurred in the provision of services for local authorities by bodies specified in regulations[96] (the educational bodies included are the National Foundation for Educational Research, the Further Education Staff College, the School Curriculum Development Committee and the National Institute of Adult Continuing Education); and

(c) the system has in part been overlaid by Part II of the Local Government Finance Act 1982, under which the Secretary of State may reduce the amount of an authority's share if their expenditure exceeds a "target" that he sets.[97]

There are some other, specific, sources of central government grant   **1–125** for local education authorities. First, each authority receive[98] grant of 90 per cent. of the aggregate amount paid[99] in any year by way of mandatory awards to persons attending first degree university courses and comparable courses. Secondly, by the 1984 Act, section 1, the Secretary of State may make education support grants to local education authorities towards expenditure for educational purposes which "it appears to him that those authorities should be encouraged to incur in the interests of education in England and Wales." The classes or descriptions of expenditure are specified in regulations[1] (to be made only after consultation with bodies representing local education authorities[2]) and the

---

[95] By s.63 and Sched. 10 to the Local Government, Planning and Land Act 1980. See below at paras. 1–130 *et seq.*

[96] See *ibid.* s.56(9) and the Rate Support Grant (Specified Bodies) Regulations 1974, 1975, 1976 and 1981 (S.I. 1974 No. 788, 1975 No. 5, 1976 No. 214 and 1981 No. 295).

[97] No targets have been set since the financial year 1985/86.

[98] Local Government Act 1974, s.8(2)(*a*).

[99] Under 1962 Act s.1(1). See below at paras. 3–43 *et seq.*

[1] The Education Support Grants Regulations 1984 (S.I. 1984 No. 1098) as amended by Amendment Regulations (S.I. 1985 No. 1070, S.I. 1985 No. 2028 and S.I. 1986 No. 1031) which, *inter alia*, specify the purposes for, or in connection with, which grants are payable. See Circ. 5/86.

[2] 1984 Act, s.3(5).

rate of grant is not to exceed 70 per cent. Grant is payable on an annual basis. The regulations may prescribe, as eligible for grant, payments made by local education authorities to other bodies. England and Wales may be treated differently. The amount of expenditure to be eligible for education support grant is not to exceed 1 per cent.[3] of the aggregate amount of education expenditure which in the Secretary of State's opinion it would be appropriate for local education authorities to incur in any financial year. The aggregate amount is determined as prescribed,[4] and excludes, *inter alia*, expenditure on awards for university and comparable courses and grants to prospective teachers.

1–126 Thirdly, grant is paid[5] towards the cost of training (or giving further training to) teachers, youth and community workers, educational psychologists and local education authority inspectors and advisers. The expenditure on which grant is payable includes the fees and expenses of trainees and the cost of providing training and of remunerating replacement staff, whether the trainee is employed by the authority or by governors of an aided school or in a designated further education establishment.[6] Conditions of payment of grant, up to maxima set for the authority, are specified, and the rate is 50 per cent., or 70 per cent. if the Secretary of State approves the training as being in a "national priority area."

1–127 Finally, the Secretary of State has made regulations[7] under which he pays grant to local education authorities and others towards the cost of Welsh language teaching, subject to various requirements which include submission of accounts and inspection of premises and which also concern staffing and equipment.

1–128 There are further, extraneous, sources of funding. Their variety is more impressive than the amount of income that they produce. Local authorities may apply to the (Home) Secretary of State for grant on approved expenditure on employing extra staff where there are substantial numbers of commonwealth immigrants in their area.[8] The grant is payable in respect of any functions but in practice a high proportion has been spent on the education service.[9] The Department of the Environment meets a proportion of the cost of approved projects under the

---

[3] 1984 Act, s.2(1) as amended by Education (Amendment) Act 1986, s.1.

[4] *Ibid.* s.2 and S.I. 1984 No. 1098.

[5] Under the Education (Training Grants) Regulations 1987 (S.I. 1987 No. 961).

[6] As to employment by governors of aided schools, see para. 4–27 and as to designated further education establishments, paras. 3–05 and 4–21.

[7] The Grants for Welsh Language Education Regulations 1980 (S.I. 1980 No. 1011), made under s.21 of the 1980 Act. See Welsh Office Circ. 37/83.

[8] See Local Government Act 1966, s.11. The amount is at discretion. At present it is 75 per cent.

[9] See Second Report of the Education, Science and Arts Committee of the House of Commons 1981–82, para. 9.27, Chartered Institute of Public Finance and Accountancy, "Financial Information Service" Chap. 2, paras. 35–6 and Home Office Circ. 97/1982; also *Education for All*, Report of the (Swann) Committee of Inquiry into the Education of Minority Groups (Cmnd. 9453).

urban social needs programme.[10] The Department of Employment meets 100 per cent. of the cost of employing careers service[11] staff appointed to deal with high unemployment. The Department of Industry has provided micro-computers in secondary schools[12] and is meeting half the cost of providing micro-processors in primary schools. The cost of education in prisons and like institutions is met by the Home Office.[13] Similarly district health authorities may make grants for the education of handicapped persons and payment towards expenditure on education functions performed for disabled persons.[14] The European Community in prescribed circumstances pays subsidy on milk supplied to school children, grants of up to 50 per cent. from the Social Fund when an education course can be construed as "training," and grants to supplement the commonwealth immigrants grant referred to above.[15]

Some of these sources of finance are more in the nature of payments for services rendered (as in the case of the letting of school buildings) than grants. Into the same category also fall payments made by the Manpower Services Commission to local education authorities for a growing range of services provided for them by local education authorities—in particular sponsored further education courses.[16]   **1–129**

Pooling of expenditure

Certain forms of education expenditure impose financial burdens inequitably as between authorities, and the law has long provided for the costs of, in particular, teacher training and advanced further education to be apportioned among local education authorities by a system of contributions to and claims upon a "pool." Schedule 2 to the Local Government Act 1974 as amended by section 32 of the Education Act 1980 remains on the statute book, but may be repealed by the Secretary of State under the Local Government, Planning and Land Act 1980,[17] and the substantive law is now contained in that Act. "Pooling" is achieved by a system of adjustments to the block grant receivable by individual local education authorities.   **1–130**

---

[10] Local Government Grants (Social Need) Act 1969, s.1. The amount of grant is at discretion. At present it is 75 per cent.

[11] As to the careers service see below at paras. 5–42 *et seq.*

[12] See Second Report of the Education, Science and Arts Committee of the House of Commons 1981–82, para. 9.30.

[13] Perhaps to be regarded as part of, or under Local Government Act 1972, s.111 incidental to, further education. See A.M. 440 and addenda, and below at para. 3–15.

[14] See National Health Service Act 1977, s.28A as substituted by Health and Social Services and Social Security Adjudications Act 1983, s.1, and Department of Health and Social Security Circ. H.C. 83/6.

[15] See Chartered Institute of Public Finance and Accountancy, "Financial Information Service" Chap. 2, paras. 48–52.

[16] See below at para. 3–31. The putting of government funds at the disposal of the Manpower Services Commission for the provision of work-related non-advanced further education affects the rate support grant total (see 53 H.C. Deb. 140, January 31, 1984).

[17] See s.53(10) and (11)(*c*), and Sched. 8. s.32 of the Education Act 1980 (education expenditure and rate support grant) and Sched. 6 are repealed by 1986 (No. 2) Act Sched. 6.

1–131   All or part of expenditure on certain education (and some other) functions may be pooled,[18] the arrangements differing according to whether expenditure is on provision of advanced further education or on other education functions. These arrangements are carried into effect by regulations made by the Secretary of State, who is obliged to consult interests as above before doing specified things.[19] He has made regulations annually since 1981, each set applying to the ensuing financial year. Separate regulations are made for England and for Wales.

1–132   The 1987 regulations,[20] following the pattern of earlier regulations, apply to expenditure on specified[21] advanced further education courses (these are in the main courses of above G.C.E. "A" level[22] and O.N.C.[23] standard) and, as respects other education functions, to listed expenditure items[24] which have in common only that they are considered to benefit local education authorities generally, and that some of them would otherwise fall inequitably as between authorities. The items include certain outgoings in connection with advanced further education (England only), specified compensation and redundancy payments to teachers, and the cost of providing primary, secondary and further education of pupils not belonging to the area of any local education authority.

1–133   A proportion (specified in regulation 5(2)) of the expenditure on each of the last-mentioned items is pooled.[25] By regulation 5(1) the Secretary of State specifies in advance for each year the aggregate amount of expenditure on advanced further education that is to be pooled[26] (*i.e.* this part of the pool is "capped"). Under regulation 7 each authority's share of the aggregate is determined by the Secretary of State after consultation with the National Advisory Body for Public Sector Higher Education (or the Wales Advisory Body for Local Authority Higher Education) and it follows that an authority who exceed their share must

---

[18] See Local Government, Planning and Land Act 1980, s.63 and Sched. 10, Pt. II.

[19] *Ibid.* Sched. 10, Pt. III. Para. 8 specifies making regulations under the Sched., adjusting the amount of the block grant as between England and Wales and specifying the amount of advanced further education expenditure that is to be pooled. There is a Pooling Committee of officer representatives of the local authority associations, under a Department of Education and Science chairman "to consider and keep under review the arrangements for pooling educational expenditure and make recommendations to the Secretary of State or to the local authority associations."

[20] The Block Grant (Education Adjustments) (England) Regulations 1987 (S.I. 1987 No. 347) and Wales Regulations (S.I. 1967 No. 359).

[21] See *ibid.* reg. 3(2) and Sched. 2 (Wales: Sched). The courses are those for the further training of teachers (except for a qualification of the City and Guilds of London Institute) or youth and community workers and others which largely correspond with those specified in Sched. 2 to the Education (Schools and Further Education) Regulations 1981 (S.I. 1981 No. 1086). See below at para. 3–23 n. 95.

[22] See below at para. 2–139.

[23] See below at para. 3–02 n. 7.

[24] See S.I.1987 No. 347 (S.I. 1987 No. 359) reg. 3(3).

[25] See Local Government, Planning and Land Act 1980, Sched. 10, para. 5.

[26] *Ibid.* para. 6. See also Local Government Act 1987, s.3 and below at para. 3–23.

themselves bear the amount of the excess. Regulation 6[27] provides how, by reference to student numbers, expenditure as ascertained in relation to individual authorities by reference to regulation 5 is to be apportioned among local education authorities, and regulation 8 for the adjustment of block grant payments to individual authorities so as to be consistent with the apportionment. Pooling adjustments are further provided for in sections 2–4 of the 1986 Act.

Areas to which pupils belong. Recoupment of expenditure between local education authorities

In order to settle where responsibility for education expenditure lies it **1–134** may be necessary to determine the area, if any, to which a pupil belongs. The Secretary of State may make regulations for this purpose and he determines any question under the regulations in case of dispute. The Education (Areas to Which Pupils Belong) Regulations 1980[28] apply to settle the question of "belonging" in three sets of circumstances: the first is the obligation upon local education authorities and school governors to publish the arrangements[29] they make for admission to schools of pupils not belonging to the area of the local education authority; the second arises where recoupment[30] of the costs incurred by one authority for providing education for a pupil who belongs to the area of another authority is prescribed; and the third is the need to identify the category of pupils who belong to no area and expenditure on whose education is to be pooled in accordance with the arrangements described above. Reference in the regulations to further education does not include advanced further education, expenditure on which, as mentioned above, is also pooled.

With the exceptions mentioned in the next paragraph, where a school **1–135** or full-time further education pupil is ordinarily resident[31] in the area of a local education authority he is to be treated as belonging to that area (regulation 5); and if he is not resident in the area of any local education authority he is to be treated as a "no-area" pupil (regulation 6). A part-time further education pupil is ordinarily to be treated as belonging to the area in which he is for the time being residing (regulation 7, which specifies the exceptions).

School pupils who are boarded out, pupils with special educational **1–136** needs[32] at boarding schools, school pupils resident in hospitals, further education pupils becoming ordinarily resident for education purposes,

---

[27] As to unlawful failure by the Secretary of State to amend the formula in reg. 6 see *R.* v. *Secretary of State for Education and Science, ex p. Inner London Education Authority, The Times*, June 20, 1985.
[28] S.I. 1980 No. 917 (as amended by S.I. 1980 No. 1862 and S.I. 1983 No. 260) made under Education Act 1980, s.38(5).
[29] See 1980 Act, s.8(3)(*d*) and below at para. 2–187.
[30] See below at paras. 1–138 and 1–139.
[31] "Ordinary residence." See below at para. 3–73.
[32] "Special educational needs"—see below at para. 2–194.

further education pupils who change ordinary residence and further education pupils in receipt of awards, are in general to be treated as belonging to the area of the person responsible for them or where they were previously ordinarily resident, while pupils in local authority care ordinarily belong to the area of the local education authority which includes the area of the "caring" local authority; but there are exceptions in relation to each category on which the regulations need to be consulted; and no-area pupils are not to be regarded as falling within any of the categories (regulations 9 to 16).

1–137　　"No-area" pupils (excluding pupils in care) are school and further education pupils whose parents are outside England and Wales, most boarding school pupils who by reason of change of circumstances cease to be treated as belonging to the area of a particular local education authority, school pupils with no fixed abode, further education pupils educated in hospitals, further education pupils who would otherwise cease to be no-area pupils, and school and further education pupils who are (a) cared for by charitable foundations, or (b) from visiting forces, or (c) resident in refugee camps, etc. Again there are exceptions that make reference to regulations 17 to 26 essential in relation to particular cases.

1–138　　Recoupment between local authorities was at one time the subject of regulations made by the Secretary of State, but his regulation-making powers have latterly been mainly restricted to circumstances in which a Scottish education authority is involved.[33] The general rule as between two authorities in England and Wales is that one authority may recoup[34] from the other the cost of providing education[35] for a pupil belonging to the other authority,[36] the amount being determined by agreement[37] or in default by the Secretary of State. An authority must make their claim within 18 months of the end of the year to which it relates.[38] The exceptions to the general rule have been that the cost of providing primary education to a pupil under five,[39] or of providing further education,[40]

---

[33] 1980 Act, s.31(5) (repealed by the 1986 (No. 2) Act and replaced by s.52 thereof). See Circ. 1/80, paras. 36–40.

[34] *Ibid.* s.31 (repealed by 1986 (No. 2) Act). s.31(1)–(3) are substituted by 1986 (No. 2) Act s.51(1) and (2). S.31(8) (as amended) of the London Government Act 1963 (recoupment in Greater London) is repealed by 1986 (No. 2) Act s.51(12) (from a date to be appointed as regards the cost of provision of further education).

[35] Widely defined by the 1980 Act, s.31(6) (so as to include, *e.g.*, in a proper case, the cost of boarding). s.31(6) is substituted by s.51(7) of the 1986 (No. 2) Act.

[36] As to parental choice of school see below at para. 2–176.

[37] Normally in accordance with the recommendations of the Inter-Authority Payments Committee (non-statutory, and comprising officers appointed by the local authority associations). The rates recommended represent the national average unit cost of providing education for school pupils of different ages and for further education students taught at different levels. The further education cost is calculated net of the average tuition fee.

[38] S.I. 1980 No. 917, reg. 27. The school year ends on March 31; the further education year on July 31.

[39] 1980 Act, s.31(2) (see n. 34 above).

[40] *Ibid.* s.31(3) (see n. 34 above).

cannot be recouped unless the provision is made with the consent of the local education authority for the area to which the pupil belongs; that advanced further education, being pooled,[41] is excluded; and that a recoupment payment may be made by one authority to the other even if no claim has been made.[42]

The provisions in the previous paragraph continue to apply under sec-   **1–139**
tions 51 and 52 of the 1986 (No. 2) Act, and with the following elabo-rations[43] and modifications. The cost of the primary education of children under five (otherwise than in hospital), and of further edu-cation of pupils within a category prescribed,[44] is also subject to recoup-ment without the consent of the authority from whom payment is claimed[45]; when the Secretary of State determines the amount of a recoupment payment in default of agreement the nature of the direction he may give is specified[46]; he is to determine disputes about entitlement to any such payment[47]; and questions about whether a pupil belongs to the area of an authority are to be decided as they would be under the 1980 Act.[48]

Capital expenditure—sources and limits

"Capital expenditure, in general terms, is expenditure on some tan-   **1–140**
gible thing which is expected to last for some years" but the law provides no strict definition, and at the margins what one authority regards as capital expenditure another may regard as current—as running costs.[49] Local education authorities incur capital expenditure on, for example, buying land and putting up and improving buildings just as do councils in their other capacities, and the law does not in the main distinguish between the capacities in which a local authority are acting.

Capital expenditure may be met from various sources including capi-   **1–141**
tal receipts, and gifts and bequests, but borrowing is the most common recourse.[50] The sources of borrowing include[51] the issue of various kinds of security, the Public Works Loans Commissioners, internal funds and bank overdrafts. Monies borrowed are secured on the authority's revenues.[52] With some exceptions, which include temporary borrowing, a local authority may borrow only with the approval of the Secretary of

---

[41] 1980 Act, s.31(7) as amended. (Substituted by s.51(8) of the 1986 (No. 2) Act).
[42] *Ibid.* s.31(4). (Substituted by s.51(9) of the 1986 (No. 2) Act.)
[43] As to acceptance of pupils at a further education establishment see below at para. 3–04.
[44] *i.e.* prescribed in regs. made by the Secretary of State.
[45] 1986 (No. 2) Act, s.51(2).
[46] *Ibid.* s.51(3) and (4).
[47] *Ibid.* s.51(11).
[48] *Ibid.* s.51(10), *i.e.* under the Education Act 1980, s.38(5) and S.I. 1980 No. 917.
[49] See General Note to s.172 of the Local Government Act 1972 in *Encyclopedia of Local Govern-ment Law.*
[50] Regulated by *ibid.* s.172 and Pt. I of Sched. 13.
[51] *Ibid.* Sched. 13 para. 2.
[52] *Ibid.* para. 11.

State, given generally or specifically.[53] Until April 1, 1981, authorities had to obtain loan sanction for capital schemes or projects, but consent for borrowing for most purposes, including the functions of local education authorities, has now been granted generally by the Secretary of State for the Environment for purposes prescribed in Schedule 12[54] to the Local Government, Planning and Land Act 1980, and for building repairs and maintenance.[55] Prescribed expenditure covers most forms of capital expenditure.

1–142   Part VIII[56] of the 1980 Act, from which Schedule 12 stems, brings not only borrowing but the totality of local government capital expenditure under central government control. For each authority the Secretary of State specifies an annual allocation of prescribed capital expenditure related to the plans submitted to him by the authority but having regard to national economic considerations. As a matter of practice, not of law, the allocation is composed of separate service blocks of which education is one; and the service block allocations may be aggregated and used for such purposes within the overall allocation as the authorities see fit. The amount in each block reflects government priorities, however, and an authority who made their allocation in ways markedly different from those indicated by the blocks would put themselves at risk as regards the subsequent year's allocation.

1–143   The amount specified for each authority may be marginally supplemented in various ways[57] (for example, by receipts from the sale of capital assets[58]), or reduced,[59] and the Secretary of State may direct[60] that part shall be spent towards a project of national or regional importance or that no part shall be spent on a specific project. If the Secretary of State believes that an authority are likely to overspend their allocation he may give them directions accordingly.[61] It remains to emphasise that allocations are permissions to spend, not grants, (though capital grants are made, in limited circumstances[62]); to add the reminder that the

---

[53] Local Government Act 1972, para. 1(*b*). Authorities must also comply with the requirements of the Treasury under the Borrowing (Control and Guarantees) Act 1946.

[54] See para. 1.

[55] See Annex A to DoE Circ. 9/83, which also qualifies the power to borrow and the extent of borrowing.

[56] See General Note to Pt. VIII in *Encyclopedia of Local Government Law.*, DoE Circ. 9/83, and Chartered Institute of Public Finance and Accountancy, "Financial Information Service" Chap. 3, paras. 28 *et seq.* Pt. VIII has been amended by the Local Government Act 1987.

[57] See Local Government, Planning and Land Act 1980, s.72 as amended.

[58] So far as authorised by *ibid.* s.75 and in the Local Government (Prescribed Expenditure) Regulations 1983 (S.I. 1983 No. 296) as amended by S.I. 1984 No. 223, S.I. 1985 No. 257 and S.I. 1985 No. 351. An authority may be restricted in the proportion of their capital receipts that they may use in any year.

[59] Local Government, Planning and Land Act 1980, s.74.

[60] *Ibid.* s.73.

[61] *Ibid.* s.78.

[62] *e.g.* by the Sports Council for the Youth Service (see below at para. 3–40) or when facilities are provided at an educational establishment for use by the public, by the Manpower Services Commission and by health authorities.

amortisation of loans is a substantial and regular part of current revenue expenditure; and to remark that it is the general control of capital expenditure that underlies the Secretary of State's control over particular educational building projects.[63]

LAND AND PROPERTY

The law relating to the land use and transactions of local education **1–144** authorities, like that concerning finance, in part relates to local authorities generally.

Acquisition

The acquisition by local education authorities of land[64] for schools **1–145** and other institutions is authorised by a general power (Local Government Act 1972, section 120) under which a council[65] may acquire by agreement, for money or money's worth, as purchaser or lessee, any land inside or outside their area for the purposes of their functions; and by acquisition subsisting restrictive covenants are overridden.[66] A local education authority may acquire land for themselves and for one or more other local education authorities. Acquisition may take place notwithstanding that the land is not immediately required for educational purposes, and in the interim it may be used for another of the council's functions. Land acquired by a local authority for one purpose may, with some qualifications, be appropriated to another purpose.[67] Also land once acquired may be disposed of.[68]

For the benefit of voluntary schools it is provided that making available land for educational institutions maintained[69] or assisted[70] by a **1–146** local education authority is a function of the authority for the purposes of the legislation governing local authority acquisition of land by agreement, notwithstanding that the land will not be held by the local education authority.[71] If a local education authority acquire land by

---

[63] See below at para. 2–52.

[64] "Land" includes any interest in land and any easement or right in, to or over land (Local Government Act 1972, s.270). See Circ. 2/60 (much of which, however, is now anachronistic because of changes in statute law).

[65] Properly, a "principal" council, which includes all local education authorities. (See Local Government Act 1972, s.270).

[66] Local Government Act 1972, s.120(3) applying the provisions (except s.31) of the Compulsory Purchase Act 1965. See *Kirby* v. *School Board for Harrogate* [1896] 1 Ch. 437.

[67] *Ibid.* s.122 as amended by Local Government, Planning and Land Act 1980, (s.90(2) of the 1944 Act was repealed by s.38(6) and Sched. 7 of the Education Act 1980). As to appropriation of land forming part of a common, *etc.* see Town and Country Planning Act 1971, s.121, as amended.

[68] Ordinarily without the consent of the Secretary of State. See *ibid.* s.123 (s.90(3) of the 1944 Act was repealed as above). See also 1973 Act, s.2 below at para. 1–157.

[69] See 1944 Act, s.114(2)(*a*), as amended, and below at para. 2–02.

[70] See 1944 Act, s.114(2)(*b*), and below at para. 2–08.

[71] 1948 Act, s.10(2) as amended. (This subsection cites s.157 of the Local Government Act 1933, now repealed and replaced by Local Government Act 1972, s.120. See also 1972 Act, Sched. 29, para. 1(2)).

agreement for a voluntary school they must not bear expenditure which would have been borne by the governors[72] had the governors themselves acquired the land.[73]

1–147   General powers (Local Government Act 1972, section 121, as amended) may also be used by local education authorities to acquire land compulsorily, but there is a specific power in the 1944 Act[74] which enables the Secretary of State to authorise a local education authority to purchase compulsorily for any school or college maintained or assisted by them or otherwise for the purpose of their functions. As in the case of voluntary acquisition, governors of voluntary schools must bear the expenditure which would have fallen to them had they bought the land themselves.

1–148   The procedure for authorising the compulsory purchase of land by local education authorities follows that in relation to compulsory purchase by local authorities generally,[75] and on a compulsory purchase order being made restrictive covenants are overridden.[76] It was held in *Darlassis* v. *Ministry of Education*[77] that the decision whether to confirm a compulsory purchase order is an administrative one, and that the Minister was therefore entitled to take into account information not available to an objector[78] to the order. Once the Secretary of State has confirmed a compulsory purchase order and notice to treat has been served it is open to the local education authority—or the trustees of a voluntary school—to enter on the land and for building operations to begin.[79]

1–149   A local education authority may accept, hold and administer any property upon trust for purposes connected with education[80]; and any intention on the part of the local education authority that a school for providing primary and secondary education (other than a nursery, or a special, school) should be vested in the authority as trustees is to be treated as an intention to maintain the school as a county school.[81]

---

[72] See below at paras. 2–70 *et seq.*

[73] 1948 Act, s.10(3) as amended by 1980 Act, s.1(3) and Sched. 1, para. 19. As to provision of sites by local education authorities for voluntary schools see below at para. 2–28.

[74] 1944 Act, s.90, as amended by Acquisition of Land (Authorisation Procedure) Act 1946 ss.6 and 10 and Scheds. 4 and 6, 1948 Act, s.10(1) and 1980 Act, s.1(3) and Sched. 1, para. 1.

[75] See Acquisition of Land Act 1981, Compulsory Purchase Act 1965, and commentary thereon in *Encyclopedia of Compulsory Purchase and Compensation.*

[76] *Kirby* v. *School Board for Harrogate* [1896] 1 Ch. 437.

[77] (1954) 118 J.P. 452. As to when the duty to "act fairly" arises see above at paras. 1–54 *et seq.*

[78] As to the rights of objectors see the Compulsory Purchase by Local Authorities (Inquiries Procedure) Rules 1976 (S.I. 1976 No. 746).

[79] Compulsory Purchase Act 1965, s.11 as amended.

[80] 1944 Act, s.85(1). As to the use to which trust funds should be put see the remarks of Jessel M.R. in *Re Poplar and Blackwall Free School* (1878) 8 Ch. 543. s.139 of the Local Government Act 1972 enables local authorities generally to accept gifts of property.

[81] 1944 Act, s.85(2) and (3) as substituted by 1980 Act, s.16(4) and Sched. 3, para. 3. The consequence is that ss.12, 14 and 16 of the 1980 Act apply as regards publication of proposals etc. See below at paras. 2–14 *et seq.*

Reverter and the School Sites Acts

In the early 19th century, before schools were provided by public **1–150** authorities, a voluntary movement grew up to provide elementary education for the poor. To facilitate the acquisition of land for this charitable purpose the School Sites Act 1841[82] made possible the conveyance of sites of up to one acre for schools and school teachers' houses out of a land-owner's estate[83] or manor where the grantor was not the absolute owner or was under some other legal disability. This legislation also provided a simplified form of conveyance[84] (which could also be used by an absolute owner) for such sites; and where[85] the grantees were an incumbent and parish officers they were treated as a corporate body; so that they and their successors became *ex officio* trustees of a charity. It also included provisos that if the land ceased to be used for the purposes for which it had been granted it would immediately and automatically[86] revert.[87]

The School Sites Acts 1844, 1849, 1851 and 1952, were passed to **1–151** explain the 1841 Act and to extend its provisions (the 1852 Act) to schools for "the sons of yeomen and tradesmen and others" and to theological training colleges. This legislation preserved the right of reverter. Its exercise has given rise to complex problems[88] and remains a live issue because many voluntary schools which may in due course be discontinued still occupy sites conveyed under the School Sites Acts. There may be more than 2,000 of these sites. The Reverter of Sites Act 1987, when brought into force by the Lord Chancellor, will resolve the major difficulty identified by a Law Commission working party[89] as follows.

It is not disputed that trustees under the School Sites Act hold a legal **1–152** estate determinable when the circumstances come about that give rise to reverter. Before the 1925 real property legislation the legal estate would automatically have shifted from the trustees to the person entitled on reverter.[90] Subsequently, it is arguable that despite saving provisions in section 7(1) and (3) of the Law of Property Act 1925 the effect of section 3(3) is that only the equitable, beneficial, interest passes. If this is the case the trustees are not divested of the legal estate but continue to hold it on trust, not now for the charity but for the person entitled on reverter until, when the person entitled is ascertained, they convey the legal estate as required by section 3(3). So it was held in *Re Clayton's Deed*

---

[82] ss.2–6 as amended. As to sale or exchange of land or buildings see s.14 as amended.

[83] "Estate" apparently in the popular, not legal, sense.

[84] In s.10 as amended.

[85] By s.7 as amended.

[86] See *Dennis* v. *Malcolm* [1934] Ch. 244, *Re Cawston's Conveyance* [1940] Ch. 27. In *Att.-Gen.* v. *Shadwell* [1910] 1 Ch. 92 it was held that land having been granted for use as a day school reverted on change of use to a Sunday School.

[87] There is no reverter provision in s.6, which is concerned with conveyances by corporations, justices, trustees, etc. See *Hornsey District Council* v. *Smith* [1897] 1 Ch. 843.

[88] See M. Scott, "Redundant School Sites," (1983) L.G.C. 600.

[89] *Property Law. Rights of Reverter* (Law Commission No. 111), Cmnd. 8410, November 1981.

[90] See *Att.-Gen.* v. *Shadwell* [1910] 1 Ch. 92.

Poll,[91] but there is more recent authority, also at first instance, (in *Re Rowhook Mission Hall*, Horsham[92]) that, as before the 1925 legislation, on reverter the trustees lose the entirety of their interest. Nourse J.'s conclusion in the last-mentioned case is consistent with two earlier decisions. In *Re Ingleton Charity*[93] a school the subject of the 1841 Act closed in 1929. In 1952 the premises were sold by the trustees (no reverter claim having been made). The court held that the statutory limitation period had run and that the trustees held a possessory title[94] free from the right of the reverter but that they had at all times been trustees for charitable (educational) purposes and that the proceeds could not be diverted from those purposes. In *Re Chavasse's Conveyance*[95] a former school site bombed during the Second World War was afterwards compulsorily purchased for other purposes by Birmingham Corporation. The court held that the trustees were not entitled to the purchase money because reverter had operated so as to leave them nothing to convey.

The Reverter of Sites Act 1987 repeals section 3(3) of the Law of Property Act 1925 and amends section 7(1). Section 1 of the 1987 Act provides that on land ceasing to be used for the purposes for which it was conveyed under the School Sites Acts no right of reverter arises, but the land becomes vested in the trustees on a trust for sale. (The provision is retrospective in applying to land in respect of which a right of reverter has already arisen). The trustees then hold the land, or the proceeds of sale, as trustees for the revertee. If they wish to apply to the Charity Commissioners under section 2 to establish a scheme which extinguishes the rights of beneficiaries they must first, under section 3, take steps to trace the revertee (unless any claim has already become statute-barred).[95a] If after three months they have failed to trace him they may make the application. The scheme will require the trustees to hold the property on trust for the charitable purposes specified in the Commissioners' order—purposes as similar in character as practicable to those for which the land was previously held, but the Commissioners are given a broad discretion. If a beneficiary makes a valid claim within five years of the making of the Commissioners' order he is to receive the value of his rights as compensation.

Section 2 also requires the Charity Commissioners to give notice of,

---

[91] [1979] 3 W.L.R. 351.
[92] [1985] Ch. 62. See (1984) 100 L.Q.R. 528. J. H. G. Sunnucks in "The Village School and the Squatting Trustees," (1984) 81 L.S. Gaz. 1851, argues persuasively in favour of the earlier of the two decisions.
[93] [1956] Ch. 585.
[94] As to possessory title and conveyance of land so held, see A. J. Balcombe and E. W. H. Christie, "Reverters under the School Sites Acts" (1953) 103 L.J. 679.
[95] April 14, 1954, (unreported, but see Cmnd. 8410 at p. 6).
[95a] Where reverter has occurred less than 12 years before the commencement of the Act, the imposition of the trust for sale (by s.1) prevents time running. Nevertheless, when more than 12 years have elapsed after reverter, s.3(4) will excuse the trustees from having to comply with the s.3 procedure.

and invite representations on, their proposed scheme, and by section 4 once the order is made it too is to be publicised, and it is subject to a right of appeal to the High Court.

The substitution of a trust for sale, under the 1987 Act, for reverter **1–153** will not, it seems, wholly dismiss the following questions:

(a) when does reverter occur;
(b) what reverts; and
(c) to whom (or what) does the land revert?

The answer to (a)—immediately upon cesser of the charitable use—leaves open the question of fact: what constitutes cesser? In *Re Chavasse* it was held that cesser did not take place when the school was bombed but some years later, upon intentional permanent discontinuance[96] of the school. In practice there may be dispute as to the date of permanent discontinuance.

Question (b)—what reverts—is material if part only of the land in **1–154** question ceases to be used for the charitable purpose. It is arguable on the wording of the 1841 Act that the whole of the land reverts, but in the absence of authority the Law Commission working party took the better view to be that part-cesser leads to part-reverter—a conclusion that is not problem-free if the site is built upon, and for example, the upper floor but not the ground floor remains in use for charitable purposes.

The 1841 Act states that the land "shall . . . revert to and become a **1–155** portion of the said estate held in fee simple or otherwise, or of any manor or land as aforesaid . . . " But this is no complete answer to question (c) if only because as in *Re Cawston's Conveyance*[97] the site of the redundant school may be an isolated one. In that case the charitable trustees argued that since the site did not form *part* of land, reverter did not arise. The Court of Appeal, however, interpreted the Act so that reverter operated in favour of the grantor's personal representatives. This decision raises the major question whether as a fixed general rule a site, even if it is not isolated, always reverts to the grantor's representatives (or to the settlement under which he held it) rather than rejoins the "estate" from which it was severed (which over the years may have been split into numerous plots in different ownerships and which may not all be contiguous). Whatever the answer,[98] identification of the persons entitled under the reverter may well be difficult.

There are additional uncertainties. Section 14 of the 1841 Act has **1–156** been understood, despite ambiguous limiting words in the reverter provisos, to give trustees the power of sale of land given or acquired under the Act so as to move the school, as an existing institution, to another

---

[96] *Att.-Gen.* v. *Price* [1912] 1 Ch. 667 is another authority for the proposition that charitable use does not necessarily cease abruptly (see note 2 below).
[97] [1940] Ch. 27.
[98] The language used by the court in *Dennis* v. *Malcolm* [1934] Ch. 244 and *Att.-Gen.* v. *Shadwell* [1910] 1 Ch. 92 seems to suggest that the general rule is "rejoinder."

site; but there is no direct authority on the point. It does seem clear, however, that trustees cannot exercise their power once the reverter proviso has taken effect. Also, events occurring between the grant and reverter may throw up problems on which the courts have not adjudicated. For example, the donor may have been tenant for life of an entailed estate and the entail may subsequently have been broken. It is not clear how a site devolves in those circumstances. Nor is it clear whether rights of common lost by the grant revive upon reverter.

Once the 1987 Act is in force, section 6 confirms that the power conferred by section 14 of the 1841 Act is exercisable at any time in relation to land which might otherwise become the subject of a trust under section 1; and the exercise of that power prevents a section 1 trust from arising.

1–157   It remains to refer to the powers of the Secretary of State, of the court and those of the Charity Commissioners that pre-date the 1987 Act. Section 2 of the 1973 Act provides that where the premises of a voluntary school have ceased to be used as such, or the Secretary of State believes that this eventuality is likely, he may by order (made by statutory instrument) make a scheme under which endowments for denominational religious education are newly used for similar purposes. Such a scheme is subject to the jurisdiction of the Charity Commissioners. The order may be made only on the application of the appropriate denominational authority, and opportunity must be given by notice to specified interested persons to make representations upon the proposed order before it is made. The order may require or authorise the disposal of land[99] or other property which is part of the endowment, including the school premises and any teacher's dwelling house.

1–158   Additionally the order may exclude the operation of the reverter proviso in section 2 of the 1841 Act if the Secretary of State is satisfied that the person to whom the land *would* revert cannot be found or, having been found, has consented to relinquish his rights gratuitously or otherwise. But for a number of reasons the Secretary of State may be able to make only limited use of this power. One is that a section 2 order may not be available because a school may have been provided to advance "Christian" education but not be attached to a particular denomination; another, that in practice the Secretary of State, so as to be seen to be acting fairly, defers enquiries for reversioners until he has reached a decision[1] about closing the school, and by that time it may be impracticable to make a section 2 order before closure—and hence reverter— takes place. This last-mentioned clog upon section 2 of the 1973 Act will be removed once the 1987 Act is in force, because section 5 enables the Secretary of State to make an order after as well as before a trust for sale

---

[99] As to conveyancing problems (under s.86(2) of the 1944 Act which was superseded by s.2 of the 1973 Act), see 96 S.J. 174.
[1] Under s.12 of the 1980 Act.

arises under section 1, provided that he has first taken steps to trace potential beneficiaries.

The court and the Charity Commissioners have powers (pre-dating 1–159 the 1987 Act) to make *cy-près* schemes for charitable purposes—but the circumstances which point to the need for a scheme may be those in which reverter comes about; and once reverter has occurred the land is released from the charitable trusts and it is too late to make a scheme which affects the revertee's rights. There are other complications, some related to the *Clayton* decision, which may make court and Commissioners reluctant to act.

Where court and Commissioners—more frequently the latter—do 1–160 make a scheme it will reflect the original trust purpose—normally to benefit a particular locality.[2] The Secretary of State has a rather wider discretion under section 2 of the 1973 Act, and when Church of England school premises are sold the diocesan education committee[3] have some choice regarding the educational purposes to which the proceeds are to be put.

Rates and charges

Land occupied by local education authorities for educational pur- 1–161 poses is rateable.[4] Voluntary schools, with the possible exception of controlled schools, are generally occupied for charitable purposes by their governors who thus take the benefit of statutory relief,[5] which is 50 per cent., or higher at the discretion of the rating authority; and the amounts payable are met by local education authorities as part of maintenance expenses.[6] The General Rate Act 1967[7] makes special provision for the ascertainment of the rateable value of county and voluntary school premises. Regulations may be made so as broadly to base the value on the number of pupils multiplied by the cost of providing a place at the school. Before regulations are made the local authority associations are to be consulted. No regulations have yet been made and in practice valuations have been derived from a formula[8] agreed with the associations. The propriety of valuation according to a formula has been

---

[2] See *Att.-Gen.* v. *Price* [1912] 1 Ch. 667, in which the Court of Appeal held that following the closure of a denominational school a *cy-près* scheme should not permit the premises to be let at a rent to be applied to church purposes generally, but that the premises should be used for the education of the poor in the locality which was the subject of the original grant.

[3] See below at para. 2–157.

[4] *West Bromwich School Board* v. *West Bromwich Overseers* (1884) 13 Q.B.D. 929 (C.A.).

[5] See General Rate Act 1967, s.40 as amended.

[6] Rating and Valuation Act 1961, s.12(6).

[7] s.30 as amended by Local Government, Planning and Land Act 1980, ss.193, 194 and Sched. 33, para. 10(2) and Sched. 34.

[8] The rateable value of schools (primary, middle, secondary, special and boarding) is assessed in accordance with an agreement made in 1961 between the Department of Education and Science, the Inland Revenue and the local authority associations. The rateable value derives from the number of places provided on the basis of an agreed uniform floor area per pupil. If in practice the number of pupils is above or below, by 5 per cent., the basic scholar place numbers, the valuation officer makes an adjustment of rateable value.

upheld by the Lands Tribunal but not so as to demand its rigid application or bind the Inland Revenue valuation officer.[9] A proportion of capital value is the basis of rateable value of further education institutions.

1–162   Trustees under section 2 of the School Sites Act 1841 have been held[10] to be owners of land for the purposes of public health legislation and hence liable for paving charges. Local education authorities and the trustees of voluntary schools appear to be owners liable for the cost of private street works under the current legislation.[11]

Planning

1–163   Local education authorities are touched by town and country planning law[12] and practice in at least three disparate ways. Development of land by local education authorities within their own area is normally deemed to be granted planning permission (where permission is required) but conditions may be attached by the Secretary of State.[13] The local planning authority (a) must draw attention, on permission being granted for educational building, to statutory provisions in aid of the disabled[14] and (b) are expected to consult local education authorities in the preparation of structure plans.[15]

---

[9] See *Dawkins* v. *Royal Leamington Spa Corporation and Warwickshire County Council* (1961) 8 R.R.C. 241 and *Henning (Valuation Officer)* v. *Croydon Corporation* (1965) 11 R.R.C. 172.

[10] In *Bowditch* v. *Wakefield Local Board* (1871) 6 L.R.Q.B. 567. A charge cannot be enforced by an order for sale (*Hornsey District Council* v. *Smith* [1897] 1 Ch. 843).

[11] Highways Act 1980, Pt. XI.

[12] "Education and Planning Law" is the title of a somewhat anachronistic article by R. P. Crompton, [1954] J.P.L. 28.

[13] See Town and Country Planning Act 1971, especially ss.40 and 270 as amended, and the regulations made thereunder.

[14] *Ibid*. s.29B inserted by the Disabled Persons Act 1981 s.3. See below at para. 2–59 and Circ. 2/82, para. 3.3.

[15] See A.M. 5/73 (W.O. 5/73).

CHAPTER 2

SCHOOLS

Grammar and "public" schools have a long history. Systematic pro-   **2–01**
vision of education for the populace dates only from the 19th century,
and was promoted in the first place by voluntary, mostly religious, societies. With the passage of time types of school have proliferated as the
following paragraphs show.

Section 9 of the 1944 Act refers to primary schools, secondary   **2–02**
schools, nursery schools, special schools and also to county and voluntary schools. By subsection (2) primary and secondary schools maintained[1] by local education authorities are either county schools, or, if
not established by them, voluntary schools (usually of a religious foundation); but the "county" and "voluntary" terminology does not extend
to nursery[2] and special[3] schools. Voluntary schools are categorised[4] as
controlled, aided or special agreement. The governors of aided and
special agreement schools meet part of the maintenance expenses[5] of
those schools, and in return, it will become apparent, enjoy wider freedom of action than the governors of controlled schools. "Maintained"
schools are to be distinguished from those schools which receive a grant
direct[6] from the Secretary of State and from other independent schools[7]
and non-maintained special schools. "School"[8]—an institution for providing primary and/or secondary education—includes all the above (but
an institution which does not so provide[9] as a sole or a principal purpose
is not a school). "Comprehensive school" appeared as a headnote to
sections 1–3[10] of the 1976 Act but those sections were repealed by

---

[1] "Maintain"—see 1944 Act, s.114(2)(*a*), as amended by 1980 Act, s.1(3) and Sched. 1, para. 1.
[2] See below at paras. 2–03 and 2–45 *et seq*.
[3] See below at paras. 2–04 and 2–203 *et seq*.
[4] 1944 Act, s.15(1) and see below at para. 2–22.
[5] See below at para. 2–24. By 1944 Act, s.65, as amended by 1980 Act, s.1(3) and Sched. 1, para. 1,
where an endowment under a trust deed produces income for a voluntary school the income is not
payable to the local education authority, but is applied by governors to meet their maintenance
obligations (if any) or as may be determined by a scheme made under the Charities Act 1960.
Exemption from registration under the 1960 Act is granted where premises are the only endowment: Charites (Exemption of Voluntary Schools from Registration) Regulations 1960 (S.I. 1960
No. 2366).
[6] See *post* paras. 2–217 *et seq*.
[7] See also below at paras. 6–27 *et seq*. (By s.34(1) of the 1980 Act amendment "direct grant" schools
are now defined as independent schools).
[8] Defined in 1944 Act, s.114(1), as amended by 1980 Act, s.34(1).
[9] See A.M. 557.
[10] As to the interpretation of these sections, see *North Yorkshire County Council* v. *Department of
Education and Science* (1978) 77 L.G.R. 457.

section 1 of the 1979 Act.[11] Other familiar school descriptions, such as "infant," "junior" and "grammar," have no place in statute[12] but derive from usage that is consistent with statutory provisions.

2–03   Most of the terms mentioned, and some others, need explanation at the outset or later in this Chapter. "Pupil"[13] where used without qualification means a person of any age for whom education is required to be provided under the Education Acts[14] but includes a junior pupil under five (in respect of whom there is no requirement). Junior pupils are children under 12.[15] Primary schools[16] provide primary education[17]—full-time[18] education suitable to the requirements of junior pupils under ten years six months and of older junior pupils whom it is expedient to educate with them.[19] Primary schools for children over two but under five are known as nursery schools.[20] Secondary schools[21] provide secondary education[22]—full-time education suitable to the requirements of senior pupils[23] (ages 12 to 18 inclusive) and junior pupils of ten years six months and over whom it is expedient to educate with them. (The overlap of the age range of primary and secondary education makes it easier to transfer pupils at the most appropriate time). A middle school is one which provides for part of the primary and part of the secondary age range. It is deemed to be primary or secondary according to how the age range of the pupils is balanced below and above the age of 11; and the Secretary of State makes a determination if the age range is evenly balanced.[24] Sixth-form college is not defined in the Education Acts but is defined specifically for the purposes of the regulations governing school premises,[25] as a school (other than a special school) which has only pupils who have attained the age of 16 years. It is to be distinguished from a tertiary college, which is a further education

---

[11] Amended by 1980 Act, s.1(3) and Sched. 1, para. 31.

[12] But some non-statutory terms appear in regulations (see, *e.g.* the Education (School Information) Regulations 1981 (S.I. 1981 No. 630), Sched. 2); and Education Act definitions are sometimes modified when used in regulations.

[13] 1944 Act, s.114(1), as amended by 1980 Act, s.24(3).

[14] Listed above at pp. xxviii *et seq.*

[15] See 1944 Act, s.114(1). There is no lower age limit.

[16] Defined in *ibid*. s.114(1), as amended by 1980 Act, s.38(6) and Sched. 7.

[17] *Ibid.* ss.8(1)(*a*), as amended by 1948 Act, s.3.

[18] "Full-time" is not defined, but see reg. 10 (as amended) of the Education (Schools and Further Education) Regulations 1981 (S.I. 1981 No. 1086) and below at para. 2–140.

[19] 1948 Act, s.4(1), authorises the compulsory withdrawal of older junior pupils for transfer to secondary education. See above at para. 1–81 n.44 and below at para. 2–240 respectively, as to attainment of, and evidence as to, age.

[20] See 1944 Act, s.9(4) and as to nursery education 1980 Act, s.24 and below at paras. 2–45 *et seq.*

[21] Defined in 1944 Act, s.114(1).

[22] See *ibid*. ss.8(1)(*b*), as amended by 1948 Act, s.3.

[23] See *ibid*. s.114(1).

[24] See 1964 Act, s.1(1), as amended by 1968 Act, s.2 and by 1980 Act, s.16(4) and Sched. 3, para. 11; 1964 Act, s.1(2), as substituted by 1980 Act, Sched. 3, para. 12; and the Education (Middle Schools) Regulations 1980 (S.I. 1980 No. 918). See also Circs. 12/64 and 12/68.

[25] Education (School Premises) Regulations 1981 (S.I. 1981 No. 909), reg. 3(1).

institution.[26] Full-time education for senior pupils under a further education scheme[27] is not secondary education.

Special schools so approved for the time being by the Secretary of State are schools organised for children whose special needs call for special provision.[28] Special schools may be maintained or non-maintained (but not "independent"). "Child" ordinarily means a person who is not over compulsory school age,[29] but, by section 20(1) of the 1981 Act, in relation to those children just mentioned extends to any pupil registered at a school who is under the age of 19; and by section 38(4) of the 1980 Act it includes any person under the age of 19 for the purpose of school admissions arrangements. There are other definitions for particular purposes. "Compulsory school age,"[30] covers only part of the age range for which primary and secondary schools may provide. A "young person" means a person over compulsory school age who has not reached 18.[31] **2–04**

Some of these definitions can be illustrated by the diagrams overleaf. **2–05**

Local education authorities are under obligation to publish a wide variety of information about the schools they maintain.[32]

PRIMARY AND SECONDARY SCHOOLS

By section 8 of the 1944 Act it is the duty of every local education authority to secure for their area sufficient schools for providing primary and secondary education,[33] but the duty does not extend to junior pupils under the age of five years.[34] **2–06**

"[T]he schools available for an area shall not be deemed to be sufficient unless they are sufficient in number, character, and equipment to afford for all pupils opportunities for education offering such variety of instruction and training as may be desirable in view of their different ages, abilities, and aptitudes[35] and of the different periods for which they may be expected to remain at school,

---

[26] See below at para. 3–11.

[27] See below at para. 3–10 and Circ. 3/87, paras. 17 to 31, 37 and 38.

[28] 1944 Act, s.9(5), as substituted by 1981 Act, s.11(1) and see below at paras. 2–192 *et seq.*

[29] See 1944 Act, s.114(1) as amended by Education (School-leaving Dates) Act 1976, s.3 and Sched.; and as to compulsory school age and registration of pupils above at para. 1–81 and below at paras. 2–109 to 2–112 respectively.

[30] See 1944 Act, s.35 and above at para. 1–81.

[31] 1944 Act, s.114(1). *Cf.* definition in Children and Young Persons Act 1969—see below at para. 2–146 n.32.

[32] See the Education (School Information) Regulations 1981 (S.I. 1981 No. 630) and below at paras. 2–186 to 2–190.

[33] See above at para. 2–03. As to the provision of secondary education as part of the provision of further education see below at para. 3–11. In *R.* v. *Secretary of State for Education and Science and Another ex p. Keating and Others* (*The Times*, December 3, 1985) it was held that s.8 had to be read in conjunction with the Sex Discrimination Act 1975 (see above at paras. 1–92 *et seq.*).

[34] 1980 Act, s.24(2). As to nursery schools and classes see below at paras. 2–45 to 2–50.

[35] "Ages, ability and aptitudes;" see above at para. 1–82.

SCHOOLS

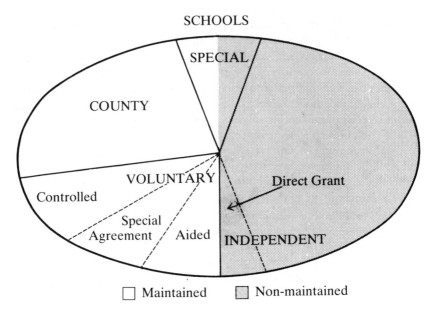

Notes to the diagrams
1. Nursery and special schools are not classified as county or voluntary
2. Special schools may, but need not, be primary or secondary
3. Nursery schools may be independent

N.B. These diagrams are included merely to illustrate the categories of
school; they are not intended to show the proportion of schools in
each of the categories.

including practical instruction and training appropriate to their respective needs."[36]

In fulfilling their duties local education authorities must have **2–07** regard[37]:

(a) to the need for securing that primary and secondary education are provided in separate[38] schools, except in the case of special schools;

(b) to the need for securing that special educational provision is made for pupils with special educational needs[39]; and

(c) to the expediency of securing boarding education, in boarding schools,[40] or otherwise,[41] for pupils for whom education as boarders is considered by parents and authority to be desirable.

The first of these three limbs has been modified to permit the provision of middle schools.[42]

To fulfil their duties local education authorities have power under sec- **2–08** tion 9 of the 1944 Act as amended, to establish primary and secondary schools, outside as well as inside their areas, and to maintain such schools, whether or not established by them. They may also assist[43] non-maintained schools, that is make grants to the school's proprietor in consideration of facilities provided; and, in particular,[44] arrange for pupils to receive primary and secondary education at non-maintained schools.

Subject to the exercise of the powers of the Secretary of State, local **2–09** education authorities enjoy a wide discretion in school provision. The discretion was temporarily curtailed by those provisions in the 1976 Act, since repealed, designed to bring about a general adoption of comprehensive

---

[36] 1944 Act, s.8(1). s.6(5) of the 1980 Act (see below at para. 2–176) seems to extend the duty of the local education authority by referring to children not in the area of the authority. As to education outside school see below at para. 5–29; and see also 1948 Act, s.4(2) (above at para. 1–81). See P. Meredith, "Individual challenge to expenditure cuts in the provision of schools" (1982) J.S.W.L. 344.

[37] 1944 Act, s.8(2). "Have regard"—see above at para. 1–46.

[38] Schools may, it seems, be "separate" although they share the same curtilage. See under "division of a school" below at para. 2–30.

[39] 1944 Act, s.8(2)(c), substituted by 1981 Act, s.2(1); and see below at paras. 2–192 et seq.

[40] See ibid. s.8(2)(d) and, as to payment of fees for board and lodging s.61 as amended and above at para. 1–90.

[41] For provision of board and lodging otherwise than at boarding schools see 1944 Act, s.50, below at paras. 5–13 and 5–14.

[42] See 1964 Act, s.1(3) and above at para. 2–03.

[43] See 1944 Act, ss.9(1) and 114(2)(b). By virtue of 1980 Act, ss.28(1), 38(6) and Sched. 7, arrangements for assistance no longer require the approval of the Secretary of State. It may be inferred from the Direct Grant School Regulations 1959 (S.I. 1959 No. 1832) as amended, reg. 5 (see below at para. 218 n. 34) that local education authorities may assist a school which receives a grant direct from the Secretary of State.

[44] See 1953 Act, s.6 as amended by 1980 Act, ss.28(1) and (2), 38(6) and Sched. 7, and by 1981 Act, s.21 and Sched. 3, para. 8. See also Circ. 268 and below at para. 5–32.

secondary education.[45] The Secretary of State retains powers over the establishment and discontinuance of schools, and in consequence over the organisation of secondary education (for instance to decide whether to permit the introduction of sixth-form colleges) under sections 12 and 13 of the 1980 Act.[46] Schools may be single-sex or co-educational, and section 8 is in terms which support a variety of types of institution, especially at the secondary stage. Before the Second World War secondary education was mostly based on the traditional grammar school model, the emphasis being placed on academic attainment. But there did exist other forms of education for pupils who had completed what was then called the elementary stage, and after the war the grammar school was joined by the secondary technical school, and by the secondary modern school. The last-mentioned was designed for the bulk of pupils who at the time of transfer[47] to secondary education did not display academic abilities or for whom places elsewhere were not available. Middle schools and sixth form colleges subsequently appeared, and there are also bilateral schools, which provide two forms of secondary education in one school. Comprehensive schools, another innovation, seek as single institutions to provide the "variety of instruction and training" which the statute demands: that a local authority may employ them for this purpose in place of a mixed system of secondary schools was confirmed by the decision in *Wood* v. *London Borough of Ealing*.[48]

2–10   The courts have considered other aspects of the obligation upon local education authorities to make schools "available" under section 8.[49] In *Watt* v. *Kesteven County Council*[50] it was held that a parent for whose child a maintained school place is not available cannot claim free education for his child at a school of his choice, but only at a school in respect of which the local education authority have made arrangements; and in *Cumings* v. *Birkenhead Corporation*[51] that "availability" refers to sufficiency of provision of schools, not to places at a school where a parent wishes to have his child educated.

---

[45] The legal problems regarding the introduction of comprehensive schools are discussed in R. Buxton, *Local Government* (2nd ed. 1973), Chapter 8.

[46] See paras. 2–16, 2–17, 2–20 and 2–35 below, circular 3/87, paras. 4 and 5 and Annex 1, and P. Meredith, "Falling Rolls and the Reorganisation of Schools" (1982) J.S.W.L. 208. The Secretary of State has resisted pressure to use his powers under ss.68 and 99 of the 1944 Act (see below at paras. 6–10 *et seq.*) on complaint of breach of s.8 by local education authorities. (See P. Meredith, "Individual Challenge to Expenditure Cuts in the Provision of Schools" (1982) J.S.W.L. 344).

[47] As to the "eleven plus" examination, formerly in general use for selecting pupils for different types of secondary education, see 120 J.P.N. 394 and 121 J.P.N. 410.

[48] [1967] Ch. 364 and see above at para. 1–75. See also *Smith* v. *Inner London Education Authority* [1978] 1 All E.R. 411.

[49] See in addition to the cases mentioned, *R.* v. *Liverpool City Council ex p. Ferguson and Others*, above at para. 1–51.

[50] [1955] 1 Q.B. 408 and see above at paras. 1–72 to 1–74.

[51] [1972] Ch. 12 see above at para. 1–77. But see now also 1980 Act, s.6 and below at para. 2–176.

Where it is alleged that a local education authority have failed in their 2–11
duty to make sufficient schools available, remedy is normally to be
sought of the Secretary of State under section 99[52] of the 1944 Act, but it
appears that a parent may apply to the courts for an injunction or
damages if the local education authority are acting *ultra vires* by temporarily closing a school without just cause or excuse. Whether closing a
school is a breach of statutory duty turns on the facts of the case. The
court reached this conclusion in *Meade* v. *London Borough of Haringey*[53] when the council had closed schools in consequence of a caretakers' strike.

In *R.* v. *Hereford and Worcester Local Education Authority, ex p.* 2–12
Jones[54] the form of words used in section 8 was held to include, as part
of the education provided, individual instrumental music tuition—with
the consequence that, by section 61,[55] charges may not be made for this
tuition when given as part of the school curriculum.

Section 11 of the 1944 Act required local education authorities to pre- 2–13
pare and submit to the Secretary of State development plans indicating
how they proposed to secure sufficient primary and secondary schools
for their areas; and section 12 obliged the Secretary of State, after
approving a development plan, to make an order defining the duties of
the local education authority in this regard. Those sections fell into
abeyance and were repealed by the 1980 Act,[56] but without affecting the
general duties of local education authorities.

Establishment and maintenance of county schools

When, under section 12 of the 1980 Act, a local education authority 2–14
intend newly to establish a county school or to maintain a school as a
county school,[57] they must first publish[58] their proposals by means of a
local newspaper and by posting them in at least one conspicuous place
and, if they relate to an existing school, at or near its main entrance.
(Minor failures to comply with publication requirements may be

---

[52] See *Wood and Others* v. *London Borough of Ealing* and *Watt* v. *Kesteven County Council* above;
also above at para. 1–49 and below at para. 6–15.
[53] [1979] 2 All E.R. 1016, C.A. as to which see D.C.M. Yardley, *Principles of Administrative Law*
(1981), pp. 71–73. See also *Gateshead Union* v. *Durham County Council* [1918] 1 Ch. 146.
[54] [1981] 1 W.L.R. 768.
[55] See above at para. 1–88.
[56] ss.30(3), 38(6) and Sched. 7.
[57] Under 1944 Act, s.85(2) and (3), as substituted by 1980 Act, s.16(4) and Sched. 3, para. 3, any
intention by a local education authority that a primary or secondary school should be vested in
them as trustees is to be treated for the purposes of 1980 Act, s.12(1) as an intention to maintain
the school as a county school; and any such school vested in a local education authority as trustees
is a county school.
[58] Before the I.L.E.A. publishes proposals it must consult the council or councils for the area or
areas which it considers will be, or are being, served by the school (Local Government Act 1985,
s.21(6)).

overlooked).[59] A copy of the published proposals must be submitted[60] to the Secretary of State.

2–15   Proposals must include date of implementation and numbers to be admitted to the school in each relevant age group,[61] and their publication must be accompanied by a statement explaining the rights of objectors.[62] An objection may be submitted to the local education authority within two months of publication by ten or more local government electors for the area, by governors of any voluntary school affected and by any other local education authority concerned. The local education authority must pass on the objections, with their own observations, to the Secretary of State.

2–16   A proposal by a local education authority newly to maintain an existing voluntary school as a county school requires the approval of the Secretary of State, and he may not give his approval unless he has first approved an agreement between authority and governors for transferring all necessary interests in the school premises.[63] The whole of the interest in the premises held by persons under a trust deed[64] does not necessarily have to be transferred; and the agreement may specify conditions, reservations and restrictions and include other agreed provisions. A third party's right to occupy or use all or part of the school premises must be left unaffected unless he agrees otherwise. Before the Secretary of State approves the transfer agreement he must be satisfied that due notice has been given to any persons other than governors who appear to be concerned, including those who have an interest in the school under a trust deed; and he must consider their representations.

2–17   Other proposals which require the approval of the Secretary of State are those of which he gives notice[65] to the local education authority to that effect within two months of submission of proposals (for example

---

[59] See *Coney* v. *Choyce* [1975] 1 W.L.R. 422 (discussed by B. Harvey in "Comprehensive Education and Parental Rights" (1975) 120 L.G.C. 691, and above at para. 1–45 n.32.

[60] See the Education (Publication of School Proposals) (No. 2) Regulations 1980 (S.I. 1980 No. 658) and Circ. 3/87. As to the adequacy of a statement of proposals see *Legg* v. *Inner London Education Authority* [1972] 3 All E.R. 177. Before the Secretary of State approves any proposals with respect to a school in the City of London or an inner London borough he must give the council for the area concerned an opportunity to make representations (London Government Act 1963, s.31(10), as amended by 1980 Act, s.16(4) and Sched. 3, para. 10).

[61] A "relevant age group" is an age group in which pupils are, or normally will be, admitted to the school in question (1980 Act, s.16(3)).

[62] 1980 Act, s.12(2) and (3); and see also *ibid*. s.15(10). Objectors are not entitled to see the observations and make further submissions. (*R*. v. *Secretary of State for Wales and Clwyd County Council ex p. Russell*, unreported, but see P. Liell and J.B. Saunders, *The Law of Education*, 9th ed. 1984, F. 80).

[63] See 1980 Act, s.12(4), and 1944 Act, Sched. 2 as amended by 1980 Act, s.1(3) and Sched. 1, para. 1. For definition see below at para. 2–20, but in this context "school premises" includes a teacher's dwelling (1944 Act, Sched. 2, para. 8). As to the law regarding school premises generally see below at paras. 2–51 *et seq*.

[64] Defined in 1944 Act, s.114(1) as amended by 1980 Act, s.1(3) and Sched. 1, para. 13.

[65] As to the giving of notice see 1944 Act, s.113, as amended by 1946 Act, s.14(1) and Sched. 2.

because they bear upon national policy), and proposals which are the subject of subsisting objections. When the Secretary of State has to approve proposals he may do so with or without modifications, in the former case after consultation[66] with the local education authority; or he may reject them. He may approve and modify only those proposals which have been specifically submitted to him: he may not substitute his own proposals.[67]

When the Secretary of State's approval is not required the local edu- 2–18
cation authority have to decide within four months of submitting the proposals to him whether to implement them. They must notify the Secretary of State of their decision. Local education authorities have a duty to implement proposals which have been approved by the Secretary of State or which they have otherwise decided to implement, but if they request the Secretary of State to modify them he may do so.[68]

Anticipatory action on proposals before the proper procedures have 2–19
been complied with is expressly prohibited, except as may be permitted by the Secretary of State as reasonable in the circumstances of the case.[69]

Establishment and maintenance of voluntary schools

Where it is proposed under section 13 of the 1980 Act to establish a 2–20
new voluntary school,[70] or it is desired that an independent school[71] should be maintained by a local education authority as a voluntary school, those concerned must first consult the authority and then publish proposals in the same way as do a local education authority in the case of a county school.[72] Similarly they must submit a copy of the proposals to the Secretary of State, and their proposals must contain the same particulars and be accompanied by a statement explaining the rights of objection by local government electors, governors of any voluntary school affected and any local education authority concerned; but objections must be submitted direct to the Secretary of State. The Secretary of State must decide[73] whether to approve or reject all such proposals and in the former case with or without modification.[74] If he thinks

---

[66] "Consultation"—see above at para. 1–45.
[67] See *Legg* v. *Inner London Education Authority* [1972] 3 All E.R. 177.
[68] The duty to implement proposals does not include the duty to admit the number of pupils stated in the proposals (s.15(10)).
[69] 1980 Act, s.16(1). See Circ. 3/87, Annex 3, paras. 32–33.
[70] New voluntary aided schools may be eligible for grant from the Secretary of State towards the cost of site and buildings: see below at para. 6–24. The Church of England maintains Diocesan Education Committees who are interested, *inter alia*, in providing new schools (see Diocesan Education Committees Measure 1955, s.2(1)(ii). See also below at para. 2–158.
[71] See 1944 Act, s.114(1), as amended by 1980 Act, s.34(1).
[72] See above at para. 2–14.
[73] As to inner London see above at para. 2–14 n.60.
[74] See *Legg* v. *Inner London Education Authority* [1972] 3 All E.R. 177.

modification desirable he must first consult the person who made the proposals and the local education authority by whom the school is to be maintained. Proposals once approved by the Secretary of State must be implemented[75] by the persons making them and by the local education authority. The former must provide the school buildings and the fittings prescribed by school premises regulations.[76] The latter are responsible[77] for otherwise equipping the school and for providing playing fields and buildings, other than school buildings, which are part of the school premises. "School building" means a building or part of a building forming part of the school premises but does not include a caretaker's dwelling and some other specified buildings used only for non-teaching purposes.[78] School "premises" include detached playing fields but not normally a teacher's dwelling house.[79] The Secretary of State may, at the request of the local education authority, modify proposals which are required to be implemented; and he may modify a trust deed or other instrument as a necessary consequence of his approving proposals after consulting governors or other proprietors.[80] Anticipatory action on proposals is prohibited as in the case of county schools.[81]

2–21   It may be claimed in proposals that a school or schools are proposed to be established in substitution for another voluntary school or schools. If the Secretary of State is satisfied that this is the case and he approves the proposals with or without modifications he may make a substitution order,[82] and the procedures relating to discontinuance[83] of voluntary schools do not apply.

2–22   Voluntary schools, as has been stated, fall into the categories of controlled, aided and special agreement. Where on application made to the Secretary of State he is satisfied that the governors of a new voluntary school are able with his contribution[84] to meet the expenditure obligations outlined below he directs by order that the school is to be an

---

[75] The duty to implement proposals does not include a duty to admit the number of pupils stated in the proposals (1980 Act s.15(10)).

[76] As to provision of controlled school buildings on a new or additional site see below at para. 2–37, and as to regulations below at paras. 2–56 to 2–58.

[77] By inference from 1944 Act, ss.8(1) and 9(1).

[78] See 1946 Act, s.4(2) as amended by National Health Service Reorganisation Act 1973, s.57 and Sched. 4, para. 9, and National Health Service Act 1977, s.129 and Sched. 15, para. 3, See also the definition in reg. 3(1) of the Education (School Premises) Regulations 1981 (S.I. 1981 No. 909).

[79] 1944 Act, s.114(1). For the exception see *ibid.* Sched. 2, para. 8. When boarding accommodation is provided as part of a school it is part of the premises—see A.M. 35.

[80] See 1973 Act, s.1, as amended by 1980 Act, ss.1(3), 16(4) and Sched. 1, para. 26 and Sched. 3, para. 17; and by 1981 Act, s.21 and Sched. 3, para. 10. See also below at para. 6–45.

[81] See above at para. 2–19.

[82] 1944 Act, s.16(2), as amended by 1980 Act, s.16(4) and Sched. 3, para. 1; and see below at para. 2–29. See School Sites Act 1841, s.14, as amended, and Reverter of Sites Act 1987, s.6(2), as to sale or exchange of land acquired under the 1841 Act.

[83] See below at paras. 2–35 and 2–36.

[84] Under 1944 Act, s.102 as amended. See below at para. 6–23; and also as regards grants and loans by the Secretary of State.

aided school; otherwise it is a controlled school.[85] During a limited period in the post-war years local education authorities entered into agreements with school promoters (reviving proposals made under the 1936 Act) under which the authority made a grant to the promoters in consideration of the establishment of, or alteration of premises for, a secondary school. The grant distinguishes these "special agreement" schools[86]: on its repayment the governors may apply to the Secretary of State for aided school status, which follows, by his order, provided that he is satisfied that they will be able and willing, with his contribution, to meet their expenditure obligations.[87]

If the Secretary of State concludes that the area to be served by a pro- **2–23** posed aided school will not also be served by a county or controlled school he must, before determining the application, consult representatives of religious denominations concerned (and, ordinarily, hold a local inquiry[88]) unless he is satisfied that the governors will be able to bear the expenditure obligations outlined below without a loan[89] from him.

Governors of aided and special agreement schools have[90]: **2–24**

   (a) to discharge liabilities incurred by them or former governors or trustees in connection with premises and equipment;

   (b) to meet the cost of altering[91] school buildings[92] to bring them up to prescribed standards[93]; and

   (c) to pay for repairs to the school buildings, save interior repairs and repairs necessary in consequence of the use of the school premises for other purposes at the instance of the local education authority.[94]

It follows that external and structural repairs to school buildings are ordinarily the responsibility of the governors, and that local education

---

[85] 1944 Act, s.15(2) as amended by 1980 Act, s.1(3), and Sched. 1, para. 1, and by 1986 (No. 2) Act Sched. 4, para. 1. As to change of status from "controlled" to "aided" see below at paras. 2–42 to 2–44.

[86] 1944 Act, s.15(2) amended as above, and Sched. 3, as amended by 1948 Act, s.11 and Sched. 1 and by 1980 Act, ss.1(3), 16(4), 38(6), Sched. 1, para. 1, Sched. 3, para. 5 and Sched. 7.

[87] *Ibid.* s.15(5), as amended by 1980 Act, s.1(3), and Sched. 1, para. 1, and see above at para. 2–02, n.5.

[88] See 1944 Act, s.93 and below at para. 6–04.

[89] *Ibid.* s.105(3) as amended, and see below at para. 6–25.

[90] 1944 Act, s.15(3) as amended by 1946 Act, s.14(1) and Sched. 2, and by 1980 Act, s.1(3) and Sched. 1, para. 1. On the interpretation of earlier legislation regarding the responsibilities of governors see *Griffiths* v. *Smith* [1941] A.C. 170. Church of England aided and special agreement schools were eligible for financial assistance under the Church Schools (Assistance by Church Commissioners) Measure 1958.

[91] "Alterations" are defined in 1944 Act, s.114(1) (as substituted by 1968 Act, s.1(3) and Sched. 1, para. 5) in relation to any school premises as including improvements, extensions and additions but excluding significant enlargement. See also below at paras. 2–31 to 2–33.

[92] Including boarding accommodation, whether in school buildings or adjacent to them. See A.M. 35.

[93] Under 1944 Act, s.10 as amended and the regulations made thereunder. See below at paras. 2–55 to 2–59.

[94] See below at paras. 2–60 to 2–62.

authorities have to pay not only for the other repairs indicated at (c) above but also for repairs to buildings forming part of the school premises which are not school buildings (for example buildings used exclusively for school meals[95]). Governors must permit local education authorities to make alterations to school buildings necessary for their school meals responsibilities.[96]

2–25   Responsibility for repairs to walls is unclear. Decisions in other branches of the law leave it uncertain whether a detached wall is a building. If a wall is structurally part of school buildings then ordinarily the governors must repair it.[97] Otherwise responsibility probably lies with the local education authority. It was held in *Ward* v. *Hertfordshire County Council*[98] that the wall forming the boundary of a school playground was not a school building; and a wall bounding a playing field is probably not a school building if only because a building for use in connection with playing fields is specifically excepted from the definition of school buildings.

2–26   Expenditure on maintenance[99] otherwise than by repair falls exclusively to the local education authority, and they must take the school as they find it,[1] but they may have recourse against governors, if the latter's default makes interior repairs necessary. If an authority default[2] in their maintenance duties and the governors act in lieu the Secretary of State may reimburse them, and the sums paid become a debt by the authority to the Crown.

2–27   It will not always be clear whether work constitutes repair or other maintenance or whether a repair is exterior or interior—and thus who is to pay for it.[3] In the absence of authority is has been suggested[4] that, for example, clearance of a blocked drain, with any necessary excavation, is maintenance rather than repair. Landlord and tenant decisions indicate that the boundary walls of a building are exterior walls whether or not they adjoin other buildings.[5]

---

[95] See 1946 Act, s.4(2), as amended by the National Health Service Reorganisation Act 1973, s.57 and Sched. 4, para. 9, and by the National Health Service Act 1977, s.129 and Sched. 15, para. 3.

[96] 1980 Act, s.22(4) and see below at paras. 5–09 to 5–11 and also A.M. 11/70.

[97] See *Lurcott* v. *Wakely and Wheeler* [1911] 1 K.B. 905 (a landlord and tenant case).

[98] [1969] 2 All E.R. 807 (but on appeal, [1970] 1 All E.R. 535, whether the wall was a school building was left open).

[99] The expenses of maintaining a voluntary school include the payment of rates (Rating and Valuation Act 1961, s.12(6)—see above at para. 1–161) and other outgoings, *e.g.* meeting the cost of repairing subsidence damage caused to adjacent property by the roots of trees growing on school premises.

[1] See *Att.-Gen.* v. *West Riding County Council ex p. Grenside* [1917] A.C. 29 and *Wilford* v. *West Riding of Yorkshire* [1908] 1 K.B. 685.

[2] 1944 Act, s.99(3), as amended by 1980 Act, s.1(3) and Sched. 1, para. 1.

[3] Problems regarding the division of responsibility between local education authority and governors are considered at 116 J.P.N. 777, and see K. Brooksbank *et. al.*, *County and Voluntary Schools* (6th ed. 1982).

[4] By K. Brooksbank *et al.* (*op. cit.*) p. 150.

[5] See *Green* v. *Eales* (1841) 2 Q.B. 225.

Maintenance includes the provision of playing fields[6] and playgrounds   **2–28**
and of a new or additional site for the school[7]; in respect of controlled
schools it also includes providing buildings which are to form part of the
school premises on that site. A "site" does not include playing fields but
otherwise includes any site which is to form part of the school premises.[8]
When a new or additional site is provided[9] by the local education authority their interest in it and in buildings on it which are to form part of
the school premises (but not, it follows from the definition of "site," in
the playing fields) is to be conveyed[10] to the trustees of the school. The
value of existing buildings on the site is taken into account[11] as between
local education authorities and governors. Where premises which have
been conveyed to trustees of a voluntary school are subsequently disposed of the Secretary of State may require[12] a proportion (as defined)
of the proceeds to be paid to the local education authority.

New schools and sites by order

The Secretary of State may by order[13] authorise the substitution of   **2–29**
one voluntary school for another, and the transfer of a county or voluntary school to a new site. A voluntary school may be transferred only by
order, and the provision[14] of the new site falls to the local education
authority. Before making an order the Secretary of State must consult
any local education authority, and the governors of any voluntary
school, which will in his opinion be affected. The order may impose conditions and provisions as he thinks fit, and he may modify a trust deed or
other instrument as a necessary consequence of his order after consulting governors or other proprietors.[15] In the case of transfer he must be
satisfied that it is not reasonably practicable, by alterations, to bring the

---

[6] See the Education (School Premises) Regulations 1981 (S.I. 1981 No. 909) and below at para.
2–56.
[7] See 1946 Act, s.3 (as amended by 1980 Act, s.1(3) and Sched. 1, para. 16) and Sched. 1, para. 1
(as amended by 1980 Act, s.16(4) and Sched. 3, para. 8) and para. 3 (as amended by 1980 Act,
s.1(4)).
[8] See 1946 Act, s.16, and as to "premises" 1944 Act, s.114(1) and above at para. 2–20.
[9] As to acquisition of land by the local education authority, see 1948 Act, s.10(3) as amended and
above at para. 1–146.
[10] 1946 Act, Sched. 1, para. 6. For a local education authority to provide in the conveyance for
reconveyance of the site to the authority if the trustees seek to dispose of it would be inconsistent
with the powers of the Secretary of State (see text below), but inclusion of an option to purchase
at a valuation would be lawful so far as not contrary to the rule against perpetuities (see Perpetuities and Accumulations Act 1964, s.9(2)).
[11] 1946 Act, Sched. 1, paras. 4 and 5 (as amended by 1980 Act s.1(4)).
[12] *Ibid.* para. 8.
[13] 1944 Act, s.16(1) (as amended by 1968 Act, s.1(3) and Sched. 1, para. 1), s.16(2) (as amended by
1980 Act, s.16(4) and Sched. 3, para. 1) and s.16(3) (as amended by 1980 Act, s.1(3) and Sched. 1,
para. 1). See School Sites Act 1841, s.14 (as amended, and clarified by Reverter of Sites Act 1987,
s.6(2)) as to sale or exchange of land acquired under that Act, and as regards Church of England
Schools the Diocesan Education Committees Measure 1955, s.2(2). See also Circ. 3/87, Annex 3,
Apps. D and E.
[14] See above at para. 2–28.
[15] Under 1973 Act, s.1(2)(*a*) as amended by 1980 Act, ss.1(3), 16(4), Sched. 1, para. 26 and Sched. 3
para. 17. See also below at para. 6–45.

premises up to the prescribed standards,[16] or that movement of population or action under (unspecified) housing and town and country planning legislation make transfer expedient. When an aided or special agreement school is transferred to a new site the expenses[17] of providing school buildings are met by the governors with the assistance[18] of a grant from the Secretary of State.

Division of a school into two or more schools

2–30 A local education authority or, after consultation with the authority, the governors of a controlled or aided (but not a special agreement) school may submit proposals to the Secretary of State that a school which is more organised in two or more separate departments be divided[19] into two or more separate schools. (A department is any part of a school organised under a separate head teacher[20]). The Secretary of State may direct accordingly by order, and when the order (which may, *inter alia*, define the premises of each of the separate schools[21]) comes into operation the local education authority must maintain each separate school as a county or voluntary school. A controlled school divides into controlled schools; an aided school divides into aided schools, unless the governors have requested that one or all of the separate schools shall be controlled schools. The creation of separate schools does not count as the establishment of a new school and thus the requirements about establishment outlined above do not apply.[22]

Alteration of schools

2–31 In *Bradbury* v. *London Borough of Enfield*,[23] which concerned the authority's plans to reorganise secondary education in the borough by introducing comprehensive schools, the court held, in relation to eight of the existing schools, that the proposed change in the age range, sex composition and use of buildings (not the switch from selective to comprehensive intake as such) was so fundamental as to constitute ceasing[24] to maintain them and as establishing new schools. Proposals of this nature should, under the law then current, have been submitted to the

---

[16] Under 1944 Act, s.10 as amended and the regulations made thereunder. See below at paras. 2–55 to 2–59.

[17] See 1946 Act, Sched. 1, para. 2.

[18] Under 1944 Act, s.103 as amended. See below at para. 6–24.

[19] See 1946 Act, s.2, as amended by 1980 Act, ss.1(3), 16(4), Sched. 1, para. 15 and Sched. 3, para. 7. As to Church of England schools see the Diocesan Education Committees Measure 1955, s.2(2).

[20] See *ibid*. s.16.

[21] *Ibid*. s.2(7). It appears that premises may be shared by separate schools.

[22] *Ibid*. s.2(2) as amended by 1980 Act, s.16(4) and Sched. 3, para. 7.

[23] [1967] 1 W.L.R. 1311 (distinguished in *Coney* v. *Choyce* [1975] 1 W.L.R. 422) applying *Wilford* v. *West Riding of Yorkshire County Council* [1908] 1 K.B. 685; and see 1968 Act, s.1(4) and (5). *Bradbury* and subsequent cases concerning school reorganisation at Enfield are discussed at 131 J.P.N. 612 and 665, and 132 J.P.N. 6. See also Buxton, *op. cit.*

[24] As to discontinuance of schools see below at paras. 2–35 to 2–36, and as to objections above at para. 1–45.

Minister and published so as to be subject to objection. Following this decision changes in the law were made to reflect the judgment of the court and introduce the notion of "significant change," as follows.[25]

A change in the age range and sex composition of a school, or **2–32** enlargement or alteration[26] of the premises, or transfer of a school to a new site,[27] do not constitute the establishment of a new school.[28] (This provision was made retrospective to permit authorities to continue to maintain schools which had been thus affected). But the intention to make a significant change in the character, or significant enlargement of the premises of a school, must be the subject of proposals by local education authority or governors in the same way as a proposal[29] for new establishment or maintenance of a county or voluntary school.[30] "Significant"[31] implies that there is a substantial change in the function or size of the school, and if a question arises whether a change in character or enlargement of premises *is* significant it is determined[32] by the Secretary of State. "Changes in character" include in particular[33] those resulting from change in age range and sex composition and from making or altering arrangements for admission by reference to ability or aptitude; and the Secretary of State stated that he would also generally regard substantial changes in the number of boarding places as "significant." "Enlargement"[34] means any modification of the existing premises which makes accommodation available for more pupils.

When voluntary school governors propose to make a significant **2–33** enlargement of, or to alter, school premises for the better provision of primary or secondary education at the premises, and/or to secure sufficient suitable primary or secondary schools for the area of the authority, the authority may provide, or assist in providing, temporary accommodation if so authorised[35] by the Secretary of State. He must be satisfied that the circumstances claimed exist and that it is not reasonably practicable, on the grounds of expense, to provide permanent accommodation. In the case of a significant enlargement his approval to

---

[25] See Circ. 12/68, and A.E. Hart, "State Education and the Rights of Parents" 113 S.J. 23.

[26] See 1944 Act, s.114(1) as amended, and note 91 above.

[27] See above at paras. 2–28 to 2–29.

[28] 1968 Act, s.1(1), as amended by 1980 Act, s.16(4) and Sched. 3, para. 15.

[29] 1980 Act, ss.12 and 13. See above at paras. 2–14 *et seq.* and *ibid.* s.16(1). See also 1973 Act, s.1 (as amended) as to modification of a trust deed (below at para. 6–45) and as respects inner London, see above at para. 2–14, notes 58 and 60. As to Church of England schools see the Diocesan Education Committees Measure 1955, s.2(2).

[30] See D.B. Southern "Maintained Schools—When a Change is not a Change" (November 8, 1985 L.G.C.). The author gives an account of the way in which the I.L.E.A. secured a reorganisation of voluntary secondary schools otherwise than on the initiative of the governors.

[31] 1944 Act, ss.67(4) and 114(1), as added by 1968 Act, s.1(3) and Sched. 1.

[32] See Circ. 3/87, Annex 3, Appendix B.

[33] 1980 Act, s.16(2).

[34] 1944 Act, s.67(4) and 114(1) as added by 1968 Act, s.1(3) and Sched. 1.

[35] 1968 Act, s.3(4), as amended by 1980 Act, ss.1(3), 16(4), Sched. 1, para. 24 and Sched. 3, para. 16.

a formal proposal as above is also required. The duties of local education authorities and governors under Schedule 1 to the 1946 Act, to which reference is made in para. 2–28, do not apply as respects temporary accommodation.

Reduction of school places

2–34　　At a time of falling school rolls local education authorities may wish to keep the size of their schools in what seems to them a proper balance. Under section 15 of the 1980 Act this may include restricting[36] the annual intake, and when an authority in the case of a county school, or the governors of a voluntary school, wish to reduce the intake to a school by 20 per cent. or more of the "standard number," they must (except in the case of primary schools with a standard number under 20) publish their proposals in the same way as if they were proposing to establish a school and submit[37] them to the Secretary of State. The same provisions about objections (and the publication of a statement explaining rights of objection) and approval (where necessary) or rejection by the Secretary of State, but not implementation, apply according as the school is a county or voluntary school. The "standard number" is normally the number that was admitted to each relevant age group[38] in the school year beginning September 1979, but the Secretary of State may by order vary the number in relation to any school or category of schools.

Discontinuance

2–35　　Where a local education authority intend to cease to maintain a county or voluntary school they must by section 12 of the 1980 Act publish[39] their proposals in the same way as if they were proposing to establish a school and submit them to the Secretary of State. The same provisions about objections (and the publication of a statement explaining rights of objection) and implementation apply, and a proposal by a local education authority to cease maintenance of a voluntary school (against which governors, amongst others, may object) always requires

---

[36] See Circ. 3/87 and P. Meredith, "Falling Rolls and the Reorganisation of Schools" [1984] J.S.W.L. 208.

[37] 1980 Act ss.15(1)–(3) and see s.16(1). See also Circ. 3/87. As to inner London see above at para. 2–14 nn. 58 and 60.

[38] A "relevant age group" is an age group in which pupils are, or normally will be, admitted to the school in question. (1980 Act s.16(3)).

[39] See above at para. 2–14 and also 1980 Act s.16(1) and Circ. 3/87. As to inner London see para. 2–14 nn. 58 and 60. See also *R. v. Secretary of State for Education and Science, ex p. Birmingham City Council and Another* 83 L.G.R. 79 regarding the invalidity of proposals to close a school when the date of closure is fixed by the chairman of a committee, and of the Secretary of State's approval of the proposals; and *R. v. Brent London Borough Council, ex p. Gunning and Others* (see above at para. 1–45) regarding the obligation of a local education authority to consult parents before proposals are adopted.

the approval[40] of the Secretary of State. He may modify[41] a trust deed or other instrument as a necessary consequence of his approving a proposal, after consulting governors or other proprietors.

Voluntary schools may alternatively be discontinued at the instance of **2–36** governors. By section 14 of the 1944 Act[42] they must serve on the Secretary of State and the local education authority by whom the school is maintained not less than two years' notice of the intended discontinuance. Once given, notice may not be withdrawn except with the consent of the local education authority. Except by leave of the Secretary of State notice may not be served if the Secretary of State or a local education authority have incurred expenditure[43] (beyond expenditure on repairs) on the premises. If leave is granted it may be subject to such requirements as he thinks just. The requirements are specified and appear to be designed to balance the public interest against rights of ownership of the premises. If the governors are unable or unwilling to carry on the school while the notice is in force the local education authority may, if they wish, conduct the school as a county school on conditions which include the governors being entitled to residual use of the premises. Once the notice runs out the duty of the local education authority to maintain the school as a voluntary school lapses.

Special provisions relating to controlled schools

There are a number of disparate provisions, as follows. Where a new **2–37** or additional site is provided for a controlled school the trustees must pay[44] the local education authority a sum determined as just by the Secretary of State out of any proceeds of sale of former premises, having regard to the value of the interest conveyed.

A local education authority and the governors of a controlled school **2–38** may come to agree that there should be a significant enlargement[45] of the school premises. The enlargement may be required wholly or mainly to provide accommodation for pupils who would otherwise have attended another voluntary school which has been discontinued, or at

---

[40] 1980 Act, s.12(4)(b). See D.B. Southern, "Maintained Schools—When a Change is Not a Change" L.G.C., November 8, 1985.
[41] See 1973 Act, s.1, as amended by 1980 Act, ss.1(3), 16(4) and Sched. 1, para. 26 and Sched. 3, para. 17, and by 1981 Act, s.21 and Sched. 3, para. 10, and below at para. 6–45; and as to the powers of the Secretary of State where premises of a voluntary school have ceased to be used as such, 1973 Act, s.2 and Reverter of Sites Act 1987 (above at paras. 1–157 and 1–158). As to Church of England schools, see the Diocesan Education Committees Measure 1955, s.2(2).
[42] 1944 Act, s.14(1), as amended by 1946 Act s.14(1) and Sched. 2, and by 1980 Act, ss.1(3), 4(5) and Sched. 1, para. 1. Failure to observe the provisions of the section might amount to breach of trust. As to substitution of one school for another see 1944 Act, s.16(2) and above at para. 2–29. Note the possible application of the School Sites Acts (see above at paras. 1–150 et seq.), and as to Church of England Schools, n. 41 above.
[43] As to cesser of use of voluntary school premises see 1973 Act, s.2 and Reverter of Sites Act 1987 (above at para. 1–157), and below at para. 2–66.
[44] 1946 Act, s.3 and Sched. 1, para. 7 (as to which see Reverter of Sites Act 1987, s.8(1)) and as to provision of new sites see above at para. 2–28.
[45] See above at para. 2–32.

which accommodation has otherwise ceased to be available, for example, because of a change in its age-range. Alternatively[46] it may be considered that enlargement would enhance primary or secondary education at the school and/or in the local education authority's area generally. If the Secretary of State is satisfied, upon the application of local education authority and governors, that any of these sets of circumstances exists, and proposals for significant enlargement are subsequently submitted, and approved[47] by him, he may by order direct[48] that the expenses shall be met by the local education authority.

2–39　The Secretary of State may also direct[49] that all or part of the cost of establishing a new controlled school shall be met by the local education authority where otherwise it would have to be met by the persons submitting the proposals to establish the school. He may so act when the latter and the local education authority satisfy him that the establishment of the school is required to provide accommodation in substitution for accommodation at another voluntary school which has been discontinued, or at which accommodation has otherwise ceased to be available; or where it is proposed to establish a new middle school for at least a substantial proportion of the pupils from the other voluntary school.[50]

2–40　A local education authority may use their own employees to carry out building, etc., works at a controlled school where they are liable to pay the expenses, and the trustees and governors must provide facilities to ensure that the work is properly executed.[51]

Change of status of voluntary schools

2–41　If the governors of an aided or special agreement school need or wish to relinquish their obligations they must apply to the Secretary of State, who must revoke his initial order, whereupon the school assumes controlled status.[52] Change of status from special agreement to aided school has already been mentioned.[53]

2–42　Section 54 of the 1986 (No. 2) Act enables the status of a controlled school to be changed to aided by order of the Secretary of State in the following circumstances. The governing body of the controlled school are to publish their proposals in the manner required by the Secretary of State in regulations[54] and submit a copy to him together with other

---

[46] See above at para. 2–33.
[47] Under s.13 of the 1980 Act. See above at para. 2–20.
[48] 1946 Act, s.1(1), as amended by 1953 Act, s.3, by 1967 Act, s.2, by 1968 Act, s.1(3) and Sched. 1, para. 6, and by 1980 Act, s.16(4) and Sched. 3, para. 6.
[49] 1953 Act, s.2, as amended by 1968 Act, s.1(3) and Sched. 2, and by 1980 Act, s.16(4) and Sched, 3, para. 9.
[50] 1967 Act, s.3, as amended by 1980 Act, s.16(4) and Sched. 3 para. 14.
[51] 1946 Act, s.6, as amended by 1980 Act, s.1(3) and Sched. 1, para. 15.
[52] 1944 Act, s.15(4), as amended by 1980 Act, s.1(3) and Sched. 1, para. 1.
[53] See above at para. 2–22.
[54] See the Education (Publication of Proposals to Change Status of a Controlled School) Regulations 1987 originally published in error as a statutory instrument (see Circ. 2/87), and Circ. 3/87, Annex 3, Appendix H.

information he reasonably requires. The published proposals are to be accompanied by a statement which specifies the proposed date of implementation and explains that within two months of publication objections may be submitted by ten or more local government electors for the area, by the governing body of any voluntary school affected and by any local education authority concerned.

The Secretary of State is not to make an order unless satisfied that the **2–43** governing body are able and willing with the assistance of his maintenance contributions[55] to defray the expenses which are met by aided school governors[56] and also to pay the compensation to which reference is made below. The order is to specify the amount of compensation, the date by which it must be paid and other conditions imposed by the Secretary of State. If the Secretary of State proposes a date for the change of status different from that proposed by the governing body he is to consult them and the local education authority about an appropriate date. On the application of (a) the local education authority or (b) the school's foundation governors (after they have consulted the other governors) the Secretary of State may after consulting (b) or (a) respectively vary his order by altering the date of changed status or the amount of compensation. The Secretary of State's order may include transitional provision relating to matters such as instrument and articles of government, appointment and dismissal of staff and admission arrangements.

On change of status compensation is payable (under section 55 of the **2–44** 1986 (No. 2) Act) by the governing body to the local education authority for any capital expenditure they have incurred in circumstances described in paras. 2–38 and 2–39 above[57] and on a new or additional site and buildings for the school,[58] but not so far as the expenditure could have been incurred had the school always been an aided school. If the amount of compensation is not agreed between governing body and authority the Secretary of State may determine it by reference to the current value of the property, and he may take advice on the valuation. The Secretary of State is not to make the governing body any contribution, grant or loan towards the compensation.

NURSERY EDUCATION

Nursery schools are primary schools which are mainly used for edu- **2–45** cating children between the ages of two and five[59] (but they are not county or voluntary schools). The Secretary of State has power to pay

---

[55] See below at para. 6–23.
[56] See above at para. 2–24.
[57] *i.e.* under 1946 Act, s.1 and 1953 Act, s.2, both as amended.
[58] Under 1946 Act, Sched. 1, para. 1—see above at para. 2–28.
[59] 1944 Act, s.9(4). As to teachers in nursery schools and classes see the Education (Teachers) Regulations 1982 (S.I. 1982 No. 106) Sched, 4, para. 4, and below at para. 4–14.

grant[60] direct to the proprietors of independent nursery schools. Local
education authorities may establish them, maintain those established by
them or by a former authority, and assist those otherwise established.[61]
Local education authorities may also provide nursery classes[62] or make
other provision[63] for pupils under five years old at primary schools
where education is provided for a wider age range of junior pupils.
There are standards to which maintained school premises must conform.[64]

2–46   Requirements about parental preference and information about
schools and admission arrangements do not apply to nursery schools or
in relation to children who will be under five at the time of their proposed admission to school, unless the authority admit to maintained
schools, under their arrangements, children who will be five within six
months of beginning school.[65]

2–47   The law regarding establishment and alteration of county and voluntary schools and their government does not, by definition, apply to nursery schools, but the provision of new premises, and alterations, require
the approval[66] of the Secretary of State; and a local education authority
who intend to cease to maintain a nursery school established by them or
a former authority must follow the same procedure as on proposing to
cease to maintain a county school.[67]

2–48   The duration of the school day and year at maintained nursery schools
and classes is subject to the same regulation[68] as applies to maintained
schools generally save that suitable activities are to be provided for a
shorter period: at least three hours on every day when a school or class
meets; or one and a half hours on a day when a class meets for only one
session, or when the pupil attends the nursery school or class for only
one session. If a school meets six days a week there may, on two days,

---

[60] 1944 Act, s.100 as amended, and the Direct Grant Schools Regulations 1959 (S.I. 1959 No. 1832).
See below at para. 2–218.

[61] 1980 Act, s.24(1), and see Circs. 2/73 (W.O. 39/73) and 1/80.

[62] "Nursery class" was defined in the Schools Regulations 1959 (S.I. 1959 No. 364) as a class mainly
for children who have attained the age of three years but have not attained the age of five years;
but those Regulations were revoked by the Education (Teachers) Regulations 1982 (S.I. 1982 No.
106), reg. 2 and Schedule 1, so far as not already revoked. The Education (Schools and Further
Education) Regulations 1981 (S.I. 1981 No. 1086), reg. 2 and Sched. 1, had revoked reg. 7 of the
Schools Regulations 1959 which imposed age restrictions on admission of children to, and reten-
tion in, nursery classes.

[63] 1980 Act, s.24(2).

[64] See the Education (School Premises) Regulations 1981 (S.I. 1981 No. 909) and below at paras.
2–55 to 2–59.

[65] 1980 Act, s.9(1) and see below at paras. 2–176 et seq. "Months" means calendar months (Interpretation Act 1978, s.5 and Sched. 1).

[66] See the Education (Schools and Further Education) Regulations 1981 (S.I. 1981 No. 1086) reg. 7
and below at para. 2–54.

[67] 1980 Act, s.12(1) and see above at p. 2–35 and *ibid.* s.16(1). As to inner London see above at
paras. 2–14 nn.58 and 60.

[68] See reg. 10 of the Education (Schools and Further Education) Regulations 1981 (S.I. 1981 No.
1086), as amended, and below at para. 2–140.

be only a single session. There are no requirements concerning religious education.[69]

The Nurseries and Child-Minders Regulation Act 1948 does not apply[70] to maintained or assisted nursery schools or to nursery schools to which the Secretary of State makes payments by section 100 of the 1944 Act or which he recognises as efficient.[71]   **2–49**

Nursery schools and classes are to be distinguished from day nurseries provided under the National Health Service Acts by a local social services authority,[72] but arrangements may be made for teachers to be employed in day nurseries, and these are referred to in Chapter 4.[73]   **2–50**

PREMISES

This section is about requirements concerning approval of premises by the Secretary of State, the standards that premises must meet, their use for public purposes, some special provisions relating to voluntary schools, and nuisance and disturbance on educational premises. Under section 42 of the 1986 (No. 2) Act articles[74] of government of county, and maintained special schools are to provide for control[75] by the governing body outside school sessions[76] subject to any direction by the local education authority; and the governors are to have regard to the desirability of making premises available to the local community.   **2–51**

Approval

Local education authorities or other persons submitting proposals[77] to the Secretary of State for (a) the establishment of a county or voluntary school; or (b) the maintenance of a school as a county or voluntary school; or (c) the making of a significant change in the character or significant enlargement[78] of the premises of such a school must under section 14 of the 1980 Act provide, for his approval, whatever particulars of the premises or proposed premises he requires,[79] and do so how and when   **2–52**

---

[69] See below at para. 2–159 n.59.

[70] By s.8(3) of that Act as amended by Local Government Act 1958, s.62 and Sched. 8, para. 30.

[71] The 1984 Act is anachronistic in that the Secretary of State no longer recognises schools as "efficient," see below at para. 6–27. As to payments under s.100 of the 1944 Act see below at para. 2–218.

[72] A local social services authority may, with the consent of the Secretary of State, (normally, for Social Services) make arrangements (and a reasonable charge) for the care of children under five not attending primary schools (the National Health Service Act 1977, s.21 and Sched. 8).

[73] 1980, Act s.26. See below at para. 4–42.

[74] As to articles see below at para. 2–107.

[75] Does not apply to schools with existing articles until September 1, 1988. As to control of voluntary school premises see below at para. 2–63.

[76] See below at paras. 2–140 and 2–141.

[77] Under 1980 Act, s.12 or s.13 (see above at paras. 2–14 and 2–20).

[78] "Significant change in the character" and "significant enlargement"—see above at para. 2–32.

[79] These requirements do not apply in respect of nursery schools—see above at para. 2–47. See A.M. 1/86 for approval procedures for building projects at county and controlled schools, maintained special schools, hostels for pupils with special educational needs and local authority further education establishments, *i.e.* those provided by a local education authority or designated as assisted establishments by or under the Education (Schools and Further Education) Regulations 1981 (S.I.

he directs. The proposals, on implementation, must conform to the approved particulars. Particulars of voluntary school premises must be the subject of consultation with the local education authority before submission to the Secretary of State. (The local education authority will be concerned about the prospective maintenance costs.)

2–53 When plans and particulars are approved by the Secretary of State the buildings and premises to which they relate are exempt[80] from building regulations made under the Building Act 1984[81] and, so far as he directs, from local Acts and bye-laws[82]; but the Secretary of State expects local education authorities to apply the standards he recommends.[83]

2–54 Unless particulars of premises have been approved by the Secretary of State as above, an authority or other persons proposing to provide new premises for a maintained school, a non-maintained special school or a hostel for pupils with special educational needs require his prior approval for construction of new premises or alteration of premises to be acquired. They must provide whatever particulars of the building work or alterations[84] he requires and do so how and when he directs.[85] He may grant exemption, as above, from local Acts and bye-laws, and his approval brings exemption from building regulations.[86]

Standards

2–55 Guidance is issued by the Department of Education and Science in the form of Building Bulletins, Design Notes, etc., and the Secretary of State makes regulations prescribing the standards to which maintained school premises must conform.[87] Local education authorities are under a duty to secure that the schools they maintain conform to the standards prescribed, which in part vary according to the type of school (including nursery schools, sixth form colleges and special schools). The duty is absolute, and its breach may thus give rise to an action for damages without proof of negligence if injury is sustained.[88] But failure to comply

---

1981 No. 1086) as amended by Amendment Regulations 1983 (S.I. 1983 No. 262). In relation to aided and special agreement schools see A.M. 13/64 and Part I of Department of Education and Science, *Building Work at Voluntary Aided and Special Agreement Schools*, 1978.

[80] *Ibid.* 1980 Act, s.14(4), as amended by Building Act 1984, s.133(2) and Sched. 7.

[81] See 1984 Act, s.4(1), and as to inner London (as defined in s.126) s.46 and Sched. 3, Pt. I as amended by Local Government Act 1985, Sched. 8, para. 14.

[82] 1944 Act, s.63(2).

[83] See A.M. 2/85, "Constructional Standards for Maintained Educational Building in England."

[84] "Alterations"—see 1944 Act, s.114(1) as substituted by 1968 Act, s.1(3) and Sched. 1, para. 5, and above at para. 2–32.

[85] 1980 Act, s.27(4) and the Education (Schools and Further Education) Regulations 1981 (S.I. 1981 No. 1086) regs. 3(*a*) and 7 as amended by Amendment Regulations 1983 (S.I. 1983 No. 262). See Circ. 7/81, paras. 11 and 12, and A.M. 1/86.

[86] *Ibid.* s.27(5) as amended by Building Act 1984, s.133(2) and Sched. 7, and *ibid.* s.4(1).

[87] 1944 Act, s.10(1) and the Education (School Premises) Regulations 1981 (S.I. 1981 No. 909). See A.M. 2/81. As to safety of premises see the Health and Safety at Work Act 1974 as amended and below at paras. 4–76 to 4–78 and 7–38 to 7–42.

[88] See *ibid.* s.10(2), *Reffell* v. *Surrey County Council* [1964] 1 W.L.R. 358 and below at para. 7–42.

with the duty is otherwise enforceable only by the Secretary of State under section 99 of the 1944 Act.[89]

Regulations specify in detail requirements concerning land, accom-   2–56
modation and structure,[90] and these are usually related to current normal numbers of pupils at different types of school or, as respects
proposed schools, the number on which the proposals are based. No
minimum site areas are prescribed but the land must be sufficient for
buildings, recreation areas (outdoor areas for recreation, play and outdoor education) playing fields[91] and "ancillary facilities" such as vehicle
service roads and parking places. Minimum recreation and (in schools
for pupils aged eight and over) playing field areas are prescribed for different types and sizes of school. Playing fields have to be suitable for
team games and grass pitches must stand up to seven hours a week of
wear during term time.

School accommodation requirements relate to teaching accommo-   2–57
dation[92]; accommodation for private study and social purposes for
pupils of 16 and over, washrooms including, in new or remodelled
schools for pupils of eight and over, changing accommodation for pupils
and staff; accommodation for medical and dental examination; and staff
accommodation including a teacher's room. Various ancillary facilities
must be provided. These include storage of various kinds and provision
for preparation of food, drink, and washing-up, but there are no
detailed requirements about kitchen and dining arrangements following
the abandonment, under the 1980 Act, of a general statutory duty to
provide school meals. Schools with boarders attract rather different,
and some additional, requirements such as a sick room and a sewing
room. Generally, there are structural requirements regarding load-
bearing, weather and safety protection, heating[93] (including energy con-
servation), lighting and acoustics, water supplies, and drainage.

Schools existing when the current regulations came into operation   2–58
(August 1, 1981) and some others in respect of which the Secretary of
State's approval was given before September 1, 1981, are not required
to meet some of the prescribed standards until September 1, 1991.[94]
Over and above these transitory provisions the Secretary of State may
exceptionally deem premises to conform to the requirements of regulations that they do not in fact satisfy while a direction made by him to

---

[89] See *Bradbury* v. *Enfield Borough Council* [1967] 1 W.L.R. 1311.
[90] As to whether a wall is part of a school building see *Ward* v. *Hertfordshire County Council* [1969] 2 All E.R. 807, and above at para. 2–25.
[91] Scheds. 2 and 3 to the Education (School Premises) Regulations 1981 (S.I. 1981 No. 909) refer to recreation areas and playing fields respectively.
[92] Specified in Sched. 4 to S.I. 1981 No. 909.
[93] In *Watts* v. *Monmouthshire County Council and Another* 66 L.G.R. 171, it was held on the equivalent (revoked) regulation (reg. 53(3) of the Standards for School Premises Regulations 1959 (S.I.
1959 No. 890)) that breach of the standard of heating specified did not give rise to any civil
remedy.
[94] S.I. 1981 No. 909, reg. 2(2) and Sched. 1.

that effect is in force.[95] He may do so if he is satisfied, with respect to any school, that it would be unreasonable to require conformity with some requirement of the regulations having regard to:

(a) the nature of the site, or existing buildings, or other special circumstances affecting the school premises; or

(b) shortage of suitable sites (where the school is to have an additional or new site)[96]; or

(c) the need to control public expenditure (where the school is to have additional buildings or is to be transferred to a new site and existing or temporary buildings are to be used).

2–59   Schools have also to comply with the law relating to the needs of the chronically sick and disabled.[97] Appropriate provision must be made for them as regards means of access to and within school buildings, parking facilities and sanitary conveniences. Appropriate provision is defined by reference to a Design Note numbered 18 and entitled "Access for the Physically Disabled to Educational Buildings." It is published by the Secretary of State for Social Services and takes effect so far as prescribed by him in regulations.[98] Exemptions may be granted where it is not reasonable or practicable[99] to make the prescribed provision.

Use for elections and other public purposes

2–60   A candidate in a parliamentary or European Assembly election may[1] on giving reasonable notice use a suitable room in a county or voluntary school at reasonable times (not including times of use for educational purposes) for holding public meetings. Use of the room is free of charge but the candidate must defray expenses incurred and any damage done. "Room" includes a hall, gallery or gymnasium. Arrangements for use of a room are to be made with the local education authority, and questions about entitlement to use, etc., are determined by the Secretary of State.[2] Local education authorities must keep lists of suitable rooms and make them available for inspection at the appropriate time. Similar provision is made in respect of local government elections.[3]

---

[95] 1944 Act, s.10(2), as amended by 1948 Act, s.7(1) and 1968 Act, s.3(3).

[96] As to new and additional sites see above at para. 2–28.

[97] Chronically Sick and Disabled Persons Act 1970, s.8 (see Circ. 13/70), and (not yet in force) Disabled Persons Act 1981, s.6. See also Town and Country Planning Act 1971, s.29B (above at para. 1–163 n.14) and Circ. 2/82, paras. 3.3 and 7.1.

[98] No regulations have yet been made.

[99] "Practicable" implies a stricter standard than "reasonably practicable" (when costs and benefits may be weighed) but is less demanding than "possible"—see *Jayne* v. *National Coal Board* [1963] 2 All E.R. 220 and *Boyton* v. *Willment Bros. Ltd.* [1971] 1 W.L.R. 1625.

[1] Representation of the People Act 1983, s.95 as amended by Representation of the People Act 1985; European Assembly Elections Act 1978, s.3 and Sched. 1, para. 2, and European Assembly Elections Regulations 1986 (S.I. 1986 No. 2209) reg. 5(1) and Sched. 1.

[2] Representation of the People Act 1983, s.95(6) and Sched. 5.

[3] *Ibid.* s.96 as substituted by the Representation of the People Act 1985. As to enforcement of the right see *Ettridge* v. *Morrell*, 85 L.G.R. 100, C.A.

For the purposes of taking the poll[4] at a parliamentary or European   **2–61** Assembly election the returning officer[5] may use free of charge a room in a maintained, assisted or grant-aided school but must defray any expenses incurred and make good any damage done.[6] The same provisions apply in substance in relation to local government elections.[7] Schools used as polling stations do not necessarily have to close for the election.

If a parish (in Wales a community) does not have its own meeting   **2–62** room a suitable room in maintained school premises may be used free of charge for specified meetings about parish affairs.[8] Use is to take place at reasonable times and after reasonable notice, and when the room is not required for educational purposes. Expenses and any damage incurred are met by the parish or community council. The Secretary of State determines what is reasonable or suitable if any question arises. A room in a maintained school may be used on similar terms for discussion of questions relating to allotments.[9]

Special provisions relating to voluntary school premises[10]

The occupation and use of voluntary schools is under the control of   **2–63** the governors[11] (or other persons specified by the trust deed[12]) save for the following powers of direction, and the requirements of other statutes (for example, for the use of schools as polling stations).

The local education authority may give such directions as they think   **2–64** fit regarding the occupation and use of controlled school premises with the following exceptions.[13] The governors may decide the use of all or part of the premises on Saturdays, so far as they are not required by the local education authority for school purposes or for a purpose connected with[14] education or the welfare of the young; and the foundation governors[15] may decide the use of all or part of the premises on Sundays.

---

[4] At European Assembly elections also counting votes and verifying ballot paper accounts. (See S.I. 1986 No. 2209 Sched. 1, modifying rule 22 of the Parliamentary Election Rules—n. 6 below).

[5] For definition see Representation of the People Act 1983, s.24.

[6] *Ibid.* s.23 and Sched. 1 (Parliamentary Election Rules) rule 22. Applied (as modified) by European Assembly Elections Act 1978, s.3 and Sched. 1, para. 2 and S.I. 1986 No. 2209, reg. 5(1) and Sched. 1.

[7] See Representation of the People Act 1983, s.36 as amended by Representation of the People Act 1985 and the Local Elections (Principal Areas) Rules 1986 (S.I. 1986 No. 2214) rule 5 and Sched. 2, rule 17; the Local Elections (Parishes and Communities) Rules 1986 (S.I. 1986 No. 2215) rule 5 and Sched. 2, rule 17; and the Parish and Community Meetings (Polls) Rules 1987 (S.I. 1987 No. 1) rule 5 and Sched, rule 7.

[8] Local Government Act 1972, s.134.

[9] See Smallholdings and Allotments Act 1908, s.35 as amended.

[10] As to temporary accommodation on alteration of premises, see above at para. 2–33.

[11] See 1944 Act, s.22(3), as amended by 1980 Act, s.1(3) and Sched. 1, para. 6. As to persons employed for the care and maintenance of premises see below at paras. 4–44 and 4–45.

[12] *Ibid.* s.22(5), amended as above. For "trust deed" see *ibid.* s.114(1).

[13] *Ibid.* s.22(1), amended as above. This power may extend so as to enable a local education authority to restrict the extent of premises in use, *e.g.* to reduce the maintenance costs.

[14] An exhibition of work done by pupils is such a purpose. See *Griffiths* v. *Smith* [1941] A.C. 170.

[15] See below at para. 2–74.

Local education authorities have a limited power to direct governors of an aided or special agreement school to provide accommodation (but not services, for example heating) for them free of charge.[16] The desired use of all or part of the premises must be for a purpose connected with education or the welfare of the young; the local education authority must be satisfied that there is no suitable alternative accommodation in their area; the direction may not be given if it conflicts with the use of the premises for school purposes; and it must relate to not more than three weekdays in any week.

2–65   Sums received by governors or trustees of a voluntary school for letting or hiring part of the school premises other than the school buildings are due[17] to the local education authority.

2–66   Apart from these provisions relating to occupation and use it is as well, in this context to add the reminder that the Secretary of State may exercise certain powers, previously referred to[18] when the premises of a voluntary school have ceased, or are likely to cease, to be used as such. And a final, very long-standing provision: when it is proposed by trustees or others to sell, exchange or mortgage school premises which have been the subject of government grant, they must first obtain the consent[19] of the Secretary of State or repay the amount of the grant to the Treasury.

Nuisance and disturbance

2–67   Section 40 of the Local Government (Miscellaneous Provisions) Act 1982 makes it an offence for a person who without lawful authority is on maintained school premises (including playgrounds and playing fields) to cause or permit nuisance or disturbance to the annoyance of those who lawfully use the premises, whether the latter are present or absent at the time.[20] It appears to be for the local education authority or governors (or, for example, the head teacher on their behalf) to determine who may lawfully be present, but it may be that the presence of parents on school premises for a legitimate purpose is lawful unless and until a person authorised by the authority has asked them to leave, or told them not to call except by appointment, or (perhaps) posted a notice to the same effect. A criminal offence occurs only in the limited circumstances stated; otherwise the remedy is a civil action in trespass.

---

[16] 1944 Act, s.22(2), as amended by 1980 Act, s.1(3) and Sched. 1, para. 6.

[17] 1946 Act, s.4(1), as amended by 1980 Act, s.1(3) and Sched. 1, para. 17.

[18] See above at para. 1–157.

[19] School Grants Act 1855, s.1, as amended. As to what amounts to consent see *Re Mill Lane Land Everton, Re Liverpool Education (Emmanuel School Purchase) Order 1929, ex p. Liverpool Corporation* [1937] 4 All E.R. 197.

[20] The nuisance might, *e.g*, consist in the fouling of school playing fields by dogs, to the annoyance of those not present at the time. See *Sykes* v. *Holmes and Another* [1985] Crim.L.R. 791, D.C., where the inhalation of solvents on school premises outside school hours and unobserved by pupils or staff was held to be contrary to s.40(1).

The existence of nuisance or disturbance appears to be a mixed ques- **2-68**
tion of fact and law—on which the courts[21] have frequently adjudicated,
as they have on the notions of "causing" and "permitting."

If a police constable or a person authorised by a local education auth- **2-69**
ority (with the consent of the governors in the case of a voluntary
school), or by the governors of an aided or special agreement school,
has reasonable cause[22] to suspect that any person is committing or has
committed an offence under section 40 he may remove him from the
premises. Proceedings may be brought only by a police constable, by a
local education authority (with the consent of the governors in the case
of a voluntary school) or by a person authorised by the governors of an
aided or special agreement school. Conviction of an offence under section 40 carries a fine on summary of conviction[23] not exceeding level 2.[24]

SCHOOL GOVERNMENT

How maintained schools are conducted is the subject of the next sec- **2-70**
tion of this chapter. Here attention is paid to the framework[25] within
which they are conducted—the making of instruments and articles of
government and the composition, proceedings, legal status and financial
position of governing bodies. Recommendations in the Taylor Report,
A New Partnership for our Schools[26] were designed to widen their membership and enhance their influence.[27] The 1980 Act[28] regulated membership but did little to clarify the role of governors. The 1986 (No. 2)
Act was still more explicit about membership and as the next section
reveals it is also concerned with role. It repealed and replaced the

---

[21] See the cases cited in *Stroud's Judicial Dictionary* (5th ed. 1986).

[22] See *ibid.*

[23] As to summary conviction, see Magistrates Courts Act 1980.

[24] See Criminal Justice Act 1982, ss.37 and 46.

[25] The 1944 Act distinguished "management" of primary schools from "government" of secondary
schools. By the 1980 Act, Sched. 1 "government" and "governor" were substituted wherever
"management" or "manager" appeared in statute or other document, without need to redraft pre-
existing documents. Similarly "rules" (of management) were superseded by "articles" (of government). Reorganisation of local governmet in 1974 necessitated special transitory intervention in
the composition and terms of office of voluntary school managers and governors and in the trust
deeds of educational charities, as to which see Local Government Act 1972, s.254(1) and (2)(*b*)
and the Local Government (Voluntary Schools and Educational Charities) Order 1973 (S.I. 1973
No. 2025) which includes for the purposes of the Order definitions of "educational charity" and
"trust deed." (See Circ. 14/73) (W.O. 298/73). See, generally K. Brooksbank and J. Revell,
School Governors (1981).

[26] Report by a Committee of Inquiry appointed by the Secretaries of State for Education and Science
and for Wales under the chairmanship of Mr. Tom (now Lord) Taylor C.B.E. (H.M.S.O. 1977).
Interest in school government was also aroused by the events at the William Tyndale junior school
in London (see report of William Tyndale Junior and Infants School Public Inquiry conducted by
Robin Auld Q.C., I.L.E.A. 1976). Disciplinary proceedings gave rise to *Ellis & Others* v.
I.L.E.A. 75 L.G.R. 382 (see above at para. 1–56 n.66) and *Haddow and Others* v. *I.L.E.A.* [1979]
I.C.R. 202 (see above at para. 1–54 n.61).

[27] See "Education: Governors and Managers" (1965) 125 J.P.N. 458; and T. Packwood, "School
Governing Bodies: A Case of Uncertainty" (July 1984) 12 No. 3 *Policy and Politics*.

[28] See Circs. 1/80 and 4/81—in part superseding A.M. 25.

government provisions in the 1944, 1968 (No. 2) and 1980 Acts,[29] but these are stated here because for schools with existing instruments and articles of government, transitional provisions in the Education (No. 2) Act 1986 (Commencement No. 2) Order 1987 postpone the date of full compliance until September 1, 1988 for county and maintained special schools and September 1, 1989 for voluntary schools. Certain of the provisions in the 1986 (No. 2) Act, however, relating to governors' proceedings, reports to the Secretary of State and access to papers of governing bodies, already apply generally.[30]

Constitution and functions of governing bodies (pre-1986 (No. 2) Act provisions)

2–71   The composition of governing bodies, the terms of office of governors, arrangements for filling casual vacancies and other constitutional matters together with the arrangements for conduct of meetings are (subject to regulations made by the Secretary of State[31]) contained in an instrument of government. There is to be an instrument relating to every county, voluntary and maintained special school, made[32] for county and special schools by an order of the local education authority and for voluntary schools by an order of the Secretary of State. (If the Secretary of State finds that no properly constituted governing body exists for a school he may rectify[33] the situation and validate defective acts and proceedings). Articles of government establish the division of functions as regards the conduct of schools between local education authority, governing body and head teacher. Articles are made in the case of primary and special schools by an order of the local education authority. Articles for county secondary schools are made[34] by order of the local education authority subject to the approval of the Secretary of State, and for voluntary schools by an order of the Secretary of State. Articles are subject to the provisions of any trust deed[35] relating to the school, but if they, or an instrument of government, are inconsistent

---

[29] As to the 1944 Act provisions see A.M. 25. The repealed provisions are 1944 Act, ss.17–21, 1968 (No. 2) Act, s.2 and 1980 Act, ss.2–4.

[30] See 1986 (No. 2) Act, ss.8(1) and (6) to (12), 56 and 62, below at paras. 2–81 and 2–88, 2–89.

[31] See below at paras. 2–100 to 2–102.

[32] 1944 Act, s.17(1) and (2) as amended by 1980 Act s.1(3) and Sched. 1, para. 2. Maintained special schools: 1968 (No. 2) Act, s.2(1) and (2). An Order may be varied or revoked under 1944 Act, s.111. A nursery school, though a primary school, is not a county or voluntary school (1944 Act, s.9).

[33] See 1944 Act, s.99(2) as amended by 1980 Act, s.1(3) and Sched. 1, para. 1, and as to the powers of a receiver in the absence of a complete governing body *Att.-Gen.* v. *Schonfeld* [1980] 1 W.L.R. 1182.

[34] 1944 Act, s.17(3) as amended by 1980 Act, s.1(3) and Sched. 1, para. 2. Maintained special schools: 1968 (No. 2) Act, s.2(3). See *Blencowe* v. *Northamptonshire County Council* [1907] 1 Ch. 504 as regards an action for trespass by managers.

[35] Defined in 1944 Act, s.114(1), amended by 1980 Act, Sched. 1, para. 13(*b*), as including in relation to any voluntary school any instrument (other than an instrument or articles of government) "regulating the maintenance, management or conduct of the school or the constitution of the body of governors thereof."

with the deed the Secretary of State may by order modify[36] it so far as seems to him just and expedient in the interests of the school.

Before he makes an order the Secretary of State must give an oppor- **2-72** tunity to make representations to the local education authority and to "any other persons appearing to him to be concerned with the government of the school." This form of words does not appear, prima facie, to be wide enough to include, for example, parents of school pupils. The Secretary of State is required to take into account the circumstances of the school and how (if not new) it has been conducted.[37] Where proposals for a significant change in the character[38] of a voluntary school are approved under section 13 of the 1980 Act and the Secretary of State by order makes consequential changes in the articles of government the opportunity to make representations does not arise.[39] Where the opportunity *does* arise a reasonable period in which to make them must be granted.[40] Orders relating to instruments and articles are local and are not statutory instruments.[41]

Sections 18 and 19 of the 1944 Act prescribed how instruments of **2-73** government were to determine the composition of the governing bodies of primary and secondary schools respectively. Those sections (and section 2(2) of the 1968 (No. 2) Act relating to maintained special schools) ceased to apply to schools in respect of which the Secretary of State made an order under section 2(11) of the 1980 Act.[42] Until an order was made instruments made before July 1, 1981 remained valid and operative and might be varied. Orders[43] now extend to all maintained schools so all instruments must now comply with the following requirements of section 2.[44]

The governing bodies of all county, voluntary and maintained special **2-74** schools are to include governors appointed by the maintaining local education authorities at their discretion as regards number and proportions, subject to the terms of the instrument and as provided in section 2. Primary schools must have at least one governor appointed by any

---

[36] 1944 Act, s.17(4), as amended by 1980 Act, s.1(3), and Sched. 1, para. 2.

[37] *Ibid.* s.17(5), amended as above.

[38] See 1980 Act, s.16(2), and above at para. 2–32.

[39] 1944 Act, s.17(6), added by 1968 Act, s.1(3) and Sched. 1, para. 2, and amended by 1973 Act, s.1(3) and (4) and Sched. 1, para. 3, and Sched. 2, Part II, and by 1980 Act, s.16(4) and Sched. 3, para. 2.

[40] *Lee and Others* v. *Department of Education and Science* 66 L.G.R. 211. This case and *Lee and Another* v. *Enfield Borough Council* (see below at para. 2–174) are discussed at 131 J.P.N. 614.

[41] See above at para. 1–42.

[42] 1980 Act, s.2(12).

[43] Three Orders were made: the Education Act 1980 (application of ss.2 and 3) Order 1981 (published in Circ. 4/81) applied s.2 to schools for which there was no provision for a governing body in an instrument of government or grouping arrangements under 1944 Act, s.20, or 1968 (No. 2) Act, s.2(4); the 1983 Order (published in Circ. 7/83) applied s.2 to any maintained special school to which that section did not already apply; and the 1984 Order (published in Circ. 7/84) applied s.2 to any remaining county or voluntary school to which it did not already apply.

[44] The Secretary of State published a model instrument for county schools in Circ. 4/81.

minor authority[45] or authorities (usually parish or district councils) whose area(s) they serve.[46] The governing bodies of all schools must contain at least one or two serving teacher governors (according to the size of the school) elected by their fellow teachers. Unless he chooses otherwise the head teacher is a governor *ex officio*,[47] and he counts as one in any event for the purpose of the following calculations. The governing bodies of voluntary schools are to include a specified proportion of foundation governors,[48] who are persons appointed (not by a local authority but under a trust deed or otherwise) to maintain the character of the school, ordinarily in accordance with the trust deed: in controlled schools the proportion is at least one fifth, and in aided and special agreement schools foundation governors must outnumber the number of the other members by two if the governing body consists of 18 governors or fewer, or by three if the governing body is larger. At least one foundation governor of an aided or special agreement school must at the time of his appointment be a parent of a registered[49] pupil. County and controlled school governing bodies must contain at least two elected parents of registered pupils, aided and special agreement schools at least one.[50] Election is by fellow parents. Administrative arrangements about elections are the responsibility of the local education authority for county and controlled schools and of governors for aided and special agreement schools.

2–75   The Secretary of State suggested that local education authorities should give consideration to the appointment of, for example, pupil governors,[51] to giving representation to industry and neighbouring local education authorities, and to granting governing bodies a limited power to co-opt. There is no objection in law to a local government officer employed by a local education authority being appointed as a member of a governing body of a school maintained by the same authority because a governing body are not a committee of a local education authority.

2–76   Where the trust deed or other instrument relating to a voluntary school was made before section 2 of the 1980 Act came into force,

---

[45] "Minor authority"—see definition in 1944 Act, s.114(1) substituted by Local Government Act 1972, s.192(4). In relation to a school maintained by I.L.E.A. (see above paras. 1–28 *et seq.*) inner London borough councils and the Common Council of the City of London are "minor authorities" (London Government Act 1963, s.31(10)).

[46] It appears that a joint appointment may be necessary if more than one minor authority is served—see Circ. 4/81, para. 7.

[47] See the Education (School Governing Bodies) Regulations 1981 (S.I. 1981 No. 809), reg. 16.

[48] 1980 Act, s.2(4). "Foundation governor" is defined in 1944 Act, s.114(1), as amended by 1980 Act, Sched. 1, para. 13(*a*). As to validity of appointment see *Meyers* v. *Hennell* [1912] 2 Ch. 256 and *Harries* v. *Crawfurd* [1918] 2 Ch. 158.

[49] Registration of pupils—see below at para. 2–109.

[50] 1980 Act, s.2(5). For modification of this requirement as regards maintained special schools see subs. (6).

[51] Circ. 4/81, para. 16. The propriety in law of appointing minors as pupil governors is in doubt: see *Re Royal Naval School, Seymour* v. *Royal Naval School* [1910] 1 Ch. 806, *Claridge* v. *Evelyn* (1821) 5 B. & Ald. 81 and *Grange* v. *Tiving* (1665) Bridgman O. 107.

section 5 provides that only foundation governors and governors appointed by the education authority and minor authorities may be *ex officio* trustees of its property.

Section 20 of the 1944 Act prescribed when a local education auth-   **2–77** ority might arrange to group two or more schools under a single govern- ing body. Section 2(4) of the 1968 (No. 2) Act applied to maintained special schools.[52] Since July 1, 1981, new arrangements have had to fol- low section 3 of the 1980 Act and prior arrangements have lapsed on a school's becoming subject to an order under section 2(11).[53] The Sec- retary of State's long term intention is that each school should have its own governing body, apart from joint bodies for two primary schools (for example, an infant and a junior school) neither of which is a special school.[54] Authorities are permitted to arrange for joint governing bodies subject to obtaining consent from governors (or promoters of a new school) in relation to a voluntary school, to the inclusion of teacher and parent governors and, except for two primary schools as above, to the approval of the Secretary of State. The Secretary of State may attach conditions to his approval. He will want to know the proposed compo- sition of the grouped governing body and when the local education auth- ority propose to substitute separate governing bodies for each school. A section 3 arrangement may be terminated by a local education authority or by the Secretary of State (and special provision is made for an arrangement which relates to voluntary schools). While it remains in force section 2 does not apply.

Governors may resign, or if appointed by a local education authority   **2–78** or minor authority[55] may be removed at their request, but the rules of natural justice apply upon dismissal before the end of a governor's term of office.[56] The minutes and proceedings of governing bodies are open to inspection[57] by the local education authority. Governors elect their own chairman.[58] Decisions taken by the governors of aided and special agreement schools with instruments made after July 1, 1981, and which are of a kind (relating to the future of the school concerned) specified, require confirmation at a second governors' meeting held not less than 28 days after the first.[59]

---

[52] As to termination of an arrangement under s.2(4), see s.3(2) (repealed as it applies to such arrangements by 1986 (No. 2) Act, Sched. 6).

[53] See n. 43 above.

[54] Circ. 4/81, para. 21.

[55] Defined in 1944 Act, s.114(1), and see note 45 above.

[56] 1944 Act, s.21(1), as amended by 1980 Act, s.1(3) and Sched. 1, para. 5 (applied to maintained special schools by 1968 (No. 2) Act, s.2(5), as amended by 1980 Act, s.4(6)). See *R.V. Brent London Borough Council, ex p. Assegai, The Times*, June 18, 1987, and as to the rules of natural justice above at para. 1–54.

[57] 1944 Act, s.21(3) amended as above.

[58] 1980 Act, s.4(2).

[59] *Ibid.* s.4(5). See *R. v. Turner* [1910] 1 K.B. 346 and *Re Hector Whaling Ltd.* [1936] Ch. 208 as to the significance of "not less than."

2–79   Other rules about tenure and procedural arrangements are in regula-tions.[60] Instruments, and arrangements made under section 3 of the 1980 Act, may incorporate matters dealt with in the regulations but must be consistent with them.[61]

Constitution and functions of governing bodies (under the 1968 (No. 2) Act[62])

2–80   Under section 1 instruments and articles of government[63] are to be made by order of the local education authority so as to regulate respect-ively the constitution of the governing body and the conduct of county, voluntary and maintained special schools. The contents of instruments are referred to below, as are the circumstances in which two or more schools may be grouped together under a single governing body and in which there are to be temporary governing bodies. As will be seen there are some differences in the provisions made for aided and special agree-ment schools[64] by comparison with those made for other maintained schools, but the general requirements stated in the next two paragraphs, with the exception mentioned, apply to all maintained schools.

2–81   All governing bodies must make the reports and returns the Secretary of State requires and give him the information he needs to exercise his functions.[65] He may make regulations requiring them to make available prescribed information regarding their proceedings.[66] Local education authorities must give governors a free copy of the instrument and articles of their school, and other information relevant to a governor's functions; also free training in how to discharge them effectively must be made available.[67]

2–82   Instruments and articles of government must be consistent with statu-tory provisions and comply with any trust deed relating to the school.[68] If it appears to the Secretary of State that a local education authority's order or proposed order is inconsistent with the trust deed and needs modification in the interests of the school he may make an order accord-ingly.[69] When an instrument provides for co-option no restriction on choice is to be imposed[70] except as regards co-opted foundation gover-nors[71]; and in the case of a county, controlled or maintained special school co-option may be necessary, under section 6, to secure some

---

[60] See paras. 2–88 and 2–100 to 2–102, and the Education (School Government) Regulations 1987 (S.I. 1987 No. 1359).
[61] 1980 Act, s.4(3).
[62] Cases cited in the preceding subsection of this Chapter may continue to be relevant.
[63] Model instruments and articles are appended to Circ. 7/87.
[64] As to transitional provisions see 1986 (No. 2) Act, Sched. 5, para. 1.
[65] 1986 (No. 2) Act, s.56.
[66] *Ibid.* s.62. See below at para. 2–101.
[67] *Ibid.* s.57.
[68] *Ibid.* s.1(5). See also s.13(1).
[69] *Ibid.* s.2(7).
[70] *Ibid.* s.15(12) and (13).
[71] See above at para. 2–74.

connection with the local business community. No person may be elected or appointed a governor unless he is aged 18 or over.[72]

Section 2 is concerned with procedural matters. Before a local edu- **2–83** cation authority make an order they are to consult the school governing body and the head teacher. In the case of a voluntary school they are to secure the body's agreement to the terms of the proposed order and the agreement of the foundation governors to any provisions of particular concern to them if the order embodies or varies an instrument of government; and the authority are also to have regard to the way in which the school has been conducted. An authority are under a duty to consider any proposal for alteration of instrument or articles of government made by any maintained school governing body or (as regards an instrument) by foundation governors in relation to matters of particular concern to them. A dispute between local education authority and governing bodies or foundation governors about instrument or articles may be referred by any party to the Secretary of State who may direct as he thinks fit.

The size of a governing body[73] depends, under section 3, on the **2–84** number of registered pupils[74] in the school. By its instrument a county controlled or maintained special school with less than 100 registered pupils is to have nine governors including the head teacher[75] *ex officio* unless he chooses not to be a governor. Two of the remaining eight are parent governors, two appointed by the local education authority, one teacher governor and three co-opted (or in the case of a controlled school two foundation governors[76] and one co-opted).[77] The number in each category increases with the size of the school up to a total of 18, or 19[78] when the head teacher is a governor. Each governor other than an *ex officio* governor is to hold office for a renewable term of four years.[79] It is provided by section 7 that in certain circumstances representative governors are to be appointed in place of co-opted governors (but not co-opted foundation governors): one by a minor authority[80] where a county or controlled primary school serves their area; one by the district health authority, for a maintained hospital special school[81]; and one (two if the school has more than 99 registered pupils) by a voluntary

---

[72] 1986 (No.2) Act, s.15(14). Younger pupils may, however, be invited to attend as observers.

[73] As to recommendations for membership by outgoing governing bodies, see *ibid*. Sched. 5, para. 3. A qualification for appointment in one of the categories specified below does not disqualify for appointment in another category, but no person is to hold more than one governorship of the same school (s.15(9) and (10)). For definitions of the categories, see s.65.

[74] "Registered pupils"—see below at para. 2–109.

[75] Or head teachers if there is more than one (1986 No. 2 Act, s.15(1)). For definition see *ibid*. s.65.

[76] The instrument is to name who is to be entitled to appoint any foundation governor, or may provide for an *ex officio* appointment (*ibid*. s.15(7) and (8)).

[77] "Parent," "teacher" and "co-opted governors" are defined at *ibid*. s.65.

[78] But see 1986 (No. 2) Act, s.3(6).

[79] *Ibid*. s.8(2) and (3) but see also s.8(10).

[80] See above at para. 2–74 and *ibid*. s.15(11).

[81] See below at para. 2–207.

organisation (or jointly[82] by more than one) designated by the local education authority as concerned with matters in respect of which a maintained special school is specially organised, unless the authority are satisfied that no such organisation exists.

2–85   There are different arrangements, specified in section 4, for aided and special agreement schools.[83] There is to be at least one governor[84] appointed by the local education authority; in the case of a primary school serving an area in which there is a minor authority[85] at least one governor appointed by that authority; foundation governors; at least one parent governor; at least one teacher—at least two when the school has 300 or more registered pupils; and the head teacher[86] *ex officio* unless he chooses not to be a governor. The instrument may provide for the appointment of additional governors. Foundation governors are to outnumber the other governors as prescribed and at least one of them, on appointment, is to be the parent of a registered pupil at the school.

2–86   Arrangements for election of parent and teacher governors, by secret ballot and otherwise as prescribed, are to be settled by governors in relation to aided and special agreement schools and by local education authorities in relation to other maintained schools.[87]

2–87   There are particular provisions, in section 5, relating to:

> (a) the appointment of parent governors by the governors of county, controlled and maintained special schools (excluding hospital special schools) where at least half of the registered pupils are boarders[88] and election would in the opinion of the local education authority be impracticable;
>
> (b) where there are vacancies and not enough parents stand for election; and
>
> (c) where, at a hospital special school, elections would be impracticable.

2–88   Further, miscellaneous, provisions about tenure and about governors' proceedings are contained in section 8 as follows. A vacancy in the governing body of any maintained school or defect in the election or appointment of a governor does not invalidate proceedings.[89] A governor may at any time resign his office. A foundation governor of a

---

[82] In the absence of agreement the Secretary of State decides (1986 (No.2) Act, s.15(11)).

[83] Following equivalent provisions in 1980 Act, s.2. See Circ. 4/81, paras. 5–16.

[84] See n. 73 above.

[85] See above at para. 2–74.

[86] See n. 75 above and note that by 1986 (No. 2) Act, s.4(4) when the head teacher has chosen not to be a governor he is, nevertheless, to be counted as one for the purpose of calculating the required number of foundation governors.

[87] 1986 (No. 2) Act, s.15(2)–(6) and (15).

[88] For definition of "boarder" see *ibid*. s.65.

[89] The decisions in *Myers* v. *Hennell* [1912] 2 Ch. 256 and *Harries* v. *Crawford* [1918] 2 Ch. 158 appear no longer to be material. See also 1944 Act, s.99(2) as amended by 1980 Act, s.1(3) and Sched. 1, para. 1, and as to the powers of a receiver in the absence of a complete governing body see *Att.-Gen.* v. *Schonfeld* [1980] 3 All E.R. 1.

voluntary school may be removed from office by the person or persons who appointed him, as may a (non co-opted)[90] governor of any county, voluntary or maintained special school, for instance because he ceases to possess the qualifications in respect of which he was appointed in the first place. The Secretary of State may make regulations (and the instrument of government may make provision consistent with them) about meetings and proceedings of governing bodies and disqualification from holding office. He has made the Education (School Government) Regulations 1987,[91] of which regulation 15 provides that a teacher governor loses office on ceasing to be employed in his school; and regulations 17 and 18 specify, respectively, the procedure to be followed in the case of resignation or removal from office of a governor, and how appointments and vacancies are to be notified. Other provisions in the regulations are in the next subsection of this chapter. Minutes of a governing body's proceedings are to be open to inspection by the local education authority.

Certain decisions of the governing body of an aided or special agreement school do not have effect unless confirmed by a second meeting of the body not less than twenty-eight days after the first.[92] These are decisions concerning the establishment, alteration[93] or discontinuance[94] of the school, revocation of an order whereby a school is an aided or special agreement school,[95] discontinuance of a school for which another school is substituted,[96] or agreement for the transfer[97] of an interest in a school to the local education authority. **2–89**

A local education authority may, under section 9, resolve to group **2–90** schools for the purposes of school government, but, by section 10, before doing so must obtain the consent of the Secretary of State unless the group consists only of two primary schools both of which serve substantially the same area, neither of them is a maintained special school and, where they are in Wales, there is no significant difference between them in the use of the Welsh language. Disputes about matters of fact in these regards are settled by the Secretary of State. The Secretary of State may give his consent subject to conditions regarding the duration of the grouping, and he may direct modifications to the requirements mentioned above concerning the size and composition of governing bodies and appointment of parent and representative governors. A grouping exempt from the need for consent may come to require it, if circumstances change so that consent would have been required in the first place. No local education authority may pass a grouping

---

[90] "Non-co-opted" includes a person appointed as explained in the previous paragraph.
[91] S.I. 1987 No. 1359.
[92] 1986 (No. 2) Act, s.8(11) and (12).
[93] Under s.13 of 1980 Act (above at para. 2–32).
[94] Under s.14(1) of the 1944 Act (above at para. 2–35).
[95] Under 1944 Act, s.15(4) (above at para. 2–41).
[96] Under 1944 Act, s.16(2) and (3) (above at para. 2–29).
[97] Under 1944 Act, Sched. 2.

resolution[98] applying to a voluntary school without first obtaining the consent of its governing body, or to a county or maintained special school without consulting the governing body.

2–91 Where schools are grouped they are to be treated for school government purposes as a single school and have a single governing body constituted under a single instrument of government.[99] A group is to be treated as an aided school if it contains at least one such school, as a special agreement school if it contains at least one special agreement school and no aided school, as a controlled school if it contains at least one such school and neither aided nor special agreement school, as a maintained special school if it consists only of such schools, and otherwise as a county school.

2–92 Where there is a proposal to transfer a school to a new site or substitute a new for an old school,[1] to establish, discontinue or alter a school[2] or change the status of a controlled school to that of an aided school,[3] or to make an alteration to arrangements approved by the Secretary of State regarding a special school[4] or the status of an aided or special agreement school,[5] if any of the schools concerned is grouped the local education authority are to review the grouping arrangement and consider whether or not to end it. They are also to report to the Secretary of State on the results of their review if his consent to the grouping was required under section 10, and provide him with information to enable him to consider whether or not to end the grouping.

2–93 Procedures[6] are laid down regarding making and varying instruments of government for grouped schools, for the election of parent and teacher governors, for governors to make an annual report to parents and for an annual parents' meeting.

2–94 A grouping may end in the following ways. The Secretary of State may end it by order if his consent was required in the first place. The local education authority may end it by resolution, but if the group includes a voluntary school the authority's resolution must needs be made with the agreement of the school's governing body. The grouping may also be ended by one year's notice either by the authority to the governing body or *vice versa*; and a group also comes to an end when it was established for a specified period at the end of that period.

2–95 The constitution of the governing body of county, controlled and maintained special schools is to be reviewed in the circumstances stated

---

[98] See 1986 (No. 2) Act, Sched. 5, para. 2 when a school is already grouped under 1980 Act, s.3.
[99] Each school must, however, have its own articles of government, though articles may be in common form.
[1] Under 1944 Act, s.16 (above at para. 2–29).
[2] Under 1980 Act, ss.12–15 (above at paras. 2–14 *et seq.*).
[3] Under 1986 (No. 2) Act, s.54 (above at para. 2–42).
[4] Under 1981 Act, s.12 (below at paras. 2–209 *et seq.*).
[5] Under 1944 Act, s.15(4) (above at para. 2–41).
[6] 1986 (No. 2) Act, s.9(9) and Sched. 1.

in section 11. The first is an increase in the number of registered pupils[7] at a school on its transfer to a new site,[8] or its alteration[9]; the second is implementation of a proposal to change approved arrangements[10] so as to increase the number of registered pupils at a maintained special school; the third is the fourth anniversary of the making of the current instrument of government when none of the events mentioned has occurred since it was made; and the fourth and last is the fourth anniversary of the latest of any of the events having taken place. Reviews required in the first two sets of circumstances mentioned, except alteration of a controlled school, are to be carried out by the local education authority; otherwise by the governing body. The review body must consider whether the governing body are properly constituted and whether the existing instrument differs from the provision a new instrument of government would be required to make. If a governing body find a difference they are to report accordingly to the local education authority.

Pending the making of an instrument of government the local education authority are, by section 12, to arrange to constitute a temporary governing body when: **2–96**

(a) the Secretary of State approves[11] their proposal to establish a new county school or to maintain a non-maintained school as a county school; or

(b) he approves[12] a proposal that an existing or contemplated non-maintained school (a "relevant school") should be maintained by a local education authority as a voluntary school; or

(c) where the authority making any of the above-mentioned proposals have determined[13] to implement it.

Where an authority propose to establish a new special school they are to constitute a temporary governing body at least a year before it opens with pupils, or when they pass their resolution to establish the school. As regards the other proposals mentioned above, the authority may arrange to constitute a governing body in anticipation of the Secretary of State's approval of their determination to implement the proposal; but in the case of a proposal that a relevant school should be maintained they must consult the promoters[14] on whether and when to do so in the case of a proposed controlled school, or get their agreement (or in default the Secretary of State's direction) in the case of a proposed aided school.

---

[7] See also 1986 (No.2) Act, s.13(2), (3) and (8).
[8] Under 1944 Act, s.16(1) (see above at para. 2–29).
[9] Under 1980 Act, ss.12(1)(d) or 13(1)(b) (see above at para. 2–32).
[10] See 1981 Act, s.12 (below at para. 2–210).
[11] Under 1980 Act, s.12 (see above at paras. 2–16—17).
[12] Under *ibid*. s.13 (see above at para. 2–20).
[13] Under 1980 Act, s.12(7) (see above at para. 2–18).
[14] Defined in 1986 (No. 2) Act, s.65.

2–97   Temporary governing bodies are to be constituted[15] in the same way *mutatis mutandis* as are substantive bodies, and provision is made, *inter alia*, for the transition from the temporary arrangements, their duration, the composition and proceedings of the temporary body, and for the organisation and functions of the school in lieu, and so as to anticipate the contents, of articles of government.

2–98   By section 13 instruments of government are to be kept up to date with a school's changing circumstances and the local education authority are to vary or renew them as necessary. Pending a review[16] changes in the number of registered pupils may be disregarded. An instrument may make provision in anticipation of change in a school's circumstances, but in relation to the number of registered pupils at the school such provision is to have effect only after change in numbers has been established by a review (if any).

2–99   Where a county, controlled or maintained special school has more governors of a particular category than the instrument of government provides for, and the excess is not eliminated by resignation, the longest serving governor or governors in the category are to cease to hold office. If governors are of equal seniority lots are to be drawn. These expedients, stated in section 14, are not to be adopted where the excess is of foundation governors; and to meet this circumstance the instrument of a controlled school is to provide a regularising procedure.

Tenure, meetings and proceedings of governing bodies

2–100   The statutory provisions outlined above are supplemented by the Education (School Government) Regulations 1987.[17–19] Ordinarily, by regulations 5–8, no person may be a member of the governing body of more than four maintained schools or groups of schools, and bankruptcy or criminal conviction, including conviction of an offence of nuisance or disturbance on school premises,[20] disqualify. An appointment as governor (other than as *ex officio* or temporary governor) may lapse after 12 months' absence from meetings. Provision is made in regulations 9 and 10 regarding chairmen and vice-chairmen—posts to which teachers, other school employees and pupils may not be elected—and in regulation 24 regarding their power to act in case of urgency.

2–101   Regulations 19 and 12 are about arrangements for convening and holding meetings, and their frequency. Termination and adjournment of meetings are the subject of regulation 21. A head teacher who decides not to be a member[21] of the governing body must by regulation 16 so notify their clerk,[22] but by regulation 11 may nevertheless ordinarily

---

[15] 1986 (No.2) Act s.12(10) and Sched. 2.
[16] Under 1986 (No. 2) Act, s.11 (see above at para. 2–95). See, however, s.13(9) and note that aided and special agreement schools are not subject to review.
[17–19] S.I. 1987 No. 1359.
[20] See above at para. 2–67.
[21] See above at paras. 2–84 and 2–85.
[22] See below at paras. 4–44 and 4–46.

attend their meetings. Regulation 13 specifies the quorum[23] in various circumstances. Regulation 14 governs the conduct of business and the taking of minutes (which, by regulation 23, are to include a record of those present). Decisions are to be made by a majority of members present and voting,[24] and the chairman has a casting vote. Schedule 2 supplements regulation 14 and requires those who have specified categories of personal interest in a matter under discussion[25] to withdraw from the meeting, or otherwise restrict their rights. Regulation 20 is about rescission and variation of resolutions passed at meetings of certain voluntary schools.

The attendance at meetings of a person who is not a member, head teacher or clerk to the governors is a matter for decision by the governing body, under regulation 22. Regulation 25 requires that papers for meetings and minutes, with confidential matters excluded, are to be available at schools for general inspection.

The regulations do not give governing bodies power to appoint com- **2–102** mittees, and where a committee act to select pupils for admission to schools the selection is presumably regarded as a ministerial act rather than the exercise of a discretion.

Status, liabilities and reimbursement of governors

Viscount Haldane L.C. in *Gillow* v. *Durham County Council*[26] stated **2–103** that the relationship between local education authority and governors "is not that of principal and agent but one of coordinate authorities between which powers are distributed." The legislation[27] which gave rise to that interpretation has long since been repealed, and although the words used still epitomise the relationship they suggest a clearer division of responsibilities than the law provides; and it has been necessary to make statutory provision[28] for the resolution of disputes between local education authorities and governors by the Secretary of State. He also has power to give directions both to governors and to local education authorities if he is satisfied that they have acted or propose to act unreasonably, and to use his default powers if they have failed to discharge their proper duties.[29]

---

[23] See D. Lanham *"The Quorum in Public Law,"* 1984 Public Law 461.
[24] "Present and voting"—see *R.* v. *Griffiths* (1851) 17 Q.B. 164 and *Everett* v. *Griffiths* [1924] 1 K.B. 941 and 953.
[25] See *Noble* v. *I.L.E.A.* 82 L.G.R. 291, C.A. (a teacher-governor participated in discussion and voted on a promotion matter in which he had a personal interest, in consequence of which the decision of the governors was held invalid); and *Lockett and Another* v. *Croydon London Borough Council, The Times,* August 6, 1986, as to the decision in which see now regs. 14(2) and (3).
[26] [1913] A.C. 54 at 65. The case concerned what would now be a voluntary school but is probably equally relevant to all maintained schools.
[27] Education Act 1902, s.7.
[28] 1944 Act, s.67(1) as amended by 1980 Act, s.1(3) and Sched. 1, para. 1, and see below at para. 6–08.
[29] 1944 Act, ss.68 and 99 (see below at paras. 6–10 and 6–15) extended to maintained special schools by 1968 (No. 2) Act, s.3(3).

2–104   In practice, articles of government may be drawn in such a way that local education authorities rather than governing bodies attract legal proceedings.[30] There is always the possibility, however, that where, for example, responsibility falls upon governors for repairs to school premises and physical injury results from a defect in the premises they could be sued for negligence[31]; and they may otherwise be subject to a claim in tort.[32] In some circumstances damages may constitute maintenance expenses[33] for which the local education authority are liable, but the cost of defending, for example, a libel action, is not maintenance. Governors may also be open to proceedings under legislation governing the welfare of employees and against sex and racial discrimination.[34] Voluntary school governors have generally wider powers than county school governors and are, therefore more at risk; also because they are probably to be regarded as managing trustees of the property of the foundation.

2–105   It seems that governors may act by a majority[35] vote, but this leaves open the question whether a minority who express dissent are thereby relieved of liability. Mere abstention may amount to acquiescence,[36] and a governor wishing to indemnify himself against the consequences of a decision of the majority (for example, because he thought it *ultra vires* or otherwise open to challenge in the courts)[37] ought in prudence to have his dissent recorded in the minutes.

2–106   Under section 58 of the 1986 (No. 2) Act a local education authority may make a scheme for the payment of travelling and subsistence

---

[30] It is not clear whether an action should be brought against governors individually or against one or more of them as representative of the whole body. See the cases cited at Chap. 2–50 of *Clerk and Lindsell on Torts* (15th ed. 1982), and also *Brown* v. *Lewis* (1896) 12 T.L.R. 455 (also *ibid*. Chap. 3.13) where the committee of a football club were held liable for injuries caused by the collapse of a stand. See also s.80 (as amended) of the Employment Protection (Consolidation) Act 1978 (and below at para. 4–84) regarding unfair dismissal of teachers at aided schools.

[31] The law regarding the liability of principals for the negligence of their agents is obscure; and in any event the better view seems to be that governing bodies are not agents. See *Griffiths* v. *Smith* [1941] A.C. 170, *Gillow* v. *Durham County Council* [1913] A.C. 54 and *Woodward* v. *Mayor of Hastings and Another* [1945] 1 K.B. 174, but also *Ching* v. *Surrey County Council* [1910] 1 K.B. 736 (where the council were held liable—see below at para. 7–39).

[32] See Chap. 7. In *Ryan* v. *Fildes and Others* [1938] 3 All E.R. 517 managers of a non-provided (in current terminology, voluntary,) school were liable for an assault by a schoolmistress in their employment, but able to claim indemnity from her under the Law Reform (Married Women and Tortfeasors) Act 1935, s.6 (now repealed and substituted by Civil Liability (Contribution) Act 1978).

[33] See above at para. 2–26.

[34] See above at paras. 1–92 *et seq*. and 1–102 *et seq*.; but note the exemption in Sex Discrimination Act 1975, s.51 as amended by 1986 (No. 2) Act, Sched. 4, para. 6 (see above at para. 1–92 n.86).

[35] See the argument in *Grindley* v. *Barker* (1798) 1 B. & P. 229 (applied in *Picea Holdings Ltd.* v. *London Rent Assessment Panel* [1971] 2 Q.B. 216).

[36] See *Re Bailey, Hay & Co.* [1971] 1 W.L.R. 1357, and *R.* v. *Hendon Rural District Council, ex p. Chorley* [1933] 2 K.B. 696 at 703 for the proposition that where no vote is taken on a resolution those present are presumed to have assented. In *Barnes* v. *District Auditor No. 11 District* 1976, (unreported), it was held that those councillors who failed to end illegal expenditure were responsible, by their inaction, for that expenditure.

[37] See above at paras. 1–48 *et seq*.

allowances to governors of maintained schools.[38] No other payment is permitted. The scheme may make different provision for different categories of school, but not for different categories of governor of the same school. An authority may also pay travelling and subsistence allowances to persons appointed to represent them on the governing bodies of independent, and non-maintained special, schools, but not if (a) they are otherwise reimbursed or (b) the authority have not made a scheme, or the arrangements would provide more generous payments than under the scheme, or would otherwise exceed what a scheme could permit. The provisions relating to maintained school governors apply equally to governors of maintained further education establishments[39]; and those relating to persons appointed to governing bodies of independent, etc., schools apply to the governors of designated establishments[40] of further education (in effect) and to governors appointed to further education establishments which are not maintained or assisted by local education authorities.

CONDUCT OF SCHOOLS

2–107 Arrangements for the conduct of maintained schools are mostly contained in articles[41] of government made, and subject to amendment, as indicated in the previous section[42]; but registration of pupils is prescribed by statute and, as will appear, there are particular statutory provisions with which articles must comply or with which they must be consistent. A White Paper, Cmd. 6523, was published in 1944 on the principles of government in maintained secondary schools. Some articles are still likely to be based on recommendations in the White Paper, and all to include provision for financial arrangements, appointment and dismissal of teachers and non-teaching staff (see Chapter 4), internal organisation and management and discipline, curriculum and (considered later in this Chapter) admission of pupils. Articles may also deal with the care and use of school premises and grounds. Many aspects of the ways in which schools are conducted (for example as regards curricula) must be made public.[43]

2–108 As indicated below Part III of the 1986 (No. 2) Act requires articles to be in certain respects more specific than formerly about the functions of local education authorities, governors, and head teachers, and the Act gave authorities some new powers and duties. Subject to statutory

---

[38] As to the expenses of governors acting as members of appeal committees on school admissions see below at para. 2–178 n.12.
[39] See below at para. 3–16.
[40] See below at para. 3–05.
[41] See A.M. 25, to which is appended a Model Instrument and Articles of Government of a County Secondary School (since superseded by those appended to Circ. 7/87).
[42] See above at paras. 2–71 and 2–80. As to amendment see below at para. 1–42.
[43] See the Education (School Information) Regulations 1981 (S.I. 1981 No. 630) and below at paras. 2–186 to 2–190.

provisions and particular provisions in articles the latter are to confer general responsibility for the conduct of schools upon governors.[44] The Secretary of State is empowered to make regulations[45] specifying the circumstances in which an authority or head teacher[46] may act as a matter of urgency without consulting the governing body or their chairman or vice-chairman.

Registration of pupils

2–109   It is the duty of a proprietor of a school to arrange for the registration[47] of pupils. The proprietor is defined in section 114(1) of the 1944 Act as the person or body responsible for the management of the school—the governors in the case of county and voluntary schools. Regulations[48] require two registers to be kept—an admission register and (except in the case of a wholly boarding independent school) an attendance register. The admission register is to contain an alphabetical index of pupils showing, in respect of each, full name, sex, parent's name and address, date of birth, date of admission or readmission and name and address of school last attended, if any; and also, where the school includes boarders, whether the pupil, if of compulsory school age, is a boarder or day pupil. The presence or absence of each pupil currently in the admission register (except boarders in independent schools) is to be recorded at the start of each morning and afternoon session[49] in the attendance register.

2–110   The regulations set out the grounds for deleting a pupil's name from the admission register. In the case of pupils not of compulsory school age these are limited to non-attendance, prolonged absence and death. In relation to pupils of compulsory school age the grounds include a parent's satisfying the local education authority[50] about the education of the pupil outside school,[51] registration at another school, prolonged absence from school, illness likely to persist during compulsory school age, and exclusion[52] from a maintained school (other than temporary) by governors or local education authority. In this last situation, if the

---

[44] 1986 (No. 2) Act, s.16(1). In parallel with school government provisions (see above at para. 2–70) the date of compliance for schools with existing articles is September 1, 1988 (county and maintained special schools) or September 1, 1989 (voluntary schools).

[45] *Ibid.* s.16(2), the Education (School Government) Regulations 1987 (S.I. 1987 No. 1359), regs. 28 and 29 and below at paras. 2–122 to 2–124, and 4–40.

[46] *Ibid.* s.16(3). Where a school is organised in separate departments, the heads of departments count as head teachers except where articles provide otherwise.

[47] 1944 Act, s.80(1) as amended by 1948 Act, ss.4, 11 and Sched. 2, and by 1980 Act, s.1(3) and Sched. 1, para. 1.

[48] The Pupils' Registration Regulations 1956 (S.I. 1956 No. 357). See A.M. 531.

[49] "Session"—see reg. 10, as amended, of the Education (Schools and Further Education) Regulations 1981 (S.I. 1981 No. 1086), below at para. 2–140.

[50] Presumably the authority for the area in which the pupil ordinarily resides.

[51] In *R. v. Gwent County Council, ex p. Perry* (1985) 129 S.J. 737, C.A., a boy was removed from school for education at home, but his name was not deleted from the register because the council's sub-committee were not satisfied that the teaching at home suited his age, abilities and aptitudes.

[52] As to exclusion from school, see below at paras. 2–118 to 2–119 and 2–122 to 2–124.

parent appeals (the nature of the appeal is not specified but the use of 1944 Act section 68[53] is perhaps intended) and the Secretary of State determines that the pupil has been excluded on other than reasonable grounds, the name of the pupil is forthwith to be reinstated in the admission register.

Registers are to be available to H.M. Inspectors,[54] and maintained **2–111** school registers are also to be open to inspection by authorised local education authority officers. Inspectors may make extracts from the registers for the purposes of the Education Acts.[55] Registers are to be preserved for three years after use. Proprietors of schools are to make returns to the appropriate local education authority showing, and where known, specifying the cause of irregular attendance and absence of two weeks or more of day pupils, except where the headmaster[56] has received a medical certificate.

Breach of the regulations is an offence carrying a fine on summary **2–112** conviction.[57]

Finance

Cmd. 6523 recommended that governors should be given reasonable **2–113** discretion within the broad headings of the expenditure budget approved by the local education authority. This is normally settled on "capitation allowances" based on the number of pupils and type of school. Articles may be drawn in general terms to cover submission of estimates, their approval (with or without amendment) and conditions of virement; or more specifically so as to refer also to the governors' power to indicate what they see to be the school's special needs and furniture and equipment requirements, and to accept and manage gifts, loans and private funds. These resources, which include the foundation income of voluntary schools and the proceeds of the activities of pupils or parent/teacher associations, supplement capitation allowances. They are not at the disposition of the local education authority, but the authority may be entitled to require governors to inform them of the existence of "voluntary" funds and to satisfy them that proper accounts are kept and audited.

Under section 29[58] of the 1986 (No. 2) Act articles are to be drawn so **2–114** as to help the governing body to judge whether expenditure on their school represents the economic, efficient and effective use of resources, and for this purpose to require local education authorities to give them

---

[53] See below at para. 6–10.
[54] See below at para. 6–05.
[55] Set out in bold type in the table of statutes towards the front of this book.
[56] "Headmaster" presumably includes any head teacher.
[57] 1944 Act, s.80(2) as amended by Criminal Law Act 1977, s.31(5) and (6) and Criminal Justice Act 1982, ss.37 and 46. The amount of the fine is level 1 on the standard scale as amended by the Criminal Penalties, etc., (Increase) Order 1984 (S.I. 1984 No. 447). As to summary proceedings see Magistrates Courts Act 1980 as amended.
[58] Foreshadowed in Green Paper, *Parental Influence at School* (Cmnd. 9242), Chap. 6.

annually an itemised statement of day-to-day running costs, and of capital expenditure incurred or proposed to be incurred. Articles are also to require local education authorities to give the governing body a sum to spend at their discretion on books, equipment, stationery and any other heads of expenditure specified by the authority or prescribed by the Secretary of State in regulations (made after consulting local authority associations[59] and, if he thinks desirable, any local education authority). In spending this sum the governing body are to comply with reasonable conditions imposed by the local education authority; they may delegate their power to spend to the head teacher; and they are not to spend inappropriately, in the opinion of the head teacher, in relation to the curriculum.

Internal organisation, management and discipline

2–115   The division of responsibility recommended in Cmd. 6523 was that the local education authority would have the right to settle the general educational character of the (secondary) school and its place in the local system, the governors would have general direction of the conduct[60] and curriculum of the school, and the head master or mistress would control internal organisation, management and discipline.[61] Some of the uncertainties concerning disciplinary matters are resolved, as explained in paras. 2–121 to 2–125 below, by sections 22–28 of the 1986 (No. 2) Act.

2–116   In *R.* v. *Manchester City Council, ex p. Fulford*[62] the court considered an article that reserved to governors "the general direction and conduct of the school" but provided that head teachers, having consulted staff, should ordinarily be entitled to attend governors' meetings. The governors had decided to abolish corporal punishment at a number of schools at a meeting of which head teachers had not been notified. The court quashed the decision because the head teachers had not been given the opportunity to explain their opposition to abolition. The governors had in fact done no more than endorse the decision of the city council, improperly because it was not one which the authority could take under their power to determine "the general educational character of the school and its place in the educational system." It is noteworthy that the combined effects of sections 2 and 3 of the 1980 Act (and the provisions

[59] See above at para. 1–36.
[60] For an example of "conduct" (the holding of an exhibition of pupils' work) see *Griffiths* v. *Smith* [1941] A.C. 170.
[61] The disciplinary powers of a head teacher are not dependent on contract (see *Wood* v. *Prestwich* (1911) 104 L.T. 388). For an example of disciplinary powers see *Spiers* v. *Warrington Corporation* [1954] 1 Q.B. 61 and above at para 1–82 n.55; and for the views of the Secretary of State as regards responsibility for discipline, see *Better Schools* (Cmnd. 9469) and p. 9 of the Second Government Response (Cmnd. 8648) to the Second Report of the Education, Science and Arts Committee 1981–1982, *The Secondary School Curriculum and Examinations* (H.C. 116–I).
[62] (1984) 81 L.G.R. 292.

in Part II of the 1986 (No. 2) Act[63] that supersede them) will, when brought fully into effect, end a practice in which the composition of governors and of a local education authority sub-committee is identical or substantially overlaps,[64] and the minds of the governors are, in consequence, not especially directed to the particular circumstances of a single school or a few.

Cmd. 6523 also contemplated that heads would have the power of suspending pupils, subject to a report being made forthwith to the governors and the local education authority. Articles have been drawn accordingly, sometimes granting parents a right of appeal, but the law has given no guidance on the action to be taken by governors and local education authorities. The question arises—and no authority is available on the point—how the practice of suspension can be reconciled with requirements as to compulsory attendance, to which reference is made elsewhere.[65] In some circumstances the suspended child may be eligible for special educational provision, to which reference is made later in this chapter, or the local education authority may transfer the child to another school or make arrangements under section 56[66] of the 1944 Act to provide education otherwise than at school. **2–117**

Not far removed from "suspension" (which is normally used as a remedy against extremes of violence and disruption) is "exclusion" from school. *Gateshead Union* v. *Durham County Council*[67] established, in words subsequently used in regulation 7(1) of the Schools Regulations 1959, that no pupil was to be "refused admission to or excluded from a school on other than reasonable grounds." The regulation has been revoked[68] and the only subsisting statutory provisions, apart from those in the 1986 (No. 2) Act, are section 54(7)[69] of the 1944 Act under which a pupil may be excluded so long as he is unclean, and section 21 of the Public Health (Control of Diseases) Act 1984 relating to notifiable diseases.[70] The exclusion of pupils from school may, however, also take place by the exercise of the disciplinary powers given to head teachers by articles of government, for example when a pupil fails to comply with school uniform requirements,[71] or will not remove earrings for physical education. But the extent of disciplinary powers is not unlimited, and it may be that, for example, the exclusion of pregnant schoolgirls is *ultra* **2–118**

---

[63] See above at paras. 2–84 to 2–85.
[64] See "School Governors and Managers" (1954) 118 J.P.N. 622.
[65] See above at para. 1–80 and below at paras. 2–222 *et seq.*
[66] See below at para. 5–29.
[67] [1918] 1 Ch. 146.
[68] By the Education (Schools and Further Education) Regulations 1981 (S.I. 1981 No. 1086).
[69] See below at para. 5–07.
[70] See below at para. 5–06.
[71] See *Spiers* v. *Warrington Corporation* [1954] 1 Q.B. 61 and below at paras. 1–82 and 2–115 but *cf.*
Mandla v. *Dowell Lee* [1983] 2 A.C. 548, H.L., above at para. 1–105.

vires and in breach of the local education authority's general duty to provide education.

2–119 Regulation 4(*a*)(*x*) of the Pupils Registration Regulations 1956[72] appears to contemplate expulsion[73] rather than exclusion, by requiring that a pupil's name be deleted from the admission register of a maintained school if he is of compulsory school age and has been excluded other than temporarily by a local education authority or governors. But if the parent appeals (1944 Act, section 68 is not specified but is presumably intended), and the Secretary of State determines that exclusion has been on other than reasonable grounds, the pupil's name is to be reinstated in the register. If no appeal is made or an appeal is unsuccessful the local education authority must, it is to be concluded, provide education elsewhere.

2–120 Suspension, exclusion and expulsion from a school are closely related and it may not always be apparent which course has been taken.[74] Any one may provoke a parent to have recourse to the Secretary of State under section 68 or section 99,[75] especially if the local education authority fail to make alternative provision for his child.

2–121 The 1986 (No. 2) Act introduced some specific duties[76] relating to school discipline. By section 22 articles are to make the head teacher responsible for taking, and publicising in the school, measures (including making and enforcing rules) for regulating the conduct of pupils, including promoting self-discipline and proper regard for authority, encouraging good behaviour and securing an acceptable standard of behaviour. What is acceptable is to be decided by the head teacher so far as not determined by the governing body. The head teacher is to act in accordance with any statement of general principles provided by the governing body and to have regard to any guidance they may offer in relation to particular matters. The governing body and the head teacher are to consult the local education authority if the measures are likely to lead to increased expenditure or affect the responsibility of the authority as employer.

2–122 Articles are to provide[77] that only the head teacher is to have power to exclude a pupil from school, and, by section 23, without delay he must take all the following steps. He must tell a parent why a pupil under 18 has been excluded and for how long, and likewise give an

---

[72] See above at para. 2–110.

[73] As to circumstances in which pupils were expelled see *Fitzgerald* v. *Northcote* (1865) 4 F. & F. 656, *Hutt & Another* v. *The Governors of Haileybury College & Others* (1888) 4 T.L.R. 623 and *Wood* v. *Prestwich* (1911) 104 L.T. 388.

[74] See M. Freeman, "Children's Education and the Law, 3 Exclusion and Other Disciplinary Measures" (1980) L.A.G. Bull. 212.

[75] See below at paras. 6–10 and 6–15.

[76] Compliance with those in paras. 2–121 to 2–124 may be postponed (see n. 44 above).

[77] 1986 (No. 2) Act, s.22(*f*). By s.65(1) "exclude" means exclude on discplinary grounds.

explanation when he decides to make permanent an exclusion that was originally for a fixed or indefinite period. If the exclusion is for more than five days in any one term or the pupil would in consequence miss taking a public examination he must inform the local education authority and governing body similarly. He must also inform the pupil (or parent if the pupil is under 18) that he may make representations to the governing body and to the local education authority.

Sections 24 and 25 require that articles are, additionally, to make **2–123** elaborate provision for the reinstatement of pupils excluded. The following is only a bare summary. The head teacher is to comply with any direction the local education authority or governing body may give. If directions conflict the head teacher is to comply with whichever leads to the earlier reinstatement of the pupil. Local education authority and governing body are to consult each other before giving directions, except that governors of aided and special agreement schools may act alone in the case of permanent (as opposed to indefinite or fixed period) exclusion. Local education authorities and governing bodies must inform each other of any directions they give, and also inform the pupil if aged 18 or over (otherwise a parent) of their decisions. Under regulation 28 of the Education (School Government) Regulations 1987,[77a] in case of urgency they may reinstate a pupil who would otherwise miss a public examination.

Local education authorities (governing bodies in the case of aided and **2–124** special agreeement schools) are to make arrangements, under section 26, to enable pupil or parent, as the case may be, to appeal against a decision not to reinstate the pupil following permanent exclusion, and for governing bodies (of other than aided and special agreement schools) to appeal against a local education authority's reinstatement direction. Appeals are to an appeal committee constituted in the same way as an admissions appeal committee.[78] Their decision is binding on all concerned. If it is reinstatement the date is to be specified. Where articles provide for an alternative form of appeal by parents against exclusion, when there is no right as above, section 27 requires that a decision on reinstatement binds the head teacher.

By section 28, where in the opinion of a local education authority the **2–125** behaviour of the registered pupils at a maintained school, other than an aided or special agreement school, or any action taken by them or their parents, is likely to prejudice severely the pupils' education, and the governing body have been so informed, the local education authority may take steps to prevent the breakdown or continuing breakdown of

---

[77a] S.I.1987 No. 1359.
[78] *i.e.* under Part I of Sched. 2 to the 1980 Act (see below para. 2–178). Sched. 3 to the 1986 (No. 2) Act takes effect in place of Part II of Sched. 2 to the 1980 Act.

discipline. These may include giving any direction to the governing body or head teacher. In the case of an aided or special agreement school the governing body and head teacher are, in the circumstances mentioned, to consider any representations made to them by the local education authority.

2–126   Generally, a wide range of decisions of significance to parents and pupils may be taken by head teachers and governors within the competence granted them by articles. Head teachers often appear to have considerable freedom in the way they run their schools and the rules they make. Articles are likely to leave open requirements and practices about some or all of, for example, school uniform[79] and games clothes, the making of reports to parents on pupils' progress, offences and punishments,[80] homework[81] and extra-curricular activities,[82] some of which involve a financial outlay. Rules requiring pupils to remain on school premises during the midday break and regarding the behaviour of pupils outside[83] school, except when clearly related to their welfare or that of the school, seem of doubtful legality—but the reasonableness of school rules, with limited exceptions as to punishments, remains largely untested in the courts.

2–127   The behaviour of pupils may amount to more than a breach of school discipline. The criminal law may be available against a pupil in the case of theft, assault against a teacher or other member of school staff, or the use of drugs; or against the vendor in the case of the sale of drugs, tobacco products and alcohol. Equally a parent may be prosecuted for assault, or a civil action for trespass on school premises may be available.[84] The police have a right of access to school premises if they are acting under a warrant, or under statutory authority, for example, the Children and Young Persons Act 1969.[85]

---

[79] See n. 71 above.

[80] See below at paras. 2–143 and, as to the limits of punishment, 7–44 *et seq*.

[81] In *Hunter* v. *Johnson* (1884) 13 Q.B.D. 225 (decided on long-repealed legislation) the court held that education was to be regarded as a statutory interference with the liberty of the subject, and that in the absence of explicit authority to impose upon children the duty of studying at home no such duty existed. The Education (School Information) Regulations 1981, contemplate that homework may be required (see below at para. 2–189).

[82] These are probably supported by s.111 of the Local Government Act 1972 (see above at para. 1–39) which would also enable the local education authority to ensure against liabilities they themselves might incur, but not to provide personal accident cover for pupils (see below at para. 5–52 n.79).

[83] Punishments for assault on another pupil on the way to school (*Cleary* v. *Booth* (1893) 1 Q.B. 465) and for breach of a rule against smoking in the street (*R.* v. *Newport (Salop) Justices, ex p. Wright* [1929] 2 K.B. 416) were upheld by the court.

[84] See above at para. 2–67 and below at para. 7–52.

[85] See Home Office Circular 89/1978, *Police Liaison with the Education Service. Report of an enquiry carried out by H.M. Inspectors of Schools in July 1982*, Department of Education and Science, 1983, and Circ. 1/84 (W.O. 1/84).

Curriculum and examinations

Articles prepared under the 1944 Act[86] and following the recommen- **2–128** dations in Cmd. 6523 gave general responsibility to governors for the school curriculum,[87] the role of the education authority being to settle the general educational character of the school and its place in the local system. Local education authorities were enabled to make (circumscribed) arrangements for giving pupils work experience as part of education in the last year of compulsory schooling under the Education (Work Experience) Act 1973,[88] and its provisions survive the introduction of those relating to the curriculum in the 1986 (No. 2) Act, which are as follows.

It is the duty of local education authorities, under section 17, to deter- **2–129** mine and keep under review their policy in relation to the secular curriculum of their maintained schools and to publish a policy statement and keep it up to date. A copy must go to every governing body and head teacher. The latter must allow it and also the statements referred to below to be inspected at reasonable times.[89] Authorities must consider in particular the range and balance of the curriculum, and their policy is to influence the performance of their statutory functions generally.

Articles of government of maintained schools, other than aided and **2–130** special agreement schools, are by section 18 to require the governing body to consider:

(a) the authority's policy statement;
(b) what in their opinion should be the aims of the secular curriculum of their school; and
(c) how the authority's policy should be modified in relation to the school.

The governing body are to make and keep up to date a written statement of their conclusions. They are to consider sex education separately and indicate in a separate statement whether it is to be part of the curriculum and, if so, their policy about content and organisation. These duties are to be carried out in consultation with the head teacher, and

---

[86] 1944 Act, s.23, as amended by 1980 Act, s.1(3) and Sched. 1, para. 7 (repealed).
[87] As to the curriculum see Green Paper, *Parental Influence at School* (Cmnd. 9242), *The School Curriculum*, published by the Secretary of State, March 25, 1981, and Government Responses (Cmnd. 8551 and 8648) to the Second Report of the Education, Science and Arts Committee 1981–1982, *The Secondary School Curriculum and Examinations* (H.C.–116–I). That Committee (see p. xvii) took the view that the Secretary of State has *duties* in regard to the curriculum. As to his powers see H.C. 116–II at p. 502. A further statement of the Secretary of State's views is in *Better Schools* (Cmnd. 9649).
See also Circ. 14/77 and report on review entitled *Local Authority Arrangements for the School Curriculum* (H.M.S.O. 1979); also Circs. 6/81 and 8/83. The Schools Council for the Curriculum and Examinations (see Circ. 13/64) (since superseded by the School Curriculum Development Committee and the Secondary Examinations Council) provided a forum for the various educational interests, but predominantly teachers, to express opinions on curricular matters. As to parental wishes see above at paras. 1–75 to 1–76.
[88] See Circ. 7/74 (W.O. 135/74), and also below at para. 5–39.
[89] Compliance with those in paras. 2–130 to 2–132 may be postponed (see para. 2–108 n. 44).

they are to have regard to representations by persons connected with the community served by the school and by the chief officer of police in connection with his responsibilities.[90] Statements are to go to head teacher and authority, and the latter must be consulted before the (general) statement is made or varied. Governors are to review their conclusions when they think fit and in specified circumstances,[91] and when they consider appropriate make a further statement.

2–131   Articles are to make the head teacher responsible for determining and organising the secular curriculum and seeing that it is followed. He must consider the statements of local education authority and governors, have regard to representations made by those mentioned in the previous paragraph, and ensure that the curriculum is compatible with the policy of the authority (modified, as need be, by the policy of the governing body)[92] and with other statutory requirements relating to education, in particular those concerning children with special educational needs.[93]

2–132   Articles of aided and special agreement schools are, by section 19, to require the contents of the secular curriculum to be under the control of the governing body, the governing body to have regard to the authority's policy statement, and the head teacher to be allocated functions by the governing body that will enable him, subject to the resources available, to determine and organise the curriculum and see that it is followed. Articles are also to impose upon governors the same requirements as above with regard to representations, the giving of a copy of a statement (if any) about policy to the head teacher and the latter's allowing it to be inspected.

2–133   Section 20 requires the Secretary of State to make regulations[94] requiring the governing body of every maintained school to make available to parents of registered pupils the information about educational provision, including syllabuses, that he prescribes.

2–134   Sections 44 and 45 impose new duties concerning political issues. Local education authorities, governing bodies and head teachers of maintained schools are:

   (a) to forbid[95] the pursuit of partisan political activities by junior pupils[96] and the promotion of partisan political views by teachers; and

---

[90] *i.e.* presumably to the exclusion of his personal opinions generally.

[91] The circumstances specified are transfer of schools to new sites under 1944 Act, s.16 (see above at para. 2–29), establishment, alteration and discontinuance of schools under 1980 Act, ss.12 or 13 (see above at paras. 2–14 *et seq.*), reduction of school places under 1980 Act, s.15 (see above at para. 2–34), where implementation of proposals materially affects the school; and change of arrangements with regard to a maintained special school (see below at para. 2–210).

[92] And conforming with their policy in regard to sex education except where the policy is incompatible with a public examination syllabus.

[93] See below at paras. 2–203 *et seq.*

[94] See also below at paras. 2–186 to 2–190.

[95] The prohibition ordinarily applies only to activities on school premises—see s.44(2).

[96] 1944 Act, s.114(1) and see above at para. 2–03.

(b) to take reasonably practicable[97] steps that where political issues are brought to the attention of pupils they are offered a balanced presentation[98] of opposing views at school or in the course of extra-curricular activities.[99]

Sex education is the subject of section 46 as follows: **2–135**

"The local education authority by whom any county, voluntary or special school is maintained, and the governing body and head teacher of the school, shall take such steps as are reasonably practicable to secure that where sex education is given to any registered pupils at the school it is given in such a manner as to encourage those pupils to have due regard to moral considerations and the value of family life."

Reported cases give little assistance in the interpretation of "moral **2–136** considerations." Under "moral" the judicial dictionary[1] refers the reader to "immoral." Winn L.J. expressed the opinion[2] that " 'immoral purposes' in their ordinary meaning connote in a wide general sense all purposes involving conduct which has the property of being wrong rather than right in the judgement of the majority of contemporary fellow citizens." A similar reference to "the consensus of general opinion" was made by Halsbury C. in an earlier case.[3] It follows perhaps that the section requires pupils to be encouraged to have due regard to what contemporary opinion takes to be right and wrong; and equally that neither teachers nor judges (nor the Secretary of State, local education authorities or governors) are entitled to substitute their own opinions for "the consensus of general opinion"; but it is not clear how teachers or courts are to establish contemporary opinion at a time of dissent about issues of sexual morality. It may be that the correct interpretation is that pupils are to be made aware that there *are* moral considerations to be taken into account even though what counts as right or wrong is today in some respects an open question.

It is possible to exaggerate the extent of controversy, as was implicitly **2–137** suggested by the Minister of State[4] when he offered the following explanation regarding "the value of family life."

"In requiring schools to reflect [it] in their work we are simply asking that pupils should be encouraged to look at personal relationships, marriage and parenthood in a positive, moral and responsible manner, to be aware not only of the problems and failures but of the possibilities and achievements to which we all aspire."

---

[97] See *Stroud's Judicial Dictionary* (5th ed., 1986).
[98] "Balanced presentation"—an analogous provision is s.2(2)(*b*) of the Broadcasting Act 1981 under which the Independent Broadcasting Authority are to ensure "a proper balance" in the subject matter of their programmes. See *R.* v. *Broadcasting Complaints Commission, ex. p. Owen* [1985] 1 Q.B. 1153.
[99] See above at para. 1–67.
[1] See n. 97 above.
[2] See *Crook* v. *Edmonson* [1966] 1 All E.R. 833 at 835.
[3] See *Beneficed Clerk* v. *Lee* [1897] A.C. 226 at 229.
[4] House of Commons Standing Committee B, July 1, 1986, col. 454.

Though lacking in incisiveness this statement is a reminder that there are basic values that are widely shared although sometimes differently interpreted.

2–138   Enforcement of the section, Lord Denning has suggested,[5] should come about by parents reporting a teacher's shortcomings to the head teacher, who should discipline the teacher. If the head teacher failed to act the courts could do so.[6]

2–139   The Secretary of State has no statutory powers regarding the nature and form of secondary school examinations, but he gives his official recognition to the certificates awarded by the independent bodies[7] who conduct the General Certificate of Education (G.C.E.) "O" and "A" level[8] and the Certificate of Secondary Education (C.S.E.) examinations; and conditions of entry of pupils at maintained schools[9] are specified (but no longer by statutory instrument)[10]:

> "For O level the Department of Education and Science requires that a candidate who is not at least 16 years of age on September 1 may not be entered unless: (a) he has completed or is about to complete a five year course of secondary education, or (b) the head teacher certifies both that it is educationally desirable for him to take the examination and that he has pursued a course of study with such a degree of competence as to make it very probable that he will pass in the subject(s) offered."[11]
>
> "Candidates for the Certificate of Secondary Education examination attending school must be in the final term of a five year course of secondary education and aged at least 16 years on September 1 in the calendar year in which the examination is taken; or aged at least 15 years on March 1 in the calendar year in which the examination is taken but have completed or be about to complete a five year course of secondary education."[12]

School day and year

2–140   Articles of government for maintained schools are, by section 21 of the 1986 (No. 2) Act, to require[13] the local education authority (governors in the case of aided and special agreement schools) to determine the times of school sessions and the dates and times of school terms and

---

[5] H.L.Deb. June 2, 1986, col. 571.

[6] But see above at paras. 1–49 and 6–15—17. 1944 Act, s.99, appears to be available.

[7] There are eight G.C.E. examination boards, mostly having close links with universities, and 12 C.S.E. Regional Examination Boards, on which teachers are in a majority but local education authorities are also represented. The Welsh Joint Education Committee (see above at para. 1–23) are an examining body for both examinations.

[8] See Second Report from the Education, Science and Arts Committee 1981–1982 (H.C. 116–I) p. lii and H.C. 116–II (Minutes of Evidence) p. 78. The G.C.E. 'O' level and C.S.E. examinations are to be superseded in summer 1988 by examinations for the General Certificate of Secondary Education.

[9] Examination fees are normally paid by the local authority as part of the cost of providing education, *i.e.* as an incident of the school curriculum. Whether they have a statutory duty to pay is not clear. If the obligation exists it is presumably not an unlimited one.

[10] Formerly under the Schools Regulations 1959.

[11] Second Report from the Education, Science and Arts Committee 1981–82 H.C. 116—I p. cxviii.

[12] *Ibid.* p. cxvii/cxviii.

[13] As to postponement of compliance see para. 2–108 n. 44.

holidays; and the local education authority (or governors) are to have power to require pupils to attend outside school premises to follow the instruction or training in the secular curriculum.

Articles are subject to the Education (Schools and Further Education **2–141** Regulations) 1981.[14] Regulation 10 requires that the school day[15] shall ordinarily be divided into two sessions[16] with a break in the middle of the day, and that in each academic year a school shall meet for at least 380 sessions. That number may lawfully be reduced by up to 20 occasional holidays in term time, and exceptionally by force of circumstances. It is noteworthy that the regulation does not specify the number of terms in an academic year, and indeed that "term" has no statutory definition.[17] Pupils under eight years of age must, each school day, receive at least three hours secular instruction, pupils over eight, four. Where a school meets on six days a week there need be only a single session on two of the days, and on those days the specified hours are halved.[18] The marking of registers[19] is to take place outside the specified periods but recreation, medical or dental examination and treatment, and time required in a voluntary school for the inspection of religious education,[20] count towards those periods.

By regulation 11, leave of absence from school is not, with certain **2–142** exceptions,[21] to be granted to enable a pupil to take up employment, but may be granted, under circumstances specified in regulation 12, for an annual holiday normally restricted to two weeks. Arrangements under regulation 12 are to be made by governing bodies.

Records and reports

Section 92 of the 1944 Act has been taken to empower[22] the Secretary **2–143** of State to require head teachers of all (except independent) schools to keep a punishment book recording all cases of corporal punishment,[23] and school annals to preserve events specially worthy of permanent record[24] in the history of the school.

---

[14] S.I. 1981 No. 1086, as amended by S.I. 1983 No. 262 and by S.I. 1987 No. 879, pursuant to 1980 Act, s.27. See Circ. 7/81, paras. 13–15. The Regulations apply to special schools but not to independent schools.

[15] "School day" is defined in 1986 (No. 2) Act, s.65.

[16] "Unless exceptional circumstances make this undesirable." See below at para. 4–55.

[17] As to the relevance of terms to school leaving dates see above at para. 1–81.

[18] Special provision is made for nursery schools and classes (see reg. 10(4) and above at para. 2–48).

[19] See above at para. 2–109.

[20] See below at para. 2–172.

[21] See Education (Work Experience) Act 1973, Children and Young Persons Act 1963, s.37, and Children and Young Persons Act 1933, s.25; also below at paras. 5–35 *et seq.*

[22] See A.M. 531. For special schools the authority is the Education (Approval of Special Schools) Regulations 1983 (S.I. 1983 No. 1499), reg. 6 and Sched. 2, para. 11(2), and for direct grant schools the Direct Grant Schools Regulations 1959 (S.I. 1959 No. 1832) reg. 14. See below at paras. 2–211 and 2–219.

[23] See below at paras. 7–44 *et seq.*

[24] See A.M. 377.

2–144   There is an obligation upon teachers, as part of their conditions of employment, to provide assessments, reports and records relating to pupils.[25] The school governing body are required to transfer, as seems appropriate to them, the records of a pupil to the educational institution he subsequently attends.[26] The Secretary of State has power[27] to make regulations about keeping and disclosure of records, but has not exercised it. Records are kept for a variety of purposes and the position in law regarding disclosure is not altogether clear in all the circumstances in which the issue may arise. Some of the circumstances are as follows.

2–145   Although it is general practice to prepare reports on pupils for parents, they have, it seems, no legal entitlement[28] to reports or to inspect records maintained about their children, unless these are computerised: the Data Protection Act 1984[29] gives those about whom automatically processed data is stored the right to inspect and if necessary correct the record—and this right perhaps extends to parents.

2–146   Section 9 of the Children and Young Persons Act 1969[30] obliges local education authorities, in care proceedings,[31] to provide such information about the school record of any child or young person[32] as appears to the authority likely to assist the court. Whether the disclosure of records to third parties is otherwise lawful without consent of pupil or parent depends on where the balance of public interest lies in the particular case[33]; and when information, for example a medical report, has been given in confidence to the authority the consent of the originator may be needed. These issues may arise when a prospective employer seeks a report on a school leaver or upon the request of a public servant such as a probation officer. Officers of the authority maintaining a school are, it may be, in a stronger position than others[34] when they seek information relevant to the education of a child, and it may be proper to draw a distinction between those concerned with the administration of the Education Acts[35] and, for example, social workers employed by the same authority.

---

[25] See the Education (School Teachers' Pay and Conditions of Employment) Order 1987 (S.I. 1987 No. 650) art. 5 and Sched. 3, para. 3(3). Circ. 151 suggested that records were necessary to enable a local education authority to comply with s.8 of the 1944 Act (see above at para. 2–06).

[26] The Education (Schools and Further Education) Regulations 1981 (S.I. 1981 No. 1086), reg. 13. See Circs. 151 and 7/81, para. 16.

[27] 1980 Act, s.27(1)(*d*).

[28] But see 1981 Act, s.7 as to statements of special needs, and below at para. 2–197.

[29] See s.21 and Pt. III generally.

[30] See also rules 10 and 20 of the Magistrates' Courts (Children and Young Persons) Rules 1970 (S.I. 1970 No. 1792).

[31] See 1969 Act, s.1, and below at para. 2–236.

[32] Defined in *ibid.* s.70. The definition of "young person" is modified by the Children and Young Persons Act (Transitional Modifications of Part I) Order 1970 (S.I. 1970 No. 1882) to include a child of ten or over.

[33] See *Campbell* v. *Tameside Metropolitan Borough Council* [1982] Q.B. 1065.

[34] They may be able to rely on 1944 Act, s.8 (see above at para. 2–06).

[35] Set out in bold type in the table of statutes, towards the front of this work.

Health hazards[36]

Specified limits to the ionising radiations from substances and appara- **2–147**
tus used in schools may be exceeded only with the approval of the Secretary of State, who may withdraw it if he considers that health and
safety arrangements at a school are inadequate. This provision does not
apply to television receivers and some other normal pieces of school
equipment.[37] There are rules concerning the keeping and use of radioactive substances on certain school premises.[38]

Copyright and licences

The purpose of this subsection is mainly to draw attention to aspects **2–148**
of the law that cannot be elaborated here[39] but are of practical significance to local education authorities.

In the absence of any copyright licence the photocopying of any sub- **2–149**
stantial part of a copyright work[40] is lawful only if done as part of an
examination question or answer. Copying otherwise than by a duplicat-
ing process (which includes photocopying) is, however, permitted if
done by a teacher or pupil in the course of instruction at school or elsewhere.[41]

The performance of a work, including playing records and showing **2–150**
films or television broadcasting, in the course of school activities, by
teacher or pupil in class or before an audience limited to teachers or
pupils or others (not including parents or guardians) directly connected
with the school's activities is not a public performance for the purposes
of the Copyright Act 1956.[42]

School plays and other entertainments are exempt from the (safety) **2–151**
licensing provisions in the London Government Act 1963, the Theatres
Act 1968 and the Local Government (Miscellaneous Provisions) Act
1982 only if members of the public are not admitted.

Every school needs one licence for television reception[43] at its prem- **2–152**
ises (irrespective of the number of sets), but closed circuit television

---

[36] As to poisonous substances in pencils, etc., see A.M. 2/65 (as amended 1968); substances that may
induce cancer, A.M. 3/70; and hazards associated with the use of trampolines etc. A.M. 2/68; of
lasers, A.M. 7/70; of dangerous pathogens in laboratories, A.M. 6/76 (W.O. 4/76); and of asbestos, A.M. 3/86 (W.O. 1/86). See also the Health and Safety at Work, etc. Act 1974 (below at
paras. 4–76 to 4–78).

[37] See the Education (Schools and Further Education) Regulations 1981 (S.I. 1981 No. 1086) reg. 6
and Circ. 7/81, para. 10.

[38] See the Radioactive Substances (Schools, etc.) Exemption Order 1963 (S.I. 1963 No. 1832) (which
also applies to further education institutions and to teacher training colleges), and A.M. 2/76.

[39] See (as regards copyright) Copinger and Skone James on *Copyright*, (12th ed. 1980).

[40] "Literary, dramatic, musical or artistic." As to computer programmes see B. Czarnota, "An apple
for the teacher" (1986) 2 E.I.P.R. 35.

[41] Copyright Act 1956, s.41(1).

[42] *Ibid.* subs. (3)–(5) as amended.

[43] Wireless Telegraphy Act 1949 (as amended), and the Wireless Telegraphy (Broadcast Licence
Charges and Exemption) Regulations 1984 (S.I. 1984 No. 1053). See A.M. 18/72 (W.E.O. 5/72).

systems[44] for school purposes will ordinarily be exempt from licensing under the Cable and Broadcasting Act 1984, section 4.

Governors' and head teachers' reports. Parents' meetings

2–153   Sections 30–32 of the 1986 (No. 2) Act introduce a new obligatory element into the articles of maintained schools.[45] Articles are to place a duty on governing bodies to report annually to parents, and to hold an annual parents' meeting except when the school is a hospital special school[46] or it consists of at least 50 per cent. boarders and the governing body considers that it would be impracticable to hold a meeting in a particular school year. Governing bodies are also to report as required to the local education authority on the discharge of their functions, and the head teacher is to report to the governing body or local education authority[47] as required on the discharge of his functions.

2–154   The governors' report[48] to parents is to summarise how they have discharged their functions since the last annual report and contain any other information the articles require, including (as briefly as is consistent with the requirements) details of the annual meeting, particulars of the governors themselves (including the address of the chairman and clerk), arrangements for the next election of parent governors, a financial statement reflecting the information referred to in paragraph 2–114 above and the same information about public examinations as is required to be published under the 1980 Act.[49]

2–155   The articles are to enable the governing body to produce their report in languages additional to English, and require them to do so in any other language the local education authority direct. It is to be the duty of the governing body to take reasonably practicable steps[50] to see that parents of registered pupils are given a free copy of the report (at least two weeks before the annual parents' meeting) and that copies are available for inspection at the school.

2–156   The annual meeting[51] is to be open to parents of registered pupils, the head teacher and others the governing body invite. The purpose is discussion of the governors' report and the discharge of the functions of governing body, head teacher and local education authority in relation to the school. The proceedings are to be under the control of the

---

[44] See the Cable Programme Services (Exceptions) Order 1984 (S.I. 1984 No. 980) and A.M. 5/70.
[45] See Circ. 8/86 paras. 10–14.
[46] See below at para. 2–207.
[47] Aided schools: see additionally 1986 (No. 2) Act, s.32(2).
[48] 1986 (No. 2) Act, s.30(1) and (2), and see transitional provisions in Education (No. 2) Act 1986 (Commencement No. 1) Order 1986 (S.I. 1986 No. 2203), Sched. 3, para. 1.
[49] See below at para. 2–189.
[50] As to "reasonably practicable" see *Stroud's Judicial Dictionary* (5th ed., 1986).
[51] 1986 (No. 2) Act, s.31(1) and see transitional provisions in S.I. 1986 No. 2203, Sched. 3, para. 1.

governing body. Resolutions may be passed, by simple majority, provided that parents of at least 20 per cent. of registered pupils are present. Only paerents may vote. (Who is to be treated as a parent is a matter for the local education authority or for the governing body in the case of aided and special schools). Resolutions are to be considered by governors, head teachers and local education authority as appropriate to their subject matter, and a brief comment on them is to be included in the next governors' report.

RELIGIOUS EDUCATION

For a predominantly secular society the provisions in the 1944 Act **2–157** regarding religious education may seem oddly extended by comparison with those relating to secular instruction. But church schools pre-dated state schools and the explanation probably lies in the lengthy development of compromise between the state and religious institutions.[52] Sections 25 to 29 must be considered a successful climax to that process to the extent that they have been only marginally amended[53] and have not given rise to reported cases. In practice the obligations imposed by the law have not always been fully met.[54]

The Department of Education and Science and its predecessors have **2–158** abstained from formal advice by circular to authorities.[55] The Church of England, however, has made formal legislative provision for the advancement of religious education. Within each diocese there is a diocesan education committee[56] whose powers and duties include[57] promoting religious education in co-operation with other religious bodies and local education authorities, and advising governors, trustees and owners of church schools, who are to consult the committee before taking major decisions.

---

[52] The strength of sectarian feeling at the turn of the century is illustrated by *Att.-Gen. and Board of Education* v. *County Council of the West Riding of Yorkshire, ex p. Grenside* [1907] A.C. 29, in which it was contended, unsuccessfully, that a local education authority were not liable to meet the costs of denominational religious instruction. And, in similar vein, see *Re Wrexham Parochial Educational Federation; Att.-Gen.* v. *Denbighshire County Council* (1910) 74 J.P. 198.
[53] By 1946 Act, s.7, as amended by 1980 Act, s.1(3) and Sched. 1, para. 18.
[54] For opinion on the current state of religious education see the memoranda of evidence contained in Vol. II of the Second Report of the Education, Science and Arts Committee, *The Secondary School Curriculum and Examinations*, 1981–82 (H.C. 116–11). See also *Report of the (Swann) Committee of Inquiry into the Education of Children from Ethnic Minority Groups* 1985 (Cmnd. 9453).
[55] Evidence of the reluctance of the Secretary of State to intervene may be found in the Government's Observations (Cmnd. 8551 pp. 6 and 7) on the Second Report from the Education, Science and Arts Committee of the House of Commons 1981–82 (H.C. 116–1).
[56] The Diocesan Education Committees Measure 1955. s.1 and Sched.
[57] *Ibid.* s.2.

In outline

2–159   It may be helpful first to give a general outline of the law. Every school day[58] in a county[59] and voluntary school must begin with collective worship,[60] but parents are allowed to withdraw their children from it and from religious instruction at the school. Collective worship and religious instruction at a county school is non-denominational but special arrangements are ordinarily made for those of particular persuasions. In controlled schools parents may, individually, ordinarily require religious instruction of a particular faith or denomination to be given to their children; otherwise it will be non-denominational. Religious instruction in aided and special agreement schools conforms to the standing practice of the particular school and arrangements are made to respect the susceptibilities of those parents who want an alternative for their children. Teachers in general are not to be required to give religious instruction and are not to be discriminated against if they do not do so.[61] To turn these general principles into acceptable practice the law makes elaborate provision, as will appear.

2–160   Subject to the requirement that in county schools the act of worship with which the school day must begin shall be non-denominational,[62] the nature of the worship is undefined. In voluntary schools it may be denominational and it need not be Christian. The act of worship must be collective on the part of all pupils not excused unless the school premises make this impracticable.[63] It is to take place on the school premises but the governors of aided and special agreement schools may on special occasions arrange for it to take place in a church or elsewhere.[64]

2–161   Religious instruction is to be given in every county and voluntary school, but attendance at any school is not to be made conditional on particular religious observances.[65] Provision is made to protect religious instruction at voluntary schools from the intrusions of the secular timetable[66] and to safeguard the confessional preferences of county and voluntary boarding school pupils on Sundays and other days of religious celebration.[67]

---

[58] "School day"—see above at para. 2–140.

[59] Nursery schools are not county schools (1944 Act, s.9(2), see above at para. 2–02): therefore in nursery schools religious worship and instruction are not mandatory. If they do take place the safeguards in ss.25–29 do not apply.

[60] 1944 Act, s.25(1). It is not specified that the act of worship or religious instruction should be Christian or Jewish but this was the intention (see 132 H.L.Deb., col. 366, June 21, 1944).

[61] 1944 Act, s.30. See below at para. 4–48.

[62] *Ibid.* s.26.

[63] *Ibid.* s.25(1).

[64] 1946 Act, s.7 as amended by 1980 Act, s.1(3) and Sched. 1, para. 18.

[65] 1944 Act, s.25(3).

[66] *Ibid.* s.25(6).

[67] *Ibid.* s.25(7). This subsection refers to "days exclusively set apart for religious observance by the religious body to which [the] parent belongs." The terminology has been carried over from repealed legislation and in *Marshall* v. *Graham, Bell* v. *Graham* [1907] 2 K.B. 112 it was held that Ascension Day was such a day for Church of England adherents.

Excusal from attendance

A parent may request that his child be excused[68] wholly or partly from **2–162** attendance at religious worship and/or instruction. To whom the request is to be made is not stated—presumably to the head teacher or competent authority. The request must be met until it is withdrawn. A difference of opinion between a child's parents could lead to receipt of conflicting requests. The law provides no guidance in this situation, but it seems probable that the request of one parent that a child be excused attendance can be countermanded only by the same parent, not by the spouse.

Where a pupil has been excused attendance he may be withdrawn **2–163** from school to receive alternative religious instruction elsewhere over the same period if the local education authority are satisfied that his own school do not provide it, that this is what the parent wishes and that arrangements have been made. But this is to happen only if the pupil cannot be sent with reasonable convenience[69] to another county or voluntary school which gives the kind of religious instruction the parent wants; and the local education authority must also be satisfied that the arrangements will interfere with school attendance only at the beginning or end of the school session[70] on any day.

In county schools

By section 26 of the 1944 Act religious instruction at a county school **2–164** is, like the collective act of worship, to be non-denominational. It is not to include any distinctive "catechism or formulary."[71] Parents of pupils at county schools may, however, wish them to have denominational instruction and may be able to take advantage of the arrangements for withdrawal referred to above. If a secondary school is so situated that arrangements for withdrawal cannot conveniently be made, and the local education authority are satisfied about the wishes of the parents, the authority may facilitate arrangements for denominational instruction within the school. But this must be done at no cost to themselves and in the absence of special circumstances making it unreasonable to provide facilities.

The non-denominational instruction at a county school is to be in **2–165** accordance with an agreed syllabus[72] adopted for the school. Elaborate arrangements are made for preparing an agreed syllabus and bringing it into operation. The local education authority are to appoint persons representative of denominations, of teachers and of the authority, as specified, who are to come together as a conference whose duty it is to

---

[68] 1944 Act, s.25(4) and (5).
[69] If another school is close at hand but a parent regards it as otherwise less satisfactory, it remains, arguably, not "reasonably convenient."
[70] "School session"—see above at para. 2–140.
[71] These words derive from the "Cowper-Temple" clause, which dates from the Elementary Education Act 1870.
[72] 1944 Act, s.29(1) and Fifth Schedule.

seek unanimous agreement upon one or more syllabuses of religious instruction for adoption by the local education authority. If the authority report to the Secretary of State that the parties to the conference are unable to reach unanimous agreement, or if it appears to him that an authority have failed to adopt a unanimously recommended syllabus, then he himself has a syllabus prepared by a representative body who are to consult the conference and the parties to it. This syllabus is then deemed to be the agreed syllabus. When a local education authority are of the opinion that an agreed syllabus should be revised they must convene another conference. If it fails to agree unanimously the Secretary of State steps in again in the same way.

2–166   A conference convened to settle an agreed syllabus may make recommendations about the expediency of the local education authority's constituting a standing advisory council on religious matters connected with the religious instruction to be given in accordance with the syllabus. If the recommendations are unanimous the authority must have regard to them,[73] and also to unanimous recommendations about council membership.[74]

In controlled schools

2–167   In the absence of any specific request from parents, under section 27 of the 1944 Act, pupils at controlled schools receive religious instruction in accordance with an agreed syllabus.[75] Parents may, however, request that their children receive instruction in accordance with the trust deed[76] of the school or, in the absence of guidance from that source, with the practice of the school before it became a controlled school.[77] The foundation governors[78] must then arrange to provide not more than two periods a week of that form of instruction, unless they are satisfied that owing to any special circumstances it would be unreasonable to do so. Separately from this obligation, where there are more than two staff in a school the local education authority must appoint[79] "reserved" teachers,[80] to a specified maximum, specifically to give the instruction; but the authority may do so only after the foundation governors have satisfied themselves in each case of the fitness and competence in this

---

[73] They are not bound to adopt them (see above at para. 1–46), but the Secretary of State might consider it unreasonable of them not to do so and invoke 1944 Act s.68 (see below at para. 6–10).

[74] 1944 Act, s.29(2) to (4).

[75] See above at para. 2–165.

[76] By *ibid*. s.67(3) any question whether the religious education given is in accordance with the trust deed (as defined in s.114(1) as amended)) is to be decided by the authority specified in the trust deed if it makes appropriate provision.

[77] As to the coming into existence of controlled schools see above at para. 2–22.

[78] "Foundation Governors"—see 1944 Act, s.114(1), as amended by 1980 Act, Sched. 1, para. 13(*a*), and above at para. 2–74.

[79] As to the appointment of teachers see below at paras. 4–27 *et seq*.

[80] When there are no reserved teachers, the arrangements made by the foundation governors may be the giving of instruction by a minister, or by the head, or an assistant teacher, if willing to do so. s.30 of the 1944 Act (see below at para. 4–48) gives some protection to teachers against religious discrimination.

respect of a person proposed to be appointed. And if the foundation governors are of the opinion that any reserved teacher has not given religious instruction efficiently and suitably they may require the local education authority to dismiss him from employment as a reserved teacher in that school[81]; but the authority may if they wish retain him on the school staff for other duties, or put him forward for employment as a reserved teacher in some other controlled school or in a special agreement school.

The local education authority must consider representations from the **2–168** governors about the proposed appointment of a head teacher of a controlled school.[82] The head teacher is not to count as a reserved teacher.

In aided and special agreement schools

The religious instruction in these schools is, by section 28 of the 1944 **2–169** Act, to be under the control of the governors and in accordance with the trust deed[83] or, if need be, the practice of the school before it became a voluntary school. If parents desire an agreed syllabus[84] for their children, and cannot with reasonable convenience[85] send them to a school which has adopted that syllabus, the governors are to make arrangements for the agreed syllabus to be taught during religious instruction periods. The authority must make the arrangements themselves if the governors are unwilling to do so. The obligation to make arrangements does not arise if the authority are satisfied that it would be unreasonable to do so owing to any special circumstances.

The governors of an aided school may without the consent of the local **2–170** education authority dismiss a teacher if he fails to give religious instruction (other than on an agreed syllabus) efficiently and suitably.[86]

Where a special agreement[87] provides for the appointment of **2–171** reserved teachers the authority may, as in the case of controlled schools, make appointments only after the foundation governors have satisfied themselves in each case of the fitness and competence to give religious instruction of a person proposed to be appointed. And foundation governors of special agreement schools have the same powers of dismissal of reserved teachers as have the foundation governors of controlled schools.

---

[81] 1944 Act, s.27(5). As to dismissal of teachers generally see below at paras. 4–27 *et seq.*

[82] *Ibid.* s.27(3) (repealed, so far as it relates to representations, *ibid.* by Education (No. 2) Act 1986, Sched. 6). As to appointment of head teachers see below at paras. 4–29 and 4–38.

[83] See as to the improper intervention of a local education authority (under legislation since repealed) *Re Wrexham Parochial Education Foundation*; *Att.-Gen.* v. *Denbighshire County Council* (1910) 74 J.P. 198, and n. 76 above.

[84] See above at para. 2–165.

[85] See n. 69 above.

[86] See (decided on earlier legislation) *Harries* v. *Crawfurd* [1918] 2 Ch. 158 and *Smith* v. *Macnally* [1912] 1 Ch. 816.

[87] See above at para. 2–22, and as to the appointment of reserved teachers, 1944 Act, Sched. 3, para. 7.

Inspection

2–172   Religious instruction in a maintained school given in accordance with an agreed syllabus may be inspected only by one of Her Majesty's Inspectors[88] or by some other person ordinarily employed by the Secretary of State, or full-time by a local education authority, as an inspector of secular instruction. Other religious instruction, in a voluntary school, may be inspected under an arrangement made by the governors—foundation governors in the case of a controlled school.[89] Pupils at voluntary schools who are excused attendance at religious worship or instruction are also excused from attending school on inspection days.[90]

ADMISSION TO SCHOOLS

2–173   On admission of pupils to schools Cmd. 6523 stated that it was important that the wishes of parents should be taken into account, and effect given to them so far as compatible with the attainments and promise of children and with the claims of other children. The ultimate responsibility must rest with the local education authority but the governors and head should play an essential part in the selection of pupils for their particular school.

2–174   This advice, as it relates to county secondary schools, was encapsulated in a model article.[91] Admissions were to be in accordance with arrangements made by the local education authority. Such arrangements are likely to give less discretion to governors than do articles for voluntary aided and special agreement schools, which may make reference to religious affiliation and provide for selection for admission to be made by governors. In primary schools selection may be made by the head teacher. Arrangements dating from the coming into force of the 1944 Act still survive and remain in effect so far as consistent with subsequent legislation which is outlined below.[92] They may pre-date the introduction of comprehensive secondary schools, and in *Lee and Anor. v. Enfield London Borough Council*[93] it was held that the authority, in endeavouring to transform a grammar school into a comprehensive school, had failed to comply with an article which required, as regards admission, that the wishes of parents, school records and the views of the headmaster should be taken into account. To permit a non-selective scheme of admissions to be introduced the article required amendment.

---

[88] See below at para. 6–05.
[89] 1944 Act, s.77(5).
[90] *Ibid.* s.77(6).
[91] See A.M. 25 (since superseded by models appended to Circ. 7/87).
[92] As to compulsory withdrawal of older junior pupils for transfer to secondary education see 1948 Act, s.4(1).
[93] (1967) 66 L.G.R. 195.

Under section 33 of the 1986 (No. 2) Act, where the governing body   **2–175**
of a county or voluntary school are responsible for determining
admission arrangements they must consult[94] the local education authority (a) once a year on whether the arrangements are satisfactory and
(b) before determining or varying them. Where the local education
authority are responsible they must consult the governing body likewise.

Admission arrangements

Admission arrangements are now subject to sections 6–8 of the 1980   **2–176**
Act[95] (most of which, by section 9, do not apply to nursery and special
schools or to children in respect of whom statements are maintained
under section 7 of the 1981 Act).[96] The powers extend and particularise
the general obligations cast upon authorities by sections 8 and 76[97] of
the 1944 Act. Every local education authority must make whatever
arrangements seem best to them[98] to enable the parents of children[99] in
the area of the authority to express a reasoned[1] preference for a particular school, whether it is maintained by the authority, by another local
education authority, or is a non-maintained school.[2] (Another authority's school may be nearer home or preferred for some other reason).
"In the area of the authority" includes travelling (for example, gypsy)
children.[3] Preferences may also be expressed by the parents of children
not in the area of the authority.[4] The expression of a preference is not
limited to normal age of admission and appears to permit parents to
seek a change of school on moving house or otherwise.

---

[94] The obligation does not arise in respect of admissions to school prior to the first day of its autumn
term in 1988 (S.I. 1986 No. 2203, Sched. 3, para. 2).

[95] As to admission of pupils to schools maintained by local education authorities in Greater London
see London Government Act 1963, s.31(8) (repealed by Education (No. 2) Act 1986, s.51(12)
from a date to be appointed, and see S.I. 1986 No. 2203, Sched. 3, para. 3). See also Circ. 1/81
paras. 3–36 and annex (superseding Ministry of Education Manual of Guidance Schools No. 1
entitled "Choice of Schools") as amended by Circ. 8/86; D. Bull 32, "School Admissions: a New
Appeals Procedure" [1980] J.S.W.L. 209; N. Harris, "Choice of School" 13 Fam.Law 192, and
"Exercising Parental Preference under the Education Act 1980, 1984 L.A.G. Bull; and generally,
P. Meredith, "Discretion and Choice of Secondary School" [1981] P.L. 52, and J. Tweedie,
"Rights in Social Programmes: the case of parental choice of school" [1986] P.L. 407. As to
unlawfulness of sex and racial discrimination relating to admission, see Sex Discrimination Act
1975, ss.22 *et seq.* and Race Relations Act 1976, s.17, both as amended (above at paras. 1–92 *et
seq.* and 1–02 *et seq.* respectively).

[96] See however, above at para. 2–46 and below at paras. 2–187 to 2–190 respectively.

[97] See above at para. 1–69 *et seq.*

[98] Arrangements might (*e.g.*) specify a time limit within which preferences are to be expressed, and
permit parents to specify an order of preference of schools.

[99] By s.38(4), "child" in this context is any person under 19.

[1] s.6(1). Preference may be based on the information about the school which is required to be published—see below at paras. 2–186 to 2–190.

[2] As to arrangements for provision of education at non-maintained schools see below at paras. 5–30
to 5–33; and as to inter-authority financial arrangements above at paras. 1–138 to 1–139.

[3] And, generally, children from overseas. See below at para. 2–191.

[4] 1980 Act, s.6(5)(*a*).

2–177   The local education authority and governors of a county or voluntary school must comply with a preference expressed in accordance with the authority's arrangements[5] (but not otherwise) unless:

(a) to do so would prejudice the provision of efficient education or the efficient use of resources[6]; or

(b) in the case of aided and special agreement schools, the preference would be incompatible with any arrangements[7] between the governors and local education authority about admission to the school; or

(c) the preference would be incompatible with arrangements for admission based wholly or partly on selection by reference to ability or aptitude.[8]

It appears that the onus of showing why a parental preference should not be respected falls upon the local education authority and governors; but it is open to an authority to adopt an admissions policy which gives priority to applicants from within a defined catchment area; and a parent who sought a departure from that policy would need to rebut the authority's claim that efficient education or the efficient use of resources would be prejudiced by respecting his choice. Both these grounds are open to wide interpretation and might relate to particular schools[9] or the authority's provision of education as a whole. The Act is silent on the problem that may arise for a local education authority when conflicting preferences are expressed by each of a child's parents.

Appeals

2–178   Parents may appeal[10] against the decision of a local education authority as regards the school their child is to attend and against the decision of governors not to admit a child. Arrangements for appeal are made by the local education authority except in the case of aided and special agreement schools, when the governors make the arrangements.[11]

---

[5] 1980 Act, s.6(2)–(4). See below at paras. 2–186 and 2–187.

[6] See *Darling and Jones* v. *Minister of Education, The Times*, April 7, 1962; and note also the powers of local education authorities as to reduction of school places (see above at para. 2–34).

[7] Such arrangements may include restrictions on admission over and above those specified in paras. (a) and (c).

[8] This exception not only protects grammar schools but also the practice of "banding" to maintain the desired balance of pupils in a comprehensive school.

[9] A local education authority might argue that admission of pupils above the number they proposed (see below at para. 2–187) would prejudice efficient education or the efficient use of resources. See P. Marston, "Parental Choice in State Education" [1980] J.S.W.L. 193 at 196; and M. Freeman, "Children's Education and the Law" [1980] L.A.G. Bull 61.

[10] 1980 Act, s.7(1). The associations of local authorities (see above at para. 1–36), in consultation with the Council on Tribunals, have prepared a Code of Practice on appeals procedures (see Appendix 1 below). For an account of the appeal system in practice, based largely on the reports of local ombudsmen (see above at paras. 1–63 to 1–65) see D. Bull "Monitoring Education Appeals" [1985] J.S.W.L. 189. See also T. Buck, "School Admission Appeals" [1985] J.S.W.L. 227 in which the *South Glamorgan* case (text below) is discussed, and P. Liell, "School Admissions Appeals under the Education Act 1980" (1985) New L.J. 274.

These include the constitution of appeals committees,[12] drawn in the case of county and controlled schools from a panel of persons nominated by the local education authority. The composition of an appeals committee is settled according to a formula.[13] Its salient requirements are that there are to be three, five or seven members; the number of local education authority and education committee members is not to exceed by more than one the number of others (persons experienced in education, acquainted with local educational conditions or parents of pupils); and (in effect) those who might be, or have been, personally concerned in the decision are excluded. It is not stated that the local education authority appoint the chairman of an appeal committee, but it may perhaps be open to them to do so, or to leave the choice to the committee themselves. It is, however, specified that a member of the education committee of the authority may not be chairman (but another member of the authority may be).

Appeal committees for aided and special agreement schools are con- **2–179** stituted in much the same way,[14] the main differences being that they are nominated by the governors and may specifically include governors, but half the members of the committee are to be drawn from a list compiled by the local education authority and the chairman is to be a person (other than a governor) selected directly by the governors, *i.e.* not drawn from the authority's list.

An appeal must be reasoned and in writing.[15] The committee must **2–180** give the parent an opportunity to appear and speak (though he is not obliged to do so) and may allow him to be accompanied by a friend or to be represented.[16] The hearing is in private[17] unless local education authority, or governors in the case of an aided or special agreement school, decide otherwise. A member of the Council on Tribunals has a right of

---

[11] 1980 Act, s.7(2) and (3).
[12] *Ibid.* s.7(4) and Sched. 2, Pt. 1. By para. 4 of the Sched., appeals committees established by governors of aided and special agreement schools are bodies to which ss.173(4) (financial loss allowance) and 174 (travelling and subsistence allowances) of the Local Government Act 1972 apply. See the Local Government (Allowances) Regulations 1986 (S.I. 1986 No. 724) and in particular reg. 9. Para. 23 of Circ. 1/81 states that members of an appeal committee set up by a local education authority are automatically entitled to payments under ss.173 and 174 as members of a committee of a local authority. This may be open to doubt since a distinction should perhaps be drawn between a committee *of* a local authority appointed (*e.g.* under the 1944 Act) to discharge one of their functions, and a committee *established by* a local authority under a special provision for a particular purpose which is not a local authority function (*e.g.* an appeals committee whose function is the making of decisions binding upon the authority). But see Local Government Act 1972, s.177(2)(*b*).
[13] 1980 Act, Sched. 2, Pt. I, para. 1.
[14] *Ibid.*, para. 2.
[15] *Ibid.* Pt. II, para. 5.
[16] *Ibid.* para. 6. Para. 8(*b*) of the Code of Practice (see n. 10 above) recommends the appeal committee also to allow the authority or governors to be represented (normally in practice by an officer of the authority's education department).
[17] The provisions of the Public Bodies (Admissions to Meetings) Act 1960, as amended, do not apply.

attendance as observer, as has a member of the local education authority.[18]

2–181 An appeal committee must take into account the parent's preference[19] and the authority's or governors' published arrangements for admission of pupils.[20] By inference they will also take into account the reasons for the decision appealed against. In *R.* v. *South Glamorgan Appeal Committee ex p. Evans*[21] the High Court considered the circumstances in which an appeal committee upheld the decision of the county council not to admit Mr. Evans's daughter to the school of his choice. The appeal committee concluded that her admission would have been prejudicial to the provision of efficient education at the school chosen. Forbes J. found that the committee had not exercised their discretion properly because they had failed to consider to what degree "prejudice" existed (they took no evidence from the head or other teachers), and having decided that prejudice did exist, to balance parental factors, namely the weight to be given to Mr. Evans's wishes against the extent of prejudice. It was held that the appeal committee had misdirected themselves, and their decision was quashed.

2–182 A particular difficulty arises when an appeal committee have to deal with a series of parental preferences for the same school. To allow one or more appeals might not prejudice the provision of efficient education at that school or the efficient use of resources, but to allow all the appeals might do so. A "first come first serve" basis of decision seems indefensible, and thus appeal committees are recommended[22] in effect to compare the merits of individual cases.

2–183 A committee's decision is to be by simple majority with the chairman exercising, if need be, a casting vote.[23] The decision is to be conveyed in writing, with the grounds stated, to parent, local education authority and, in the case of aided and special agreement schools, the governors.[24] Some other procedural details are specified: otherwise local education authority or governors settle the arrangements.[25] They are likely to include the time within which an appeal has to be made.

2–184 If not all (seven or five) nominated members of an appeal committee are available for a hearing it may be practicable for the authority or governors to constitute, alternatively, a smaller committee (of five or

---

[18] 1980 Act, Sched. 2, Part II, para. 10.
[19] *Ibid.* para. 7, and see R. Taylor "Can parents interfere with education provisions" (1982) *Local Government Chronicle* 1008.
[20] 1980 Act, s.8. See above at para. 2–177 and below at 2–187.
[21] Unreported but see P. Liell & J.B. Saunders, *The Law of Education* (9th ed., 1985 F.75) and see P. Liell "Why appeals must be looked at afresh" *Education* June 8, 1984.
[22] In para. 7(1) of the Code of Practice (see n. 10 above). The recommendation is based on a generous interpretation of the jurisdiction of appeal committees.
[23] 1980 Act, Sched. 2, Pt. II, para. 8.
[24] *Ibid.* para. 9.
[25] *Ibid.* para. 11. An appeal committee are bound by the rules of natural justice. (See above at para. 1–54).

three).[26] If during the course of the hearing a member absents himself he may not on his return vote on the issue before the committee. If the absence is improper and sustained it is arguable that the remaining members may reach a decision.

The decision of an appeal committee is binding on the local education **2–185** authority or governors against whom the appeal lay and (when it lay against an authority) on the governors of a county or controlled school who by the committee's decision are to admit the child.[27] The committee, it seems, may allow an appeal even though there has been no breach of duty to admit the child. No explicit right of appeal to the High Court on a point of law is granted but the case cited shows that judicial review[28] is not excluded. Appeals committees are subject to the supervision of the Council on Tribunals[29] and, as regards county and controlled schools, to the jurisdiction of the Local Commissioners for Administration.[30] The latter have found maladministration by local education authorities and appeal committees in the following sets of circumstances: composition of appeal committee effectively confined to members of the majority party; failure on the part of the local education authority to give adequate information to appeal committees and to explain that each appeal should be considered on its merits; failure on the part of the appeal committee to place the "onus of proof" upon the local education authority; failure to give parents proper opportunity to put their case; and failure to consider on its merits an application in respect of a child not belonging to the authority's area.[31] Additionally parents may have recourse to the Secretary of State under section 68[32] of the 1944 Act, not to appeal against the merits of an appeal committee's decision but to complain about any unreasonable action of local education authority or governors in connection with an appeal, for example, by giving inaccurate information to the committee. No doubt a direction given by the Secretary of State in such circumstances would be drafted so as not to place the local education authority under conflicting obligations.

---

[26] See the opinions expressed in paras. 21 and 22 of Circ. 1/81 and in para. 3 of the Code of Practice; also D. Lanham, "The Quorum in Public Law" [1964] P.L. 461.

[27] 1980 Act, s.7(5).

[28] "Judicial review"—see above at para. 1–50.

[29] 1980 Act, s.7(6). See Annual Report for year ended July 31, 1983. The application of the Tribunal and Inquiries Act 1971 to appeals committees places them under an obligation, upon request, to give reasons for decisions (1971 Act, s.12).

[30] 1980 Act s.7(7) and see above at paras. 1–58 et seq. See also para. 26 of Circ. 1/81 for examples of circumstances in which the Commissioner might be invited to intervene.

[31] See The Local Ombudsmen, Report for the year ended March 31, 1984, report of an investigation into complaint 610/Y/85, the article by D. Bull cited at note 10 above and above at para. 1–63. "Belonging to the authority's area": see above at paras. 1–34 to 1–136 and 2–176.

[32] See Times Educational Supplement June 25, 1982, p. 6, and as to s.68 generally, below at paras. 6–10 et seq. Over the period 1977–1984 inclusive over 5,000 representations were made to the Secretary of State: 3 were successful—see the article by D. Bull cited at n. 10 above.

Information about schools

2–186   The rights of parents under sections 6 and 7 of the 1980 Act are made the more effective by the requirements of section 8. Local education authorities, as regards county and controlled schools, are to publish particulars of their arrangements for:

(a) admission of pupils to their own and other authorities' schools and to non-maintained schools[33];

(b) enabling parents to express a preference under section 6(1); and

(c) appeals against admission decisions under section 7(1).

Governors of aided and special agreement schools are to publish their arrangements for admissions and appeals or arrange for publication by the local education authority on their behalf but on their own responsibility.

2–187   Particulars of admission arrangements must include the number[34] of pupils to be admitted to each school in each age group, the respective admissions functions of local education authority and governors, the policy[35] followed in deciding admissions and the arrangements made for pupils "not belonging to the area of the local education authority."[36] Local education authorities must also publish their criteria for offering places at non-maintained schools and the names of, and number of places at, those non-maintained schools with which they have standing arrangements.[37–38] Local education authorities, and governors of aided and special agreement schools, have also to publish such other information[39] about each of their schools "as they think fit"[40] and as the Secretary of State may require. He may also require the publication[41] of general information about primary, secondary and maintained special schools, and specify time and manner of publication.

2–188   Under the Education (School Information) Regulations 1981,[42] the general information to be published[43] includes:

(a) number of pupils and age range in each school;

---

[33] See below at paras. 5–30 to 5–33.

[34] In the Department's view (para. 30 of Circ. 1/81 as amended by para. 18 of Circ. 8/86) the number must be specified precisely, and should be the number beyond which the authority or goverors would normally refuse to make further admissions.

[35] The policy includes how priorities are determined when a school is oversubscribed (*e.g.* by reference to state of health, subling connection, residence in catchment area and denominational membership in the case of voluntary schools) and, when selection is by ability or aptitude, how the procedure operates.

[36] For the meaning of this expression see the Education (Areas to which Pupils Belong) Regulations 1980 (S.I. 1980 No. 917) and above at paras. 1–134 to 1–136.

[37–38] As to arrangements with non-maintained schools see below at para. 5–32.

[39] Circ. 15/77 advised local education authorities on the sort of information that might be made available (in advance of the statutory requirements).

[40] See above at para. 1–47.

[41] As regards nursery schools see 1980 Act, s.9(1).

[42] S.I. 1981 No. 630, as amended by Amendment Regulations 1983 (S.I. 1983 No. 41).

[43] *Ibid.* reg. 3 and Sched. 1. As to additional information regarding special educational provisions see below at para. 2–203.

(b) its classification[44] and its affiliation, if any, to a religious denomination;

(c) the authority's arrangements for transfer between maintained schools otherwise than at normal admission age;

(d) their policy regarding entering pupils for public examinations;

(e) their arrangements and policies regarding
  (i) transport,[45]
  (ii) school milk and meals,[46]
  (iii) provision of school clothing[47] (including uniform and physical training clothes),
  (iv) other payments for pupils at maintained schools,[48] and
  (v) special educational provision.[49]

Welsh local education authorities have additionally to publish information about the teaching and use of Welsh in other than aided and special agreement schools.

Information about particular schools[50] must include: **2–189**

(a) particulars of any specific arrangements for enabling parents to visit the school in advance of a child's possible entry;

(b) the school curriculum;

(c) arrangements for excusing a pupil's attendance at religious worship or instruction[51];

(d) the organisation of the school;

(e) homework requirements;

(f) pastoral care;

(g) discipline (including practice as regards corporal punishment)[52];

(h) extra-curricular activities;

(i) requirements concerning dress, including school uniform and its cost; and

(j) career guidance.[53]

Additionally, where a school other than a special school has pupils aged 15 or over, its policy about public examinations and its own examination record must be published.

Regulations also make detailed requirements about manner of publi- **2–190**
cation[54] to ensure that parents have free copies of up-to-date information about schools and admission arrangements in good time to make

---

[44] See above at para. 2–02.
[45] See below at paras. 5–21 to 5–24. This information may be specially material in helping parents to express a preference for a particular school.
[46] See below at paras. 5–09 to 5–12.
[47] See below at paras. 5–15 to 5–19.
[48] See below at para. 5–20.
[49] See below at paras. 2–203 *et seq.*
[50] S.I. 1981 No. 630, reg. 4 and Sched. 2.
[51] See above at paras. 2–162 to 2–163.
[52] See below at paras. 7–44 *et seq.*
[53] See below at paras. 5–43 to 5–46.
[54] S.I. 1981 No. 630, regs. 5–8.

use of it, and that copies are available for reference at schools and offices.

Children from overseas[55]

2–191   The statutory duties placed on local education authorities regarding the provision of education[56] do not discriminate against children from overseas by, for example, stating a length of residence qualification. But the offer of a place at a maintained school does not as such qualify a child under the Immigration Rules[57] for admission to this country. An exception is normally made for children visiting under a recognised short-term exchange scheme. Children who are admitted with their parents under the Immigration Rules qualify for education at a maintained school[58] provided that their stay is likely to be long enough for education to be reasonably practicable. European Community nationals are in a favourable position with regard to the issue of residence permits, and "the children of a national of a Member State who is or has been employed in the territory of another Member State shall be admitted to that state's general educational . . . courses under the same conditions as the nationals of that State if such children are residing in its territory."[59]

EDUCATION OF HANDICAPPED CHILDREN

2–192   "As with ordinary children, education of the handicapped began with individual and charitable enterprise."[60] Following the Elementary Education Act 1870, public provision of education for children with specific handicaps or disabilities developed, until under the 1944 Act[61] local education authorities were required to identify and provide special educational treatment for handicapped children as part of the general duty to provide sufficient primary and secondary schools for children according to their ages, abilities and aptitudes. Education for children falling into specified categories of handicap was provided either in a special school (maintained or non-maintained) in the case of serious handicap or, if that was impracticable or the disability not serious, at an ordinary school; or if attendance at school was impracticable, elsewhere, for

---

[55] See Annex to Circ. 1/81.

[56] 1944 Act, s.8 and 1980 Act, s.6. On the education of immigrants, see Circ. 7/65.

[57] The Rules are made by the (Home) Secretary of State under s.3(2) of the Immigration Act 1971 for the guidance of immigration officers and tribunals. They are not statutory instruments (see above at paras. 1–41 to 1–43). They are laid before both Houses of Parliament and if disapproved must be amended by the Secretary of State. Current rules are contained in House of Commons Papers, 1972–1973, Nos. 79–82, 313 and 437 and 1973–1974, No. 102.

[58] See below at para. 3–14 as regards fees at further education institutions.

[59] Article 12 of EEC Reg. 1612/68 (J.O. 1968, L257/2; O.J. 1968, 475). (See above para. 1–114).

[60] From *Special Educational Needs*, the Report of the Committee of Inquiry into the Education of Handicapped Children and Young People under the chairmanship of Mrs. Mary Warnock, H.M.S.O. 1978 (Cmnd. 7212), from which the 1981 Act derives.

[61] ss.33 and 34 (repealed).

example, at home or in hospital. Child guidance services and the employment of educational psychologists and remedial teachers became an accepted part of educational provision; and continues as such despite the transfer of medical inspection and treatment functions from the education to the health service in 1974.[62]

The substance of the law relating to handicapped children is now con-   **2–193** tained in the Education Act 1981.[63] But the term "handicapped children" and the language of "handicap" have now been abandoned (as was earlier, the concept of children being ineducable by reason of mental handicap)[64] to acknowledge the belief that treatment is best related not to specific handicaps—handicap may be complex—but to the special educational needs of children with problems over and beyond those of the generality of children. This approach also both extends the category of children for whom special educational provision (rather than "treatment") is requisite and makes it appropriate to formulate the obligation upon local education authorities and others so that, with necessary exceptions and safeguards, children with special educational needs are to be educated alongside[65] other children in ordinary schools, defined[66] as schools which are not special schools. The parents of children of compulsory school age who have special educational needs are subject to the duty[67] to secure their education, but the 1981 Act is generous in the rights it gives to parents[68]—to be kept informed and to appeal against decisions affecting their children.

Section 1 of the 1981 Act defines special educational needs in terms of   **2–194** a learning difficulty which calls for special educational provision. A child has a learning difficulty if:

(a) he has a significantly greater difficulty in learning than the majority of his contemporaries; or

(b) he has a disability that prevents or hinders him from making use of the normal local school facilities for his own age-group; or

(c) he is under the age of five but would be likely, if older, to fall within (a) or (b) above.

---

[62] See below at para. 5–03. As to child guidance see Circ. 3/74 (W.O. W.H.S.C.(15)5), and as to staffing of special schools and classes generally Circ. 4/73 (W.O. 47/73) (partly anachronistic).

[63] The Act is based on *Special Needs in Education* (Cmnd. 7996). See Circ. 8/81. Some transitional arrangements remain in force: see Sched. to the Education Act 1981 (Commencement No. 2 Order) Order 1983 (S.I. 1983 No. 7). See also V. Hannon, "The Education Act 1981: new rights and duties in special education" [1982] J.S.W.L. 275; J.C. Morris, "Education Act 1981: a critique" 126 S.J. 23, I. Goultry, "The Education Act 1981 in Practice" 81 L.S. Gaz. 2928, B. Cox, *The Law of Special Educational Needs* (1986) and *Special Educational Needs: Implementation of the Education Act 1981*, 3rd Report of the Education, Science and Art Committee 1986–87, H.C. 201–I.

[64] See 1970 Act.

[65] See W. Swann, "Statistics of Segregation," (1984) 8 *Childright* 18.

[66] In 1981 Act, s.20(1).

[67] As to the duty to secure education, see 1944 Act, s.36 (above at para. 1–80) and as to its enforcement below at paras. 2–222 *et seq*.

[68] As defined in 1944 Act, s.114(1) and see above at para. 1–70.

But a difficulty arising from a difference between the teaching language and the language used at home does not constitute a learning difficulty. Special educational provision means,[69] for children aged two and above, provision additional to or different from ordinary maintained school provision; or, for still younger children, any kind of educational provision.

Identification and assessment. Appeals

2-195   By section 4 a local education authority must identify those of the children for whom they are responsible who have special educational needs of a kind that call for special educational provision to be determined by the authority rather than left to the discretion of the school.[70] (The Secretary of State expects[71] that these will be children for whom, in an ordinary school, extra staffing or equipment would be required—approximately the category who would have been classified as handicapped under section 34 (repealed) of the 1944 Act). The responsibility extends to children in the authority's area who are either:

(a) pupils of any age registered[72] at a school maintained by the authority or at a non-maintained school with which the authority have made arrangements[73]; or

(b) have been brought to the attention of the authority as having, or probably having, special educational needs and are registered at some other school, or are not registered pupils but are not under two or over compulsory school age.[74]

The responsibility is thus not limited by reference to "ordinary residence"[75] in the authority's area, but it does not extend to young people between the ages of 16 and 19 who are not registered school pupils.

2-196   Children so identified must be assessed as prescribed in section 5 of the 1981 Act.[76] Before deciding to make an assessment the local education authority must notify[77] the parent, informing him of the procedures to be followed, of the name of the officer of the authority who has further information, and of his right to make representations within a period of less than 29 days. If the local education authority do decide to make an assessment they must notify the parent in writing and explain their reasons. Copies of the notification are to be sent to the

---

[69] "Speech therapy" is not "special educational provision," it is "non-educational provision." See *R. v. Oxfordshire Education Authority, ex p. W., The Times*, November 22, 1986.

[70] 1981 Act, s.4(1).

[71] See Circ. 8/81, para. 9.

[72] See 1944 Act, s.80, as amended, and above at para. 2–109.

[73] Under 1953 Act, s.6, as amended by 1980 Act ss.28, 38(6) and Sched. 7, and by 1981 Act, s.21(4) and Sched. 3, para. 8. See below at para. 5–32.

[74] "Compulsory school age," see above at para. 1–81.

[75] As to "ordinary residence" see below at para. 3–73.

[76] As to assessments and statements of special educational needs, see Circ. 1/83.

[77] As to service of notices see 1944 Act, s.113 as amended.

social services authority and to the district health authority.[78] The rights and duties of parents in connection with examination of a child for the purposes of assessment are prescribed.[79] The Secretary of State may make regulations about the conduct of assessment,[80] and he requires local education authorities to take into consideration representations and evidence from the parent, information received from social services and district health authorities, and educational, medical, psychological and other advice.

If upon assessment the authority conclude that they do not need to **2–197** specify special educational provision[81] the parent must be notified of his right of appeal to the Secretary of State, who may direct the local education authority to reconsider their decision.[82] If the authority conclude that they do need to determine special educational provision they must by 1981 Act, section 7, make, and maintain, a statement of the child's special educational needs, and they must make reassessments as often as the Secretary of State prescribes.[83] They must arrange the special educational provision unless the parent has made suitable arrangements.[84] Before making the statement the authority must send it in draft to the parent and inform him in writing of his right to make representations about it within 15 days, and to discuss it with an officer of the authority. The parent may within a further 15 days require a further meeting or meetings with whoever advised the authority about the part of the assessment with which he disagrees, or some other person able in the opinion of the authority to discuss the advice. Thereafter the authority may make the statement as drafted or modified, or decide not to make a statement. They must notify the parent in writing of their decision and, on making a statement, serve[85] a copy on him, and notify him of his

---

[78] The Education (Special Educational Needs) Regulations 1983 (S.I. 1983 No. 29), reg. 3. By Local Authorities Social Services Act 1970, s.1, as amended by the Local Government Act 1972, s.195, social services authorities are non-metropolitan county, metropolitan district and London borough councils and the Common Council of the City of London. For district health authorities see National Health Services Act 1977, as amended.

[79] In 1981 Act, Sched. 1, para. 2. The same rights and duties arise if the Secretary of State decides to examine a child (*ibid.* s.18). It is an offence not to comply with the requirements of a notice under para. 2 requiring a child's attendance "without reasonable excuse," having regard to the circumstances.

[80] See 1981 Act, Sched. 1, para. 1, and the Education (Special Educational Needs) Regulations 1983 (S.I. 1983 No. 29) regs. 4–8.

[81] In *R. v. Hampshire County Council ex p. J., The Times*, December 5, 1985, the Council misdirected themselves as to the meaning of "special educational needs" (dyslexia was a disability) and also "special educational provision" and also as to the circumstances in which they should pay fees under the 1953 Act, s.6(2)(*a*)(iii) (see below at paras. 2–207 and 5–32).

[82] The Secretary of State may decline to direct the local education authority to reconsider their decision (*R. v. Hereford and Worcester County Council and Another, ex p. Lashford, The Times*, November 10, 1986).

[83] Reassessment must take place within a year of a child's reaching the age of $13\frac{1}{2}$ unless he was assessed during the previous year (S.I. 1983 No. 29 reg. 9).

[84] What arrangements are "suitable" appears to be left to the judgment of the local education authority.

[85] See 1944 Act, s.113, as amended.

right of appeal[86] against the special educational provision specified. They must also notify him of the name of the person to whom he can turn for information and advice, and this person will not necessarily be a local authority officer.

2–198   The Secretary of State may make regulations about the keeping, disclosure and transfer of statements, and he prescribes their form and content.[87] They must include details of the authority's assessment and specify the special educational provision to be made. Statements are to be reviewed annually by the local education authority. If a local education authority propose to amend or cease to maintain a statement they must ordinarily give the parent the right, within 15 days, to make representations, which they must consider before taking a decision. (When sections 5 and 6 of the Disabled Persons (Services, Consultation and Representation) Act 1986 have been brought into force local education authorities are to keep under review the dates when disabled persons (as defined in section 16) who have been the subject of a statement under section 7 of the 1981 Act are expected to leave full-time education. With some exceptions their needs for statutory welfare services are to be assessed as prescribed once the leaving date has been established).

2–199   Under section 8 a parent may appeal[88] against special educational provision specified in a statement to an appeal committee constituted in the same way, and following the same procedure (with appropriate modifications), as a committee set up to consider school admission appeals.[89] The appeal committee may either confirm the special educational provision specified in the statement, or require the local education authority to reconsider it in the light of their observations.[90] If the special educational provision is confirmed, or after a reconsidered decision by the local education authority, the parent may appeal to the Secretary of State, who may confirm the special educational provision specified, amend the statement, or direct the local education authority to cease to maintain it.

2–200   A parent for whose child no statement is maintained may, by section 9, ask the responsible local education authority[91] to arrange for an assessment of his educational needs. The authority must comply unless they consider the request unreasonable.[92] But the assessment need not follow the section 5 procedure if the local education authority consider a

---

[86] See below at para. 2–199.
[87] See 1981 Act, s.7(11) and Sched. 1, Pt. II, and S.I. 1983 No. 29, regs. 10–12.
[88] In *R.* v. *Surrey County Council Education Committee, ex p. H.*, 83 L.G.R. 219, C.A., an unsuccessful application was made for judicial review (see above at para. 1–50) of the decision of an appeal committee.
[89] See below at para. 2–178.
[90] The appeal committee do not, unlike appeal committees established under the 1980 Act, make a binding decision.
[91] "Responsible local education authority": see above at para. 2–195.
[92] "Unreasonable": see below at para. 6–11. Presumably the request would be unreasonable if there were no *prima facie* evidence of severe handicap.

statement of special educational needs to be unnecessary; and even if the authority agree that a child has special educational needs they are not obliged to make and maintain a statement if they believe that the needs can be met in an ordinary school.[93] A parent for whose child a statement *is* maintained may ask for an assessment under section 5, and the local education authority must comply unless an assessment has been made within six months or the local education authority are satisfied that a section 5 assessment would be inappropriate.[94]

If a district health authority form the opinion that a child under five **2–201** has, or probably has, special educational needs they must, by section 10, so inform the parent. They must also inform the appropriate local education authority—presumably the authority where the child is ordinarily resident—after giving the parent the opportunity of discussion with an officer of the health authority. Additionally the health authority must inform the parent of any voluntary organisation which may be able to help.

By section 6, if a local education authority are of the opinion that a **2–202** child in their area under the age of two has, or probably has, special educational needs of a kind that merit formal assessment they may, with the parent's consent, or must at his request, make one. The section 5 assessment procedures do not apply and the authority may make the assessment, and make and maintain a statement of the child's special educational needs, as they consider appropriate.

Provision of special education. Special schools and independent schools

In fulfilling their duties to secure provision of primary and secondary **2–203** schools local education authorities are to have regard "to the need for securing that special educational provision is made for pupils who have special educational needs,"[95] and local education authorities must keep under review their arrangements for special educational provision.[96] They must also, in accordance with regulations[97] made by the Secretary of State, publish information about their policy and arrangements for the education of children with special educational needs, and about maintained schools, including special schools,[98] where special educational

---

[93] R. v. *Hereford and Worcester County Council, ex p. Lashford, The Times*, May 13, 1987.

[94] A request could be "inappropriate" without being "unreasonable."

[95] 1944 Act, s.8(2)(c) as substituted by 1981 Act, s.2(1). "Have regard to": see above at para. 1–46.

[96] 1981 Act, s.2(4). Advice about implementing the 1970 Act concerning mentally handicapped children is in Circ. 15/70.

[97] See the Education (School Information) Regulations 1981 (S.I. 1981 No. 630) as amended by the Education (School Information) (Amendment) Regulations 1983 (S.I. 1983 No. 41).

[98] See definition in 1944 Act, s.9(5), as substituted by 1981 Act, s.11(1), and above at para. 2–04. Maintained special schools are, with some exceptions, subject to the requirements that apply to county and voluntary schools regarding premises, government, conduct and compulsory attendance, as to which see other sections of this Chapter. See, as to unreasonable exercise of governors' functions, below at para. 6–10 n.38.

provision is made; and they may complement the information specified as they think fit.[99] The requirements[1] largely follow those in relation to ordinary maintained schools, but additionally[2] general information must include the authority's detailed arrangements and policies particularly as respects identification and assessment of children with special educational needs; provision made for them in, and otherwise than in, maintained schools; the use made of non-maintained special schools[3] and independent schools[4]; advice to parents; and transport.

2–204   A child for whom a statement, as above, is maintained is, by section 2, to be educated at an ordinary school provided that account has been taken of the parent's views, and that education there "is compatible with:

   (a) his receiving the special educational provision that he requires;
   (b) the provision of efficient education for the children with whom he will be educated; and
   (c) the efficient use of resources" by the local education authority.[5]

2–205   Responsibilities are placed upon maintained school governors (local education authorities in the case of maintained nursery schools) to endeavour to secure that in their schools special educational needs are recognised and met, and in particular that the "responsible person"— head teacher or governor—makes known the needs of which he has been informed to those who are likely to teach the pupils concerned. Teachers are to be made aware of the importance of identifying and providing for special educational needs. So far as compatible with the objectives (a) to (c) above, and reasonably practicable,[6] children with special educational needs are to engage in school activities with other children.

2–206   Where boarding hostels are provided for children with special educational needs they are open to inspection[7] on behalf of the Secretary of State.

---

[99] 1980 Act, s.8 and s.9(2) as amended by 1981 Act, s.21(4) and Sched. 3, para. 14. Information about aided and special agreement schools must be published by or on behalf of the governors.

[1] See above at para. 2–189.

[2] S.I. 1981 No. 630, Sched. 1, Pt. II.

[3] As to grants for non-maintained special schools see below at para. 2–216.

[4] "Independent School"—see 1944 Act, s.114(1) as amended by 1980 Act, s.34(1) and below at para. 6–27. As to rateability of an independent school providing facilities for deaf children, see *Royal Cross School for the Deaf* v. *Morton* [1975] 1 W.L.R. 1002.

[5] These provisions supersede s.10 of the 1976 Act, which is repealed, having never been brought into force, by the 1981 Act, s.21 and Sched. 4.

[6] See *Stroud's Judicial Dictionary* (5th ed., 1986).

[7] The Education (Schools and Further Education) Regulations 1981 (S.I. 1981 No. 1086), regs. 5 and 8 as amended by Amendment Regulations (S.I. 1983 No. 262). As to inspection see below at para. 6–05.

For children for whom ordinary schools are inadequate special edu-   **2–207**
cational provision may be made at maintained or non-maintained
special schools (including hospital special schools)[8] or independent
schools; or if the local education authority are satisfied in relation to any
child in their area that it would be inappropriate[9] for provision to be
made at a school they may make other provision after consulting the
parent. Where a local education authority are satisfied that in the interests of the pupil special educational provision should be arranged for
him at a non-maintained special school or an independent school, they
are under obligation to pay the fees,[10] including boarding fees if boarding is essential. The parent of a pupil of compulsory school age registered at a special school in accordance with arrangements made by a
local education authority may not withdraw[11] him without the consent
of the authority, but on their refusal may refer the question for decision
by the Secretary of State.

Local education authorities may not make arrangements at an inde-   **2–208**
pendent school (which is an "ordinary" school) unless the Secretary of
State has approved[12] it as suitable for children for whom statements are
maintained under section 7, or he otherwise consents, normally in particular instances. An approval or consent may be subject to conditions
imposed upon the local education authority and may be withdrawn if the
conditions are not complied with.[13]

The Secretary of State may make regulations[14] about the conditions   **2–209**
under which he approves and continues to approve a school (a) as a
special school, or (b) as a suitable independent school, and about withdrawal of approval. Regulations may require a special school to be
organised as a primary or secondary school (notwithstanding the discretion to the contrary granted by the 1944 Act)[15] and are to secure, so

---

[8] Local education authorities may provide schools at hospitals or, under s.26 of the National Health
Service Act 1977, as amended, make use of hospital premises. See (regarding mentally handicapped children and young people) Circ. 5/74. The explicit power of former hospital authorities to
make arrangements with local education authorities (National Health Service Act 1946, s.62) was
repealed by the National Health Service Reorganisation Act 1973, s.57 and Sched. 5.

[9] 1981 Act, s.3. This provision runs in parallel with s.56 of the 1944 Act. See below at para. 5–29 and
Circ. 8/81, para. 7. As to payment by local education authorities of the cost of parental visits to
handicapped children away from home see A.M. 6/66.

[10] 1953 Act, s.6 as amended by 1980 Act, ss.28, 38(6) and Sched. 7, and by 1981 Act, s.2(4) and
Sched. 3, para. 8. See *R. v. Hampshire County Council ex p. J, The Times,* December 5, 1985.

[11] 1981 Act, s.11(2), and see s.18 which empowers the Secretary of State to have the child examined.

[12] 1981 Act, s.11(3) and see Circ. 8/81, para. 32. Formerly the Secretary of State approved those
independent schools that were "recognised as efficient," but procedures for "recognition" were
discontinued in 1978 (see Circ. 6/78, W.O. 60/78).

[13] 1981 Act, s.13(2)–(4).

[14] 1981 Act, ss.12(1) and (2) and 13(1) and as regards any necessary modifications of trust deeds
under 1973 Act, s.1(2)(*b*) as amended by 1981 Act, s.21(4) and Sched. 3, para. 10, see below at
para. 6–45.

[15] 1981 Act, s.12(3) and see proviso to 1944 Act, s.8(2)(*a*). See above at para. 2–07.

far as practicable, respect for parental wishes concerning religious worship and instruction.[16]

2–210   The regulations regarding special schools[17] provide that as a condition of approval (which may be conditional or for a limited period) the Secretary of State must approve the arrangements at the school for the special educational provision made for pupils, specified by number, age and sex and whether day or boarding, according to their special educational needs, and in the case of non-maintained schools the arrangements as respects the governing body.[18] Such schools are not to be conducted for profit; and their premises are ordinarily to conform to the standards prescribed for maintained special schools.[19]

2–211   There are further, continuing, requirements.[20] *Inter alia* the Secretary of State has to approve changes in the arrangements for special educational provision and (non-maintained schools) as respects the governing body; provision is made[21] for health care, religious worship and instruction and (non-maintained schools) in relation to milk, meals and other refreshments; there are to be incident and punishment books, and a report is to be made at least annually to education authorities on each pupil for whom they maintain a section 7 statement; and requirements are laid down regarding non-teaching staff at residential schools and at maintained schools whether or not residential, and to safeguard staff against religious discrimination.

2–212   Teachers[22] are not to be employed in non-maintained special schools over the age of 65 except when the Secretary of State approves in a particular case; and as regards such schools the Secretary of State has reserve powers concerning remuneration of teachers, the keeping of accounts and the provision of reports and returns. Access to non-maintained schools is to be given to persons acting for authorities who place children there.

2–213   The governing body of a non-maintained special school have to publish a prospectus annually[23] containing information analogous to that required under the 1980 Act as regards maintained schools.[24]

2–214   The Secretary of State may withdraw his approval[25] of a special school if it fails to comply with the requirements outlined above or other relevant

---

[16] 1981 Act, s.12(4) and the Education (Approved of Special Schools) Regulations 1983 (S.I. 1983 No. 1499) Sched. 2, para. 9.

[17] S.I. 1983 No. 1499. See Circ. 6/83. By reg. 8 requirements apply, with some modifications, to special schools in hospitals. No regulations have yet been made regarding independent schools.

[18] S.I. 1983 No. 1499, Sched. 2, paras. 1 and 2. As to governing bodies of maintained special schools see above at paras. 2–74 and 2–84.

[19] S.I. 1983 No. 1499, Sched. 2, paras. 3 and 4. See the Education (School Premises) Regulations 1981 (S.I. 1981 No. 909) made under s.10(1) of the 1944 Act, and above at paras. 2–55 to 2–59.

[20] S.I. 1983 No. 1499, reg. 6 and Sched. 2, paras. 5–19.

[21] As to the provision of clothing of pupils at special schools see below at paras. 5–15 to 5–16.

[22] See, generally, Chap. 4.

[23] S.I. 1983 No. 1499, reg. 6 and Sched. 3.

[24] See above at para. 2–189.

[25] See S.I. 1983 No. 1499, reg. 7.

regulations,[26] but ordinarily only after consultation and giving time for requirements to be complied with.

Discontinuance of maintained special schools

A local education authority who intend to cease[27] to maintain a   **2–215**
special school may do so only in accordance with proposals approved by the Secretary of State. He expects proposals to explain in particular how alternative special educational provision is to be made. Notice of proposals is to be served on the Secretary of State, the parents of all registered pupils, any other local education authorities who take up places in the school, and other persons the maintaining authority think appropriate. The notice must specify when it is intended to implement the closure proposals, (time will need to be allowed for the amendment of section 7 statements) and also specify a period of not less than two months during which objections to them may be made to the local education authority. The right to object of interested persons (for example, members of staff) upon whom no notice is served is not specifically stated in the statute but the Secretary of State has made it clear that no limitation of the right is intended. Copies of objections and observations on them must be sent by the local education authority to the Secretary of State, who may approve or reject the proposals, and in the former case require that the closure takes place at a time different from that specified in the notice.

Grants for non-maintained special schools

The Secretary of State may pay grants to persons other than local edu-   **2–216**
cation authorities who maintain special schools or propose to do so.[28] Capital grants go towards relevant expenditure (expenditure approved by the Secretary of State) on acquiring land or buildings, providing or altering buildings and new provision of furniture or equipment: maintenance grants on their upkeep. The Secretary of State may make capital grants conditional on the school's serving the category of pupils (by age, sex and type of disability or learning difficulty) that he directs or on its combining with some other school for the more efficient provision of facilities for pupils with special educational needs.

---

[26] The Education (Schools and Further Education) Regulations 1981 (S.I. 1981 No. 1086) as amended, (see above at paras. 2–54, 2–140, 2–144, 2–147 and 2–206). The Education (Teachers) Regulations 1982 (S.I. 1982 No. 106) (see Circ. 7/82 and below at paras. 4–10 to 4–19 and 4–21 to 4–25) and the Education (School Premises) Regulations 1981 (S.I. 1981 No. 909) (see above at paras. 2–55 to 2–59).

[27] 1981 Act, s.14. See Circ. 3/82.

[28] See 1944 Act, s.100, as amended and the Education (Grant) Regulations 1983 (S.I. 1983 No. 74). See Pt. V of S.I. 1983 No.74 as to general conditions of payment, etc., also below at para. 6–20).

DIRECT GRANT SCHOOLS

2–217   In the inter-war years local authority provision of grammar schools was supplemented by schools to which, subject to certain conditions, the Minister of Education paid a direct grant in return for the allocation of places to pupils who had previously been educated at the public expense. In accordance with the recommendations of the Fleming Committee,[29] the direct grant grammar schools were perpetuated under the 1944 Act and subsequent legislation, until a government decision in 1975 (associated with the move at that time—in the event uncompleted—towards a universal system of comprehensive secondary education) led to the gradual withdrawal of grants.[30] Some of the schools failed to survive; most were assimilated into the maintained school system, or continued in existence as wholly independent schools and may now be eligible to participate in the assisted places scheme.[31]

2–218   The authority for payment of direct grant is section 100 of the 1944 Act; and the fees of pupils filling places at a direct grant school which the proprietors have put at the disposal of a local education authority are paid by the authority.[32] The present tense is used because although direct grant grammar schools have been eliminated some few other non-maintained schools (not including special schools)[33] continue to be eligible for direct grant in accordance with regulations made under section 100.[34] These are nursery schools and other[35] schools which on November 6, 1959, were already in receipt of grant under pre-existing regulations. Nursery school proprietors receive from the Secretary of State grant of up to one half of the cost of maintaining the school as

---

[29] *The Public Schools and the General Education System* H.M.S.O. 1944, and see Circ. 32.

[30] See the Direct Grant Grammar Schools (Cessation of Grant) Regulations 1975 (S.I. 1975 No. 1198) as amended by the Scholarships and other Benefits Regulations 1977 (S.I. 1977 No. 1443), the Direct Grant Grammar Schools (Cessation of Grant) (Amendment) Regulations 1979 (S.I. 1979 No. 1552) and the Direct Grant Schools (Amendment) Regulations 1981 (S.I. 1981 No. 1788). See Circ. 7/75 (W.O. 126/75).

[31] See below at paras. 6–35 to 6–43.

[32] See 1953 Act, s.6 as amended by 1980 Act, ss.28, 38(6) and Sched. 7 and by 1981 Act, s.21(4) and Sched. 3, para. 8; and below at para. 5–32. A contract between a local education authority and a direct grant school whereby the authority took up a quarter of the places at a school could be validly determined only on reasonable notice being given (*Birkenhead School* v. *Birkenhead County Borough, The Times*, March 16, 1973).

[33] As to grants in respect of non-maintained special schools see the Education (Grant) Regulations 1983 (S.I. 1983 No. 74) reg. 6 and above at para. 2–216.

[34] See Direct Grant Schools Regulations 1959 (S.I. 1959 No. 1832), which now take effect as amended by the Direct Grant Schools Amending Regulations 1963 (S.I. 1963 No. 1379) and 1965 (S.I. 1965 No. 1), the Direct Grant Schools (Amendment) Regulations 1968 (S.I. 1968 No. 1148), 1973 (S.I. 1973 No. 1535), 1978 (S.I. 1978 No. 1145), 1980 (S.I. 1980 No. 1861) and 1981 (S.I. 1981 No. 1788), and reg. 2(2) of the Education (Grant) Regulations 1983 (S.I. 1983 No. 74). See also (below at paras. 6–19 to 6–20) the Education (Grants) (Music and Ballet Schools) Regulations 1985 (S.I. 1985 No. 684), as amended by Amendment Regulations (S.I. 1986 No. 989).

[35] There is now only one such school: The Royal Hospital School, Holbrook, Suffolk.

approved by the Secretary of State, net of any sums received from local education authorities for the areas served and of payments made on behalf of pupils. Proprietors of other schools receive grants the amount of which the Secretary of State determines having regard to what was paid under the pre-existing regulations. Grants are payable in respect of a financial year and may be withheld or reduced if specified conditions are not fulfilled.

The conditions in the Direct Grant Schools Regulations are wide **2–219** ranging. They relate to the probity of governors; the condition of premises (new premises and alterations require the approval[36] of the Secretary of State); the conduct of the school (it must be efficient and not be conducted for profit and be free of specified health hazards); medical inspection and the supply of midday meals; the keeping of records and supply of information to the Secretary of State; the transfer of educational and medical information to another educational institution; approval of fees and boarding or other charges by the Secretary of State[37]; and teachers. Teachers are to be paid adequate and reasonable salaries, not to be disadvantaged because of religious opinions or attendance or non-attendance at worship, and to be given a hearing before dismissal. Schools other than nursery schools are subject to further conditions, relating to entry of pupils for external examinations and to the provision of, and excusal from, religious worship and instruction.

Those conditions also applied to direct grant grammar schools. There **2–220** are additional conditions in relation to other schools. The total number of pupils on the register is subject to the Secretary of State's approval; for primary and secondary schools there is to be a governing body including, if the Secretary of State so requires, local education authority representatives (but not so as to exceed one third of the total unless the proprietor otherwise agrees); and places in the school are to be reserved for pupils from its normal catchment area, the number to be agreed between governing body and local education authorities or in default determined by the Secretary of State. Also no teacher is to be employed who would be disqualified[38] from employment in a maintained school because, for example, of failure to satisfy his employer during his probationary period.[39]

If conditions or requirements contained in regulations run contrary to **2–221** the trust deed or other instrument relating to a direct grant school, the Secretary of State may, after consulting the persons responsible for the

---

[36] See A.M. 2/79.
[37] Mobility allowances under the Social Security Act 1975, s.37A are by subs. (8) to be disregarded in calculating income for assessing entitlement to fee remission. See Circ. 1/76 (W.O. 18/76).
[38] See the Education (Teachers) Regulations 1982 (S.I. 1982 No. 106) and below at paras. 4–19 and 4–24.
[39] See A.M. 9/78 as amended by Circ. 7/82.

management of the school, by order modify the deed or instrument accordingly.[40]

2–222   The duty of parents under section 36 of the 1944 Act to secure the education of children of compulsory school age has been explained in Chapter 1.[41] Here the consequences of failure to secure the attendance at school of a registered pupil and the means of enforcing attendance are outlined.

Failure to attend school

2–223   Failure by a parent to secure regular attendance[42] of a child of compulsory school age at a school where he is a registered pupil is an offence under section 39(1)[43] of the 1944 Act (whether or not the child is the subject of a school attendance order)[44] unless[45] the absence is with leave[46] granted by a person authorised by governors or school proprietor to grant it; or by reason of sickness[47] or any unavoidable cause; or on any day exclusively set apart for religious observance by the religious body to which the parent belongs; or the parent proves that the school is not within walking distance of the child's home and that the local education authority have made no suitable arrangements for transport or boarding accommodation or for enabling him to attend a school nearer his home.[48] It is a defence[49] to proceedings under section 39 when a medical officer of a local education authority, suspecting that the person or clothing of a maintained school pupil is infested with vermin or in a foul condition, directs the pupil, in his own or others' interest, to be excluded from school until examined or cleansed. The defence lapses if the direction is necessitated by wilful default of pupil or parent.

2–224   "[I]t is unnecessary in order to create the offence [under section 39] to show any knowledge on the part of the parents of the child's absence or any neglect on their part to ensure that the child did regularly

---

[40] 1973 Act, s.1 as amended by the 1980 Act, ss.1(3), 16(4) and Scheds. 1, para. 26 and 3, para. 17, and by the 1981 Act, s.21 and Sched. 3, para. 10.

[41] See above at paras. 1–80 to 1–85. For a comment on analogous Scottish provisions, see F. Doran, "School Attendances and Exclusions" (1980) SCOLAG Bull. 66.

[42] See above at para. 1–82.

[43] See *Spiers* v. *Warrington Corporation* [1954] 1 Q.B. 61, and above at para. 1–82 n. 55.

[44] See below at paras. 2–230 to 2–233.

[45] See s.39(2) and, as regards the defences, T.I. McLeod, "Aspects of School Attendance Reports" (1981) 145 J.P.N. 133.

[46] Under s.39(5) as amended by 1980 Act, s.1(3) and Sched. 1, para. 10 (and subject to regs. 11 and 12 of the Education (Schools and Further Education) Regulations 1981 (S.I. 1981 No. 1086), above at para. 2–141) or by direction of a medical officer (see note 49 below).

[47] As to exclusion from school of a child liable to convey notifiable disease see Public Health (Control of Disease) Act 1984, s.21 and below at para. 5–06.

[48] Note that a local education authority are now under a prima facie duty to respect parental preference as to choice of school. See 1980 Act, s.6 and above at para. 2–177.

[49] 1944 Act, s.54(7), and see below at para. 5–07 as to the power to ensure cleanliness.

attend . . . Those . . . were matters wholly in mitigation"—*per* Lord Parker of Waddington C.J. in *Crump* v. *Gilmore*.[50] It is no defence to send a child to a school of the parents' choice to which he is properly refused admittance.[51]

In *Happe* v. *Lay*[52] a father withheld his son from school because the   **2–225** school refused to readmit him unless he received two strokes of the cane for misbehaviour. The boy was then suspended[53] from school and stayed at home for the rest of the term. On appeal against conviction of the father under section 39(1) the court held that suspension did not constitute "leave" under section (2). Refusal to admit children because their mother objected to any form of physical punishment similarly gave rise to an offence of non-attendance (*Jarman* v. *Mid-Glamorgan Education Authority*).[54]

In *Jenkins* v. *Howells*[55] a girl stayed at home to perform domestic   **2–226** duties at her widowed mother's farm. The mother was chronically ill. The court held that sickness of a parent or "family responsibilities" did not amount to an "unavoidable cause" of absence. The "unavoidable cause," *per* Goddard L.J., must actually affect the child. It meant something in the nature of an emergency such as the burning down of the parent's house. The fact that a child is refused admission to school because he is sent in a verminous condition[56] does not constitute an "unavoidable cause" of absence (*Walker* v. *Cummings*).[57] Evidence is admissible on the question whether the presence of dirty or verminous children at school justifies withholding a child from attendance and constitutes an "unavoidable cause" (*Symes* v. *Brown*).[58]

An example of a day "exclusively set apart for religious observance"   **2–227** is Ascension Day for Church of England adherents.[59] "Walking distance" means two miles for children under eight and three miles for those of eight and over, by the nearest available route.[60] For a route to be "available" it has to be one along which a child, accompanied as necessary, can walk with reasonable safety to school: it does not cease to

---

[50] 68 L.G.R. 56 D.C. and see *London County Council* v. *Hearn* (1909) 78 L.J.K.B. 414 (truancy is no defence).

[51] *Jones* v. *Rowland* (1899) 80 L.T. 630 and see *Bunt* v. *Kent* [1914] 1 K.B. 207.

[52] 76 L.G.R. 313, D.C. As to corporal punishment see below at paras. 7–44 *et seq.*

[53] "Suspension"—see above at para. 2–117.

[54] (1985) 82 L.S. Gaz. 1249, D.C.

[55] [1949] 2 K.B. 218.

[56] See below at para. 5–07.

[57] (1912) 107 L.T. 304 and see *Fox* v. *Burgess* [1922] 1 K.B. 623 (below at para. 5–07 n.26) and *Spiers* v. *Warrington Corporation* [1954] 1 Q.B. 61 (above at para. 1–82 n.55). As to the circumstances in which it is unreasonable to refuse a child admission see *Bowen* v. *Hodgson* (1923) 93 L.J.K.B. 76.

[58] (1913) 109 L.T. 232.

[59] See *Marshall* v. *Graham, Bell* v. *Graham* [1907] 2 K.B. 112.

[60] s.39(5). In *Hares* v. *Curtin* [1913] 2 K.B. 328 the measurement was made from house porch to school porch, and "road" (a narrower term than "route") was held to include a cart track.

be available because dangerous for an unaccompanied child (*Rogers* v. *Essex County Council*).[61] As to distance the burden of proof lies on the parent. "Suitable arrangements" for transport[62] to and from a school which is not within walking distance must be arrangements which take the child "from a point reasonably near his home to a point reasonably near the school" (*per* Lynskey J. in *Surrey County Council* v. *Ministry of Education*).[63] Transport to a point where the child is within walking distance of home or school is not a "suitable arrangement."

2–228 Under section 39(3) where a child has no fixed abode the defence relating to walking distance is not available. The parent is, however, to be acquitted on proof that his trade or business requires him to travel from place to place, that the child has attended a school at which he was a registered pupil as regularly as the nature of the parent's occupation permits and, if the child is six or over, that he has made at least 200 attendances over the 12 months ending with the date of institution of proceedings.

2–229 A child who is a boarder at the school where he is a registered pupil is, by section 39(4), deemed to have failed to attend regularly if he is absent without leave and cannot plead sickness or unavoidable cause.

School attendance orders[64]

2–230 If it appears[65] to a local education authority that a parent of a child of compulsory school age in their area is *not* performing his duty under section 36 of the 1944 Act they must, unless the child is severely handicapped,[66] serve notice under section 37 requiring him to satisfy them within a period of not less than 14 days that he *is* doing so.[67] If the

---

[61] See *Rogers* v. *Essex County Council* [1987] A.C. 66, affirming *Shaxted* v. *Ward* (1954) 118 J.P., D.C., *sub nom. Farrier* v. *Ward* [1954] 1 W.L.R. 306. See "Children's Safety and the Walk to School" (1986) 150 L.G.Rev. 813. *Rogers* does not appear to have been directly overruled by s.53 of the 1986 (No. 2) Act (see below at para. 5–22) which was added following the decision. An authority who followed *Rogers* might be open to complaints of acting unreasonably, under s.68 of the 1944 Act (see below at para. 6–10), but see *R.* v. *Devon County Council, ex p.* C. The Independent, April 29, 1987; also C.E. Bazell "School attendance—recent changes in the law" 151 J.P.N. 151.

[62] As to the provision of transport by local education authorities see s.55 of the 1944 Act as amended and below at paras. 5–21 to 5–23. See also P. Liell, "School Transport" 82 L.S. Gaz. 2250.

[63] [1953] 1 W.L.R. 516. See also *Rootkin* v. *Kent County Council* [1981] 1 W.L.R. 1186, C.A.

[64] See Circ. 1/80, paras. 12 and 13, Circ. 1/81 paras. 37–39 and Circ. 2/86 (school attendance and the education welfare service).

[65] "If it appears"—see *Phillips* v. *Brown* (unreported, but see P. Liell and J.B. Saunders, *The Law of Education* (9th ed., 1984) F. 82).

[66] *i.e.* has special educational needs in respect of which the local education authority maintain a statement under s.7 of the 1981 Act. As to the making of an order in relation to a severely handicapped child see below at para. 2–232; and see 1980 Act, s.10(5) as amended by 1981 Act, s.21 and Sched. 3, para. 15.

[67] 1944 Act, s.37(1), as amended by 1981 Act, s.21 and Sched. 3, para. 2. This subsection places no obligation on a local education authority to compel the parent to send his child to school. See *Chapman and Others* v. *Essex County Council* (1956) 55 L.G.R. 28. As to service of notice, see 1944 Act, s.113 as amended.

parent fails to satisfy the authority and the authority conclude that it is expedient that the child should attend school, they must, under section 10 of the 1980 Act, notify him in writing of their intention to make a school attendance order specifying the school they intend to name in the order, and, if they think fit, a suitable alternative or alternatives. An aided or special agreement school[68] may not be specified without the consent of the governors. The authority's notice must also explain that if within 14 days the parent selects an alternative specified, it will be named in the order, and that he has further options as follows. He may apply within the same period:

(a) for the child to be admitted to another maintained school (and notify the maintaining authority if different from the authority serving the notice); or

(b) for education to be provided for the child at a non-maintained school; or

(c) for[69] the child to be admitted at the parent's own expense to a non-maintained school (and notify the authority serving the notice).

If a place is offered (in the case of (c) suitable to the child's age, ability and aptitude or special educational needs)[70] then the school in question is named in the school attendance order. In the case of (a) and (b) the local education authority are under a *prima facie* duty to comply with the parental preference.[71] If they do not do so, for the reasons stated in section 6(3) of the 1980 Act,[72] then the parent may appeal under the same arrangements as apply when, in ordinary course, a preference for admission to a particular school is rejected.[73]

If the parent fails to respond to the authority's notice, or his application for a place at a school not named by the authority is unsuccessful, then the authority will make a school attendance order[74] naming the school they originally specified.[75] The order requires the parent to cause the child to become a registered pupil at that school. The order, once made, ordinarily[76] continues in force as long as the child is of   **2–231**

---

[68] See above at para. 2–02.

[69] 1980 Act, s.10(4) as amended by 1981 Act, s.21 and Sched. 3, para. 15.

[70] "Special educational needs." See 1981 Act, s.1 and above at para. 2–194.

[71] 1980 Act, s.6(2) and (5)(*b*). See above at para. 2–176.

[72] See above at para. 2–177 and (on a comparable, repealed, provision) *Darling and Jones* v. *Minister of Education, The Times*, April 7, 1962.

[73] See above at para. 2–178.

[74] In the form prescribed by the School Attendance Orders Regulations 1944 (S.R. and O. 1944 No. 1470).

[75] 1944 Act, s.37(2) as amended by 1981 Act, s.21, Sched. 3, para. 2 and Sched. 4. Exceptionally it may be permissible for the local education authority to inspect the home (*R.* v. *Surrey Quarter Sessions Appeals Committee, ex p. Tweedie* (1963) 107 S.J. 555.

[76] *Ibid.* s.37(7). See below at para. 2–237 as to discharge by a juvenile court.

compulsory school age, but it is open to amendment[77] by the local education authority (for example, at the time of transfer from primary to
secondary education) or if the parent subsequently applies for a place at
a different school. The application is dealt with under procedures analogous to those described above. A parent may also apply for a school
attendance order to be revoked[78] on the ground that arrangements have
been made for the child to receive suitable full-time education otherwise
than at school. If the local education authority are not satisfied with the
arrangements and decline to revoke the order, the parent may refer the
question to the Secretary of State, who may at his discretion require the
child to be medically examined[79] and may give directions as he thinks
fit.

2–232   There are special provisions in section 15 of the 1981 Act[80] regarding
school attendance orders in relation to children who are the subject of
statements under section 7 of that Act. The local education authority
must notify[81] the parent of their intention to serve the order, and the
notice is to state that if within 15 days he selects a school for his child
that school will be named in the order unless the Secretary of State
directs otherwise. If the local education authority believe that the
selected school is unsuitable for the child, or would prejudice the provision of efficient education or the efficient use of resources, they must
notify the parent of their intention to require the Secretary of State to
direct what school is to be named in the order. His direction may make
consequential amendments to the section 7 statement. If the named
school is maintained by a local education authority they and the governors must admit him to the school. There are matching provisions in section 16[82] for amendment and revocation of school attendance orders
made as above, and an aggrieved parent may refer the question to the
Secretary of State, who may give directions to the local education authority as he thinks fit.

2–233   Failure to comply with a school attendance order is an offence unless the
person upon whom the order is served proves that the child is taking the
benefit of section 36 of the 1944 Act otherwise than at school.[83] If proceedings end in acquittal the court may direct that the school attendance

---

[77] 1980 Act, s.11 as amended by 1981 Act, s.21 and Sched. 3, para. 16.

[78] 1944 Act, s.37(4) as amended by 1981 Act, s.21, Sched. 3, para. 2 and Sched. 4 (and see 1944 Act,
s.111 as to revocation and variation of orders generally).

[79] 1944 Act, s.69(2) (as amended) which refers in terms to "pupil", rather than "child" as in s.37, but
in the present context the discrepancy seems immaterial. Failure without reasonable excuse to
comply with s.69(2) is an offence punishable on summary conviction by a fine not exceeding level
1 on the standard scale (see nn. 87 and 88 below).

[80] See Circ. 8/81, paras. 35–37. As to statements under *ibid.* s.7, see above at para. 2–197.

[81] As to service of notice, see 1944 Act, s.113 as amended.

[82] As regards medical and other examinations see s.18. As regards revocation s.16 appears to duplicate, but without inconsistency, s.37(4) of the 1944 Act as amended by 1981 Act, s.21, Sched. 3,
para. 2, and Sched. 4.

[83] 1944 Act, s.37(5), as amended by 1981 Act, s.21 and Sched. 3, para. 2. Proof that the child is
attending a school other than that named in the order appears to be no defence.

order lapse; but the local education authority on any change of circumstances may restart the procedure for obtaining an order.[84]

Enforcement of school attendance

Proceedings[85] may be instituted[86] only by a local education authority. **2–234** Any person found guilty (under section 37 of the 1944 Act) of failing to comply with a school attendance order, and a parent guilty (under section 39) of failing to secure the regular attendance at school of a registered pupil of compulsory school age, is liable on summary conviction[87] to a fine, the maximum of which is level three on the standard scale.[88] Upon conviction for failure to comply with a school attendance order, the order is spent. Continued default on the part of a parent obliges the local education authority to initiate new proceedings under section 37.[89] Third and subsequent offences under sections 37 or 39 carry up to one month's imprisonment as alternative, or additionally, to the fine.

The definition of parent[90] being wide the question may arise against **2–235** whom to bring proceedings. In *Hance* v. *Burnett*[91] it was held that in the absence of the father the mother had actual custody of the child and proceedings could be brought against her. This decision was followed in the rather more recent case of *Woodward* v. *Oldfield*[92] where the father was in prison. If the father is present, however, *London County Council* v. *Stansell*[93] indicates that he is the right person to be charged. The fact that the definition includes persons other than natural parents does not relieve the latter from responsibility for securing school attendance even if they are not exercising actual custody (*London School Board* v. *Jackson*).[94] In *Hance* v. *Fairhurst*[95] it was held that an attendance order made against a husband cannot be enforced against his widow.

Before instituting proceedings the local education authority must con- **2–236** sider whether they should also, or alternatively, bring the child before a

---

[84] 1944 Act, s.37(6).
[85] See 1944 Act, s.40, as amended, and N. Harris, "Tackling Truancy—the Legal Questions", 17 Fam. Law 21.
[86] 1944 Act, s.40(2) as substituted by Children and Young Persons Act 1969, Sched. 5, para. 13. A local education authority may not bring proceedings so as to make a child a ward of court (*Re B. (Infants)* [1961] 3 W.L.R. 694).
[87] As to summary proceedings see Magistrates Court Act 1980 as amended, and see C.E. Bazell, "Prosecutions under s.37 and s.39 of the Education Act 1944," 150 J.P.N. 295.
[88] Under 1944 Act, s.40(1) as amended by Criminal Law Act 1977, s.31 and Sched. 6, Criminal Justice Act 1982, ss.37 and 46 and the Criminal Penalties (Increase) Order 1984 (S.I. 1984 No. 447). It is not open to justices to find that an offence is so trifling that the person charged should not be convicted (*Rennie* v. *Boardman* (1914) 111 L.T. 713).
[89] *Enfield London Borough Council* v. *Forsyth* (1987) 17 Fam. Law 163. See C.E. Bazell, "School attendance—recent changes in the law" 151 J.P.N. 151.
[90] See 1944 Act, s.114(1), and above at para. 1–70.
[91] (1880) 45 J.P. 54, D.C.
[92] [1928] 1 K.B. 204. See above at para. 1–70.
[93] (1935) 154 L.T. 241.
[94] (1881) 7 Q.B.D. 502.
[95] (1882) 47 J.P. 53.

juvenile court in care proceedings[96] under section 1 of the Children and Young Persons Act 1969; and the court which convicts a person of an offence under section 37, or before which a person is charged under section 39, may direct[97] the local education authority to bring the child concerned before a juvenile court.

2–237   If a juvenile court conclude[98] that the child is

(a) of compulsory school age and not receiving efficient full-time education suitable to his age, ability and aptitude and to any special educational needs he may have; and

(b) is also in need of care and control which he is unlikely to receive unless the court make an appropriate[99] order, then the court may make such an order.[1]

The court will find[2] that condition (a) is satisfied if it is proved that a school attendance order has not been complied with, or that the child is a registered pupil at a school and not attending regularly, or that he is a person whom another person[3] habitually wandering from place to place takes with him. Condition (a) will not be satisfied it is proved that the child *is* receiving efficient full-time education; and in that case if the child is the subject of a school attendance order the court may direct[4] that the order cease to be in force.

2–238   Condition (b) may be satisfied if the court conclude that the child is not receiving proper education. "Care applies not only to the physical condition of the child—his meals and his comfort at home—but also to his proper education" *per* Lord Denning M.R. in *re S (a minor) (Care Order: Education)*.[5] This was an appeal (unsuccessful) against a care order made by a juvenile court because a school attendance order had not been complied with, the parent objecting to education at a

---

[96] See 1944 Act, s.40(2), as substituted by Children and Young Persons Act 1969, Sched. 4, para. 13. Care proceedings in relation to failure to receive education may be instituted only by a local education authority (Children and Young Persons Act 1969, s.2(8)(*a*)); and care proceedings may be instituted by a local education authority in circumstances other than failure to receive education. See Children and Young Persons Act 1969, ss.1 and 2, as amended. See Circ. 19/70, also R. Grimshaw and J. Pratt, "Truancy and the Juvenile Court" 147 J.P.N. 571. As to investigations by local education authorities in connection with proceedings under *ibid*. s.1, see s.9, and C. Ball, "School Reports in the Juvenile Court" 147 J.P.N. 808.

[97] 1944 Act, s.40(3), as substituted by Children and Young Persons Act 1969, Sched. 5, para. 13.

[98] Children and Young Persons Act 1969, s.1(2), as amended.

[99] One of the five specified in Children and Young Persons Act 1969, s.1(3), *e.g.* a supervision order or a care order.

[1] As to allocation of functions between local authority and local education authority where a child is placed in the care of a local authority, see the Local Authorities and Local Education Authorities (Allocation of Functions) Regulations 1951 (S.I. 1951 No. 472) as amended, and Circ. 232.

[2] Children and Young Persons Act 1969, s.2(8)(*b*).

[3] It is, separately, an offence for a vagrant to prevent a child from receiving education (Children & Young Persons Act 1933, s.10, as amended).

[4] 1944 Act, s.40(4), as substituted by Children and Young Persons Act 1969, Sched. 5, para. 13.

[5] [1978] Q.B. 120, and see R.E.C. Jewell, "School Attendance and Child Care" (1977) 141 L.G.Rev. 190 and 442, and P. Meredith "Executive Discretion and Choice of Secondary School", [1981] P.L. 42 at 79.

comprehensive school—the only form of education offered to his son by the local education authority.

In proceedings[6] relating to school attendance proof of age may be **2–239** required. Any person may obtain[7] a copy of the entry in the register of births[8] certified by a registrar[9] upon payment of a fee[10]; and a local education authority may obtain particulars of entries free of charge.

For the purposes of prosecuting a parent under section 37 or section **2–240** 39 of the 1944 Act a child shall be presumed to be of compulsory school age (if that is material) unless the parent proves the contrary[11]; and documents, certificates and extracts from minutes signed by authorised local education authority officers, head teachers and chairmen of governors or their clerks are to be received in evidence and accepted for what they purport to be unless the contrary is proved.[12]

---

[6] ss.94 and 95 (as amended) of the 1944 Act apply generally in relation, respectively, to certificates of birth and registrars' returns, and the provision of evidence in legal proceedings under the Education Acts. Reference is made to them here because of their particular relevance to school attendance proceedings.

[7] 1944 Act, s.94 as amended. A written requisition must be made in the form specified in the Certificates of Births, Deaths and Marriages (Registration) Regulations 1937 (S.R. & O. 1937 No. 885). Forms are free.

[8] See Births and Deaths Registration Act 1953, s.25.

[9] A registrar of births and deaths or a superintendent registrar. See the Births and Deaths Registration Act 1953 and the Registration Service Act 1953, both as amended.

[10] The amount is revised from time to time. See the Registration of Births, Deaths and Marriages (Fees) Order 1987 (S.I. 1987 No. 50).

[11] 1944 Act, s.95, as amended by 1980 Act, s.1(3) and Sched. 1, para. 1, and as partly substituted by 1948 Act, s.9. The court must be satisfied that all reasonable diligence has been used to obtain evidence as to age.

[12] But the heavier burden is upon the prosecution to prove the offence. See *R. v. Carr-Briant* [1943] K.B. 607 and *R. v. Dunbar* [1958] 1 Q.B. 1.

CHAPTER 3

FURTHER EDUCATION

3–01   "Further education" is the general term used to embrace a variety of activities, for those above compulsory school age, which are provided by local education authorities or supported by them or by the Department of Education and Science. Technical education, often part-time and at "night school," gained public support from the middle of the 19th century.[1] Technical colleges[2] were the forerunners of what are now the crowning institutions of the public sector—polytechnics, where courses of up to degree level are taught and are not confined to technology but rival the diversity of those offered at the universities.[3] Colleges of education, formerly limited to teacher training,[4] prepare students for degrees and professional qualifications. Institutions which provide full-time school, as well as further education, courses are sometimes called tertiary colleges. A minority of institutions are specific to a particular form of training (for example, farm institutes, the Royal College of Music and the London School of Nautical Cookery). Vocational courses may be full-time, "sandwich,"[5] or part-time, by day or block release, or held in the evenings. Adult education is generally provided part-time, often in institutions separate from those which offer full-time courses; but adult education equally falls within the scope of further education. So does the youth service, for which local education authorities run youth clubs or centres and give assistance to voluntary youth organisations. Other further education institutions, courses and qualifications defy ready classification.

3–02   As will appear, the statutory basis for these wide-ranging activities is slender—even fragile—and many of the bodies that influence the nature and extent of further education do not derive from the Education Acts. Examples are the Council for National Academic Awards,[6] who award

---

[1] "Compulsory school age." See 1944 Act, s.35 and above at para. 1–81.

[2] "A school or college is not a factory and the scholars or pupils are employed neither by those who own or those who teach at the school"—*per* Wrottesley J. in *Weston* v. *London County Council* [1941] 1 K.B. 608 at 613—so the Factories Act (now the Act of 1961) does not apply.

[3] Universities, though largely publicly funded, are regarded as part of the "private sector." They constitute, with public sector institutions, the two halves of the so-called "binary system" of higher education. For the origins of polytechnics see *A Plan for Polytechnics and Other Colleges* (Cmnd. 3006) 1966. For the future see *Higher Education: Meeting the Challenge* (Cm. 114) 1987.

[4] As to teacher training see below at paras. 4–04 to 4–09.

[5] A "sandwich course" is a course of alternate periods of full-time study in an institution and of practical experience. It is defined for the purposes of the Education (Mandatory Awards) Regulations 1986 (S.I. 1986 No. 1306) in para. 1(1) of Sched. 5 to those Regulations.

[6] The Council was established on a recommendation in the report of the (*Robbins*) *Committee on Higher Education* (Cmnd. 2154) 1963. See A.M. 9/64. The Council have assumed the responsibilities of the former National Council for Diplomas in Art and Design. See A.M. 14/74.

degrees and validate the academic content of degree courses outside the universities, the Business and Technical Education Council,[7] who plan courses and set award standards within the areas which their name indicates, the Further Education Unit (formerly part of the Department of Education and Science), concerned with curriculum matters, and advisory bodies representative of local education authority and other interests, on whom the Secretary of State relies to a greater or lesser extent in deciding how to exercise his statutory functions.

Particular reference must be made to the regional advisory councils for further education and to the National Advisory Body for Public Sector Higher Education. There are ten regional advisory councils: nine in England and the Welsh Joint Education Committee[8] acting as the council for Wales. The councils operate in accordance with terms of reference agreed between the participating local education authorities, who meet their staffing and other expenses. Their membership usually includes representatives from local education authorities, polytechnics and universities, principals of, and teachers at, further education institutions, and employers and employees in industry and commerce. H.M. Inspectors[9] attend as assessors. The National Advisory Body for Public Sector Higher Education (established in 1982 as the N.A.B. for Local Authority Higher Education) derives from the (Oakes) Report of the Working Group on the Management of Higher Education in the Maintained Sector.[10] The Body consists of a board on which a wide range of higher education and other interests are represented, and a committee chaired by the Parliamentary Under Secretary of State at the Department of Education and Science and comprising the chairman of the Board and representatives of local education authorities. The functions of the Board include keeping in touch with the world of higher education, professional bodies and industry and commerce, and receiving instructions from, and making recommendations to, the committee to help them fulfil their terms of reference. These include considering the academic provision to be made in higher education institutions; advising the Secretary of State about the apportionment of the advanced further education pool,[11] allocation of resources for capital expenditure for local authority higher education, allocation of resources to voluntary colleges and the approval of advanced courses; monitoring implementation of the "dispositions" made by the Secretary of State; and

---

[7] See A.M. 7/73. Formerly the Business Education Council and Technical Education Council were separate bodies. B.T.E.C. qualifications are superseding the Ordinary National Certificate (part-time) and Ordinary National Diploma (full-time) of about G.C.E. "A" level standard, and the Higher National Certificate (part-time) and Higher National Diploma (full-time) of university pass degree standard, which were administered by a committee representative of the Department of Education and Science, professional institutions and technical college teachers.

[8] See para. 1–23.

[9] See paras. 6–05 et seq.

[10] Cmnd. 7130. See A.M. 3/78.

[11] See para. 1–133.

contributing to the co-ordination of the provision of higher education in its several sectors and between the provision in England and the other countries of the United Kingdom.[12]

The Statutory Basis[13]

3–03   Section 7 of the 1944 Act refers to further education as one of the three progressive stages[14] of public education, and section 8 contemplates that the full-time education of senior pupils may be part of further education provision,[15] but the main further education provisions in the 1944 Act are in six sections—41 to 46.[16] It is the duty of every local education authority to secure the provision for (but not necessarily in) their area of adequate facilities for further education:

(a) full-time and part-time education for persons over compulsory school age; and

(b) leisure-time occupation, in organised cultural training and recreative activities suited to the requirements of persons over compulsory school age who are able and willing to profit by the facilities provided for that purpose.[17]

The wide terms in which the law is cast help local education authorities to reflect in their provision the particular needs of their area.

3–04   "Secure the provision" indicates that local education authorities may not only provide services themselves, but may also assist voluntary bodies (for example, teacher training institutions and youth organisations) to do so. "For their area" might seem to exclude an obligation to accept pupils belonging to another area or to no area, but the power to provide further education for them as an incident of executing the local duty is implicit in the Education (Areas to which Pupils Belong) Regulations 1980[18]; and under section 51(5) and (6) of the 1986 (No. 2) Act it is not a ground for refusing to admit a pupil to, or excluding him from, a further education establishment that he does not belong to the area[19] of the local education authority maintaining or assisting[20] that establishment,

---

[12] See 72 H.C. Deb. 192–4, January 30, 1985.

[13] See *The Legal Basis of Further Education*, a review by officers from the Department of Education and Science, the Welsh Office and the local authorities, D.E.S. 1981.

[14] See above at para. 1–66.

[15] See above at para. 2–03 and below at para. 3–11.

[16] s.47 is spent. As to duties in relation to recreation and social and physical training see s.53, below at para. 5–27. The Technical and Industrial Institutions Act 1892 is concerned with the government and land transactions of such institutions, but is now of very limited application. As to the effect of the 1892 Act upon the construction of a will and trusts thereby created for the maintenance of a school, see *Re Stanley's Trust Deed* (1910) 26 T.L.R. 365.

[17] *Ibid*. s.41(*a*) and (*b*). As to recreation see also below at para. 5–27.

[18] S.I. 1980 No. 917, as amended.

[19] "Belong to the area"—see para. 1–134. As to London, s.31(8) of the London Government Act 1963 remains unrepealed as regards further education until the Secretary of State brings 1986 (No. 2) Act, s.51(12) fully into force.

[20] "Assist"—see 1944 Act, s.114(2)(*b*).

except in relation to pupils who do not fall within a category prescribed by regulation, or where the admission of a pupil would cause a pupil belonging to the area to be refused admission. "Facilities for further education" are deemed to include facilities for vocational and industrial training.[21]

Section 27(6) of the 1980 Act enables the Secretary of State to make   **3–05** regulations[22] with respect to the provision of further education courses at establishments provided by local education authorities and, by section 27(7), establishments designated by regulation as substantially dependent for maintenance or assistance from a local education authority on grants by the Secretary of State under section 100(1)(*b*) of the 1944 Act.[23] Two of the current regulations are concerned with advanced further education and are referred to under that heading. The regulations require local education authorities who provide further education establishments, in consultation when appropriate with the regional advisory council for further education, to try to secure that so far as may be reasonable the courses at their establishments do not duplicate those provided at the establishments of neighbouring authorities, and that any fees are comparable.[24]

There are a number of miscellaneous provisions. Those further edu-   **3–06** cation establishments provided or designated as above are subject to the regulations (and advice)[25] concerning health hazards[26] and approval of premises[27] that apply to schools; and the law regarding nuisance and disturbance on school premises[28] applies equally to the premises of a further education establishment provided by a local education authority. Provision must be made, as in schools, for the chronically sick and disabled[29] in establishments provided under a further education scheme.[30] Reference in statute to "further education establishments" may be taken to include, when not inappropriate, youth clubs and community centres.

---

[21] Industrial Training Act 1964, s.16. See below at para. 3–29.

[22] See the Education (Schools and Further Education) Regulations 1981 (S.I. 1981 No. 1086), as amended by Amendment Regulations S.I. 1983 No. 262, and Circ. 7/81.

[23] See S.I. 1981 No. 1086, reg. 3(*b*) and Sched. 3 as amended/added by the Education (Schools and Further Education) (Amendment) Regulations 1983 (S.I. 1983 No. 262). There are 12 assisted and 42 grant-aided establishments (two fewer than in the otherwise identical list in Sched. 1 to S.I. 1983 No. 973—see below n. 66). As to the making of grants by the Secretary of State otherwise than to local education authorities see the Education (Grant) Regulations 1983 (S.I. 1983 No. 74) and below at paras. 3–19 *et seq.*

[24] See S.I. 1981 No. 1086, reg. 17.

[25] See Circ. 7/81, para. 10.12.

[26] See S.I. 1981 No. 1086, reg. 6 and the Radioactive Substances (Schools etc.) Exemption Order 1963 (S.I. 1963 No. 1832). See above at para. 2–147 and A.M. 2/76.

[27] S.I. 1981 No. 1086, reg. 7 as amended by S.I. 1983 No. 262 and see above para. 2–54.

[28] See Local Government (Miscellaneous Provisions) Act 1982, s.40, and above at paras. 2–67 to 2–69. A youth and community centre is among further education establishments to which s.40 applies.

[29] See Chronically Sick and Disabled Persons Act 1970, s.8, as amended, and above at para. 2–59.

[30] See below at para. 3–10.

3–07   The tenancies of students and prospective students at universities, and further education establishments in general are not "protected tenancies"[31] under the Rent Acts; and the repairing obligations in short leases do not apply to leases granted to those institutions.[32]

3–08   The law relating to copyright and licensing for various purposes applies to further education establishments as it does to schools.[33] So does the law relating to sex and racial discrimination.[34]

3–09   The provisions about disputes between local education authorities and governors,[35] unreasonable exercise of functions[36] and default[37] apply to maintained colleges[38] of education and other further education establishments and their governors as they apply[39] in relation to schools and their governors.

Schemes

3–10   Local education authorities are not empowered or required to carry out their duties except in accordance with schemes[40] of further education or at county colleges.[41] The making and approval of schemes was accomplished by the mid-1950s, but most schemes do not now reflect actual provision made for further education by local education authorities; and county colleges have never been brought into being.[42] It seems to follow that much if not most of the provision made by local education authorities for further education may be *ultra vires*.[43] It might be argued that regulations made under the wide terms of section 27(6) of the 1980 Act supersede, even perhaps repeal by implication, parts of the earlier legislation, but the regulations so far made[44] are of very

---

[31] See the Rent Act 1977, s.8 and the Protected Tenancies (Exceptions) Regulations 1986 (S.I. 1986 No. 541) and A.M. 17/74 (W.O. 5/74).
[32] Landlord and Tenant Act 1985, s.14(4).
[33] See above at paras. 2–148 to 2–152 and also below at para. 3–25.
[34] See above at paras. 1–92 *et seq.* and 1–102 *et seq.*
[35] 1944 Act, s.67(1) as applied by 1968 (No. 2) Act, s.3(3). See above at para. 2–103 and below at para. 6–08.
[36] *Ibid.* s.68, applied as above. See below at para. 6–10.
[37] *Ibid.* s.99, applied as above. See below at para. 6–15.
[38] See below at para. 3–16.
[39] See above at para. 2–103.
[40] See proviso to 1944 Act, s.41, and s.42. Circ. 133 required submission of schemes by March 31, 1948. As to schemes relating to the Greater London Area, see London Government Act 1963 s.31(1)(*c*) and (4).
[41] See 1944 Act, ss.43–46 as amended; also *The Legal Basis of Further Education*, (see note 13 above) para. 6.
[42] The County Colleges Order 1947 (S.R. & O. 1947 No. 527) determined April 1, 1947, as the date after which it would be the duty of local education authorities to establish and maintain county colleges. The duty does not take effect because of failure of the Secretary of State under s.43(3) of the 1944 Act to specify colleges.
[43] As to the unwillingness of the Government to legislate as recommended in *The Legal Basis of Further Education* (see note 13 above) see 58 H.C.Deb. 164, April 10, 1984.
[44] The Education (Schools and Further Education) Regulations 1981 (S.I. 1981 No. 1086) as amended by S.I. 1983 No. 262.

limited application, so the argument is not a persuasive one. Equally it is difficult to construe the designation by the Secretary of State of polytechnics[45] and of advanced courses[46] as a limited variation[47] and approval of a scheme.

Further education and secondary education

The law on the relationship between further education and secondary **3–11** education[48] is also in doubt. Under section 8 of the 1944 Act it is "the duty of every local education authority to secure that there shall be available for their area sufficient schools . . . for providing secondary education . . . other than such full-time education as may be provided for senior pupils in pursuance of a [further education] scheme . . . " It is arguable that the terms of the section oblige local education authorities to provide places for all those who wish to remain at school beyond compulsory school age[49] and up to their 19th birthday, but it seems a more straightforward interpretation that places are to be made available *either* at school *or* in a further education institution. It is not in doubt, however, that local education authorities who permit senior pupils to transfer to a tertiary college or other further education institution before attaining the upper limit of compulsory school age are in breach[50] of the law.

Fees and charges

It has long been general practice for local education authorities to **3–12** charge adults fees for further education courses, but the 1944 Act does not authorise the charging of fees for further education—unless authorisation is to be deduced from the prohibition[51] of fees for education at maintained schools. Section 27(6) and (7) of the 1980 Act enable the Secretary of State to make regulations with respect to fees to be charged for further education courses at establishments provided or assisted by local education authorities or to which he makes grants, but he has not used regulations to authorise fee-paying generally. Evidence that the charging of fees is normal practice, however, comes from, for example, the requirement as to coordination of fee levels,[52] and the recoupment

---

[45] Designation of polytechnics is an executive act by the Secretary of State, for which there is no legislative provision. It was a condition for designation that any amendment to the instrument of government (see below at para. 3–16) should be submitted to the Secretary of State for approval.
[46] See S.I. 1981 No. 1086, reg. 14 and below at para. 3–23.
[47] See *The Legal Basis of Further Education* (see n. 13 above) para. 7.
[48] See *ibid.* para. 3. As to provision for 16–19 year olds see Circ. 3/87 paras. 17 to 31, 37 and 38.
[49] See above at para. 1–81.
[50] See *The Legal Basis of Further Education* (see n. 13 above) para. 10.
[51] See 1944 Act, s.61(1) and above at para. 1–87.
[52] S.I. 1981 No. 1086, reg. 17.

provisions of sections 51 and 52[53] of the 1986 (No. 2) Act. But it is arguable that none of the provisions that relate to fees constitutes the "express words [that] are necessary to empower a public authority to raise money from the subject."[54] The issue has not been taken to the courts, but may become a live one now that some authorities have begun the practice of levying fees for 16–19 year olds in further education.

3–13   Subject to the regulation regarding comparability,[55] local education authorities have discretion regarding the levels of fees charged for the further education courses they provide, but in practice they are guided by the Secretary of State and C.L.E.A.[56] as follows. The Secretary of State specifies the fees[57] which he will recognise for the purpose of making awards to students following designated (first degree and comparable) courses.[58] He has also recommended fees for postgraduate and other further education courses. C.L.E.A. recommend fees relating to advanced[59] and non-advanced further education (but not including non-vocational adult education) courses and separately in relation to full-time and part-time courses.

3–14   Separate fee levels are recommended by the Secretary of State and C.L.E.A. in relation to home and European Community students, and to other overseas students. A local education authority may charge higher fees[60] to those students attending a full-time or "sandwich"[61] course at a further education establishment[62] who have no relevant

---

[53] See above at paras. 1–138 to 1–139.

[54] See S.A. de Smith, *Judicial Review of Administrative Action* (4th ed. 1980) p. 100. The cases there cited are, however, mostly in support of the proposition that no power may be implied to charge for a licence: they do not relate to the taking of fees for services rendered.

[55] See S.I. 1981 No. 1086, reg. 17 and above at para. 3–05.

[56] See above at paras. 1–36 to 1–38.

[57] These are specified in the Education (Mandatory Awards) Regulations 1986 (S.I. 1986 No. 1306) Sched. 1. See below at para. 3–46.

[58] See *ibid* reg. 10 and below at para. 3–43.

[59] Courses listed in Sched. 2 to S.I. 1981 No. 1086. See below at para. 3–23.

[60] The fees are "relevant fees," defined as fees for tuition, etc., in regs. 5 and 7 of the Education (Fees and Awards) Regulations 1983 (S.I. 1983 No. 973) as amended by Amendment Regulations S.I. 1984 No. 1201 and S.I. 1985 No. 1219 and made under s.1 of the Education (Fees and Awards) Act 1983. The Regulations make lawful under s.41(1) of the Race Relations Act 1976 what would otherwise be a prohibited discriminatory practice under that Act and supersede the making of a formal discrimination determination by the Secretary of State under s.41(2). See also above at para. 1–104 and *The Funding and Organisation of Courses in Higher Education: Interim Report on Overseas Student Fees* (First Report from the Education, Science and Arts Committee H.C. 1979–1980, 552–1) and Government Observations thereon (Cmnd. 8011 (1980)).

[61] See above at para. 3–01 n. 5.

[62] Defined in S.I. 1983 No. 973, Sched. 1 as an establishment provided by a local education authority or substantially dependent for its maintenance on assistance from a local educaton authority or grants under s.100(1)(*b*) of the 1944 Act, and specified in the Schedule. There are 12 assisted and 44 grant aided establishments, which with the addition of Cranfield Institute of Technology and the Royal College of Art correspond with those listed in S.I. 1981 No. 1086, Sched. 3 (see above n. 23).

connection[63] with the United Kingdom or Islands (the Channel Islands and the Isle of Man) unless they come within the categories of excepted students. The categories include (subject to conditions) European Community nationals and their children, refugees, and persons whose parents were temporarily employed outside the United Kingdom and Islands or outside the European Community.[64]

Although an authority are not bound in law by the fees specified or   **3–15**
recommended, or by the recommendations of C.L.E.A. on catering and residence charges, departure from them would create problems for the authority in relation to one or more of inter-authority recoupment payments,[65] the pooling of expenditure[66] and the amount of block grant receivable.[67] Courses provided at the request of industrial firms and commercial organisations, or an industrial training board or the Manpower Services Commission[68] are ordinarily at full cost, as are training courses for certain professions supplementary to medicine,[69] the cost of which is met by the National Health Service authorities. Similarly the Home Office meet the cost of teaching provided in prisons: local education authorities have power, but no obligation, to educate prisoners.[70]

Government and conduct of maintained institutions[71]

For every institution, including colleges of education, maintained by a   **3–16**
local education authority and providing full-time further education under a further education scheme, section 1 of the 1968 (No. 2) Act requires that there must be an instrument of government, establishing a body of governors.[72] The instrument is made by order of the local education authority, and in the case of colleges of education the order requires the approval of the Secretary of State. It provides for the

---

[63] A student has a relevant connection if he has been ordinarily resident (see below at para. 3–73) therein for three years preceding his course otherwise than to receive full-time education (see *ibid.* reg. 6). See *Orphanos* v. *Queen Mary College* [1985] 2 All E.R. 233 and above at para. 1–102 n.32.

[64] See S.I. 1983 No. 973, Sched. 2 as amended by S.I. 1984 No. 1201, and by S.I. 1985 No. 1219. For definitions see reg. 2. In *University College London* v. *Newman, The Times* January 8, 1986, it was held that a New Zealand student who has spent most of the three years preceding a course beginning January 1, 1984, "bumming around" the United Kingdom and other European Community states had been ordinarily resident in the European Community.

[65] See above at paras. 1–138 to 1–139.

[66] See above at paras. 1–130 *et seq.*

[67] See above at paras. 1–123 *et seq.*

[68] See below at paras. 3–29 *et seq.*

[69] See A.M. 10/76.

[70] See s.116 of the 1944 Act (as amended). See A.M. 440 and addenda, *Prison Education* (First Report from the Education, Science and Arts Committee, H.C. 1982–1983 45–1), Government Reply, Cmnd. 9126 and Second Report H.C. 1983–1984, 453; also *Prison Education* (Second Report from the Education, Science and Arts Committee H.C. 1986–87 138–I and II).

[71] See Circs. 22/68 and 7/70. The annex to the latter contains model articles for different categories of college (see Appendix 2 below).

[72] As to status and liabilities of governors see above at para. 2–103. As to payment of allowances see Local Government Act 1972 s.177 as amended and the Local Government (Allowances) Regulations 1986 (S.I. 1986 No. 724) reg. 8 and Sched. 3, Pt. I, and above at para. 2–106.

number and method of appointment of governors,[73] who are likely to include local education authority representatives, the principal and other college staff *ex officio*, staff and students by election, and representatives of local interests, including industry and commerce. By section 61 of the 1986 (No. 2) Act a member of a governing body must be aged 18 or over, or be a student at the institution; if the latter, his participation in their proceedings may be restricted by regulations made by the Secretary of State, and the regulations may authorise the imposition of additional restrictions by the instrument. With the approval of the Secretary of State a local education authority may constitute[74] a single governing body for two or more institutions but may end the arrangement at any time.

3–17 There must also be articles[75] of government made by order of the local education authority with the approval of the Secretary of State. The articles give a degree of autonomy and academic freedom to the Institution, according to its size and status. They allocate functions to the local education authority, board of governors, the principal and the academic board (loosely equivalent to a university senate) if any. They may go on to regulate the constitution and functions of committees and sub-committees.[76] Under section 56 of the 1986 (No. 2) Act governing bodies must provide the information the Secretary of State requires to exercise his functions; and section 62 empowers the Secretary of State to make regulations requiring governing bodies to make available information regarding their meetings and proceedings as prescribed.

3–18 The arrangements for considering applications for admission to an educational institution ought perhaps to be "fair," but there is no obligation to act judicially and applicants are not entitled to a hearing. Disappointed applicants have no right to demand reasons for the refusal of any general claim to redress in the courts.[77] Admission of overseas students to courses of further education and the conditions under which they are permitted to remain in the United Kingdom are subject to rules made under the Immigration Act 1971 as amended.[78]

---

[73] The courts may be unwilling to intervene in a dispute concerning the composition of a governing body. See *Dixon* v. *Chairman of the Governors and the Govenors of the Huddersfield Polytechnic* [1979] C.L.Y. 93 (unreported) and *The Times H.E.S.*, March 10, 1978.

[74] 1968 (No. 2) Act, ss.1(4) and 3(2).

[75] *Ibid.* s.1(3). As to the operation of an article relating to dismissal of full-time members of the teaching staff and the residual powers of a local education authority, see *Winder* v. *Cambridgeshire County Council* (1978) 76 L.G.R. 549, C.A.; also below at para. 4–34 n. 12.

[76] *Ibid.* s.3(1). As to the propriety of procedures relating to expulsion of students see *Ward* v. *Bradford Corporation and Others* (1971) 70 L.G.R. 27, and *Herring* v. *Templeman* [1973] 3 All E.R. 569. See also above at paras. 1–54 *et seq.*—"natural justice."

[77] See *Central Council for Training in Social Work* v. *Edwards and Others, The Times*, May 5, 1978 and above at para. 1–55.

[78] See Circ. 14/78 (W.O. 131/78) (and Circ. 15/78 (W.O. 110/78) regarding the welfare of overseas students).

Further education establishments and facilities not provided by local education authorities

Further education establishments[79] not provided by local education   **3–19**
authorities may be eligible for grants or loans from the Secretary of
State,[80] unless they are conducted for profit or are part of the university
sector. Capital grants may be paid to the governing bodies of those
establishments in respect of relevant expenditure (expenditure
approved by the Secretary of State[81]) on land or buildings, the provision
or alteration of buildings and new provision of furniture and equipment.[82] There is a restriction on the amount of capital grant for certain
purposes payable to some denominational further education establishments other than establishments for the further education and training
of disabled persons.[83] Where a restricted grant is paid in respect of a
teacher training college the Secretary of State may lend the governing
body up to 75 per cent. of the relevant expenditure to which the grant
relates.[84] Maintenance grant[85] may be paid in respect of relevant expenditure on the maintenance, including running expenditure, of further
education establishments and on account of scholarships, etc., tenable
at eight specified establishments.[86]

Before he makes a grant or loan payments the Secretary of State has   **3–20**
to satisfy himself[87] about the courses provided, fees and other charges,
remuneration of teachers, compliance with requirements (for example,
as regards health hazards) corresponding to those contained in regulations[88] in force under section 27 of the 1980 Act (if the regulations do
not apply to the establishment in question), and the absence (with specified exceptions) of religious discrimination. Changes in the constitution

---

[79] These include (mostly teacher training) establishments and establishments for the further education and training of disabled persons and the Cambridge Institute of Education. See reg. 10 of
the Education (Grant) Regulations 1983 (S.I. 1983 No. 74).

[80] See 1944 Act, s.100(1)(b), 1967 Act, s.4 (which makes specific provisions for loans for capital
expenditure incurred in relation to colleges of education) and S.I. 1983 No. 74, regs. 24–30 of
which specify general conditions of payment, etc. (see below at para. 6–20).

[81] S.I. 1983 No. 74, reg. 3 "Relevant expenditure" so defined is not to be confused with relevant
expenditure for rate support grant purposes (as to which see above at para. 1–123).

[82] Ibid. regs. 11 and 12.

[83] Ibid. reg. 14.

[84] Ibid. reg. 15.

[85] Ibid. regs. 11 and 13.

[86] Ibid. Sched. 3. The institutions are Coleg Harlech, Wales; Cooperative College, Loughborough;
Fircroft College, Birmingham; Hillcroft College, Surbiton; Northern College, Barnsley; Plater
College, Oxford; Royal College of Art; and Ruskin College, Oxford.

[87] S.I. 1983 No. 74, reg. 16. This regulation does not apply to the institutions specified in Sched. 4:
Cranfield Institute of Technology, Royal Academy of Music, Royal College of Art and Royal College of Music, but the Secretary of State may specify requirements as to conditions of payment of
grant to these institutions.

[88] See the Education (Schools and Further Education) Regulations 1981 (S.I. 1981 No. 1086), above
at paras. 2–54, 2–140, 2–144, 2–147 and 2–206.

of the governing body or in the conduct of the establishment are to be notified in advance to the Secretary of State, and grant payments are conditional on the changes being withdrawn, postponed or modified if he so requires.

3–21   The Secretary of State may also make grants to persons other than local education authorities who provide certain further education facilities otherwise than for profit.[89] The facilities are in leisure-time occupations[90] and, when provided under 1944 Act, s.53 in co-operation with a local education authority, for the recreation and social and physical training of those receiving education. Capital grants go towards relevant expenditure on acquiring land and buildings, provision and alteration of buildings and new provision of furniture or equipment; maintenance grants on their upkeep. Capital grants to trustees and others responsible for the management of a village hall or community centre used wholly or in part to provide the facilities mentioned may extend to the provision of the hall or centre.

Freedom of speech

3–22   Section 43 of the 1986 (No. 2) Act is designed to secure freedom of speech in further education establishments[91] maintained by local education authorities or designated by regulations, as well as in universities. Every individual and body of persons concerned in the government of the establishment must take reasonably practicable[92] steps to ensure that freedom of speech within the law[93] is secured for members, students, employees and visiting speakers, and that, in particular, use of the premises of the establishment and of students' union premises is not denied to any individual or body because of his or their beliefs or the policy or objectives of the body. The governing body are to issue and keep up to date a code of practice that sets out procedures at meetings and other activities specified, and the conduct required. All concerned in the government of the establishment, including local education authorities in the case of those they maintain or assist, are to take reasonably practicable steps (including disciplinary measures where appropriate) to secure compliance with the code of practice.

---

[89] S.I. 1983 No. 74, reg. 20—and see also reg. 23 and the general conditions specified in Pt. II of the Regulations (see below at para. 6–20). See also Circ. 13/71. Capital grants for voluntary youth service, village hall and community centre projects have ceased except towards youth service projects of national or regional significance.

[90] As explained in 1944 Act, s.41(*b*). See above at para. 3–03.

[91] See 1986 (No. 2) Act, s.43(5). Maintained establishments are those which are the subject of the penultimate subsection of this section of this Chapter. As to designated establishments see n. 23 above.

[92] See *Stroud's Judicial Dictionary* (5th ed., 1986).

[93] See S.A. de Smith *Constitutional and Administrative Law* (5th ed., 1985) Chap. 23.

ADVANCED FURTHER EDUCATION

Courses of advanced further education (or "higher education"[94] as it **3–23** is often called) at establishments to which the Secretary of State makes grants, or which are provided or assisted by local education authorities, are designated[95] as such by the Secretary of State. They are courses for the further training of teachers[96] and other courses which last full-time for at least four weeks or, part-time, involve more than 60 hours of instruction. They include first degree and postgraduate courses,[97] courses for Diploma of Higher Education, Higher National Diploma and Certificate courses, courses in preparation for professional examinations and other courses[98] of above G.C.E. "A" level or Ordinary National Certificate standard.[99] They are provided at polytechnics, colleges of education and other further education institutions.

Advanced further education courses may not be provided at a further **3–24** education establishment without the approval[1] (which may be subject to conditions) of the Secretary of State, and must be discontinued[2] if he so decides. He receives advice from the regional advisory councils for further education,[3] the National Advisory Body for Public Sector Higher Education,[4] the Voluntary Sector Consultative Council and the local authority associations[5] in reaching what may be decisions of consequence; the discontinuance of courses may in effect lead to the closure of the establishment where they are provided. Year by year the Secretary of State has given his general approval by circular[6] to the provision of courses on terms which may include obtaining the agreement of the regional advisory council concerned; and he may outline his general policy on applications to introduce new courses.

Although polytechnics and other establishments offering advanced **3–25** further education are no doubt to be considered primarily as teaching institutions, the law, while offering no formal encouragement, places no

---

[94] See, generally, *The Funding and Organisation of Courses in Higher Education* (Fifth Report from the Education, Science and Arts Committee, H.C. 1979–1980, 787–1) and Government Observations thereon (Cmnd. 8139 (1981)).

[95] See 1980 Act, s.27(6) and the Education (Schools and Further Education) Regulations 1981 (S.I. 1981 No. 1086) reg. 14(1) and Sched. 2. The courses correspond only in part with those designated under S.I. 1986 No. 1306 (see n. 58 above) but do so largely with those specified for "pooling" purposes in Sched. 2 to the Block Grant (Education Adjustments) (England) Regulations 1987 (S.I. 1987 No. 347). See above at para. 1–132.

[96] As to teacher training courses see below at paras. 4–07 to 4–09.

[97] In *D'Mello* v. *Loughborough College of Technology* (1970) 114 S.J. 665, it was held that the prospectus was part of the contract between students and college.

[98] By S.I. 1981 No. 1086, Sched. 2, para. 2(1)(f) "other courses" may be taken only by students of 18 and above who hold specified qualifications.

[99] See above at para. 3–02 n. 7.

[1] S.I. 1981 No. 1088, reg. 14(2).

[2] *Ibid*. reg. 15.

[3] See above at para. 3–02.

[4] *Ibid.*

[5] See above at para. 1–36.

[6] See *e.g.* Circ. 4/87.

bar on research[7] activities or on the undertaking of consultancy work; and indeed such activities are regarded as properly incidental to a thriving institution.[8] But public funds (and time paid for out of public funds) are not to be used for private gain, or to meet liabilities incurred by teachers otherwise than when engaged on activities within their terms of employment[9]; nor do teachers retain the copyright of literary, dramatic, musical or artistic works made in the course of employment (but students, unless apprenticed, appear to do so) unless there is an agreement to the contrary.[10]

3–26   To put consultancy work on a more secure[11] legal basis and otherwise to facilitate co-operation with the world of commerce and industry through sponsored or joint research projects, exploitation of inventions and testing of equipment and materials, the 1985 Act made specific provision in section 1[12] for the supply of goods and services through a further education establishment if they result from its educational activities (defined as teaching, industrial and vocational training and research), from the use of its facilities and the expertise of staff, and from ideas of students and staff arising from educational activities. Local education authorities are empowered by section 2 to enter into agreements for the supply of goods and/or services through the further education establishments they provide or assist,[13] and to lend money for the purposes of the agreement to a body corporate—a limited company— in which they (or those assisted) hold 20 per cent. or more of voting shares. The supply of goods and services is to be at open market value except where the supply arises in the normal course of educational activities[14] or is made to a specified public body.[15] A financial and accounting[16] framework is laid down by section 3[17] within which

---

[7] Circ. 94 commended research in technical colleges and began "the main function of technical colleges is the advancement and dissemination of knowledge, especially knowledge of value to industry and those engaged in industry."

[8] A.M. 14/78 (W.O. 4/78) offers advice about research and experiments on volunteers in non-medical institutions, and A.M. 3/79 about experiments in genetic manipulation as part of further education research.

[9] As to terms of employment see below at para. 4–98.

[10] See Copyright Act 1956, s.4.

[11] *i.e.* more secure than under s.111 of the Local Government Act 1972. See (Muir Wood) Report of Joint Working Group of the Advisory Council for Applied Research and Development and the Advisory Board for the Research Councils, *Improving links between Higher Education and Industry* H.M.S.O. 1983.

[12] See Circ. 6/85 (W.O. 52/85).

[13] "Assist"—see 1944 Act, s.114(2)(*b*).

[14] *e.g.* in training restaurants and hairdressing courses where the "product" arises incidentally out of the teaching.

[15] A Research Council under the Science and Technology Act 1965 (see below at para. 3–71 n. 11) or a body specified by an order made by statutory instrument.

[16] The accounts of companies established under the Act are subject to company law.

[17] As amended by Local Government Reorganisation (Miscellaneous Provision) (No. 4) Order 1986 (S.I. 1986 No. 452) art. 5(7).

commercial activities are to take place; in particular accounts are to be kept, separate from those required under section 23 of the Local Government Finance Act 1982, an annual surplus on revenue account is to be sought, and interest on loans is to be at a minimum rate determined by the Secretary of State with the consent of the Treasury.

NON-ADVANCED FURTHER EDUCATION

Into this residual category fall both non-vocational "adult" education **3–27** (to which separate reference is made below) and vocational education, often leading to nationally recognised qualifications, in colleges of further education and technical colleges among establishments variously named. Farm institutes (or schools of agriculture) perhaps deserve special mention. They provide a particular form of further education (courses in agriculture, horticulture, poultry-keeping, etc.) responsibility for which passed from the Ministry of Agriculture, Fisheries and Food to the Department of Education and Science and local education authorities in 1964.[18]

As already mentioned, vocational and industrial training are to be **3–28** regarded as part of further education,[19] but in recent years statutory responsibilities have been placed on bodies other than local education authorities that enable those bodies in part to settle the pattern of education and training courses that are provided in further education establishments.

Vocational and industrial training. The Manpower Services Commission

Industrial training boards[20] exist, as stated in section 1 of the Indus- **3–29** trial Training Act 1982, "for the purpose of making better provision for the training of persons over compulsory school age for employment in any activities of industry and commerce." They have no power to provide or pay for further education, but they may pay fees to its providers in respect of persons who receive further education in association with

---

[18] See Circ. 275 (and addenda).
[19] Industrial Training Act 1964, s.16. See above at para. 3–09. A.M. 11/76 (W.O. 6/76) and 12/78 (W.O. 6/77) (now partly anachronistic) advise local education authorities about the links between the training and further education services. A local education authority who wished to go beyond training and provide work for young unemployed persons would have to rely upon s.137 of the Local Government Act 1972 (see above at para. 1–39).
[20] By the Industrial Training Act 1982, s.1(3) and Sched. 1, boards consist of a chairman, representatives of both sides of industry and persons concerned with education. The Agriculture Board is similarly constituted under s.1(3) and Sched. 1 of the Agricultural Training Board Act 1982. Boards cover agriculture, civil air transport, clothing and allied poducts, construction, engineering, hotel and catering, petroleum, road transport and rubber and plastics processing.

training provided or approved by a board.[21] Thus industrial training boards pay for the training element in "integrated courses" provided in consultation with local education authorities at further education establishments.[22]

3-30   The Manpower Services Commission were established in 1974 under the Employment and Training Act 1973[23] as a non-departmental public body accountable to the Secretaries of State for Employment and for Wales. Their membership derives from both sides of industry, from local government and (one member) from organisations (other than local authorities) concerned with education, and their responsibilities include assisting persons to train for employment. "Training" includes any education with a view to employment. Co-operation between the Commission and local education authorities is facilitated nationally by consultative bodies representative of the Commission, the Department of Education and Science and Welsh Office and the local authority associations; and locally by the Commission's Area Manpower Boards[24] and the regional advisory councils for further education.

3-31   The growth of unemployment has stimulated the provision of courses of education and training by local education authorities at the request of the Commission or of employers supported by it. By section 45 of the Local Government (Miscellaneous Provisions) Act 1982 local authorities have power, and are deemed always to have had power, to enter into arrangements with the Commission. The Commission's schemes have included Unified Vocational Preparation[25] and the Youth Opportunities Programme,[26] but now, in particular, the Training Opportunities Scheme for unemployed persons[27] of 19 and over; the Youth Training Scheme, which provides a two year course of work experience and work-related training or further education for 16-year-old school leavers and some older persons; and, for 14 to 18-year-olds, the Technical and Vocational Education Initiative which links general and vocational education to work experience. The cost of courses provided by local education authorities and sponsored by the Commission is met by

---

[21] Industrial Training Act 1982, s.5(4)(c).

[22] The Committee on Industrial Training (representative of the Department of Education and Science, local authority associations, Confederation of British Industry, employees, Manpower Services Commission and industrial training boards) made national recommendations regarding the division of cost between industrial training boards and further education providers. They have not met for several years.

[23] See the Employment and Training Act 1973 as amended by the Employment and Training Act 1981.

[24] See Circ. 6/82.

[25] See Circ. 6/76.

[26] See Circ. 10/77.

[27] See A.Ms. 2/82 and 3/84 as to the effect upon entitlement to supplementary benefit of unemployed young people participating in part-time courses of further education. See M. Freeland, "Labour law and leaflet law: the Youth Training Scheme of 1983" (1983) 121 L.J. 220.

payment of fees[28] and, in certain circumstances, capital grants for provision of accommodation.[29]

An increasing proportion of vocational education and training is **3–32** being provided at the instance of the Manpower Services Commission, and the availability of government funds to local education authorities and the Commission respectively is being adjusted accordingly.[30]

Adult education

The term "adult education"[31] is usually taken to refer to non- **3–33** vocational education. The line between non-vocational and vocational is sometimes an arbitrary one, but one which so far as the law is concerned does not need to be drawn because, as has already been made clear, the statutory basis is in very general terms. The adult education provision of local education authorities tends to be in practical and creative subjects, and courses do not normally prepare students for examinations leading to recognised qualifications. They are generally followed in weekly classes held in establishments with names such as "evening institute" and "adult education centre" and are often housed in schools. Some local education authorities maintain residential colleges. The practical and administrative arrangements made by authorities for adult education provision are very diverse.

Certain bodies that provide courses of "liberal adult education"— **3–34** undefined but broadly corresponding to non-vocational education as described in the previous paragraph—may be eligible for grants[32] from the Secretary of State. The bodies comprise any body responsible for meeting expenses in respect of a university or university college and any national association (or district committee thereof) having as a principal object the promotion of liberal education for adults. Grant may be paid to meet all or part of relevant expenditure[33] incurred by a body on providing liberal adult education tuition for courses which are included in a programme approved by the Secretary of State. Grants include remuneration of teaching or organising staff only where posts are approved by the Secretary of State for the purposes of the programme. National associations may also receive grants for relevant expenditure

---

[28] See Employment and Training Act 1973, s.2(2)(d). Fees for schemes sponsored by employers with the financial support of the Commission may be payable direct by employers. Unless fees are recommended nationally by agreement between the local authority associations and the Confederation of Britsh Indusry local education authorities need to negotiate direct with employers.

[29] See Circ. 6/82, para. 8.

[30] See *Training for Jobs* (Cmnd. 9135) 1984.

[31] See (Russell) Report entitled *Adult Education: A Plan for Development*, H.M.S.O. 1973. The National Institute of Adult Continuing Education (supported by block grant—see above at para. 1–124) is concerned with the provision of adult education, and there is an Advisory Council for Adult and Continuing Education.

[32] See 1944 Act, s.100(1)(b) and the Education (Grant) Regulations 1983 (S.I. 1983 No. 74) regs. 4 and 18 (see also below at para. 6–19). Under reg. 23 grants are subject in each case to the Secretary of State's satisfying himself on the requirements he specifies, and regs. 24–30 specify general conditions of grant (as to which see below at para. 6–20).

[33] Defined in *ibid*. reg. 3 (see above at para. 3–19 n. 81).

on other educational services.[34] The Secretary of State may also pay grants to the Trades Union Congress or any independent trade union in respect of relevant expenditure on trade union studies and on training teachers in those studies.[35]

3–35   The main providers of liberal adult education, apart from local education authorities, are the extra-mural or "continuing education" departments of universities and the Workers Educational Association, but other national voluntary organisations may be concerned with local provision of adult education, for example, the National Federation of Women's Institutes and the National Federation of Community Associations.[36] All the providers of adult education are eligible for assistance from local education authorities in performing their function of "securing the provision"[37] of further education. Assistance may take the form of, for example, contributing towards administrative and organising costs, provision of accommodation for courses, and financial help in hiring premises.

YOUTH SERVICE

3–36   There is no fixed age-range for the youth service (to which indeed no express reference is made in statute) but in practice it looks to those aged between 11 and 21. It includes the provision by local education authorities of, and support of voluntary, youth clubs and centres; work with young people not based on such places; information, advice and counselling work; and social service by young people within the community.[38] Sometimes the service has been named by local education authorities "Youth and Community Service" to acknowledge this last-mentioned activity.[39] The operation of the youth service in any local education authority area generally reflects the opinions of a local advisory committee, who include teachers and the representatives of church and voluntary organisations. Assistance by local education authorities to voluntary bodies includes making available premises, playing fields, etc., paying grants in aid of capital or current expenditure, and guidance given by youth service staff.

---

[34] Education (Grant) Regulations 1983 (S.I. 1983 No.74) reg. 19.

[35] *Ibid.* reg. 22. "Independent trade union" is defined in s.153(1) of the Employment Protection (Consolidation) Act 1978.

[36] See 126 J.P.N. 172 for a somewhat dated, but still illuminating, account of the part played by the W.E.A., and of the case for diversity of provision of liberal adult education.

[37] 1944 Act, s.41. See above at para. 3–03.

[38] The youth service may also be linked with the Manpower Services Commission Youth Training Scheme (see Circ. 6/82, para. 17).

[39] See Youth Service Development Council, *Youth and Community Work in the 1970s* (1969) Department of Education and Science. See also the report of the (Albermarle) Committee, *The Youth Service in England and Wales* (Cmnd. 929) 1960.

The authority for youth service expenditure and activities by local **3–37**
education authorities is regarded as being contained in section 41[40] of
the 1944 Act (though the section applies only to persons over compulsory school age[41]) and section 53,[42] which places a duty on local education authorities to secure that further education facilities include
adequate facilities for recreation and social and physical training.[43] Formal departmental advice has related mainly[44] to the training of youth
leaders and community centre wardens,[45] the involvement of immigrants[46] in the service and the arrangements under which the Secretary
of State formerly paid capital grants[47] for youth service projects.

Youth workers and others whose work brings them regularly into con- **3–38**
tact with those under 19 are subject to Part II of the Education
(Teachers) Regulations 1982.[48] The Secretary of State recognises as
having qualified status[49] as youth workers those who have successfully
completed one of a variety of training courses, mostly of two years'
duration, and all who satisfy his requirements for the status of qualified
teacher.[50] The Joint Negotiating Committee for Youth Leaders and
Community Centre Wardens consider the suitability of qualifications for
recognition as conferring qualified status, and make recommendations
to the Secretary of State. The Joint Negotiating Committee also negotiate[51] salary scales and conditions of service for those youth workers
who are employed by local education authorities, and like other negotiating bodies within the local government service comprise an
employers' and a staff panel and work within the framework of the
Local Authorities' Conditions of Service Advisory Board.[52]

---

[40] See above at para. 3–03.
[41] Further education provision for those under compulsory school age (see above at para. 1–81)
seems to be *ultra vires* unless incidental to the provision for those over compulsory school age.
[42] See below at para. 5–27.
[43] This legal basis seemed inadquate in the opinion of the (Thompson) Review Group on the Youth
Service in England in 1982. See Chapter 11 of their Report *Experience and Participation* (Cmnd.
8686) 1982. But the Secretary of State rejected this view (see 63 H.C. Deb. 1035, July 11, 1984).
[44] But see Circ. 1/85 arising out of the Thompson Report (see n. 43 above).
[45] See Circ. 13/78 and National Youth Bureau, "Realities of Training 1978—Review of the Training
of Part-Time Workers in the Youth and Community Service" carried out for the (widely representative) Consultative Group on Youth and Community Work Training.
[46] See Circ. 8/67.
[47] The grants have mostly been discontinued. See above at para. 3–21 n. 89, and Thompson Report
para. 10.21.
[48] S.I. 1982 No. 106, regs. 6–11. See below at paras. 4–21 to 4–25.
[49] Qualifications, for the purposes of "pooling" expenditure by local education authorities on training youth and community centre wardens, are listed in Sched. 1 to the Block Grant (Educational
Adjustment) (England) Regulations 1987 (S.I. 1987 No. 347) and the Wales Regulations (S.I.
1987 No. 359) (see above at para. 1–132). See also Thompson Report (see note 43 above) paras.
9.22 *et seq*. The Council for Education and Training in Youth and Community Work was established in 1982 and undertakes the professional endorsement of initial and further training courses.
[50] See below at paras. 4–12 to 4–15.
[51] As to the effect of J.N.C. agreements see below at para. 4–99 n. 20.
[52] See K.P. Poole, *The Local Government Service in England and Wales* (1978) Chap. 4.

3–39   The Secretary of State may pay grants[53] to any body (other than a local education authority) responsible for meeting expenses in respect of a university or university college, and to any national youth organisation,[54] in respect of relevant expenditure[55] on courses for training youth leaders and community centre wardens.

3–40   Grants may be made in aid of youth service projects under the urban social needs programme[56] and by the Sports Council, a publicly funded non-departmental body sponsored by the Department of the Environment.

<h3 style="text-align:center">AWARDS AND GRANTS</h3>

3–41   Arrangements for financial assistance to students in further education (under review[57]) stem from the report[58] of the (Anderson) Committee, *Grants to Students*, and are authorised by the opening sections of the 1962 Act.[59] Section 1 provides that local education authorities shall make (mandatory) awards to appropriately qualified persons following higher education (including teacher training) courses, section 2 that they may make (discretionary) awards to persons over compulsory school age in respect of other further education courses, and section 3[60] that the Secretary of State shall have complementary powers to make grants and awards in specified circumstances outside the competence of local education authorities. The making of mandatory awards[61] and the exercise of the Secretary of State's powers are governed by regulations. Awards and grants in the three categories are considered in the following three subsections of this section; in the fourth subsection reference is made to awards from other sources; and the final subsection is concerned with residence qualifications.

3–42   Member states of the Council of Europe have agreed that awards and grants made by the appropriate authority in one state should continue to be available in another state for courses of study or research approved by the authority.[62]

---

[53] See the Education (Grant) Regulations 1983 (S.I. 1983 No. 74) reg. 21, and see also reg. 23 and Pt. V of the Regulations (see below at para. 6–20) regarding conditions as to payment of grant.

[54] *e.g.* The Young Men's Christian Association and the National Association of Youth Clubs.

[55] See above at para. 3–19 n. 81.

[56] See above at para. 1–128.

[57] Announced by the Secretary of State on June 8, 1986. See 99 H.C. Deb., 1046–55; also First Report from the Education, Science and Arts Committee, *Student Awards*, H.C. 28 1986–7.

[58] Cmnd. 1051 (1960).

[59] As substituted by s.19 of and Sched. 5 to the 1980 Act, and amended by s.4 of the 1984 Act. Circular 11/75 contains a commentary on the duties and powers of local education authorites as at October 1975, some of which is still a useful aid to construction of the current law.

[60] Amended by 1986 (No. 2) Act, Sched. 6.

[61] See 1962 Act, s.4(1); and above at para. 1–125 as regards recovery of 90 per cent. of the cost of making mandatory awards from the Secretary of State. The Education (Mandatory Awards) Regulations 1986 (S.I. 1986 No. 1306) as amended by Amendment Regulations 1986 (S.I. 1986 No. 1397) are current at the time of writing.

[62] See European Agreement on Continued Payments of Scholarships to Students Studying Abroad (Treaty Series no. 51 (1972) Cmnd. 4966).

Mandatory awards

Mandatory awards are bestowed on persons who are ordinarily resi- **3–43**
dent[63] in the area of a local education authority and attend courses[64]
which are provided by a United Kingdom university,[65] college or other
institution (including those provided, in conjunction, in an institution in
another country) and are designated by regulation as being full-time
first degree and comparable[66] courses, full-time courses for the diploma
of higher education, courses for initial training of teachers and full-time
courses for the Higher National Diploma or for the H.N.D. of the Business and Technical Educational Council.[67] The regulation is as follows:

10.—(1) The following are prescribed as designated courses—
(*a*) a first degree course, that is to say—
    (i) a course provided by an establishment for a first degree of a univer-
    sity or for the degree of Bachelor of Medicine or an equivalent
    degree;
    (ii) a course provided by an establishment of further education for a first
    degree of the Council for National Academic Awards;
    (iii) a course provided either by the Cranfield Institute of Technology or
    by the Information Technology Institute for a first degree of the
    former;
(*b*) a Dip HE course, that is to say—
    (i) a course provided by an establishment for the Diploma of Higher
    Education;
    (ii) a course provided by an establishment for the Diploma of Higher
    Education or a first degree as the student may elect after the com-
    mencement of the course;
(*c*) a course provided by an establishment of further education for the Higher
    National Diploma, or the Higher National Diploma of the Business &
    Technical Education Council;
(*d*) a course of initial training for teachers, that is to say—
    (i) a course for the initial training of teachers (other than a course for
    the degree of Bachelor of Education) provided by an establishment;
    (ii) a part-time day course of teacher training, involving not less than 3
    days' attendance a week during the course, for the time being pre-
    scribed for the purposes of this provision by the Secretary of State;
    (iii) any other course of teacher training, whether part-time or partly full-
    time and partly part-time, for the time being so prescribed;
(*e*) a course comparable to a first degree course, that is to say—

---

[63] For definition see 1962 Act, s.1(8) and Sched. 1, reg 8 of the Education (Mandatory Awards) Regulations 1986 (S.I. 1986 No. 1306), and below at para. 3–73 to 3–74. See 1962 Act, s.1(6) as to the power of a local education authority to waive this requirement and make an award at their discretion (as to which see *R.* v. *Lancashire County Council, ex p. Huddleston* [1986] 2 All E.R. 941).
[64] 1962 Act, s.1(1) to (3) and (6), and S.I. 1986 No. 1306, reg. 7.
[65] See definition in S.I. 1986 No. 1306, reg. 2.
[66] In *R.* v. *Leeds City Council, ex p. Datta, The Times*, November 25, 1982, it was held that a two year L.L.B. course at Leeds University limited to graduates of that university, or of some other university accepted by the senate, was not a first degree course. By 1962 Act, s.1(4) regulations may prescribe the qualifications a person is to hold before becoming entitled to a mandatory award for a "comparable" course.
[67] See above at para. 3–02 n. 7.

> (i) a course of at least 3 academic years' duration provided by a university for a certificate, diploma or other academic award;
>
> (ii) a course for the time being prescribed for the purposes of this provision by the Secretary of State;
>
> (f) an international course, that is to say a course provided by an establishment in the United Kingdom in conjunction with a university, college or other institution in another country for a first degree of a university or a course so provided comparable to a first degree course being, in either case, a course prescribed for the purposes of this provision by he Secretary of State.   ·
>
> (2) In this Regulation references to an establishment and an establishment of further education do not include references to establishments of further education which are neither maintained nor assisted by recurrent grants out of public funds.

Regulations prescribe[68] the conditions under which awards are bestowed, the exceptions to the duty to bestow, what payments are to be made and the circumstances of payment, and power to suspend or terminate awards.

3-44   In practice, regulations have been revised and reissued annually, and sometimes more frequently, if only—but not only—to revise the amounts[69] payable in respect of fees and maintenance. They are as elaborate as might be expected having regard to the extent of public expenditure that they authorise. For practical purposes it is especially necessary to have regard to their detail. Parts I and II of the regulations are mainly concerned with interpretation, conditions, exceptions, transfer and termination of awards, miscellaneous procedural matters, and designation of the courses in respect of which the duty to bestow an award arises. Some of these topics need further brief mention, after which there follows an account of the main substantive content of the regulations—Part III, payments.

3-45   Provision[70] is made for ascertaining which local education authority are responsible for bestowing awards on persons who have been ordinarily resident in more than one authority's area, and on European Community[71] nationals and children of European Community nationals who meet specified conditions and who would otherwise[72] be excluded because not ordinarily resident in the area of any authority. Procedures regarding application for an award are laid down.[73] It must be in writing and ordinarily[74] reach the authority before the end of the first term of

---

[68] 1962 Act, s.1(5) and (7).

[69] Because of the annual revisions no sums are stated in the following account of the regulations.

[70] 1962 Act, Sched. 1, paras. 3 and 4 and S.I. 1986 No. 1306, regs. 8 and 9.

[71] Defined in S.I. 1986 No. 1306, reg. 2.

[72] S.I. 1986 No. 1306, reg. 9 brings the law into consistency with the decision in *MacMahon* v. *Department of Education and Science* [1982] 3 W.L.R. 1129 (see above at para. 1–115). See *R.* v. *Inner London Education Authority, ex p. Hinde* (1984) 83 L.G.R. 695, concerning successful applications by E.C. nationals for awards for courses at vocational schools under Art. 7 of Council Regulation (EEC) No. 1612/68. See also reg. 5(4) and below at para. 3–73.

[73] S.I. 1986 No. 1306, reg. 11.

[74] Exceptional circumstances are specified in reg. 11(2), and see *R.* v. *West Glamorgan County Council, ex p. Gheissary, The Times*, December 18, 1985.

the course; and an undertaking must be given to repay overpayments. The obligation to bestow an award does not ordinarily arise when the prospective applicant has already attended a specified course,[75] or he falls within one of three specified categories[76]: two of these relate to residence,[77] the third to conduct. In certain circumstances, and subject to conditions, an award may be transferred so as to be held for a course other than for that for which it was first held.[78] Awards ordinarily terminate at the end of the normal course period, but there are provisions for extension, and for termination if the course has been abandoned, the academic authorities do not permit completion, or the student[79] has "shown himself by his conduct to be unfitted to hold the award."[80]

The bestowal[81] of an award obliges the authority to pay specified **3–46** annual fees[82] in respect of the student. The fees include admission, tuition and graduation fees, college fees or dues at specified universities, and fees charged by an external body for examinations, course validation or otherwise to meet its proper requirements. As will appear there are some exceptions[83] to this obligation and also to the second obligation—to pay annual maintenance grants[84] (part of which are to be treated as being in respect of the Easter and Christmas vacations[85]). The maintenance grant is to be the amount by which the student's resources[86] (as assessed by the authority[87]) fall short of his requirements.[88] The requirements consist (so far as applicable in the particular case) of ordinary maintenance, supplementary maintenance, maintenance of dependants, and additional sums in the case of students who are 26 or older before their course starts.

---

[75] S.I. 1986 No. 1306, reg. 12.
[76] *Ibid.* reg. 13.
[77] See below at para. 3–73.
[78] S.I. 1986 No. 1306, reg. 14.
[79] Defined in *ibid.* reg. 2.
[80] *Ibid.* reg. 15, and see also reg. 16.
[81] As to method of payment, see *ibid.* reg. 25, and below at para. 3–64.
[82] *Ibid.* reg. 17 and Sched. 1.
[83] See *ibid.* regs. 16, 23, 26 and 27 and in relation to maintenance grants regs. 20, 21, 22 and 24; and also below.
[84] See *ibid.* regs. 17 and 18. In certain circumstances students may also be entitled to social security benefits under the relevant legislation. See in particular the Supplementary Benefit (Conditions of Entitlement) Regulations 1981 (S.I. 1981 No. 1526), which as amended by Amendment Regulations 1986 (S.I. 1986 No. 1010) define and redefine respectively "course of advanced education" and "student."
[85] But see S.I. 1986 No. 1306, Sched. 2, para. 14 as regards supplementary vacation payments. A student may be able to claim supplementary benefit under the Supplementary Benefits Act 1976 as amended (to be superseded by income support under s.20 of the Social Security Act 1986 when brought into force). See *R.* v. *Barnsley Supplementary Benefits Tribunal, ex p. Atkinson* [1977] 1 W.L.R. 917, C.A. and D. Lasok, "Student Grants and Supplementary Benefit" 126 New L.J. 647, for discussion of the decision of the Divisional Court in that case and generally.
[86] "Resources"—see S.I. 1986 No. 1306, Sched. 3 and below at paras. 3–51 *et seq.*
[87] See *ibid.* reg. 19 (which, to enable the authority to make the calculation, requires the student to provide information on the resources of any person whose means are relevant).
[88] "Requirements"—see *ibid.* Sched. 2.

3–47   The amount of ordinary maintenance[89] differs broadly according as the student does or does not reside at his parents' home,[90] and is lower in the former case. In the latter case the amount exceeds that specified as the norm if the student: (a) is at London University or attending an establishment within the Metropolitan Police District,[91] or (b) attends a course at an extra-United Kingdom institution for at least one term.

3–48   Supplementary maintenance[92] (of specified amounts which may vary according to circumstances) is payable where a student:

(a) attends his course for a longer period than the usual period in any academic year,[93] or for not less than 45 weeks in any continuous period of 52 weeks[94];

(b) (except in the circumstances immediately last-mentioned) is at a further education establishment[95] which is not maintained wholly out of public funds and undertakes authorised vacation study[96] or attends a period of term-time residential study[97] away from the establishment but normally within the United Kingdom;

(c) incurs travelling expenses in connection with his studies[98] (in closely prescribed circumstances) and/or each term in getting to and from his home[99] which is outside the United Kingdom;

(d) insures[1] against the cost of medical treatment outside the United Kingdom;

(e) has to purchase special equipment[2] for specified courses, for example in architecture and medicine;

(f) suffers in the opinion of the authority undue hardship[3] during the vacation; or

(g) being disabled,[4] is obliged, to the satisfaction of the authority, to incur additional expenditure to attend his course.

3–49   Only an independent student[5] may claim for maintenance of dependants[6]—dependent child,[7] spouse or adult dependant. The provisions are

---

[89] See S.I. 1986 No.1306, Sched. 2, Pt. 1.

[90] See *ibid*. Sched. 2, Pt. 5, para. 23.

[91] Roughly the area of Greater London, and see below at para. 5–25 n. 88.

[92] See S.I. 1986 No. 1306, Sched. 2, Pt. 2.

[93] See *ibid*. Sched. 2, para. 6, and see definition of "year" in reg. 2.

[94] *Ibid*. Sched. 2, para. 7.

[95] See definition in *ibid*. reg. 2. Also included is the Royal Naval Engineering College, Manadon.

[96] *Ibid*. Sched. 2, para. 8.

[97] *Ibid*. para. 9.

[98] *Ibid*. para. 10.

[99] *Ibid*. para. 11.

[1] *Ibid*. para. 12.

[2] *Ibid*. para. 13 (applies only to courses which began before September 1, 1986).

[3] *Ibid*. para. 14, and see n. 85 above.

[4] *Ibid*. para. 15.

[5] Defined in *ibid*. reg. 3.

[6] See *ibid*. Sched. 2, Pt. 3, and definitions in para. 17(1).

[7] The marriage which allows a student to make a claim for grants for child dependants must be a marriage which is relevant to the claim, and the child dependants must be children of the marriage *R*. v. *Kent County Council, ex p. Ahmed, The Times*, October 22, 1981.

so elaborate as to defy more than bare summary: the sums payable to the student as his requirements differ according to his circumstances and those of his dependant(s)[8]; and persons who would prima facie fall into the dependant category are excluded in specified circumstances.[9] A student, whose wife, husband or child is excluded (because the student is not independent, or for other reason) may, nevertheless be able to take advantage of section 3 of the 1973 Act, which enables the Secretary of State by regulation, for the avoidance of hardship, to make allowances which supplement local education authority payments up to the level at which they would have been made had the wife, husband or child[10] not been excluded. Regulations[11] define eligible dependants,[12] the circumstances in which no allowance is payable to a student,[13] and the amount of the allowance.[14] The income of the student's family[15] and the capital resources[16] of the student's household are taken into account.

Extra payments are made to meet the requirements of older students[17] (aged 26 or more) who have been in full-time employment for three out of the six years before the first year of the course to which their award relates or who have earned specified sums over the preceding three years, and to certain older students who have attended a previous course for which they have held[18] an award or a teacher training grant and have met the full-time employment requirement. **3–50**

The resources of a student in any year of his course are the aggregate of his income for that year and any contribution by parent[19] or spouse applicable in his case—but not necessarily paid. Payment is not enforceable and the contribution is essentially a notional sum used for the purposes of calculating the amount of grant. Similarly there is no power to require parents or spouse to submit a statement of their income, but if they fail to do so the student's maintenance payments are at risk.[20] **3–51**

In calculating a student's income[21] all sources are taken into account but the total is reduced by income tax and social security contributions, **3–52**

---

[8] S.I. 1986 No. 1306, Sched. 2, Pt. 3, paras. 18–20.

[9] *Ibid.* para. 17(2), (3) and (4).

[10] By s.3(5) "child" includes a step-child or illegitimate child.

[11] See the Education (Students' Dependants Allowances) Regulations 1983 (S.I. 1983 No. 1185) as amended by Amendment Regulations (S.I.s 1984 No. 1179 and 1985 No. 1160 and 1986 No. 1325). Note (reg. 2) that the definitions of *e.g.* "child" and "spouse" for the purposes of these Regulations are not identical with the definitions in Pt. 3 of Sched. 2 to S.I. 1986 No. 1306.

[12] S.I. 1983 No. 1185, reg. 4.

[13] *Ibid.* reg. 5.

[14] *Ibid.* reg. 6 as amended by S.I. 1986 No. 1325.

[15] S.I. 1983 No. 1185, reg. 7 as amended by S.I.s 1984 No. 1179, 1985 No. 1160 and 1986 No. 1325.

[16] S.I. 1983 No. 1185, reg. 6(5).

[17] S.I. 1986 No. 1306, Sched. 2, Pt. 4, paras. 21 and 22.

[18] Under 1962 Act, s.2(3) as first enacted.

[19] "Parent" ordinarily includes the parent of an adopted or stepchild. See S.I. 1986 No. 1306, Sched. 3, Pt. 2, para. 2.

[20] By the combined effect of regs. 19 and 27 of S.I. 1986 No. 1306.

[21] See *ibid.* Sched. 3, Pt. 1, para. 1, as amended by Amendment Regulations 1986 (S.I. 1986 No. 1397). As to the method of reduction see S.I. 1986 No. 1306, reg. 5(2).

and a variety of resources are disregarded. The "disregards" include the first £n of scholarship or employer's payments, social security benefits of various kinds, remuneration for vacation work, payments under covenant by a parent and the first £n from sources not specified. The general rules of calculation are varied in the case of students particularly specified.[22]

3–53　　Parental contributions[23] are not applicable in respect of all categories of student. The exceptions[24] include independent students,[25] students whose parents are beyond reach, and certain students who have been in the care of a local authority or voluntary organisation. Where parental contributions are applicable the amount,[26] which is subject to a maximum, otherwise varies according to the residual income[27] of the parent and is reduced by £n in respect of each other child[28] of the parent who is wholly or mainly dependent on him, and by a larger sum if the child holds a statutory award.[29]

3–54　　Residual income is what remains after prescribed deductions[30] from gross income have been made. The deductions fall into seven categories and include mortgage interest and, up to a prescribed limit, the cost of domestic assistance when a parent is incapacitated. Gross income[31] ordinarily means the income of the student's parent in the financial year preceding that in respect of which the student's resources are assessed, but there are departures from this general rule—for instance when income in the current financial year is likely to be not more than 85 per cent. of income in the preceding financial year, where one of the student's parents has died after a parental contribution has been assessed, and where parents do not ordinarily live together; and there are rules for determining what is to count as income. Personal tax relief[32] and deductions from income for income tax[33] purposes are ignored for the purpose of determining[34] gross income.

3–55　　The amount[35] of parental contribution may be reduced by the authority as they think just (after consultation with any other authority concerned) where a statutory award is held by more than one child[36] of a parent, by the parent himself or by the student's step-parent. Where a

---

[22] See S.I. 1986 No. 1306, Sched. 3, Pt. 1, para. 1(2) and (3).
[23] See *ibid*. Sched. 3, Pt. 2.
[24] See *ibid*. Sched. 3, Pt. 2, para. 3.
[25] As defined in *ibid*. reg. 3 and see above at para. 3–49.
[26] See *ibid*. Sched. 3, Pt. 2, para 4.
[27] Defined in *ibid*. Sched. 3, Pt. 2, para. 2.
[28] Defined in *ibid*. Sched. 3, Pt. 2, para. 2.
[29] Defined in *ibid*. reg. 2.
[30] See *ibid*. Sched. 3, Pt. 2, para. 6(2) and (3).
[31] *Ibid*. Sched. 3, Pt. 2, para. 5; and see para. 2(2) and (3).
[32] Under Chap. 2 of Pt. 1 of the Income and Corporation Taxes Act 1970 (as amended).
[33] Under Acts passed after the Finance Act of the preceding year (1985 in S.I. 1986 No. 1306).
[34] See S.I. 1986 No. 1306, Sched. 3, Pt. 2, para. 6(1).
[35] *Ibid*. para. 4(2).
[36] As defined in *ibid*. para. 2, to include an adopted child and a step-child.

contribution is ascertained in respect of more than one child the aggregate amount of contribution in respect of each child is not to exceed the amount that would be applicable if only one child held an award.

Spouses' contributions[37] are applicable when a student and his/her **3–56** spouse are living together, except in the case of a student in whose case a parental contribution is applicable or whose child holds an award in respect of which a parental contribution is applicable.[38] In general, calculation of spouse's contributions follows that of parental contribution, and the amount[39] varies according to the residual income and is reduced by £n in respect of each child of a student who is dependent on him or his spouse. Provision is made for cases in which the student marries, or his marriage ends,[40] in any year.

Special provisions apply to students who are widows, widowers, **3–57** divorced or separated.[41] Any such student who has dependants[42] enjoys a more generous "disregard" than does an "ordinary" student, and has enhanced requirements[43] which, if applicable, include those of older students.[44]

Maintenance payments are made to sandwich course students[45] during a year which included periods of full-time study as well as periods of **3–58** industrial, professional or commercial experience outside the establishment where the full-time study takes place. Various specified kinds of unpaid work do not count as periods of experience.[46] Payments are calculated by modifying, as prescribed,[47] the calculation of the requirements and resources of full-time students, except in the case of students who are members of religious orders[48] and following the courses mentioned in the next following paragraph.

Maintenance payments to students who are members of religious **3–59** orders (except on courses under (b) in the next paragraph) are specially prescribed[49] and differ according as the student lives at home or, as respects other students, to where he is studying. Such students on sandwich courses, and on part-time day teacher training courses prescribed[50]

---

[37] S.I. 1986 No. 1306, Sched. 3, Pt. 3.

[38] *Ibid.* para. 7.

[39] *Ibid.* para. 8.

[40] Termination of marriage may come about simply "by virtue of the parties . . . ceasing ordinarily to live together (*ibid.* reg. 5(3)).

[41] *Ibid.* Sched. 4. These provisions do not apply to lone parents, who have never married. They are thus in breach of European Council Directive 76/207 (see above at para. 1–117) (*R.* v. *Secretary of State for Education and Science, ex p. Schaffter, The Times*, August 18, 1986).

[42] As defined in S.I. 1986 No. 1306, Sched. 2, Pt. 3, para. 17 and to whom para. 18 applies (see above at para. 3–49).

[43] *Ibid.* Sched. 4, paras. 2 and 3.

[44] See *ibid.* Sched. 2, Pt. 4, para. 21, and above at para. 3–50.

[45] See *ibid.* reg. 20 and Sched. 5, para. 1.

[46] Defined in *ibid.* Sched. 5, para. 1.

[47] See *ibid.* Sched. 5, paras. 2 and 3.

[48] See *ibid.* reg. 20(1).

[49] In *ibid.* reg. 21.

[50] Under *ibid.* reg. 10(1)(*d*)(ii).

by the Secretary of State and involving not less than three days attendance a week, receive reduced payments; and those taking courses[51] in, for example, architecture or medicine receive a supplementary payment of up to a specified amount for purchasing special equipment.

3–60 Special provisions for maintenance payments[52] apply to students on certain teacher training courses (except students who are members of a religious order following courses falling under (a) below and to whom the previous paragraph applies). The courses are:

(a) the part-time day courses mentioned in the previous paragraph;

(b) other part-time (or partly full-time and partly part-time) courses prescribed[53] by the Secretary of State, except initial training— non B.Ed.-courses.

The maintenance payments for students on courses under (a) are three-quarters of full maintenance grant[54]; and on courses under (b) the amount differs according to the nature of the course and the circumstances of the student.[55]

3–61 No payments in respect of fees or towards maintenance[56] are to be made to students classed as "assisted."[57] Assisted students are those who receive in aggregate, from scholarships, etc. (other than under section 1 of the 1962 Act) and from remuneration[58] (net of income tax and social security contributions) during leave of absence from employment, not less than the aggregate of fees[59] and maintenance requirements.[60]

3–62 A student who is provided with free board and lodging[61] by the academic authority,[62] in accordance with arrangements under which charges are raised only against students whose resources exceed their requirements,[63] receives a maintenance grant[64] calculated[65] so as to take account of the benefit received.

3–63 Discretionary payments[66] may be paid to students who repeat part of their courses and to certain other students who have previously attended

---

[51] Specified in S.I. 1986 No. 1306, Sched. 2, Pt. 2, para. 13 (applies only to courses which began before September 1, 1986).

[52] *Ibid*. reg. 22.

[53] Under *ibid*. reg. 10(1)(*d*)(iii).

[54] *Ibid*. reg. 22(2).

[55] *Ibid*. reg. 22(3) to (6).

[56] Under *ibid*. reg. 17(*a*) or (*b*).

[57] *Ibid*. reg. 23.

[58] Excluding payments received by a student on a course described under (b) in the previous paragraph.

[59] Payable under S.I. 1986 No. 1306, Sched. 1.

[60] Ascertained in accordance with Pts. 1, 3, 4 and paras. 6 and 7 of Pt. 2 of *ibid*. Sched. 2.

[61] *Ibid*. reg. 24. (Where reg. 21 applies, see above at para. 3–59, reg. 24 does not.)

[62] Defined in *ibid*. reg. 2.

[63] Ascertained under *ibid*. reg. 18. See above at para. 3–46.

[64] Under *ibid*. reg. 17(b).

[65] Under *ibid*. reg. 18 and Sched. 2, Pt. 1, para. 4.

[66] *Ibid*. reg. 26.

specified advanced further education courses[67]; and there is provision for withholding and reducing payments[68] where students withhold information,[69] are absent from their courses (other than for up to 28 days on account of illness) or for other specified reasons.

As to the method[70] of payment, fees may be paid by the authority **3–64** direct to the academic authority, but all other payments must be made to the student. Payments may be in instalments at times the authority consider appropriate, and provisional payments may be made pending final calculation of an award. When provisional payments or payments in advance are made any subsequent overpayments may be deducted from subsequent payments due, or over- or under-payment may be adjusted by payment between student or academic authority and the authority. There is no other provision under which an authority may seek a refund.[71]

Discretionary awards[72]

A local education authority may[73] bestow awards on persons over **3–65** compulsory school age (including those undergoing teacher training) in respect of attendance at courses[74] of full-time or part-time education (in Great Britain or elsewhere) other than

(a) primary or secondary education courses;
(b) courses for which mandatory awards may be bestowed; and
(c) designated[75] postgraduate[76] or comparable courses (except a course taken by a teacher as training) provided by a university, college or other institution.

The local education authority may "make such payments as are payable in pursuance of such awards" a form of words which appears to confer a wide discretion.[77] "Training" in relation to teacher training includes further training whether the person undergoing the further training is already qualified as a teacher or not.[78]

---

[67] "Advanced further education course" by reg. 4(4) refers to a course listed in the Education (Schools and Further Education) Regulations 1981 (S.I. 1981 No. 1086) Sched. 2, para. 2 (and see above at para. 3–23 n. 95).

[68] S.I. 1986 No. 1306, reg. 27.

[69] When information is required under *ibid*. reg. 19.

[70] *Ibid*. reg. 25 and see also reg. 11(1)(*b*).

[71] An action such as *London County Council* v. *Mead* (1954) 118 J.P. 514 (recovery of part of a grant) could therefore not now be brought.

[72] See J.E. Alder, "Fettering a Discretion. Local Education Authorities and Students' Grants" 141 L.G.Rev. 525.

[73] 1962 Act, s.2, and see below at para. 3–75.

[74] As to responsibility for support of students in professions supplementary to medicine see A.M. 10/76.

[75] There are no regulations subsisting under s.2 to designate such courses.

[76] As to postgraduate awards generally see Circ. 11/70 (which has, however, been partly overtaken by statutory and other changes).

[77] See Circ. 11/75, paras. 113–4.

[78] 1962 Act, s.4(5) as amended by the 1986 (No. 2) Act, Sched. 4, para. 3 and Sched. 6.

3–66 Local education authorities may[79] also make allowances to students pursuing further education correspondence courses but only to relieve hardship and where the authority are satisfied that the course is suitable for the pupil.

Grants and awards by the Secretary of State

3–67 The Secretary of State is authorised by regulation to pay grants or bestow awards in three sets of circumstances. First, he may pay grants[80] to local education authorities and others to facilitate and encourage the training of teachers, youth and community workers,[81] education welfare officers, educational psychologists, local education authority inspectors and education advisers, and other categories he prescribes. "Training" includes further training, whether or not the person undergoing it is already qualified, the provision of experience relevant to the employment engaged in, training for employment in a different capacity in education, and the study of matters connected with, or relevant to, education.

(1) One set of regulations[82] authorises the Secretary of State to make grants to local education authorities in respect of expenditure incurred in connection with the training of the teachers and others mentioned above.

(2) Another set[83] authorises him to make grants (known as training awards) to persons undergoing initial or further training as teachers. Training awards are tenable only for full-time courses lasting up to two academic years which are provided by an establishment in England and Wales named by the Secretary of State, and which are designed to prepare persons to teach craft, design and technology in secondary schools.[84] Awards are made only to persons who satisfy conditions[85] relating to:

(a) age (between 26 to 49 inclusive);
(b) attendance at previous courses;
(c) the nature of their initial training (if any, not to have been in the subjects mentioned);
(d) acceptance by the training establishment; and
(e) suitability and intention to teach in a maintained secondary or middle school.

When considering whether to make an award the Secretary of State has

---

[79] See the Scholarships and Other Benefits Regulations 1977 (S.I. 1977 No. 1443) regs. 4(*e*)(ii) and 6 made under 1944 Act, s.81(1).

[80] 1986 (No. 2) Act, s.50.

[81] Defined in the Education (Training Grants) Regulations 1987 (S.I. 1987 No. 96) reg. 3.

[82] See S.I. 1987 No. 96 and above at para. 1–126.

[83] The Education (Teacher Training Awards) Regulations 1983 (S.I. 1983 No. 481) as amended by Amendment Regulations 1986 (S.I. 1986 No. 1346) (sums have been revised annually). See A.M.s 3/83, 1/84 and 1/85 (W.O. 1/83, 1/84 and 1/85).

[84] S.I. 1983 No. 481, *ibid.* reg. 5, and see definition in reg. 2.

[85] *Ibid.* reg. 4 and Sched. 1.

to take account of other financial support available for the period of training.[86] Awards are for the ordinary duration of the course but may be extended or terminated in specified circumstances.[87] They cover fees, maintenance expenditure, lodging and travelling expenditure and when appropriate payments in respect of dependent relatives.[88]

(3) A third set of regulations[89] authorises the Secretary of State to pay training bursaries of a fixed sum in similar circumstances, but without age-limit and extending additionally to mathematics and physics. Persons who have previously completed a course of initial teacher training are not eligible.

(4) A fourth set[90] empowered the Secretary of State to make grants (known as scholarships) for certain postgraduate Certificate of Education courses beginning between September 1, 1982 and August 31, 1984.

Secondly the Secretary of State may bestow awards on persons **3–68** attending postgraduate or comparable courses[91] who satisfy him about their educational qualifications[92] and fitness in other respects, and who meet residence requirements.[93] The awards are state studentships and state bursaries.[94] Studentships[95] are tenable for full-time humanities courses leading to higher degrees[96] at universities and other institutions in England and Wales, other courses designated by the Secretary of State in the United Kingdom or abroad, and courses at the European University Institute.[97] Bursaries (but not studentships) are tenable for courses, mainly professional or vocational in character, designated by the Secretary of State.[98] The maximum period of a state studentship or bursary is ordinarily three years[99] but it may be suspended or cancelled

---

[86] S.I. 1983 No. 481, reg. 3.

[87] *Ibid.* reg. 6.

[88] *Ibid.* reg. 7 and Scheds. 2 and 3 as amended by S.I. 1986 No. 1346.

[89] The Education (Bursaries for Teacher Training) Regulations 1986 (S.I. 1986 No. 1324), as amended by the Amendment Regulations (S.I. 1987 No. 499), under which one part-time course is included.

[90] The Education (Teacher Training Scholarships) Regulations 1981 (S.I. 1981 No. 1328).

[91] 1962 Act, s.3(*b*), and see the State Awards Regulations 1978 (S.I. 1978 No. 1096) as amended by S.I.s 1983 No. 188 and No. 920.

[92] S.I. 1978 No. 1096, reg. 8.

[93] See *ibid.* Sched. 2 (added by S.I. 1983 No. 920). The requirements discriminate in favour of those ordinarily resident in the United Kingdom and Islands and certain European Community nationals (as defined in Sched. 2, para. 1, and see below at para. 3–73).

[94] *Ibid.* reg. 4(1)(*a*) and (*b*).

[95] There are major state studentships and one-year studentships. The awards are limited in number and are therefore competitive. The awards scheme is administered by the British Academy as agent for the Secretary of State (see British Academy, *Postgraduate Awards 2*). Awards for postgraduate courses in the social sciences and natural sciences are made by the Economic & Social Research Council and the Science and Engineering Research Council respectively (and see below at para. 3–71).

[96] The degrees of Doctor, Master, B.Litt and B.Phil.

[97] See S.I. 1978 No. 1096 (as amended) reg. 5 and definition in reg. 2.

[98] See *ibid.* reg. 6 and Department of Education and Science, *Postgraduate Awards 1*.

[99] See *ibid.* reg. 9, as amended by S.I. 1983 No. 188, reg. 3.

for unsatisfactory progress or conduct. Awards payments[1] are made by the Secretary of State as he thinks fit towards fees, maintenance (including maintenance of dependants) and travelling and other expenses, and he takes account of any income of the award holder, his dependants and, in the case of a state bursary, parental income.

3–69   Thirdly, the Secretary of State may bestow[2] awards on persons above a prescribed age in respect of courses at institutions receiving payments under section 100 of the 1944 Act[3] and which are designated under regulations as colleges providing long term residential courses of full-time education for adults. Regulations[4] provide that state bursaries for adult education may be bestowed on persons of 20 and over who meet the residence requirements specified[5] (and who are not ordinarily resident in Wales) for long term residential courses at eight specified institutions.[6] The duration of the awards and payments[7] are subject to the same regulations as apply in the case of state studentships and bursaries generally. Similar arrangements[8] are made for the bestowal of state bursaries on persons ordinarily resident in Wales.

3–70   Additionally[9] the Secretary of State may award, or by making payments enable other persons to award, industrial scholarships tenable for relevant full-time higher education courses including sandwich courses, at universities, colleges or other institutions in the United Kingdom (or in another country in conjunction with a United Kingdom institution). Industrial scholarships may be held as a supplement to mandatory awards, and, known as National Engineering Scholarships, are administered by the Department of Education and Science under a committee representative of government, industry, schools and higher education.

Awards for other sources

3–71   Awards (variously described) for education, training and research[10] are made by research councils,[11] the British Museum (Natural History), the Royal Society, a number of further education establishments[12] and

---

[1] See S.I. 1978 No. 1096, reg. 10 as amended by S.I. 1983 No. 188, reg. 4.

[2] 1962 Act, s.3(c).

[3] See above at paras. 3–34 and 3–35.

[4] S.I. 1978 No. 1096 (as amended) regs. 4 and 7.

[5] See ibid. Sched. 2 and n. 93 above.

[6] Cooperative College, Loughborough; Fircroft College, Birmingham, Hillcroft College, Surbiton; Northern College, Barnsley; Plater College, Oxford; Ruskin College, Oxford; Coleg Harlech, Wales; Newbattle Abbey, Dalkeith, Scotland.

[7] See S.I. 1978 No. 1096 (as amended) regs. 9 and 10 and para. 3–68, above.

[8] See State Awards (State Bursaries for Adult Education) (Wales) Regulations 1979 (S.I. 1979 No. 333 as amended by S.I.s 1983 No. 1274 and No. 1747).

[9] See 1980 Act, s.20 and Circ. 1/80, para. 21.

[10] See the Education (Fees and Awards) Regulations 1983 (S.I. 1983 No. 973) reg. 11.

[11] The Agricultural Research Council, Economic and Social Research Council, Medical Research Council, Natural Environment Research Council and Science and Engineering Research Council.

[12] Coleg Harlech, Gwynedd; Co-operative College, Loughborough; Fircroft College, Birmingham; Hillcroft College, Surbiton; Northern College, Barnsley; Plater College, Oxford; Royal College of Art, London; and Ruskin College, Oxford.

the National Film and Television School, Beaconsfield. Rules of eligibility,[13] may be adopted by those institutions which subject to prescribed extensions and restrictions, confine awards to candidates who have a relevant connection with the United Kingdom and Islands[14] or specified parts of the United Kingdom, or who are "excepted candidates"— European Community migrant workers or their children or refugees ordinarily resident in the United Kingdom who do not have a relevant connection but who meet specified requirements.[15] A relevant connection[16] means being ordinarily resident for three years preceding the date of application for the award otherwise than (during any part of that period) wholly or mainly for the purpose of receiving full-time education.

Similar rules of eligibility may be adopted by the Minister of Agriculture, Fisheries and Food in respect of the awards he makes (postgraduate agricultural studentships[17]), and candidates may be restricted to those British or Commonwealth citizens who have a relevant connection with England and Wales or are "excepted candidates" (as above). **3–72**

Residence qualifications

The obligation upon local education authorities to bestow mandatory awards does not (with an exception in favour of refugees[18]) extend to persons not ordinarily resident throughout the three years preceding the first year of the course in the British Islands or, in specified cases, the European Community; or to persons who although so resident were, for any part of the three years, resident wholly or mainly for the purposes of receiving full-time education.[19] "Ordinary residence" means belonging to the area of the authority.[20] There is prima facie some circularity here because "belonging to the area" is defined primarily by reference to "ordinary residence." In R. v. *Barnet London Borough Council, ex p. Shah*,[21] Lord Scarman reviewed the authorities on the meaning of **3–73**

---

[13] See S.I. 1983 No. 973, reg. 13 and Sched. 3 as amended by S.I. 1984 No. 1201.

[14] The Channel Islands and the Isle of Man (S.I. 1983 No. 973, reg. 2).

[15] See S.I. 1983 No. 973, Sched. 3, and, for definitions reg. 2 and S.I. 1985 No. 1219 as amended by S.I. 1984 No. 1201.

[16] S.I. 1983 No. 973, reg. 12.

[17] *Ibid*. regs. 14–16.

[18] Defined in the Education (Mandatory Awards) Regulations 1986 (S.I. 1986 No. 1306) reg. 2.

[19] S.I. 1986 No. 1306, reg. 13, In R. v. *Hereford and Worcester County Council ex p. Wimbourne* 82 L.G.R. 251, it was held that British citizens as well as others might properly be refused an award on falling within the terms of (now) reg. 13(1)(*b*). See also reg. 5(4), under which a person is to be treated as ordinarily resident in the British Islands even if not so resident because of temporary employment abroad of spouse or parent, and R. v. *Lancashire County Council, ex p. Huddleston* [1986] 2 All E.R. 941.

[20] See 1962 Act, Sched. 1, para. 2 (as modified by S.I. 1986 No. 1306 reg. 8), 1986 (No. 2) Act, s.51 (above at paras. 1–138 and 1–139) and the Education (Areas to which Pupils Belong) Regulations 1980 (S.I. 1980 No. 917) as amended by S.I. 1980 No. 1862 and S.I. 1983 No. 260 (above at para. 1–134). As to "no area" students see S.I. 1986 No. 1306, reg. 9.

[21] [1983] 2 A.C. 309. In R. v. *Hampshire County Council, ex p. Martin, The Times*, November 20, 1982, it was held that the place where a minor's parents were ordinarily resident was not in itself a decisive factor.

"ordinary residence" and concluded that it meant habitual and normal residence from choice and for a settled purpose (including education) throughout the prescribed period, apart from temporary or occasional absences.[22] (He added that a student who fails to establish eligibility for a mandatory award must be understood to be asking the local education authority to exercise their discretion[23] to waive the eligibility requirements, and that the authority are under a duty to consider the request).

3–74   It was following the *Shah* decision that the mandatory award regulations were revised to render ineligible, as stated above, persons wholly or mainly resident for the purposes of full-time education. Previously local education authorities had generally followed the practice, wrongly in the light of *Shah*, of excluding students who failed a "real home" test; and the Secretary of State advised[24] that local education authorities should, in the interests of good administration (and to anticipate applications for judicial review,[25]) reconsider cases where awards had been refused on residence grounds for courses beginning in 1979/1980 or later, and earlier only in exceptional circumstances. The propriety of the Department's advice was challenged in *R. v. Hertfordshire County Council, ex p. Cheung* and *R. v. Sefton Metropolitan Borough Council, ex p. Pau*.[26] The Court of Appeal directed the councils to reconsider making awards to the two applicants, who had undertaken courses beginning in the academic year 1978/1979, on the ground that Mr. Akbarali, who had been party to the *Shah* decision, had begun his course in that year, and "good public administration required all 1978 students to be treated in the same way as Mr. Akbarali."

3–75   By section 2 of the 1983 Act the Secretary of State took power to enable local education authorities to confine discretionary awards[27] to persons having a connection with the United Kingdom specified by regulations.[28] A relevant connection exists if the candidate for the award has been ordinarily resident in the United Kingdom or Islands[29] for three years preceding his intended course otherwise than (during any part of that period) wholly or mainly to receive full-time education. An

---

[22] As an example of what may amount to "ordinary residence" see *R. v. Inner London Education Authority, ex p. Palomar* (1982) 126 S.J. 673.

[23] Under s.1(6) of the 1962 Act.

[24] See Department of Education and Science Circular letter dated March 30, 1983.

[25] "Judicial review"—see above at paras. 1–50 *et seq.* As to the effect of the *Shah* decision on applications made by students in respect of courses beginning in Autumn 1982 see *R. v. Haringey London Borough and Others, ex p. Lee and Others, The Times*, July 31, 1984 and *R. v. West Glamorgan County Council, ex p. Gheissary, The Times*, December 18, 1985 in which the local education authority unfairly refused to consider an application made out of time.

[26] *The Times*, April 4, 1986. As to fairness and consistency see *H.T.V. v. Price Commission* [1976] I.C.R. 170 and above at para. 1–57.

[27] Under 1962 Act, ss.1(6) and 2. See above at para. 3–65.

[28] See the Education (Fees and Awards) Regulations 1983 (S.I. 1983 No. 973) regs. 8–10.

[29] The Channel Islands and the Isle of Man (*ibid.* reg. 2).

exception is made in favour of "excepted candidates"—European Community migrant workers and their children, and refugees ordinarily resident in the United Kingdom, who do not have a relevant connection but who meet specified requirements.[30]

---

[30] See S.I. 1983 No. 973, Sched. 3, and for definitions, reg. 2, as amended by S.I. 1984 No. 1201 and S.I. 1985 No. 1219.

CHAPTER 4

TEACHERS AND OTHERS

4–01   This Chapter is mostly about the law relating to the employment of
teachers at establishments maintained by local education authorities.
"Teacher" in context includes lecturers at further education establishments. "Others" in the title is not derogatory but rather recognises the
range and extent of non-teaching staff employed in the education service. In 1984 of 803,000 over 30 per cent. were not teachers.[1] They
included administrative staff, careers officers,[2] inspectors,[3] education
welfare officers and educational psychologists and others, as well as
manual employees such as caretakers, cleaners, and ground maintenance and school meals staff. They are local government officers,
appointed under section 112 of the Local Government Act 1972, and
their terms of employment follow those negotiated in bodies[4] established for the local government service generally, and their pensions are
provided under the local government superannuation scheme.[5]

4–02   By contrast with, for example, France and Germany teachers are not
normally employees of the state. Most are employed by local education
authorities and in law, though not by usage, are, also, their officers.
Authorities are therefore required to appoint teachers for the proper
discharge of their education functions on such terms as they think fit,
subject to other statutory intervention. This is extensive both under
general employment legislation[6] and under the Education Acts and the
powers[7] those Acts grant the Secretary of State. As a preliminary he

---

[1] See "C.I.P.F.A. Financial Information Service" *Education*, Vol. 20, para. 16.04.
[2] See Employment and Training Act 1973, s.8, as amended and below at para. 5–43.
[3] See 1944 Act, s.77 as amended, and below at para. 6–05.
[4] Salaried employees: the National Joint Council for Local Authorities' Administrative, Professional, Technical and Clerical Services (*the Purple Book*); inspectors, advisors and educational
psychologists: the Soulbury Committee (*Purple Book* except in relation to salaries and leave);
youth leaders: the Joint Negotiating Committee for Youth Leaders and Community Centre Wardens; manual employees, National Joint Council for Local Authorities' Services (Manual
Workers) (*the Green Book*).
[5] Youth and community workers employed for the purposes of ss.41 and 53 of the 1944 Act, as
amended (see above at paras. 3–36 to 3–39) are within the teachers' superannuation scheme (see
below at paras. 4–135 to 4–153).
[6] See especially the fourth section of this Chap. in which, and elsewhere in context, references to
statutes by year are to the Employment Protection Act 1975, the Employment Protection (Consolidation) Act 1978, the Employment Act 1980 and the Employment Act 1982. For the most part
citation of cases is restricted to those directly concerning the education service, and reference
should also be made to (*e.g.*) B.A. Hepple & P. O'Higgins, *Encyclopedia of Labour Relations
Law* (1972). In the White Paper, *Building Businesses—not Barriers* (Cmnd. 9794) the Government announced proposals to make wide-ranging changes in employment law.
[7] See above at pp. xxviii *et seq.*

requires[8] that "at any[9] school or further education establishment there shall be employed by the authority or body concerned a staff of teachers suitable and sufficient in numbers" to provide education appropriate to the ages, abilities and aptitudes of pupils at each establishment. This requirement is less rigid than might appear because arrangements may be made to utilise the services of teachers employed otherwise[10] than at the school or establishment or by the authority or other[11] employing body. Additionally[12] schools are specifically required to have a head teacher.

The Secretary of State has the power[13] to make payments to encour- **4–03** age teachers to take temporary employment in Commonwealth countries, and there is a scheme for exchange and interchange of teachers and assistants with overseas countries, administered formerly by the Department of Education and Science but now by the Central Bureau for Educational Visits and Exchanges.

TRAINING

Intending school teachers need to train for the qualifications referred **4–04** to in the next section of this Chapter. The normal pattern is a three or four year course leading to the degree of Bachelor of Education (B.Ed.) provided at a local education authority or voluntary further education institution[14] or, following graduation, a one-year course leading to the Postgraduate Certificate in Education (P.G.C.E.).

Reference has already been made: **4–05**

(a) to the arrangements for pooling[15] the teacher training costs of local education authorities;

(b) to the duties and powers of the Secretary of State and local

---

[8] Under reg. 7(1) of the Education (Teachers) Regulations 1982 (S.I. 1982 No. 106). Previously statutory authority for ministerial intervention in the appointment of teachers appears to have been an adjunct of grant-making powers, in the first place regulations made under s.100 of the 1944 Act (as originally enacted), and subsequently provisions relating to the making of non-specific grants to councils which were local education authorities: s.3(4) of the Local Government Act 1958 empowered the making of regulations "for prescribing standards and general requirements for the administration of any of the services giving rise to relevant expenditure"; and reg. 16 of the Schools Regulations 1959 (S.I. 1959 No. 364), which survived the repeal of the 1958 Act (but were revoked by the 1982 regulations), imposed requirements concerning the appointment of teachers.

[9] By S.I. 1982 No. 106, reg. 3 the Regulations apply to maintained schools, special schools (whether or not maintained) and further education establishments provided by local education authorities, or not provided but designated in the Regulations (see below at para. 4–21). As to teachers in non-maintained special schools, see above at para. 2–212.

[10] Local education authorities employ "supply" teachers to stand in for those absent from school in case of (e.g.) sickness.

[11] An "other" employing body is ordinarily the governing body of an establishment.

[12] S.I. 1982 No. 106, reg.7(2)(a).

[13] Overseas Development and Co-operation Act 1980, s.14(1)(b) and see Circ. 10/60 and A.M. 18/61.

[14] See Chap. 3, especially para. 3–19.

[15] See above at paras. 1–130 to 1–133.

education authorities concerning awards and grants[16] to, or in respect of,[17] those in training for the teaching profession or undertaking further training;

(c) to the requirements concerning the government[18] of colleges of education (in common with other further education establishments); and

(d) to the making of grants and loans to persons[19] other than local education authorities towards capital and maintenance expenditure on further education, including teacher training, establishments.

4–06   The foregoing supplement the principal provision relating to the training of teachers, 1944 Act, section 62, under which the Secretary of State is to "make such arrangements as he considers expedient for securing that there shall be available sufficient facilities for the training of teachers for service in schools . . . and other establishments maintained by local education authorities . . . ." For that purpose he may give directions to a local education authority "requiring them to establish, maintain or assist any training college[20] or other institution or to provide or assist in the provision of any other facilities specified in the direction." Local education authorities may be directed to contribute as the Secretary of State thinks just towards his requirements—in practice through the pooling arrangements referred to above.

4–07   The Secretary of State may give directions[21] as to the number and categories of students to be admitted to teacher training courses at further education establishments provided by local education authorities and by designated[22] assisted or grant-aided establishments. B.Ed. courses and courses for further training of teachers (full-time lasting for four or more weeks or part-time involving more than 60 hours of instruction) are advanced further education courses and so[23] may not be provided without the approval of the Secretary of State and must be discontinued at his direction. He may concur in arrangements for enabling persons from the Commonwealth to attend teacher training courses in the United Kingdom at the public expense.[24]

---

[16] See above at paras. 3–41 *et seq.*

[17] See above at para. 1–126 (reimbursement to local education authorities by the Secretary of State of the cost of employing teachers released to attend in-service training courses).

[18] See above at paras. 3–16 to 3–18.

[19] See Pt. III of the Education (Grant) Regulations 1983 (S.I. 1983 No. 74) made under 1944 Act, s.100 and 1967 Act, s.4, and above at para. 3–19.

[20] Provision must be made, as in schools, for the chronically sick and disabled. See Chronically Sick and Disabled Persons Act 1970, s.8, as (prospectively) amended, and above at para. 2–59.

[21] Under the Education (Schools and Further Education) Regulations 1981 (S.I. 1981 No. 1086) reg. 16.

[22] Under, and listed in *ibid.* Sched. 3 (added by Amendment Regulations 1983 (S.I. 1983 No. 262)) (see above at para. 3–05 n. 23).

[23] *Ibid.* regs. 14 and 15 and Sched. 2; and see above at para. 3–24.

[24] Overseas Development and Co-operation Act 1980, s.14(1)(*a*).

The Secretary of State's powers to determine the qualifications[25] of **4–08** teachers enable him also to determine what courses are suitable as professional training,[26] and on the recommendation of the Advisory Committee on the Supply and Education of Teachers[27] he has established the Council for the Accreditation of Teacher Education to advise him on the approval of initial training courses. (The members are practising teachers, teacher trainers, and officers and members of local education authorities). Entrants to an initial teacher training course must normally have attained the academic requirements for admission to first degree studies, including G.C.E. "O" level (grade C or above) or C.S.E. (grade 1) standard in Mathematics and English, and for a postgraduate course must hold a degree of a British university or the Council for National Academic Awards (C.N.A.A.)[28] or a recognised equivalent. Further recommendations are made to training institutions regarding selection and admission; and there are also recommendations about medical examination[29] of entrants to teacher training, and about the relationship between colleges of education and schools as regards teaching practice.[30]

The Secretary of State is able to encourage the release of teachers to **4–09** attend courses in subjects which he regards of particular importance by paying local education authorities the cost of employing replacement teachers[31]; and his grants and awards are designed to help persons to qualify in such subjects.[32]

QUALIFICATIONS AND PROBATION

The Secretary of State is authorised by section 27 of the 1980 Act to **4–10** make regulations[33] concerning the qualifications and probation of teachers at maintained, including special, schools, non-maintained special schools, and further education establishments provided by local education authorities, or not provided but designated[34] in regulations. Apart from the requirement[35] that teachers at further education establishments are to have qualifications appropriate to giving adequate

---

[25] See below at paras. 4–12 to 4–15.

[26] See Circ. 3/84 (W.O. 21/84) and Teaching Quality (Cmnd. 3386) s.5; also Circs. 9/78, 2/83 (W.O. 13/83) 4/85 (W.O. 32/85) and, as regards further education teachers, Circ. 11/77.

[27] Representative of the local authority and teachers' associations and of the universities, polytechnics and churches concerned with teacher training (lapsed 1985).

[28] See above at para. 3–02.

[29] See Circ. 11/78 (W.O. 111/78) as amended by Circ. 7/82.

[30] See Circ. 24/66.

[31] See Circ. 1/86 and above at para. 1–126.

[32] See below at para. 3–67.

[33] The Education (Teachers) Regulations 1982 (S.I. 1982 No. 106). See Circ. 7/82.

[34] See S.I. 1982 No. 106, Sched. 3. The list of establishments corresponds with that in the Education (Schools and Furher Education) (Amendment) Regulations 1983 (S.I. 1983 No. 262) (see above at para. 3–05) save for the omission of the Royal Academy of Music and the Royal College of Music.

[35] See Circ. 11/77.

instruction in the subjects in which courses are provided, the current teachers' regulations, in relation to qualifications and probation, apply only to school teachers.

4–11 With some exceptions teachers from overseas, other than EEC nationals, need a work permit as well as to comply with the regulations.[36]

Qualifications

4–12 Employment as a school teacher is ordinarily—the exceptions will be stated—restricted to those whom the Secretary of State has notified in writing as being "qualified."[37] Since April 8, 1982, in order to qualify a person has either:

(a) to have completed successfully a course of initial training approved[38] by the Secretary of State for the degree of B.Ed. the Certificate in Education, the P.G.C.E. or a comparable academic award of a United Kingdom university or the C.N.A.A.[39]; or

(b) (i) to have completed successfully (within or outside the United Kingdom) an approved comparable course and

(ii) (unless the course was completed before September 1, 1984) to have reached G.C.E. grade C standard (or C.S.E. grade 1) in English and mathematics; or

(c) to possess an approved special qualification[40] and meet the conditions in (b)(ii); or

(d) to have completed 20 years' service as a teacher, and before April 1, 1945, to have been recognised as eligible for recognition by the Board of Education as an uncertificated teacher or have been classified as a supplementary teacher; or

(e) (i) to possess a qualification approved in the person's case by the Secretary of State on the recommendation[41] of a local education authority,

(ii) meet the conditions in (b)(ii), and

(iii) have at least ten years' service (less if the Secretary of State approves for special reasons) as a teacher or of other experience similarly approved by the Secretary of State; or

(f) to have obtained a prescribed qualification to teach the mentally

---

[36] See Circ. 1/81, Annex, para. 12.

[37] See S.I. 1982 No. 106, reg. 13(1) and Sched. 5 and Circ. 11/73 as amended by Circ. 7/82.

[38] See above at para. 4–08.

[39] See above at para. 3–02.

[40] See Circ. 11/73, para. 9. The approved special qualifications are a degree of a university of the British Isles or C.N.A.A. and certain other qualifications which have for the time being been accepted by the Secretary of State. The other qualifications are listed in Appendix 3 to Circ. 11/73, which is divided into the following categories: art, handicraft, music, needlecraft and domestic subjects, science subjects, speech and drama, Higher National Diplomas and Certificates and National Froebel Union or Foundation.

[41] See Circ. 2/83 (W.O. 13/83) paras. 8 and 9.

handicapped and have had at least five years' satisfactory service as a teacher in a special school since doing so.

In the case of a person who is qualified under paragraph (c) above the **4–13** Secretary of State's notification is to state this, and will be given only if he is satisfied that the person will be employed as a teacher at a school to which the regulations apply. Moreover persons so qualified (or who hold special qualifications under revoked regulations)[42] are not qualified[43] for employment at either a primary school or a special school unless they acquired their special qualification before January 1, 1970, or at a secondary school (which is not a special school) unless either the qualification was obtained before January 1, 1974, or it was recognised at the time of notification of "qualified" status as a qualification for teachers of subjects for whom there was then a special need. It follows that most graduates wishing to enter the teaching profession have to take a teacher training course unless their degree is a B.Ed.

In certain cases unqualified persons may be employed[44] as school **4–14** teachers in specified circumstances. The first two categories of unqualified persons are rapidly dwindling in numbers—teachers who served in maintained, etc., schools before April 1, 1945 and teachers who served before the same date in secondary schools for the blind. The third category are unqualified teachers who served as teachers in special schools before April 8, 1982, and who would fall within (f) above had they the service mentioned. They may be employed at a special school notwithstanding that they do not satisfy the requirements[45] (where relevant) about employment to teach the deaf and blind. The fourth category are unqualified teachers serving as assistant teachers in nursery classes and at nursery schools immediately before April 8, 1982, who have completed a course of instruction in the care of young children. They may continue in that employment but not be newly appointed to it after that date. The fifth category are student teachers—unqualified teachers over the age of 18 who are either awaiting admission to a course of initial training for which they have been accepted or who, having failed to complete a course satisfactorily, are continuing it with a view to completion within a further year. Student teachers may be employed as school teachers but only for up to two years (or longer if approved by the Secretary of State in individual cases) and without responsibility for a class or for teaching a subject which is not also taught by a qualified teacher at the school. The final category are instructors who satisfy the employers about their special qualifications and

---

[42] The Schools Regulations 1959 (S.I. 1959 No. 364) reg. 16, para. 2(*b*) as amended, or para. (2) as originally made.
[43] S.I. 1982 No. 106, reg. 13(2).
[44] *Ibid*. Sched. 4.
[45] See below at para. 4–15.

experience, and no qualified teacher is available[46] for appointment or to give the particular form of instruction (including vocational training). These unqualified teachers may be employed until a suitable qualified teacher is available or, if appointed before April 8, 1982, for a specified period or an unspecified period if the appointment was not expressed to be a temporary one.

4–15   There are special rules applying to employment of teachers of the deaf and blind.[47] No person is to be employed at a school as the teacher of a class for deaf or partially hearing pupils or, at a special school, of a class of blind pupils (except to give instruction in a craft, trade or domestic subject) unless he possesses a specified qualification[48] as well as otherwise being a qualified teacher; but he may be so employed at a special school[49] for up to three years by one or more employers if the employers are satisfied that it is his intention to acquire one of the specified qualifications. Unqualified teachers in the first and third categories mentioned in the last paragraph (and as respect teachers of the blind the second category as well) may also be so employed. And a person may[50] be employed at a special school as a teacher of a class of pupils who are both deaf or partially hearing and also blind if he could be employed as the teacher of the class were it one for pupils who were only deaf or partially hearing or only blind.

Probation

4–16   Qualified teachers have ordinarily to serve a probationary period,[51] and the requirements concerning probation override anything to the contrary in a contract of service. The normal period of probation is one year (two years in the case of part-time teachers) at a maintained school (or a non-maintained special school), or, without any break, at more than one school maintained by the same local education authority. Probation starts when the qualified teacher first takes up a relevant appointment—and this may be postponed indefinitely.

---

[46] For a case on a similarly worded regulation, now revoked, and discussion of the distinction between "appointment" and "employment" see *Birmingham City Council* v. *Elson* (E.A.T.) 77 L.G.R. 743.

[47] S.I. 1982 No. 106, regs. 15–18.

[48] Respectively, the Teacher's Diploma of the British Association of Teachers of the Deaf or the University of Manchester Certificate for Teachers of the Deaf; and the School Teacher's Diploma of the Association for the Education and Welfare of the Visually Handicapped or the University of Birmingham Diploma in Special Education (Visually Handicapped); or comarable qualifications approved by the Secretary of State.

[49] As to further requirements regarding employment of teachers at non-maintained special schools see above at para. 2–212.

[50] S.I. 1982 No. 106, reg. 18.

[51] *Ibid.* reg. 14 and Sched. 6. See A.M. 9/78 (W.O. 5/78) as amended by Circular 7/82, A.M. 1/83 and also, generally, Second Report from the Education, Science and Arts Committee 1981–82 *The Secondary School Curriculum and Examinations* (H.C. 116–1) para. 8.19, and *Government Response* (Cmnd. 8551) pp. 9–10.

The duties[52] assigned to a probationary teacher, his supervision and **4–17** the conditions under which he works, are to be such as to facilitate fair and effective assessment of his conduct and efficiency as a teacher. In certain circumstances the period of probation may be varied—doubled in the case of teachers qualified otherwise than under (a) or (b) in paragraph 4–12 or abbreviated[53] if the relevant authority or body[54] so decide on account of the teacher's previous experience and the particular circumstances of his case. If the conduct and efficiency of a teacher leads the relevant authority or body to think it appropriate to extend his probationary period they may do so after considering any representations he may wish to make. Sick-leave or maternity leave[55] in term-time which in aggregate exceeds six weeks in any probationary year does not count towards completion of the period of probation.

If it appears to the relevant authority or body that a teacher is not fit- **4–18** ted for employment as such, and is unlikely to be an efficient and satisfactory teacher, they may report accordingly to the Secretary of State during his probationary period or up to a month after it expires; but before doing so they must consider any representations he wishes to make, and on doing so they must inform the teacher, the employers[56] (if other than the relevant authority or body) and Her Majesty's Inspector.[57] Unless an adverse report is made the teacher (and, if appropriate as above, the employers) are to be given written notice by the relevant authority or body that he has satisfactorily completed his probation period.

If the Secretary of State receives an adverse report he is to give the **4–19** teacher an opportunity to make representations, and to make any appropriate enquiries. To comply with the rules of natural justice[58] the gist of the report is to be given to the teacher so that he knows what is alleged against him. If on consideration the Secretary of State finds an adverse report well-founded he must give written notice accordingly to the teacher, the relevant authority or body and employers if other than one of the last mentioned. Once notice has been given the teacher's services are to be dispensed with as soon as reasonably practicable. He is to be given at least one month's notice, or salary in lieu, and the opportunity to resign when or before his notice expires; and he is not to be re-employed as a teacher in any school without the consent of the Secretary of State. If the Secretary of State is not satisfied that the report is

---

[52] See *Inner London Education Authority* v. *Lloyd* [1981] I.R.L.R. 394.

[53] Although a probationary period may not be served in an independent school, service in such a school may be taken into account under this subparagraph.

[54] The local education authority by whom the school is maintained, or the employers in the case of a non-maintained special school.

[55] See below at paras. 4–73 to 4–74 and 4–105.

[56] *e.g.* governors of aided schools.

[57] See below at para. 6–05.

[58] *R.* v. *Department of Education and Science, ex p. Kumar, The Times,* November 23, 1982 and see above at paras. 1–54 to 1–57.

well-founded he is to give notice as above directing that the teacher's probation be extended for the period he specifies.

EMPLOYMENT. PARTICULAR STATUTORY REQUIREMENTS

4–20   The contract between teacher and local education authority (or governors in the case of a voluntary aided school)[59] is ordinarily a contract of service,[60] enforceable in the courts[61] except when statute prescribes adjudication by an industrial tribunal. It no longer[62] has to take any particular form and is typically achieved[63] by the teacher's signing a copy of his letter of appointment in which the terms are specified. The contract may be open-ended or temporary (to end on the occurrence of a specified event) or for a fixed period.[64] It is likely to incorporate a nationally negotiated collective agreement[65] on conditions of service supplemented by terms negotiated locally between the authority and local branches of unions[66]; and it is subject to the wide variety of statutory interventions described in this section and later in this Chapter. Until the Teachers' Pay and Conditions Act 1987[67] was passed, the national conditions of service of school teachers were settled wholly separately from remuneration, and the negotiated conditions contain no reference, except as regards the midday break, to the scope of teachers' duties.

Fitness for teaching. Appraisal

4–21   The Education (Teachers) Regulations 1982[68] apply to the employment of teachers at maintained (including special) schools, non-maintained special schools[69] and further education establishments provided

---

[59] See below at para. 4–27.

[60] *Smith* v. *Martin and Kingston upon Hull Corporation* [1911] 2 K.B. 775.

[61] But see 1978 Act, s.131 under which jurisdiction may be conferred on industrial tribunals. See also *R.* v. *Liverpool City Corporation, ex p. Ferguson and Ferguson* [1985] I.R.L.R. 501 regarding improper discrimination in the payment of teachers (above at para. 1–51).

[62] Sched. 2, to the Schools Regulations 1959 (S.I. 1959 No. 364) (revoked by the Education (Teachers) Regulations 1982 (S.I. 1982 No. 106)) prescribed terms of employment for most teachers, who were to "be employed under a written agreement, or in the case of a teacher appointed by an authority, either under a written agreement or under a minute of the authority." The agreement or minute had to define conditions of service either expressly or by reference to specified regulations or minutes.

[63] A resolution by employers to make an appointment does not complete the contract until communicated to the applicant (*Powell* v. *Lee and Others* (1908) 99 L.T. 284).

[64] See below at para. 4–84.

[65] See below at para. 4–98.

[66] "Recognition" (of a trade union) and "collective bargaining" are defined in 1975 Act, s.126, as amended by the 1980 Act. As to a claim for recognition see *Cleveland County Council* v. *Springett and Others* [1985] I.R.L.R. 131 (E.A.T.).

[67] See below at paras. 4–52 and 4–115. The omission of remuneration from the terms of reference of a negotiating body was exceptional and open to criticism. See Second Report from the Education, Science and Arts Committee 1981–82 (H.C. 116–I), *The Secondary School Curriculum and Examinations* para. 8.19, and *Government Response* (Cmnd. 8648) p. 14.

[68] S.I. 1982 No. 106 made under s.27 of the 1980 Act. See Circ. 7/82 and above at para. 4–02.

[69] As to employment of teachers in non-maintained special schools see also the Education (Approval of Special Schools) Regulations 1983 (S.I. 1983 No. 1499) Sched. 2, Part II, paras. 15 and 16 and above at para. 2–212.

by local education authorities, or not provided but designated[70] in the regulations. They also apply to the employment elsewhere by local education authorities of teachers and others whose work regularly brings them into contact with persons under 19[71]; and no teacher may be employed at a direct grant school which is not a grammar school if his employment would be precluded by the regulations.[72]

No person to whom the regulations apply is to be appointed[73] unless **4–22** the authority or (teachers at schools or further education establishments) other appointing body (the employers) are satisfied about his health[74] and physical capacity for this "relevant"[75] employment; but in the case of teachers on first appointment the employers may, where it appears reasonable to do so, accept the Secretary of State's conclusion in the matter, and in other cases they may rely upon the medical record in previous relevant employment.

If the employers believe that an employee may no longer[76] have the **4–23** health or physical capacity for his employment they must give him the opportunity to submit medical evidence and make representations to them. They must consider the evidence and representations and any other medical evidence available to them, and may require him to undergo a medical examination (or arrange one at his request). The employers and/or employee may submit evidence in advance to the practitioner conducting the examination, and this may be attended by a practitioner appointed by the person being examined. If the employers are satisfied that an employee has not the health or physical capacity for his employment he is not to continue in relevant employment.

The Secretary of State has "barring" powers[77] in relation to relevant **4–24** employment which he may exercise, after consulting the employers, on medical grounds, on grounds of misconduct[78] (whether or not evidenced by criminal conviction) or, in the case of teachers, on educational grounds.[79] On any of these grounds the Secretary of State may direct the

---

[70] Under S.I. 1982 No. 106, reg. 3(1) and Sched. 3 (see para. 4–10 n. 34).

[71] See also the Rehabilitation of Offenders Act 1974 (Exceptions) Order 1975 (S.I. 1975 No. 1023) as amended by Amendment Order 1986 (S.I. 1986 No. 1249) regarding disclosure of "spent convictions;" and Circ. 4/86 (W.O. 28/86).

[72] The Direct Grants Schools Regulations 1959 (S.I. 1959 No. 1832) reg. 27 as substituted by the Direct Grant Schools (Amendment) Regulations 1981 (S.I. 1981 No. 1788) reg. 3. See above at para. 2–220.

[73] S.I. 1982 No. 106, reg. 8.

[74] See Circ. 11/78 (W.O. 111/78) as amended by Circ. 7/82. In *Watts* v. *Monmouthshire County Council and Another* 66 L.G.R. 171 it was held that the report of a medical examination conducted prior to a teacher's employment was a confidential report to the county education officer, and the employing authority were under no duty to inform the teacher of its contents.

[75] Defined in S.I. 1982 No. 106, reg. 6.

[76] *Ibid*. reg. 9. See Circ. 11/78 (W.O. 111/78) as amended by Circ. 7/82.

[77] *Ibid*. reg. 10. As to teachers in schools which participate in the assisted places scheme, see below at para. 6–42.

[78] "Misconduct" is undefined but includes pederasty and misappropriation of funds. The Secretary of State's procedures are explained in A.M. 3/82. See also n. 71 above.

[79] "Educational grounds"—see *Mitchell* and *Hanson* cited at n. 84 below.

employers to suspend or terminate the employment or to continue it only on specified conditions. Where he is considering exercising his powers on medical grounds the procedures referred to in the previous paragraph must be followed. Where the other grounds are material he must give the employee an opportunity to make representations, and consider them and other relevant information available. The Secretary of State's direction may also apply to subsequent relevant employment by a person who is (or is not at the time) in relevant employment. A direction may be withdrawn or varied by the Secretary of State but otherwise binds employers.

4–25 When employers dismiss a person from relevant employment for misconduct (whether he is convicted of a criminal offence or not), or would have dismissed him, or considered doing so, but for his resignation, they are to report[80] the facts of the case to the Secretary of State.

4–26 Under section 49 of the 1986 (No. 2) Act the Secretary of State may make provision by regulation[81] for regular appraisal of the performance of teachers' duties and related activities. Before making regulations he is to consult relevant local authority associations and representatives of teachers, and any other person with whom he believes consultation to be desirable. Regulations may apply to teachers employed in various specified categories of school and further education establishment or elsewhere, and may make provision in particular:

(a) for requiring governing bodies to secure, so far as reasonably practicable,[82] that appraisal arrangements are complied with, and to help local education authorities to perform their appraisal obligations;

(b) regarding disclosure to teachers of the results of appraisals and the opportunity for them to make representations; and

(c) requiring authorities to have regard to appraisal results in exercising prescribed functions.

Appointment and dismissal

4–27 In every county and maintained special school the appointment of teachers is under the control of the local education authority, except so far as articles[83] of government provide otherwise, and only the authority may dismiss a teacher.[84] ("Dismissal" includes termination of contract

[80] S.I. 1982 No. 106, reg. 11.

[81] Arrangements may in practice be made voluntarily between representatives of teachers and employees.

[82] See *Stroud's Judicial Dictionary*, (5th ed. 1986).

[83] As to the making of articles see above at paras. 2–71 *et seq.*

[84] 1944 Act, s.24(1) as amended, applied to maintained special schools by 1968 (No. 2) Act, s.2(5) as amended (repealed by the 1986 (No. 2) Act but see para. 4–35). As to grounds for, and exercise of power of, dismissal under pre-1944 Act legislation, see *Perry* v. *Pardoe and Others* (1906) 50 S.J. 742 (right of teacher to be heard); *Martin* v. *Eccles Corporation* [1919] 1 Ch. 387 (teacher absenting herself); *Mitchell* v. *East Sussex County Council* (1913) 109 L.T. 778 and *Hanson* v. *Radcliffe U.D.C.* [1922] 2 Ch. 490 ("educational grounds"); *Richardson* v. *Abertillery U.D.C., Thomas* v. *Abertillery U.D.C.* (1928) 138 L.T. 688 (reasons of financial economy); and *Price* v. *Rhondda*

by notice: it does not necessarily carry derogatory overtones. The expiry of a fixed-term contract is not dismissal at common law though it may give rise to the statutory rights referred to in the next section of this Chapter). In voluntary controlled and special agreement schools the position is the same apart from the requirements placed upon local education authorities regarding appointment and dismissal of "reserved" teachers.[85] In voluntary aided schools appointment and dismissal of teachers is regulated by the articles of government. These have to meet the following requirements.[86] The governors are the employers and are to make teaching appointments. The local education authority are to decide teacher numbers; to have power to prohibit the dismissal of teachers without their consent,[87] and to be able to require the dismissal[88] of any teacher, except those appointed to give denominational religious instruction[89]; and by agreement with the governors (or in default as determined by the Secretary of State) to be able to prohibit the appointment without their consent of teachers to be employed on secular instruction,[90] and to direct[91] what are to be the educational qualifications[92] of teachers thus employed. The provisions outlined apply to maintained special schools[93] as they do to county and voluntary schools, but not to further education establishments maintained by local education authorities, where appointment and dismissal are regulated wholly by the articles of government.[94]

Current regulations, unlike earlier versions, do not prescribe the   **4–28** method of appointment of teachers. This, together with dismissal procedures, is to be found in each establishment's articles of government, which must of course embody or otherwise be consistent with statutory provisions (as must the terms of employment of teachers be consistent with both). As regards schools, the Department offered advice in *Principles of Government in Maintained Secondary Schools*.[95] It is likely to have been heeded if only because the Secretary of State's approval of

---

Urban Council [1923] 2 Ch. 372, *Short* v. *Poole Corporation* [1926] Ch. 66 and *Fennell* v. *East Ham Corporation* [1926] Ch. 641 (discrimination against married women teachers, as to which see now the Equal Pay Act 1970, the Sex Discrimination Acts 1975 and 1986 and above at paras. 4–62 to 4–67).

[85] See 1944 Act, ss.27(3), (repealed in part by 1986 (No. 2) Act), (4) and (5), and 28(3) and (4) as amended, and above at paras. 2–167 and 2–171.

[86] See *ibid.* s.24(2) as amended by 1980 Act, s.113 and Sched. 1.

[87] See *Jones* v. *Lee* [1981] I.C.R. 310, C.A., (purported dismissal of head teacher of a voluntary aided school without the consent of the local education authority).

[88] See 1978 Act, s.80 as amended, as regards the application of the law governing unfair dismissal, and para. 4–84.

[89] See 1944 Act, s.28(2) as amended, and above at para. 2–170.

[90] Not defined but presumably, by exclusion, all instruction that is not religious instruction.

[91] Revocation and variation of directions—see 1944 Act, s.111 and above at para. 1–42.

[92] See above at paras. 4–12 to 4–15.

[93] 1968 (No. 2) Act, s.2(5) as amended.

[94] See *ibid.* s.1(3), above at para. 3–17 and Appendix 2, below.

[95] Cmd. 6523, 1944, and see above at para. 2–107; but see also the Government's proposals in *Parental Influence at School*, (Cmnd. 9242), subsequent to the recommendations in Chap. 8 of *A New Partnership for our Schools*, H.M.S.O., 1977.

secondary school articles has been required. Nevertheless, there are wide differences between the practices of local education authorities. Many of these will be eliminated when sections 34 to 41 of the 1986 (No. 2) Act to which reference is made in paras. 4–35 to 4–41, below, are fully implemented.

4–29   The terms of articles will differ according as they relate to head or assistant teachers, to primary or secondary or special schools or further education establishments, and to county or to voluntary schools in their three categories, but they are likely to be on similar lines. Those concerning the appointment[96] and dismissal of a head teacher of a secondary school other than a voluntary aided school will serve as a basis for exposition and vehicle for some of the case law. It is likely to be provided that, after advertisement by the local education authority, representatives of the school governors and local education authority shall meet to draw up a short list and subsequently to conduct interviews and recommend the local education authority to make an appointment. The head teacher will be employed under a contract of service with the local education authority terminable by written notice[97] on either side to take effect at the end of a term—three months' notice preceding the end of the spring or autumn term and four months preceding the end of the summer term.

4–30   Dismissal,[98] by the local education authority, will ordinarily be on recommendation of the governors[99] confirmed at a second meeting of governors at least 14 days after the first. For misconduct or other urgent cause, the governors are likely to be given powers to recommend more peremptory dismissal and to suspend[1] the head teacher from office pending the decision of the local education authority. The head teacher

---

[96] As to the appointment of the head teacher of a controlled school see 1944 Act, s.27(3) (repealed in part by 1986 (No. 2) Act) and above at para. 2–168.

[97] In *Watts* v. *Monmouthshire County Council and Another* 66 L.G.R. 171, it was held that although failure of the teacher to perform his duties by reason of illness or accident did not frustrate the contract of employment, acceptance of a statutory gratuity did so, and so no notice determining the contract was necessary and no breach had been committed by the employers. As to a general dismissal of teachers not for proper educational purposes see *R.* v. *Liverpool City Council, ex p. Ferguson and Others, The Times*, November 20, 1985, and see above at para. 1–51.

[98] See also *Burgundy Book*, para. 8 (below at para. 4–103). As to the effect of imprisonment upon a contract of service and appeal against dismissal by a local education authority see *R.* v. *Powys County Council, ex p. Smith* 81 L.G.R. 342. Some unreported cases are considered in G.R. Barrell and J.A. Partington, *Teachers and the Law*, (6th ed., 1985), Chap. IV.

[99] See *Curtis* v. *Manchester City Council, The Times*, May 27, 1976, as to whether: (1) a local education authority may dismiss otherwise than on the recommendation of the governors (no governors having been appointed); (2) a sub-committee of an education committee may act as a tribunal to hear complaints against a head teacher; (3) procedures pursuant to an article relating to misconduct are apt for use where allegations are of incapacity. In *Honeyford* v. *Bradford Metropolitan City Council* [1986] I.R.L.R. 32, the Court of Appeal held that the Council had power to dismiss a head teacher notwithstanding a contrary recommendation by governors, (see also n. 87 above).

[1] Suspension must be with pay unless the contract of employment (see *Burgundy Book*, para. 8.1.5 and below at para. 4–103) specifically authorises otherwise. See *Gorse* v. *Durham Council* [1971] 1 W.L.R. 775 and other cases cited at para. 1–303 of B.A. Hepple and P. O'Higgins, *Encyclopedia of Labour Relations Law* (1972). Compare the rights of the employer in circumstances of "industrial action" (see below at para. 4–56).

will be entitled to appear,[2] accompanied if he wishes by a friend, at any meeting of governors and local education authority at which his dismissal is considered, and to be given some days notice of the meeting. It was decided in *R. v. Governors of Litherland High School, ex p. Corkish*[3] that the committee of the local education authority must consider the proposed dismissal as a rehearing and not merely whether the governors' recommendation can reasonably be supported. This decision contrasts with that in *R. v. Staff Committee of London County Council's Education Committee, ex p. Schonfeld and Others*[4] where it was held that the sub-committee were acting administratively in refusing consent to the dismissal of the headmaster of a voluntary aided school and that in consequence *certiorari* was not available. Failure by governors to find facts which supported the decision by a local education authority to suspend a head teacher, and the governors' recommendation of reinstatement, do not preclude a fresh investigation into the facts by the authority's disciplinary subcommittee (*McGoldrick v. Brent London Borough Council*).[5]

Provisions similar to the above are likely to appear in articles relating **4–31** to aided secondary schools except that the governors are likely to advertise a vacancy for a head teacher, and the appointment will be to their service. Dismissal by the governors will be subject to a power of prohibition[6] by the local education authority, who will also be empowered to require dismissal.

The provisions in articles relating to assistant teachers at other than **4–32** aided secondary schools are likely to be broadly as follows. On a vacancy being notified by the governors to the local education authority the latter will advertise the post and submit the names for consideration by the governors[7] in consultation with the head teacher. The local education authority may, if they think fit, after consultation with governors and head teacher, require the governors to appoint a teacher on transfer from another school or from a pool of new entrants to the profession. Appointments will be made to the service of the local education authority (so that the authority reserve the right to transfer teachers between schools) and subject to their confirmation. The provisions for dismissal

---

[2] As to disciplinary hearings by governors, see the Education (School Government) Regulations 1987 (S.I. 1987 No. 1359), reg. 14 (above at para. 2–101); and as to the (non-statutory) right to a hearing before dismissal see *Blanchard* v. *Dunlop* [1971] 1 Ch. 165, *Malloch* v. *Aberdeen Corporation* [1971] 1 W.L.R. 1578, *Scott* v. *Aberdeen Corporation* [1975] S.L.T. 167 and decisions generally on the requirements of natural justice, as to which see above at para. 1–54. See also I.S. Dickinson, "Parliament, Natural Justice and The Unregistered Teacher" (1975) L.G.C. 879.

[3] *The Times*, December 4, 1982, C.A.

[4] *The Times*, October 29, 1955.. The case is of doubtful authority, the distinction between "judicial" and "administrative" decisions having subsequently been eroded (see above at paras. 1–54 to 1–57).

[5] *The Times*, November 20, 1986. See below at para. 6–14.

[6] See above at para. 4–27.

[7] See *Noble* v. *I.L.E.A.* (1983) 82 L.G.R. 291, C.A. as to the invalidity of an appointment where the procedure was improper; also above at para. 2–101 n. 25.

and suspension[8] are likely to be similar to those relating to head teachers, except that the periods of notice may be shorter by one month[9] and two meetings of governors may not be required.

4–33   Articles regarding vacancies for assistant teachers at aided secondary schools are likely to provide for advertisement by governors, and for appointment to be made to their service by them in consultation with the head teacher; and otherwise to follow the pattern of articles relating to other secondary schools. As in the case of head teachers, the local education authority will be empowered to require dismissal, and dismissal by governors will be subject to prohibition by the local education authority, except in the case of teachers appointed to give denominational religious instruction.[10] In *Hannam* v. *Bradford Corporation*[11] it was held that the local education authority committee who consider whether or not to prohibit dismissal ought not to include members of the governing body of the school where the teacher has been employed because of the risk, or appearance, of bias, but that there is no contract of service between local education authority and teacher and therefore no right to damages against the authority for breach of contract on wrongful dismissal.

4–34   Articles relating to the procedure for appointment and dismissal of teachers at primary schools are (as part of the articles of govenment generally) not subject to approval by the Secretary of State, but in practice are likely to be found largely to conform to those outlined above for secondary schools, although perhaps somewhat less elaborate. More elaborate are the provisions in articles for further education institutions.[12]

4–35   Sections 34 to 41 of the 1986 (No. 2) Act supersede section 24(1) of the 1944 Act in relation to the appointment and dismissal of staff, but the foregoing, including most of the case law, will remain relevant as regards aided schools, and so far as consistent with the new provisions. Schools with existing articles are not required to comply with the new provisions until September 1, 1988 in the case of county and maintained special schools and September 1, 1989 in the case of voluntary schools. The local education authority are, by section 34, to determine the complement of teaching and non-teaching posts for all, except aided, maintained schools. The complement is to include all full-time teaching posts, and part-time teaching posts where employment is confined to a particular school. It excludes the authority's school meals and midday supervisory staff.

---

[8] Note that if power to suspend is granted to governors in the articles no such power can be conferred on a head teacher in a contract of service (though he might be given power to exclude and to recommend suspension).

[9] But see the 1978 Act, s.49, as amended and below at para. 4–81.

[10] 1944 Act, s.28(2) as amended. See above at para. 4–27.

[11] [1970] 1 W.L.R. 937.

[12] See above at para. 3–17 and Appendix 2. In *Winder* v. *Cambridgeshire County Council* 76 L.G.R. 549, C.A. the procedures attending dismissal of further education teacher were considered.

The appointment and dismissal of all staff at maintained (except   **4-36**
aided) schools are, by section 35, under the control of the local education authority, subject to the terms of sections 27 and 28 of the 1944
Act (religious education)[13] and to a number of specific provisions to
which reference is made below or which apply when there is a temporary governing body.[14] Articles of government are to require the local
education authority to consult the governing body and head teacher
before appointing any person to work solely at the school otherwise
than (a) in a teaching post; or (b) in a non-teaching post which is part of
the complement of the school; or (c) solely in connection with meals
and/or midday supervision.

The articles of government of maintained (except aided) schools are   **4-37**
to provide for the local education authority not to appoint[15] a person as
head teacher unless his appointment has been recommended by a selection panel constituted in accordance with the articles as provided by section 36. The selection panel (members of which may be replaced at any
time) is to consist of not less than three persons appointed by the local
education authority and not less than three governors appointed by the
governing body; and the number appointed by the governing body is not
to be less than that appointed by the local education authority. The chief
education officer or his representative is to have the right to attend[16] all
panel proceedings, including interviews, to advise the members. The
Secretary of State has made regulations[17] about meetings and proceedings of selection panels.

Articles are to require[18] the local authority to appoint an acting head   **4-38**
teacher, after consulting the governing body, on a vacancy occurring,
and the vacancy is to be advertised in papers circulating throughout
England and Wales as the authority consider appropriate. The selection
panel are to interview such applicants as they think fit, and if they fail to
agree about who is to be interviewed the governor members may nominate up to two applicants for interview, and the other members up to
two different applicants. If the panel are unable to agree to recommend
for appointment by the local education authority any of the applicants
interviewed they are to consider interviewing other applicants. If they
do so and are still unable to make a recommendation, or decide not to
do so, they may require the local education authority to re-advertise the
vacancy. If an authority decline to appoint a person recommended the
panel must consider interviewing applicants not previously interviewed
and recommending one of them, and if necessary ask the authority to

---

[13] See above at paras. 2–167 to 2–171.
[14] See 1986 (No. 2) Act, Sched. 2 and above at paras. 2–96 and 2–97.
[15] *Ibid.* s.37(1)(*a*). By s.37(2) the requirement does not apply to "acting" appointments. See also the
definition of "head teacher" in s.65(1).
[16] *Ibid.* s.37(1)(*j*).
[17] See the Education (School Government) Regulations 1987 (S.I. 1987 No. 1359) regs. 26 and 27.
[18] 1986 (No. 2) Act, s.37(1)(*b*)–(*i*).

re-advertise the vacancy. The authority must comply with the request to
re-advertise, and may do so on their own account if they have advertised
the post and the panel have failed to make an acceptable recommendation or a request to re-advertise, after having had sufficient time to do
so.

4–39   By section 39, deputy head teachers are to be appointed either

  (a) under the arrangements for head teachers as above[19] (and the
      head teacher, if not a member of the panel is entitled to be pres-
      ent to advise at their proceedings, including interviews, and is in
      any event to be consulted before a recommendation is made to
      the authority); or
  (b) in accordance with the following arrangements.

4–40   The articles of government of maintained (other than aided) schools
are, under section 38, to require local education authorities to deal with
vacancies in the school complement by first deciding whether to retain
an existing post, and then, if they decide to do so or the post is a new
one, either advertising the vacancy or filling it with an existing or prospective employee. (The procedures specified do not apply in the case of
a temporary appointment made pending the return to work of the
holder of the post or the taking of any steps the articles require concerning the vacancy). When the post is advertised much the same procedures
apply as in the case of a head teacher but advertisement does not have to
be nationwide and the governing body fill the role of the panel; and once
the post has been advertised a local education authority may make an
appointment only after the proper procedures have been followed or
they decide to fill it with an existing or prospective employee. When the
post is not advertised the governing body are entitled to determine a
specification for it in consultation with the head teacher. The authority
are to have regard to the specification and to consult the governing body
and the head teacher when considering whom to appoint. In case of
urgent need to make an appointment the authority may act without consulting the governing body if they are unable to contact the chairman or
vice-chairman.[20] If the authority make an appointment with which the
governing body disagree, they must report accordingly to their education committee. Whether the post is advertised or not articles are to
enable the governing body to delegate their functions to one or more
governors or to the head teacher, or to both acting together.

4–41   Section 41 requires articles of maintained (other than aided) schools
are also to make provision in relation to dismissal or other ending of
employment. The local education authority are to consult the governing
body and head teacher (except when he is the person concerned) before

---

[19] But by 1986 (No.2) Act, s.39(3) there is no requirement to appoint an acting deputy.
[20] Education (School Government) Regulations 1987 (S.I. 1987 No. 1359) reg. 29, made under
s.16(2) of the 1986 (No. 2) Act.

dismissing any person (except a reserved teacher)[21] holding a post in the school complement[22] or otherwise requiring him to cease work at the school, or permitting him to retire so that he would be entitled to premature retirement compensation.[23] The authority are also to consult similarly before extending a teacher's initial period of probation or deciding whether he has completed it successfully; and to consider the recommendation of a governing body that a person should cease to work at their school. It does not follow from the requirement to consult that the local education authority may act only upon a recommendation of the governing body. Both governing body and head teacher are to have power to suspend any person from working at a school (without loss of emoluments) when one or other are of the opinion that his exclusion is required, and on doing so the one must inform the other and the local education authority, who may direct the end of suspension. This provision appears to be without prejudice to a local education authority's power to suspend, as employer.

Employment of teachers in day nurseries

Both local education authorities and governors of county and volun- **4-42** tary schools may make arrangements[24] for teachers employed by them to serve in day nurseries provided by local social services authorities.[25] The conditions are:

(a) that the teacher is employed in a nursery school or a nursery class[26] in a primary school;
(b) that he consents to provide his services;
(c) that arrangements made by a local education authority are, in respect of a teacher at a voluntary school, concurred in by the governors;
(d) that no arrangements are to be made by governors except at the request of a local education authority and on terms they approve; and
(e) that the teacher continues to be a member of his school's teaching staff and subject to the general directions of his head teacher.

The arrangements may make provision for the supply of teaching **4-43** equipment; for regulating the functions of the teacher, the head teacher of his school and the person in charge of the day nursery; and for supplementary or incidental matters, including financial adjustments between

---

[21] See 1944 Act, ss.27(5) and 28(4), above at paras. 2–167 and 2–171.
[22] And certain other posts. See 1986 (No. 2) Act, s.41(3), and above at para. 4–35.
[23] See below at para. 4–147.
[24] See Education Act 1980, s.26.
[25] Under National Health Service Act 1977, s.21 and Sched. 8 charges may be made for the use of day nurseries. Social services authorities—see above at para. 2–196 n. 78.
[26] See above at para. 2–45.

local education authorities when the school and day nursery are in different areas.

Non-teaching staff

4-44   Under the 1944 Act, the persons employed for the care and maintenance of voluntary controlled and special agreement (as well as of county) school premises are to be appointed and dismissed by the local education authority; and local education authorities may give directions to the governors of voluntary aided schools regarding their number and conditions of service.[27] School meals staff at all maintained schools are in the employment of the local education authority.[28] Beyond this, arrangements for the appointment and dismissal of non-teaching staff, for example, in addition to those above-mentioned, nursery assistants and technicians, will be found in articles of government. In aided schools power to appoint or dismiss is likely to be granted to governors. In other maintained schools they may be entrusted with selection for appointment. Aided school governors may appoint a clerk to deal with foundation business and sometimes other school business as well; otherwise the general practice is for the chief education officer or his representative to act as clerk to the governors.

4-45   These provisions will be superseded so far as inconsistent with those referred to in paragraphs 4–35 to 4–41 above when the latter are fully implemented.[29] The power to give directions to governors of voluntary aided schools about the persons employed for the care of maintenance of premises is retained, and special provision is made about clerks to governing bodies, as follows.

4-46   Articles of maintained (except aided) schools are, by section 40 of the 1986 (No. 2) Act,[30] to provide that the clerk is to be appointed by the local education authority in accordance with arrangements determined by them in consultation with the governing body, except in the case of controlled and special agreement schools when the articles already make provision for his appointment. The authority may dismiss a clerk only in accordance with like arrangements and with the same exception. The authority must consider any representations by the governors as to their clerk's dismissal. When the clerk fails to attend a meeting of the governing body a governor may act as clerk, without prejudice to his position as a governor.

4-47   The cost of employing non-teaching (as of teaching) staff falls in all cases to the local education authority provided that it is part of the expense of maintaining the school and not related, for example, to the administration of the foundation income of a voluntary school.

---

[27] 1944 Act, s.22(4), as substituted by 1986 (No. 2) Act, Sched. 4, para. 2.
[28] This follows by implication from 1980 Act, s.22.
[29] See para. 4–35 as to postponement of compliance with these provisions.
[30] See para. 4–35 as to postponement of compliance with these provisions.

Religious opinions

By section 30 of the 1944 Act, no person is to be disqualified from   **4–48**
being employed as a teacher or otherwise in a county school, or as a
non-reserved teacher[31] or otherwise in a voluntary controlled or special
agreement school, because of his religious opinions or because he
attends or omits to attend religious worship. Nor is a teacher in any such
school to be disadvantaged (for example, in relation to pay or promotion) on those grounds or because he does or does not give religious
instruction. Only a teacher in an aided school or a reserved teacher in a
controlled or special agreement school may be required to give religious
instruction, and he is not to be disadvantaged because he does so or
because of his religious opinions or attendance at worship.

In *Ahmad* v. *I.L.E.A.*[32] it was held that the right to manifest religion   **4–49**
under article 9(1) of the European Convention on Human Rights[33] did
not avail a teacher who took time off in breach of contract in order to
undertake religious observances.

Extent of duties. Breach of contract

A teacher's job description may until recently have been in general   **4–50**
terms. For example the contract might provide that the teacher is to be
employed under the direction of the head teacher[34] exclusively in the
capacity of a teacher and only on duties connected with the work of the
school. Where the duties were so described it was held[35] that the headmaster was entitled to require a teacher to do work other than the particular work for which she had been engaged, provided that the request
was reasonable. What was reasonable would depend on the circumstances, and differ from time to time and place to place. It would be relevant to take account of the custom and practice of the profession. But
custom and practice cannot override a specific term: if the number of
teaching hours per week is specified in the contract there can be no
implied term[36] that the teacher shall work longer hours for preparation
of lessons, marking, etc.

It has been a matter of dispute whether activities customarily per-   **4–51**
formed by teachers are undertaken by virtue of an implied term of the

---

[31] "Reserved teacher" see 1944 Act, s.27(2) and above at paras. 2–167 and 2–171.
[32] [1978] Q.B. 36, C.A. See A. Hofler, "Religious Discrimination. A Loophole to be Closed," 80 L.S. Gaz. 1043.
[33] See above at para. 1–109. An appeal to the European Human Rights Commission failed (1982) 4 E.H.R.R. 126.
[34] Limited control over a teacher's dress may, under this form of words, probably be exercised by the head teacher.
[35] *Redbridge London Borough Council* v. *Fishman* (E.A.T.) 76 L.G.R. 408.
[36] *Lake* v. *Essex County Council* [1979] I.C.R. 577, C.A. See, however, the remark, *obiter*, of Scott J. in *Sim* v. *Rotherham Metropolitan Borough Council*, 85 L.G.R. 128, that "it was accepted by both sides that in order to do his or her job properly a teacher would have to spend some time outside school hours in marking school work and in preparing for classes."

contract[37] or as a voluntary expression of professional goodwill. In *Sim* v. *Rotherham Metropolitan Borough Council*[38] Scott J. remarked that failure to detail obligations was to be expected in a contract to serve in a professional capacity and he held it to be obligatory for teachers to provide "cover" for absent colleagues as part of a (not unlimited) "professional obligation . . . to co-operate in running the school during school hours in accordance with the timetable and other administrative regulations or directions from time to time made or given" by the head teacher.

4–52 The Teachers' Pay and Conditions Act 1987 has enabled the Secretary of State, by order under prescribed procedures, to import conditions[39] into school teachers' contracts of employment.[40] Teachers are to carry out professional duties under the reasonable direction of the head teacher (whose own duties are also specified). The duties are to include those listed under 12 headings, and working time—days and hours in a year—is also defined. When a listed duty is specified in some detail, for example, the period over which a teacher may be required to provide cover, the maxim *expressio unius exclusio alterius* would seem to apply, in this instance to defeat a head teacher's requirement of cover for a longer period; but the use of "include" appears otherwise to empower a head teacher to impose additional duties, and thus leaves room for dispute over the reasonableness of his requirements.

4–53 In advance of statutory intervention by the Secretary of State teachers have taken "industrial action" of which the following are examples: refusal to take classes for absent colleagues for whatever period is customary in the local education authority; refusal to work to timetables[41] which differ from those drawn up at the beginning of the school year; refusal to attend consultations with parents arranged outside the pupils' timetabled day; refusal to stay in a staff meeting, or invigilate an examination, which starts outside the pupils' timetabled day or runs on beyond that period; refusal to undertake duties at the beginning of the morning session and the end of the afternoon session; refusal to mark the attendance register[42]; and refusal to undertake the marking of work and the preparation and writing of reports on pupils. To the extent that

---

[37] Teachers can probably be required, as a contractual obligation, to supervise pupils for a limited period on, or in the immediate vicinity of, school premises at the beginning and end of school sessions, *e.g.* as they alight from or board a bus. See the cases cited below at paras. 7–09 to 7–16 and 7–31 *et seq.* and *Donnelly* v. *Williamson* [1981] I.R.L.R. 533. (attendance by teacher at parents' evenings). For examples of extra-curricular activities see above at paras. 1–87 to 1–88.

[38] 85 L.G.R. 128, and see L.W. Blake, "Professional Obligations and Contractual Duties in the Teaching Profession" 150 L.G.Rev. 623.

[39] See s.3(6)(*b*) and the Education (School Teachers' Pay and Conditions of Employment) Order 1987 (S.I. 1987 No. 650), Circ. 5/87, and Appendix 3 to this work; also below at paras. 4–115 to 4–117.

[40] See definitions in s.7(1).

[41] See *Sim* v. *Rotherham Metropolitan Borough Council* (above at para. 4–51).

[42] See above at para. 2–109.

action of this kind is in breach of contract a union who incite it commit a tort unless authorised by a members' ballot.[43]

"Working to rule" has been held to be a breach of contract,[44] but in **4–54** the case of teachers there has been no rule book and the issue is rather whether refusal to perform services of the kind exemplified, or otherwise obstructing the work of the school, constitutes breach of implied terms of contract or "withdrawal of good will." Employers have taken the view that breach of contract is committed where it can be shown that it has been normal practice for teachers to carry out the services exemplified without reasonable excuse for failing to do so, provided that the demands made upon them are reasonable. It would not, for example, be reasonable to require a teacher to take on an absent colleague's duties as an additional burden for an unlimited period of time,[45] or *a fortiori*, to undertake "domestic" tasks because of a strike by non-teaching staff. Whether a head teacher in such circumstances may lawfully refuse to open school premises to which he has the keys is perhaps an open question.

As a practical means of dealing with the consequences of strike **4–55** action,[46] whether for the whole or only for part of the school day (or in some of the circumstances mentioned), it has sometimes been the practice to exclude children from school by rota and to adopt a "totting up" procedure under which the loss of teachers' services is aggregated and the loss of teaching time to pupils averaged over the school as a whole. But it is doubtful whether this practice is lawful having regard to a local education authority's statutory duties.[47] If pupils would otherwise be unsupervised during the break between morning and afternoon sessions it might be proper to close the school at that time or to organise it temporarily on a "one session a day" basis.[48]

When employers conclude that there has been a breach of contract it **4–56** will be for consideration whether the breach is so fundamental as to amount to repudiation of the contract and thus to justify[49] dismissal. In practice the breach is unlikely to be so regarded, and for the contract to be taken to subsist but, in the absence of a satisfactory alternative

---

[43] See Trade Union Act 1984, s.10(1) and *Metropolitan Borough of Solihull* v. *National Union of Teachers* [1985] I.R.L.R. 211.
[44] *Secretary of State for Employment* v. *Association of Locomotive Engineers and Firemen* (No. 2) [1972] I.C.R. 19, C.A.
[45] See now S.I. 1987 No. 650, Sched. 3, para. (9).
[46] It is not proposed to consider civil action against trade unions themselves. The immunities of trade unions are now subject to the ballot requirements of the Trade Union Act 1984. As to the effect of strikes on the computation of periods of employment under the 1978 Act, see *ibid.* Sched. 13, para. 15.
[47] See especially 1944 Act, s.8, as amended, *Meade* v. *London Borough of Haringey* [1979] 2 All E.R. 1016, C.A. and above at para. 2–11.
[48] See reg. 10(1) of the Education (Schools and Further Education) Regulations 1981 (S.I. 1981 No. 1086) (above at para. 2–140) and 1980 Act, s.22 (below at paras. 5–09—10) regarding a local education authority's school meals obligations.
[49] See *Simmons* v. *Hoover* [1976] I.R.L.R. 266 (refusal to work during a strike is not "self-dismissal").

response,[50] for the employer to deduct pay as a measure of damages[51] in respect of the breach. In the case of strike action, where the teacher does not work for the whole or part of the school day no pay is due[52] in respect of the strike period; in other cases an estimate must be made of the extent of the loss suffered by the employers.

4–57   In *Royle* v. *Trafford Metropolitan Borough Council*[53] a teacher refused to take a class which included five pupils additional to the 31 in the class before industrial action started. The court held that the employers had accepted the duties which the teacher continued to perform, and had not suffered any financial loss by reason of his breaches of contract. They were not entitled, therefore, to stop his pay altogether. He would, however, have been entitled to his full salary only if he had "properly and fully performed his duties under his contract of employment." He had not done so and thus it was appropriate to make a deduction[54] representing the notional value of the services he had not rendered. It was held that a proportionate deduction of $\frac{5}{36}$ of salary (*i.e.* based on the number of children excluded from the class) was a reasonable estimate of damages, given that no replacement teacher had been employed to teach the children excluded from the class, and no claim had been made against the local education authority by a parent on grounds of failure to educate his child.

4–58   Mr. Royle was employed in a county school: where an aided school teacher is in breach of contract it appears that deductions from salary are lawful only with the concurrence of the governors, because the latter are the employers and there is no privity of contract between teacher and local education authority. The latter, however, have to meet salary payments as part of the expenses of maintaining[55] the school, and a

---

[50] Suspension seems inappropriate in cases of collective action and when no separate misconduct takes place. Salary paid during prolonged suspension might be expenditure contrary to law under Local Government Finance Act 1982, s.19. See also above at para. 4–30 n. 1 and below at para. 4–103.

[51] A "penalty" will be unlawful, but the propriety of making a deduction from salary as an equitable set-off was established in *Sim* v. *Rotherham Metropolitan Borough Council* (above at para. 4–51). It is arguable that continuance of full salary where there is breach of contract is "wilful misconduct" under Local Government Finance Act 1982, s.20, with the consequences for which that section provides.

[52] *Henthorn and Taylor* v. *Central Electricity Generating Board* [1980] I.R.L.R. 361, C.A. See *Burgundy Book*, para. 5.2.2 (below at para. 4–100). There is no standard formula for calculating the salary deduction where the strike is for a period shorter than a school session: authorities have adopted a variety of methods.

[53] [1984] I.R.L.R. 184. See also *Miles* v. *Wakefield Metropolitan District Council* [1987] 2 W.L.R. 795. B.W. Napier in "Teachers and their Contracts" (1985) 129 S.J. 181, is critical of the *Royle* decision, but see now *Sim* (note 51 above).

[54] What will be an appropriate deduction depends on the circumstances. One authority have deducted the nominal sum of £2 in respect of each occasion on which a teacher refuses to cover a lesson for an absent colleague.

[55] 1944 Act, s.114(2)(*a*) as amended. In addition, under s.5 of the Remuneration of Teachers Act 1965 (repealed) and the document (*i.e.* the Burnham Committee report) to which it refers, authorities were under a duty to pay all teachers in maintained schools whether or not employed by the authority. (See below at para. 4–114).

difference of opinion between local education authority and governors as to whether a contract had been breached, or as to the propriety of making salary deductions, might need to be resolved under sections 67[56] or 68[57] of the 1944 Act, so as to protect the authority from the imputation of having made payments in excess of proper maintenance expenses.

Ascertainment of the rights and duties of teachers and employers **4–59** becomes even more complex in situations where teachers are properly on leave before the start of collective action, where a school is closed because of a strike by, for example, caretakers as in *Meade* v. *London Borough of Haringey*,[58] or where picketing[59] is taking place. In the case of ordinary or sick leave, and in the absence of evidence to the contrary, the teacher is probably not to be regarded as on strike during the proper period of absence; and similarly if a school is closed by the authority. In these circumstances the teacher remains entitled to remuneration or sick pay[60] and (except where he is ill) the employer probably to use his services at an institution not affected by the action. Refusal to cross picket lines may be the equivalent of strike action, but inability to do so after an attempt has been made, and perhaps on reasonable fear for personal safety, would leave the employer with a continuing obligation to remunerate. Express terms in a contract of employment of course override these conjectures and the uncertainties referred to earlier.

The performance of contracts entered into with third parties, for **4–60** example in connection with school journeys, may be put in jeopardy by refusal of teachers to participate, and precipitate proceedings against local education authority or teachers.

EMPLOYMENT. GENERAL STATUTORY REQUIREMENTS

The statute law which moderates the relationship between employer **4–61** and employee applies to teachers and the non-teaching staff of local education authorities largely as it does in employment generally. Its main features are outlined in this section.

Sex and racial discrimination

The relevant legislation[61] is the Equal Pay Act 1970,[62] the Sex Dis- **4–62** crimination Acts 1975 and 1986 and the Race Relations Act 1976. The 1970 Act requires that men and women engaged upon like or equivalent

---

[56] See above at para. 2–103.

[57] See below at para. 6–10.

[58] [1979] 2 All E.R. 1016, C.A., and see above at para. 2–11.

[59] Explained in Trade Union and Labour Relations Act 1974, s.15, as substituted by Employment Act 1980, and amended by Employment Act 1982.

[60] Statutory as well as contractual sick pay. As to the effect of strikes on sick pay see Social Security and Housing Benefits Act 1982, s.3(3) and Sched. 1.

[61] The "1970," "1975," "1976" and "1986" Acts in this subsection. See also above at paras. 1–92 *et seq.*

[62] As amended by, and re-enacted in, Sched. 1 to the 1975 Act, and amended by, *inter alia*, the Employment Protection Act 1975, the Wages Councils Act 1979, the 1986 Act and the Equal Pay (Amendment) Regulations 1983 (S.I. 1983 No. 1794).

work are to be given equal treatment disregarding any special legal protection or treatment enjoyed by women: an "equality clause" to secure the right, if not expressly included in a contract of employment, is deemed to be included.[63] Disputes are to be referred to and determined by industrial tribunals.[64]

4–63   The 1970 Act is concerned with contractual terms of employment, the 1975 and 1986 Acts with non-contractual terms. With specified exceptions, it is unlawful to discriminate[65] against a woman[66]:

(a) in arrangements for recruitment of staff;
(b) in the terms on which employment is offered;
(c) by refusing or deliberately omitting to offer her employment;
(d) by the way in which she is given access (or by not giving her access) to promotion, transfer or training or other benefits, etc.;
(e) by dismissing her or subjecting her to any other detriment[67]; and
(f) by setting different retirement ages for men and women.

Terms in collective agreements must be non-discriminatory.[68]

In general, discriminatory practices which are unlawful under the 1970 Act are not to be challenged under the 1975 Act.

4–64   It is lawful to discriminate where sex is a genuine occupational qualification for a job.[69] Among the circumstances listed are where for reasons stated "the job needs to be done by a man to preserve decency or privacy"[70] and where "the holder of the job provides individuals with personal services promoting their welfare or education . . . and those services can most effectively be provided by a man."[71]

4–65   The law against racial discrimination[72] in employment is closely modelled on that relating to sex discrimination, and it is unlawful[73] to discriminate on racial grounds in relation to (a)–(e) in paragraph 4–63 above. As might be expected there are fewer exceptions[74] for "genuine occupation" than in the case of sex discrimination, but there is a "personal services" exception of which a local education authority might wish to take advantage, for example to employ an education welfare

---

[63] 1970 Act, ss.1 and 6, as amended.
[64] *Ibid.* s.2 and see s.2A (inserted by the Equal Pay (Amendment) Regulations 1983 (S.I. 1983 No. 1794)) as to procedure before an industrial tribunal.
[65] 1975 Act, s.6 as amended by 1986 Act, ss.1 and 2. As to the meaning of "discrimination," see s.1 and above at para. 1–93.
[66] The discriminatory treatment of men is equally unlawful (1975 Act, s.2) and the statutory provisions should be read accordingly.
[67] Including "sexual harassment"—see *Porcelli* v. *Strathclyde Council* [1985] I.C.R. 177, E.A.T.
[68] See 1986 Act, s.6, applying 1975 Act, s.77.
[69] 1975 Act, s.7 as amended by 1986 Act, s.1, and see also s.46 (communal accommodation). "Job" is not defined in the 1975 Act (but see note 84 below).
[70] *Ibid.* s.7(2)(*b*).
[71] *Ibid.* s.7(2)(*e*).
[72] Defined in 1976 Act, s.1 (and see above at para. 1–102).
[73] *Ibid.* s.4.
[74] *Ibid.* s.5.

officer of the same racial group as form a significant proportion of the pupils at a school.

A complaint of unlawful sex or racial discrimination in the employ- **4–66** ment field is to be made to an industrial tribunal[75] and may be the subject of conciliation[76] by an A.C.A.S. conciliation officer to endeavour to promote a settlement in advance of a tribunal hearing. The remedy[77] granted by a tribunal for a well-founded complaint is to be whichever (one or more) of the following they consider just and equitable:

(a) an order declaring rights;
(b) an order for monetary compensation;
(c) a recommendation that the respondent take action to obviate or reduce the adverse effect of the act of discrimination on the complainant.

Both the Equal Opportunities Commission and the Commission for **4–67** Racial Equality may prepare, for approval by Parliament and the Secretary of State, codes of practice[78] designed to eliminate unlawful discrimination and promote equality of opportunity in the field of employment; and an industrial tribunal may take codes into account when considering any question to which they are relevant.

Particulars of terms of employment

Within 13 weeks of employment beginning, the employers are to give **4–68** the employee a written statement[79] (unless he is employed normally for less than 16 hours weekly).[80] The particulars specified in the statement, or by reference to an accessible document,[81] are to include[82] scale or rate of remuneration and intervals at which remuneration is to be paid, holidays, sick pay, length of notice, disciplinary[83] and grievance procedures (except as to health or safety at work) and the title of the job[84] which the employee is employed to do. The employers are also to inform the employee of changes[85] in terms of employment within a month of their taking place. Such changes must of course be agreed

---

[75] 1975 Act, s.63, 1976 Act, s.54, and see also above at paras. 1–100 and 1–107.
[76] 1975 Act, s.64, and 1976 Act, s.55.
[77] 1975 Act, s.65 and 1976 Act, s.56 (both as amended).
[78] See 1975 Act, s.56A (added by 1976 Act) and 1976 Act, s.47. Codes of practice under both sections have been issued and came into effect on April 30, 1985, and April 1, 1984, respectively. (See S.I. 1985 No. 387 and S.I. 1983 No. 1081).
[79] 1978 Act, s.1(1), as amended by 1982 Act, and see ss.5 and 5A, also so amended, regarding excluded contracts.
[80] *Ibid.* s.146(4) as amended by 1982 Act.
[81] *Ibid.* s.2(3).
[82] *Ibid.* s.1(2)–(4) and s.2, as amended by 1982 Act. As to deductions from wages, see Wages Act 1986, Pt. I.
[83] A.C.A.S. have issued a Code of Practice under 1975 Act, s.6. See the Employment Protection Code of Practice (Disciplinary Practice and Procedures) Order 1977 (S.I. 1977 No. 867).
[84] "Job" means the nature of the work which the employee is employed to do in accordance with his contract, and the capacity and place in which he is so employed (*ibid.* s.153(1)).
[85] 1978 Act, s.4, as amended by 1982 Act. See Circ. 5/87, paras. 16–18.

changes, because the particulars only record—they do not create—
terms of employment; but they may constitute evidence of terms of
employment, and moreover changes may come about as a result of the
variation of a collective agreement[86] incorporated into a contract of service.

4-69   Employees (except part-timers as above) also have the right to be
given itemised pay statements,[87] which are to include gross and net pay
and particulars of deductions from gross pay.

4-70   If employers fail to comply with their obligations as regards statements the employee may refer[88] the matter to an industrial tribunal for
determination.

Trade union membership and activities

4-71   Action (short of dismissal) is not to be taken[89] against an employee
for joining an independent trade union[90] or taking part in its activities
outside working hours (or within by agreement with employers) or to
compel him to join a trade union or to penalise him for not being in
membership of one. Appropriate exceptions are made where a "closed
shop" exists. Complaint[91] may be made to an industrial tribunal against
breach of these provisions, and if the tribunal find it well founded they
may award compensation[92] to the employee. The employers may not
exculpate[93] themselves on the ground of actual or threatened industrial
action, but in an appropriate case the award may be made against a third
party[94] instead of against the employer.

Time off work. Maternity leave

4-72   Officials of independent trade unions are to be given time off[95] with
pay for their industrial relations duties and members (without a right to
pay) for trade union activities. Limited time off (whether or not with
pay seems to be left open) is also to be given to employees for public
duties[96]—as Justice of the Peace or member of a local authority, statutory
tribunal, health or water authority or governing body of a maintained

---

[86] See below at paras. 4–98 *et seq.*

[87] *Ibid.* ss.8 and 9.

[88] *Ibid.* s.11.

[89] *Ibid.* s.23 as amended by 1980 and 1982 Acts. "Action short of dismissal" includes disciplinary action, *e.g.* demotion, which is within the contract of employment. See B. A. Hepple and P. O'Higgins, *Encyclopedia of Labour Relations Law* (1972) para. 2–1817.

[90] "Trade union" is defined in s.28 of the Trade Union and Labour Relations Act 1974, and "independent trade union" in s.153(1) of the 1978 Act.

[91] 1978 Act, s.24.

[92] Assessed under *ibid.* s.26.

[93] *Ibid.* s.25 as amended by 1980 Act.

[94] *Ibid.* s.26A as substituted by 1982 Act.

[95] *Ibid.* ss.27 and 28. See *Beal and Others* v. *Beecham Group Ltd.* [1982] I.C.R. 460. For the amount of time off and purposes to which it may be put see Code of Practice issued by A.C.A.S. under s.6, as amended, of the 1975 Act and the Employment Protection Code of Practice (Time Off) Order 1977 (S.I. 1977 No. 2076).

[96] 1978 Act, s.29 as amended. See *Corner* v. *Buckinghamshire County Council*, 77 L.G.R. 268 (time off to carry out duties as J.P.).

educational establishment. On redundancy,[97] time off[98] with pay is to be given to look for work or make arrangements for training; and it is also to be given for ante-natal care.[99] All the time off rights can be asserted by complaint[1] to an industrial tribunal. Only the two last-mentioned are ordinarily available[2] to those who are employed normally for less than 16 hours weekly.

An employee who is absent from work wholly or partly because of **4–73** pregnancy or confinement is entitled to maternity pay[3] and the right to return to work. To take advantage of the latter right an employee[4] has:

(a) to continue to be employed (whether or not at work) until immediately before the beginning of the eleventh week before the expected week of confinement;

(b) to have been continuously employed[5] for not less than two years before the beginning of the eleventh week; and

(c) to give notice as specified to her employers about her forthcoming absence, the (expected or actual) time of confinement and her intention to return to work.

An employee who has been dismissed[6] on grounds of pregnancy (because incapable of carrying out her duties or where statute would be contravened if they were carried out) may have the same entitlement if, but for the dismissal, she would have satisfied (a) and (b) above.

An employee who meets the requirements mentioned above has the **4–74** right[7] to return to her previous job within 29 weeks from the week of confinement. If this is not practicable by reason of redundancy she is to be offered alternative employment if there is a suitable vacancy. In either case conditions of employment are to be not less favourable than before. An employee exercises[8] her right by giving notice in writing to

---

[97] See below at paras. 4–91 *et seq*.

[98] *Ibid*. 1978 Act, s.31.

[99] *Ibid*. s.31A (inserted by 1980 Act).

[1] *Ibid*. ss.27(7), 28(4), 29(6), 31(6) and 31A(6). As to the jurisdiction of the tribunal see ss.30, 31(7) and 31A(7). See also *Corner* v. *Buckinghamshire County Council* (n. 96 above), as to tribunals generally s.128, and as to conciliation s.133, both as amended by 1980 Act.

[2] *Ibid*. s.136(4).

[3] *Ibid*. ss.34–44 and consequential provisions have been repealed and replaced by Social Security Act 1986, ss.46–50, and related provisions. (As to circumstances in which the Secretary of State refused to pay rebates to employers under the 1978 Act, see *Secretary of State for Employment* v. *Newcastle-upon-Tyne City Council* [1980] I.C.R. 407, E.A.T.). Remuneration paid under contract (see para. 4–105) goes towards meeting the statutory obligation and *vice versa*. As to conflict between statutory and contractual rights see *I.L.E.A.* v. *Nash* [1979] I.C.R. 229.

[4] 1978 Act, s.33, as amended.

[5] "Continuous employment"—see *ibid*. s.151, and substituted by 1982 Act and Sched. 13 as amended and below at para. 4–81. "Supply" teachers employed at a daily or hourly rate may not qualify.

[6] Under *ibid*. s.60(1)(*a*) or (*b*), and see below at para. 4–87.

[7] *Ibid*. s.45. As to enforcement see s.46.

[8] *Ibid*. s.47, as amended by 1980 Act.

the employers at least 21 days before the day on which she proposes to return. The employers may for reasons they specify postpone the return for up to four weeks. If before the 29 weeks expire, or before the date for return notified by the employer, she is certified to be unwell and not fit for work she may have a further four weeks absence from work. These general rules are modified if work is interrupted by industrial action or for some other reason. An employee who has a right both under the Act and under a contract of employment or otherwise to return to work may not exercise the two rights separately, but may take advantage of whichever right is in any particular respect the more favourable.[9]

4–75 Provisions in the Employment Act 1980, in particular those against unfair dismissal[10] and giving rights to redundancy payments,[11] are adapted[12] so as to apply during the period of absence from work and on refusal of employers to permit return to work.

Health and safety at work
4–76 It is the duty[13] of employers to ensure, so far as is reasonably practicable,[14] the health, safety and welfare at work[15] of employees and others, such as school pupils, and this duty is particularised to include provision of systems of work that are without risk to health; provision of information, training and supervision; and a safe and healthy place of work and working environment. Employers are to prepare, keep up-to-date and bring to the notice of employees, a written statement of their general policy with respect to health and safety at work and how they propose to implement it.

4–77 Employers are to consult elected "safety" representatives[16] of employees about co-operation to ensure health and safety at work, and if at least two safety representatives ask for a safety committee to be established the employers must comply. Employees must[17] take reasonable

---

[9] 1978 Act, s.48.

[10] *Ibid.* s.56, as amended by 1980 Act; and see s.56A, inserted by 1980 Act; also below at para. 4–84.

[11] *Ibid.* s.86, and below at para. 4–93.

[12] *Ibid.* Sched. 2, as amended by 1980 and 1982 Acts.

[13] ss. 2, 3 and 4 of the Health and Safety at Work etc. Act 1974, as amended by 1975 Act. See Circ. 11/74 (W.O. 226/74). As to enforcement of the Act, obtaining disclosure of information and offences, see ss.18 *et seq.*, 27–28, and 33 *et seq.* respectively. A.M. 20/61 is on industrial safety and the education service. See G. Cox, "Contractors in Schools: a need for basic standards" L.G.C. November 21, 1986.

[14] See *Stroud's Judicial Dictionary* (5th ed., 1986).

[15] For the meaning of "work" and "at work" see Health and Safety at Work etc. Act 1974, s.52, as amended by 1975 Act.

[16] See the Safety Representatives and Safety Committees Regulations 1977 (S.I. 1977 No. 500), and, as to the recognition of a union for the appointment of representatives, *Cleveland County Council* v. *Springett and Others* [1985] I.R.L.R. 131, E.A.T.

[17] Health and Safety at Work etc. Act 1974, s.7, and see also ss.8 and 9, and below at paras. 7–05 *et seq.*

care for the safety of themselves and others likely to be affected by their acts and omissions at work, and co-operate with their employers regarding statutory obligations. This requirement applies not only to teachers and other employees of local education authorities (in relation to children and others) but to employees of contractors at work on school etc. premises. The self-employed must also take care.[18]

Persons who have "to any extent, control" of non-domestic premises **4–78** such as schools and other educational establishments, or of access to them or plant or substances in them, must ensure,[19] so far as reasonably practicable,[20] that they are safe and not a risk to the health of those other than their employees who work there. This provision appears to place responsibility on head teachers and some non-teaching staff as well as on local education authorities and governors.

Regulations[21] require notification to the enforcing authority of acci- **4–79** dents at work resulting in death or specified major injury and of dangerous occurrences.

Breaches of the health and safety requirements outlined above do not **4–80** as such give rise to civil liability, but the circumstances of an accident or injury to health may be actionable in separate proceedings.[22]

Dismissal: general requirements

The terms of articles of government outlined in the previous section **4–81** are consistent with the general statutory provisions regarding dismissal. In brief,[23] these are as follows. A person who has been continuously employed[24] for a month or more must be given[25] at least one week's notice if he has been employed for less than two years; at least one week's notice for each year of continuous employment if he has been employed for between two and 12 years; and at least 12 weeks' notice if the continuous employment has been for 12 years or more. The employee must give at least a week's notice if he has been continuously employed for a month or more.[26] Articles, as has been indicated, are likely to require longer periods of notice than the minimum specified except in the case of a long period of continuous employment.

A working week of less than 16 hours does not count in computing a

---

[18] Health and Safety at Work etc. Act 1974, s.3(2).
[19] *Ibid*. s.4. *e.g.*, failure by a caretaker to report a material defect would appear to be a breach of the statutory duty. See also below at para. 7–38.
[20] (See n. 14 above).
[21] The Reporting of Injuries, Diseases and Dangerous Occurrences Regulations 1985 (S.I. 1985 No. 2023) made under *ibid*. s.15 as amended by 1975 Act.
[22] Health and Safety at Work etc. Act 1974, s.47, as amended by 1975 Act.
[23] For fuller treatment see Hepple & O'Higgins, *Encyclopedia of Labour Relations Law* (1972).
[24] "Continuous employment" is explained in 1978 Act, s.151 as substituted by 1982 Act and computed in accordance with that section and Sched. 13, as amended.
[25] 1978 Act, s.49(1). See subs. (4) and (4A) in respect of contracts for limited periods.
[26] *Ibid*. s.49(2).

period of continuous employment unless it is of at least eight hours and employment has been for five years or more. Short breaks between classes are part of working hours (*Girls' Public Day School Trust* v. *Khanna*.[27] When working hours are specified in the contract of employment (as in *Lake* v. *Essex County Council*)[28] voluntary overtime for preparation and marking does not count in the calculation. Nor do periods on strike count. There is a presumption of continuity, and a period of employment with the same employer is continuous even though the capacity in which the employee works and his terms of employment change, unless one of the exceptions in Sched. 13 to the 1978 Act applies (*Wood* v. *York City Council*).[29] Employment under several different contracts of employment with the same employer may be aggregated (*Surrey County Council* v. *Lewis*).[30] The breaks in employment between July and September when a teacher has been employed year by year over a series of academic years do not break the continuity of employment within the period of employment as a whole (*Ford* v. *Warwickshire County Council*).[31] A teacher "starts work" at the beginning of employment under the contract, not later when she actually begins teaching (*General of the Salvation Army* v. *Dewsbury*).[32]

4–82   During the period of notice the employee ordinarily has specified rights[33] to receive pay, and these rights are to be taken into account[34] in assessing an employer's liability for breach of contract if he fails to give the required period of notice. The right to notice may be waived or payment may be accepted in lieu.[35] The notice provisions are without prejudice to subsisting rights[36] of either party to terminate[37] the contract without notice by reason of the conduct of the other party.

4–83   An employee is entitled to receive a written statement giving particulars[38] of the reasons for his dismissal within 14 days of requesting it, whether the dismissal takes place on or without notice, or a fixed term contract expires without being renewed, provided that he has been continuously employed for six months. Unreasonable refusal to provide a written statement may give grounds for complaint to an industrial tribunal.

---

[27] (1987) 84 L.S. Gaz. 189, E.A.T.
[28] [1979] I.C.R. 577.
[29] [1928] I.C.R. 840, C.A.
[30] [1981] I.C.R. 232, C.A.
[31] [1983] I.C.R. 273, H.L.
[32] [1984] I.C.R. 498, E.A.T.
[33] *Ibid.* s.50 and Sched. 3 as amended.
[34] *Ibid.* s.51.
[35] *Ibid.* s.49(3).
[36] *i.e.*, at common law or under the contract of service.
[37] 1978 Act, s.49(5).
[38] *Ibid.* s.53 as amended by 1982 Act. As to part-timers see Sched. 13 as amended. As to what constitutes an adequate statement see *Gilham and Others* v. *Kent County Council (No. 1)* [1985] I.C.R. 227, C.A.

Unfair dismissal

A common law claim for redress upon wrongful dismissal[39] is to be distinguished from the right[40] granted by statute not to be unfairly dismissed. The right does not in general extend to those who have been continuously employed[41] by the same employer for less than (normally) two years, or who have reached the normal retiring age for the position held or the age of 65[42]; nor does it extend to those who have agreed in writing to exclude the right before the end of a fixed term contract of one year or more.[43] Dismissal[44] for the purposes of statutory protection arises: **4–84**

(a) when the employer terminates a contract of employment with or without notice;

(b) when a fixed term contract[45] expires;

(c) when the employee, properly, terminates the contract of employment by reason of the employer's conduct[45a]; and

(d) when, with exceptions in certain circumstances, a woman is not permitted to return to work after confinement.[46]

Where the employers are the governors of an aided school and dismissal is required by the local education authority[47] the unfair dismissal provisions apply as if the local education authority were the employers.[48]

To resist the claim that dismissal was unfair, employers have first to show[49] what the reason (or principal reason) was and: **4–85**

(a) that it specifically related to the capability or qualifications[50] of

---

[39] As to claim by a college registrar for wrongful dismissal and the effect of the authority's disciplinary regulations upon the contract see *Gunton* v. *Richmond-upon-Thames London Borough Council* 79 L.G.R. 241, C.A.

[40] 1978 Act, s.54.

[41] "Continuous employment"—see para. 4–81.

[42] ss.64 and 64A (inserted by 1980 Act) as amended by 1982 Act, the Sex Discrimination Act 1986, s.3 and the Unfair Dismissal (Variation of Qualifying Period) Order 1985 (S.I. 1985 No. 782) made under 1978 Act, s.149(1)(c). (The qualifying period is one year for those whose continuous period of employment began before June 1, 1985). The qualifying period and upper age limits do not apply when the complaint is governed by 1978 Act, s.58—see below at para. 4–87 n. 59. As to the relationship between normal retirement age and upper age limits see *Nothman* v. *London Borough of Barnet* [1977] I.R.L.R. 489, C.A. and [1979] I.R.L.R. 35, H.L. and *Waite* v. *Government Communications Headquarters* [1983] I.R.L.R. 161, C.A.

[43] 1978 Act, s.142(1), as amended by 1980 Act.

[44] *Ibid.* s.55, as amended by 1982 Act.

[45] As to the distinction between a fixed term contract and a contract for a specific task see *Wiltshire* v. *National Association of Teachers in Further Education and Guy* [1980] I.R.L.R. 1981, *Ford* v. *Warwickshire County Council* [1983] I.C.R. 273, H.L. and *Brown and Others* v. *Knowsley Borough Council* [1986] I.R.L.R. 102.

[45a] As to constructive dismissal see *Bridgen* v. *Lancashire County Council* [1987] I.R.L.R 58.

[46] 1978 Act, ss.56 and 56A (amended/inserted by the 1980 Act). As to teachers employed by the governors of an aided school, see the Employment Protection (Employment in Aided Schools) Order 1981 (S.I. 1981 No. 847) made under 1978 Act, s.149(1)(a)).

[47] Under para. (a) of the proviso to s.24(2) of the 1944 Act. See above at para. 4–27.

[48] 1978 Act, s.80, as amended by Education Act 1980, s.1(3) and Sched. 1 para. 30.

[49] 1978 Act, s.57(1) and (2).

[50] "Capability" and "qualifications" are defined in *ibid.*, s.57(4). See *Cohen* v. *London Borough of Barking* [1976] I.R.L.R. 416.

the employee for performing work of the kind for which he was employed; or

(b) to his conduct[51]; or

(c) that he was redundant[52]; or

(d) that he could not continue to work in the position which he held without some statutory provisions being contravened[53]; or

(e) that some other[54] reason existed so substantial as to justify dismissal.

The expiry of a fixed term contract may be a substantial other reason, but whether the employee knew the job was not likely to be renewed would be material in the decision whether he was unfairly dismissed.[55]

4–86   If the employers can comply with these requirements, whether or not the dismissal counts as unfair depends[56] on whether in the circumstances (including the employers' size and administrative resources) they acted reasonably[57] or not in treating the reason as sufficient for dismissing the employee. The question is to be determined "in accordance with equity and the substantial merits of the case." Pressure put on employers by threat of industrial action is to be discounted in determining whether or not dismissal was unfair.[58]

4–87   Dismissal is to be regarded as unfair in specified circumstances relating to the employee's taking part, or failing to take part, in trade union activities.[59] Dismissal on ground of pregnancy[60] is unfair except where:

(a) the employee is incapable of adequately carrying out her duties

---

[51] See *Haddow & Others* v. *Inner London Education Authority* [1979] I.C.R. 202 (dismissal following strike), *Gardiner* v. *Newport County Borough Council* [1974] I.R.L.R. 262 (indecency), and *Nottinghamshire County Council* v. *Bowly* [1978] I.R.L.R. 252 (indecency).

[52] Dismissal for redundancy is unfair if the employee is discriminated against (1978 Act, s.59 as amended by 1982 Act). See also below at para. 4–96.

[53] This reason was advanced, erroneously it was held, in both *Birmingham City Council* v. *Elson*, 77 L.G.R. 743, and *Sandhu* v. *Department of Education and Science and London Borough of Hillingdon* [1978] I.R.L.R. 208.

[54] As to when the dismissal of a teacher who has been employed as a replacement for another teacher absent on pregnancy or suspended on medical grounds is dismissal within this category, see 1978 Act, s.61.

[55] *Terry* v. *East Sussex County Council* [1976] I.C.R. 536, E.A.T.; *North Yorkshire Council* v. *Fay* [1985] I.R.L.R. 247, C.A.

[56] 1978 Act, s.57(3), as amended by the 1980 Act. See *Redbridge L.B.C.* v. *Fishman*, 76 L.G.R. 408, E.A.T. (reasonableness of request to teacher), *Neale* v. *Hereford and Worcester County Council* [1986] I.C.R. 471 (misconduct by teacher), *Pendlebury* v. *Christian Schools North West Ltd.* [1985] I.C.R. 174 (dismissal by mistake), *Norfolk County Council* v. *Bernard* [1979] I.R.L.R. 220 (drugs offences), *Wiseman* v. *Salford City Council* [1981] I.R.L.R. 202 (indecency), and *I.L.E.A.* v. *Lloyd* [1981] I.R.L.R. 395 (unsatisfactory probation).

[57] See A.C.A.S. Code of Disciplinary Practice and Procedure, brought into effect by S.I. 1977 No. 867 (see above at para. 4–68 n. 83).

[58] 1978 Act, s.63.

[59] *Ibid.* s.58 as substituted by 1982 Act, and see as to union membership agreements ("closed shops"), s.58A as substituted by *ibid.* See also above at paras. 4–71 and 4–72.

[60] 1978 Act, s.60.

or where statute would be contravened if they continued to be carried out; and
(b) the employers offer a new and not substantially less favourable contract of alternative employment.

Complaint against unfair dismissal is made to an industrial tribunal,[61]   **4–88** but may not be made when the dismissal took place during a lockout or strike or other industrial action,[62] unless the employee can show that he personally has been discriminated against.[63] When an industrial tribunal find a complaint well-founded[64] they are to explain to the employee what orders for reinstatement or re-engagement may be made and in what circumstances they may be made, and ask him whether he wishes the tribunal to make an order.[65] If no order is made the tribunal may make an award for compensation[66] to be paid by employer (or, exceptionally, a third party) to employee. In certain circumstances interim relief may be granted by an industrial tribunal before the complaint is determined.[67]

Complaints of unfair dismissal have been made against local   **4–89** education authorities by school meals staff.[68] The Education Act 1980 having removed[69] the duty upon local education authorities to provide a comprehensive school meals service, some authorities under financial pressure, decided to employ staff upon terms less favourable than those in national collective agreements. To achieve this result staff were dismissed and offered new engagements.

Staff have had recourse to industrial tribunals, who, in applying the   **4–90** provisions of the 1978 Act, have sought to ascertain the reasons for council decisions and the manner in which they were implemented, in order to discover whether the action was unreasonable under section 57(3). Kent County Council[70] were found to have failed the tests in both

---

[61] 1978 Act, ss.67 and 128 (as amended, respectively, by 1982 and 1980 Acts), and s.134 (as amended by 1980 Act) as to conciliation to anticipate proceedings before a tribunal.

[62] "Lock-out" and "strike" are undefined for the purposes of *ibid.* s.62, but see the definition of those terms in Sched. 13, para. 24.

[63] *Ibid.* s.62, as amended by 1982 Act.

[64] *Ibid.* s.68, as amended by 1982 Act.

[65] As to orders for reinstatement and re-engagement, see *ibid.* ss.69, 70 and 71, as amended by 1982 Act.

[66] As to the award of compensation see ss.72–76A, as amended and substituted by 1980 and 1982 Acts and (s.73) amended by Sex Discrimination Act 1986, s.3. In the calculation of continuous employment (by contrast with the position on redundancy) only service with the "dismissing" authority counts (*Merton London Borough Council* v. *Gardiner* [1981] I.C.R. 186). As to the method of calculating compensation see *Gilham and Others* v. *Kent County Council (No. 3)* [1986] I.C.R. 52, E.A.T.

[67] *Ibid.* ss.77–79, as amended by 1982 Act.

[68] See R. Lewis, "School Meals—the Current Legal Challenges" (February 1985) *County Councils Gazette* 342.

[69] See below at para. 5–09.

[70] *Gilham and Others* v. *Kent County Council (No. 2)* [1985] I.C.R. 233, C.A.

section 57(1) and (3) of the Act,[71] and thus to have acted unfairly by reason, *inter alia*, of having set aside a national agreement (notwithstanding that national agreements are no longer imported into the contracts of employment by statute)[72]; and their appeals to the Employment Appeal Tribunal and Court of Appeal failed on the ground that the decision of the industrial tribunal had been one of fact, not of law, and thus not open to review. Devon and Somerset county councils were, in similar circumstances, held by industrial tribunals not to have acted unfairly—their decisions having been held to be matters of policy on which the councils had properly decided. Other authorities[73] taking similar action have been challenged in the High Court under the procedure for judicial review, unsuccessfully except[74] where it was possible to show procedural *ultra vires*.[75]

Dismissal on redundancy

4–91   A shrinking school population and public expenditure economies give rise to the dismissal of teachers and others because they are redundant.[76] Redundancy[77] can come about through closure of a teaching establishment or reduction in the need for staff there, or in a local education authority's maintained schools as a whole.[78] Dismissal includes the expiry of a fixed-term contract, and failure to renew such a contract may, but does not necessarily, prove redundancy.[79] The legislation is modified[80] so as to apply it to employees who by statute are remunerated by persons other than the employer—in the present context teachers and others who are remunerated by local education authorities but employed by governors of aided schools.

4–92   A local education authority or other employer proposing to dismiss[81] employees as redundant must consult[82] representatives of the relevant

---

[71] See above at paras. 4–85 and 4–86.

[72] See para. 4–99 n. 20.

[73] See *R.* v. *Hertfordshire County Council, ex p. National Union of Public Employees and Others*, and *R.* v. *Essex County Council, ex p. Same* [1985] I.R.L.R. 258, C.A.

[74] See *R.* v. *Birmingham City Council, ex p. National Union of Public Employees and Another, The Times*, April 24, 1984, and above at para. 1–27.

[75] Procedural *ultra vires*—see above at para. 1–53.

[76] See, generally, Second Report from the Education, Science and Arts Committee, *The Secondary School Curriculum and Examinations*, 1981–82 (H.C. 116–1) and *Government Response* (Cmnd. 8648).

[77] Defined similarly in s.126(6) of the 1975 Act and s.81(2) of the 1978 Act.

[78] 1978 Act, s.81(2A) inserted by 1982 Act, Sched. 3.

[79] See *Lee* v. *Notts. County Council* [1980] I.R.L.R. 284, C.A., *North Yorkshire County Council* v. *Fay* [1985] I.R.L.R. 247, C.A. and *Brown* v. *Knowsley Borough Council* [1986] I.R.L.R. 102, E.A.T.

[80] See 1978 Act, s.117, as amended by Wages Act 1986, s.27(A) and Sched. 8.

[81] "Dismiss," by 1975 Act, s.126(1) as amended, is to be defined in accordance with s.55 of the 1978 Act as amended (see above at para. 4–84).

[82] 1975 Act, s.99 (as amended) and see s.119(7) (as amended by the 1978 and 1982 Acts), and also below at para. 4–96. In *National Union of Teachers* v. *Solihull Metropolitan Borough Council* (unreported) an industrial tribunal held that failure to renew fixed term contracts amounted to dismissal for redundancy. The council were in breach of s.99, having failed formally to consult unions

trade unions[83] about the dismissal at the earliest opportunity (before giving individual notices of dismissal)[84] and must put in writing to the union representatives the reason for the proposals, the numbers and description of employees whom they propose to dismiss as redundant, the total number of those employees employed at the establishments concerned, the proposed method of selection for dismissal and how and over what period the dismissals are to take effect. The employer must consider union representations and give reasons if he rejects them. All these obligations placed on the employer are subject to their being reasonably practicable in the circumstances. A union may complain[85] to an industrial tribunal that the requirements specified have not been complied with in relation to particular dismissals, and if the tribunal find the complaint well founded they may require the employer to pay remuneration for a "protected" period. If the employer fails to comply the employee may complain to an industrial tribunal.[86] Multiple dismissals are to be notified[87] to the Secretary of State under sanction of a fine.

An employee who has been continuously employed[88] for at least two   **4–93** years[89] by one or more local education authorities, or by certain other bodies, and who is dismissed[90] wholly or mainly by reason of redundancy, is entitled[91] to a redundancy payment from his employers. Employment, to qualify,[92] must be for 16 or more hours weekly, or eight hours if employment has been for five years or more. No

---

in advance. See also *National Association of Teachers in Further and Higher Education* v. *Manchester City Council* [1978] I.C.R. 1190, E.A.T. and the cases cited at n. 79 above. As to the meaning of "consultation" see above at para. 1–45.

[83] *i.e.*, independent trade unions as defined in ss.28 and 30, as amended, to the Trade Union and Labour Relations Act 1974.

[84] See *National Union of Teachers* v. *Avon County Council* [1978] I.R.L.R. 55, E.A.T.

[85] 1975 Act, ss.101–102 and 106 as amended.

[86] *Ibid.* ss.103 and 108, as amended by the 1978 Act.

[87] *Ibid.* s.100 as amended by Employment Protection (Handling of Redundancies) Variation Order 1979 (S.I. 1979 No. 958) and s.105, as amended by Wages Act 1986.

[88] See above at para. 4–81.

[89] Ending with the date on which notice expires or other relevant date as defined in 1978 Act, s.90.

[90] As defined in *ibid.* s.83 (and following the definition in s.55 for the purposes of unfair dismissal— see above at para. 4–84); and see s.31 as to time off to look for work, etc.; s.84 and the Redundancy Payments (Local Government) (Modification) Order 1983 (S.I. 1983 No. 1160) Sched. 2, para. 3, renewal of contract or re-engagement; s.85, anticipation by employee of expiry of employer's notice; and s.86, failure to permit women to return to work after confinement treated as dismissal. Retirement under an early retirement scheme does not constitute dismissal for redundancy (*University of Liverpool* v. *Humber and Birch* [1984] I.R.L.R. 54).

[91] *Ibid.* s.81 as amended by 1982 Act, and S.I. 1983 No. 1160, as amended by S.I. 1985 No. 1872. The "other bodies" include the governing body of a voluntary school and of an assisted or grant-aided further education establishment. As to employees in Lancashire see The Redundancy Payments (Exemption) Order 1980 (S.I. 1980 No. 1052). See ss.92 and 110 as to when a dismissed employee goes on strike, and ss.106 and 107, as amended, as to the circumstances in which payment may be made by the Secretary of State. In *Lee* v. *Nottinghamshire County Council* [1980] I.R.L.R. 284, C.A. a fixed term contract was not renewed: this was dismissal on account of redundancy even though the lecturer knew on appointment that a run-down of staff was taking place.

[92] See 1978 Act, Sched. 13. as amended.

payment[93] is due to a man of 65, or a woman of 60, or more, or where under specified circumstances and conditions there has been misconduct or where re-engagement or renewal of suitable employment is offered but not accepted. In *Taylor* v. *Kent County Council*[94] it was held that an offer to a former headmaster of a post at the same salary in a mobile pool of teachers was not suitable, because not substantially equivalent to the employment that had ceased; and in *Spencer and Griffin* v. *Gloucestershire County Council*[95] that, the council having to reduce their costs and lower school cleaning standards, it was not unreasonable for school cleaners to refuse re-engagement for rather fewer hours a week than they had previously worked on the ground that they would be unable to do their work to a standard satisfactory to themselves.

4–94   The amount[96] of the redundancy payment is calculated by reference to continuous employment of up to 20 years. Written particulars of the calculation are to be provided by the employer.[97] Teachers and other employees who have served more than one authority or governing body have their periods of employment aggregated. For each year of service from the (inclusive) ages of 41 to 64 (men) or 59 (women) the entitlement[98] is one and a half weeks' pay,[99] from 22 to 40 one week's pay and from 18 to 21 half a week's pay. For the purposes of calculating the redundancy payment a week's pay is not to exceed £145. Employers may pay teachers additional compensation on the basis that the £145 limit does not apply.[1] They also have power, in certain circumstances where the employee has pension or compensation rights, to exclude or reduce a redundancy payment.[2] Employers may claim out of the Redundancy Fund established by the Secretary of State for Employment a rebate[3] on the amount of redundancy payment made only if their employees number less than ten. Questions about the right to redundancy payment or its amount or about rebates are determined by industrial tribunals.[4]

---

[93] 1978 Act, s.82 (and see S.I. 1983 No. 1160, Sched. 2, para. 2).
[94] [1969] 3 W.L.R. 156.
[95] [1985] I.R.L.R. 59.
[96] See 1978 Act, ss.81 and 151(4) and Sched. 4, 13 and 14 as amended, and S.I. 1983 No. 1160, Sched. 2, para. 5.
[97] *Ibid.* s.102, as amended.
[98] As to caims for redundancy payments see *ibid.* s.101. As to calculation of payment due to part-time, hourly paid, teachers, see *Cole* v. *Birmingham City District Council* [1978] I.C.R. 1004.
[99] "A week's pay"—see *ibid.* s.152, and Sched. 14 as amended.
[1] See reg. 5 of the Teachers (Compensation for Redundancy and Premature Retirement) Regulations 1985 (S.I. 1985 No. 1181).
[2] 1978 Act, s.98 and the Redundancy Payments Pensions Regulations 1965 (S.I. 1965 No. 1932). See 1978 Act, s.118 and the Redundancy Payments Statutory Compensation Regulations 1965 (S.I. 1965 No. 1988) as regards set-off of redundancy payments against compensation granted under certain statutory provisions which include s.98 of the 1944 Act, and s.12 of the 1946 Act (both repealed).
[3] 1978 Act, s.104 as amended in particular by Wages Act 1986, Part III and Scheds. 4 and 5.
[4] See *ibid.*, ss.91, 108 and 128 as amended.

For teachers aged between 50 and 59 (inclusive) the lump sum pay-   **4-95**
ment may be supplemented by a pension on early retirement[5]; certain
further education teachers who lost their employment before September
1, 1985 because of contraction in provision of further education courses,
who are entitled to a redundancy payment and are aged 41 to 49 (inclusive), may claim[6] a lump sum in compensation calculated as prescribed;
and teachers (and others) at teacher training establishments who
between August 1, 1975, and September 1, 1981, suffered loss of
employment, or loss of diminution of emoluments, as a result of
reorganisation of teacher training facilities, are eligible[7] for compensation of various kinds which extends to widows, children and other
dependants.

An agreement was reached in 1976 between C.L.E.A. and teachers'   **4-96**
organisations[8] on procedures for consultation between individual local
education authorities and local representatives of the teachers' organisations when redundancy and premature retirement compensation were
contemplated. It is in Appendix VIII of the *Burgundy Book*[9] and supplements the statutory consultation requirements to which reference has
been made.[10] Authorities are to seek volunteers for premature retirement and to consult their teachers on policy regarding enhancing the
level of premature retirement compensation. The policy should not
involve discrimination between teachers in similar professional circumstances, which include length of service. Use of the premature retirement compensation provisions for the efficient exercise of the
authority's functions is to be the subject of similar consultations, which
should establish the circumstances in which the authority would act (for
example, on reorganisaton of schools or redeployment of teachers for
other reasons), and involve consideration of the same issues as in redundancy cases and the same disclosure of information.

---

[5] Teachers' Superannuation Regulations 1976 (S.I. 1976 No. 1987) reg. 53A (added by reg. 12 of
the Teachers' Superannuation (Amendment) Regulations 1978 (S.I. 1978 No. 422)) made under
s.9 of the Superannuation Act 1972, and the Teachers' (Compensation for Redundancy and
Premature Retirement) Regulations 1985 (S.I. 1985 No. 1181) made under s.24 of the Superannuation Act 1972. See below at para. 4–147.

[6] See the Teachers' (Compensation) (Advanced Further Education) Regulations 1983 (S.I. 1983
No. 856) made under s.24 of the Superannuation Act 1972, and Circ. 5/83 (W.O. 43/83).

[7] See Circular 6/75 and the Colleges of Education (Compensation) Regulations 1975 (S.I. 1975 No.
1092) and Amendment Regulations 1981 (S.I. 1981 No. 1088) made under s.24 of the Superannuation Act 1972, the Pensions Increase (Compensation to Staff of Teacher Training Establishments) Regulations 1975 (S.I. 1975 No. 1478) made under s.5(2) of the Pensions (Increase) Act
1971, *Pearson* v. *Kent County Council* 77 L.G.R. 604, Q.B.D. and, as to calculation of emoluments, *Leeds City Council* v. *Pomfret* [1983] I.C.R. 674.

[8] National Union of Teachers, Incorporated Association of Assistant Masters, Incorporated Associ-
ation of Assistant Mistresses, Incorporated Association of Headmasters, Incorporated Associ-
ation of Headmistresses, National Association of Head Teachers, National Association of
Schoolmasters/Union of Women Teachers, National Association of Teachers in Further and
Higher Education, Association of Principals of Colleges, National Society of Art Education and
Association of Agricultural Education Staffs.

[9] See below at paras. 4–100 and (as to provision for compensation) 4–147.

[10] See above at para. 4–92.

4-97   The agreement also incorporates[11] one made in 1973, and revised in 1975, on redundancies in further education institutions under which:

   (a) the need for and implications of proposed redundancies are to be discussed;
   (b) the possibility of alternative employment is to be explored;
   (c) not less than a year's notice; and
   (d) a hearing is to be given;
   (e) secondment for up to 12 months is to be granted on full pay for retraining for other educational posts and, as now provided by statute[12];
   (f) service in more than one authority is to be regarded as continuous for calculating redundancy payments.

EMPLOYMENT. NEGOTIATED CONDITIONS OF SERVICE

4-98   Since 1944 a succession of agreements has been negotiated between bodies representative of teachers and their employers[13] covering various aspects of service conditions other than remuneration. The agreements have now been consolidated in the *Burgundy* and *Silver Books* in relation to primary and secondary school teachers, and further education teachers, respectively. The terms of the agreements have been varied from time to time.[14] A major distinction between the books is that the *Burgundy Book* fails to provide any definition of the teacher's day or duties except as regards the school midday break.[15] (As explained earlier[16] that omission has been made good by the Secretary of State). Otherwise the books cover much the same ground, and the *Silver Book*, the terms of which have been negotiated by the National Joint Council for Teachers in Further Education,[17] must be left to speak for itself.

4-99   The conditions of service for teachers[18] (including head teachers) in primary and secondary schools are negotiated in a body known as the

---

[11] As Appendix C of Appendix VIII.
[12] See above at para. 4–94.
[13] As to the (qualified) duty of employers to disclose information for purposes of collective bargaining, see the Employment Protection Act 1975, ss.17–21 as amended; and as to unlawful sex discrimination in collective agreements, see Sex Discrimination Act 1986, s.6.
[14] The second edition of the *Burgundy Book* was published in 1985.
[15] See below at para. 4–110.
[16] See above at para. 4–52.
[17] See now Teachers' Pay and Conditions Act 1987, s.4 (and below at para. 4–115). The Council have consisted of representatives of the Association of County Councils, Association of Metropolitan Authorities, Welsh Joint Education Committee, National Association of Teachers in Further and Higher Education, Association of Principals of Colleges, National Society for Education in Art and Design, and Association of Agricultural Education Staffs. Observers from the following bodies have had the right to attend: Department of Education and Science, Catholic Education Council, Church of England Board of Education, Methodist Church Division of Education and Youth, and Courts of Governors of the five I.L.E.A. polytechnics. There are also Joint Negotiating Committees for further education teachers assigned by local education authorities to Prison Department establishments, and for teachers in social service establishments.
[18] For definition of "teacher" and other definitions see *Burgundy Book*, para. 4.

C.L.E.A./School teachers (S.T.) Committee. The committee comprise C.L.E.A. and representatives of all save one of the teachers organisations which were represented on the Burnham Committee.[19] The number of representatives of each organisation is not specified. Agreements are reached when a majority of each side agree. In the foreword to the *Burgundy Book* it is stated that "both sides of the Committee expect[20-21] individual local education authorities to adopt the agreements negotiated in C.L.E.A./S.T. and to incorporate them in the contracts of service of their members." As also stated in the foreword the negotiated provisions are not exhaustive. They are supplemented by, and are subject to, the authority's own conditions of contract, articles of government of schools and, of course, the statutory provisions outlined elsewhere in this Chapter.

Appointment, resignation and retirement

Paragraph 5 of the *Burgundy Book* states the arrangements for payment of salary by monthly instalments, and in particular the arrangements on appointment and on resignation. Provision is made for deduction[22] of salary in the case of absence in various circumstances.[23] Periods of notice on termination of employment are specified, consistent with those likely to be included in articles of government and with the statutory requirements.[24] Attention is drawn to the powers of the Secretary of State regarding dismissal on medical grounds,[25] and an obligation is placed on local education authorities to make known any other circumstances in which they dismiss teachers on those grounds. Retirement is to be automatic at the age of 65 or postponed by mutual agreement. Reference is made to the arrangements for premature retirement compensation.[26] An obligation is placed on the pregnant teacher to give notice to the local education authority of the expected date of confinement. Attention is drawn to the negotiated[27] maternity leave scheme and to the statutory[28] provisions; and the date of termination

4–100

---

[19] Namely the Association of County Councils, Association of Metropolitan Authorities, Welsh Joint Education Committee, National Union of Teachers, National Association of School Masters/Union of Women Teachers, Assistant Masters and Mistresses Association, Secondary Heads Association and National Association of Head Teachers. The Professional Association of Teachers is not represented (although it was represented on the Burnham Committee) on C.L.E.A./S.T. nor are the Churches, even though the governors of voluntary aided schools are the employers of teachers at those schools (see above at para. 4–27). As to the Burnham Committee see below at para. 4–113.

[20-21] Negotiated agreements have not been incorporated by law in contracts of service since the repeal of Sched. 11 to the Employment Protection Act 1975 by the 1980 Act.

[22] As to deductions from salary in circumstances of industrial action see *Royle* v. *Trafford Borough Council* [1984] I.R.L.R. 184 and above at para. 4–57.

[23] As to strikes see above at paras. 4–55 to 4–59.

[24] See above at para. 4–81.

[25] See above at para. 4–24, and also para. 10, which refers to suspending powers.

[26] See Appendix VIII, above at para. 4–96 and below at para. 4–147.

[27] See below at para. 4–105.

[28] See above at paras. 4–73 to 4–75.

of employment is specified if no application is to be made for maternity leave.

Individual grievances and collective disputes

4–101   Paragraph 6 introduces procedures[29] for the settlement of individual grievances[30] and collective disputes. The former can arise in a variety of circumstances ranging from disputes between teachers to grievances involving governors or the local education authority. Sometimes grievances can be resolved informally but on other occasions a formal procedure may be appropriate. Both formal and informal procedures are laid down, differing according to whether head teachers or other members of staff are concerned; and the procedures are modified so as to apply to voluntary aided schools.

4–102   Collective disputes may arise concerning the conditions of service of teachers employed by a particular local education authority, or the general relations between teachers' associations and authorities. Recommendations are made for consultative procedures at local level and conciliation procedures[31] at national level.

Discipline. Dismissal

4–103   Paragraph 7 records that there is no national agreement on disciplinary procedures but that teachers should be informed of any local procedures.[32] Paragraph 8 on dismissal, refers to the statutory provisions to which reference has already been made[33] and lays down a formal procedure for hearing cases that may involve dismissal. Suspension[34] is provided for, normally on full salary, "in the event of emergency on allegation of misconduct or for any other urgent cause." It appears not to be an appropriate response to strike action or other disruption unaccompanied by separate misconduct. The procedures elaborate those likely to be included in articles of government and are to conform to the terms of articles.

---

[29] See Appendix II.

[30] See above at para. 4–68. The propriety of using the individual grievance procedure on a complaint by a number of teachers against a headmistress has been doubted: see *Curtis* v. *Manchester City Council, The Times*, May 27, 1976 (above at para. 4–30 n. 99).

[31] In practice the procedure is used only on agreement between the two sides; and a single conciliator is appointed.

[32] See *Ellis* v. *I.L.E.A.*, 75 L.G.R. 382 regarding disciplinary procedures and the need to observe the rules of natural justice (see above at para. 1–54) in proceedings. Disciplinary procedures are designed to deal with individual cases of misconduct, not with collective action (as to which see above at paras. 4–53 *et seq.*). They are likely to follow the Code of Practice issued by A.C.A.S. under s.6 of the Employment Protection Act 1975. A case may in practice have to be heard three times—by governors, by a local education authority disciplinary sub-committee and by a differently constituted local education authority appeal committee. Acquittal of a criminal offence does not preclude the taking of proceedings under a staff disciplinary code (*Saeed* v. *I.L.E.A.* [1985] I.C.R. 637).

[33] See above at paras. 4–81 *et seq.*

[34] See above at paras. 4–30, 4–32 and 4–41. As to suspension on medical grounds see *Burgundy Book*, para. 10 and above at para. 4–24.

Leave of absence

Paragraph 9 provides for leave of absence in various circumstances. A   **4–104**
teacher absent from duty owing to illness receives sick pay on a scale
which reaches its maximum on absence during the fourth and successive
years of service: full pay for 100 working days followed by half pay for
the same period, with discretion to the authority to extend the entitlement. The conditions of entitlement, and the amount due, are elaborately specified. Normally, sick pay counts towards the employers'
statutory sick pay liability[35] and, equally, statutory benefits received are
normally deductible from the amount of sick pay due.

A maternity leave scheme, which in origin antedates the statutory   **4–105**
provisions, operates without prejudice to statutory rights[36] and obligations. It lays down in particular the procedures to be followed by a
teacher who wishes to apply for maternity leave, the duration of absence
and the amount of, and conditions of entitlement to, salary during
absence.

Principles have been settled[37] for local agreements about granting   **4–106**
leave to teachers who undertake duties in connection with public examinations: not less than ten days for chief examiners and chief moderators
and five days for assistant examiners and moderators. Fees paid to
teachers should be in recognition of additional work outside the
teacher's normal responsibilities. Some payment of fees should also be
made to teachers undertaking public examining duties in their own
schools, if the duties are similar to those of external examiners and take
up extra time.

Teachers are to have leave entitlements for jury and other public ser-   **4–107**
vice[38] comparable with those of other local authority officers.[39]

Teachers who are accredited representatives of recognised teachers'   **4–108**
organisations are to be given union facilities and rights[40] consistent with
the *Industrial Relations Code of Practice* issued by A.C.A.S.[41]; and local
education authorities are recommended as far as possible to appoint
additional staff to avoid the over-burdening which may arise as a consequence of absence of teachers on union activities. Authorities are asked
to recognise the volume of work of representatives and to give paid
leave of absence accordingly. Authorities are advised to encourage and
support those representatives who wish to attend training courses on
their duties; teachers' organisations to pay regard to the needs of the

---

[35] See Pt. I of the Social Security and Housing Benefits Act 1982 as amended, especially s.10 and
Sched. 2, para. 2; and as to the effect of strikes on statutory sick pay *ibid*. s.3(3) and Sched. 1.
[36] See above at paras. 4–73 to 4–75. As to conflict between statutory and contractual rights see
I.L.E.A. v. *Nash* [1979] I.C.R. 229.
[37] *Burgundy Book*, para. 9.3, and Appendix IV.
[38] There is also a statutory entitlement (see above at 4–72).
[39] Local authorities are to consider granting paid leave (N.J.C. for Local Authorities' A.P.T. and C.
Services Scheme of Conditions of Service—*the Purple Book*, para. 47).
[40] See *Burgundy Book*, para. 9.5 and Appendix V.
[41] See above at para. 4–72 n. 95.

schools in arranging when the courses are to take place—in consultation with the authority if term time is proposed.

4–109   Authorities are to make known to teachers any arrangements they have—none are agreed nationally—for leave with or without pay[42] in other circumstances, for example, participation in a parliamentary election or as a national representative in sport.

The midday break

4–110   Paragraph 11 refers to an agreement made between teachers' unions and local authority associations in 1968[43] which resulted in revocation of the regulation which entitled local education authorities to require teachers to supervise school midday meals,[44] but recognised that the head teacher retained responsibility for the conduct of meals, and recommended that supervisory assistants should be employed.[45] Teachers who undertook the oversight of pupils during the midday break should be entitled to a free meal. They should, however, be able to enjoy a proper break and to leave the school premises.[46] (Provision was subsequently made for teachers to enter into separate contracts to supervise at midday for additional remuneration).[47]

Insurance

4–111   Under this heading[48] paragraph 12 specifies the amount of an indemnity for the teacher or his dependants in the case of death or total disablement caused by violence or criminal assault suffered in the course, or as a consequence, of employment. Where the teacher is a victim of a violent crime[49] any compensation paid by the Criminal Injuries Compensation Board is to be in addition to any sick pay entitlement, and sick leave may be extended. Authorities are recommended to pay compensation[50] for loss or damage to personal property, and in certain

---

[42] Holiday pay is payable notwithstanding that the holiday is incorporated in a period of leave of absence without pay (*Evans* v. *Gwent County Council* 1982 Ch.D. (unreported)).

[43] See Circ. 16/68 which forms Appendix VII of the *Burgundy Book*; also Circ. 3/78 (W.O. 186/77) paras. 13–17.

[44] In *Price and Others* v. *Sunderland Corporation* [1956] 1 W.L.R. 1253 it was established that s.49 (repealed) of the 1944 Act did not empower the local education authority to require teachers to collect money for school meals. Breach of contract by failure to supervise school meals, (*Gorse* v. *Durham County Council* [1971] 1 W.L.R. 775) might still arise, (*Metropolitan Borough of Solihull* v. *National Union of Teachers* [1985] I.R.L.R. 211).

[45] The costs may be met out of education support grant (see above at para. 1–125). The risks to which inadequate supervision can give rise are exemplified in a case reported in *The Times Educational Supplement*, November 13, 1981. A boy's eye was damaged by a paper clip "fired" at him. There was only one "dinner lady" to supervise two classrooms, and the authority were held negligent. (As to negligence generally see below at paras. 7–05 *et seq.*).

[46] See now the Education (School Teachers' Pay and Conditons of Employment) Order 1987 (S.I. 1987 No. 650), Sched. 3, para. 4(*e*).

[47] By s.8(2A) of the 1965 Act inserted by 1986 (Amendment) Act, s.2 (both now repealed by Teachers' Pay and Conditions Act 1987).

[48] See also below at paras. 5–49 to 5–53.

[49] *Burgundy Book* para. 12.2. As to assaults on teachers by pupils and others see above at para. 2–127.

[50] *Ibid.* para. 12.3 and 12.4, and Appendix IX, ss.1 and 2.

circumstances for death, personal loss or injury sustained in voluntary, *i.e.* non-contractual, "out of school" activities.

Travelling and other allowances

These are the subject of paragraphs 13 to 15. There are national **4–112** recommendations[51] on travelling allowances for teachers who use their own cars when required to undertake journeys to facilitate the discharge of their duties. Teachers at residential special schools who are required to carry out duties additional to normal teaching duties may be eligible for allowances which are the subject of annual national agreements.[52] National agreements may also make them liable to pay certain charges. There are no national agreements for allowances or charges in respect of teachers at boarding establishments associated with primary and secondary schools.

REMUNERATION

The negotiation between representatives of employers and teachers **4–113** of national salary scales dates from 1919, and the giving of statutory force to the recommendations of Burnham[53] negotiating committees from the coming into operation of the 1944 Act.[54] The interest of the Secretary of State in the outcome of negotiations was formalised by the Remuneration of Teachers Act 1965, when for the first time he was represented on the Management Panel of the Burnham committees. The 1965 Act was repealed on the passing of the Teachers' Pay and Conditions Act 1987. At that time there were two Burnham committees, one for primary and secondary school teachers and one for further education (including college of education) teachers, each consisting of an independent chairman, Management Panel and Teachers' Panel, and on which were represented the local authority associations and teachers' organisations.[55]

---

[51] As regards the use of vehicles for school activities see below at para. 5–24, and as to insurance, below at para. 5–53. A travelling allowance payable in respect of an out-of-school activity is not an emolument of office and therefore is not taxable (*Donnelly* v. *Williamson* [1981] I.R.L.R. 533).

[52] The agreements are concluded between the bodies represented on C.L.E.A./S.T. (see above at para. 4–99).

[53] After Lord Burnham, the first chairman.

[54] Separate committees were established for teachers in: (1) primary and secondary schools, (2) further education, (3) farm institutes, (4) teacher training institutions (the Pelham Committee). s.89 of the 1944 Act, on remuneration of teachers, was repealed by the 1965 Act.

[55] Primary and Secondary Schools Committee: National Union of Teachers, Assistant Masters and Mistresses Association, Secondary Heads Association, National Association of Head Teachers, National Association of School Masters/Union of Women Teachers, Professional Association of Teachers. Further Education Committee: The National Association of Teachers in Further and Higher Education, Association of Principals of Colleges, National Society for Art Education, Association of Agricultural Education Staffs and Association of Polytechnic Teachers. The omission of one of the bodies represented on the Teachers' Panel from a Panel Sub-Committee was held to be "wholly unreasonable" in *R.* v. *Burnham Primary and Secondary Committee, ex p. Professional Association of Teachers, The Times*, March 30, 1985.

4–114   Under the 1965 Act when a committee agreed[56] on recommendations
the Secretary of State prepared a draft document (a Burnham report) to
give effect to them. The draft was submitted for the approval of the
committee and if necessary modified to satisfy them. The document,
once settled, was published by Her Majesty's Stationery Office and
accompanied by an order of the Secretary of State, made by statutory
instrument, directing that teachers should be remunerated in accordance[57] with the scales and other provisions the document contained. The
document could be amended by a subsequent order. There was provision for arbitration in default of agreement.

Arrangements for settling remuneration

4–115   Under the 1987 Act the remuneration of teachers continues to be
based on subsisting orders until they are superseded,[58] in the case of
school teachers,[59] by provisions taking effect under the 1987 Act, and in
the case of further education teachers[60] by provisions agreed between
teachers and employers. The remuneration and conditions of employment of further education teachers are to be settled by a process in
which the organisations previously represented on the Burnham Further
Education Committee are to participate.[61] Section 2 provides that the
remuneration (and other conditions of employment)[62] of school
teachers are to be considered by an Interim Advisory Committee[63] of
between five and nine members including persons with knowledge or
experience in education,[64] who may be full-time or part-time. The Secretary of State appoints the chairman and deputy chairman. He may

---

[56] s.2 did not specify what form "agreement" was to take. By convention each panel took their
decision by majority vote and only agreement between the two panels constituted an agreement
by the committee. The rules and procedures for determining teachers' remuneration were so elaborate as to lay the Burnham committees open to challenge. In *Lewis* v. *Dyfed County Council*, 77
L.G.R. 339, C.A. it was held that an order of the Secretary of State was valid notwithstanding
certain imperfections in drafting or in the mode of action adopted by the committee. Substantial
compliance with the Act was enough. Doubts remained however, whether the degree of sub-
delegation adopted (*e.g.* to panel sub-committees) breached the rule *delegatus non potest delegare*
and whether provisions in the documents relating to establishment matters (*e.g.* the determinaton
of the number of teachers at a school to be placed on a particular scale) were properly authorised
by s.2(1), (2) and (3) of the 1965 Act.
[57] Arrangements were made for interpretation of a report, as in the case of further education
teachers (see below at para. 4–133).
[58] s.1(2). The subsisting orders are the Remuneration of Teachers (Primary and Secondary Education) Order 1983 (S.I. 1983 No. 1463) as amended by Amendment Orders S.I.'s 1984 No. 1650,
1986 No. 559, 1987 No. 137, 1987 No. 236 and 1987 No. 398. See also the Education (School
Teachers' Pay and Conditions of Employment) Order 1987 (S.I. 1987 No. 650) and Circ. 5/87. For
orders relating to further education teachers see note 79 below.
[59] As defined in s.7(1).
[60] As defined in s.7(1).
[61] s.4 and see above paras. 4–98 and 4–113.
[62] See above at para. 4–52 and Appendix 3, below.
[63] s.2(1), (3) and Sched. 1. Provision is made for resignation and removal from office; remuneration,
pension, etc.; disqualification from membership of the House of Commons; and regarding the
proceedings of the Committee.
[64] See above at para. 1–17.

give the Committee directions with respect to the matters he refers to them, the considerations to which they are to have regard, the financial or other constraints to which their recommendations are to be subject and the time within which they are to report to him. The Committee are to give local authority associations, teachers' organisations, bodies representing voluntary school governors and any local education authority with whom consultation appears desirable a reasonable opportunity to submit evidence and make representations to them before they make a report to the Secretary of State containing their recommendations and advice on the matters referred to them. The Secretary of State is to have the report published.

After himself consulting the bodies mentioned above the Secretary of **4–116** State may, under section 3, by order made by statutory instrument give effect to the recommendations of the Committee with or without modification, or he may make such other provision as he thinks fit. An order which gives effect to recommendations without material modification is subject to the negative resolution procedure[65] in Parliament; any other order[66] requires approval in draft by resolution of each House.

An order may: **4–117**

(a) take effect by reference to provisions contained in a document published by Her Majesty's Stationery Office or (a subsequent order) by amendment of those provisions;
(b) make different provision for different cases and areas; and
(c) as regards remuneration,[67] make particular provision as follows.

The order may confer discretion on the local education authority with respect to any matter, and provide for:

(a) the aggregate of allowances payable to teachers in a school;
(b) the number or proportion of teachers in a school to be paid on specified scales or specified allowances;
(c) the designation of schools to which special provisions apply;
(d) the determination of questions arising on the order;
(e) retrospective increases, but not decreases, in pay; and
(f) matters specified to be settled by teachers and local education authorities.

The effect of an order is to require local education authorities to remunerate teachers in accordance with the scales and other provisions in, or referred to in, the order.

The 1987 Act expires on March 31, 1990 unless continued in force, **4–118** from year to year, by order approved in draft by each House of

---

[65] See above at para. 1–41.
[66] The Secretary of State was empowered to make an order to come into effect before October 1, 1987, without consulting the Advisory Committee, and the negative procedure applied to it (s.3(7) and (8)). See S.I. 1987 No. 650.
[67] Section 3(9) enabled the first order (S.I. 1987 No. 650) to make provision for remuneration to make retrospective to January 1, 1987.

Parliament.[68] Orders relating to remuneration (and other conditions of employment) then subsisting continue in force until superseded by provisions agreed between teachers and their employers. For the future, after 1990, a new system of determining teachers' pay is expected to be established.

Remuneration of primary and secondary school teachers

4–119   In March 1987 the Secretary of State published[69] a pay structure designed to take effect from October 1. It contains elaborate assimilation arrangements from old to new scales, and "safeguarding" of salaries of teachers who as a result of educational reorganisation have lost their posts[70] or had them down-graded is to continue; but some simplification of the complexities of Burnham reports will perhaps be achieved. The proposals are in outline as follows.

4–120   There is to be a single, 11 point, basic scale[71] for teachers other than head and deputy head teachers. Graduates enter at the second point and good honours graduates at the fourth. Progress up the scale is by annual increments on September 1. An innovation is the introduction of incentive allowances, to be paid in recognition of one or more of the following: responsibilities beyond those common to the majority of teachers, outstanding classroom teaching, shortage skills and recruitment to posts difficult to fill. Incentive allowances are at five different rates and initially are to be distributed to teachers according to the scale on which they were previously paid. Allowances at the highest rate go to senior teachers, at lower rates to teachers on scales 4 and 3 and at a lower rate still to teachers selected for promotion from scales 2 or 1.

4–121   Teachers in special schools[72] are to be paid in accordance with the same salary structure as has been devised for those in ordinary schools, and this, it is claimed, will facilitate movement between the two types of school. But teachers in special schools currently on scales 1, 2(S) and 3(S) are to receive a pay advantage (£1,000 at October 1987), in recognition of their distinctive position, over teachers on scales 1, 2 and 3 in ordinary schools.

4–122   Head and deputy head teachers receive "spot" salaries according to the group within which their school falls. There are 14 groups, determined by the size[73] of the school, for ordinary schools and eight for

---

[68] s.6 and see above at para. 1–41.

[69] *School Teachers' Pay and Conditions of Employment. The Government's Proposals.* See also Circ. 5/87.

[70] See *Stott* v. *Oldham Corporation*, 67 L.G.R. 520, C.A. (temporary appointment as deputy head teacher—loss of post).

[71] Amounts of pay and allowances are not specified because of the frequency of changes.

[72] As to the reserve powers of the Secretary of State regarding remuneration of teachers in non-maintained special schools see the Education (Approval of Special Schools) Regulations 1983 (S.I. 1983 No. 1499) Sched. 2, para. 16, and above at para. 2–212.

[73] Calculated, in Burnham reports, by reference to both numbers and ages of pupils at the school.

special schools, whose heads and deputies, like their teaching staffs, enjoy a financial advantage over their colleagues in ordinary schools.

With effect from January 1, 1987, unqualified teachers currently on **4–123** scale A as instructors[74] are to be placed on a new ten point incremental scale in which discretionary (but not London or social priority school)[75] allowances are consolidated. Student teachers[76] are to be paid one of two "spot" salaries according as they are awaiting admission to a course of initial teacher training[77] or have failed a course and are retaking it. Unqualified teachers on scales B and C are to be paid the "spot" salaries specified.

In addition to the incentive allowances already mentioned there are **4–124** London allowances at inner, outer and fringe rates, allowances for teachers at social priority schools, for unqualified teachers (a) in special schools and (b) undertaking special responsibilities, and for qualified[78] teachers of the blind and partially sighted and of the deaf and partially hearing.

The proposals make no reference to remuneration of teachers in reg- **4–125** ular part-time service or of "supply" teachers employed on a day-to-day or other short notice basis. Currently they are paid, respectively, the appropriate proportion of a full-time annual salary and by the day or hour.

Remuneration of teachers in further education

Until the current Burnham report[79] is superseded further education **4–126** teachers are remunerated as follows. The salary and grading arrange- ments differ according to whether or not the teacher teaches agricultural and horticultural subjects (in an agricultural or horticultural establish- ment or elsewhere), and there are some special rules for calculating the salaries of teachers in separate adult education establishments.[80]

---

[74] See above para. 4–14.

[75] These schools (other than special schools) were designated as such by members of the Burnham Primary and Secondary Education Committee acting as a Designating Committee (see 1983 report s.11). The Committee had regard to "the social and economic status of the parents of children at the school; the absence of amenities in the homes of children attending the school; the proportion of children in the school receiving free meals and belonging to families in receipt of supplementary benefits under the Supplementary Benefits Act 1976; the proportion of children in the school with serious language difficulties; and the proportion of retarded, disturbed and handicapped chil- dren."

[76] See above at para. 4–14.

[77] See above at para. 4–04.

[78] See above at para. 4–15.

[79] Brought into effect by the Remuneration of Teachers (Further Education) Order 1983 (S.I. 1983 No. 1464) and amended by Amendment Orders, S.I. 1984 No. 2043, S.I. 1985 No. 495, S.I. 1985 No. 1248 and S.I. 1986 No. 176. By the Orders (and see s.1(1) of the Report) further education teachers are those paid by local education authorities who are employed in further education establishments and other teachers whom they employ for further education functions (excluding teachers seconded to bodies which reimburse the employing authorities the amount of their salar- ies).

[80] *Burnham Report*, s.8.

4–127   In a further education establishment which is not an agricultural or a horticultural establishment the grading[81] of lecturer posts[82] (grade I, grade II, senior lecturer and principal lecturer) turns on the classification of courses according to five categories of work, ranging from I (postgraduate) to V (below courses leading to Ordinary National Certificate[83] or equivalent). The proportion of senior posts rises in step with work category and there is no provision at all for appointment of principal lecturers when no work falls into category III or above, or for lecturers in grade I where all work falls within those categories. There are various qualifications and exceptions which augment the discretion of local education authorities[84] in settling grading proportions, and they may appoint a reader or readers or academic posts above[85] reader where work in a department is wholly or mainly in categories I or II/III.

4–128   There are separate scales[86] for each of the posts above-mentioned and rules[87] about starting pay and increments (paid ordinarily on September 1). Progression on the scales by a grade I (or IA or IB) lecturer may be accelerated on his obtaining a qualification or completing a course specified.

4–129   In order to fix the remuneration of heads of departments[88] and principals and vice-principals[89] "unit totals"[90] are calculated by reference to the number of student hours in each category of work. One unit is earned for each 100 student hours in category I, 300 in category II/III and 600 in categories IV and V (and there are rules for calculating student hours). A department falls into grade I if its unit total is 76–140, and into higher grades with higher unit totals. The highest grade is VI, where the unit total is over 900. There are salary scales[91] for heads of departments (and academic posts above reader) in relation to each grade.

4–130   Unit totals are also used to place establishments into 12 groups for the purposes of determining the salary range of vice-principals and principals, group 1 when the total is up to 250, rising to group 12 when the total is over 13,500. Principals and full time vice-principals are paid a fixed salary within the appropriate range.[92]

---

[81] *Burnham Report*, Appendix 11A, Part I. See *Bridgen* v. *Lancashire County Council* [1987] I.R.L.R. 58 regarding the date of appointment to a grade.

[82] *Ibid.* s.4.

[83] See above at para. 3–02 n. 7.

[84] By s.3 of the Report reference to local education authorities in the document includes governors where the latter exercise the relevant function under articles of government (see above at para. 3–17).

[85] *Ibid.* s.5 and Appendix IIA Pt. II.

[86] *Ibid.* Appendix IA, para. 2.

[87] *Ibid.* Appendix III.

[88] *Ibid.* s.6.

[89] *Ibid.* s.7.

[90] *Ibid.* Appendix IIA, Pt. III.

[91] *Ibid.* Appendix IA, para. 3, and Appendix IIA, Pt. IV.

[92] *Ibid.* Appendix IA, para. 4 and Appendix IIA, Pt. V(A).

Lecturers[93] Grade 1A and 1B in agricultural and horticultural estab-   **4–131**
lishments (or teaching those subjects on the staff of local education
authorities) are paid on incremental scales.[94] 1A is the basic grade and
1B normally appropriate where the teacher has particular administrative
or practical responsibilities. Teachers appointed on lecturer grade II,
vice-principals and principals[95] are paid on a scale of five consecutive
points on the appropriate salary range[96] determined by the local education authority having regard to duties and responsibilities.

There are provisions[97] relating in particular to additional allow-   **4–132**
ances,[98] "safeguarding" and remuneration[99] of part-time further education teachers, some of which are the counterpart where appropriate,
of those applicable to primary and secondary school teachers.

The Burnham Committee were empowered to meet as a Joint Com-   **4–133**
mittee of Reference to consider questions relating to the report brought
forward by a local education authority or teachers' association through
the Management and Teachers' Panels, or by consent of the chairman.
The Committee did not, however, constitute a body of arbitrators. They
did not oust the jurisdiction of the courts where a teacher was in dispute[1] with his employing authority; and "there is no statutory provision
for settling disputed questions as to teachers' remuneration."[2]

Errors in remuneration

The complexity of salary calculations (among other reasons)[3] is such   **4–134**
that inevitably from time to time errors are made in the amount of
remuneration paid to teachers. Whether or not subsequent adjustments
are to be made may turn on whether the error was one of fact or of law.
For example if a teacher has been underpaid by his local education authority because of an error of fact in computing his length of service[4] then
the authority are under a duty to pay the difference in the accrued salary[5] when the error is discovered—this is not a case of a retrospective
increase in remuneration. And if as a result of a mistake of fact a local

---

[93] *Burnham Report*, s.9 and Appendix IIB.
[94] *Ibid*. Appendix IB, para. 2.
[95] *Ibid*. s.10.
[96] *Ibid*. Appendix IB, para. 3.
[97] *Ibid*. Pts. IV and V, ss.11–17.
[98] See also *ibid*. Appendix V: Secondment of teachers employed on teacher training courses.
[99] See *ibid*. Appendix IV.
[1] See *Vaughan and Another* v. *Solihull Metropolitan Borough Council, The Times*, May 25, 1982
(dispute between headmasters and local education authority regarding the proper level of their
remuneration) and *Baron* v. *Sunderland Corporation* [1966] 2 Q.B. 56.
[2] *Per* Kilner Brown J. in *R.* v. *Central Arbitration Committee, ex p. Gloucestershire County Council*
[1981] I.C.R. 95 at 99.
[3] As to a claim for arrears and associated damages arising from a strike see *R.* v. *Liverpool City
Council, ex p. Coade and Another, The Times*, October 10, 1986, when an order of *mandamus*
(see above at para. 1–50 n. 89) was granted to the applicants directing the council to comply with
their obligations to remunerate in accordance with the 1965 Act.
[4] As to teachers' records, see A.M.s 1/64 22/70 and below at para. 4–140 n. 21.
[5] See *Brown* v. *Dagenham Corporation* [1929] 1 K.B. 737.

education authority overpay they may recover the overpayment[6]; but if it arises from misinterpretation of a salary document their mistake is probably one of law, so that unless the contract of employment provides otherwise the excess amounts paid are not recoverable.[7] The authority would then be liable at the instance of the auditor, but the Secretary of State would probably sanction the overpayment under the Local Government Finance Act 1982, section 19(1), if the authority reasonably believed that they had not acted *ultra vires*.

PENSIONS

4–135   The teachers' superannuation scheme is so complex that it will be as well to begin with a bare outline. Those who must join the scheme are mostly[8] full-time teachers in maintained schools and further education establishments who are over eighteen and under fifty-five when they begin teaching; some others, including part-time teachers, may do so. Teachers in service which counts towards the reckoning of benefits (reckonable service)[9] pay basic contributions of 6 per cent.[10] of salary, and employers a percentage sufficient to keep the account in balance.

4–136   Subject to minimum qualifying periods, the basic benefits, related to the amount of reckonable service, are a pension and lump sum on retirement at 60 or over, or earlier on health breakdown, or on the teacher's being prematurely retired. There is also a death gratuity and a widow's pension payable while the widow is on her own, and pensions for dependent children. Women teachers and unmarried men teachers may nominate a close and financially dependent relative to receive the pension otherwise payable to a widow. Pensions are indexed to the cost of living.

4–137   There are arrangements to deal with breaks in service, for "freezing" pension benefits when a teacher leaves employment with enough qualifying service before a pension falls due, for transfer values[11] "out" and "in," and for repayment of contributions on leaving employment

---

[6] But not necessarily the whole of the overpayment because of the operation of the doctrine of estoppel (*Avon County Council* v. *Howlett* [1981] I.R.L.R. 447).

[7] See *Chitty on Contracts* (25th ed. 1983) para. 1956, and the cases there cited. In practice the contract of employment will often provide that salary overpayment is to be recoverable either by deduction from subsequent salary or as a debt.

[8] See the list in the Teachers' Superannuation Regulations 1976 (S.I. 1976 No. 1987) Sched. 1, as amended by S.I. 1978 No. 1512, reg. 6, S.I. 1980 No. 919, reg. 29, S.I. 1982 No. 496, reg. 5 and S.I. 1985 No. 1844, reg. 9. The list includes teachers in non-maintained special schools and youth and community workers employed by local education authorities. The local government superannuation scheme cannot apply to teachers (*Secretary of State for the Environment* v. *Cumbria County Council* [1983] I.C.R. 52, H.L.

[9] See S.I. 1976 No. 1987 regs. 3, 4, 8 and 72, as amended by S.I. 1978 No. 1422, reg. 19, S.I. 1980 No. 919 regs. 4 and 27 and S.I. 1985 No. 1844, regs. 13, 17 and 28.

[10] The increase from 5 per cent. to 6 per cent. under the Teachers' Superannuation Act 1956 was a source of much contention. See 120 J.P.N. 133.

[11] See S.I. 1976 No. 1987, regs. 80–84 as amended by S.I. 1978 No. 1422, reg. 24 and Sched. 7 as amended by S.I. 1978 No. 1422, reg. 26, S.I. 1980 No. 919, regs. 14 and 15 and S.I. 1980 No. 1043, regs. 5 and 6.

covered by the scheme; also for reconciling the scheme with the national insurance system.[12]

The scheme springs from section 9 of the Superannuation Act 1972. It **4–138** is incorporated in regulations made by the Secretary of State with the consent of the Treasury[13] and after consultation with the representatives of local education authorities, teachers and others likely to be affected. Regulations may, by section 12(1) of the 1972 Act, take effect retrospectively. Previous schemes, made under successive Teachers' Superannuation Acts, go back to the Elementary School Teachers (Superannuation) Act 1898,[14] and regulations under the 1972 Act are, by section 12(4), not to detract from superannuation rights acquired under previous schemes. The Secretary of State is given various powers to make determinations under the regulations, but, by section 11, may put questions of law to the High Court or may be directed by the court to do so.[15]

The regulations operative since January 1, 1977, are the Teachers' **4–139** Superannuation Regulations 1976,[16] which have been heavily amended. To expound them in full detail would be impracticable, but the outline given in the last few paragraphs can usefully be elaborated to provide (not more than) a general guide.

Contributions

Teachers' contributions,[17] mainly by deduction from salary,[18] are the **4–140** aggregate of 6 per cent. of salary and other contributions referred to below. They are normally allowed as a deduction in calculating income for tax purposes. If a teacher suffers a reduction in salary he may be permitted to pay contributions on his former salary to improve his benefit entitlement.[19] Contributions cease when a teacher has completed 45 years' service counting for an annual pension or at the age of 70 if

---

[12] S.I. 1976 No. 1987, reg. 10 as substituted by S.I. 1980 No. 1043, reg. 4, and Sched. 9, as amended by S.I. 1980 No. 1043, regs. 7 and 8 and by S.I. 1985 No. 1844, reg. 8. Modification of contributions and benefits (as explained in Circular 172) does not apply in respect of reckonable service done after March 31, 1980. See also the Contracted Out Employment (Teachers) Regulations 1977 (S.I. 1977 No. 1678).

[13] By the Transfer of Functions (Minister for the Civil Service and Treasury) Order 1981 (S.I. 1981 No. 1670) the Treasury now exercises the functions of the Minister for the Civil Service as regards superannuation.

[14] Under which were made the Elementary School Teachers Superannuation Rules 1919 (S.R. & O. 1920 No. 2298) (as amended, still extant).

[15] See S.I. 1976 No. 1987, reg. 97.

[16] S.I. 1976 No. 1987 (see A.M. 1/77) as amended by S.I.'s 1978 No. 422, No. 1422 and No. 1512, 1979 No. 1206, 1980 No. 919 and No. 1043, 1982 No. 496 and No. 967, and 1985 No. 1844. See also the Teachers' Superannuation (Policy Schemes) Regulations 1979 (S.I. 1979 No. 47, as amended by S.I. 1980 No. 919, reg. 32, the Teachers' Superannuation (Notional Salaries) Regulations 1981 (S.I. 1981 No. 934), the Teachers' Superannuation (War Service) Regulations 1982 (S.I. 1982 No. 46), and the Teachers (Compensation for Redundancy and Premature Retirement) Regulations 1985 (S.I. 1985 No. 1181) (made under s.24 of the Superannuation Act 1972).

[17] S.I. 1976 No. 1987, reg. 12(2)(a).

[18] Ibid. reg. 15, as substituted by S.I. 1980 No. 919, reg. 6 and amended by S.I. 1985 No. 1844, reg. 10, and as to the definition of "salary," reg. 3(7).

[19] S.I. 1976 No. 1987, reg. 14.

earlier.[20] Employers'[21] contributions are determined as a result of periodic actuarial inquiry[22] and are to be sufficient to meet the likely cost of benefits and any deficiency in the teachers' superannuation account.[23] From April 1, 1984, the employers' contribution has been 9.45 per cent. of teachers' salaries. Contributions[24] are payable to the Secretary of State (but by contrast with the "funded" local government superannuation scheme, there is no actual, only a notional, teachers' superannuation fund). Dilatoriness on the part of the employers in making contributions over incurs the payment of interest.

4–141   To augment benefits, teachers may[25] purchase added years up to specified maxima[26]—past[27] added years before employment in reckonable service and current[28] added years. The latter are not more than six years up to the age of 60 following discontinuance of, or a break in, employment in reckonable service. The amount and methods of making contributions are specified,[29] as are requirements concerning election[30] to purchase.

4–142   Reckonable service from April 1, 1972 counts automatically for family benefits: those referred to below at paras. 4–149 and 4–150. Earlier reckonable service does not count unless the teacher has, on election, paid contributions in respect of such service.[31] The amount, method and duration of the contributions of teachers in different categories are prescribed, together with the rules regarding election and determinations by the Secretary of State.

---

[20] S.I. 1976 No. 1987, reg. 18.

[21] See *ibid*. reg. 12(2)(*b*). By reg. 12(3) local education authorities are deemed to be the employers of all maintained school teachers. By *ibid*. reg. 92 employers must keep appropriate records of teachers (see A.M. 1/64 and 22/70).

[22] S.I. 1976 No. 1987, reg. 91. In *ex p. Hill, The Times*, October 13, 1965, the Divisional Court refused, on the facts, an application for leave to appeal for an order of *mandamus* directed to the Treasury in respect of an overdue actuarial enquiry. As to the actuarial valuations 1971–1976 and 1976–1981 see A.M.s 1/79 and 2/84 respectively.

[23] See S.I. 1976 No. 1987, reg. 85 as substituted by S.I. 1979 No. 1206, reg. 5; 86 as amended by *ibid*. reg. 6; 87 as amended by *ibid*. reg. 7; 88 as substituted by *ibid*. reg. 8; 89 and 90, and Sched. 8 as substituted by *ibid*. reg. 9.

[24] S.I. 1976 No. 1987, regs. 12(1), 16, 17, 21 and 91(3) and (4). By reg. 13 there are special provisions relating to the contributions of service education officers as defined in reg. 3, and by reg. 14 to those of teachers on reduced salary during absence on sick or maternity leave.

[25] Teachers with war service (defined in S.I. 1976 No. 1987, reg. 7) *must* purchase added years.

[26] See S.I. 1976 No. 1987, reg. 22, as amended by S.I. 1978 No. 422, regs. 5, 23 as substituted by S.I. 1980 No. 919, regs. 17 and 34.

[27] S.I. 1976 No. 1987, reg. 24 as substituted by S.I. 1982 No. 967, reg. 3, and amended by S.I. 1985 No. 1844, reg. 18.

[28] S.I. 1976 No. 1987, reg. 30 as amended by S.I. 1978 No. 422, reg. 10. This provision also enables short breaks in service (*e.g.* during a strike) to be made "reckonable."

[29] S.I. 1976 No. 1987, reg. 26 as amended by S.I. 1982 No. 967, regs. 4, 27, 28, 29, as amended by S.I. 1978 No. 422, regs. 9, 31, 32 and 33 and Sched. 2A inserted by S.I. 1982 No. 967 and amended by S.I. 1985 No. 1844 reg. 31.

[30] S.I. 1976 No. 1987, reg. 25, as substituted by S.I. 1982 No. 967, reg. 3, and Sched. 3.

[31] S.I. 1976 No. 1987, regs. 35, 36, as amended by S.I. 1980 No. 919, regs. 18, 37–44, 45, as amended by S.I. 1978 No. 422, reg. 11 and S.I. 1982 No. 967, reg. 5; and Sched. 4.

On leaving reckonable service a teacher may, if he wishes, not seek to   **4–143**
recover his contributions, and provided that he has served for a minimum period may claim a "frozen" pension at the age of 60. Alternatively, after he has not been employed in reckonable service for at least
three months (or less if he is emigrating) he is entitled to be repaid[32] the
balance of his contributions reduced by tax, provided that he satisfies
stated conditions.[33] A teacher who reaches the age of 70 without having
qualified for any allowance or gratuity is also entitled to repayment of
contributions. Personal representatives of a deceased teacher may be
entitled to repayment.[34] There are further provisions[35] regarding repayment of contributions to teachers who:

(a) could have elected to pay contributions for family benefits but
did not do so;
(b) paid them under the Teachers' Superannuation Act 1922; and
(c) were employed in further reckonable service after retirement.[36]

Benefits

Local education authorities collect contributions: benefits are paid by   **4–144**
the Secretary of State. All benefits must be applied for,[37] and supported
by the particulars he requires. A pension (annual allowance) and a lump
sum (additional allowance) is payable[38] to a teacher who has attained
the age of at least 60 or has become incapacitated[39] earlier due to infirmity. He must have served for a minimum qualifying period. This is normally[40] five years, but in certain specified circumstances it is ten years,
and in others the requirement is waived. Current, but not past, added
years count towards the qualifying period.

The pension[41] is $\frac{1}{80}$ of average salary for each year of reckonable ser-   **4–145**
vice, which may include added years and service earned in another

---

[32] A trustee in bankruptcy cannot claim such a repayment (*In re Duckett, ex p. Minister of Education* v. *The Trustee* [1964] 1 Ch. 398.
[33] S.I. 1976 No. 1987, reg. 46, as amended by S.I. 1978 No. 1422, reg. 5, S.I. 1980 No. 919, reg. 19, and S.I. 1985 No. 1844, reg. 19, and 49 as amended by S.I. 1978 No. 1422, reg. 6, S.I. 1980 No. 919, reg. 21 and S.I. 1985 No. 1844, regs. 6 and 21.
[34] S.I. 1976 No. 1987, reg. 48.
[35] S.I. 1976 No. 1987, regs. 50–52 as amended by S.I. 1978 No. 1422, reg. 7 and S.I. 1985 No. 1844, regs. 5 and 22–24.
[36] As to the return of repaid contributions to the Secretary of State, see S.I. 1976 No. 1987, regs. 19 and 20 and S.I. 1985 No. 1844, regs. 5 and 10–14.
[37] S.I. 1976 No. 1987, regs. 71 and 93.
[38] *Ibid.* reg. 53, as amended by S.I. 1978 No. 1422, reg. 8 and S.I. 1980 No. 919, reg. 22, and Sched. 5. As to benefits after re-employment see reg. 61 as amended by S.I. 1980 No. 919, reg. 7 and S.I. 1985 No. 1844, regs. 5 and 27; as to modifications for teachers on reduced salary, see reg. 73 as substituted by S.I. 1980 No. 919, reg. 28, and reg. 73A inserted by S.I. 1985 No. 1844, reg. 29; as to abatement on re-employment reg. 75; and as to abatement on account of sick pay reg. 76, as amended by S.I. 1978 No. 1422, reg. 20; and reg. 79A as inserted by S.I. 1978 No. 1422, reg. 23.
[39] Defined in S.I. 1976 No. 1987, reg. 3(6). As to suspension and resumption of infirmity allowance see reg. 78.
[40] As to part-time service see S.I. 1976 No. 1987, reg. 5, as amended by S.I. 1980 No. 919, reg. 16.
[41] S.I. 1976 No. 1987, reg. 54 as amended by S.I. 1978 No. 1422, reg. 10 and S.I. 1985 No. 1844, reg. 25.

approved scheme approved by the Inland Revenue, provide that a transfer value is paid.[42] Up to 45 years of service are reckonable, or 40 years if retirement takes place at the age of 60. The reckonable service of a teacher who retires incapacitated before the age of 60 is enhanced. Average salary means[43] the highest amount of a teacher's full salary over any period of 365 days during his last 1095 days of service before retirement. The lump sum[44] is ordinarily $\frac{3}{80}$ of average salary for each year of reckonable service (enhanced for the incapacitated) since the beginning of October 1956 plus $\frac{1}{30}$ for each year of earlier reckonable service. The pension starts,[45] and the lump sum is payable, at the age of 60; later if retirement is postponed or earlier upon incapacity. Pension ordinarily[46] continues until death.

4–146   A teacher who has at least one year's reckonable service, becomes incapacitated before the age of 70 and does not qualify for a pension may apply for a short service gratuity.[47] The gratuity is $\frac{1}{12}$ of average salary for each year of reckonable service.

4–147   A teacher aged between 50 and 59 (inclusive) who is retired prematurely on grounds of redundancy or in the interests of the efficient discharge of his employers' functions, and who has completed a minimum qualifying period, is entitled[48] to pension and lump sum as if he had retired at 60 or over. His benefit may, at the discretion of his last employer be supplemented,[49] by a notional additional period of service up to a specified maximum. The supplement is normally paid by the employer and does not derive from the superannuation scheme as such.

4–148   A death gratuity is payable[50] to the personal representatives of a teacher who dies while in reckonable service or, having retired by reason of ill-health, within a year of retirement, but not if he had received a pension because he was incapacitated. It is also payable in respect of ex-teachers who have done more than five years service and die under the age of 60 having left the profession.

4–149   In addition to the death gratuity a short term pension[51] (according to the size of the family) is payable for up to six months to the widow of a

---

[42] See S.I. 1976 No. 1987, regs. 82–84, and Sched. 7, Pt. 2, as amended by S.I. 1980 No. 919, reg. 15. See also the Teachers' Superannuation (Notional Salaries) Regulations 1981 (S.I. 1981 No. 934).

[43] S.I. 1976 No. 1987, reg. 9 as amended by S.I. 1982 No. 496, reg. 4 and S.I. 1985 No. 1844, reg. 4.

[44] S.I. 1976 No. 1987, reg. 56 as amended by S.I. 1978 No. 422, reg. 14, S.I. 1978 No. 1422, reg. 12 and S.I. 1985 No. 1844, reg. 26.

[45] S.I. 1976 No. 1987, reg. 55 as amended by S.I. 1978 No. 422, reg. 13 and S.I. 1978 No. 1422, reg. 11.

[46] See S.I. 1976 No. 1987, reg. 70 as amended by S.I. 1978 No. 1422, reg. 18 and S.I. 1980 No. 919, reg. 26.

[47] *Ibid.* reg. 57 as amended by S.I. 1978 No. 1422, reg. 13 and S.I. 1980 No. 919, reg. 23.

[48] S.I. 1976 No. 1987, reg. 53A (added by reg. 12 of S.I. 1978 No. 422) as amended by S.I. 1978 No. 1422, reg. 9.

[49] Under the Teachers (Compensation for Redundancy and Premature Retirement) Regulations 1985 (S.I. 1985 No. 1181) and see above at para. 4–95.

[50] S.I. 1976 No. 1987, regs. 58–60.

[51] *Ibid.* reg. 63, as substituted by S.I. 1980 No. 919, reg. 24 and amended by S.I. 1985 No. 1844, reg. 7.

teacher who dies in service, at the rate of his annual salary, followed by a long term pension.[52] This will at most be half of the pension to which the teacher would have been entitled had he retired upon incapacity on the day he died. It may be much less. The pension is augmented in respect of children,[53] or paid on their behalf where there is no widow. There is also provision for pension when the teacher is not in service at the time of death.

A widow's pension normally ceases[54] on remarriage or cohabitation **4–150** but may revive on renewed widowhood; and a child's pension ceases when he becomes 17 unless he is receiving full-time education or training or is incapacitated.[55] An unmarried male teacher may, while employed in reckonable service, nominate[56] a financially dependent close relative to receive the benefits which would otherwise go to a widow. The nomination lapses if he marries. A female teacher may similarly nominate, and if married nominate her financially dependent husband.

A male teacher may add to benefits otherwise receivable by allocat- **4–151** ing[57] not more than one third of his annual pension to his widow or other dependant, or as an annuity for the joint lives of himself and his widow and on his death as a pension for his widow. The same option is open to female teachers in relation to widowers and other dependants.

Teachers' pensions are official pensions under the Pensions (Increase) **4–152** Act 1971[58] as applied by regulations,[59] and orders[60] confer annual cost of living increases. Pensions beginning before 1971 were scaled up as a basis for further increases.[61] Increases are not payable in the case of premature retirement (as distinguished from retirement on account of incapacity) before the age of 55[62] but once that age is reached they are

[52] S.I. 1976 No. 1987, reg. 64 as amended by S.I. 1978 No. 1422, reg. 15 and S.I. 1980 No. 919, reg. 25; and reg. 66 as amended by S.I. 1978 No. 1422, reg. 16. See also regs. 68 as amended by S.I. 1980 No. 919, reg. 9, and 69.
[53] S.I. 1976 No. 1987, reg. 63 as substituted by S.I. 1980 No. 919, reg. 24, and 67 as amended by S.I. 1981 No. 1422, reg. 17; and see definition of "child" in S.I. 1976 No. 1987, reg. 3 as amended by S.I. 1985 No. 1844, reg. 16.
[54] See S.I. 1976 No. 1987, reg. 70 as amended by S.I. 1978 No. 1422, reg. 18 and S.I. 1980 No. 919, reg. 26.
[55] See S.I. 1976 No. 1987, reg. 62(b).
[56] Ibid. reg. 65.
[57] Ibid. reg. 74, as amended by S.I. 1978 No. 422, reg. 15, S.I. 1980 No. 919, reg. 10 and S.I. 1985 No. 1844, reg. 30; and Sched. 6, as amended by S.I. 1978 No. 422, reg. 16, S.I. 1980 No. 919, reg. 30 and S.I. 1985 No. 1844, reg. 32.
[58] See s.5 as amended and Sched. 2, paras. 17–20A.
[59] The Pensions (Increase) Act 1971 (Modification) (Teachers) Regulations 1972 (S.I. 1972 No. 1676), Increase of Pensions (Teachers' Family Benefits) Regulations 1971 (S.I. 1971 No. 1614) and 1972 (S.I. 1972 No. 1905), the Pensions Increases (Compensation to Staff of Teacher Training Establishments) Regulations 1975 (S.I. 1975 No. 1478) and, under the Pensions (Increase) Act 1974, s.1, the Pensions Increase (Teachers) Regulations 1974 (S.I. 1974 No. 813).
[60] Made under the Social Security Pensions Act 1975, s.59 as amended. See the Pensions Increase (Review) Order 1984 (S.I. 1984 No. 1307).
[61] Pensions (Increase) Act 1971, as amended.
[62] Ibid. s.3 as amended by Pensions (Increase) Act 1974 s.3, and Pensions Increase (Reduction of Qualifying Age) Order 1972 (S.I. 1972 No. 1299).

taken into account in calculating subsequent pension payments.[63] "Frozen" lump sums also attract cost of living increases.[64]

4–153   The Secretary of State may defer, suspend or reduce payment of benefit to teachers convicted of treason or other specified offences.[65]

---

[63] Pensions (Increase) Act 1971, s.3, as amended by S.I. 1972 No. 1299.
[64] Pensions (Increase) Act 1971, s.9, as amended by Superannuation Act 1972, s.25.
[65] S.I. 1976 No. 1987, reg. 79, as amended by S.I. 1978 No. 1422, reg. 22 and S.I. 1980 No. 919, reg. 11, and reg. 79A inserted by S.I. 1978 No. 1422, reg. 23.

CHAPTER 5

SUPPLEMENTARY FUNCTIONS OF LOCAL EDUCATION AUTHORITIES

"Supplementary," "complementary," "ancillary," "miscellaneous" **5–01** or just "other" functions? "Other" is too dismissive, "miscellaneous" a confession of taxonomic failure, "ancillary" implies subordination, and "complementary" claims too much: the transfer of the careers service to the Manpower Services Commission, for example, would scarcely damage the integrity of educational provision. So the modest "supplementary" must do.

IN RELATION TO MAINTAINED SCHOOLS AND OTHER INSTITUTIONS

In this section "complementary" would be appropriate because the **5–02** functions referred to are bound up with the principal duties of local education authorities. They include some, for instance cleansing verminous children, and provision of meals, that have been part and parcel of the education service since at least the first decade of the present century.

Health

Until April 1, 1974, local education authorities provided medical and **5–03** dental inspection and treatment services for pupils[1] at the schools and other educational establishments they maintained. Subsequently that responsibility has passed[2] to the Secretary of State for Social Services, but child guidance staff[3] not providing medical treatment remain in the employment of local education authorities to give advice about pupils with behavioural, emotional or learning difficulties. Joint consultative committees exist[4] to promote co-operation between health authorities and local authorities. A local education authority who, exceptionally, wished to provide a health care service not provided by a health authority might find enabling power in the Local Government Act 1972, section 137.[5] The Department of Education and Science continue to offer advice[6] on health matters of concern to local education authorities. The

---

[1] "Pupil"—defined in 1944 Act, s.114(1) as amended by 1980 Act s.24(3). See above at para. 2–03. As to education in hospital see Circ. 5/74 and above at para. 2–207; also below at para. 5–29.
[2] See Circ. 1/74 (W.O. 35/74) and A.M.2/74.
[3] See Circ. 3/74 (W.O. W.H.S.C (15) 5).
[4] See National Health Service Act 1977, s.22 as amended.
[5] As to Local Government Act 1972, s.137 see above at para. 1–39. There is no obligation upon a local education authority to provide a health care service—see *R.* v. *Oxfordshire Education Authority, ex p. W., The Times*, November 22, 1986.
[6] *e.g.* A.M. 20/67 (asbestos dust), A.M. 15/77, (W.O. 8/77) health education in schools), Circ. 12/78 (W.O. 112/78) (control of tuberculosis), A.M. 2/86 (AIDS).

residual duty[7] of local education authorities is to make arrangements for encouraging and assisting pupils (except when parents give notice[8] of objection) to take advantage of the following services that the Secretary of State for Social Services provides.

5–04   District health authorities[9] on behalf of the Secretary of State[10] provide medical and dental inspection and treatment[11] of maintained school pupils. Local education authorities and governors of voluntary schools make available[12] appropriate accommodation. By arrangement with the local education authority the Secretary of State may also[13] provide the same services for:

(a) senior pupils in any educational establishment, other than a school, maintained by a local education authority at which full-time further education is provided (with the agreement of the governors); and

(b) any child or young person who is receiving primary or secondary education otherwise than at school under special arrangements[14] made for him by the authority.

The same services may be provided for junior or senior pupils in attendance at a non-maintained educational establishment, by arrangement with the proprietor, which may include payment by him.

5–05   The Secretary of State must make available to local authorities, *inter alia,* the use of premises and the services of medical and dental practitioners and nurses in the health service (and may make available those of, in particular, staff in professions supplementary to medicine) "so far as is reasonably necessary and practicable to enable local authorities to discharge their functions relating to . . . education . . . ."[15]

---

[7] 1944 Act, s.48(4) as amended by National Health Service Reorganisation Act 1973, s.57 and Sched. 4, para. 7, and by National Health Service Act 1977, s.129 and Sched. 15, para. 2. As to enforcement, see 1944 Act, s.99 as amended and below at para. 6–15.

[8] "Notice"—see 1944 Act, s.113 as amended by 1946 Act, s.14.

[9] See National Health Service Act 1977, Pt. I as amended by Pt. I of Health Services Act 1980.

[10] 1977 Act, s.5(1)(a).

[11] The definitions of "medical inspection" and "medical treatment" in 1944 Act, s.114(1) were repealed by s.57 and Sched. 5 of the National Health Service Reorganisation Act 1973. A local education authority are not obliged to supervise treatment (*e.g.,* the taking of medicine in school) and if a teacher does so negligently he and the authority may incur liability unless an appropriate agreement has been made in advance with the parent.

[12] National Health Service Act 1977, s.5(1) and Sched. 1, para. 3 as amended by Education Act 1980, s.1(3) and Sched. 1, para. 29.

[13] 1977 Act, Sched. 1, para. 1, as amended by the 1981 Act, s.21 and Sched. 3, para. 13, and Sched. 2.

[14] Under 1944 Act, s.56, as amended by the 1948 Act, and the 1981 Act. See below at para. 5–29 and above at para. 2–207.

[15] National Health Service Act 1977, s.26, as extended by Health Services Act 1980, s.3. For definition of "medical practitioner" and "dental practitioner" see s.128(1) as amended, and for the procedure to be followed by the Secretary of State, s.27. Local education authorities may require premises for the purposes of s.56 of the 1944 Act (see below at para. 5–29), and are likely to require the services specified to carry out their duties under, (*e.g.*), s.54 of the 1944 Act (see below at para. 5–07) and s.5 of the 1981 Act (see above at para. 2–196).

Once notice has been received from the proper officer[16] of a local **5–06** authority, a child who is, or has been, suffering from a notifiable disease[17] or has been exposed to infection is not to attend school[18] until a certificate permitting attendance has been obtained. It is an offence[19] for the person having care of a child to contravene this requirement. The principal[20] of a school in which any pupil is suffering from a notifiable disease must, if required, provide a list[21] of the names and addresses of day pupils. Failure to do so is also an offence.

Cleanliness

In the interests of cleanliness[22] a local education authority may auth- **5–07** orise their medical officer[23] to have examined the persons and clothing of pupils attending any of their maintained schools that they have named in a written direction.[24] On reasonable suspicion a medical officer may act on his own initiative. Examinations are made by a person authorised[25] by the local education authority, and if the pupil or his clothing is found to be infested with vermin or in a foul condition any officer of the authority may serve a notice on his parent requiring him to have the pupil and clothing cleansed. The notice is to convey that unless the cleansing has been carried out satisfactorily within a stated period (not less than 24 hours) it will be done under the local education authority's arrangements[26]; and if need be the medical officer may by order direct accordingly. The local education authority must provide suitable premises, persons and appliances for carrying out cleansing; and where district councils[27] have premises and appliances the local education

---

[16] "Proper officer" is defined in s.74 of the Public Health (Control of Diseases) Act 1984 and "local authority" in *ibid.* s.1.

[17] Those listed in 1984 Act, s.10 together with others made notifiable by a local authority under s.16, and others, including measles, whooping cough and scarlet fever specified in the Public Health (Infectious Diseases) Regulations 1968 (S.I. 1968 No. 1366) reg. 4 and Sched. 2 as amended.

[18] 1984 Act, s.21. "School" includes a Sunday or sabbath school.

[19] On summary conviction (see Magistrates' Courts Act 1980) a fine is payable at level 1 on the standard scale. (See Criminal Justice Act 1982, s.75.)

[20] The "principal" is the person in charge of a school or, if none, the head of any department (1984 Act, s.22(4)).

[21] 1984 Act, s.22.

[22] 1944 Act, s.54. See A.M. 156. As to exclusion from school see subs. (7) and above at para. 2–118.

[23] By *ibid.* s.114(1) as amended by the National Health Service Reorganisation Act 1973, Sched. 4, para. 8 (continued in effect by National Health Service Act 1977, Sched. 14, para. 13) "a duly qualified medical practitioner employed or engaged, whether regularly or for the purposes of any particular case, by that authority or whose services are made available to that authority by the Secretary of State." See also Circ. 1/74. (W.O. 35/74).

[24] As to revocation and variation of directions and orders see 1944 Act, s.111 and above at para. 1–42.

[25] A girl is to be examined or cleansed only by a duly qualified medical practitioner or a woman authorised for the purpose by the local education authority (*ibid.* s.54(8)).

[26] If a parent withholds his child from examination and the child is in consequence excluded from school that parent is guilty of an offence against school attendance requirements. See *Fox* v. *Burgess* [1922] 1 K.B. 623 and above at para. 2–226 n. 57.

[27] Including inner London boroughs and the Common Council of the City of London. (London Government Act 1963, s.32(7).

authority may require permission to use them, on terms settled by agreement or in default by the Secretary of State for Social Services. The medical officer's order may cover conveyance to, and detention at, the premises where the cleansing is to be carried out.

5–08   If, after cleansing, the pupil or his clothing is again found to be in need of cleansing, and this is proved to be due to the parent's neglect, on summary conviction[28] the parent is liable to a fine at level 1[29] on the standard scale. Where a child lives with both parents the court may hold one or other liable for the neglect on the facts of the case.[30]

Meals and milk

5–09   The functions of local education authorities as respects the provision[31] of meals and milk[32] at maintained schools are now, under section 22 of the 1980 Act, exercised[33] largely at discretion. An authority may provide registered pupils with meals, milk or other refreshments[34] at such charges[35] as they think fit. They may do so on school premises or elsewhere[36] where education is provided; and they are also to provide free facilities for the consumption of meals or other refreshments brought to school.

5–10   Local education authorities must consider whether it is appropriate to remit all or part of the charge to meet the circumstances of any pupil or class or description of pupils. An obligation arises only in relation to a pupil whose parents are in receipt of supplementary benefit[37] or family income supplement.[38] Provision as appears to be requisite must be made for him in the middle of the day free of charge. These provisions for remission of charges are replaced by section 77(2) of the Social Security Act 1986, and once that section is brought into force authorities must charge for whatever is provided, and charge every pupil the same, except that midday provision free of charge as above is to be made for a

---

[28] As to summary proceedings see Magistrates' Courts Act 1980 as amended.

[29] 1944 Act, s.54(6) as amended by Criminal Law Act 1977, s.31(5) and (6), Criminal Justice Act 1982, ss.37 and 46 and the Criminal Penalties etc. (Increase) Order 1984 (S.I. 1984 No. 447).

[30] See *Plunkett* v. *Alker* [1954] 1 Q.B. 420 distinguishing *London County Council* v. *Stansell* (1935) 154 L.T. 241.

[31] As to the supervision of school meals see Circs. 16/68, 3/78 (W.O. 186/77) and above at para. 4–110, and as to the Report of the Committee on Catering Arrangements in Schools, and of the working party on nutritional aspects of school meals, A.M. 15/75 (W.O. 2/75).

[32] As to grants to authorities from the EEC towards the cost of milk and milk products see above at para. 1–128.

[33] See Circ. 1/80, paras. 2–9, Circ. 3/78 (W.O. 186/77) and Circ. 5/74, paras. 22–25 as regards provision for children in hospitals (the two latter are partly anachronistic); also, seventh Report from the Education Science and Arts Committee 1981–1982 (H.C. 505) and Government response (Cmnd. 8740). Information about policy with regard to school meals must be published under the Education (School Information) Regulations 1981 (S.I. 1981 No. 630) Sched. 1, para. 9.

[34] Breakfasts and sandwiches may be provided.

[35] Charges may be recovered as a civil debt.

[36] This provision applies when s.77(1) of Social Security Act 1986 is brought into force.

[37] "Supplementary benefit"—defined in Supplementary Benefits Act 1976, s.34 as amended (see Social Security Act 1980, Sched. 2, Pt. II).

[38] "Family income supplement"—see Family Income Supplements Act 1970 as amended.

pupil whose parents are in receipt of income support under that Act (or who is in receipt of it himself).

Governors of maintained schools are to afford local education auth- **5–11** orities facilities for school meals and to allow them as necessary to make use of school premises and equipment, and to alter school buildings.[39] Governors of voluntary schools are not to be required to incur expenditure.

With the consent of the proprietor of a non-maintained school in their **5–12** area and upon agreed, including financial, terms, a local education authority may make arrangements for securing the provision[40] of meals, milk and other refreshments for pupils there. So far as practicable the expense is not to exceed that which would have been incurred had the pupils been at a maintained school.

Board and lodging

A local education authority may, under section 50 of the 1944 Act,[41] **5–13** make arrangements to provide board and lodging for a pupil for whom they are satisfied, having regard to his age, ability, aptitude and any special educational needs,[42] that primary or secondary education or special educational provision can best[43] be provided at a particular county, voluntary or special school, but cannot otherwise be provided for him there. In making the arrangements the local education authority are so far as practicable to give effect to the wishes of the pupil's parents with respect to the religious denomination of the person with whom he will reside.

Unless the local education authority conclude that they are unable to **5–14** provide education suitable to the pupil's age, ability and aptitude or special educational needs without also providing board and lodging, they are to require[44] the parent to pay as much (if any) of the cost as he

---

[39] See A.M. 11/70.

[40] Under 1944 Act, s.78(2), as amended by 1948 Act, s.11 and Sched. 2 and National Health Service Act 1973, s.57 and Sched. 5, and extended by 1980 Act, s.22(5).

[41] As amended by 1946 Act, s.14(1) and Sched. 2, Pt. I, 1948 Act, s.11 and Sched. 1, Pt. I, and 1981 Act, s.21 and Sched. 3, para. 3. As to the provision of boarding accommodation at primary and secondary schools see 1944 Act, s.8(2)(*d*) and above at para. 2–07; as to payment of fees for board and lodging *ibid.* s.61(2) and (3) as amended and above at para. 1–90; and as to boarding at non-maintained schools 1953 Act, s.6 and below at para. 5–32. Where the child is in the care of a local authority that authority must provide the board and lodging (see the Local Authorities and Local Education Authorities (Allocation of Functions) Regulations 1951 (S.I. 1951 No. 472) reg. 4 and Circ. 232).

[42] "Special educational needs" and "special educational provision" are defined in 1981 Act, s.1 (see above at para. 2–194).

[43] The implication is that it would not necessarily be wholly impracticable to provide suitable education elsewhere; and this may be material having regard to the terms of 1944 Act, s.52, as to which see below at para. 5–14.

[44] 1944 Act, s.52 as amended by 1948 Act, s.11 and Sched. 2, and by 1981 Act, s.21 and Sched. 3, para. 4.

is able without financial hardship. Sums payable are recoverable summarily as a civil debt.[45]

Clothing

5–15 Under section 5 of the 1948 Act[46] a local education authority may provide clothing[47] in a variety of circumstances: first, for pupils (a) boarding at educational institutions maintained by the authority (b) at maintained nursery schools and classes[48] and (c) for whom special educational provision[49] is made and the authority are providing board and lodging elsewhere than at a maintained institution.

5–16 Secondly, where it appears to a local education authority that a pupil at a maintained school or a special school, whether or not maintained, who does not fall within any of the categories above is unable, because his clothing is inadequate or unsuitable, to take full advantage of the education provided at the school, they may provide him with clothing to ensure that he is sufficiently and suitably clad while he remains a pupil there.

5–17 Thirdly, with the consent of the proprietor of a non-maintained (other than a special) school and upon agreed, including financial, terms, a local education authority may make arrangements to the same end as that stated in the last paragraph for a pupil in the same circumstances. So far as is practicable the expense is not to exceed that which would have been incurred had the pupil been at a maintained school.

5–18 Finally, an authority may provide physical training clothes for pupils at maintained schools and further education establishments,[50] and for persons who make use of physical training facilities made available by the authority under section 53[51] of the 1944 Act.

5–19 Provision of clothing may confer[52] a right of property, or of user, at the option of the providing authority unless the Secretary of State prescribes[53] one way or the other. When a right of property is conferred the

---

[45] See Magistrates' Courts Act 1980, s.58.

[46] As amended by 1953 Act, s.17(1) and Sched. 1, the 1980 Act, s.29 and the 1981 Act, s.21 and Sched. 3, para. 7.

[47] By 1944 Act, s.114(1) includes boots and other footwear. Information about policy and arrangements with regard to provision of clothing must be published, under the School Information Regulations 1981 (S.I. 1981 No. 630) Sched. 1, para. 10.

[48] "Nursery schools and classes"—see 1980 Act, s.24 and above at paras. 2–45 to 2–50.

[49] "Special educational provision"—see 1981 Act, s.1 and above at para. 2–194.

[50] "Further education establishments"—see *ibid.* s.41 and above at para. 3–03. What counts as a "maintained" further education establishment is unclear: apart from those provided by local education authorities Sched. 3 to the Education (Schools and Further Education) Regulations 1981 (S.I. 1981 No. 1086) (see above at para. 3–05) lists 12 which are "substantially dependent" for their maintenance on assistance from local education authorities.

[51] See below at para. 5–27.

[52] 1948 Act, s.5(5).

[53] Prescription is by regulation made by the Secretary of State (1944 Act, s.114(1)).

authority have power[54] to require the parent of the pupil, or the other persons mentioned in the last paragraph, to pay as much of the cost of provision as they are able to pay without financial hardship, or a lesser sum. Those aged 18 and over who are not registered school pupils pay instead of their parents. Any sum required to be paid is recoverable[55] summarily as a civil debt.[56]

Payment of expenses[57]

To enable pupils to take advantage of educational facilities[58] without   **5–20** hardship to themselves or their parents local education authorities may defray[59] the expenses of children at county, voluntary or special schools to enable them to take part in any school activities. "School activities" in this context may be taken to include activities out of school hours, including those organised as part of recreation and social and physical training.[60] The expenses may include the purchase of uniform or other clothing, and of transport, though the particular powers mentioned elsewhere[61] may be available. Authorities may also grant scholarships[62] or other allowances to school pupils over compulsory school age, but not[63] in respect of higher education, including teacher training courses, to which the 1962 Act applies. Payments[64] may be made only to relieve financial hardship and are to be related to parental means; and the authority must be satisfied that the education to which the payment relates is suitable for the pupil.

---

[54] 1948 Act, s.5(6) and the Education (Provision of Clothing) Regulations 1980 (S.I. 1980 No. 545) (overriding the decision in *Clements* v. *Williams* (1837) 8 Car. & P. 58). A child in the care of a local authority is to be treated as a child of parents with sufficient resources to pay the whole cost (see the Local Authorities and Local Education Authorities (Allocation of Functions) Regulations 1951 (S.I. 1951 No. 472, reg. 8 and Circ. 232).

[55] 1948 Act, s.5(6) and subs. (6A) inserted by 1980 Act, s.29. See Circ. 1/80 para. 28.

[56] See Magistrates' Courts Act 1980, s.58.

[57] Information about a local education authority's policy must be published under the School Information Regulations 1981 (S.I. 1981 No. 630) Sched. 1, para. 11.

[58] Speech therapy is not an educational facility. See *R.* v. *Oxfordshire Education Authority, ex p. W.*, *The Times*, November 22, 1986, and above at para. 5–03, n. 5.

[59] See 1944 Act, s.81(*a*) and the Scholarships and Other Benefits Regulations 1977 (S.I. 1977 No. 1443) reg. 4(*a*) as amended by Amendment Regulations 1979 (S.I. 1979 No. 260) reg. 2. Children in the care of a local authority are not to be aided under s.81(*a*). (See the Local Authorities and Local Education Authorities (Allocation of Functions) Regulations 1951 (S.I. 1951 No. 472) reg. 7(1)(*a*) and Circ. 232.)

[60] See below at para. 5–27.

[61] See above at paras. 5–16 and 5–18, and below at paras. 5–21 *et seq.*

[62] 1944 Act, s.81(*c*) and S.I. 1977 No. 1443, reg. 4(*e*)(i). See "School Uniform: Grants and Discipline" 118 J.P.N. 102. The local education authority are to pay the whole of the cost in the case of children in the care of a local authority, but not to exercise their functions under s.81(*c*) to pay maintenance allowances in respect of such children over compulsory school age. (See S.I. 1951 No. 472, reg. 7(1)(*c*) and proviso and reg. 7(2), and Circ. 232.)

[63] See 1962 Act (as first enacted), s.4(4)–(6) and above at paras. 3–41 *et seq.*

[64] S.I. 1977 No. 1443, reg. 6.

Transport

5–21   By section 55(1) of the 1944 Act local education authorities are to make arrangements for provision of free transport and otherwise as they consider necessary[65] (or as the Secretary of State may direct[66]) to facilitate the attendance of pupils at schools (including boarding schools) or further education courses or classes; and by subsection (2)[67] they may pay the whole or part, as they think fit, of reasonable travelling expenses of pupils to whom the arrangements under subsection (1) do not apply. The use of "otherwise" in subsection (1) covers the provision of staff[68] to take care of children during the journey.

5–22   Authorities may consider it "necessary" that their arrangements should deprive a parent of one of his defences against failure to secure his child's attendance at school under section 39(2)(*c*)[69] of the 1944 Act—that the authority have failed to make suitable[70] arrangements for his transport to and from the school at which he is a registered pupil and which is not within walking distance[71] of his home. By an added subsection (3) to section 55, introduced by section 53 of the 1986 (No. 2) Act, in considering the necessity of making arrangements authorities are to have regard, *inter alia,* to the age of a particular pupil and the nature of the route or alternative routes that he could reasonably be expected to take. There is, however, no positive obligation on authorities to provide transport for all pupils (for example, pupils at independent schools) at schools beyond walking distance from their homes, and the defence is material only in respect of children of compulsory school age.[72] On the other hand authorities may consider necessary under section 55(1) arrangements which extend beyond defeasance of the section 39(2)(*c*) defence, and under which free transport is provided, for example, for

---

[65] "Consider necessary"—see above at para.1–47. Government legislative proposals based on the report of a Working Party (see A.M. 22/73) to increase the discretion of local education authorities were withdrawn after parliamentary opposition in 1980. An authority's general arrangements and policies in respect of transport are to be published under the Education (School Information) Regulations 1981 (S.I. 1981 No. 630) Sched. 1, para. 8.

[66] As to revocation and variation of directions see 1944 Act, s.111 and above at para. 1–42.

[67] As amended by 1948 Act, s.11(1) and Sched. 1, Pt. I. Cash payments may be made and exceptionally it may be economical for a local education authority to pay a parent to use his own car to take his child to school. Where a child is in the care of a local authority that authority make the payments. (See the Local Authorities and Local Education Authorities (Allocation of Functions) Regulations 1951 (S.I. 1951 No. 472) reg. 5, and Circ. 232.)

[68] Failure to provide staff may constitute negligence (*Shrimpton* v. *Hertfordshire County Council* 104 L.T. 145), but supervision by prefects may be adequate (*Jacques* v. *Oxfordshire County Council and Another,* 66 L.G.R. 440) (see below at para. 7–31). A local education authority were held not liable for the negligence of a taxi driver who was their independent contractor (*Myton* v. *Woods and Others,* 79 L.G.R. 28).

[69] See above at para. 2–227, where reference is made to *Rogers* v. *Essex County Council* [1987] A.C. 66.

[70] See *Surrey County Council* v. *Minister of Education* [1953] 1 W.L.R. 516 and above at para. 2–227; also "The Provision of Free Transport for School Children" 117 J.P.J. 821.

[71] See 1944 Act, s.39(5) and above at para. 2–227. A bus pass having been granted may be withdrawn if on recalculation the distance is found to be less than that specified in the authority's arrangements (see *Rootkin* v. *Kent County Council* [1981] 1 W.L.R. 1186).

[72] See 1944 Act, s.35 and above at para. 1–81.

pupils of above compulsory school age, for some of those whose homes are within walking distance from school (perhaps for health reasons), and for particular categories of pupils, for instance those whose parents are receiving family income supplement.[73] Similarly the walking distance test does not restrict the exercise of their discretion under subsection (2).

Free transport under section 55(1) is mostly secured by purchase of   **5–23** season tickets or "bus passes" for use on public transport,[74] by contract hire of buses or other vehicles, or by use of the authority's own vehicles. A school bus[75] may be used[76] to carry fare-paying passengers when it is being used to provide free school transport. The passengers may, but need not, be pupils who do not fall within the authority's arrangements. Fares are at the authority's discretion and some general requirements[77] relating to public service vehicles[78] do not apply.

Separate statutory provisions (for example, 1944 Act, s.53)[79] support   **5–24** the use of vehicles[80] by local education authorities to take pupils to playing fields and on other school journeys. It is arguable that charges may be made only where the activity is extra-curricular.[81] Where charges are made the ordinary licensing requirement[82] for public service vehicles do not apply where a permit[83] is granted to a local education authority or school[84] for the use of a bus (a separate permit for each bus) otherwise than for profit and when members of the general public are not being carried. Permits in respect of small buses (between eight and 16 passengers—minibuses) may be granted by councils who are local education authorities (and by the Inner London Education Authority), and in respect of large buses by a traffic commissioner.[85] Regulations[86]

---

[73] "Family income supplement"—see Family Income Supplements Act 1970 as amended.

[74] Three seated children all under 14 count as two passengers (the Public Service Vehicles (Carrying Capacity) Regulations 1984 (S.I. 1984, No. 1406) reg. 5).

[75] By s.46 of the Public Passenger Vehicles Act 1981 a school bus is "a motor vehicle which is being used by [a local education authority] to provide free school transport"; and see also Transport Act 1985, ss.6–9. As to grants towards the duty on bus fuel see Fuel Duty Grant (Eligible Bus Services) Regulations 1985 (S.I. 1985 No. 1886), Sched.

[76] *Ibid.* s.46(1)(*a*).

[77] Namely *ibid.* ss.6 (initial fitness), 8 (inspection), 9 (prohibition on driving unfit vehicles), 12(1) (operators' licences) and 22 (drivers' licences) all as amended or substituted by Transport Act 1982 and Transport Act 1985.

[78] See definition in Public Passenger Vehicles Act 1981, s.1.

[79] See below at para. 5–27.

[80] See below at para. 5–53 as to vehicle insurance.

[81] See 1944 Act, s.61(1) and above at paras. 1–87 *et seq.* Work experience under the 1973 Work Experience Act (see below at para. 5–39) is probably extra-curricular.

[82] See Public Passenger Vehicles Act 1981, ss.12(1) and 22 as amended by Transport Act 1985.

[83] See Transport Act 1985, ss.18–21. As to the grant of permits see the Minibuses (Permits) Regulations 1977 (S.I. 1977 No. 1708) as amended.

[84] Also to bodies which fulfil the duty of the local education authority (or the I.L.E.A.) with respect to the provision of education, and bodies connected with such schools or bodies. See the Minibus (Designated Bodies) Order 1980 (S.I. 1980 No. 1356) as amended.

[85] "Traffic commissioner"—see Transport Act 1985, s.3.

[86] See the Minibuses (Conditions of Fitness, Equipment and Use) Regulations 1977 (S.I. 1977 No. 2103) as amended.

prescribe conditions of fitness for small buses. For large buses the fitness requirements[87] in relation to public service vehicles apply; and the traffic commissioner must be satisfied about the adequacy of facilities or arrangements for keeping them in a fit and serviceable condition.

School crossing patrols

5–25   County and metropolitan district councils (in London, the Common Council of the City and the metropolitan police commissioner)[88] may make arrangements[89]—the function is permissive—for patrolling, between 8 a.m. and 5.30 p.m.,[90] places where children cross roads on their way to and from school or from one part of a school to another. In taking decisions about making arrangements they must have regard to representations received from local authorities[91] within their area. The councils appointing patrols must satisfy themselves that the persons appointed are adequately qualified, and must give them the requisite training. It is customary that when arrangements are made the county or metropolitan district council act in their capacity as local education authority. Should a teacher stand in for a school crossing patrol, in an emergency, and by his negligence[92] an accident to a child occurs, he will himself be liable, as will also, vicariously, his employing authority unless perhaps he is not acting at their instance. To safeguard themselves against an emergency, or in any event, councils' arrangements may include an agreement with the local police authority[93] for the performance of specified functions by that authority—by a police officer or traffic warden.[94]

5–26   By exhibiting[95] the prescribed[96] sign a uniformed school crossing patrol has power to require a vehicle to stop before it reaches the crossing place and not to impede the children crossing[97]; and it is not to start again while the sign continues to be exhibited. Failure to comply is an offence[98]; and it is to be presumed in the absence of proof to the contrary

---

[87] See the Public Passenger Vehicles Act 1981, ss.6–11 as amended by Transport Act 1982 and Transport Act 1985.

[88] See Road Traffic Regulation Act 1984, s.27 as to expenses under s.26 in the metropolitan police district, which is roughly, but not wholly, coterminous with Greater London, which extends to the boundaries of the outer London boroughs.

[89] *Ibid.* s.26, as amended by Local Government Act 1985, s.8 and Sched. 5, para. 4(10).

[90] Greenwich Mean Time or Summer Time as appropriate (Interpretation Act 1978, s.9).

[91] Namely, parish (in Wales community) councils; in counties, additionally, district councils; and, within the metropolitan police district, London borough and other councils.

[92] A school crossing patrol may, of course, himself be held negligent. See *Toole* v. *Sherbourne Poufees Ltd. and Another*, 70 L.G.R. 52 and below at para.7–32.

[93] As defined in Police Act 1964, Sched. 8 as amended, the police committee of a non-metropolitan county and the policy authority of a metropolitan county.

[94] As to employment of traffic wardens, see Road Traffic Regulation Act 1984, s.95(4)(*a*).

[95] *Ibid.* s.28. The word "stop" must be visible. See *Hoy* v. *Smith* [1964] 1 W.L.R. 1377.

[96] See Traffic Signs Regulations and General Directions 1981 (S.I. 1981 No. 859) reg. 37 and Sched. 1, Pt. II, Diagram 605.1.

[97] As to the nature of the obligation see *Franklin* v. *Langdown* [1971] 3 All E.R. 662, distinguishing *R.* v. *Greenwood* [1962] Crim. L.R. 639 and *Wall* v. *Walwyn* [1974] R.T.R. 24.

[98] Road Traffic Regulation Act 1984, s.98 and Sched. 7.

that the patrol's uniform and sign were not defective and that the children were on their way to or from school or from one part of the school to another.

RECREATION AND SOCIAL AND PHYSICAL TRAINING

Local education authorities are under a duty[99] to secure that the primary, secondary and further education provided for their area (by themselves or otherwise) includes adequate facilities for recreation and social and physical training.[1] Accordingly they may (and they may assist[2] others to) establish, maintain and manage camps, holiday classes, playing fields, play centres and other places at which those facilities are available. (The "other places" include playgrounds, gymnasiums and swimming baths not appropriated[3] to any school or college). They may also organise games, expeditions and other activities, and defray, or contribute towards, the expenses. In making their arrangements local education authorities are to have regard to the expediency of co-operating with voluntary societies and bodies, and this may include making grants[4] or providing them with free accommodation.   **5–27**

The facilities provided by local education authorities are to be available to any persons receiving primary, secondary or further education; and playing fields[5] and other facilities may be made yet more widely available by the exercise of the powers to provide recreational facilities that are granted[6] to all local authorities.   **5–28**

EDUCATION OUTSIDE SCHOOL

A child or young person may be unable to attend a suitable primary, secondary or special school by reason of "extraordinary circumstances." The term is not elaborated but would include a child's being in hospital[7] or unable to leave home because of illness or physical disability. If a local education authority are satisfied that such circumstances exist they have power,[8] with the approval of the Secretary of State, to make   **5–29**

---

[99] 1944 Act, s.53 as amended; and see also *ibid*. s.41(*b*) above at para. 3–03.

[1] As to the provision of clothing for physical training see 1948 Act, s.5(3) as amended and above at para. 5–18.

[2] "Assist" see 1944 Act, s.114(2)(*b*).

[3] "Appropriation" is not defined for the purposes of the 1944 Act, but see Local Government Act 1972, s.122 as amended and above at para. 1–145.

[4] As to government grants see the Education (Grant) Regulations 1983 (S.I. 1983 No. 74) and above at para. 3–19; and as to the youth service, above at paras. 3–36 *et seq.*

[5] Provided in accordance with the Education (School Premises) Regulations 1981 (S.I. 1981 No. 909) reg. 6. See above at para. 2–56.

[6] By s.19 of the Local Government (Miscellaneous Provisions) Act 1976. See Circ. 11/64. By para. 53 of Sched. 14 to the Local Government Act 1985, the I.L.E.A. may exercise the powers under s.19(1)–(3) for the benefit of persons under 26.

[7] See Circ. 5/74 and above at para. 5–05.

[8] Under 1944 Act, s.56 as amended by 1948 Act, s.11 and Pt. I of Sched. 1. See also 1981 Act, s.3 in relation to a child with special educational needs (above at para. 2–207).

special arrangements for him to receive primary or secondary education otherwise than at school, full-time or part-time.

EDUCATION AT NON-MAINTAINED SCHOOLS

5–30   The assisted places scheme,[9] introduced by the 1980 Act, is administered and funded by the Secretary of State. Local education authorities may give parents financial assistance[10] under the Scholarships and Other Benefits Regulations 1977 and under the 1953 Act. Additionally, by means of section 137 of the Local Government Act 1972, it is lawful[11] for a local authority who are not a local education authority (but not for a local education authority) to establish a trust for the purpose of providing free or assisted places at independent schools for children resident in their area.

5–31   To enable pupils to take advantage without hardship of educational facilities available to them, local education authorities may pay[12] the whole or part of the tuition and board and lodging fees and attendance (including transport) expenses at fee-paying schools, provided[13] that payment is required in order to prevent or relieve financial hardship, that it is related to the means of the pupil's parents, and that the authority are satisfied that the education is suitable for the pupil.

5–32   A local education authority may arrange[14] for a pupil to receive primary and secondary education at a non-maintained school, and where they are satisfied that because of shortage[15] of places at reasonably convenient maintained schools they cannot otherwise provide education suitable[16] to his age, ability, aptitude and any special educational needs he may have, they must pay the whole of his tuition fees. The arrangements may be in respect of individual pupils, to take account, for example, of musical ability, or alternatively provide for a number of

---

[9] See below at paras. 6–35 *et seq.* It is open to a local education authority, in a proper case, to supplement an assisted place by paying board and lodging fees under the Scholarships and Other Benefits Regulations 1977. See below para. 5–31.

[10] See Circ. 1/81, para. 32.

[11] As to the Local Government Act 1972, s.137 see above at para. 1–39. See also *Manchester City Council* v. *Greater Manchester County Council*, 78 L.G.R. 560, H.L. and G. Tideswell. "The Education Trust Case at Manchester" (1979) 125 L.G.C. 772, and C.A. Cross (1980) 126 L.G.C. 841.

[12] Under the 1944 Act, s.81(*b*) and reg. 4(*d*) of the Scholarships and Other Benefits Regulations 1977 (S.I. 1977 No. 1443) as amended by S.I. 1979 No. 542. The Secretary of State has complementary powers under 1944 Act, s.100(1)(*c*) (see below at para. 6–19). As to assistance towards the cost of boarding education for service children (which is in part met by the Ministry of Defence Boarding Schools Allowance) see Circular 3/81. See also "Boarding Education: Assistance by Authorities", 118 J.P.J. 607. The local education authority pay the whole of the fees and expenses of a child in the care of a local authority (see the Local Authorities and Local Education Authorities Allocation of Functions Regulations 1951 (S.I. 1951 No. 472) reg. 7(1)(*b*) and Circular 232.

[13] S.I. 1977 No. 1443, reg. 6.

[14] 1953 Act, s.6(1) elaborating 1944 Act, s.9(1), both as amended by 1980 Act, s.28. See Circ. 1/80, para. 27.

[15] 1953 Act, s.6(2)(*a*)(ii) as amended by 1981 Act, s.21, Sched. 3, para. 8.

[16] See *Watt* v. *Kesteven County Council* [1955] 1 Q.B. 408 and above at para. 2–10.

places to be taken up at a non-maintained school because of a shortage of maintained school places. When boarding[17] is necessary fees for board and lodging are to be paid as well. Authorities are under the same obligation in respect of pupils taking up places provided at direct grant schools[18] and those for whom special educational provision[19] needs to be made otherwise than at a maintained school.

Local education authorities must publish their criteria for offering **5–33** places at non-maintained schools, and the names of, and number of places at, those non-maintained schools with which they have standing arrangements.[20]

EMPLOYMENT

There have long been general restrictions[21] on the employment of **5–34** children and young persons in industrial undertakings and ships which are not of direct concern to local education authorities. Local education authorities do, however, have responsibilities for their welfare as regards employment, not mainly under the Education Acts but under children and young persons legislation of which the other provisions[22] are mostly otherwise enforced. Substantial changes in the law regarding employment of children are contained in the Employment of Children Act 1973 but at present there seems little prospect of that Act being brought into force.

Restrictions

No child is to be employed[23] so long as he is under 13,[24] or before the **5–35** close of school hours on a school day, or before 7 a.m. or after 7 p.m., or for more than two hours on any school day, or for more than two hours on any Sunday, or to lift, carry or move anything so heavy as to be

---

[17] 1953 Act, s.6(2)(*b*) as amended by 1981 Act, s.21, Sched. 3, para. 8(2). See Report of the Working Party on Assistance with the Cost of Boarding Education, H.M.S.O., 1959, Circ. 14/60, and above at para. 2–08.

[18] 1953 Act, s.6(2)(*a*)(i) and see above at para. 2–218. Paras. (*b*) and (*c*) of S.I. 1977 No. 1443, reg. 4, were material in relation to places at a direct grant grammar school that were additional to those provided as grant-aided places.

[19] 1953 Act, s.6(2)(*a*)(iii) as substituted by 1981 Act, s.21, Sched. 3, para. 8, and see *R.* v. *Hampshire County Council, ex p., J., The Times*, December 5, 1985, and above at para. 2–207.

[20] 1980 Act, s.8(4).

[21] See Employment of Women, Young Persons and Children Act 1920, s.1 as amended. "Young person" means a person who is not a child but is under 18, and "child" by 1944 Act, s.58, is a person not over compulsory school age, as to which see *ibid.* s.35 and above at para. 1–81.

[22] Enforcement of conditions of employment (hours and holidays) are not the responsibility of local education authorities. (See Young Persons (Employment) Acts 1938 and 1964 as amended).

[23] Children and Young Persons Act 1933, s.18 (as amended by, *inter alia*, Children Act 1972, s.1) and as to offences, s.21. (These sections are extended and further amended by the Employment of Children Act 1973 from a day to be appointed.) If and when s.19 of the Children and Young Persons Act 1933 is brought into force (and it is prospectively repealed by the Employment of Children Act 1973) local education authorities will be able to make byelaws restricting the employment of persons under 18 other than children.

[24] A person attains a particular age at the start of the anniversary of date of birth (Family Law Reform Act 1969, s.9).

likely to injure him. These restrictions may be modified by byelaws[25] made by the local education authority,[26] enabling children under thirteen to be employed in light agricultural or horticultural work and for not more than one hour before school begins. Byelaws may also prohibit the employment of children in specified occupations, and they may prescribe various conditions of employment. Restrictions do not apply to performance in entertainments when, as explained below, no local education authority licence is required or when a licence has been granted[27] by a police magistrate to permit a child, under specified conditions to give a performance abroad[28] for profit. Leave of absence from school may be given[29] in those circumstances and when a local authority licence is granted.

5–36 Performance of children in entertainments[30] of various kinds is prohibited[31] except under licence granted by a local education authority, but a licence is not required when the number of performances over a period of six months is minimal, or where the performance is given under arrangements made by a school or approved body[32] and no payments are made except for defraying expenses. A licence is not to be granted unless the authority are satisfied about the child's fitness for the performance, that his health and kind treatment will be secured and that his education will not suffer. If they are so satisfied they must grant the licence. The conditions which licences are to specify are laid down, and they must also comply with the provisions of regulations[33] made by the Secretary of State. These include stringent education requirements. There are particular restrictions[34] in relation to the granting of licences for performances by children under 14; there is an absolute prohibition[35] against persons under 16 taking part in performances that might endanger life or limb; and there are restrictions[36] on training for performances of a dangerous nature.

---

[25] As to the confirmation of byelaws by the Secretary of State see Children and Young Persons Act 1933, s.27, as amended.

[26] 1933 Act, s.96 as amended. By s.97 as amended, in the City of London the Common Council have the powers and duties otherwise exercised by a local education authority in relation to street trading and employment but not performance in entertainments.

[27] Under 1933 Act, s.25 (in which "police magistrate" is defined) as amended by Children and Young Persons Act 1963, in particular by s.42. As to offences see 1933 Act, s.26, and as to powers of entry s.28, both as amended.

[28] *i.e.*, outside the United Kingdom (which does not include the Channel Islands and Isle of Man).

[29] Under the Education (Schools and Further Education) Regulations 1981·(S.I. 1981 No. 1086) reg. 11. See above at para. 2–141.

[30] 1963 Act, s.37 (as amended by Licensing Act 1964 and by Cable and Broadcasting Act 1984, s.57(1) and Sched. 5, para. 12) and s.39.

[31] As to offences, see 1963 Act, s.40.

[32] "A body of persons approved for the purposes of [s.37] by the Secretary of State or by the local [education] authority in whose area the performance takes place."

[33] See the Children (Performances) Regulations 1968 (S.I. 1968 No. 1728), especially reg. 10.

[34] See 1963 Act, s.38.

[35] 1933 Act, s.23 as amended by 1963 Act.

[36] 1933 Act, s.24 and 1963 Act, s.41.

Local education authorities also have power to make byelaws to **5–37**
restrict the employment of young persons under 17 in street trading.[37]

Over and above[38] these provisions a local education authority may by **5–38**
notice[39] in writing served on parent or employer obtain from him information concerning the employment of a child who is a registered pupil
at a county, voluntary or special school. If it appears to a local education
authority that the child's health or capacity fully to benefit by education
is being prejudiced they may by notice served upon the employer prohibit or restrict his employment. Contravention of this provision is an
offence carrying a fine[40] on summary conviction.[41] To prove it a local
education authority need to adduce, for example, evidence[42] by a school
teacher of a decline in the pupil's work performance.

Work experience

So as to provide children with work experience[43] in the last year[44] of **5–39**
compulsory schooling (and not to the exclusion of older pupils), local
education authorities are empowered to lift most of the restrictions
mentioned above where the employment is in pursuance of arrangements made or approved by them, and leave of absence from school
may be granted[45] accordingly. But no child is to be employed (a) contrary to an enactment[46] which in terms applies to persons of less than, or
not over, a specified age or (b) (with very limited exceptions) in a ship.[47]
Nor are any arrangements to permit a child to be employed contrary to
the law prohibiting or regulating the employment of young persons; and

---

[37] 1933 Act, s.20 as amended by 1963 Act, s.35. In the City of London the Common Council are the byelaw-making authority. "Street trading" is defined in 1933 Act, s.30. As to offences see 1933 Act, s.21 (as amended by the Employment of Children Act 1973 from a day to be appointed).
[38] Under 1944 Act, s.59, to be repealed by the Employment of Children Act 1973 from a day to be appointed. Powers of entry are granted as under 1933 Act, s.28 as amended.
[39] As to service of notices see 1944 Act, s.113 as amended.
[40] 1944 Act, s.59(3). The amount of the fine increases after the first offence.
[41] As to summary proceedings see Magistrates' Courts Act 1980 as amended.
[42] See *Margerison* v. *Hind* [1922] 1 K.B. 214.
[43] Under the Education (Work Experience) Act 1973, s.1. See Circ. 7/74 (W.O. 135/74) and Chap 9. of *Half our Future*, a report of the Central Advisory Council for Education (The Newsom Report) H.M.S.O., 1963.
[44] *i.e.* during the period of 12 months before the child attains the upper limit of compulsory school age (*ibid.* s.1(4)). The Education, Science and Arts Committee (1981–1982, H.C. 116–1, para. 4.17) recommended extension to the last two years. In reply the Government pointed out (Cmnd. 8648) that the effect of the 1973 Act and the Education (School Leaving Dates) Act 1976 (see above at para. 1–81) taken together was that "pupils may undertake work experience courses at any time during the 12 months before the date on which they become eligible to leave school— which, depending on their date of birth, will be either the end of the spring term in their fifth year, or the Friday before the last Monday in May of that year. It follows that it is already open to all pupils to undertake work experience not only at any time during their fifth year but also during a substantial part (and in many cases throughout the whole) of the final term of the fourth year."
[45] Under the Education (Schools and Further Education) Regulations 1981 (S.I. 1981 No. 1086) reg. 11. See above at para. 2–141.
[46] Including byelaws, regulations, etc. (Education (Work Experience) Act 1973, s.1(4)).
[47] *i.e.* contrary to s.1(2) of the Employment of Women, Young Persons and Children Act 1920 or, when it comes into force, s.51(1) of the Merchant Shipping Act 1970.

the regulations applying to young persons apply to children employed under the arrangements.

RESEARCH, UNIVERSITIES, CONFERENCES

5–40   To improve the educational facilities provided for their area a local education authority may make provision for conducting research,[48] or for assisting its conduct, as appears to them desirable; and to improve the further education facilities they may assist financially any university[49] or university college.

5–41   A local education authority may organise, or participate in organising, conferences[50] for discussion of educational questions, and pay the expenses of those they authorise to attend, all at reasonable cost.

THE CAREERS SERVICE

5–42   Formerly vocational guidance and employment placing were functions performed in most areas by local education authorities—the youth employment service—but elsewhere by the Department of Employment. As from April 1, 1974, all local education authorities have had to provide[51] what are now called careers services.[52]

5–43   Local education authorities are under a duty to make arrangements to help those[53] at educational institutions in Great Britain other than universities: (a) to decide what employment,[54] and training for it, are suitable for, and available to, them (*i.e.* to give vocational advice); and (b) to find them that employment and training. Officers are to be appointed to administer the arrangements, which are also to be available to university students. Additionally local education authorities may (and must, when the Secretary of State[55] directs) make similar arrangements to assist others as well: young people may wish to use the service after taking up employment.

---

[48] 1944 Act, s.82 as amended by 1980 Act, s.38(6) and Sched. 7, and see below at para. 6–19 as regards the powers of the Secretary of State.

[49] 1944 Act, s.84 amended as above.

[50] *Ibid.* s.83 amended as above. As to conferences organised by local authority associations see above at para. 1–36.

[51] Under the Employment and Training Act 1973, s.8 as amended by the Employment and Training Act 1973 (Repeals) Order 1981 (S.I. 1981 No. 494). Sex and racial discrimination in the performance of functions under s.8 are unlawful (Sex Discrimination Act 1975, s.15(2) and Race Relations Act 1976, s.14(2). See above at paras. 1–94 and 1–102 n. 30 respectively). Under the Local Government (Miscellaneous Provisions) Act 1982, s.45 local education authorities have power to enter into arrangements with the Manpower Services Commission (see above at para. 3–30) and the Secretary of State (see n. 13 below), but the nature and extent of the arrangements are unspecified.

[52] As to the administrative arrangements adopted by local education authorities see Education, Science and Arts Committee, minutes of evidence (H.C. 1981–1982 116–11) p. 385.

[53] Except part-timers at evening classes, or as otherwise specified by the Secretary of State, unless their attendance is with a view to employment. (1973 Act, s.8(7).)

[54] "Employment" and "training" are defined in *ibid.* s.13(1), as amended.

[55] "The Secretary of State"—normally the Secretary of State for Employment, but see above at para. 1–05 n. 9.

The arrangements are to consist of giving assistance by collecting and **5-44** providing information about prospective employees, employers and training facilities, and of providing advice and guidance for the purposes mentioned. Services in support of these arrangements may also be provided.

Local education authorities are to consult and co-operate with one **5-45** another to perform their functions effectively, and they may on terms (including financial terms) make agency[56] arrangements or act jointly.

They are to keep[57] records of the vocational advice given to students **5-46** at educational institutions (other than universities) and to pass them on at the request of another authority, together with any earlier records they may have received, if the student transfers to an institution in the other authority's area. When they know that a person has left school altogether they are to give him a written[58] summary of the vocational advice given, to keep a copy of it for two years from the date he left school, and during that period let him and, while he is under 18, his parent or guardian each have (not more than) one copy on request. There is no obligation to provide a summary if a comprehensive written statement has already been supplied.

Careers services are provided under the general guidance[59] of the Sec- **5-47** retary of State who may require from local education authorities information about the way they perform their functions and facilities for obtaining it. The Secretary of State may in conjunction with other Ministers make arrangements to constitute a body[60] comprised of departmental officers (and others too if the arrangements so provide) to carry out his own functions. To provide himself with advice he established the representative Careers Service Advisory Committee as an advisory body,[61] but it has lapsed and he now consults *ad hoc.*

A further statutory obligation[62] upon local education authorities is to **5-48** give the Secretary of State the information he specifies in connection with claims for social security benefits.

---

[56] *i.e.* one authority may perform any function for another over the whole or part or the other's area. Also the Agricultural Training Board or an Industrial Training Board (see above at para. 3–29) may take part in arrangements (Agricultural Training Board Act 1982, s.4(1)(*f*) and Industrial Training Act 1982, s.5(3)(*e*)).

[57] Employment and Training Act 1973, s.9(1).

[58] "Writing" is defined in the Interpretation Act 1978, Sched. 1.

[59] 1973 Act, s.10. The Guidance is contained in a document, *The Careers Service. Guidance to Local Education Authorities in England and Wales,* published by the Department of Employment (revised, 1980). In para. 98 it refers to inspection.

[60] At least one person must have special responsibility for the employment of young disabled persons (Chronically Sick and Disabled Persons Act 1970, s.13(1) as amended by Employment and Training Act 1973, s.14(1) and Sched. 3, para. 11). No such body (in succession to the Central Youth Employment Executive) exists, but co-operation between the Department of Employment, Manpower Services Commission (see above at para. 3–30) and Department of Education and Science is promoted by a Careers Service liaison committee.

[61] Under the Employment and Training Act 1973, s.5(2).

[62] *Ibid.* s.12(2) as amended.

INSURANCE

5-49   It is the general practice of local authorities to insure against the risks that attend the discharge of their functions—against the "perils" to which property is subject; against claims by the public where legal liability may be incurred as a result, for instance, of negligence by employees (vicarious liability)[63] or of disrepair of buildings; and against compensation claims by employees[64] for injury or loss arising out of and in course of employment for which they might be held liable. The authority for insurance is section 111 of the Local Government Act 1972— the power to do things calculated to facilitate, or conducive or incidental to, the discharge of any of their functions[65]—taken together with the statutory authority for the function in question. If "incidental" is read as "necessarily" incidental then the power is curtailed (significantly as will appear as regards the education service) but cases[66] decided on the common law principle that section 111 superseded do not support so restrictive an interpretation.

Teachers and others
5-50   Thus some authorities have taken a generous view of their powers, notably in support of their employees, for example to make employer contributions to a voluntary group life assurance scheme. The statutory basis here, as for employers' liability insurance, is section 112 of the Local Government Act 1972 (under which local authorities may employ officers on such terms and conditions including conditions as to remuneration as they think fit) supported if necessary by section 111. The terms of service of school teachers are elaborately specified in statutory instruments[67] and the nationally negotiated (*Burgundy Book*) conditions of service[68]; but teachers, it has been suggested,[69] are local government officers and there seems no obstacle in law to local education authorities supplementing their conditions of service in ways (for example, as above) consistent with statutory and contractual provisions.
5-51   The *Burgundy Book* recommendations[70] place specific obligations upon local education authorities to meet liabilities they might not otherwise incur. To the extent that the compensation payable to the teacher arises out of an incident in the performance of his contract of employment, sections 111 and 112 are again the authority's recourse for *vires*, but if the cover extends, as contemplated, to out-of-school activities

---

[63] As to vicarious liability and negligence see the opening paragraphs of Chap. 7.
[64] The Employers' Liability (Compulsory Insurance) Act 1969, s.1 obliges most employers (including the governors of aided schools) to insure against liability for employees.
[65] See above at para. 1.39.
[66] *e.g. Att.-Gen.* v. *Smethwick Corporation* [1932] 1 Ch. 562, C.A.
[67] See above at paras. 4–52 and 4–113 *et seq*.
[68] See above at para. 4–98.
[69] See above at para. 4–02.
[70] See above at para. 4–111.

(which by definition are outside the teachers's contract of employment) then the authority must rely, it seems, on section 111 in support of sections 8[71] or 53[72] of the 1944 Act. These are the provisions which also support the further *Burgundy Book* recommendation that local education authorities insure teachers engaged in out-of-school activities[73] on their behalf against personal accident, and indemnify them against third party claims not covered by the teacher's own insurance arrangements.

Third party claims

The status of teachers *vis-a-vis* their employing authority in the last-mentioned circumstances is not entirely clear, partly because of the uncertain compass[74] of the teacher's contract of employment. Even if teachers are to be considered agents rather than employees it is not improbable that a court would hold a local authority vicariously liable[75] on, for instance, a negligence claim by a parent against injury to a child engaged in out-of-school activities and in the care of a teacher; and a local education authority would need to insure[76] accordingly. By contrast it might be less easy for a parent to sustain a claim against a local education authority where the child was injured in the course of work experience[77] or otherwise[78] outside a teacher's care; and to extend insurance beyond a certain point might be to exceed the liberality of section 111.[79] Local education authorities may attempt to limit their liabilities by the conditions which they impose for admitting children to extra-curricular activities, but the scope for doing so has been drastically curtailed by section 2 of the Unfair Contract Terms Act 1977.

5–52

Vehicle insurance

The statutory provisions above-mentioned are available to enable local education authorities to pay teachers and other employees a mileage allowance[80] when they are authorised, and willing, to use their own cars in furtherance of their duties. An insurance policy for a private vehicle may limit third-party cover to domestic and professional purposes to the exclusion of "use for hire and reward." Receipt of a

5–53

---

[71] See above at para. 2–06.
[72] See above at para. 5–27.
[73] See above at para. 4–111.
[74] See above at paras. 4–50 *et seq.*
[75] "Vicarious liability"—see below at para. 7–02.
[76] In A.M. 22/67 local education authorities were advised to insure against liability for accidents or damage to property taking place during educational visits to industrial firms or work experience.
[77] See above at para. 5–39.
[78] See *Brown* v. *Nelson and Others* 69 L.G.R. 20 and below at para. 7–43.
[79] It would probably be *ultra vires* for a local education authority to take out personal accident insurance cover for children engaging in out-of-school activities. See, generally, C. A. Cross and S. H. Bailey, *Cross on Local Government Law* (7th ed. 1986) paras. 1–10 to 1–12.
[80] See *Burgundy Book,* para. 13, above at para. 4–112.

mileage allowance could conceivably be so construed. A policy thus restricted nevertheless validly covers[81] use of a car[82] where passengers pay separate fares in advance of the journey and the fares do not in aggregate exceed running costs.

---

[81] See Transport Act 1980, s.61.
[82] Not adapted to carry more than eight passengers.

CHAPTER 6

SUPPLEMENTARY FUNCTIONS OF THE SECRETARY OF STATE

The extent to which the Secretary of State has surrendered[1] powers of **6–01** control over the performance of the functions of local education authorities has, by omission, gone unremarked. But his rights to intervene, explicable in the terms of section 1[2] of the 1944 Act, remain pervasive, as a glance at the index to this book shows. This Chapter records those of his supervisory powers and duties, and the functions he exercises in his own behalf, that have not already been noted.

SUPERVISION

Section 27 of the 1980 Act gives the Secretary of State power to make **6–02** regulations on a wide variety of matters concerning maintained[3] schools, special schools (whether or not maintained) and further education establishments provided by local education authorities or substantially dependent on assistance[4] from local education authorities or grants[5] from the Secretary of State. The provisions of the regulations[6] are referred to elsewhere but it may be helpful to mention here the main topics to which they may relate: teachers' qualifications and probation[7]; the provision of teaching staff[8]; materials or apparatus which may give rise to health risks[9]; educational records of pupils[10]; the school day and year[11]; the health, and restrictions on employment, of teachers and others[12]; approval of premises[13]; and provision of, and fees for, further education courses.[14]

The nature of other supervisory powers and duties is sufficiently indi- **6–03** cated by the titles of the subsections that follow.

---

[1] Notably under ss.30 and 38(6) of, and Sched. 7 to, the 1980 Act.
[2] See above at para. 1–06.
[3] "Maintain"—see 1944 Act, s.114(2)(*a*) as amended by 1980 Act, and above at para. 2–02.
[4] Under 1944 Act, s.114(2)(*b*).
[5] Under *ibid*. s.100(1)(*b*)—see above at para. 3–05.
[6] The principal regulations are the Education (Schools and Further Education) Regulations 1981 (S.I. 1981 No. 1086) as amended and the Education (Teachers) Regulations 1982 (S.I. 1982 No. 106).
[7] See above at paras. 4–10 to 4–19.
[8] See above at para. 4–02.
[9] See above at para. 2–147.
[10] See above at para. 2–144.
[11] See above at para. 2–140.
[12] See above at paras. 4–21 to 4–25.
[13] See above at para. 2–54.
[14] See above at paras. 3–05 and 3–24.

Reports, returns, inquiries

6–04   The Secretary of State may require from local education authorities reports and returns[15] giving him the information he needs to exercise his functions, for which purpose he may also cause a local inquiry[16] to be held.

Inspection

6–05   Inspection of educational establishments is one of the most long-established governmental activities in relation to education. Under section 77 of the 1944 Act it is the duty of the Secretary of State to have inspections made[17] of every educational establishment, in particular schools (maintained and independent) and further education establishments,[18] and training colleges[19] maintained by local education authorities; and inspections are also made of other institutions on request to the Secretary of State or to a local education authority by the persons responsible for their management. Inspections take place at intervals the Secretary of State considers appropriate (and special inspections when he considers them desirable). They are carried out by inspectors (H.M.I.s[20]) appointed by the Crown on his recommendation; and he may appoint assistant and additional inspectors. Hostels for pupils with special educational needs may be inspected[21] by an H.M.I. or a person authorised for the purpose by the Secretary of State. Inspection of the careers service[22] is carried out by inspectors of the Department of Employment and Welsh Office in conjunction with H.M.I.s. Local education authorities may appoint their own officers[23] to carry out inspections of the establishments they maintain. Obstruction of an inspector is

---

[15] 1944 Act, s.92. This section has been regarded as authority for the requirement that school punishment books and annals shall be kept (see above at para. 2–143).

[16] *Ibid.* s.93 as amended by Local Government Act 1972, s.272(2). The Secretary of State may act, alternatively, under the Local Government Act 1972, s.250 and in either case the inquiry is subject to the Tribunals and Inquiries Act 1971, ss.1, 11 and 12 and (under s.19(2)) the Tribunals and Inquiries (Discretionary Inquiries) Order 1975 (S.I. 1975 No. 1379) arts. 3 and 4 and Sched. 1, Pt. 1. According to P. Meredith, "Individual Challenge to Expenditure Cuts in the Provision of Schools" ((1982) J.S.W.L. 344) only one inquiry has been carried out under s.93— see Report of Local Inquiry under the chairmanship of Sir David Hughes Parry (1950) concerning the establishment of a Roman Catholic primary school in Haverfordwest.

[17] Unless he is satisfied that other suitable arrangements for inspection are in force. As to inspection of religious instruction see above at para. 2–172.

[18] Those establishments used for further education under a further education scheme made and approved under the 1944 Act. See s.42 and above at para. 3–10.

[19] See 1944 Act, s.62 and above at para. 4–06.

[20] As to the status of H.M.I.s, see Second Report from the Education, Science and Arts Committee, *The Secondary School Curriculum and Examinations*, 1981–1982 (H.C. 116–1) paras. 9.19 to 9.21 and Government Response (Cmnd. 8648) pp. 13–14. See also n. 27 below.

[21] Education (Schools and Further Education) Regulations 1981 (S.I. 1981 No. 1086) reg. 8 as amended by S.I. 1983 No. 262, reg. 4(2), and see above at para. 2–206.

[22] See above at paras. 5–42 *et seq.*

[23] s.77(3). See H.C. 116–1, para. 9.21 and Cmnd. 8648, p. 15.

an offence incurring a fine[24] on summary conviction.[25] Up to three months' imprisonment may be imposed for a second or subsequent offence.

It is the practice[26] of the Secretary of State to publish H.M.I.s' reports **6–06** and to seek from local education authorities and others information about action taken in consequence of their contents.

The role of H.M.I.s[27] is much wider than can be inferred from a bare **6–07** paraphrase of the statutory provisions. It includes organisation of, and participation in, in-service training for teachers, and the publication of material to keep them informed of developments in the educational scene. H.M.I.s enable the Secretary of State to assess standards of performance and trends in education, and inform him about the outcome of his policies.[28]

Disputes and questions

As mentioned above[29] a dispute between a local education authority **6–08** and governors of a maintained school (including a special school) or further education institution regarding their respective powers and duties may be referred[30] for determination by the Secretary of State, and this is the case "notwithstanding any enactment rendering the exercise of the power or performance of the duty contingent upon the opinion of the authority or the governors." This general provision is superseded by particular provisions, for example, concerning disputes over the appointment[31] of teachers to give secular instruction in aided schools.

It is not clear that in all circumstances the jurisdiction of the courts is ousted. Their jurisdiction has been considered[32] in relation to earlier legislation (1902 Act, s.7(3)) providing for adjudication by the Board of Education of disputes between local education authorities and

---

[24] Not exceeding level 4 for first or subsequent offences—see Criminal Law Act 1977, s.31(5)–(7) and Criminal Justice Act 1982, ss.37 (as amended by Criminal Penalties etc. (Increase) Order 1984 (S.I. 1984 No. 447)), 39, 46 and Sched. 3.

[25] See Magistrates' Court Act 1980, as amended.

[26] See A.M. 2/83 and Amendment No. 1 (1983) and Circ. 1/87.

[27] See *The Work of H.M. Inspectorate in England and Wales.* A Policy Statement by the Secretary of State for Education and Science and the Secretary of State for Wales, D.E.S. 1983; and S. Browne, "The Accountability of H.M. Inspectorate (England)" in J. Lello (ed.) *Accountability in Education,* Ward Lock Educational, 1979, p. 35.

[28] The article by P. Meredith (see n. 16 above) refers to H.M.I.'s reports on the effect of local authority expenditure policies on the education service in England in the financial years 1980–1981 and 1981–1982.

[29] See above at paras. 2–103 and 3–09.

[30] Under 1944 Act s.67(1) as amended by 1980 Act, s.1(3) and Sched. 1, para. 1(2), and extended by 1968 (No. 2) Act, s.3(3) and by 1986 (No. 2) Act, Sched. 4, para. 4. As to the Secretary of State's obligation to determine the dispute see *Board of Education* v. *Rice* [1911] A.C. 179.

[31] 1944 Act, s.24(2)(*b*) as amended by 1980 Act, s.1(3) and Sched. 1, para. 8; and see above at para. 4–27.

[32] See also *Martin* v. *Eccles Corporation* [1919] 1 Ch. 387. As to the manner of adjudication by the Board see *Board of Education* v. *Rice* [1911] A.C. 179; and see also *R.* v. *Hull Prison Board of Visitors, ex p. St. Germain and Others* (*No. 2*) [1979] 3 All E.R. 545.

managers. In *Blencowe* v. *Northamptonshire County Council*[32a] a disputed direction by the local education authority concerning the hour of commencement of secular instruction was held to be outside the jurisdiction of the court, as was in *West Suffolk County Council* v. *Olorenshaw*,[32b] a dispute about the amount of a school cleaner's wages; but in *Wilford* v. *West Riding County Council*[32c] a disputed direction (in effect) to restrict the age range of a school was held to be within jurisdiction, and in *Gillow* v. *Durham County Council*,[32d] Viscount Haldane L.C. expressed *obiter* the view that a far-reaching question of law was outside section 7(3).

6–09   The Secretary of State also determines[33] disputes between local education authorities about which of them are responsible for providing education for a pupil, and whether any contribution[34] is payable by one local education authority to another. The methods of settling questions whether religious education complies with a trust deed and whether a change in the character of a school or enlargement of its premises is significant have already been considered.[35]

Unreasonable exercise of functions
6–10   Section 68[36] of the 1944 Act reads:

"If the Secretary of State is satisfied, either on complaint by any person or otherwise, that any local education authority[37] or the governors[38] of any county or voluntary school have acted or are proposing to act unreasonably with respect to any power conferred or the performance of any duty imposed by or under this Act, he may,[39] notwithstanding any enactment rendering the exercise of the power or the performance of the duty contingent upon the opinion of the authority or of the governors, give such directions[40] as to the

---

[32a] [1907] 1 Ch. 504.
[32b] [1918] 2 K.B. 687.
[32c] [1908] 1 K.B. 685.
[32d] [1913] A.C. 54.
[33] s.67(2).
[34] The second limb of s.67(2) is repealed by 1986 (No. 2) Act, Sched. 6 and replaced by s.51(11) of that Act. See above at para. 1–139.
[35] s.67(3) and (4). See, respectively, above at para. 2–167 n. 76 and para. 2–32.
[36] As amended by 1946 Act, s.14 and Sched. 2, Local Government Act 1972, s.272(1) and Sched. 30, and 1980 Act, s.1(3) and Sched. 1, para. 1(2), and extended by Sex Discrimination Act 1975, s.25 and Race Relations Act 1976, s.19 to include the duties imposed on local education authorities and governors by those Acts (see above at paras. 1–96 and 1–103 respectively). s.68 applies to all the Education Acts, since Acts subsequent to the 1944 Act are to be construed as one with that Act (see above at para. 1–01 n. 1).
[37] Or, as amended by 1946 Act, s.14 and Sched. 2 and by Local Government Act 1972, s.272(1) and Sched. 30, a joint education board or a committee exercising the authority's functions under 1944 Act, Sched. 1 (see above at para. 1–23).
[38] Also by s.3(3) of the 1968 (No. 2) Act as amended by 1986 (No. 2) Act, Sched. 4, para. 4 governors of maintained special schools and of further education institutions (see above at paras. 2–203 and 3–09).
[39] Expressed as a discretion, but probably to be regarded as an obligation (see above at para. 1–47).
[40] "Directions"—see 1944 Act, s.111 and above at para. 1–42. Directions appear to be enforceable by *mandamus* (see above para. 1–50 n. 52) without separate recourse to s.99 (*Secretary of State for Education and Science* v *Metropolitan Borough of Tameside* [1977] A.C. 1014.

exercise of the power or the performance of the duty as appear to him expedient . . . "

The inclusion of "otherwise" indicates that the Secretary of State may **6–11** act on his own initiative; and use of the subjective terminology "is satisfied" seems *prima facie* to give him unrestricted discretion[41] in determining the reasonableness of a local education authority's actions. The House of Lords decided otherwise, however, in *Secretary of State for Education and Science* v. *Metropolitan Borough of Tameside.*[42] Following an election and change of power the authority withdrew plans to introduce comprehensive secondary education. The Secretary of State directed that they should adhere to the plans: to change them when they were "designed to come into effect less than three months later must in his opinion give rise to considerable difficulties."[43] On appeal by the authority the court applied the *"Wednesbury"*[44] test and concluded on the facts that they were not guilty, in Lord Diplock's words,[45] of "conduct which no sensible authority acting with due appreciation of its responsibilities would have decided to adopt." Therefore the Secretary of State could not properly have reached the conclusion that the local education authority had acted unreasonably. It followed that his direction to the council to revert to their predecessors' plan was *ultra vires*.

Earlier decisions[46] had established that the courts would not deal with **6–12** a complaint of unreasonable action by a local education authority or governors unless the action was *ultra vires,* for example, because of breach of the rules of natural justice.[47] Recourse should be had to the Secretary of State under section 68. The consequence of *Tameside* seems to be that the scope for ministerial intervention, for example, at the instance of dissatisfied parents is, equally, restricted to those cases where an authority have acted so unreasonably—perversely or in bad faith—as to exceed their powers. It is not enough that the Secretary of State personally regards their action as misguided.[48] "He must be very

---

[41] See above at para. 1–47.
[42] [1977] A.C. 1014. On this decision see D.C.M. Yardley, *Principles of Administrative Law* (1981) pp. 66–71; H. R. W. Wade, *Administrative Law* (5th ed. 1982) pp. 398–399; J. F. Garner, *Administrative Law* (6th ed. 1985) pp. 134–35; S. A. de Smith, *Constitutional and Administrative Law* (5th ed. 1985) pp. 601–02; O. Hood Phillips, *Constitutional and Administrative Law* (6th ed. 1978) pp. 601–02; P. P. Craig, *Administrative Law* (1983) pp. 364–366; C. Harlow & R. Rawlings, *Law and Administration* (1984) pp. 330–34. (1977) 93 L.Q.R. 4 and [1977] C.L.J. 1. For a contrasting decision under Scottish Law see *Lord Advocate* v. *Glasgow Corporation* [1973] S.L.T. 153; [1973] S.L.T. 33, H.L., and J.S. Dickinson, "Ministerial powers under the Education Acts in England and Scotland" (1977) L.G.C. 374.
[43] *Tameside* (above) at 1018.
[44] *Associated Provincial Picture Houses Ltd.* v. *Wednesbury Corporation* [1948] 1 K.B. 223.
[45] *Tameside* (above) at 1064.
[46] See *Cumings and Others* v. *Birkenhead Corporation* [1972] Ch. 12 and *R.* v. *Powys County Council, ex p. Smith*, 81 L.G.R. 342.
[47] See *Herring* v. *Templeman and Others*, 71 L.G.R. 295 and above at para. 1–54.
[48] But see below at para. 6–16; and as to allegations of maladministration against the Secretary of State for failing to give directions, above at para. 1–62. See also Second Report from the Education Science and Arts Committee, *The Secondary School Curriculum and Examinations*, 1981–1982, (H.C. 116–1) paras. 9–3 to 9.18 and Government's Observations (Cmnd. 8511)

careful then not to fall into the error—a very common error—of thinking that anyone with whom he disagrees is being unreasonable . . . . He must ask himself: 'Is this person so very wrong? May he not quite reasonably take a different view?' "[49]—*per* Lord Denning M.R.

6–13 Thus before issuing a direction, and in anticipation of challenge, the Secretary of State must needs attempt to predict judicial opinion in relation to the particular circumstances of the case. His "satisfaction" may more readily be accepted as conclusive when the issue is one of pure judgment and does not turn on how he has applied his mind to the facts. In the words[50] of Lord Wilberforce:

> "If a judgment requires, before it can be made, the existence of some facts, then, although the evaluation of those facts is for the Secretary of State alone, the court must inquire whether those facts exist, and have been taken into account, whether the judgment has been made upon a proper self-direction as to those facts, whether the judgment has not been made upon other facts which ought not to have been taken into account. If these requirements are not met, then the exercise of judgment, however *bona fide* it may be, becomes capable of challenge."

6–14 Despite the narrow scope for intervention under section 68, its use by the Secretary of State went unchallenged by Derbyshire County Council[51] in 1982 when he directed that a sixth-former should be allowed to take up an assisted place[52] at an independent school, and by Brent London Borough Council[53] in 1986 when he directed the council to drop what he regarded as unreasonable disciplinary proceedings against a teacher.

Default by local education authorities and governors

6–15 The opening words of section 99(1)[54] of the 1944 Act follow those of section 68 above but relate to default in place of unreasonable action. If the Secretary of State is satisfied that an authority or governors[55] have failed to discharge a statutory duty he may[56] make an order declaring

---

pp. 11–13; D. Foulkes, "Tameside and the Education Act 1944" 125 New L.J. 649, in which the appropriateness of the *Wednesbury* test is doubted in relation to the exercise of the Minister's powers; P. Meredith, "Individual Challenge to Expenditure Cuts in the Schools" (1982) J.S.W.L. 344, regarding Ministers' resistance to using s.68 in relation to alleged breaches of s.8 of the 1944 Act; P. Meredith, "Executive Discretion and Choice of Secondary School" [1981] P.L. 52 at 77 (recourse to the Secretary of State in his appellate capacity); and D. Bull, "Monitoring Education Appeals" (1985) J.S.W.L. 189 at 222 (representations in respect of school allocations—as to which see above at para. 2–185).

[49] *Tameside* (above) at 1026.
[50] *Ibid.* at 1047.
[51] See 36 H.C. Deb. 1099–1100 (February 9, 1983).
[52] See below at paras. 6–35 *et seq.*
[53] See 107 H.C. Deb. 531 (December 17, 1986).
[54] s.99 has been amended by 1980 Act, s.1(3) and Sched. 1, para. 1(2) so as to omit reference to "managers," and extended by Sex Discrimination Act 1975, s.25 and Race Relations Act 1976, s.19 to include default by local education authorities and governors under those Acts (see above at paras. 1–96 and 1–103 respectively). s.99 applies to all the Education Acts since Acts subsequent to the 1944 Act are to be construed as one with that Act (see above at para. 1–01 n. 1).
[55] "Governors"—see n. 38 above.
[56] See n. 39 above.

the default and giving directions for remedying it, and he may apply if need be for mandamus.[57] The same section gives the Secretary of State power to secure[58] a properly constituted school governing body, to validate governors' defective acts or proceedings and to recover[59] from a local education authority sums paid by him to voluntary school governors who have incurred expenditure because of the authority's failure to discharge their duty to maintain the school.

In *R. v. Secretary of State for Education and Science, ex p. Chance,*[60] **6–16** an action for *mandamus* seeking reconsideration of the Secretary of State's decision not to declare an authority in default, the court followed *Tameside*[61] in concluding that before the Secretary of State could make a default order he would need to be satisfied that the authority were guilty of conduct as described by Lord Diplock in that case; but it was held that he had not properly addressed the facts of the case in the light of the relevant statutory provision (whether a child required special educational treatment under section 8(2)(c) of the 1944 Act) and ought therefore to reconsider his decision. In *Chance,* Woolf J. thus appeared to be "rehabilitating" both section 68 (to which he also referred) and section 99 in demonstrating the possibility of challenging the manner in which the Secretary of State makes a decision not to give directions where at least initially it may be impracticable to challenge the decision itself.

The remedy under section 99 of the 1944 Act ordinarily excludes **6–17** application to the courts. For example,[62] an application for judicial review was rejected where a person sought to challenge the propriety of the election of parent governors to the governing body of a county school. " . . . the appropriate and constructive remedy was provided by section 99"—*per* Mann J. in *R. v. Northampton County Council, ex p. Gray.*[63] If, however, a person suffers special damage as a result of breach of statutory duty he may, as in *Meade v. Haringey London Borough Council,*[64] apply to the court for damages or an injunction notwithstanding the statutory enforcement provision. *Meade* was a private

[57] See above at para. 1–50 n. 52.
[58] 1944 Act, s.99(2) and see above at para. 2–71.
[59] 1944 Act, s.99(3) and see above at para. 2–26.
[60] Unreported, but see P. Liell & J. B. Saunders, *The Law of Education,* (9th ed. 1985) F.77.
[61] See above at para. 6–11.
[62] See also *Watt* v. *Kesteven County Council* [1955] 1 Q.B. 408 (above at para. 1–74); *Wood and Others* v. *Ealing London Borough Council* [1967] Ch. 364 (above at para. 1–75); *Cumings and Others* v. *Birkenhead Corporation* [1972] 1 Ch. 12 (above at para. 1–77); M. Freeman, "Children's Education and the Law, 1, Parents' Rights" (1980) L.A.G. Bull. 61 (the author claims that there is no example of the Secretary of State ever having acted under s.99); the Report, observations and article by P. Meredith cited at n. 48 above; S. A. de Smith, *Judicial Review of Administrative Action* (4th ed. 1980) pp. 531–2; and H. W. R. Wade, *Administrative Law* (5th ed. 1982) pp. 626–9. The powers of the courts are considered above at paras. 1–48 *et seq.*
[63] *The Times,* June 10, 1986.
[64] [1979] 1 W.L.R. 637, C.A. (See above at para. 2–11) See also *Lee* v. *Enfield Borough Council,* 66 L.G.R. 195 (see above at para. 1–76) and, for a Scottish analogy, I. S. Dickinson, "Enforcing statutory duties in the field of education" [1979] S.L.T. 289.

law claim: where no private rights are at stake the general rule applies that the specific remedy under the statute should be sought rather than recourse made to the courts. It appears[65] that if the court entertain an application for judicial review they are unlikely to act so as to overrule the Secretary of State's decision, but may direct him to review it if he failed to give proper consideration to its consequences.

GRANTS, LOANS AND CONTRIBUTIONS

6–18   The making of grants[66] to local education authorities and of awards[67] to students has already been considered. In this section reference is made to the power of the Secretary of State to make (a) grants for research and services provided otherwise than by local education authorities, and towards schools fees and expenses; and (b) contributions, grants and loans in respect of aided and special agreement schools. The assisted places scheme is described in the next section of this Chapter.

Research, services, school fees and expenses

6–19   Section 100 of the 1944 Act authorises the Secretary of State to make regulations under which he may make payments to persons and bodies in various circumstances. Over the years the section has been heavily amended,[68] but its two remaining substantive provisions—subsections (1)(b) and (1)(c)—authorise a variety of payments. Most of these have already been mentioned in the appropriate context: direct grants[69] to a now severely restricted number of schools; and grants towards further education (including teacher training) establishments and the provision of facilities for leisure-time occupation and social and physical training,[70] to bodies concerned with adult education[71] and with the training of youth leaders and community centre wardens,[72] and in respect of non-maintained special schools.[73] The Secretary of State may also pay grants[74] towards relevant expenditure[75] on educational research and development or organising or advisory services; and to certain music

---

[65] *R. v. Secretary of State for the Environment and Others, ex p. Ward* [1984] 2 All E.R. 556.

[66] See above at paras. 1–121 *et seq.*

[67] See above at paras. 3–41 *et seq.*

[68] Subs. (1)(a)(i) and (ii) were repealed by 1980 Act, s.38(6) and Sched. 7; subs. (1)(a)(iii) was repealed by the Education Act 1944 (Termination of Grants) Order 1980 (S.I. 1980 No. 660); subs. (1)(c) was amended by 1962 Act, s.13 and Sched. 2; subs. (2) was repealed and subs. (3) was amended by Local Government Act 1958, s.67(a) and Sched. 9; and subs. (4) was repealed by 1973 Act, s.1 and Sched. 2. S.100 has been extended by Sex Discrimination Act 1975, s.27 and Sched. 2, para. 3—see above at para. 1–99.

[69] See above at paras. 2–45 and 2–218.

[70] See above at paras. 3–19 to 3–21.

[71] See above at paras. 3–33 to 3–35.

[72] See above at para. 3–39.

[73] See above at para. 2–216.

[74] Under the Education (Grant) Regulations 1983 (S.I. 1983 No. 74) reg. 17, subject to the requirements he specifies under reg. 23 and to the general conditions specified in Pt. V of the Regulations (as to which see below at para. 6–20).

[75] Relevant expenditure is that approved by the Secretary of State. See *ibid.* reg. 3.

and ballet schools[76] to reimburse them for operating the aided pupils scheme[77] for children at those schools.

Payment of the grants last-mentioned is subject to conditions[78] relat-   **6–20** ing, *inter alia,* to the number of places and level of fees. Payment of all the other grants mentioned in the preceding paragraph (except direct grants to schools) is subject to the same set of general conditions.[79] H.M.I.s or other persons authorised by the Secretary of State are to have a right of inspection, records and accounts are to be kept as the Secretary of State requires and be open to inspection by the Comptroller and Auditor General, and the Secretary of State is to be satisfied as to efficiency. The mode of payment of grant is specified, as are the circumstances in which repayment is required and the matters the Secretary of State is to take into account on deciding whether to make a grant (or loan), and its amount.

Under section 21 of the 1980 Act the Secretary of State may pay   **6–21** grants towards expenditure on teaching the Welsh language to persons other than local education authorities as well as to authorities[80]; and under section 1 of the 1986 Act he may pay grants to the Fellowship of Engineering and to the Further Education Unit[81] subject to the conditions he imposes.

Financial assistance to voluntary aided and special agreement schools

The substance of the law is contained in sections 102, 103 and 105 of   **6–22** the 1944 Act, which have been heavily amended, and in section 1(2) of the 1967 Act. Since 1944 the generosity of the state towards the churches has grown.

The Secretary of State pays[82] to governors of aided schools mainten-   **6–23** ance contributions of 85 per cent. of their expenditure on (a) the alterations[83] and repairs to schools for which they are responsible[84] and (b) the provision of a site or school buildings where school premises are to

---

[76] The Chetham's School of Music, Manchester; the Purcell School, Harrow; The Royal Ballet School, London; The Wells Cathedral School, Somerset; The Yehudi Menuin School, Surrey. See the Education (Grants) (Music and Ballet Schools) Regulations 1985 (S.I. 1985 No. 684) as amended by Amendment Regulations 1986 (S.I. 1986 No. 989).

[77] S.I. 1985 No. 684, Sched. 1., as amended by S.I. 1986 No. 989, reg. 4.

[78] See *ibid.* Sched. 2.

[79] See Pt. V of the Education (Grant) Regulations 1983 (S.I. 1983 No. 74) (which also applies to loans made to the governing body of a teacher training college under reg. 15, as to which see above at para. 3–19).

[80] See above at para. 1–127.

[81] See above at para. 3–02.

[82] 1944 Act, s.102 as amended by 1946 Act, s.14 and Sched. 2, 1968 Act, s.1 and Sched. 1, 1975 Act, s.3 and 1980 Act, ss.1(3) and 16(4), Sched. 1, para. 1 and Sched. 3, para. 4. The payment is mandatory in respect of expenditure under (a), optional under (b).

[83] "Alterations" are defined in 1944 Act, s.114(1) (substituted by 1968 Act, s.1(3) and Sched. 1, para. 5). See above at para. 2–24.

[84] Under 1944 Act, s.15(3)(*a*) as amended (see above at para. 2–24). A.M. 13/64 introduced a Code of Procedure—*Building Work for Aided and Special Agreement Schools.*

be significantly enlarged under proposals he has approved.[85] The same maintenance contributions are paid to the governors of special agreement schools[86] unless the agreement itself relates to the relevant expenditure.

6–24   When an aided or special agreement school is to be established[87] under proposals approved[88] by the Secretary of State, or is transferred[89] to a new site by his order,[90] he may pay the governors a grant of up to 85 per cent. of their expenditure on the provision of the site or (by construction or adaptation) of the school buildings, unless in the case of a special agreement school the agreement itself is material. In the case of transfer the local education authority provide the site.[91] Where governors or trustees dispose[92] of a site the proceeds of sale are taken into account in settling the amount of the grant. Grants may be repayable[93] in certain limited circumstances.

6–25   Governors of aided and special agreement schools may apply[94] to the Secretary of State for a loan towards the capital cost of their share of initial expenses on school premises, the grants and maintenance contributions mentioned above having been taken into account. "Initial expenses" means expenses:

    (a) to meet the cost of alterations required by the Secretary of State arising out of the development plan[95] approved for the area;

    (b) to be incurred under a special agreement;

    (c) (i) on providing a site or school buildings or a significant enlargement of school premises on which a maintenance contribution[96] may be paid,

        (ii) on providing school buildings on a site to which a school is transferred by order,[97]

        (iii) on providing a site or school buildings for a new school which by order[98] is deemed to be in substitution for a discontinued school or schools,

---

[85] Under 1980 Act, s.13 (see above at para. 2–32).
[86] "Special agreement" school—see above at para. 2–22.
[87] 1967 Act, s.1(2) (as amended by 1968 Act, s.1 and Sched. 2, by 1975 Act, s.3, and by 1980 Act, ss.1(3), 16(4), Sched. 1, para. 23 and Sched. 3, para. 13). See Circ. 3/67 (which refers to grant on the cost of "new places"). No new special agreement schools may be established.
[88] Now under s.13 of the 1980 Act (see above at para. 2–20).
[89] Under 1944 Act, s.103 as amended by 1953 Act, ss.8 and 17(2) and Sched. 2, by 1967 Act, s.1(5), by 1975 Act, s.3 and by 1980 Act, s.1(3) and Sched. 1, para. 12.
[90] Under 1944 Act, s.16 as amended (see above at para. 2–29).
[91] See above at paras. 2–28 to 2–29.
[92] See, as to disposal, the School Sites Act 1841 and above at paras. 1–150 *et seq.*
[93] See the School Grants Act 1855 and above at para. 2–66.
[94] 1944 Act, s.105(1) and (2) as extended by 1959 Act, s.1(4) and 1967 Act, s.1(4), and amended by 1968 Act, s.1(3) and Sched. 1, and by 1980 Act s.1(3) and Sched. 1, para. 1.
[95] No longer extant—see 1980 Act, s.38(6) and Sched. 7 and above at para. 2–13.
[96] See 1944 Act, s.102, above at para. 6–23.
[97] Under *ibid.* s.16(1) (see above at para. 2–29).
[98] Under *ibid.* s.16(2) (see above at para. 2–29).

(iv) on providing a site where a new school is to be established under proposals approved[99] by the Secretary of State,

(d) certified by the Secretary of State as being attributable to the provision of education of displaced pupils.[1]

If after consulting the governors' representatives the Secretary of **6–26** State agrees that borrowing is appropriate he may with the consent of the Treasury enter into a loan agreement with them which specifies the amount, rate of interest and other terms and conditions.

INDEPENDENT SCHOOLS

An independent school[2] is any non-maintained school at which full- **6–27** time education is provided for five or more pupils of compulsory school age[3] (whether or not also provided for pupils under or over that age) but excluding a special school. As from April 30, 1978, there has been no category of independent schools recognised as efficient by the Secretary of State,[4] but independent schools remain subject to inspection by H.M.I.s. Financial assistance to parents by local education authorities has already been considered[5]: this section gives an account of the law[6] relating to the conduct of independent schools—registration, complaints and Independent Schools Tribunals—and of the assisted places scheme introduced by the 1980 Act.

Conduct

There is a Register of Independent Schools[7] kept by an officer of the **6–28** Secretary of State—the Registrar. It is open to public inspection. The proprietor of an independent school may apply[8] to have his school included in the Register and in doing so must state, *inter alia,* numbers and particulars of pupils and teaching staff. An independent school will not be registered[9] if the proprietor or the premises are disqualified,[10]

---

[99] Under 1980 Act, s.13 (see above at para. 2–20).

[1] Under 1944 Act, s.104 (repealed) "displaced pupils" are those for whom education would in the Minister's opinion have been provided in some other aided or special agreement school had it not ceased to be available to them for specified reasons.

[2] Defined in 1944 Act, s.114(1), as amended by 1980 Act, s.34(1).

[3] "Compulsory school age"—see 1944 Act, s.35 and above at para. 1–81.

[4] See Circ. 6/78 (Circ. 60/78).

[5] See above at paras. 5–30 *et seq.*

[6] See A.M. 557.

[7] 1944 Act, s.70, as amended by 1980 Act, s.34 (on the coming into effect of which certain schools were entered in the Register without application). The law relating to the conduct of independent schools is administered by the Secretary of State for Education and Science or the Secretary of State for Wales as the case may be; and there are separate registers and registrars for England and for Wales. As to changes brought about by the 1980 Act, see Circ. 1/80, paras. 50–54.

[8] See the Education (Particulars of Independent Schools) Regulations 1982 (S.I. 1982 No. 1730) reg. 4.

[9] "Registered (and 'provisionally regstered') school" is defined in 1944 Act, s.114(1).

[10] See below at paras. 6–33 and 6–34.

and it is only provisionally registered until, after inspection,[11] the Secretary of State notifies[12] the proprietor that registration is final.

6–29   It is an offence[13] to conduct an independent school which is not registered or provisionally registered (unless an application for registration has been made within one month from when the school was first conducted) or to dissemble a provisionally registered school as a registered school. On summary conviction[14] a fine[15] is payable and up to three months' imprisonment may follow a subsequent offence.

6–30   Regulations[16] require the proprietor of a registered or provisionally registered school to submit particulars to the Registrar. The particulars are contained in an annual return and include those required in the application for registration and information about the number of pupils following examination courses. The proprietor is also to give the Registrar notice of certain changes—of proprietor, head teacher, name and location of the school and discontinuance of the school; and he is to give the Secretary of State the facts of the case where a teacher is dismissed on grounds of misconduct, or would or might have been dismissed but for his resignation.

If the Secretary of State is satisfied that the proprietor of a school has failed to comply with the requirements of the regulations he may, on at least two months' notice in writing which specifies the failings, order the deletion of the school from the Register unless the proprietor satisfies him that the regulation in question has been complied with within the period of notice.

6–31   The Secretary of State has to attend not only to procedural failings but to substantial complaints[17]—that the school premises, in whole or part, are unsuitable, that the accommodation is inadequate, or that efficient and suitable instruction[18] is not being provided, having regard to the numbers, age and sex of pupils; or that the proprietor of the school or any teacher employed there is not as such a proper person (a question of fact in each case). If the Secretary of State is satisfied that any registered or provisionally registered school is objectionable upon

---

[11] See 1944 Act, s.77 as amended, and above at para. 6–05.

[12] "Notice"—see *ibid.* s.113 as amended.

[13] 1944 Act, s.70(3) and s.70(3)(A) inserted by 1980 Act, s.34(6).

[14] "Summary conviction"—see Magistrates' Courts Act 1980 as amended.

[15] Not exceeding level 4 for first and subsequent offences—(see Criminal Law Act 1977, s.31(5)–(7) and Criminal Justice Act 1982, s.37 (as amended by Criminal Penalties etc. (Increase) Order 1984 (S.I. 1984 No. 447)), and ss.39 and 46 and Sched. 3.

[16] S.I. 1982 No. 1730 made under 1944 Act, s.70(4) and (5) as substituted and inserted by 1980 Act, s.34(7).

[17] 1944 Act, s.71.

[18] Education catering for the special characteristics of a minority sect is suitable if it primarily equips a child for life within his own community, provided that it leaves him free in later years to adopt some other form of life—*dicta* of Woolf, J. in *R.* v. *Secretary of State for Education and Science, ex p. Talmud Torah Machzikei Hadass School Trust, The Times,* April 12, 1985. Attendance at an independent school is not, *ipso facto,* evidence that efficient and suitable instruction is being provided—see A.M. 557.

any of those grounds he serves[19] a notice of complaint on the proprietor in which the grounds and full particulars of the matters complained of are stated. The notice specifies how and by what time (not less than six months) the complaints are to be remedied unless the Secretary of State considers them irremediable. If the notice alleges that any teacher is not a proper person he is named and the grounds of the allegation are specified. A copy of the notice is served on him.

Notices specify the time (not less than one month) within which the **6–32** complaint may be referred on appeal[20] to an Independent Schools Tribunal. Under the Independent Schools Tribunal Rules 1958[21] appeals are made by sending written notice to the Secretary of State stating the grounds, and if the complaint is that the teacher is not a proper person (when the teacher, as well as the proprietor, may appeal) a copy of the notice of appeal is to be sent to the proprietor of the school or the teacher as the case may be. The Secretary of State then requests the Lord Chancellor and Lord President of the Council to constitute an impartial Independent Schools Tribunal consisting of a chairman from the legal panel and two members from the educational panel. By 1944 Act, Sched. 6, members of the legal panel are appointed by the Lord Chancellor and possess legal qualifications he considers suitable; members of the Educational Panel are appointed by the Lord President of the Council and possess experience he considers suitable in teaching or the conduct, management or administration of schools. No officer of a government department or a local government officer (other than a teacher) may be appointed to either panel. Remuneration is by the Secretary of State (1976 Act, s.6). The Lord Chancellor appoints a secretary of the Tribunal.

The Rules prescribe, *inter alia,* arrangements for the time and place of the hearings, rights of audience, procedures and interlocutory applications to the chairman. The decision of the Tribunal, by majority if need be, may be given orally at the hearing or in writing as soon as may be thereafter. The secretary sends a copy of the Tribunal's order with a statement of the findings to every appellant and to the Secretary of State. Tribunals are under the supervision of the Council on Tribunals, and otherwise subject to the Tribunals and Inquiries Act 1971.[22] The reasons for their decision are thus to be stated on request and the decision is subject to appeal[23] on a point of law.

---

[19] As to service of notices see 1944 Act, s.113 as amended.
[20] *Ibid.* s.72(1).
[21] S.I. 1958 No. 519 as amended by Amendment Rules 1972 (S.I. 1972 No. 42). By 1944 Act, s.75(1), as amended by 1976 Act, s.6(2), rules are made by the Lord Chancellor with the concurrence of the Lord President of the Council; and by s.75(2) the Arbitration Acts do not apply to proceedings before a tribunal except so far as the rules specifically apply them.
[22] See Tribunals and Inquiries Act 1971, s.12 and s.13 (as amended by 1980 Act, s.7(6)) and Sched. 1.
[23] For an unsuccessful appeal by a school proprietor against disqualification see *Byrd* v. *Secretary of State for Education and Science* (1968) 112 S.J. 519.

6–33   Orders[24] are of five kinds:

(a) that the complaint be annulled;

(b) that the school be struck off the Register;

(c) that the school be struck off unless it complies with the requirements of the notice (as may be modified by the order) within the
period specified in the order and to the satisfaction of the Secretary of State;

(d) that the premises be disqualified as unsuitable in whole or part
for use as a school or from being used as accommodation for
more than a number of pupils specified by age and sex; and

(e) that the proprietor or teacher be disqualified[25] respectively from
being the proprietor of an independent school or a teacher in any
school (and unless the order directs otherwise, that the proprietor be also disqualified from being a teacher, and vice versa).[26]

Any of these orders may be made[27] by the Secretary of State himself if
the notice of complaint is not referred by the proprietor to an Independent Schools Tribunal within the time specified, unless the allegation
was that a teacher was not a proper person, in which case the Secretary
of State may not make an order if the teacher refers the complaint to an
Independent Schools Tribunal in due time.

6–34   The Registrar of Independent Schools must act[28] on an order striking
a school off the Register as from the date when it takes effect. Fines and
terms of imprisonment on summary conviction[29] are specified[30] for use
of premises for purposes for which they are disqualified, and for acting
as the proprietor of an independent school or accepting or endeavouring
to obtain employment as a school teacher while disqualified.[31] Proceedings may be instituted[32] only by or on behalf of the Secretary of State. If,
on application, he is satisfied that any disqualification is no longer
necessary by reason of change of circumstances he may by order
remove[33] it. Should he fail to remove a disqualification the person

---

[24] 1944 Act, s.72(2). By s.75(3) every order of an Independent Schools Tribunal is to be registered
by the Registrar of Independent Schools and open to public inspection.

[25] For circumstances in which a proprietor was disqualified as not being a proper person see *Byrd* v.
Secretary of State for Education and Science (1968) 112 S.J. 519 and (a teacher) *Gedge* v. *Independent Schools Tribunal, The Times*, October 7, 1959.

[26] 1944 Act, s.72(4).

[27] *Ibid.* s.72(3).

[28] *Ibid.* s.73(1).

[29] See Magistrates' Courts Act 1980 as amended.

[30] 1944 Act, s.73(2) and (3). As to fines see n. 15 above.

[31] Under the foregoing provisions or, by 1944 Act, s.73(5), their equivalent in Scottish legislation
(Education (Scotland) Act 1980). Employment in a further education or other establishment not
being a school as defined in 1944 Act, s.114(1) as amended (see above at para. 2–02) appears to be
lawful.

[32] 1944 Act, s.73(4).

[33] *Ibid.* s.74.

aggrieved[34] may appeal to an Independent Schools Tribunal in the same way as an appeal is made against a complaint notice.

Assisted places

Under section 17 of the 1980 Act, the Secretary of State has estab-　**6–35** lished, and operates, a scheme[35] to enable "pupils who might not otherwise be able to do so to benefit from education at independent schools." The scheme may be regarded as the successor to the allocation of places at direct grant grammar schools. Under it, participating schools remit the whole or part of tuition fees[36] of pupils selected for assisted places, and are reimbursed by the Secretary of State. The scheme excludes boarding fees[37] but includes entrance fees for public examinations paid by a participating school for their candidates.

Participating[38] schools are those independent schools[39] providing　**6–36** secondary education with which the Secretary of State makes an agreement. He is to have regard to the desirability of securing an equitable distribution of assisted places throughout England and Wales and as between boys and girls. An agreement[40] refers to the number of assisted places available at the school and may contain conditions additional to those prescribed in regulations.[41] An agreement may be terminated only as prescribed[42]—by school proprietors ordinarily on three years' notice, and by the Secretary of State also on three years' notice, or at any time if he is not satisfied about the educational standards of the school or is satisfied that a condition has been contravened. He must state his reasons.

The regulations,[43] which give substance to the scheme, must be the　**6–37** subject of prior consultation[44] with the representatives of participating schools, and of review every two years. To be eligible for selection for

---

[34] "Person aggrieved"—prima facie to be interpreted generously in its natural sense, but see *e.g.* H. W. R. Wade *Administrative Law* (5th ed. 1982).

[35] Under 1980 Act, s.17(1). See Circ. 1/80, para. 46. (No further circular has been issued).

[36] *Ibid.* s.17(3). Tuition and "other fees the payment of which is a condition of attendance" are covered.

[37] By agreement between the Secretary of State and a participating school other fees may also be excluded, but specified incidental expenses are covered. See the Education (Assisted Places) (Incidental Expenses) Regulations 1985 (S.I. 1985 No. 830) as amended and below at para. 6–43. Boarding fees may be paid by a local education authority in a proper case, under the Scholarships and Other Benefits Regulations 1977 (S.I. 1977 No. 1443)—see above at para. 5–31.

[38] 1980 Act, s.17(2).

[39] *Ibid.* s.17(10) under which participation is restricted to schools which are finally registered (see 1944 Act, s.70 and above at para. 6–28) and conducted for charitable purposes only. References to a school include references to proprietors (see 1944 Act, s.114(1)) and persons acting with their authority.

[40] 1980 Act, s.17(4).

[41] *Ibid.* s.17(6) and (7). See s.35(2) as to parliamentary procedure (and above at para. 1–41).

[42] *Ibid.* s.17(5) and Sched. 4.

[43] The Education (Assisted Places) Regulations 1985 (S.I. 1985 No. 685) as amended by Amendment Regulations 1986 (S.I. 1986 No. 991).

[44] 1980 Act, s.17(8) and (9).

an assisted place at a participating school[45] a child[46] must satisfy a number of conditions. First,[47] he must either (a) have been ordinarily resident[48] in the British Islands[49] throughout two years preceding January 1, in the calendar year in which his first assisted year[50] begins, or (b) have been resident in the British Islands on that date and ordinarily resident in the European Community[51] throughout the preceding two years, and be the child of a European Community national who on that date was employed or who was last employed in the British Islands, or (c) be a refugee[52] who has not been ordinarily resident outside the British Islands since he was recognised as such or was granted asylum.

6–38   The second condition[53] is that the child must have reached the age of at least eleven and, ordinarily, the normal school entry age, or will have reached both before August 1 in his first assisted year.

6–39   Thirdly,[54] if following selection the child would be in the sixth form, either the participation agreement must provide expressly for sixth form selection and the child must satisfy any conditions specified or, if he is already attending the school, the sixth form must include assisted pupils admitted in an earlier school year.

6–40   Fourthly,[55] when applying to the school for an assisted place the parents[56] must provide information about their income; and lastly[57] a school are not to select a child for an assisted place unless they are satisfied that he is capable of benefitting from the education provided. Subject to any provisions in the participation agreement the method of selection is at the school's discretion.

6–41   The extent of remission[58] of fees[59] is calculated by reference to the income[60] of the parents, reduced in respect of dependants, and of the pupil himself. Where relevant[61] income does not exceed a stated sum

---

[45] "School"—see S.I. 1985 No. 685, reg. 2(1).
[46] "Child" under S.I. 1985 No. 685, reg. 2(1) includes, *inter alios*, a child over compulsory school age (notwithstanding the definition in 1944 Act, s.114(1)).
[47] S.I. 1985 No. 685, reg. 4.
[48] "Ordinary residence"—see above at para. 3–73.
[49] "British Islands"—defined in the Interpretation Act 1978 as the United Kingdom, Channel Islands and Isle of Man.
[50] "First assisted year"—see S.I. 1985 No. 685, reg. 3(3).
[51] "European Community," "national" and "employment"—see *ibid.* reg. 2(1).
[52] "Refugee"—as defined in *ibid.* reg. 4(3).
[53] *Ibid.* reg. 5.
[54] *Ibid.* reg. 6.
[55] *Ibid.* reg. 7.
[56] Defined in *ibid.* reg. 2(2), as amended by S.I. 1986 No. 991, reg. 4. As to a child or assisted pupil without parents and in care see reg. 2(3), amended by *ibid.*
[57] S.I. 1985 No. 685, reg. 8.
[58] See *ibid.* regs. 9 to 15 and Sched. 2 as amended by S.I. 1986 No. 991, reg. 6.
[59] See definition in S.I. 1985 No. 685, reg. 2(1), reg. 20, and reg. 21 as amended by S.I. 1986 No. 991, reg. 3.
[60] See S.I. 1985 No. 685, reg. 11 and Sched. 1 as amended by S.I. 1986 No. 991, reg. 5.
[61] "Relevant income" is defined in S.I. 1985 No. 685, reg. 11(2).

fees are wholly remitted. The method of calculation of, and rules as to, entitlement to remission are elaborate. Questions[62] about entitlement are settled by the school. The Secretary of State may specify[63] various administrative arrangements, and the method of submitting and dealing with reimbursement claims[64] by schools is laid down.

Each school are to publish[65] particulars of the assisted places scheme, **6-42** annual particulars of the number of places likely to be offered, and their examination results. Ordinarily at least 60 per cent.[66] of assisted pupils in any school year are to come from publicly maintained schools. Participation agreements rather than regulations now determine under what circumstances teachers are excluded from employment in schools participating in the assisted places scheme.

Under separate regulations[67] participating schools meet certain **6-43** incidental expenses of assisted pupils and are reimbursed[68] by the Secretary of State. Parents are paid grants for uniform[69] and other (including sports) clothing, and towards expenditure on journeys[70] actually made to and from school or to visit a parent, guardian or other relative, and to universities and further education establishments regarding admission. The amount of the grant is determined by reference to parental relevant income and (travel grants) according as the pupil is a boarder or day pupil. Distance[71] and mode of transport are also material in the calculation. The means of the parents also determine whether, or to what extent, a school remit part or the whole of the charges they would otherwise make for meals[72] provided for day pupils. Questions[73] about the grants and remission of meals charges are settled by the school in the same way[74] as questions about remission of fees. Charges for specified field study courses[75] leading to G.C.E. examinations are remitted if the parents are entitled to whole or part remission of fees. There are general and administrative provisions along the lines of those in the principal regulations.[76]

---

[62] S.I. 1985 No. 685, reg. 13.

[63] *Ibid.* regs. 16, 22, and 23.

[64] *Ibid.* reg. 17.

[65] *Ibid.* reg. 18.

[66] *Ibid.* reg. 19.

[67] The Education (Assisted Places) (Incidental Expenses) Regulations 1985 (S.I. 1985 No. 830) as amended by S.I. 1986 No. 990, made under 1980 Act, s.18 (Note: the sums specified are likely to be subject to further amendment).

[68] Under S.I. 1985 No. 830, reg. 9 and in accordance with reg. 17 of S.I. 1985 No. 685.

[69] S.I. 1985 No. 830, reg. 3, as amended by S.I. 1986 No. 990, reg. 3.

[70] S.I. 1985 No. 830, reg. 4 as amended by S.I. 1986 No. 990, reg. 4.

[71] "Walking distance" may be material. See above at paras. 2–227 and 5–22.

[72] S.I. 1985 No. 830, reg. 5 as amended by S.I. 1986 No. 990, reg. 5.

[73] S.I. 1985 No. 830, reg. 6.

[74] Under S.I. 1985 No. 685, reg. 13.

[75] S.I. 1985 No. 830, reg. 7.

[76] *i.e.* S.I. 1985 No. 685. See S.I. 1985 No. 830, regs. 8 and 10.

EDUCATIONAL TRUSTS[77]

6–44   Section 1 of the 1973 Act[78] revised the powers of the Secretary of
State in relation to educational trusts generally. It first repealed section
2 of the Charities Act 1960[79] and the Endowed Schools Acts 1869–1948
so that he might no longer exercise concurrently the functions of the
Charity Commissioners[80] regarding charitable trusts, or make educational endowment schemes[81]; and his approval became no longer
required for the appointment of new trustees under a scheme made
before the Education Act 1918 came into operation.[82]

6–45   Secondly the section enables the Secretary of State after consultation
with governors or proprietor by order to modify a trust deed[83] or other
instrument relating to a school (a) to take account of an order he makes
under section 16[84] of the 1944 Act or the implementation of proposals[85]
concerning the establishment of schools or changes affecting them and
(b) to enable governors or proprietors to meet any requirement necessary for approval[86] of the school as a special school or as an independent
school suitable for those needing special educational provision. Similarly, after consultation with those managing an institution concerned
with the provision of educational services or research, he may modify
the trust deed or other instrument to enable them to comply with the
conditions or requirements of regulations.[87] Modifications may be permanent or for a period specified.

---

[77] As to s.2 of the 1973 Act, which gives the Secretary of State powers in relation to certain trusts for
denominational religious education, see above at para. 1–157.

[78] As amended by 1980 Act, ss.1(3) and 16(4) and Sched. 1, para. 26 and Sched. 3, para. 17, and by
1981 Act, s.21 and Sched. 3, para. 10.

[79] Other, contingent, parts of the 1960 Act were also repealed. For transitional and supplementary
provisions see Sched. 1 to the 1973 Act.

[80] "Charity Commissioners"—see Charities Act 1960, s.1. Their consent is required for the sale or
exchange of land acquired under the Technical and Industrial Institutions Act 1892, by s.9 of that
Act.

[81] Where a scheme makes provision for the benefit of county or voluntary school pupils it is to extend
to pupils in an army school—a school established to educate the children of "other ranks" (see the
Army Schools Act 1891 as amended by, inter alia, 1944 Act, s.120(1)(a)).

[82] 1918 Act, s.47, as amended by 1973 Act, s.1(4) and Sched. 2.

[83] "Trust deed" defined in 1944 Act, s.114(1) as amended by 1980 Act, s.1(3) and Sched. 1, para.
13(b).

[84] See above at para. 2–29.

[85] Under ss.12 or 13 of the 1980 Act—see above at paras. 2–14 to 2–38. On discontinuance of a
school (one of the forms of "change" under s.12) a local education authority will remain bound by
a trust created by a conveyance of land to their predecessors in title unless the Secretary of State
makes an appropriate order.

[86] See 1981 Act, ss.12 and 13 and the Education (Approval of Special Schools) Regulations 1983
(S.I. 1983 No. 1499), as to which see above at paras. 2–209 to 2–214.

[87] Made under 1944 Act, s.100—see Education (Grant) Regulations 1983 (S.I. 1983 No. 74),
especially regs. 17 and 23.

By section 78 of the Sex Discrimination Act 1975 trust deeds concern- **6–46**
ing property used for educational purposes[88] may, on the application of
the trustees, and subject to the conditions stated in that section, be
amended by the Secretary of State so as to advance education without
sex discrimination.

---

[88] At establishments listed in the table in s.22 of the 1975 Act (see above at para. 1–94).

CHAPTER 7

LOCAL EDUCATION AUTHORITIES, TEACHERS AND TORT

7–01 A tort[1] is a wrong which may give rise to civil proceedings, characteristically an action for damages, although an injunction may be the appropriate remedy. The operation of the education system may give rise to torts of various kinds and this Chapter is divided into sections accordingly.

7–02 Teachers and non-teaching staff of local education authorities (or of governors or others responsible for educational institutions) ordinarily stand in the legal relationship of servant to master (or in current terminology, employee to employer, but it must be remembered that persons other than servants may be "employed"). A servant who commits a tort in the course and within the scope of his employment[2] renders his master vicariously liable[3] for it under the doctrine *qui facit per alium facit per se*. An action may of course be brought against a local education authority (or others) in circumstances where there is no intervention by a teacher or other servant or where the act of the servant is merely ministerial, but most claims are in respect of an employee's tort, and, if it is proved, the employers[4] are liable unless they can show that it was committed outside the scope of his duties. Where there is vicarious liability the master may be able to look to the servant to indemnify him.[5]

7–03 In conducting an extra-curricular activity[6] a teacher may be surpassing his contractual duties but if he is acting as agent of the authority again they will, prima facie, be vicariously liable. A student teacher might be held to be an agent and similarly render the authority liable if he commits a tort.

7–04 Children are liable in tort but their age is likely to be taken into account in determining the extent of their liability—in which parents do not share.

---

[1] See textbooks on tort, *e.g.* Clerk and Lindsell, (15th ed., 1982); Salmond and Heuston, (18th ed., 1981); and Winfield and Jolowicz, (12th ed., 1984).

[2] See *Smith* v. *Martin and Kingston-upon-Hull Corporation* [1911] 2 K.B. 775 and below at para. 7–23.

[3] See Clerk and Lindsell, *op. cit.,* Chap. 3; Charlesworth and Percy, *Negligence* (7th ed., 1983) paras. 2.96 *et seq.*; and for an example of action outside the scope of employment, see *Dixon* v. *Roper, The Times,* February 3, 1922.

[4] Where governors are the employers (in the case of a voluntary aided school) they, and not the local education authority, are liable, but see above at para. 2–104.

[5] See *Ryan* v. *Fildes and Others* [1938] 3 All E.R. 517; the Civil Liability (Contribution) Act 1978; and generally Clerk and Lindsell, *op. cit.*

[6] See examples above at paras. 1–87 and 1–88.

NEGLIGENCE

Negligence is the breach of a duty to take care.[7] The standard of care   **7–05**
the law requires is that of a reasonably prudent man in reasonably foreseeable circumstances. This principle derives from the decisions of the
courts and its application in the field of education needs to be illustrated
by reference to decided cases.[8] Sometimes a pupil's injury is self-
inflicted, sometimes another pupil or third party is involved, sometimes
an authority's general rules and practices are alleged to be at fault. More
often than not supervision[9] by teachers is at issue. Although reported
cases relate to injury, negligence may give rise to other claims, for
example, a teacher—and hence, usually, his employer—may be liable if
he fails to take reasonable care of property accepted by him for safe custody, and loss ensues. From time to time teachers or others rather than
pupils are the injured parties: loss of services may result but gives no
right of action to the employers against the tortfeasor.[10]

Williams v. *Eady*,[11] decided in 1893, remains the leading case, in   **7–06**
which Lord Esher approved the statement by the judge at first instance
of the *in loco parentis* rule—that a "schoolmaster was bound to take
such care of his boys as a careful father would take of his boys . . . he
was bound to take notice of the ordinary nature of young boys, their
tendency to do mischievous acts and their propensity to meddle with
anything that came in their way." Here, through the intervention of
another pupil, a boy was injured by phosphorus which it was the practice to put on hockey balls to make them luminous at night. The schoolmaster had not kept the phosphorus sufficiently out of harm's way.

The doubts that have been expressed by judges in reaching their con-   **7–07**
clusions and the extent of reversals on appeal emphasise the subjective
nature of the "careful father" test, the difficulty of applying it[12] and its
inadequacy in certain circumstances. Moreover as the years pass parental opinion may change on what standard of care is appropriate. Judges
who forty or more years past survived the rigours of a public school education may take a more robust view of the risks to which a child may
reasonably be exposed than does the representative contemporary
parent—or, to be fair, today's public school.

---

[7] See Charlesworth, *op. cit.,* especially paras. 9–66 to 9–80. As to the statutory duty of employees to take care see Health and Safety at Work etc. Act 1974, s.7 and above at para. 4–77.

[8] Some of the cases are reviewed in D. Brown, "Injuries at School" (1970) 114 S.J. 216; K. T. Watson, "Liability for Injuries at School" (1960) 110 L.J. 363; and "Accidents to Schoolchildren" (1953) 97 S.J. 55., and A. N. Khan (1986) 5 Lit. 102.

[9] As to negligence in relation to medical treatment, see above at para. 5–04 n.11.

[10] See, *e.g. Receiver for Metropolitan Police District* v. *Croydon Corporation* [1957] 2 Q.B. 154.

[11] (1893) 10 T.L.R. 41, C.A.

[12] See *Ricketts* v. *Erith Borough Council*, 42 L.G.R. 471, below at para. 7–11; *Lyes* v. *Middlesex County Council*, 61 L.G.R. 443, below at para. 7–41; and *Nicholson* v. *Westmorland County Council, The Times,* October 25, 1962, C.A. where in finding a teacher not negligent for an accident to a little girl who was scalded by the teacher's cup of tea, the Master of the Rolls referred to "a reasonably careful parent looking after a family of twenty."

7–08   It is not surprising that the decisions of the courts have mostly turned on the particular facts at issue, frequently without reference to earlier cases, but it remains possible to state some general propositions that the decisions appear to uphold:

(1) Unless *res ipsa loquitur*—the facts speak for themselves—it is for the plaintiff (or if he is under age his representative) to prove that the defendant has been negligent. However serious a mishap, unless failure to take proper care is proved, the injured party has no right to any recompense at common law. Accidents can happen without negligence, or with negligence by the victim only.

(2) Only a reasonable standard of supervision of pupils is required; their age will be relevant to what is reasonable; continuous supervision may not be called for; and warnings given to children may be material in assessing whether care is adequate. Removal of all potential sources of danger goes beyond what is reasonable: the proper development of children entails their taking some risks and this applies to even quite young children. The duty to supervise does not ordinarily extend beyond school hours.

(3) The "careful father" (or "prudent parent") test may be inappropriate where a pupil is injured by another pupil. Here the question may be whether there was any departure from the standard of care that would have been prudent in the circumstances and whether the consequences of that departure were reasonably foreseeable.

(4) It is not always necessary for the plaintiff to show that any particular teacher was at fault—a system of supervision or arrangements with regard to safety on school premises may be defective. In assessing the arrangements what is reasonably practicable for the smooth running of a school will be material, and failure to meet the "careful father" test will not render the authority liable if their practice is in accordance with that generally adopted and approved in schools.

(5) What kind of accident is reasonably foreseeable turns in part on the age of pupils and their experience in the activity in which they are engaged at the time of the accident. Against an older pupil an authority may be able to plead *volenti non fit injuria*.[13] An accident to a third party where inadequate care is exercised over a child may be held to be reasonably foreseeable.

(6) The more dangerous the article in a school the higher the standard of care required: articles such as teapots and oil cans are not dangerous *per se*.

(7) A pupil does not become a servant of the local education authority (and hence potentially render the authority vicariously liable for his negligence) just because from time to time he does some act in support of the life of the school community; and it is reasonable that pupils should be required to perform such acts.

---

[13] This maxim may be roughly translated: "where there is consent there is no injury."

In the playground

In *Langham* v. *Wellingborough School Governors and Fryer*[14] a pupil **7–09** walking along a school corridor passed an open door and was injured by a golf ball struck from the playground. It was held that this was not an example of *res ipsa loquitur,* that the headmaster had not been shown to have failed in his supervisory duties and that satisfactory arrangements for supervision would in any event not have prevented the accident. The same case went to show that the "careful father" test is somewhat strained when a third party is involved, and attention was also drawn to its inadequacy in *Beaumont* v. *Surrey County Council*[15] where horseplay in a playground with a long piece of heavy-gauge elastic resulted in a severe eye injury to a pupil. Lane J. preferred "to use the ordinary language of the law of negligence" and found that it was the headmaster's duty, bearing in mind the known propensities of pupils of secondary school age, to take all reasonable and proper steps to prevent any of the pupils under his care from suffering injury from inanimate objects, from the action of their fellow pupils, or from a combination of the two. The plaintiff Beaumont was successful because he was able to show that the elastic, an attractive object which might very well cause injury, had been abandoned by a master in a waste-paper basket adjacent to the playground, and that supervision in the playground had been defective during the break when the incident occurred.

In *Martin* v. *Middlesbrough Corporation*[16] the prudent parent test was **7–10** found appropriate. A pupil fell during midday break and injured her hand on a piece of glass, probably part of a milk bottle. Her claim was sustained on the ground that an accident of that kind was foreseeable, and better arrangements should have been made for the disposal of empty milk bottles.

In *Ricketts* v. *Erith Borough Council*[17] a boy left the school play- **7–11** ground without permission and returned having bought a toy bow and arrow. He discharged an arrow which struck the spectacles of a little girl, splintering the glass so that she lost her eye. There was no continuous supervision in the playground but one of the teachers went out from time to time to see that all was well. This the court held was a standard of supervision which might be expected from a reasonably careful parent—having regard to the much larger number of children in the care of schoolteachers. The accident in *Rawsthorne* v. *Ottley*[18] arose from the presence in the playground of a lorry with a load of coke. A boy's leg was crushed as a result of his jumping on to the lorry at the back of the

---

[14] (1932) 96 J.P. 236.
[15] 66 L.G.R. 580.
[16] (1965) 109 S.J. 576.
[17] 42 L.G.R. 471. *cf. Smith* v. *Hale, The Times,* October 27, 1956, where an arrow thrown in a playing field struck a boy in the eye, and on the facts all reasonable care was found to have been taken by the masters.
[18] [1937] 3 All E.R. 902.

cab (out of sight of the driver) and of interference with the tipping part of the lorry by other pupils. The headmaster was held not to have failed to meet the duty of care of a careful parent. He had no reason to suppose that the lorry was in the playground, but in any event in the opinion of the judge he would not have been negligent in leaving boys in the playground when coke was being tipped, and it was not the law "that a schoolmaster should keep boys under supervision during every moment of their school life." A lorry was not "an allurement or trap." Neither were the owners of the lorry or their driver negligent, the latter having failed to look to see what was happening as he drove off.

7–12 In *Rich v. London County Council,*[19] a piece of coke was thrown as a result of which a young child lost an eye. The coke was stored in the playground at a time when the shortage of fuel threatened regular delivery. The Court of Appeal held that storage on the premises was reasonable in the circumstances and that supervision by the teachers and warnings given to children had been adequate. They disagreed with the judge at first instance who took the view that, applying the "careful father" test, the coke should have been fenced off. They doubted whether fencing would have been effective, and in the words of Morris L.J.[20] "it cannot be said that it is the duty of a reasonable, careful and solicitous parent . . . to seek to remove from [a child's] reach anything that may conceivably be used by him to indulge his mischievous propensity, always provided that reasonable, proper, and adequate supervision over the child is exercised." The circumstances of this case were distinguished from those in *Jackson v. London County Council and Chappell*[21] where an eye injury was caused by the throwing of "rough stuff" taken from a truck left in the corner of a playground. The headmaster had recognised a danger and asked the contractor to remove the truck, but the latter had not done so. Both the contractor and the local education authority were held to have been negligent. In this case something unusual had been brought on the premises—the coke in *Rich* had become a permanent feature.

7–13 During the morning break, in the course of a playground scuffle a boy of 13 was accidentally stabbed in the leg (which had subsequently to be amputated). The allegation (in *Clark v. Monmouthshire County Council and Others*[22]) was that the masters at the school ought to have known that the culprit (of about the same age) had a sheath knife with him and should have removed it, or alternatively that there was no proper supervision in the playground. The Court of Appeal concluded that though knives were sometimes brought to school this was not in all cases

---

[19] [1953] 2 All E.R. 376.
[20] See at 381.
[21] 28 T.L.R. 359. Distinguished in *Prince and Another v. Gregory and Another* [1959] 1 W.L.R. 177 where a pile of mortar left in a gutter was held not to be a dangerous thing or allurement to children.
[22] (1954) 118 J.P. 244, C.A.

exceptionable (it was reasonable, for example, that boys should have knives to take to camp and staff would have regard to age and treat each case on its merits); nor had the staff been negligent in not observing that the culprit was carrying a knife under his lumber jacket on the day in question; and although on that day—the last day of term—supervision was not at the usual level this did not prove negligence. Only reasonable supervision was called for and supervision, however good, could not prevent a sudden and unexpected accident of this kind.[23]

The reasonableness of supervision was also at issue in *Jefferey* v. *London County Council*[24] where a child aged nearly six climbed a water pipe and was killed as a result of falling through the glass roof of the playground lavatory. The court held that the lavatory was not unsafe because of possible access to its glass roof via the pipe, and that to leave a child of five and upwards in the playground at the end of school hours to wait for his mother was not negligent. In the words of McNair J.[25] "school authorities . . . must strike some balance between the meticulous supervision of children every moment of their time when they are under their care and the very desirable object of encouraging the sturdy independence of children as they grow up." There was a general propensity of small children to climb but it was not "the duty of school authorities, in all circumstances, to keep children under such detailed observation that they cannot climb." **7–14**

A similar conclusion was reached in *Ward* v. *Hertfordshire County Council*[26] when a boy of eight in running across the playground before the start of the school day tripped and injured his head against a low flint boundary wall. The Court of Appeal declined to follow the judge at first instance who concluded that the wall was inherently dangerous. It had stood there for more than a hundred years and though minor accidents had occurred parents, including the mother of the plaintiff, had not regarded it as dangerous. Nor was failure to supervise the children negligence, and moreover had a supervisor been present it would have been unreasonable for him to prevent children running races between the walls. **7–15**

An analogous case is *Mays* v. *Essex County Council*[27] where a boy of the same age, arriving early at school, lost his balance on a frosty slide in the playground and fractured his skull. Sliding had taken place in an orderly manner and "no average prudent father in the playground at **7–16**

---

[23] The same general conclusion was reached in *Newton* v. *East Ham Corporation* [1963] C.L.Y 2426, where a boy was hit in the eye by a piece of coke thrown by another boy, and in *Price* v. *Caernarvonshire County Council, The Times,* February 11, 1960, where a boy lost his eye from a rounders bat which accidentally slipped out of the hand of another player.

[24] (1954) 119 J.P. 45. See also *Good* v. *Inner London Education Authority* (1980) 10 Fam. Law 213, C.A., in which a child's eye was injured by sand in horseplay just after school hours, and the authority were found not negligent.

[25] See at 46.

[26] [1970] 1 All E.R. 535. See also above at para. 2–25.

[27] *The Times,* October 11, 1975.

that time would have thought it necessary to stop the children playing on it." There was no duty to provide supervision in the playground or to have had the playground salted.

In and around the classrooms

7–17   Several cases have to do with eye injuries.[28] In *Crouch* v. *Essex County Council*[29] the court considered the circumstances in which a 15 year old boy received an eye injury from a strong solution of caustic soda squirted into his eye from pipettes. The master had warned pupils that a strong solution was dangerous but some had been inattentive, and the girls responsible for the accident had thought that the solution, in an unlabelled beaker, was water. It was held that the chemistry master had not been negligent in allowing pupils with some background in chemistry to use caustic soda without direct supervision, provided that, as was the case, there had been proper warning; failure to label the beaker was acceptable since there was no other liquid from which it had to be distinguished; the standard of discipline maintained was sufficient for safety; and the irresponsible acts of the pupils had not been reasonably foreseeable by a master approaching his duties as would a prudent and careful parent.

7–18   In *Butt* v. *Cambridgeshire and Isle of Ely County Council*[30] a geography class of 37 girls aged nine-to-ten years were issued with pointed scissors four and a half inches long. Sandra, scissors in hand, whispered to Winifred in front of her. Winifred turned round and the point of Sandra's scissors entered her eye. On evidence from experienced teachers the trial judge concluded that the council could not be found negligent for providing pointed rather than rounded scissors—the former were educationally desirable—but that the system was at fault in not ensuring proper supervision. The Court of Appeal decided that the class had been conducted efficiently: children were told by the mistress to put scissors down if they were not cutting, and it was not practicable for her to keep her eyes on all the children all the time. Nor would it be practicable, as had been suggested, for children who sought the teacher's particular attention to be told to wait until the end of the class or, if they were attended to, for other children to be required to put down their scissors. The onus, Edmund-Davies, L.J. pointed out, was not on the defendants to show that the accident had occurred despite

---

[28] In addition to those mentioned in the text, see *Kubach and Another* v. *Hollands and Another* [1937] 3 All E.R. 907 in which an explosion in a chemistry class caused a severe eye injury, and liability was held to rest not with the proprietress of the school but with the supplier of the chemicals; and *Foster* v. *London County Council, The Times,* March 2, 1928, in which a teacher was found negligent in ordering a pupil to remove a pen nib from its holder with a pair of pincers: the nib broke and splinters injured the pupil's eye.

[29] 64 L.G.R. 240. See also *Shepherd* v. *Essex County Council* (1913) 29 T.L.R. 303 where phosphorus had been made available for a classroom experiment and a boy burned himself with a piece: he had received adequate warning and there was no negligence.

[30] 68 L.G.R. 81, C.A.

their having taken reasonable care. Similarly in *Elsmere and Another* v. *Middlesex County Council*,[31] during a mid-morning break, and in the absence of a teacher, scissors being used by a girl in unravelling silk slipped and entered a boy's eye. The court held that the danger was unforeseeable and not one against which the teacher should have taken precautions. By contrast in *Black* v. *Kent County Council*[32] the Court of Appeal held, on rather similar facts, that the authority had been negligent. A boy aged seven using sharp-pointed scissors in an art class had his chair jogged as a result of which the scissors jabbed his right eye. The court held that it was reasonably foreseeable that pointed scissors involved greater risk than blunt-ended ones, and that staff ought to avoid such risks unless there was a valid countervailing reason.

In *Harris* v. *Guest and Others*[33] an eye injury was caused by the dis-   **7–19** charge of an air pistol during a fight in a classroom during an unsupervised period. The court held that it was not negligent for boys and girls aged about 16 with prefects present to be left unsupervised. Adequate general warnings had been given by the headmaster. The class was also unsupervised in *Suckling* v. *Essex County Council*.[34] A knife used for modelling was taken from an unlocked cupboard and during horseplay a boy of eleven received an injury as a result of which he lost an eye. Vaisey J. held that if such implements had to be locked up not only would it be difficult to run a school successfully "but it would run the serious risk of turning these children into the votaries of the principle of safety first. It is better that a boy should break his neck than allow other people to break his spirit."

In *Wray* v. *Essex County Council*,[35] John aged 12 was "trotting"   **7–20** around a blind corner to get from one classroom to another. He collided with Arthur who was carrying an oil-can by the handle. The spout, projecting about six inches, struck John in the eye and he was severely injured. It was alleged that the master who asked Arthur to take the can to a colleague had been negligent in giving the can, a dangerous article, to a boy to carry, or alternatively that he should have given Arthur special instruction on how to carry the can and should have foreseen the possibility of an accident. The Court of Appeal endorsed the opinion of the county court judge that no such accident as occurred was foreseeable and that the oil-can, unlike a bottle containing phosphorus or a

---

[31] *The Times,* December 12, 1956.
[32] *The Times,* May 23, 1983.
[33] *The Times,* October 25, 1960.
[34] *The Times,* January 27, 1955.
[35] [1936] 3 All E.R. 97. *Cf. Cooper* v. *Manchester Corporation, The Times,* February 13, 1959, in which a boy was scalded on coming into collision with a girl carrying a large teapot through a passage in a school. The Court of Appeal held that carrying the teapot was an ordinary domestic duty, an accident was not forseeable at a time when classes were being held, and accordingly there was no negligence. And see also *Baxter* v. *Barker and Others, The Times,* April 24, and November 13, 1903 where the plaintiff was injured having collided in a school cloister with boys carrying vitriol.

gun,[36] was not dangerous in itself. The more dangerous the article the higher the standard of care appropriate. Lord Wright M.R. made reference to earlier cases and besides citing *Williams* v. *Eady*[37] mentioned, *inter alia, Chilvers* v. *London County Council*[38] in which a child lost his eye by falling on the point of a toy lance which was part of a toy soldier. In that case the teacher had been held not negligent in allowing the child to play with the toy. Toy soldiers were commonplace.

7–21   It is the duty of an employer to take reasonable care for his servants' safety in all the circumstances of the case.[39] In *Watts* v. *Monmouthshire County Council*[40] the issue was whether the council had taken reasonable care for the plaintiff teacher's safety, having regard to their knowledge of his peculiar susceptibility to injury from collision or jostling. The court found the council not negligent in their system of supervising the distribution of milk and in not excusing the teacher from milk duty altogether. The risk of the jostling which he suffered while on milk duty was small and no greater than the same risk on other duties to which he was exposed.

7–22   In *Watkins* v. *Birmingham City Council*[41] the injured party was also, exceptionally, not a pupil. A teacher fell over a child's tricycle which had been left outside her classroom, in default of school rules, by a boy of 10 who had been given the task of delivering milk to classrooms. The teacher was injured and claimed against the local education authority on the ground that the boy had acted as their servant and that accordingly they were vicariously liable for his negligence. The Court of Appeal held that despite the existence of certain aspects of the master and servant relationship the boy was not the authority's servant: he was a pupil, his duties as a milk boy derived from that status, and he could not be held to alternate between the role of pupil and of servant. He might well have been acting as agent of the school authority, but any vicarious liability on that account was negatived by his having broken the school rule against movement of toys (of which the tricycle was one) from the centre of the school hall. Had the work of milk delivery been beyond his capacity or had he been inadequately supervised the authority would have been directly liable.

7–23   In *Smith* v. *Martin and Kingston-upon-Hull Corporation*[42] a teacher was found to have been negligent in sending a pupil aged 14 to attend to the fire in the teachers' common room as a result of which her pinafore caught fire and she was seriously burned. The defendant corporation

---

[36] See *Dixon* v. *Bell* (1816) 5 M. & S. 198 (loaded gun) and *King* v. *Ford* (1816) 1 Stark N.P. 421 (fireworks).
[37] See above at para. 7–06.
[38] (1916) 80 J.P. 246. Similarly *Dixon* v. *Roper, The Times,* February 3, 1922, where a child swallowed a whistle from a cracker.
[39] See *Paris* v. *Stepney Borough Council* [1951] A.C. 367.
[40] 65 L.G.R. 171, C.A.
[41] *The Times,* August 1, 1975, C.A.
[42] [1911] 2 K.B. 775. See above at para. 4–20 n.60.

appealed on the ground that the relationship of master and servant did not exist between corporation and teacher, and that in any event the act of the teacher was outside the scope of her authority. The court had no difficulty in finding that the master and servant relationship existed: the teacher was engaged and paid by the corporation, was under their control and could be dismissed by them. The second argument rested on drawing insupportable distinctions between teaching and education and between orders which should and should not be obeyed. Small acts of courtesy were educational; and if the teacher had gone herself to look after the fire she would have left her class unattended. Alternatively since children are expected to obey all the orders of the teacher it would be unreasonable to limit the liability of the education authority to circumstances in which orders were of a kind that they intended the teacher to give. Since the court would not disturb the negligence verdict they held the corporation liable.

In *Smerkinich* v. *Newport Corporation*[43] the plaintiff, aged 19, while **7–24** attending a technical class injured his hand on a small circular electric saw. It was possible that a guard could have been provided but it did not necessarily follow that it was the duty of the authority to provide one. And even if they were negligent in that respect the plaintiff was not a child, he was conscious of the danger of using the saw, and the maxim *volenti non fit injuria*[44] applied. *Butt* v. *Inner London Education Authority*[45] provides a contrast. A printing apprentice while operating a printing machine at a school of further education caught and injured his hand in it. He claimed that the authority were negligent by, *inter alia*, failing to provide some kind of guard on the machine as would have been required had the machine been installed in a factory.[46] But practice in factories was not in conformity with the law and it was argued that apprentices should be trained to meet the conditions they would find in employment. The Court of Appeal decided, however, that it was the duty of the school to provide for the safety of the pupils.[47]

Two cases which further illustrate the proposition that accidents may **7–25** happen without negligence are *Crisp* v. *Thomas*,[48] in which there was no finding of *res ipsa loquitur* when a blackboard fell from an easel and injured a pupil, and *Perry* v. *King Alfred School Society*[49] where horse-play led to injury caused by the fall of a radiator: the accident was not reasonably forseeable.

---

[43] (1912) 76 J.P. 454.

[44] See n. 13 above.

[45] 66 L.G.R. 379, C.A.

[46] "A school or college is not a factory and the scholars or pupils are employed neither by those who own or those who teach in the school"—*per* Wrottesley J. in *Weston* v. *London County Council* [1941] 1 K.B. 608 at 613—so the Factories Act (now the Act of 1961) does not apply.

[47] Failure to provide a guard to a gas stove was held negligent in *Fryer* v. *Salford Corporation* [1937] 1 All E.R. 617 when the apron of a girl aged 11 caught fire.

[48] (1890) 63 L.T. 756, C.A.

[49] [1961] C.L.Y. 5865.

Physical training and organised games

7–26   During a supervised game of "touch" in a school assembly hall the pupil plaintiff in *Ralph* v. *London County Council*[50] put a hand through one of the class partitions which formed one of the sides of the hall. The Court of Appeal held that the injury he sustained arose from the negligence of the authority. A reasonable and prudent father would have foreseen such an accident. But in similar circumstances (*Cahill* v. *West Ham Corporation*[51]) the authority were found not negligent because the instructions to the plaintiff pupil in a relay race had been to touch the master not the glass partition.

7–27   In *Wright* v. *Cheshire County Council*[52] a boy of 12, having vaulted a buck in a school gymnasium, was injured by falling on his arm. Another boy, who should have been waiting to support him if necessary, had disappeared at the ringing of a bell to mark the end of the lesson. It was claimed that an adult should have been present at the end of the buck. The Court of Appeal found that the authority had not been negligent: the boys concerned were experienced and proficient in performing the exercise, which was carried out under the general supervision of a master. The system adopted was a general and approved one and this sufficed as a defence even if, as the judge at first instance had decided, it did not conform to the standard of care required by a reasonably careful parent. Moreover that standard did not totally exclude the possibility of mishap. By comparison, in *Gibbs* v. *Barking Corporation*[53] a master present at a vaulting horse did nothing to assist a boy to land. The boy successfully claimed damages against the authority for the master's negligence.

7–28   An unemployed boy of 17 was required as a condition of receiving benefit to attend a course of instruction provided by the London County Council on behalf of the Ministry of Labour. The course included physical exercises which in turn included playing "horses and riders." The boy, a "horse," fell down on a wooden floor and was injured. His claim in negligence (*Jones* v. *London County Council*[54]) was unsuccessful on

---

[50] (1947) 63 T.L.R. 546, C.A.

[51] (1937) 81 S.J. 630.

[52] (1952) 2 T.L.R. 641. See also *Turner (a Minor)* v. *Somerset County Council* [1974] C.L.Y. 2581 in which a games master divided his time between supervising games separately played by boys and girls and was held not negligent when an 11-year-old girl collided with another girl and fell over, hurting herself. The risk of an accident was too remote. The same principle was illustrated in *Clarke and Another* v. *Bethnal Green Borough Council* (1939) 50 T.L.R. 519.

[53] [1936] 1 All E.R. 115, C.A. *Cf.*, on similar facts, *Baker* v. *Essex County Council, The Times,* December 11, 1952, where however, no negligence was found, *Thornton et al.* v. *Board of School Trustees of School District No. 57 et al.* (1976) 57 D.L.R. (3d) 438; *Bills* v. *State of South Australia* (1985) 38 S.A.S.R. 80; and *Moore* v. *Hampshire County Council,* 80 L.G.R. 481, C.A.

[54] (1932) 96 J.P. 371. *Jones* was applied in *Cooke* v. *Kent County Council* (1949) 82 Ll.L. Rep. 823 where the injured party was again a "horse." Harman J. found that supervision had been adequate and remarked: "It does seem to me that the notion which has grown up that whenever anybody suffers injury he must necessarily be able to get compensation from somebody else must not be encouraged." See *Gillmore* v. *London County Council* [1938] 4 All E.R. 331 as to circumstances in which a polished wooden floor was found to be unsafe for a physical training exercise.

appeal. The exercises were under the supervision of a well-qualified instructor, the game had no accident record and to play it on a wooden floor was not dangerous, the boy's rider was about his own weight and size and there was no occasion to give him any particular instruction or to put him to act as a rider on taking part in the game for the first time.

Towards the end of his first judo class a young man of good physique   7–29
suffered an injury while in practice combat with another participant. He alleged (*Conrad* v. *Inner London Education Authority*[55]) that the instructor had been negligent by not making clear that the method of combat should be confined to the "O-Goshi" throw which had been taught and demonstrated. The Court of Appeal held that the instruction to the class had not been ambiguous but, even if it had been, the cause of the accident was failure on the part of one of the participants to submit, as they had been warned, when the other achieved domination in the practice: they were doing their best to use the "O-Goshi" throw. The instructor was competent and had not been negligent in his instruction and supervision.

In *Affutu-Nartoy* v. *Clarke and Another*[56] it was held to be wrong and   7–30
a breach of the duty of care for a teacher taking part in a game of rugby football with 15-year-old schoolboys to have any physical contact with the boys. The teacher and his employers were liable in damages for the injuries caused to the plaintiff.

Outside school

Three cases have to do with accidents on school buses. In *Shrimpton*   7–31
v. *Hertfordshire County Council*[57] a child injured herself by falling while alighting from a school bus, as she might not have done had a supervisor been present. The court held that the authority, having provided the bus, must ensure its reasonably safe use. The fact that they were under no statutory obligation to carry Miss Shrimpton, who lived within a mile of the school, was immaterial. In *Ellis* v. *Sayers Confectioners*[58] a supervisor was employed but failed to take sufficient care—as much as a reasonable parent would take—that a deaf and dumb child having alighted from the bus could cross the road safely. The authority were held 20 per cent. liable when he was knocked down (the balance of responsibility being with the owner and driver of the vehicle). In *Jacques* v. *Oxfordshire County Council*[59] in the course of a school bus journey a paper pellet damaged a child's eye. The flicking of pellets was generally stopped by the prefects and the pupils were not particularly boisterous or undisciplined. The standard of care of a reasonably

---

[55] 65 L.G.R. 543, C.A.
[56] *The Times,* February 9, 1984.
[57] 104 L.T. 145.
[58] (1963) 107 S.J. 252.
[59] 66 L.G.R. 440.

      prudent parent had, the court held, been met: the education authority
had not failed in their duty by leaving supervision to prefects.

7–32   In *Toole* v. *Sherbourne Pouffes*[60] a crossing warden was standing on
the pavement with arm outstretched motioning the children back. He
was held negligent in failing to do enough to ensure that a child aged six
did not dart out on to a pedestrian crossing where he was knocked down
by a van.

7–33   A five-year-old child who left a playground unattended and was
knocked down on a main road nearby claimed successfully (*Barnes* (*An
Infant*) v. *Hampshire County Council*[61]) on the ground that she had
been released from school five minutes before the normal time (at which
she would have been met by her mother). The early release of the children amounted to negligence. The failure of the school authorities to
ensure that young children on leaving school were paired off with
responsible adults was also put in question. This case contrasts with
Jefferey v. *London County Council*[62] where the authority were held not
liable for failure to supervise in the playground a child of about the same
age.

7–34   *Carmarthenshire County Council* v. *Lewis*[63] is another case of a straying child where the authority were found liable. A four-year-old boy
attending a nursery school strayed from a classroom through a playground on to the highway causing a lorry in avoiding him to strike a tele-
graph pole, so that the driver was killed. The driver's widow sought
damages on grounds of negligence by the responsible teacher or authority. The teacher had temporarily left the children in the classroom
unattended but on the facts was held not to have been negligent in doing
so. The fact that the gate between playground and street was unlocked
and free to be pushed open was, however, evidence of negligence on the
part of the authority, who should reasonably have foreseen the possibility of an accident: the fatal consequence of their negligence was not
too remote. The law relating to the straying of animals on the highway
was not material.

7–35   The duty of a headmaster to take care of boys while absent, properly,
from school was considered in *Camkin* v. *Bishop*.[64] Boys, in wartime,
were allowed to help a farmer by working in his fields. A senior boy was
apparently in authority. In the absence of the farmer, horseplay ensued
during which a clod of earth thrown at one boy hit another, who in consequence lost his eye. In rejecting a negligence claim based on absence
of supervision the Court of Appeal took the view that such an accident
might equally have occurred on any outing on which the boys, in accordance with normal practice, were allowed to go without supervision; and

---

[60] 70 L.G.R. 52.
[61] [1969] 1 W.L.R. 1563. The case is reviewed at (1969) 119 New L.J. 939.
[62] (1954) 119 J.P. 45 and see above at para. 7–14.
[63] [1955] A.C. 549.
[64] [1941] 2 All E.R. 713.

even if a master had accompanied the boys he might have been temporarily absent when the accident occurred. An ordinary parent would not regard the weeding of beet a dangerous practice. There was no analogy to cases in which boys were allowed to handle dangerous chemicals or to be in proximity to dangerous machinery.

In *Trevor* v. *Incorporated Froebel Educational Institute*[65] a boy of 12, **7–36** while on a form picnic, fell from the top of an ornamental grotto and injured his leg. The court found no reason why he should not have been allowed to play there. He might have created a danger for himself by climbing, but should have foreseen this and was the author of his own misfortune. No one could reasonably have foreseen that he would have sought to encounter such a danger.

Premises and equipment: breach of statutory duty

To prove a breach of statutory duty by a local education authority, or **7–37** others with responsibility under the Education Acts, there is no need to prove any breach of the duty of care. Though the circumstances which give rise to a breach of statutory duty may equally support an action for negligence (and for that reason "breach of statutory duty" appears here as a "negligence" subsection) the two torts are to be regarded as independent.[66] An action for breach of statutory duty may be brought when[67] the statute is intended to prevent the kind of harm that has been suffered, the plaintiff is one of a class the statute desires to protect and no special remedy provided by the statute is adequate for the protection of the person injured.

The main relevant statutory provision is section 10(2) of the 1944 Act **7–38** which, subject to provisos,[68] places a duty on local education authorities to secure that the premises of every school maintained[69] by them conform to the standards prescribed by regulations; and the material regulation is reg. 24(1) of the Education (School Premises) Regulations 1981[70] under which every part of the school building[71] is to be of such a design and construction that the safe escape of occupants in case of fire, and their health and safety in other aspects, are reasonably assured. It will be noted that the Regulations refer not to premises but to buildings, and that, for example, the standard of maintenance of the paved

---

[65] *The Times*, February 11, 1954.
[66] See Charlesworth (*op. cit.*) para. 12.01 and H. W. R. Wade, *Administrative Law*, (5th ed., 1982) pp. 665 *et seq.*
[67] There are the tests stated in Charlesworth (*op. cit.*) para. 12.07 and adopted by Veale J. in *Reffell* v. *Surrey County Council* [1964] 1 W.L.R. 358 at 362 (below at para. 7–42).
[68] See above at para. 2–58.
[69] "Maintained" see above at para. 2–02. It follows that this duty extends to voluntary aided and special agreement schools (where responsibility for external and structural repairs lies with the governors), see above at para. 2–22, as well as other maintained schools.
[70] S.I. 1981 No. 909.
[71] As defined in *ibid.* reg. 3.

recreation areas[72] is not specified. But section 2(2) of the Occupiers' Liability Act 1957 places a duty on the occupier of premises[73] "to take such care as in all the circumstances of the case is reasonable to see that the visitor[74] will be reasonably safe in using the premises for the purposes for which he is invited or permitted by the occupier to be there." Both local education authorities and governors in the case of voluntary schools[75] are occupiers and potentially liable at the suit of visitors—pupils and others such as parents—in case of default. Section 4 of the Health and Safety at Work etc. Act 1974[76] may also be material, but breach of duty under that section does not as such give rise to civil liability.[77]

7–39   The case law is limited and decisions mostly turn on provisions no longer in force, but they settle principles which are still relevant. In *Ching* v. *Surrey County Council*[78] the Court of Appeal decided that under section 7 of the Act of 1902 it was the duty of the local education authority to keep the school premises in a proper condition.[79] It was established that the plaintiff, a boy of nine, had injured himself by his foot being caught in a hole in the tar paving of a playground. The court held that neglect of a statutory duty with regard to a place where children were expected to play made those upon whom statute placed the duty responsible for injuries sustained.

7–40   *Ching* was followed in *Morris* v. *Carnarvon County Council*[80] where a girl aged seven caught and injured her finger in a classroom door. The door, heavy and with a strong spring, was unsuitable. It should have been replaced. In both cases the school had been transferred to the county council from the former school board but this did not detract from their responsibilities.

7–41   In *Lyes* v. *Middlesex County Council*[81] a pupil aged 15 sustained injuries to hand and wrist when they went through the panel of a swing door in the school. The "prudent parent" test in negligence was applied and it was held that it extended to the state of the school premises. The glass panel was deficient because the glass was not thick enough; and the authority, in addition to being found negligent were in breach of a

---

[72] See S.I. 1981 No. 909, Sched. 2.

[73] As extended by s.1.

[74] "Invitee" or "licensee" under the common law which was superseded by the 1957 Act—see Charlesworth (*op. cit.*) paras. 7.04 to 7.05. As to the common law liability of governors for negligence in relation to the state of premises, see *Woodward* v. *Mayor of Hastings* [1945] K.B. 174 and *Griffiths* v. *Smith* [1941] A.C. 170. As to the duty of an occupier to persons other than visitors, see Occupiers' Liability Act 1984.

[75] Under 1944 Act, s.22(3) as amended (see above at para. 2–63).

[76] See above at para. 4–76 n.13.

[77] 1974 Act, s.47.

[78] [1910] 1 K.B. 736.

[79] A successful action against managers was brought under the same provision by a headmaster when he was injured on the bursting of a boiler (*Abbott* v. *Isham* (1920) 90 L.J.K.B. 309).

[80] [1910] 1 K.B. 840.

[81] 61 L.G.R. 443.

provision in Regulations[82] (now revoked) requiring that premises be kept on a satisfactory level of efficiency.

In *Reffell* v. *Surrey County Council*[83] a girl aged 12 put out her hand **7–42** to stop a partly glazed door swinging towards her and was injured as a result of her hand penetrating the glass. The glass was thinner than the toughened glass being newly fitted or replaced in schools. The claim for breach of the duty imposed by section 10 of the 1944 Act and the Regulations then current[84] was appropriate because the pre-conditions stated above[85] were met. The duty to secure safety was absolute and the glass was not reasonably safe. Equally the authority were in breach of section 2(2) of the 1957 Act.

An authority will not be liable under the 1957 Act for injuries to a **7–43** pupil if he is one of those taken to apparently safe premises staffed by competent and careful persons, and uses equipment apparently safe and under the control of those persons (*Brown* v. *Nelson and Others*[86]).

TRESPASS TO THE PERSON

Trespass to the person may be permissible when it takes the form of **7–44** reasonable punishment, but where the bounds of reasonableness are overstepped, corporal punishment amounts to assault (usually coupled with battery) and detention to false imprisonment.[87] The employers of a teacher will be vicariously[88] liable if expressly or by implication they have authorised the act complained of.

The nature of punishment[89] in schools turns on policies or decisions **7–45** made under powers either allocated to governors or head teacher or reserved to the local education authority by articles[90] of government; but articles cannot authorise any punishment that is otherwise unlawful. Equally, though local rules may exist governing, for example, whether and by whom corporal punishment[91] is to be administered, breach of a

---

[82] Reg. 5 of the Schools Grant Regulations 1951 (S.I. 1951 No. 1743).
[83] [1964] 1 W.L.R. 358.
[84] Reg. 51 of the Standards for School Premises Regulations 1959 (S.I. 1959 No. 890) (in terms similar to those in the 1981 Regulations cited above at para. 2–57).
[85] See above at para. 7–37.
[86] 69 L.G.R. 20.
[87] For definitions, and generally, see Clerk and Lindsell (*op. cit.*) Chap. 4.
[88] See above at para. 7–02.
[89] See, generally, P. Newell (ed.), *A Last Resort? Corporal Punishment in Schools*, (1972), esp. Chap. 2; A. K. Scutter, "Schoolteachers' Position as to Corporal Punishment" 122 S.J., 671 and 692; M. Dutchman-Smith, Schoolteachers, Classroom Teachers and the Law" 134 J.P.N. 698; M. Freeman, "Children's Education and the Law 3: Exclusion and other Disciplinary Measures" [1980] L.A.G. Bull. 212; G. J. McGarry, "Some Legal Aspects of Punishment in Schools" 58 A.L.J. 707; and P. Wallington, "Corporal Punishment in Schools" (1972) Juridical Review 124.
[90] See above at para. 2–126.
[91] All schools (other than independent schools) are to keep a book in which all cases of corporal punishment are recorded (see above at para. 2–143). The Education (School Information) Regulations 1981 (S.I. 1981 No. 630) Sched. 2, para. 10 requires publication of the practice of the school as respects corporal punishment.

rule does not, as such, ordinarily constitute a breach of the common law (though a teacher may risk disciplinary action by his employers).

7–46   "The authority of the schoolmaster is, while it exists, the same as that of the parent. A parent when he places his child with a schoolmaster delegates[92] to him all his own authority so far as it is necessary for the welfare of the child" *per* Cockburn C.J. in *Fitzgerald* v. *Northcote.*[93] In *R.* v. *Hopley*[94] the same judge said "a parent or a schoolmaster (who . . . has the parental authority delegated to him) may inflict moderate and reasonable corporal punishment" but added that a father cannot be held to authorise excessive chastisement. As the last-mentioned case indicates, assault may be a crime[95] as well as a tort (and the same is true of false imprisonment). It has been suggested that because section 1(7) of the Children and Young Persons Act 1933 refers to "the right . . . of a teacher . . . to administer [corporal] punishment" that subsection of itself grants such a right. On the contrary it is sub-mitted that the subsection assumes a pre-existing right. But the right does not necessarily depend on the notion of delegation by the parent, which may be inapt now that education is compulsory. Rather it has been presumed to arise from the very act of sending a child to school, and to permit a teacher to administer in good faith reasonable corporal punishment for breach of reasonable school rules.[96]

7–47   What punishment is reasonable will depend, *inter alia,* on the age and physical condition of the child (so far as is known to the teacher) and the method of carrying out the punishment. Caning on the hand has been held to be lawful,[97] as have two strokes of the cane on the buttocks, the boy wearing trousers and underpants.[98] In *R.* v. *Newport (Salop.) and*

---

[92] See *Goldney* v. *King, The Times,* February 7, 1910 (parent made stipulations in effect as to the extent of delegation of authority to administer corporal punishment) and *Price* v. *Wilkins* (1888) 58 L.T. 680 (no right to keep pupil at school against parent's wishes).
[93] (1865) 4 F. & F. 656, para. 690.
[94] (1860) 2 F. & F. 202. A schoolmaster obtained a father's permission to chastise his son severely and then beat him to death.
[95] As to the distinction between crime and tort see the works cited above at n. 1. Under the Children and Young Persons Act 1933, s.1(1) any person of 16 or more is guilty of a misdemeanour if he, *inter alia,* wilfully assaults a child (a person under 14) in his care in a manner likely to cause him unnecessary suffering or injury to health but, (s.1(7)) not so as to affect "the right of any parent, teacher or other person having the lawful charge of a child to administer punishment to him." For examples of alleged criminal assaults see *R.* v. *Byrd* [1968] Crim. L.R. 278, *R.* v. *Taylor, The Times,* December 28, 1983, and news items in *The Times,* January 14, 1955 (*Cook* v. *Attock*), June 16, 1961 (*R.* v. *Reid*), July 11, 1961 (*R.* v. *Gilchrist*), January 11, 1965 (*R.* v. *Jeffs*), August 23, 1966 (*Walsh* v. *Bolwell*), February 17, 1967 (*Asquith* v. *Proctor*) and March 17, 1972 (*R.* v. *Higgitt*) some of which are summarised at (1978) 122 S.J. 671. As to assault upon teachers, see above at para. 2–127.
[96] See *Mansell* v. *Griffin* [1908] 1 K.B. 160 and 947, *R.* v. *Newport and Salop Justices and Others, ex p. Wright* [1929] 2 K.B. 416 and *Ryan* v. *Fildes* [1938] 3 All E.R. 517.
[97] *Gardner* v. *Bygrave* (1889) 53 J.P. 743 and *Scorgie* v. *Lawrie* (1883) 10 R. (Ct. of Sess.) 610.
[98] *Ridley* v. *Little, The Times,* May 26, 1960. The boy was a resident pupil at a school for the sub-normal. The case was brought under s.1(1) of the Children and Young Persons Act 1933 (see note 95 above) and in the judgment attention was drawn to the test being whether the assault was likely to cause unnecessary harm and not whether in fact it had done so.

Others, ex p. Wright[99] the nature of the assault—the boy bent over and was administered five strokes of the cane—was not at issue but rather whether on the facts there was proper occasion for punishment. In *Ryan* v. *Fildes*,[1] Tucker J., following the statements of law in *R.* v. *Hopley*[2] and *Mansell* v. *Griffin*,[3] concluded that a blow to a boy's head, in which his ear may have been hit, though not very violent was an immoderate punishment, and that an action for damages arising from the boy's subsequent deafness therefore succeeded against Miss Fildes' employers.

The opinion was expressed in *Fitzgerald* v. *Northcote*[4] that a school- **7–48** master was entitled to assault a pupil to the extent of taking a book from him if the master could reasonably believe it to contain evidence of misbehaviour, and to imprison[5] the pupil in a room pending expulsion if expulsion was reasonable in the circumstances.

The question arose in *Mansell* v. *Griffin*[6] who may inflict corporal **7–49** punishment, and it was held that an assistant teacher[7] as well as a head teacher may inflict it as part of the ordinary means of preserving discipline in his class, provided that there is no bad motive, the punishment is usual in the school and it is within the contemplation of the parent. The assistant teacher was in breach of the local education authority's regulations that permitted only the head teacher to inflict corporal punishment, but the breach did not make him liable for assault. The outcome might have been otherwise had the parents known the nature of the regulations.

In *Hunter* v. *Johnson*[8] a child was "kept in" for three quarters of an **7–50** hour as punishment for failure to do homework. There was no lawful authority to impose homework and it followed that the punishment was unlawful. Although explicit provision for homework remains absent in current legislation the Education (School Information) Regulations 1981[9] contemplate that it may be required. A reasonable period of detention, say up to half an hour, is probably within the law—but may give rise to practical difficulties where the pupil is entitled to free

---

[99] [1929] 2 K.B. 416 and above at para. 2–126 n.83.

[1] [1938] 3 All E.R. 517. The employers, the school managers, were able to recover the whole of the damages from Miss Fildes, as joint tortfeasor, under s.6 of the Law Reform (Married Women and Tortfeasors) Act 1935 (now repealed and replaced by the Civil Liability (Contribution) Act 1978).

[2] See above at para. 7–46.

[3] [1908] 1 K.B. 160 at 947, and see below at para. 7–49.

[4] (1865) 4 F. & F. 656.

[5] A pupil cannot be falsely imprisoned if he is unaware that he is under a restraint (*Herring* v. *Boyle* (1834) 1 C.M. & R. 377).

[6] [1908] 1 K.B. 160 at 947.

[7] In *Re Basingstoke School* (1877) 41 J.P.N. 118 the view was tentatively expressed that it was not unreasonable or necessarily illegal for a prefect to administer moderate corporal punishment in accordance with practice laid down by a headmaster.

[8] (1884) 13 Q.B.D. 225 and see also, on similar facts, *R.* v. *Watson and Others, Justices* (1884) 48 J.P.N. 149. Detention at a public boarding school was held to be a reasonable punishment in *Hutt* v. *Haileybury College (Governors)* (1888) 4 T.L.R. 623.

[9] S.I. 1981 No. 630, Sched. 2, para. 8. See above at para. 2–189.

transport[10] home; and there are other relevant considerations such as the availability of crossing patrols and the time of nightfall.

7–51   Many of the cases referred to above are not drawn from the public system of education and were decided long ago: they may not in all respects still provide reliable guidance to the current state of the law. It appears that those relating to corporal punishment have lost their relevance for most schools and pupils, by virtue of section 47 of the Education (No. 2) Act 1986. This provision reconciles domestic law with the decision in *Campbell and Cosans* v. *United Kingdom,*[11] where the European Court of Human Rights found the United Kingdom to be in breach of Article 2 of Protocol 1 of the European Convention on Human Rights. To meet this decision the Education (Corporal Punishment) Bill was introduced[12] in Parliament by the Government in 1985 and would have given parents the option whether or not their children should be subject to corporal punishment. The House of Lords[13] rejected the principle of making differences in punishment as between pupils in a school and the Bill was not proceeded with; but section 47 of the 1986 (No. 2) Act, although elaborated in ten material subsections, does appear absolutely to prohibit corporal punishment of pupils under 18 and thus to close the issue, except as regards pupils at independent schools which receive no assistance from public funds, or who themselves receive no such assistance. To those pupils the prohibition does not apply.[13a] Section 47(3) makes clear that the use of reasonable physical force to avert danger of injury to persons or property is not unlawful, and section 47(4) that reasonable corporal punishment is not a criminal offence.

Nuisance and Trespass

7–52   "The essence of nuisance is a condition or activity which unduly interferes with the use or enjoyment of land" while "trespass to land consists in any unjustifiable intrusion by one person upon land in the possession of another."[14] The distinction in practice may be a fine one. Local education authorities may have occasion to bring proceedings under either head in relation to the schools and other establishments they maintain.

7–53   Oddly, if may be thought, educational institutions do not feature in reported cases within the jurisdiction but in *Matheson and Another* v.

---

[10] See above at para. 5–21.

[11] (1982) 4 E.H.R.R. 293 and see above at para. 1–112 n. 58.

[12] Following publication by the D.E.S. in 1983 of a consultative document "Corporal Punishment in Schools."

[13] See H.L. Deb. Vol. 465, Col. 1314 (July 4, 1985) following in effect the dissenting opinion of Judge Sir Vincent Evans in *Campbell*—see (1982) 4 E.H.R.R. 293 at 308.

[13a] The prohibition also, exceptionally, may not apply to pupils (a) in certain independent schools which do receive assistance and (b) whose assistance derives from funds otherwise than under the Education Acts; but see s.47(7).

[14] Clerk & Lindsell *op. cit.* at paras. 23.01 and 22.01 respectively. See also para. 23.22 and note the difference between public nuisance (which is a crime) and private nuisance.

Northcote College Board of Governors,[15] the New Zealand Supreme Court considered preliminary points of law arising from allegations of the "throwing of fire-crackers and striking of golf-balls on to the plaintiff's land and trespassing thereon, stealing fruit and interfering with the plaintiff's use and enjoyment of land and causing nuisance, annoyance and damage thereto." English case law and authorities were reviewed and the decision was reached that the allegations, if proved, might constitute actionable nuisance[16] arising out of individual acts of trespass by pupils, for which acts—as such, as distinct from the nuisance—the school governors would not be liable.

DEFAMATION

It is defamatory to publish to a third person words which "tend to   **7–54** lower the plaintiff in the estimation of right-thinking members of society generally,"[17] slander where the words are fugitive (*i.e.* normally spoken) and libel where the words are written or in some other permanent form. Mere vulgar spoken abuse is not defamatory. An indeterminate class or category of persons cannot be defamed; but if the defamatory statement can be taken to refer to particular persons or to each and every person (for example, all the teachers at a school) all could sue.[18] Libel is actionable *per se,* but proof of special damage[19] is required in the case of slander unless the slander is, *inter alia,* of the person in his calling or office.[20] Defences to publication of defamatory matter are justification, privilege and fair comment.

Most of the reported cases within the field of education concern alle-   **7–55** gations against school teachers in their calling, and the defence has often been that of qualified (not absolute[21]) privilege which exists when on the occasion of the communication the person who makes it "has an interest or a duty, legal, social or moral, to make it to the person to whom it is made and the person to whom it is so made has a corresponding interest or duty to receive it[22];" but the existence of malice or indirect motive will negative this defence. The burden of proof of malice lies on the plaintiff.

---

[15] [1975] 2 N.Z.L.R. 106.

[16] And possibly negligence but not a tort under the rule in *Rylands* v. *Fletcher.* See Clerk & Lindsell, *op. cit.,* Chap. 24.

[17] Lord Atkin in *Sim* v. *Stretch* (1936) 52 T.L.R. 669 at 671, and see generally Clerk and Lindsell, *op. cit.,* Chap. 20 and Gatley on *Libel and Slander* (8th ed., 1981).

[18] See *Browne and Others* v. *D. C. Thomson & Co.* [1912] S.C. 359.

[19] *i.e.,* sums actually lost by the plaintiff or which he is obliged to pay.

[20] See below at para. 7–59.

[21] As to absolute privilege of a statement made in evidence concerning grounds for dismissal of a teacher, see *Trapp* v. *Mackie* [1979] 1 All E.R. 489.

[22] Lord Atkin in *Adam* v. *Ward* [1917] A.C. 309 at 334.

Of assistant teachers

7–56   In *Hume* v. *Marshall*[23] the defendant, second master at Dulwich College, made allegations to the headmaster and governors about the drunkenness of the plaintiff, an assistant master at the school. The court held that the communication, if *bona fide* and without malice, was privileged. Similar allegations in *Goslett* v. *Garment*[24] (at a different school) were not privileged, though made *bona fide*, because the master against whom the allegations were made had left the school and thus the defendant was not under a duty to make the communication.

7–57   In *Reeve* v. *Widderson*[25] a headmistress wrote to the chief education officer in a way that the plaintiff, a teacher at the school, took to suggest her unfitness for work at the school, and thus, she claimed, her reputation as a teacher was injured. The House of Lords held that the occasion was privileged and the jury found no malice. By contrast, when a headmaster wrote to the directors of a school making false charges about the conduct of a teacher out of school his remarks were held not to be privileged (*Milne* v. *Bauchope*[26]). In *M'Carogher* v. *Franks*[27] when the secretary of an old boys' society made allegedly defamatory remarks about a mistress at the school to a group of pupils the court held that the occasion was privileged because the remarks were made without malice and for the good of the school.

Of head teachers

7–58   In *Ripper* v. *Rate*[28] the letters of the defendant, a subscriber to a Church of England school, to the secretary of the Surrey Education Committee alleging cruelty by a headmaster were held to be privileged and there was no evidence of malice. The action of the headmaster therefore failed.

7–59   In *Jones* v. *Jones*[29] a headmaster claimed that he had been slandered by allegations of adultery. No special damage was suffered by the headmaster and it was found that the slanderous words were not spoken of him in the way of his calling. His action therefore failed. The common law has since been altered by section 2 of the Defamation Act 1952 under which "in any action for slander in respect of words calculated[30] to disparage the plaintiff in any office, profession, calling, trade or business held or carried on by him at the time of the publication, it shall not be necessary to allege or prove special damage whether or not the words are spoken of the plaintiff in the way of his office . . . "

---

[23] (1877) 37 L.T. 711.

[24] (1897) 13 T.L.R. 391.

[25] *The Times*, April 24, 1929.

[26] [1867] Sessions Cases 1114.

[27] *The Times*, November 25, 1964.

[28] *The Times*, January 17, 1919.

[29] [1916] 2 A.C. 481.

[30] Not defined, but from decisions in different contexts it appears that words are calculated to have a particular effect if that is the natural result of their being used.

The defendants in *Baraclough* v. *Bellamy*[31] protested in writing to the **7–60**
education authority about the way in which a headmaster celebrated
Empire Day in 1927. Whether or not the jury found the occasion privileged and, if so, whether there was malice the report leaves unclear, but
Swift J. ruled that the defence of fair comment was not open to the
defendants (who did not gain the verdict) as the protest consisted only
of statements of fact.

In *Hardwick* v. *Daily Express*[32] that newspaper alleged that the head- **7–61**
master plaintiff had banned a girl aged six from the school's Christmas
party for having come to school wearing a trouser-suit. The judge said
that the report painted the headmaster as an unreasonable and unfeel-
ing man so as to bring him within Lord Atkin's dictum[33] regarding the
nature of defamation. The headmaster was successful in his claim for
damages.

Of pupils

In *Bridgman* v. *Stockdale and Others*[34] an allegation of cribbing by a **7–62**
candidate at an examination was made by the invigilator in a remark to
the rest of the class. The candidate brought an action for slander.
Ormerod J. decided "after anxious consideration" that the occasion was
privileged because there was a common interest of invigilator and the
whole of the class that the examination was fairly conducted and that no
one person had an advantage over the others. There was no malice and
the action therefore failed, unfortunate though the remarks had been.
The judge went on to say that even had he found the occasion not to be
privileged, in the absence, as he found, of special damage he would, for
the plaintiff to succeed, have had to find that the slander was in the way
of the candidate's profession or business. But he took the innuendo to
be that the plaintiff was dishonest or a fraud—it reflected on his general
character rather than being said of him by way of trade or business as a
trainee, qualifying for a particular appointment. (He was already qualified as an electrical engineer but this does not appear to affect the argument).

Remarks written by teachers on reports to parents or made, for **7–63**
example, to a doctor or social worker are covered by qualified privilege
unless malice is proved, and the same applies to the contents of references.

---

[31] *The Times*, July 18, 1928.
[32] A news item in *The Times*, December 22, 1972.
[33] See above at para. 7–54.
[34] [1953] 1 W.L.R. 704.

CODE OF PRACTICE AS TO THE CONSTITUTION AND
PROCEDURES OF APPEAL COMMITTEES ESTABLISHED UNDER
THE EDUCATION ACT 1980 AND THE EDUCATION ACT 1981.
FEBRUARY 1985.

Introduction

Section 7 of the Education Act 1980 gives parents the right to appeal against decisions on the schools their children should attend. Each local education authority (or the governors of aided or special agreement schools) has to set up appeal committees to consider those appeals. Schedule 2 to the Act sets out the constitution and procedures of the appeal committees. This Code is a guide to making arrangements for appeals which are intended to be used when informal procedures have been exhausted and have failed to produce agreement. It has been prepared by representatives of the local authority associations and of voluntary schools, in consultation with the Council on Tribunals. Annex 2 to the Code deals with appeals relating to special education under the Education Act 1981.

Parents must have confidence that they will receive a fair hearing from an impartial appeal committee. Local education authorities and governors must take care to avoid any choice of members that may give an appearance of bias. Appeal committee members should be reminded on appointment and induction that they act independently of the local education authority or governors.

Department of Education and Science Circular 1/81 emphasises that hearings should normally be conducted in as informal an atmosphere as possible. Any attempt to reproduce the atmosphere and formal procedures of a court of law would be totally out of place in appeal committees.

[*Where there is a direct quotation from the Act in the code the words are underlined.*] "Authority" means the local education authority, "Act" means the Education Act 1980. This Code supersedes that dated August 6, 1981 and its addenda.

1. Membership of appeal committees for county and voluntary controlled schools

 (a) The authority should establish a panel of persons from whom appeal committees can be constituted, including parents whenever possible. Sufficient persons may be appointed to enable two or more appeal committees to sit at the same time. Panel members shall comprise:

  (i) members of the authority or of any education committee of the authority; and

  (ii) persons who are not members of the authority or of any education committee of the authority but who have experience in education, are acquainted with the educational conditions in the area of the authority or are parents of registered pupils at a school;

 but shall not include any person employed by the authority otherwise than as a teacher.

 (b) An appeal committee shall consist of three, five or seven members nominated by the authority.

 (c) The members of an appeal committee who are members of the authority or of any education committee of the authority shall not outnumber the others by more than one.

(d) A person who is a member of an education committee of the authority shall not be chairman of an appeal committee. Similarly, a member of an education sub-committee dealing with admission policies should not be chairman of an appeal committee.

(e) A person shall not be a member of an appeal committee for the consideration of any appeal against a decision if he was among those who made the decision or took part in discussions as to whether the decision should be made. Authorities should have particular regard in formulating their admissions procedures to the manner in which they are handled to avoid any conflict of interest or suggestion of bias in the event of appeals. For example, a person married or closely related to a person excluded from membership of an appeal committee, should not normally be a member; husbands and wives should not serve on the same committee.

(f) A person who is a teacher at a school shall not be a member of an appeal committee for the consideration of an appeal involving a question whether a child is to be admitted to that school. This includes a teacher at the school to which the child has been allocated.

(g) An authority should establish by resolution the procedure for selection of the membership of panels and thereafter of appeal committees, and for the appointment of chairmen. In appointing chairmen it would be helpful to look for previous experience in the conduct of hearings.

2. Membership of appeal committees for voluntary aided or special agreement schools

(a) The governors of such a school, or of two or more schools where joint arrangements are entered, shall appoint a panel of persons from whom appeal committees can be constituted. Sufficient persons may be appointed to enable two or more appeal committees to sit at the same time. Panels:

(i) may include one or more of the governors;

(ii) shall include persons appointed from a list drawn up by the local education authority by whom the school is maintained; and

(iii) shall not include any person employed by the authority or the governors otherwise than as a teacher.

(b) Half the members of an appeal committee (excluding the chairman) shall be nominated from among those in paragraph 2(a)(ii) above.

(c) None of the governors shall be chairman of an appeal committee.

(d) A person shall not be a member of an appeal committee for the consideration of any appeal against a decision if he was among those who made the decision or took part in discussions as to whether the decision should be made. Governors should have particular regard in formulating their admissions procedures to the manner in which they are handled to avoid any conflict of interest or suggestion of bias in the event of appeals. For example, a person married or closely related to a person excluded from membership of an appeal committee, should not normally be a member; husbands and wives should not serve on the same committee.

(e) A person who is a teacher at a school shall not be a member of an appeal committee for the consideration of an appeal involving a question whether a child is to be admitted to that school.

(f) The governors, and all those responsible where joint arrangements are made, should establish the procedure for selection of membership of panels and thereafter of appeal committees, and for the appointment of a chairman. In appointing chairmen it would be helpful to look for previous experience in the conduct of hearings.

3. Size of appeal committee

The Act requires that appeal committees consist of three, five or seven persons, but experience shows that too large a number can be daunting to parents. If an appeal committee member has to leave during an appeal, the committee can continue (if everyone agrees) so long as there are still three of five members and the composition still complies with paragraph 1 or 2 above. However, if there are fewer than three members left, the appeal must be reheard by a fresh appeal committee. The 14 day notice requirement for the fresh hearing (see paragraph 7 (b)) need not apply if the parent agrees.

It is important to remember that the authority members of the committee must never outnumber the other members by more than one.

4. Clerk to the committee

(a) Each appeal committee should have the services of a clerk. If the committee withdraws or invites the parties to do so when it wishes to consider its decision, the clerk should remain with the committee but only for the purpose of offering advice on procedure or law, assisting by reference to notes of evidence and recording decisions and reasons. The role of the clerk should be explained to parents when the committee retires to consider its decision.

(b) In the case of county or voluntary controlled schools, the clerk may be the chief executive, secretary or appropriate officer of the local authority, and he will be responsible for supplying the necessary staff, for allocating appeals to appeal committees, and for ordering the business. In the case of voluntary aided or special agreement schools, the clerk should be a person appointed by the governors of the school or schools concerned after consultation with the authority and subject to the authority's approval of any remuneration payable to him. In either case, the person attending an appeal committee as clerk to that committee should be seen as an independent source of advice on procedure. He or she should not be an employee who in the course of his employment by the authority or the school or schools concerned deals with the admission of children to schools.

5. Procedures before notice of appeal

(a) Every effort should be made to use informal procedures with a view to encouraging settlement of admissions decisions without the need for an appeal under the Act. An authority's admissions procedures should identify two stages to ensure that the point of appeal is not reached until all other means of settlement have been exhausted:

    (i) a period of fixed length, during which informal discussions can take place. During that period, allocations may be made in all those cases where parental preference is being satisfied; and

    (ii) a date which final and formal decision will be made in any outstanding cases, following which formal notice of appeal may be given. It must be made clear to the parent when this point has been reached, and how an appeal can be made.

(b) While it may be possible in each case to stagger the dates in (a)(i) and (ii) above for individual schools or groups of schools, authorities should seek to arrange their timetable so that notices of appeal must be lodged will before customary holiday periods, so that all appeals are normally decided in the case of secondary schools before the end of the summer term, and in the case of primary schools before the commencement of any relevant term of entry.

(c) In the case of voluntary aided or special agreement schools, governors should have regard to the admission arrangements for all maintained schools in their areas, and arrangements will need to be agreed in each authority area with regard to the respective timetables for admission decisions. Appeals against governors' decisions should usually be heard before the authority's appeal procedure commences. The inability of governors of individual schools to offer alternative placements suggests that any period for negotiation in advance of a decision will be limited and early decisions will enable parents to seek alternatives. In this situation a parent has two separate rights of appeal; one is against a decision of governors to refuse admission to an aided or special agreement school, the other is against an authority's decision not to meet a parental preference in respect of a county or controlled school.

(d) The notice of the final decision not to meet a parental preference should give the full reasons for the decision. Authorities or governors should provide with that notice a form on which an appeal can be made, information about how to make it and a request that any documents the parent wishes to submit should be sent in with the form.

6. Notice of appeal

(a) An appeal shall be by notice in writing setting out the grounds on which it is made.

(b) An appeal should be lodged within the period specified by the authority or governors, as the case may be, but that period should not be less than 14 days from the notification of the decision; provision may be made for this period to be extended in exceptional circumstances.

7. Hearings

(a) An appeal committee shall afford the appellant an opportunity of appearing and making oral representations, and in all cases a time and place of hearing should be appointed. Parents should be encouraged to attend to present their case, but can however be advised:–

(i) that they may elect not to attend but rely on their written statements;
(ii) that otherwise, if they do not attend and it is not reasonably practicable to offer an adjourned hearing date, the appeal will have to be decided on what information is available.

(b) Unless the parent consents in writing to a lesser period, he should be given at least 14 days (from the date of posting) written notice by first class post of the meeting of the committee at which the appeal is to be heard. Hearings should be in premises reasonably accessible to the parents concerned; and, while consideration should be given to convening hearings at times of day convenient to parents, the volume of appeals and local circumstances may prevent such flexibility. When arranging appeal hearings, in particular for annual secondary school transfer, the authority should have regard to the incidence of holiday arrangements. Ideally, hearings would not be held in the education department's offices.

(c) At least 7 days before the hearing, the chief education officer or governors of the school, as the case may be, should supply to the clerk and send to the parent by first class post:–

(i) a written statement summarising the application of the admissions policy to the case in question, with any relevant background information;
(ii) a written statement summarising the reasons for the decision, explaining why a factor given in section 6(3) of the Act applies; and

    (iii) copies of any information or documents which are to be put before the committee at the hearing.

(d) The matters to be taken into account by an appeal committee shall include:

    (i) any preference expressed by the appellant in respect of the child as mentioned in section 6 of the Act; and

    (ii) the arrangements for the admission of pupils published by the authority or the governors under section 8 of the Act.

(e) At the start of the hearing the chairman or clerk should welcome the parties and introduce those present. The procedure should be explained and it should be stated that the committee is independent of the authority or governors.

(f) The clerk may be called on to give legal or procedural advice to the appeal committee during the course of the hearing and when they retire to consider a decision. Annex 1 to the code is a suggested summary of the two stage process by which the appeal committee should make its decisions.

(g) The conduct of proceedings is in the discretion of the committee and the emphasis should be on informality coupled with fairness. One method of proceeding is set out below but this may be varied as the committee thinks fit, so long as both parties have the opportunity to put their case:

    (i) case for the authority (or governors);
    (ii) questioning by the parent;
    (iii) the case for the parent;
    (iv) questioning by the authority (or governors);
    (v) reply and summing up by the authority (or governors);
    (vi) summing up by the parent.

The committee may adjourn any case to enable a parent to attend, to receive further significant evidence, because of the illness or absence of a member of the committee, or for any other appropriate reason. It should not normally be necessary for a child or other witness to attend although the committee may consider it appropriate to allow witnesses who have attended to give evidence, provided it is relevant and not repetitive. Sufficient time must be allowed for each party to put forward its case. The committee should ensure that parents are given the opportunity to comment on information obtained from the authority or governors in the course of hearing other appeals where the committee considers this information will be relevant to its decision. Neither party attending the hearing should be present alone with the appeal committee in the absence of the other.

(h) Appeals shall be heard in private except when otherwise directed by the authority or governors by whom the arrangements are made but, without prejudice to paragraph 6 of Schedule 2 to the Act, a member of the local education authority may attend as an observer any hearing of an appeal by an appeal committee established by the authority, and a member of the Council on Tribunals may attend as an observer any meeting of any appeal committee at which an appeal is considered. If practicable it is open to the authority or governors to direct that the committee may hear more than one appeal in relation to one school at the same time. In that case the authority (or governors) may present its general case in the presence of all the parents. Thereafter, unless any parent objects in relation to his own appeal, the appeals may be heard in the presence of other parents and the authority's (or governors') case can be limited to the application of its admission policies to each particular parent.

(i) Injustice could result if the appeal of one parent at an oversubscribed school were to be decided before the appeal of another for the same school had been considered. Where it is not possible to hear all appeals in relation to one school at the same time, the appeal committee should therefore, if practicable adjourn its decisions in relation to that school until all have been heard, and then issue them. In such instances of grouped appeals, the grounds for the decision should preferably include the committee's views about the whole of the circumstances disclosed by those appeals as well as a decision on each case in question.

(j) In the case of authority appeals, the appeal is against a decision as to the school at which education is to be provided for the child; however many parents will appeal in effect because their preferred school has not been offered. If arrangements are made to group appeals along the lines envisaged in paragraph 9(h) and (i), it needs to be borne in mind that a particular parent may wish to concentrate on a school at which a place has not been offered rather than the one at which a place has been offered.

8. Representation

(a) An appeal committee may allow the appellant to be accompanied by a friend or to be represented, and an appeal committee should normally do so unless there are good reasons to the contrary which should be given to the parent. However legal representation will seldom be necessary or appropriate.

(b) The appeal committee should also allow the authority or governors to be appropriately represented.

9. Decisions of the appeal committee

(a) In the event of disagreement between the members of an appeal committee the appeal under consideration shall be decided by a simple majority of the votes cast and in the case of an equality of votes the chairman of the committee shall have a second or casting vote. It would be preferable, however, for unanimous decisions to be reached.

(b) The decision of the appeal committee and the grounds on which it is made shall be communicated by the committee in writing to the appellant and to the authority or governors as the case may be. The decision should be communicated by the clerk. It is important that the decision is fully and clearly expressed and capable of being understood by a lay person. It is important that the decision and the reasons for it are fully and clearly expressed and capable of being understood by a lay person. The reasons should reflect the stages suggested in Annex 1.

(c) The decision of an appeal committee on any such appeal shall be binding on the local education authority or governors by or on whose behalf the decision under appeal was made and, in the case of a decision made by or on behalf of a local authority, on the governors of any county or controlled school at which the committee determines that a place should be offered to the child in question.

(d) Where an appeal committee is minded not to uphold any of the parent's preferences, but wishes to suggest that another school is considered by the authority and the parents, it may be appropriate to adjourn the case to enable this consideration to take place. If the parent is still not satisfied, the hearing should be resumed and the committee should hear further representations before making its decision. That decision, however, can only be either for or against giving effect to the parental preference originally expressed under the authority's admission arrangements.

10. Organisation of appeals

(a) Each decision on the allocation of school places will be based on the individual circumstances of each case, and this principle must govern the conduct of each appeal. However, there are several sets of circumstances in which the appeals machinery might be invoked and each will give rise to particular or organisational difficulties. This code does not attempt to suggest detailed procedures for all the sets of circumstances which will arise in the operation of admission arrangements under the Act. It is important, however, to emphasize the overriding need for fairness to each individual parent and the need to ensure that each parent has a genuine right of appeal as intended by the Act. Some of the circumstances which may require particular consideration are referred to below.

(b) The appeals machinery will have to accommodate not only appeals arising in connection with the annual transfer to secondary schools but also those occurring in primary schools admission procedures or brought by parents who wish their child to change school at other than the normal admission times.

(c) The appeals machinery will have to take account of the arrangements made for the expression of parental preference. For example, a system which enables parents to express a number of preferences in order of choice will call for particular consideration to ensure that the arrangements for appeals fit fairly into the overall system.

11. Record of the proceedings of an appeal committee

The clerk of an appeal committee should keep brief notes of the proceedings, the attendance, the voting and the decisions in such form as the authority or governors may agree is appropriate. Such documents will not be public.

12. Service of documents

Documents required to be served under this code may be sent by first class post or delivered to a parent addressed to him at the address given by him to the authority or governors in the course of the admissions procedure.

ANNEX 1

SUGGESTED GUIDANCE ON REACHING A DECISION

There are two stages:–

1. It is for the authority (or governor) to satisfy the committee that the duty to allocate the child to the school preferred by the parent does not apply for one or more of the following reasons:–

(a) compliance with the preference would prejudice the provision of efficient education or the efficient use of resources; or

(b) (if applicable) the preferred school is an aided or special agreement school and compliance with the preference would break arrangements for admissions made between the governors and the authority; or

(c) (if applicable) the arrangements for admission to the preferred

313

school are based wholly or partly on selection by reference to ability or aptitude and the child does not meet the criteria for selection.

If the authority (or governors) fail to satisfy the committee on one of the above points, the committee must allow the appeal by allocating the child to the school of the parent's choice.

2. If the authority (or governors) does satisfy the committee that one of the factors (i), (ii) or (iii) applies than the committee must balance this against the parent's preference and decide which should prevail. This involves consideration of the reasons given for the parent's preference and the authority's (or governors') published admission arrangements. It will then be necessary to consider the consequences for the authority or governors of complying with the parental preference and how serious they would be. The committee must then balance these conflicting factors and reach a decision. Where two or more appeals are being decided together in respect of the same school, this process may involve considering the consequences of allowing all or only some appeals. If, as a result, it is thought right to allow some, but not all the appeals, this may involve comparing the circumstances of one parent with another to establish which appeals should succeed.

ANNEX 2

APPEALS RELATING TO SPECIAL EDUCATION

1. This annex has been drawn up to assist authorities in dealing with the provisions of the Education Act 1981 whereby parents may appeal against the educational provision set out in an authority's statement of special educational needs made for a child. This annex is intended to be read in conjunction with the code of practice. The guidelines outlined below suggest ways in which the authority may interpret the code of practice in relation to appeals under the 1981 Act and where appropriate reference is made to paragraphs of the main body of the code.

2. The statutory provisions governing the membership of appeal committees considering appeals under the 1981 Act are the same as for committee considering appeals under the 1980 Act (see para 1 of the code). However, the DES has expressed the view that an appeal committee dealing with an appeal under the 1981 Act should contain at least one person with some knowledge of special education, and the authority will no doubt wish to include a person with this expertise whenever possible.

3. Parents may appeal to an appeal committee in accordance with arrangements made by the authority under section 8 of the 1981 Act where the authority maintains a formal statement of their child's special educational need following the first or any subsequent formal assessment of the child's educational needs under section 7 of the Act. The appeal committee can therefore only consider whether the special educational provision specified in the statement is appropriate after a formal assessment has been made. It should be noted that where the authority do not maintain or propose to maintain a formal statement no appeal to the committee can be made. There is however a right of appeal to the Secretary of State against a decision not to determine special educational provision (section 5(6), 1981 Act), and parents should have already been advised of this right in appropriate cases. The length of time allowed between assessment and appeal has not been specified, and it is recommended that authorities fix a reasonable period of not less than 14 days within which parents may lodge an

appeal as one of the arrangements made under section 8(1) of the 1981 Act. Parents should be advised of this time limit when they are told of their right to appeal. The Education (Special Educational Needs) Regulations 1983 specify the frequency with which assessments are to be repeated. When a statement is maintained, parents may also request re-assessment after a period of six months and the authority shall comply with the request unless they are satisfied that an assessment would be inappropriate.

4. Paragraph 5 of the code suggests non-statutory discussions to avoid the need for an appeal. The emphasis of the procedures under the 1981 Act is also on co-operation and the DES has expressed the hope that the appeal procedure will be used as little as possible; clearly authorities will wish to accommodate the wishes of parents wherever possible. The continuation of established good practices in this respect by way of a "non-statutory" extension to the discussions envisaged by the Act would, therefore, be desirable though clearly each authority will have to fix a reasonable limit in each case beyond which they feel further discussion would be fruitless. The procedure for the preparation of a formal statement under section 7 of the 1981 Act and the Education (Special Educational Needs) Regulations 1983 amounts to a statutory consultation process with the parent. The parent must be served with a copy of the proposed statement and has the right to make representations to the authority about its contents. The parent may require a meeting with an officer of the authority and may then require a further meeting or meetings if necessary. Section 7(7) of the 1981 Act specifies a time limit of 15 days within which each of these parental rights may be exercised.

5. An appeal under the 1981 Act must be in writing setting out the grounds on which it is made, and local education authorities should devise a pro-forma including guidance for parents which should be given to those parents who express dissatisfaction with the formal statement in accordance with section 7 of the 1981 Act (see paragraph 6 of the code). It should be remembered that the requirement of section 7(3)(b) of the 1981 Act covering the duty of an authority to give a written explanation of the parents' rights under section 7(4) to 7(7) does not relate to a parent's right of appeal under section 8 of the 1981 Act. This pro-forma should therefore give additional, clear guidance to parents on the "next stage" in the proceedings and should set out clearly their rights in respect of an appeal and should encourage them to attend any hearing if they wish to do so. In addition, as referred to in paragraph 3 above, they should fix a time limit of not less than 14 days for parents to lodge an appeal after they have received the authority's formal statement.

6. The DES has expressed the wish that the appeals procedure under the 1981 Act should be as close as possible to that used under the 1980 Act and the procedure used in the hearings should, therefore, be that set out in paragraph 7(g) of the code. However authorities should consider the following points of particular concern and relevance to appeals under the 1981 Act:

(a) the person conducting the appeals on behalf of the authority will very often be different from the person who conducts appeals under the 1980 Act and it will be important to ensure that he or she is fully familiar with the relevant procedures. Furthermore, the nature of the cases under the 1981 Act will often mean that witnesses are called much more often than under 1980 Act appeals; this will apply equally to parents who may wish to call their own experts to challenge professional judgments which have been given and so the guidance in paragraph 7(g) of the code should be adapted accordingly.

(b) because there is an increased likelihood of parents seeking their own expert evidence in connection with these appeals, authorities should point out to them at some stage prior to the hearing that appeal committees will wish to come to a fair decision based upon a full understanding of all the evidence before them and this will be greatly assisted if parents provide copies of medical reports etc., to the clerk to the appeal committee in good time before the hearing. The clerk will then be able to circulate such written documentation to members before a hearing and so the risk of time consuming adjournments will be minimised.

(c) because of the nature of some of the appeals under the 1981 Act, and of the assessments made by various professionals in connection with the preparation of a formal statement, the need for rigorous control over, for example, the production and dissemination of copies of documents associated with appeals will be essential in order to maintain the confidentiality which is essential with appeal cases.

7. (See paragraph 7 of the code). The matters to be taken into account by an appeal committee in considering an appeal shall include any representations made by the appellant under section 7 of the 1981 Act, and since it is a statement of the authority's proposed special educational provision which is the subject of the appeal, the authority will wish to ensure that copies of the statement are provided for the parents, if they do not still have copies, and for the appeal committee. Parents and appeal committee members will of course be entitled to be given copies of any reports which it is intended to present to the committee.

8. (See paragraph 9 of the code). The appeal committee may confirm the special educational provision specified in the statement or remit the case to the authority for reconsideration in the light of their observations. Any observations the committee wishes to make should therefore be clear, and in writing. Parents should be informed of the appeal committee's decision in every case. It should be noted that unlike an appeal under the 1980 Act any decision made by an appeal committee does not bind the authority.

9. Parents who are dissatisfied with the decision of an appeal committee, or of an authority after it has been requested to reconsider a case following its remission by an appeal committee, may appeal to the Secretary of State. Parents should be informed of this further right of appeal and of the address to which they should write at the same time as they are informed of the decision of the appeal committee or the authority.

APPENDIX 2
(See para. 3–16)

MODEL ARTICLES OF GOVERNMENT OF ESTABLISHMENTS OF FURTHER EDUCATION (ANNEX TO D.E.S. CIRCULAR 7/70)

1. *The following is reproduced with the permission of the Controller of Her Majesty's Stationery Office.*
2. *The Groups referred to in the model articles, as defined in paragraph 10 of the Circular, are as follows:*

(a) *Group A—Colleges with a substantial proportion of advanced work;*
(b) *Group B—Other colleges with a significant amount of advanced work, whether full-time or part-time;*
(c) *Group C—Colleges with little or no advanced work.*

3. *Although Circular 7/70 was expressed not to apply to polytechnics the model articles are used by the Department of Education and Science for reference when proposals for amendment of polytechnic articles are received.*

Model articles and notes
(The notes are printed in smaller type)

In exercise of the powers conferred upon them by Section 1 of the Education (No 2) Act 1968, the .... Council, acting as Local Education Authority, hereby order as follows:

Interpretation
1. a. In these Articles, unless the context otherwise requires, the following expressions shall have the meanings indicated in this paragraph:

"The College" means ....;

"The Governors" means the Governing Body of the College;

"The Authority" means ....;

"The Secretary of State" means the Secretary of State for Education and Science;

....;

....

b. The Interpretation Act 1889 shall apply for the interpretation of these Articles as it applies for the interpretation of an Act of Parliament.

Conduct of the college
2. a. The College shall be conducted in accordance with the Education Acts 1944 to 1968, as amended by any subsequent enactment, with any relevant regulations made by the Secretary of State and, subject thereto, with the provisions of these Articles.
b. The Authority, in consultation with the Governors, shall be responsible

317

for determining the general educational character of the College and its place in the local educational system.

c. The Governors shall be responsible for the general direction of the College.

d. The Principal shall be responsible to the Governors for the internal organisation, management and discipline of the College.

e. The Chief Administrative Officer of the College shall act as Clerk to the Governors.

Notes:
 i. In the case of colleges in Group A and some colleges in Group B it will normally be appropriate for the Chief Administrative Officer of the college to act as Clerk.
 ii. In other cases the authority will need to consider the appropriate provision in the light of all the circumstances of the particular college; it will no doubt often be considered appropriate that this duty should be performed by the Chief Education Officer.

Committees

3. The Governors shall establish such committees as they think fit (including, where appropriate, committees with a membership which includes representatives of the students) and shall determine their membership and functions. Any committee of the Governors may establish sub-committees and determine their membership and functions.

Academic organisation

4. a. There shall be an Academic Board of the College comprising:

    (i) The Principal (who shall be Chairman);

    (ii) The Vice-Principal, if any;

    (iii) All Heads of Departments and other teaching staff with comparable responsibilities;

    (iv) The Chief Administrative Officer of the College;

    (v) The College Librarian;

    (vi) Such number of members of the teaching staff of the College, being not less than [6] as may be determined by the Governors, elected by the teaching staff under arrangements devised by them and approved by the Academic Board;

The Board shall have power to co-opt not more than ...... additional members.

b. Subject to the overall responsibilities of the Governors, the Academic Board shall be responsible for the planning, co-ordination, development and oversight of the academic work of the College, including arrangements for the admission and examination of students.

c. The Academic Board shall establish such committees as they think fit (including, where appropriate, committees with a membership including representatives of the students) and shall determine their membership and functions. Any committee or the Board may establish sub-committees and determine their membership and functions.

d. So far is practicable, the Academic Board shall delegate its functions to Departments in matters not affecting other Departments or the College as a whole.

Notes:
 i. Provision on the lines of this model article will normally be appropriate for colleges in Group A. The desirability of providing for students to be represented, or to attend as observers, on the Board should be considered. Where such provision is not included in the Article, the power of co-option should be drawn widely enough to permit the co-option of students as well as additional members of the college staff.

ii. In other cases the question of making provision for an Academic Board and, in that event, appropriate provision for its composition and its functions will need to be considered.

iii. For colleges in Group B provision for an Academic Board will usually be thought desirable. Its membership might be defined in terms of the Principal (who shall be Chairman), the Vice-Principal (if any) and ...... other members of the teaching staff appointed in accordance with arrangements made by the Governors at a duly constituted meeting.

iv. There may be colleges in Group C, with a substantial number of students over the age of 18 engaged on full-time courses, in respect of which authorities may wish to include specific provision for an Academic Board. Where such provision is not made, the Articles should require the Governors to make arrangements for the teaching staff to be consulted regularly about the organisation and regulation of the academic work of the College.

Appointment, promotion and dismissal of staff

5. a. Upon the occurrence of a vacancy in the post of Principal, Vice-President (if any) or Chief Administrative Officer, the post shall be advertised and a short list of candidates to be interviewed shall be prepared by a committee consisting of such number of Governors as the Governors may decide and 1 person [2 persons] appointed by the local education authority. The committee shall interview the candidates on the short list and, unless it decides that re-advertisement of the post is desirable, shall make an appointment subject to confirmation by the Authority.

   b. Under arrangements made by the Governors after consultation with the Academic Board, the Principal shall have a general responsibility for the appointment of other members of the teaching staff; provided that in the case of the appointment of a Head of Department the Governors shall be represented on the selection committee and the appointment shall be subject to confirmation by the Governors.

   c. Responsibility for appointments within the approved establishment of non-teaching staff (other than that of the Chief Administrative Officer) shall be delegated to the Principal in accordance with arrangements approved by the Governors after taking the advice of the Principal.

   d. All staff shall be appointed to specified posts in the College in the service of the Authority subject to such conditions of service as the Authority may determine.

   e. The Governors, or their Chairman, shall be empowered to suspend the Principal, Vice-Principal (if any) and the Chief Administrative Officer provided that the Chairman shall immediately report his action to the Governors. The Principal shall be empowered to suspend any member of the College staff other than the Vice-Principal (if any) or the Chief Administrative Officer but shall immediately report such action to the Governors or their Chairman. Any action taken under this paragraph shall be notified immediately to the Authority.

   f. The Governors shall be empowered to recommend to the authority the dismissal of the Principal, Vice-Principal (if any) and Chief Administrative Officer, and to dismiss any other member of the staff, subject to confirmation by the Authority.

   g. A member of staff shall be entitled to a personal hearing (accompanied by a friend if he so wishes) at any meeting of the Governors or of the Authority or of any committee of sub-committee thereof at which his dismissal is to be considered.

Notes:

i. The provisions of this article will be appropriate for Colleges in Group A.

ii. The general pattern of the article will be suitable for other colleges but authorities will wish to consider, in the light of the circumstances of individual colleges, the extent to which particular provisions need to be varied. One question they may wish to consider is the extent to which, and the way in which, the Governors might best be associated with the appointment of different grades of teaching staff.

Finance, premises and supplies

6. a. The annual financial estimates of the College shall be prepared under the direction of the Principal and in the form laid down by the Authority for submission by the Governors to the Authority by such a date and with such supporting data as the Authority may require.

   b. Within the estimates as approved by the Authority, the Governors shall be entitled to incur expenditure without further reference to the Authority and shall be empowered:

      i. To exercise virement within the headings shown in the Appendix to these Articles.

      ii. To determine, subject to the provisions of the Burnham Further Education Report, the numbers and grades of teaching staff.

      iii. To carry out repairs, maintenance and minor alterations up to a figure of £500 per job [or such higher figure as the Authority may determine] by what they judge, having regard to economical management, as the best means.

      iv. To place orders for supplies (including equipment) and services at their discretion, subject in the case of items costing more than £100 each [or such higher figure as the Authority may determine] to their making use of any central purchasing arrangements of the Authority where this would be more economical.

      Provided that the Governors shall not, without the consent of the Authority, undertake in any financial year any commitment which would involve the Authority in continuing expenditure after the end of that year.

   c. Subject to the provisions of these Articles, the financial administration of the College shall be conducted in accordance with financial rules to be made by the Authority after consultation with the Governors.

Notes:
i. This article will be appropriate for most colleges in Group A. A suggested list of headings for virement purposes is to be found in Appendix B of the Report of the Study Group on the Government of Colleges of Education.

ii. In the case of other colleges, the aim should be to give the Governors the maximum responsibility for incurring expenditure within approved estimates which is reasonable and appropriate in relation to the particular circumstances of the college. Special consideration will be necessary in the case of agricultural colleges with trading departments.

Students

7. a. The Governors shall make arrangements for the Students' Union or other body representing the students to conduct and manage its own affairs and funds in accordance with a constitution approved by the Governors.

   b. They shall also make arrangements whereby representations on matters of proper concern to the students may be made by their representatives to the Governors, the Academic Board or the Principal as may be appropriate.

   c. The Governors shall establish a disciplinary committee with a membership that includes representatives in equal numbers of the staff and of the students of the College, provided that if Governors other than staff and student Governors are appointed to this committee their members shall not exceed one third of the total.

    d. After consultation with the Academic Board and representatives of the students the Governors shall make rules governing the procedures to be followed in the College in matters concerning student discipline. These rules shall provide, inter alia:

        i. For the Principal to be empowered to suspend a student for good cause, pending consideration of his case by the disciplinary committee within a period to be stated, and for the Principal to report any such action promptly to the Chairman of the Governors.

        ii. For any decision to expel or, subject to the Principal's powers under i. above, to suspend a student to be taken by the disciplinary committee.

        iii. For a student to have a right of appeal against the decision of the disciplinary committee to the Governors or to a committee of the Governors appointed by them for this purpose.

        iv. For any Governor who has been concerned in the proceedings of the disciplinary committee as a member of that committee to take no part in the meeting of the Governors or their committee at which any appeal from the disciplinary committee's decision is considered.

        v. For a student to have the right to appear and be heard (accompanied by a friend if he so wishes) at any meeting of the disciplinary committee at which his case is to be considered and at any meeting of the Governors or their committee at which his appeal is to be dealt with.

    e. The Governors may exclude a student from the College for an unsatisfactory standard of work on the recommendation of the Academic Board subject to his having a right of hearing (accompanied by a friend if he so wishes) before the Governors or a committee of the Governors. OR: The Academic Board shall be empowered to exclude a student from the College for an unsatisfactory standard of work, provided that he shall have a right of hearing (accompanied by a friend if he so wishes) before the Governors or a committee of the Governors).

Notes:

i. As indicated in paragraph 12 of the Circular the above article will be suitable for any college with a substantial proportion of (full-time equivalent) adult students.

ii. Modifications may be considered necessary in the case of other colleges. For example, while it can be assumed that most colleges (in particular those with a substantial number of adult students) will have a Students' Union, there will be some that will not. In those cases the Articles should at least require arrangements to be made whereby representations on matters of proper concern to the students may be made by their representatives to the Governors, the Academic Board, if any, or the Principal, as appropriate. They might also make provision for the establishment of a Joint Consultative Committee which might include equal numbers of representatives of the Governors, the teaching staff and the students. (Such a committee might also be appropriate in colleges with a Students' Union).

iii. And, while the general provisions of paragraphs c. and d. of the article will be appropriate for colleges that do not have a substantial proportion of adult students, authorities may wish to consider whether or not the disciplinary committee should include student representatives.

iv. The intention behind paragraph e. of the model article is that a student should have a right of hearing before the Governors or their committee where he is of the opinion that his exclusion is based in part on criticism of his personal behaviour.

Consultative Committees

8. The Governors shall make appropriate arrangements to establish machinery for consultation with representatives of industry, art and design, commerce

and the professions, including, as desirable, consultative committees with members drawn from these fields.

Copies of Articles

9. A copy of these Articles shall be given to every Governor, every member of the full-time teaching staff and the Chief Administrative Officer on appointment and shall be available upon request to every part-time teacher, every member of the non-teaching staff and every student.

Date of Articles

10. These Articles shall come into operation on [. . . .]

APPENDIX 3

(See paras. 4–52 and 4–115)

STATUTORY CONDITIONS OF EMPLOYMENT OF SCHOOL TEACHERS

(Schedules 1, 2 and 3 of The Education (School Teachers' Pay and Conditions of Employment Order 1987)

SCHEDULE 1

CONDITIONS OF EMPLOYMENT OF HEAD TEACHERS

Overriding Requirements

1. A head teacher shall carry out his professional duties in accordance with and subject to—

(a) the provisions of the Education Acts 1944 to 1986;

(b) any orders and regulations having effect thereunder;

(c) the articles of government of the school of which he is head teacher, to the extent to which they content is prescribed by statute;

(d) where the school is a voluntary school, any trust deed applying in relation thereto;

and, to the extent to which they are not inconsistent with these conditions,—

    (i) provisions of the articles of government the content of which is not so prescribed;

    (ii) any rules, regulations or policies laid down by his employers; and

    (iii) the terms of his appointment.

General Functions

2. Subject to paragraph 1 above, the head teacher shall be responsible for the internal organisation, management and control of the school.

Consultation   **3.** In carrying out his duties the head teacher shall consult, where this is appropriate, with the authority, the governing body, the staff of the school and the parents of its pupils.

Professional duties

4. The professional duties of a head teacher shall include—

School Aims   (1) Formulating the overall aims and objectives of the school and policies for their implementation;

Appointment of Staff   (2) Participating in the selection and appointment of the teaching and non-teaching staff of the school;

Management of Staff   (3) (a) Deploying and managing all teaching and non-teaching staff of the school and allocating particular duties to them (including such duties of the head teacher as may properly be delegated to the deputy head teacher or other members of the staff) in a

323

manner consistent with their conditions of employment, maintaining a reasonable balance for each teacher between work carried out in school and work carried out elsewhere;

(b) Ensuring that the duty of providing cover for absent teachers is shared equitably among all teachers in the school (including the head teacher), taking account of their teaching and other duties;

Liaison with staff unions and associations

(4) Maintaining relationships with organisations representing teachers and other persons on the staff of the school;

Curriculum

(5) Determining, organising and implementing an appropriate curriculum for the school, having regard to the needs, experience, interests, aptitudes and stage development of the pupils and the resources available to the school;

Review

(6) Keeping under review the work and organisation of the school;

Standards of teaching and learning

(7) Evaluating the standards of teaching and learning in the school, and ensuring that proper standards of professional performance are established and maintained;

Appraisal, training and development of Staff

(8) (a) Supervising and participating in any arrangements within an agreed national framework for the appraisal of the performance of teachers who teach in the school;

(b) Ensuring that all staff in the school have access to advice and training appropriate to their needs, in accordance with the policies of the maintaining authority for the development of staff;

Management information

(9) Providing information about the work and performance of the staff employed at the school where this is relevant to their future employment;

Pupil Progress

(10) Ensuring that the progress of the pupils of the school is monitored and recorded;

Pastoral Care

(11) Determining and ensuring the implementation of a policy for the pastoral care of the pupils;

Discipline

(12) Determining in accordance with any written statement of general principles provided for him by the governing body, measures to be taken with a view to promoting, among the pupils, self-discipline and proper regard for authority, encouraging good behaviour on the part of the pupils, securing that the standard of behaviour of the pupils is acceptable and otherwise regulating the conduct of the pupils; making such measures generally known within the school, and ensuring that they are implemented;

(13) Ensuring the maintenance of good order and discipline at all times during the school day (including the midday break) when pupils are present on the school premises and whenever the pupils are engaged in authorised school activities, whether on the school premises or elsewhere;

Relations with parents

(14) Making arrangements for parents to be given regular information about the school curriculum, the progress of their children and other matters affecting the school, so as to promote common understanding of its aims;

Relations with other bodies

(15) Promoting effective relationships with persons and bodies outside the school;

Relations with governing body

(16) Advising and assisting the governing body of the school in the exercise of its functions, including (without prejudice to any rights he may have as a governor of the school) attending meetings of the governing body and making such reports to its in connection with the discharge of his functions as it may properly require either on a regular basis or from time to time;

Relations with authority

(17) Providing for liaison and co-operation with the officers of the maintaining authority; making such reports to the authority in connection with the discharge of his functions as it may properly require, either on a regular basis or from time to time;

Relations with other educational establishments

(18) Maintaining liaison with other schools and further education establishments with which the school has a relationship;

Resources

(19) Allocating, controlling and accounting for those financial and material resources of the school which are under the control of the head teacher;

Premises

(20) Making arrangements, if so required by the governing body or the maintaining authority, for the security and effective supervision of the school buildings and their contents and of the school grounds; and ensuring (if so required) that any lack of maintenance is promptly reported to the maintaining authority or, if appropriate, the governing body;

Appraisal of head teacher

(21)(a) Participating in any arrangements within an agreed national framework for the appraisal of his performance as head teacher;

(b) Participating in the identification of areas in which he would benefit from further training and undergoing such training;

Absence

(22) Arranging for a deputy head teacher or other suitable person to assume responsibility for the discharge of his functions as head teacher at any time when he is absent from the school;

Teaching

(23) Participating, to such extent as may be appropriate having regard to his other duties, in the teaching of pupils at the school, including the provision of cover for absent teachers.

Daily break

5. A head teacher shall be entitled to a break of reasonable length in the course of each school day, and shall arrange for a suitable person to assume responsibility for the discharge of his functions as head teacher during that break.

SCHEDULE 2

CONDITIONS OF EMPLOYMENT OF
DEPUTY HEAD TEACHERS

[including second masters and mistresses]

A person appointed deputy head teacher in a school, in addition to carrying out the professional duties of a school teacher, including those duties particularly assigned to him by the head teacher, shall—

(1) assist the head teacher in managing the school or such part of its as may be determined by the head teacher;

(2) undertake any professional duty of the head teacher which may be delegated to him by the head teacher;

(3) undertake, in the absence of the head teacher and to the extent required by him or his employers, the professional duties of the head teacher;

(4) be entitled to a break of reasonable length in the course of each school day.

SCHEDULE 3

CONDITIONS OF EMPLOYMENT OF
SCHOOL TEACHERS

[these conditions, with the exception of paragraph 4, apply to deputy head teachers]

Exercise of general professional duties

1. A teacher who is not a head teacher shall carry out the professional duties of a school teacher as circumstances may require—

(a) if he is employed as a teacher in the school, under the reasonable direction of the head teacher of that school;

(b) if he is employed by an authority on terms under which he is not assigned to any one school, under the reasonable direction of that authority and of the head teacher of any school in which he may for the time being be required to work as a teacher.

Exercise of particular duties

2. (a) A teacher employed as a teacher (other than a head teacher) in a school shall perform, in accordance with any directions which may reasonably be given to him by the head teacher from time to time, such particular duties as may reasonably be assigned to him;

(b) A teacher employed by an authority on terms such as those described in paragraph 1(b) above shall perform, in accordance with any direction which may reasonably be given to him from time to time by the authority or by the head teacher of any school in which he may for the time being be required to work as a teacher, such particular duties as may reasonably be assigned to him.

Professional duties

3. The following duties shall be deemed to be included in the professional duties which a school teacher may be required to perform—

STATUTORY CONDITIONS OF EMPLOYMENT

Teaching

(1)(a) Planning and preparing courses and lessons;
(b) Teaching, according to their educational needs, the pupils assigned to him, including the setting and marking of work to be carried out by the pupil in school and elsewhere;
(c) Assessing, recording and reporting on the development, progress and attainment of pupils;

Other activities

(2)(a) Promoting the general progress and well being of individual pupils and of any class or group of pupils assigned to him;
(b) Providing guidance and advice to pupils on educational and social matters and on their further education and future careers, including information about sources of more expert advice on specific questions; making relevant records and reports;
(c) Making records of and reports on the personal and social needs of pupils;
(d) Communicating and consulting with the parents of pupils;
(e) Communicating and co-operating with persons or bodies outside the school;
(f) Participating in meetings arranged for any of the purposes described above;

Assessments and reports

(3) Providing or contributing to oral and written assessments, reports and references relating to individual pupils and groups of pupils;

Appraisal

(4) Participating in any arrangements within an agreed national framework for the appraisal of his performance and that of other teachers;

Review: Further training and development

(5) (a) Reviewing from time to time his methods of teaching and programmes of work;
(b) Participating in arrangements for his further training and professional development as a teacher;

Educational methods

(6) Advising and co-operating with the head teacher and other teachers (or any one or more of them) on the preparation and development of courses of study, teaching materials, teaching programmes, methods of teaching and assessment and pastoral arrangements;

Discipline, health and safety

(7) Maintaining good order and discipline among the pupils and safeguarding their health and safety both when they are authorised to be on the school premises and when they are engaged in authorised school activities elsewhere;

Staff Meetings

(8) Participating in meetings at the school which relate to the curriculum for the school or the administration or organisations of the school, including pastoral arrangements;

Cover

(9) Supervising and so far as practicable teaching any pupils whose teacher is not available to teach them:
Provided that no teacher shall be required to provide such cover—

(a) after the teacher who is absent or otherwise not available has been so for three or more consecutive working days; or

327

      (b) where the fact that the teacher would be absent or otherwise not available for a period exceeding three consecutive working days was known to the maintaining authority for two or more working days before the absence commenced;

unless—

      (i) he is a teacher employed wholly or mainly for the purpose of providing such cover ("a supply teacher"); or

      (ii) it is not reasonably practicable for the maintaining authority to provide a supply teacher to provide cover; or

      (iii) he is a full-time teacher at the school but has been assigned by the head teacher in the time-table to teach or carry out other specified duties (except cover) for less than 75 per cent of those hours in the week during which pupils are taught at the school;

Public examinations

(10) Participating in arrangements for preparing public examinations and in assessing pupils for the purposes of such examinations; recording and reporting such assessments; and participating in arrangements for pupils' presentation for and supervision during such examinations;

Management

(11)(a) Contributing to the selection for appointment and professional development of other teacher and non-teaching staff, including the induction and assessment of new and probationary teachers;

      (b) Co-ordinating or managing the work of other teachers;

      (c) Taking such part as may be required of him in the review, development and management of activities relating to the curriculum, organisation and pastoral functions of the school;

Administration

(12)(a) Participating in administrative and organisational tasks related to such duties as are described above, including the management or supervision of persons providing support for the teachers in the school and the ordering and allocation of equipment and materials;

      (b) Attending assemblies, registering the attendance of pupils and supervising pupils, whether these duties are to be performed before, during or after school sessions.

Working time

4(1) After 1st August 1987—

      (a) a teacher employed full-time, other than in the circumstances described in subparagraph (c), shall be available for work for 195 days in any year, of which 190 days shall be days on which he may be required to teach pupils in addition to carrying out other duties; and those 195 days shall be specified by his employer or, if the employer so directs, by the head teacher;

(b) a teacher shall be available to perform such duties at such times and such places as may be specified by the head teacher (or, where the teacher is not assigned to any one school, by his employer or the head teacher of any school in which he may for the time being be required to work as a teacher) for 1265 hours in any year, those hours to be allocated reasonably throughout those days in the year on which he is required to be available for work;

(c) subparagraphs (a) and (b) do not apply to a teacher employed wholly or mainly to teach or perform other duties in relation to pupils in a residential establishment;

(d) time spent in travelling to or from the place of work shall not count against the 1265 hours referred to in subparagraph (b);

(e) unless employed under a separate contract as a midday supervisor, a teacher shall not be required to unertake midday supervision, and shall be allowed a break of reasonable length either between school sessions or between the hours of 12 noon and 2.00 p.m.;

(f) a teacher shall, in addition to the requirements set out in subparagraphs (a) and (b) above, work such additional hours as may be needed to enable him to discharge effectively his professional duties, including, in particular the marking of pupils' work, the writing of reports on pupils and the preparation of lessons, teaching material and teaching programmes. The amount of time required for this purpose beyond the 1265 hours referred to in subparagraph (b) and the times outside the 1265 specified hours at which duties shall be performed shall not be defined by the employer but shall depend upon the work needed to discharge the teacher's duties;

(2) In this paragraph, "year" means a period of 12 months commencing on 1st September unless the school's academic year begins in August in which case it means a period of 12 months commencing on August 1.

INDEX

The abbreviations l.e.a. *and* S. of S. *are used for* local education authority *and* Secretary of State.

[Roman page numbers refer to the Preface]

331

allowances—*cont.*
  co-opted members of education
    committees, for, 1–17 n.43
  meetings and conferences of local
    authority associations, for, 1–36
  pupils over compulsory school age, for,
    5–20
  school admission appeal committee
    members, for, 2–178 n.12
  students pursuing further education
    correspondence courses, for, 3–66
  see also **awards, grant**
alteration of schools, 2–31
  new school, constituting, 2–31
  nursery schools, 2–47
  S.of S., functions in relation to, 2–32,
    2–47
  "significant change", 2–32
  see also **school buildings, school premises**
Anderson Committee on *Grants to Students*,
  3–41
appeal, rights of, 1–48
  see also **disputes, representations, school
    admission appeal committees, special
    educational provision**
area committees, 1–14 n.32
areas to which pupils belong, 1–134
  see also **ordinary residence**
army school, 6–44 n.81
articles of school government, 1–76, 2–71,
    2–80, 2–82, 2–107
  admission to school, on, 2–174
  clerk to governing body, on, 4–44, 4–46
  conduct of school, general reponsibility
    for, on, 2–108
  curriculum and examinations, on,
    2–128
  finance, on, 2–113
  making and revision of, 2–83
  model, 2–80 n.63, 2–170 n.41, 2–174
  non-teaching staff, on, 4–44
  organisation, management and
    discipline, on, 2–115
  parents' meetings, on, 2–153, 2–156
  premises, control of, on, 2–51
  reports to parents, on, 2–153
  school sessions, terms and holidays, on,
    2–142
  teachers, on, 4–27
assisted places scheme, 2–217, 6–14, 6–35
  fees, extent of remission of, 6–41
  incidental expenses, 6–43
  participation agreement, termination of,
    6–36
  participation agreement under, 6–36
  particulars, publication of, 6–42
  selection conditions, 6–37, 6–42
  see also **independent schools**
assisted schools, 2–08, 2–45
Association of County Councils, 1–36
  see also **local authority associations**

Association of Metropolitan Authorities,
  1–36
  see also **local authority associations**
awards,
  Council of Europe, member states and,
    3–42
  grants and, to students in further
    education, 3–41
  miscellaneous, 3–71
  see also **discretionary awards, grants,
    industrial scholarships, mandatory
    awards, non-teaching staff,
    postgraduate courses, teacher
    training**

B.Ed. degree, 4–04, 4–12
  courses, 4–07
Bains report on *The New Local Authorities*,
  1–26
ballet schools, aided pupils scheme, 6–19
"belonging to the area of a l.e.a.",
  ordinary residence as test, 1–135
  questions about, determination of, 1–139
  see also **ordinary residence**
binary system, 3–01 n.3
birth certificate, 2–239
block grant, 1–123
  deductions from aggregate of, 1–124,
    1–133
  distribution to l.e.as., 1–123
  I.L.E.A., for, 1–33, 1–123
  pooling adjustments, 1–130
  see also **finance of l.e.as., rate support
    grant**
board and lodging, 5–13
  cost of, 5–14
  maintained school at, fees for, 1–90
  non-maintained school at, payment of
    fees by l.e.a., 5–31
  provision of, 5–13
boarder,
  school attendance of, 2–229
boarding,
  accommodation, as part of school
    premises, 2–20 n.79, 2–57
  education, 2–07
  education for service children, 5–31
    n.12
  fees, excluded from assisted places
    scheme, 6–35
  places, change in the number of, 2–32
  schools, 2–07
  schools, provision of clothing for pupils
    at, 5–15
  see also **assisted places scheme,
    independent schools, non-
    maintained schools**
Burgundy Book — *see* **teachers' conditions
  of service**
Burnham Committees and reports, 4–99,
  4–113, 4–126

nuisance, 7–52
see also **playgrounds, playing fields,
school premises**
nursery,
class,
clothing, provision for pupil at, 5–15
primary school, at, 2–45
teachers at, 4–14, 4–42
day, 2–50
teachers' employment in, 4–42
education, 2–45
school, 2–02, 2–05, 2–45
clothing, provision for pupils at, 5–15
defined, 2–03, 2–45
direct grant, 2–218
independent, grant payable to, 2–45
maintained, discontinuance of, 2–47
maintained, recognition of special
educational needs at, 2–205
premises, new, 2–47
religious education in, 2–159 n.59
teachers, 4–14, 4–42

objections, 1–45
see also **appeal, right of, disputes, school
admission appeal committees**
officers,
appointment of, 1–26
delegation to. 1–27
member of school governing body as,
2–75
teachers as local government, 4–02
see also **non-teaching staff**
ombudsmen, 1–58
local, school admission appeal
committees, and, 2–185
orders,
local and personal, 1–42
revocation and variation of, 1–42
service of, 1–42 n.25
see also **statutory instruments**
ordinary residence, 2–195, 3–73
adult education awards and, 3–69 n.5
belonging to the area of a l.e.a., as test of,
1–135, 3–73
discretionary awards and, 3–75
mandatory award condition, as, 3–43,
3–45
meaning of, 3–73
miscellaneous awards and, 3–70
postgraduate awards and, 3–68 n.93
racial discrimination and, 1–104
out-of-school activities — *see* **extra-
curricular activities**
overseas students,
further education courses, admission of,
3–18
further education courses, fees for, 1–102
n.32, 3–14
see also **discretionary awards, mandatory
awards**

parents,
board and lodging of pupil, wishes and
obligations of, 5–13
cleanliness of pupil, responsibility of, for,
5–07
clothing, payment of cost by, 5–19
contribution to student's resources, 3–51,
3–53
criminal offence, by, 2–127
education duty of, to secure, 1–80, 2–230
exclusion of pupil, appeal by, against,
2–110, 2–119, 2–124
governor of school — *see* **instrument of
school government**
information about educational provision,
to be made available to, 2–133
information about schools, for, 2–186
meaning of, 1–70
meetings, 2–153, 2–156
religious education,
right to withdraw child from, 2–159,
2–162
request for agreed syllabus by, 2–163
request for denominational by, 2–164,
2–167
reports to, by governors, 2–153
respect for wishes of, 1–69, 2–173, 2–209
school admission preferences of, 2–176,
2–230
school admission appeals by, 2–178
school attendance order, and, 2–230,
2–234, 2–238
school attendance, prosecution of,
regarding, 2–234, 2–240
school premises, on, 2–67
school, visit to, by, 2–189
suspension of pupil, appeal by, against,
2–117, 2–120
see also **special educational needs, special
educational provision**
Parliament, laying of documents before,
1–24, 1–41
**Parliamentary Commissioner for
Administration** — *see* **ombudsmen**
physical training,
clothes, provision of, by l.e.as., 5–18
courses, sex discrimination and, 1–97
see also **recreation and social and physical
training**
planning law, 1–163
playgrounds, 5–27
accidents in, 7–09
nuisance and disturbance in, 2–67
voluntary schools, provision of, at, 2–28
playing fields, 5–27
accidents in, 7–11 n.17, 7–39
nuisance and disturbance on, 2–67
school buses, for journeys to, 5–24
standards, 2–56
voluntary schools, provision of, at, 2–20,
2–28

343

school premises—*cont.*
controlled school, significant
enlargement of, 2–38
criminal offences at, 2–100, 2–127
defined, 2–20
elections and other purposes, use for,
2–60
enlargement of, 2–32
fittings prescribed, 2–20
maintained (other than voluntary),
control of, 2–51
nuisance and disturbance on, 2–67, 2–100
nursery, 2–47
parents on, 2–67
police on, 2–69, 2–127
sale of Church of England, 1–160
site, controlled school, for, 2–28
site, tranfer to new, 2–32
special, non-maintained, 2–210
standards, 2–55, 7–38
trespass on, 2–67, 2–127
voluntary school, dealings in, 2–66
voluntary school, occupation and use of,
2–63, 7–38
voluntary school significant enlargement
or alteration of, 2–33
voluntary school, to be maintained as
county school, 2–16
see also **aided schools, school buildings,
special agreement schools**
school proprietor,
defined, 2–109
independent school, of, 6–29, 6–33
leave of absence, grant by, 2–223
non-maintained school of, grant to, 2–08
registration of pupils, duty concerning,
2–109
school attendance, obligations regarding,
2–111
School Sites Acts, 1–150
school uniform, 2–118, 2–126
information about, 2–189
pupils under assisted places scheme, for,
6–43
purchase of, by l.e.a., 5–20
sex discrimination and, 193 n.94
schools,
age range, change in, 2–32
admission to — *see* **admission to school**
allocation of children to, complaints
about, 1–62, 1–78
alteration — *see* **alteration of schools**
annals of, 2–143
arrangements with independent, 1–72
availability of, 2–10
categories of, diagrams illustrating, 2–05
character, change of, 2–32
closure, sex discrimination in, 1–95
conduct of, 2–107
co-educational, 2–09
day and year, length of, 1–82, 2–48, 2–140

schools—*cont.*
defined, 2–02
department of, 2–30
development plan for, 2–13
discontinuance of, 2–35
division of, 2–30
education outside, 5–29
enlargement of, 2–32
exclusion from, 2–110, 2–118, 2–122,
2–223
finance, 2–113, 2–154
grouping, for government, 2–77, 2–90
holidays, 2–140
infant, 2–02
information about, 2–05, 2–186
inspection of, 6–05
junior, 2–02
leave of absence from, 2–141, 5–39
leaving dates, 1–81
management, 2–115
midday break, 4–110
new — *see* **county school, voluntary
school, establishment of**
ordinary, 2–193, 2–204
organisation, 2–115
places, reduction of, 2–34
plays and entertainments at, 2–151
provision, S. of S.'s powers in relation to,
2–09
punishments, 2–126, 2–143
reinstatement of pupil in, 2–123
reports on pupils, 1–70, 2–126, 2–145,
7–63, Appendix 3 p.323
reports on special school pupils, 2–211
rules, 2–126
sessions, 2–48, 2–109, 2–140
sex composition, change in, 2–32
single-sex, 2–09
sites, reverter of, 1–150
sites, sale or exchange of land acquired
under School Sites Acts, 2–21 n.82
sufficient, duty to secure, 1–73, 2–06
television licences for, 2–152
terms, 1–81, 2–140
trustees of, 1–149
see also **admission to school, boarding,
clothing, maintenance of schools,
non-teaching staff, school
attendance, school discipline,
teachers**
**Schools Council for the Curriculum and
Examinations**, 2–128 n.87
Scilly, Isles of, 1–16
Scottish education authorities,
recoupment of expenditure, 1–138
secondary education, 2–06
assisted place for, 6–36
defined, 2–03
further education, relationship with, 3–11
l.e.a., duty of, to provide, 2–06
non-maintained school, at, 2–08, 5–32

voluntary schools—*cont.*
  premises, powers of Charity
    Commissioners, 1–157, 1–159
  premises, powers of S. of S., 1–157, 1–160
  private street works, liability of trustees,
    1–162
  property, trustees of, 2–76
  rate relief for, 1–161
  School Sites Acts and, 1–150
  significant change in, 2–32, 2–72
  site, provision for additional or new, 2–28
  status, change of, 2–41
  substitution of one school for another,
    2–21, 2–29
  temporary accommodation at, 2–33
  trustees, site conveyed to, 2–28
  see also **aided schools, articles of school
    government, controlled schools,
    governing bodies and governors,
    instruments of school government,
    religious education, special
    agreement schools, teachers**
Voluntary Sector Consultative Council,
  3–24

Wales,
  adult education awards for residents in,
    3–69
  local ombudsman for, 1–64
  see also **Secretary of State for Wales**
**Wales Advisory Body for Local Authority
  Higher Education**, 1–133
walking distance, 2–223, 2–227, 5–22
  see also **transport**
Warnock report, *Special Educational
  Needs*, 2–192 n.60

Welsh Joint Education Committee, 1–23
  as examining body, 2–139 n.7
  as local authority association, 1–37 n.14
Welsh language teaching, grants for, 1–127,
  6–21
Welsh Office, 1–11 n.22, 3–30
  administrative memorandums and
    circulars, p.vi n.4
  see also **circulars**
work experience, 2–128, 5–39
  see also **employment of children**
Workers' Education Association, 3–35

young persons, defined, 2–04, 5–34 n.21
  see also **employment of children and
    young persons**
youth clubs, 3–06, 3–36
youth leaders and workers,
  Joint Negotiating Committee for, 3–38,
    4–01 n.4
  pay and conditions of service of, 3–38
  qualifications of, 3–38
  S. of S.'s powers as to, 3–38
  superannuation of, 4–01 n.5
  training of, 3–37, 3–39
Youth Opportunities Programme, 3–31
youth service, 3–01, 3–36
  national organisations, 3–39
  urban social needs programme, grants
    for, under, 3–40
  Sports Council grants for, 1–143 n.62,
    3–40
  voluntary bodies, assistance by l.e.as. to,
    3–36
  Youth Training Scheme and, 3–36 n.38
Youth Training Scheme, 3–31, 3–36 n.38